Early Utah Journalism

Utah State Historical Society

THE FIRST DESERET NEWS PRESS
June 15, 1850

EARLY UTAH JOURNALISM

A half century of forensic warfare. waged by
the West's most militant Press.

By

J. CECIL ALTER

Eighty-one Illustrations

GREENWOOD PRESS, PUBLISHERS
WESTPORT, CONNECTICUT

Originally published in 1938
by the Utah State Historical Society, Salt Lake City

Reprinted from an original copy in the collections
of the University of Illinois Library

First Greenwood Reprinting 1970

Library of Congress Catalogue Card Number 79-98803

SBN 8371-3065-4

Printed in the United States of America

Illustrations

Introduction

The pioneer editor usually considered himself a weakling if he did not stand positively and aggressively for or against something, monitoring the thoughts and actions of the community with the dignity and severity of a Dictator—even if at the same time he was guilty of neglecting to print news items in his columns, or to meet his creditor's bills when due! Only in the perspective of Time can such self-appointed leadership be correctly appraised, for while most of them more or less honestly believed themselves to be Davids setting forth to slay the Giant Error with a newspaper sling, they very often proved in the sequel to be Don Quixotes shouting at the wind, or "Wilkins Micawbers," whose heads in the dreamy clouds of imagined success did not know their feet were mired in the slough of despond!

Such an editor often had a hard time convincing the ·people he was their leader or spokesman; and he expended enough effort, and displayed enough intellectual power, to have set himself up as a successful merchant or professional man. But our pioneer journalist, under the persuasion that he must mold public opinion in the hard and quick way, often very shortly found himself manning his ship alone. As a result, there are more wrecks on the shoals and shores of the sea of newspaper journalism, than of any other business of equal investment, turnover or importance. Seven or eight country newspapers have perished in Utah for every one that remains in existence today.

There were a few altruistic, devoted editors like Johnson and Carpenter of St. George, who preferred to write and print, rather than to eat; but on crucial occasions they reluctantly chose to eat—or their families forced them to do so—thus effecting the demise of the newspapers instead of their publishers! Many others, feeling for the first time the intoxicating power of the press in their hands, learned swiftly to their sorrow, of its two-edged responsibilities, and gave up their ideal, surrendered their liberty, and forfeited their precious presses. (As proof, consult the index for "bankruptcy", "trials in court", "jailed", and so forth!)

But the far greater number of frontier editors were singularly capable, courageous journalists, who placed Utah's pioneer newspapers among the Nation's most distinguished and respected spokesmen and historians of those early days. They portrayed the propaganda and public sentiment of earnest groups of people having sharply conflicting views, undergoing a slow but far reaching change through the years. No newspapers of any section of the country, or of any period in the Nation's history, were ever more eagerly awaited or more closely read than those hailing from Utah through the anti-polygamy crusade of the last half of the Nineteenth Century.

There is therefore, reposing in the files of the old Utah newspapers, and reflected in the following pages, some of the most vivid factual pictures of pioneer public and private life available anywhere in the West—because those old time editors very often laid all the cards on the table so as to leave their hands and heads free for more persuasive arguments!

As indicated, the frontier newspaper was usually a personal organ, played enthusiastically by the editor, as long and as loud as the people pumped the bellows of support! As a consequence, many editors and newspapers sprang up and expanded until they burst with their own sense of supremacy; while others, perhaps with slightly different motives, or at a different stage of events or public sentiment, went vigorously and successfully on, to become permanent institutions in the community.

The personal organs that became outstanding and long-standing, were not the most rabid and unrelenting word-fighters; for we usually noticed that the more intense the feeling displayed, and the more radical the language used, the nearer was "the hook" extended from the wings to snatch the performer from the stage of action. But the editors who did not take themselves too seriously, who did not expect nor try to "overcome all evil" in a day, and who really admired a good retaliation or come-back in an adversary, and who wrote themselves most deeply into their papers in the form of "homey" gossip and philosophy, kindly hints and suggestions, tinctured with plenty of good humor, are the "boys" who were permitted by public sentiment to grow up in the business!

Most of the personal editors at one time or another, ran pell mell down the lane of their editorial columns smack into a libel suit, or more frequently, into that quicker and "hurtier" obstacle—a sledge-hammer fist! (As evidence, note the frequency in the index of "libel" and "fighting"!) But the editor with a sense of justice and fair play, who willingly accepted the invitation of the midnight visitors to accompany them on a hazing expedition to a ducking place in the river, either became a good sport, a better citizen, and a wiser newspaper man, or he disappeared beyond the horizon, calling vile names over his shoulder as he ran! These are references to actual incidents reported in the text that follows!

Gunshot wounds, broken bones, coats of tar and feathers, blazing night-time duels, imprisonments, conflicts and quarrels galore are also reported in the following pages—all in the name of a free press and a free speech, too freely interpreted! (For emphasis, note in the index "Vigilantes", "tar and feathers", "banished", and so forth.) Personal combats were looked upon as necessary discipline, and frequently the recipient editor lived to tell the tale in his own paper! Also at one time in the 1880's, when feeling was running especially high, a Salt Lake newspaper "congratulates its contemporaries in Zion who have libel suits on their hands. Like the diseases of childhood—measles, mumps and the like—they seem to be necessary to tone down the gushing utterances of precocious infantiles!"

10

Usually, however, the editors defined their policies with precision, as if it were a virtue for the newspaper to be Republican, Democratic, Independent, Mormon or Anti-Mormon, and to be bitterly opposed to all other factions and groups in the community; and they set out to espouse these causes with vigor, and with prejudice, placing themselves at the head of imaginary armies, battling for the principles outlined on the newspaper masthead!

The columns of the pioneer newspapers were said to be bright or spicy, dull or commonplace, depending on how daring or timid the editor might be. But since most persons in the community were usually found (sometimes before it was too late!) to be either prospective subscribers or advertisers, discretion came to dictate that the editor's venom, sarcasm or other "spice" be sprinkled chiefly upon contemporaneous publishers, or upon vaguely defined "principles." Usually the greatest applause for these contestants came from far-away exchanges, with no money to spend! As a consequence, the editor was sometimes easily misled into addressing himself to the wrong audience. Thus the real freedom of speech of those early days became the father of the libel laws on the books today!

Many a new editor has gone in with a new heart and a new determination to succeed, where another with similar determination— aye, and possibly with more ability—was giving up the struggle. The real bitter heart-aching story of the downs and ups, especially the downs, can never be fully told; nor would the chief sufferer wish them told, significant and helpful as they might be to others, anymore than a sufferer would wish to re-live a dreadful illness. (For emphasis, consult "suicide" in the index!) Many newspapers were doomed to fail from the start, by the braggadocio, half-preparedness of the would-be editor, and his willingness to let everyone concerned take a chance with him for the rent, print paper, ink, and other necessaries; and thus the biggest news of the community often never got into the newspapers—that is, when the newspapers got out!

Country newspapers are different today, largely because the country editor tries to make his newspaper in some respects a miniature of the metropolitan "big brother." His personal prejudices are engulfed, and he very wisely displays a minimum of personal attributes that would set him apart from Mr. Merganthaler's robot in the back room. But if you had thought such a policy would not pay, just compute the tenure of the existing editors today—averaging two or three times as long as in any period in the past!

DESERET NEWS.

BY W. RICHARDS.   G. S. L. CITY, DESERET, JUNE 15, 1850.   VOL. 1.--NO. 1.

LAT. 40° 45' 44" LON. 111° 26' 34"

PROSPECTUS.
DESERET NEWS.

Motto—"Truth and Liberty."

We propose to publish a small weekly sheet, as large as our local circumstances will permit, to be called "*Deseret News*," designed originally to record the passing events of our State, and in connexion, refer to the arts and sciences, embracing general education, medicine, law, divinity, domestic and political economy, and every thing that may fall under our observation, which may tend to promote the best interest. welfare, pleasure and amusement of our fellow citizens.

We hold ourselves responsible to the highest Court of truth for our intentions, and the highest Court of equity for our execution. When we speak, we shall speak freely, without regard to men or party, and when, like other men, we err, let him who has his eyes open, correct us in meekness, and he shall receive a disciple's reward.

We shall ever take pleasure in communicating foreign news as we have opportunity; in receiving communications from our friends, at home and abroad; and solicit ornaments for the "*News*" from our poets and poetesses.

The first number may be expected as early in June as subscriptions will warrant—waiting the action of 300 subscribers.

Terms, 6 months, $2,50; *invariably in advance.*

Single copy, 15 cents.

Advertising, $1,50 per square lines, and 50 each succeeding insertion. $1 for half square, or 8 lines.

Travellers and Emigrants, 25 cents per copy, with the insertion of their names, place of residence, time of arrival and leaving.

Companies of 20, and upwards, entered at once, 20 cents each.

A paper that is worth printing, is worth preserving; if worth preserving, it is worth binding; for this purpose we issue in pamphlet form; and if every subscriber shall preserve each copy of the "News," and bind it at the close of the volume, their children's children may read the doings of their fathers, which otherwise might have been forgotten; ages to come.

U. S. SENATE.

"Sketch of debate," in the Senate, for Feb. 6, 8, 12, inclusive, 1850, on the Right of Petition; represent Messrs. Seward, Hale & Chase as chief speakers. Mr. Mangum presented the proceedings of a meeting at Wilmington, N. C., denouncing the fanaticism of the North, threatening a dissolution of the Union, in a certain contingency, &c.—Laid on the table.— Several petitions were presented by Mr. Hale, from various sections, "for promotion of the abolition of slavery; improving the condition of the free people of color; to prevent the increase of slavery by the non-admission of new States into the Union; for abolishing slavery in the District of Columbia; to prevent the introduction of slavery in the Territories; to prevent internal slave trade between the States; and respectfully ask Congress to propose, without delay, some plan for the immediate and peaceful dissolution of the American Union."

The Germantown ladies address Congress, as "Dear Friends," and after an appropriate prayer, "we bid you an affectionate farewell." Many joined the above gentlemen in debate, which was generally warm, criminative and recriminative; somewhat dramatic, with some symptoms of the tragic.

Query; If the people, the whole people, want the Union peacefully dissolved, why not dissolve it? Why ask Congress to do a thing they have no power to do? Congress did not make the Union; the Union made Congress, and the people made the Union; consequently, on the principles of federal republicanism, the same power that makes must unmake, if unmade at all; and if the Union is ever peacefully dissolved, it will be by the sovereign people who made it; for they alone possess the rightful power of dissolution within themselves, and not in their Senators or Representatives; and we hope we shall never again hear of any portion of the American people petitioning Congress to do what it has no power to do, even if it had the disposition. Let our Union remain forever, peacefully!

TERRIBLE FIRE IN SAN FRANCISCO.

An appalling and destructive fire occurred on the 24th of December, which threatened for a time to reduce the famous city of San Francisco to a heap of smoking ruins. The fire broke out in Dennison's Exchange, and in two hours, nearly a million of dollars worth of property was destroyed The Parker House was among the buildings burned. All the buildings, except the Delmonico Hotel, on Portsmouth square, and all on Washington street, commencing at the "Eldorado," and running to Montgomery street, were burned.

The Parker House, U. S. Restaurat, Exchange, Eldorado, Merchant's Exchange, Our House, Central House, Washington Arcade, Pollard & Co. Auction Room, Guerschard & Van Buren's Establishment, and many more valuable buildings were burned, or blown up, to stop the progress of the fire.

12

Foreword

This monograph on the activities of Utah's pioneer newsmen, and the fortunes of their editorial "other-selves" (the newspapers), was initiated with the lurking belief it might yield a few "man-bites-dog" stories of unique interest; and it is gratifying to have found those expectations far more than fulfilled. The men-who-bite-dogs do not always report their achievements, nor confine their doings to the biting of dogs; consequently this interesting research has unwittingly opened an entirely new field of pioneer endeavor—a fresh and intriguing chapter in the history of the far West, which depicts its greatest activity within the Utah State boundary lines.

Restricted as was this project, to Early Utah Newspapers, only the merest mention of personnel and paper changes since 1900 has been permissible. There also remain untold a great many tales and legends in the memories of early newspapermen still living, which we could not here reproduce. Also, the remarkable stories of the state's printing establishments are yet to be told—of the quaint old time hand presses first used; of the steam and gasoline power successors, and finally the magnificent electrical typesetting and press running equipment of today owned by the country weeklies, with auxiliary job printing establishments that are the show places of the town!

Little effort has been made to trace the many tangled ownerships— the names of local citizens, banks, merchants, politicians, friends and even enemies who have held minor interests, if not the upper hand. Though invisible, this influence has sometimes swung suspended like the Sword of Damocles above the head of "Ye Modest Ed." It is therefore a charity to omit these names—a kindness alike to the editor who is openly supposed to own the paper, and to the banker who equally ardently wishes he didn't.

In those days, a contemporary newspaper was an important visitor in the newspaper office, and made up much of the news. Had it not been so, much of this present history could not have been written, because of the dearth of newspaper files. When a Utah County newspaper suspended, and courteously notified its exchanges to drop it from their "Ex" lists, at least thirty editors "noticed" the demise with tender and touching editorials. It was an unwritten law of the fraternity that a newspaper birth or death should be acknowledged. What editor knew how soon he would be cribbing news from it, or missing it when it was gone—or how soon he himself might exist only in the kindly plaudits of his contemporaries! In the spirit of the fraternity it was practically mandatory that every newspaper be on the mailing list of every other newspaper—that the network of exchanges be complete. The receipt of a new paper was tantamount to a request to be placed on the exchange list; and friend or foe, it went as faithfully as if paid for!

While Salt Lake City has always been a fertile spot for newspapers, and supported five dailies back in 1885, with only one-fifth its present population, and Beaver with only 1,700 population at one time supported three newspapers, several towns of 1,500 to 4,000 population remained without papers. "They're no good," an old timer told us; "The newspaper asks us for the news, prints it, and then asks us to buy it!" And maybe that is why his town of 2,000 population has never had a newspaper of its own.

The Printer's Auxiliary for September 7, 1897, says: "We shall expect to see newspapers established in the other thirty towns in the State that are all larger than Randolph, and without papers. It is a surprising fact that there are 21 towns in Utah, each with a population of from one to three thousand, without an established newspaper. In no other state in the Union are there nine county seat towns that are newspaperless!"

Nevertheless more than 1,200 editors and publishers are named in the ensuing text, counting neither "Devils" nor "Darlings." And be it remembered that a very large percentage of the 585 publications mentioned herein, were manned, front office and back, by one omnipresent person! More than a hundred of these journals are credited to Salt Lake City, fifty to Ogden, twenty-five to Provo, and twelve to Beaver! Sketches of 326 papers are given herewith, not counting seventy newspapers that have come and gone since the World War!

The labor involved in the gathering and preparation of the material for this monograph proved to be so prodigious it would have been abandoned when its intricacies first appeared, had it been in production for profit, even though it promised best seller prospects! And it would not have been completed as a labor of love, had all its proportions and problems been revealed at one time. Begun five or six years ago, at which time most of the work was done and many of the cuts were made, the work was stalemated for four years, due to the curtailment of the Society's regularly appropriated funds.

To accomplish the task of compiling this work, every book of history, travel, biography, diary, gazetteer and directory in print was gleaned for references, including scores of photostat pages from volumes available only in distant respositories. Every city and town in Utah that has now or ever has had a newspaper, was visited, and from a few hours to several days time were spent searching the existing newspaper files and canvassing the place for a look at stray volumes or single copies of old newspapers and interviewing old settlers.

Every column of every Utah newspaper still preserved has thus been minutely examined for material concerning the Utah newspapers themselves, and mention of their contemporaries.

The pursuit of this history has been a fascinating lure, following long forgotten trails strewn with comedy, drama, and with tragedy; but nearly all the trails have discouragingly frayed out and ended like an old road in the desert. To reconstruct the history of a newspaper without its files, is like writing the biography of a man long dead, with no relatives or friends left in the land!

14

The old newspaper files, like the human lives they represent, are precious beyond valuation, for they cannot be replaced; and within their aging covers are the records of the chief events of every person that ever lived in the community, from the birth to the funeral—besides the stories in intimate detail of every event of public importance in the history of the town and country. It is one of the tragedies of the newspaper business in Utah, that less than five per cent of the papers existing prior to 1900 left any files whatsoever! May Heaven bless the precious tomes at Logan, Park City, Heber, Manti and elsewhere; and may the Fire Demon ever be baffled in the presence of such historical treasures!

The brief story of each newspaper's inception, progress and demise as presented in this work, is almost exclusively restricted to the documentary evidences uncovered in this search, all duly quoted and credited, with but a slender thread of connecting comment. There were altogether between 8,000 and 9,000 separate original items, consisting of about 350,000 words, from which the material in these pages has been condensed.

Acknowledgment of valued assistance is gratefully given to the many institutions and individuals mentioned at appropriate places in the text. The members of the Society's Board of Control have all been very patient, kind and helpful, especially Dr. Wm. J. Snow, Wm. R. Palmer, and Herbert S. Auerbach. Dr. Snow conceived the original idea for this monograph, and as President, promoted the plan. Many relatives and friends of early editors kindly furnished pictures and newspapers; and especially helpful privileges were accorded by the Public Librarians in Salt Lake City, Ogden, Provo and Brigham City, Utah, and New York, N. Y.; and by the Tribune-Telegram, Deseret News, and University of Utah Librarians in Salt Lake City, and the Bancroft Library, Berkeley, and the Library of Congress, Washington.

Others deserving special mention are H. Lorenzo Reid, at Dixie College, St. George, for the use of his remarkable collection of early southern Utah newspapers; John E. Jones, of the Western Newspaper Union, in Salt Lake City, for access to important records and historical material; Andrew Jenson for halftone cuts, and access to foreign language newspaper material; Alvin F. Smith and A. William Lund of the L. D. S. Church Historian's Office Library, who placed many precious newspaper files at our disposal, and assisted with reproductions. My last acknowledgment of indebtedness is to my wife, Jennie G. Alter, without whose capable and untiring assistance the original notes could not have been compiled.

J. CECIL ALTER

Salt Lake City,
August, 1938.

ALBERT CARRINGTON
Born January 8, 1813
Died September 19, 1899

ELIAS SMITH
Born September 6, 1804
Died June 24, 1888

The First Deseret News Building (with smoke) looking Northeast at Hotel Utah Corner—June 15, 1850. "Council House" under construction at right.

—From Stansbury's Great Salt Lake.

16

Early Utah Journalism

ALTA, Salt Lake County

Population 1873, about 800 in winter, 1,500 in summer; since 1905,
none to 25, approximately.

Alta Daily Independent. First issue, Saturday evening, May 3,
1873; 4 pages, 4 columns; every evening except Sunday; $8 per
annum; Kenner & Edmiston, editors and proprietors. No copies found.
A prospectus was circulated in March, promising the first number about
April 5, 1873. The paper was "as lifey and spicy as two enterprising
young men accustomed to the business can make it," said the Salt Lake
Tribune, May 6, 1873. It has "symptoms of vitality rarely seen in a
premature bantling," added the Salt Lake Herald, May 7, 1873; and
"It presents a neat, typographical appearance," commented the Deseret
News that evening.

Almost immediately followed the untimely epitaph in the Salt
Lake Daily Journal of May 27, 1873; "The Alta Independent has
gone the way of such ventures. Whom the Gods love, die young!" And
a kindly eulogy in the Deseret News of June 2, 1873: "We understand
that the Alta Independent, after a somewhat limited probation, has
ceased to breathe. Alta is too small, too young, or too something else
to support a newspaper." The final contemporary reference is in the
Salt Lake Journal of June 10, 1873, "The material of the Alta Independent is to be sold at constable sale. Parties are ready to buy it and
start a tri-weekly paper."

Editor Kenner wrote in the Wasatch Wave (Heber), March 3,
1889: "It is a great thing to run a newspaper . . . I remember having
a paper up in the summits of the Wasatch range at Alta . . . and the
people became so attached to it, I couldn't raise enough money to lift
the attachment. It is probably there yet."

About seventy-five business houses are listed at Alta in the 1874
State Gazetteer, including a drug store, four clothing stores, five groceries, six hotels, fifteen saloons and a shooting gallery. The railroad
to Alta was completed in May, 1873 and the mining camp seemed like
good newspaper territory, consequently another rose up at once.

The Cottonwood Observer. First issue Saturday morning, July
12, 1873, four tall pages, five columns, a semi-weekly, published
every Wednesday and Saturday morning, by R. Webb and H. Simcockes at $5 a year "with malice toward none, with charity for all,
and with firmness in the right," evidently not realizing that the good
die young as recently stated. The Bancroft Library has the only num-

bers in existence, dated July 16, 19, 26, and 30, 1873, being numbers
2, 3, 5, and 6.   Advertising patronage was drawn from Alta, Granite,
Sandy, Salt Lake City, and San Francisco to support front page fiction
features, appropriate to that region: "Blue Ridge Bandits" and "The
Touching Romance of Lady LaVere."   The editors explain (July 16)
"owing to press of advertisements, we are compelled to hold over our
editorial remarks and several contributions.   Advertisers will receive
notice in our next."

   There were no geologists' advertising cards but: "Mrs. A. Johnson, Colorado Lodging house, clairvoyant, gives descriptions, ledges,
samples of ore, etc."   True to promise the editor in the July 19th issue,
gave a column or so on "Life in Alta" describing the personal and business intimacies of the people, more especially the advertisers, being
reading-notices, par excellence!   The non-paying news was of this
type: "Street Organ: A street organ has made its appearance in the
streets of Alta.   A crippled Italian is the proprietor, who thus publicly
appeals to the charity of the people.   On Thursday he made his debut
and collected a large crowd, attracted more from curiosity than anything else."

   The community was new—new on the map, and its people new
to one another; hence they were unamalgamated, and probably duly
secretive about their mines, their finds, their fortunes and misfortunes;
hence the diminishing amount of news run in the Observer from a
notable dearth in the beginning.   "We wish the Observer a more fortunate career than fell the lot of its predecessor, the Alta Independent,"
was a sendoff repeated July 19th, from the Salt Lake Tribune.   But
editor Simcockes had evidently traded out the clairvoyant advertising
account and promptly disappeared.   Richard Webb became editor and
publisher July 26, 1873.

   The news caught by the Webb was mostly from outside of Alta,
showing where he had been in search of it; and it may be noted that
three kinds of meat were advertised as follows: "The Cricket Saloon
at Sandy," "The Sandy Meat Market," and "The Granite Trout House."
The issue of July 30th may have been the last one; it certainly was
the last one an editor would wish to produce of the kind, for there
were but a few stickfuls of news and no new advertising cards.   Thus
the record closes, and the expressed hopes of the Salt Lake Herald
were not realized, of gleaning a wealth of interesting news from the
columns of the Alta newspaper!

AMERICAN FORK, Utah County

Population: 1890, 1,942; 1900, 2,732; 1910, 2,797; 1920, 2,732; 1930, 3,047.

   Weekly Gazette (Pen-and-Ink-manuscript form).   The Salt Lake
Telegraph, March 11, 1868, says: "From American Fork.   We are
pleased to receive number 12 of the American Fork Weekly Gazette,
edited by Brother R. G. Eccles.   It is published in neat manuscript.   Its

KIRK ANDERSON'S VALLEY TAN.

BY KIRK ANDERSON. EIGHT DOLLARS IN ADVANCE.

VOLUME 1. GREAT SALT LAKE CITY, U. T., FRIDAY, DECEMBER 24, 1858. NUMBER 8.

THE VALLEY TAN.

IS PUBLISHED EVERY FRIDAY BY

KIRK ANDERSON.

TERMS:

Single copy for one year, $8, invariably in advance.

Toll the Bell for Lilla Dale.

My Lilla dear is sleeping
'Neath the old chestnut tree
The spot where oft she wandered,
When innocent and free.
The wild rose and the myrtle
Still cluster round the spot;
But my heart's filled with sorrow,
And lonely is my lot.

Chorus.
Toll, toll the bell, for gentle Lilla Dale,
And let its tones echo through the vale;
Our Lilla dear we've lost, so loving, kind and true;
Sing to-day one sad lay—lost Lilla Dale!

'Tis spring; the birds are warbling
A sad and mournful tale.
Of beauty once so blooming,
Now lying cold and pale.
The streamlet ripples onward,
So quiet through the vale;
The wild rose drops a dewy tear
For earth-lost Lilla Dale.

Chorus.—Toll, toil the bell, &c.

My Lilla dear, I'm watching;
O! wilt thou never come,
To greet me with a blessing
From thy far, angel home?
My sad heart now is aching,
With heavy care oppressed;
O! may I quickly greet thee,
In that pure land of rest!

Chorus.—Toll, toll the bell, &c.

The Triumphs of Peace.

The following passage will be read with interest at the present time, when the whole civilized world is exulting over the greatest scientific victory of the age. It is extracted from a speech of that eminent and far-seeing statesman, John C. Calhoun, in the Senate of the United States, March 16th, 1846, on the bill for terminating the joint occupancy of Oregon Territory. After using many weighty objections to an appeal to arms for the settlememt of the question, Mr. Calhoun drew a vivid picture of the marvelous progress of the arts of peace, which would be arrested by war:

But I have still higher reasons. I am opposed to war as a friend of human improvement, to human civilization, to human progress and advancement. Never in the history of the world has there occurred a period so remarkable as the peace which followed the battle of Waterloo for the great advances made in the condition of human society. The chemical and mechanical powers have been investigated and applied to increase the comforts of human life in a degree far beyond what was ever known or hoped before. Civilization has been spreading its influence far and wide, and the general progress of human society has outstripped all that has been previously witnessed. The invention of man has seized upon and subjugated two great agencies of the natural world which were never before made the servants of man. I refer to steam and electricity, under which, of course, I include magnetism in all its phenomena.

Steam has been controlled and availed of for all the purposes of human intercourse, and by its resistless energies has brought nations together whom Nature seemed to seperate by insurmountable barriers. It has shortened the passage across the Atlantic more than one half, while the rapidity of traveling on land has been three times greater than was ever known before. Within the same time man has chained the very lightning of Heaven, and brought it down and made it administer to the transmission of human thought, insomuch that it may with truth be said that our ideas are not only transmitted with he rapidity of lightning, but by lightning itself. Magic wires are stretching themselves in all directions over the earth, and when their mystic meshes shall at length have been perfected our globe itself will be endowed with a sensitiveness which will render it impossible to touch it on any one point and the touch not be felt from one end of the world to the other. * * * And this work is as yet but commenced; it is but the breaking of the dawn of the world's jubilee. It promises a day of more refinement, more intellectual brightness, more moral elevation, and consequently of more human felicity than the world has ever seen from its creation.

The Late Flogging by an Army Officer.

A few days since we copied from a Texas paper a statement respecting a person who had been sevevely flogged by order of Lieut. Barton, of the U. S. Army. The Alexandria Gazette now publishes a statement, which, if true, places the transaction in a far different light. The following are the particurlars:

About two months previous to the flogging, the man who was flogged, Heid by name, (not Head,) a German by birth, and a private in the band of the 1st. Infantry, in which Lieut. Barton was adjutant, was tried by Court Martial for disobedience of orders, convicted, and punished. On receiving his discharge, he engaged his seat in the mail ambulance for San Antonio; but, just before starting, he armed himself with a six shooter and a bowie knife, and stole into the quarters of the band, where the Corporal who had reported him was writing.

Heid reminded the Corporal of his trial, and, without provocation, seized him by his hair of the head, pulled him back on the bed, thence to the floor, beat him with his fist, and stamped on him. The Corporal was a feeble old man, while Heid is a young, athletic fellow. For this Heid, who had fled, was captured tied and whipped, receiving thirty lashes, which did not draw one drop of blood, and instead of being confined to his bed for three weeks, he overtook the mail ambulance that same day, at a distance of eighteen miles. Lieut. Barton, was tried before a jury composed principally of Germans, Heid's countrymen, convicted and fined as before stated, which fine was remitted by the Governor, on the facts of the case being made known to him, but only to be mulct in much higher damages by a civil court, unless the verdict is set aside by a higher court:

The Gazette justifies Lieut. Barton's conduct, on the ground of the lawlessness of the population, and the notoriety of the fact that soldiers have been beaten and treated in the most shameful manner, and even killed, for which not one conviction has been had, and asks, what non-commissioned officer would perform his duty, if discharged soldiers, in this lawless frontier country, should be permitted to assault and beat them with impunity?

☞ Patience is a tree whose roots are bitter—but the fruit is very sweet.

[*Card from Postmaster Weller.*]

Mails to the Atlantic.

Editors Alta: As a matter of public information and general interest, will you please announce in your paper that hereafter I shall dispatch from this office on the 5th and 20th of each month, a mail *via* Tehuantepec to New Orleans.

I am directed by the Postmaster General to request writers of letters destined to places in the Atlantic States, to endorse thereon the route by which they wish them sent, as to-wit: "*via* Los Angelos, Overland;" "*via* Salt Lake, Overland;" "*via* Tehuantepec."

Letters with no such endorsements upon them, and all newspapers, will be sent "*via* Panama."

Three cents will pay the postage on a single letter "*via* Overland" as far as Chicago, Ill., and Cincinnatti, Ohio. Beyond these points the postage will be ten cents.

Newspapers throughout the State will do the public a favor by inserting this in their columns.

C. L. WELLER, Postmaster.

San Francisco Post Office, Nov. 15th, 1858.

Miner's Meeting at Lower Agua Frio.

A meeting of miners in the Agua Frio District, [illegible] Saloon, on Saturday evening, Nov. 20, 1858, at which Jas. McCrory was chosen chairman and Sam. W. Smith appointed Secretary.

Mr. Giltner stated the object of the meeting and offered the following preamble and resolutions, which were unanimously adopted.

Believing that we, as miners, have certain rights granted us by the General Government with regard to the working of the mines in California therefore be it *Resolved*, That we, the miners of the Agua Frio District, *will* always maintain the *privilege* to make our own laws and regulations without consulting the miners or other districts.

Further be it *Resolved*, That we *will enforce* our laws and regulations until new ones are regularly instituted by a majority of the miners in the district.

Resolved,, That the regulation and mining law of our district, which has been in vogue for two years and a half, prohibiting Chinamen from working within our district, and not allowing white men to work them, *shall* still be the law and rule in this district,

Resolved, If any Chinese stop within the district for the purpose of mining, they *must* leave within forty-eight hours, after being notified by at least three miners; if not, the miners in the locality or district shall compel them to leave and inflict such punishment as they may deem proper.

Resolved, That the above laws of our mining district shall hold good for one year and longer if not repealed.

Resolved, That after this the Chinese question shall be acted upon, once every fall in this district.

Resolved, That we will always abide by the decisions of a majority of the regular placer miners in the district.

It was then moved that a committee of five be appointed to warn the Chinamen, who are now on the creek, to leave—which was unanimously adopted.

The following gentlemen were appointed said committee—Messrs. Purdy, White, Paix, Alexander and Allen. On motion, the meeting adjourned.

JAS. McCRORY, Chairman.

Sam. W. Smith, Secretary.—*Mariposa Star.*

Man Drowned.—On the afternoon of last Tuesday [26th ult.] as Lieut. Collins, who has been stationed on the Klamath Reservation, was moving down the coast with his command, he met with an accident in crossing the mouth of the big lagoon, above Trinidad. He had twenty seven in his command, all of whom were some distance ahead of him, and crossed in safety before the tide came up. He started over, accompanied by his lady, being himself on one side of her, and having one of his men on the other. Although several seas broke over them, the animals stood firm, and Mrs. Collins holding fast to her saddle, kept her seat, and the party crossed in safety. Whitman, with the animals, twelve in number, five of which were carried into the lagoon, and two were lost. Mr. Whitman's animal was carried in among the number, and he was drowned. He was from Crescent City, and had charge of the train which was moving the command down. Lieut. Collins sent men back to search for his body, but had not learned yesterday evening whether it had been recovered or not.

Aid for the Stockton Route.—We are happy to learn that the gallant Gen. Clarke, Commander in Chief of the Pacific Department, has ordered four companies of the Sixth Infantry, 240 men, to the Mojave country, where they will be of great service in protecting the mails between Stockton and Kansas City [illegible] as our [illegible] them, will be taught a lesson that they will be likely to remember, and travelers on our route in future will be free from annoyance from them. It is rather hard upon soldiers, who after a long and severe march have arrived in comfortable quarters, to post them off 400 miles into a wilderness, but the army is small and the U. S. territory large, and there is no help for it. We are not advised who will be in command, or whether they will proceed by way of Stockton or Los Angelos to their place of destination. Two other companies are ordered to San Bernardino, one to San Diego, one to Humboldt and two will be stationed at the San Francisco Presidio.

[*San Joaquin Republican.*

The Crossing at Tehauntepec.—A correspondent of the Union, writing from Ventosa, Nov. 3d, forwards us the following intelligence in relation to the Isthmus route:

We arrived here on the steamer Oregon yesterday, and leave this morning for Acapulco, with twelve passengers and mails from New Orleans. The passengers from New Orleans left that city Oct. 27th, at 10 a. m., and arrived at Minititlan on the 30th at 12 m. From Minititlan to Suchel is ninety-three miles by the river Coatzacoalcos, which they traveled in nine hours. From Suchel to Ventosa is 116 miles, which they made in twenty-five hours. They all speak in glowing terms of the route.

A portion of the route was made with mules, which arrangement will soon be changed.

In a short time measures will be taken to give several hundred persons convenient passage.

Bordering on the Personal.—The editor of the *Constitutionalist*, published at Doniphan, K. T., pitched into the editor of a Black Republican sheet after the following manner:

The editor of the *Chief* wishes us to bring him into notice, but we do not wish to pollute our columns with such trash, unless forced to do so. We would gently hint to the cross-eyed, crank-sided, peaked and long razor-nosed, blue-mouthed, nigger-lipped, white-eyed, soft-headed, long-eared, crane-necked, blobber-lipped, squeaky-voice, empty-headed, snaggle-toothed, filthy-mouthed, boxancled, pigeon-toed, reel-footed, ignoble Black Republican, abolition editor to attend to his own affairs, or we will pitch into him in earnest.

A Profitable Forty Acre Farm.—To show what "much labor on little land" accomplishes, we present a brief statement drawn from the Hampshire County (Mass.,) Agricultural Society's Transactions, there given in the statement of Mr. Stebbins, of South Deerfield, on entering his farm for the premium of the Society.

The farm in question contains 41 acres, ten of it worn-out sandy land, when it came into his possesion, over twenty years ago. But he "resolved to have a better farm." To this sandy field (three acres the first year) he applied clay at the rate of fifty loads per acre, followed by twentyfive loads of manure and 200 lbs. of plaster. This was all ploughed in together, the land planted to corn, and a fair crop was the result. After corn, oats were sown, and the ground seeded to clover. By the use of clay and manure," he says, "I have made all my land as good as the best, and increased my pasture one hundred per cent., in quantity and quality of product." [illegible]

As to deep plowing, he finds [illegible] soil plow.—He turns under his manure four or five inches deep, and then subsoils the bottom of the furrow as deeply as possible.—Corn is planted two years in succession, the better to mix soil and manure and to fit the land for grass, and he now sows barley instead of oats, as a more profitable crop.

The secret of his succuss lies in the fact that instead of one hundred loads of manure, as formerly, he now makes three hundred and fifty loads, supplying his yards freely with absorbent earths, and using salt, lime and plaster to a considerable extent.

In 1854, the products of the forty-one acre farm, in the usual farm crops, were worth a fraction under $1,000, and the net profits $1.116 75. There were twenty-three acres in mowing; thirteen acres in corn and potatoes, three in barley and two in wheat. The reader may here see that a large farm is not essential to profitable management.—*Telegraph.*

Spicy.—One of the young ladies of Jefferson Female College, in a composition prepared for a recent occasion of public exercise in that institution, indulged her pen and hearers in a spicy paragraph something like the following:

"*Common sense*'—Surely there never was a greater misnomer, since it seems to be the most *uncommon* kind of sense. When I graduate, and get my diploma, I intend establishing an Acadamy in which Common Sense shall be the only branch taught. Both ladies and gentlemen shall be eligible to participotion in the benefits of this institution. Charges moderate,—as much so as the procurement of an ample store of good advice will allow; and since this commodity is so often to be had gratis, parents need have no fears of ruinous bills. Tobacco positively eschewed. Punsters shall be *pun*-ished with the utmost rigor known to the tan. Young ladies who sail into this Common Sense Academy looking like a small schooner under a heavy press of canvass, may sail in at the front door and out at the back, provided the navigation is not too much obstructed. All lessons will be illustrated and enforced by brilliant lectures from the [illegible]".

Courtesy L. D. S. Church Historian's Office Library

pages are filled with instructive and interesting matter, comprehending the scientific, useful, and amusing, such as: "An Essay on Astronomy; Original Poetry by J. Crystal; Local Items; .Wit and Humor; and Various Selected Matter."

American Fork Independent began March 21, 1890; every Friday; $2 a year. J. F. Bledsoe and James McCoard, publishers. Only one copy found, (in personal file of A. F. Gaisford, Jr.) June 13, 1890, 4 pages, 6 columns, plus 2-page supplement, all home print. American Fork Independent Publishing Co., McCoard & Riddell. It contains more inches of advertising than of home news, much if not most of both relating to the mines in American Fork Canyon. The paper is said to have been printed on an Army press.

"The paper is small in dimensions but large in expectations," said the Provo Daily Enquirer, March 24, 1890. Then, "Dr. Ed. Isaacson, editor of the American Fork Independent . . . has bright hopes for the future of his paper, which was shortly issued twice a week," the Enquirer reported further May 3, 1890. "We think it is a very creditable paper," says the Home Sentinel, Manti, May 28, 1890. "Mr. Heskel of Grand Junction has purchased the American Fork Independent" says the Provo Enquirer, July 5, 1890. "He will take charge about July 15th."

Still another change is indicated: "The American Fork Independent under its new management, is a great improvement . . . and will hereafter give a great deal of attention to mining matters," says the Park (City) Record, May 2, 1891, doubtless quoting an Independent statement. "Mr. Pribyl, the new editor and proprietor of the American Fork Independent is a thorough and experienced newspaper man and is getting out a good paper," we learn from the Provo Enquirer, May 13, 1891. The Price Telegraph states November 20, 1891, that "The American Fork Independent reached us in a new dress last week, as a 7-column folio." A. F. Gaisford's notes say John F. Pribyl purchased the plant and in 1892 moved it to Corinne. The Heber Herald of March 14, 1892 closes the record: "The American Fork Independent has discontinued—another case of journalism unappreciated."

American Fork Item: 8 pages, 4 columns, every Saturday, $1.25 a year; date of first issue not ascertained. "The American Fork Item is the latest thing in newspaperdom," says the Bingham Bulletin, September 23, 1893. "It is an independent weekly, published by M. L. Scott. It starts out without one 'ad' from the business men of the town, to whom the paper comes as a surprise, no patronage having been solicited. We trust American Fork's new paper will meet with more liberal patronage than the several which today lie in restless graves." The American Newspaper Directory for 1896 shows: "Dunkley & Scott, editors and publishers." The Item was occasionally quoted by its exchanges, we noticed, as late as February 8, 1896, but no copies were found. The next and last news concerning it is in the

Wasatch Wave (Heber) of April 24, 1896: "The American Fork Item has again changed hands and the new man at the helm has changed the name of the paper to: . . . . **American Fork World**": q.v. (table).

The Advance. First issue, April 25, 1901; 8 pages, 5 columns, 4 home print, every Thursday, John R. Wallis, editor and proprietor. "It will be a paper of the people and for the people" proclaims the editor in his Salutatory. "We hope the people will patronize us and encourage us, if our labors are found worthy of support." The Salina Sun says: "John R. Wallis, who formerly edited a bright little paper at St. George, and had to quit work because of poor health, is about to start a new paper at American Fork. We can't just exactly understand why editing a paper in American Fork can be more healthful than the same kind of slavery at St. George. This much we will say, however, for a sick man, John Wallis can do more and better newspaper work than some of the pencil pushers in Utah county who pose as intellectual giants."

Wallis ran an exceptionally fine newspaper for three months, the last number, July 11, 1901, bearing this Valedictory: "With this issue The Advance will retire. We regret to make this announcement, but after publishing for 12 weeks at considerable loss, without making any headway with a subscription list, we have reluctantly come to the conclusion that it would avail nothing to publish any longer."

The Salina Sun of July 19, 1901, says: "American Fork, one of the largest towns in Utah county, has just demonstrated that it is the bummiest place in the State. Three months ago John R. Wallis, a good newspaper man, and a loyal Saint, a moral and upright fellow, started 'The Advance' at American Fork. . . . He put in an entirely new plant, and at once proceeded to issue one of the neatest and newsiest local papers in the State. It seems that John made an awful mistake. Last week The Advance closed down because of no patronage. . . . At any rate some one should take a bucket of black paint and a brush and blot out the name of American Fork from the map of Utah." And the Park Record of July 20, 1901, says: "American Fork has allowed its only newspaper, The Advance, to die of starvation at the tender age of 12 weeks. If you ever hear of a hearse running over anything that looks like a man, it is a 10-to-1 bet it hails from American Fork."

The Citizen was entered May 27, 1903, as second class mail matter. W. D. Loveless was proprietor May 30, 1908. In 1914 the paper included "The Lehi Department," and "The Pleasant Grove Department," both page-width headings. That made three headings for one newspaper! In 1915, L. W. Gaisford and S. W. Ross bought the hydraheaded sheet, rechristening at least one-third of it "The American Fork Citizen." Ross sold his interest to Gaisford in 1919, who thereupon became editor and manager. Gaisford's "Adieu" appeared November 24, 1923, when he was succeeded by A. F. Gaisford and A. F. Gaisford, Jr., the present publishers.

BEAVER, Beaver County

Population: 1870, 1,207; 1880, 1,732; 1890, 1,752; 1900, 1,701; 1910, 1,899; 1920, 1,827; 1930, 1,673.

It seems worthy of preliminary remark that more first-class, two-fisted, paying newspapers have flourished, and died with their boots on, in Beaver than in many other cities of several times the size. Moreover the Beaver newspapers, because of the isolation yet prominence of that city in the early history of the State, furnished to the city dailies and other exchanges more column inches by far than any other single set of news sources before the days of syndicates and press associations. It was a place of rival interests, particularly Mormon and Gentile. Thus each section of the population felt assured of the facts only in a newspaper published by its own people. There were mining and political interests galore. The John D. Lee trial for complicity in the Mountain Meadows Massacre was held in the United States court at Beaver; and Fort Cameron, a strongly garrisoned United States military post, for some years frowned upon the city. Dignitaries of note came and went as from a metropolis. Little wonder then, that opposing dailies, tri-weeklies and weeklies vied simultaneously with one another for patronage, while other Utah towns of much greater population permitted lone newspapers of high quality to starve!

"The Beaver Enterprise, is the name of a new Daily that has reached us," says the Salt Lake Herald, August 16, 1873. "It is a live-looking little paper, presents a neat appearance typographically, and is edited with considerable ability," by George W. Crouch; the Carrigan brothers were business managers. As there are no files, we must depend on the notices in exchanges for our history. The Salt Lake Tribune of September 13, 1873, credits a news item to the Enterprise.

Then something happened, for The Deseret News (Salt Lake City) of November 21, 1873, says: "We learn from A. M. Musser, Esq., that he received information over the Deseret Telegraph wire this morning that Mr. Joseph Field, and other prominent citizens of Beaver, had bought the Enterprise material; that the resumption of that paper commenced yesterday; and that it would be issued tri-weekly hereafter."

An advertisement in the St. George Enterprise, April 24, also July 10, 1874, says: "The Beaver Enterprise, an independent tri-weekly newspaper, published at Beaver City, U. T., by James Field, proprietor, and contains all the news and items of interest to southern Utah." The Salt Lake Tribune for December 29, 1874, (then anti-Mormon) says: "The Beaver Enterprise comes to us semi-occasionally, and every number announces a change of proprietors. The paper is a fossil concern, muzzled by the priesthood, and good Saints even sicken at the diet its columns furnish them. . . . An old friend, Daniel Tyler, comes to the surface again as editor of the delectable sheet. . . . He shook himself rid of this journalistic incubus a few months ago under the plea of

ill-health, but he is called to the helm again by his worshipful masters.
. . . This poor scribe does not start out with very brilliant expectations.
Hear his dolorous squeal: 'One of our principal typos having left,
whose place of necessity has to be filled by apprentices, should typographical errors occur, or an issue fail to appear in time, we trust
our patrons will bear with us' . . . . Like all other Church papers, there
is no revenue to the Enterprise office, and typos become starved out
and leave."

The American Newspaper Directory for 1875 says: "Beaver City
Enterprise; tri-weekly; Tuesdays, Thursdays and Saturdays; 4 pages;
size 20 by 24; subscription $6; established 1873. Beaver Publishing
Co., editors and publishers; circulation 533; only paper in southern
Utah; largely devoted to local and mining interests; good circulation in surrounding mining camps." The Deseret News, June 29,
1875, says: "Better late than never. The following items are from
the Beaver Enterprise of June 22, which was received this morning.
'Having disposed of an interest in the Enterprise to Mr. S. A. Kenner,
the paper will hereafter appear under his exclusive management. Mr.
K's labor commenced on this number. Jos. Field.' "

"The celebration of the Fourth at Beaver . . . Brother Kenner of
the Enterprise read the Declaration," we find in the Salt Lake Tribune,
July 10, 1875. The Deseret News, Friday, August 20, 1875, says:
"No. 1, Vol. 3, of the Beaver Enterprise 'enlarged and improved' came
to hand this morning." And the Utah Evening Mail (Salt Lake City)
January 12, 1876, says: "The Beaver Enterprise has finally resumed
again. Cause of delay, failure of the supply of paper." While the
Deseret News of January 28, 1876, adds: "Going ahead: The Beaver
Enterprise of January 22 came to hand with 28 columns, and boasting
5 months' paper on hand." On May 29, 1876, the Utah Evening Mail
says: "The idiot who dishes up the editorial hash for his victims at
Beaver, is at least consistent with his record as a tool of the priests
who own him." The American Newspaper Directory for 1876 gives
S. A. Kenner, editor, and Joseph Field, publisher; circulation 810.
"Only Democratic paper in Utah; only paper in southern Utah."

A new era is reported in the Deseret News January 29, 1877:
"The Beaver Enterprise is to be transformed into a daily and weekly
paper under the title of The Square Dealer. Mr. Joseph Field, the proprietor, recently bought the material of the Mail, formerly published
in this city." The Provo Enquirer puts it this way: February 14, 1877:
"We learn that a new paper will make its appearance, semi-weekly, in
Silver Reef, Leeds mining district. The first issue will begin on the
first of March; it will be called The Silver Age, and published by Mr.
Joseph Field, proprietor and publisher of the Beaver Enterprise. Mr.
Field is certainly an enterprising man, as well as a man of faith. He
will publish a Daily at Beaver called the Square Dealer and now con-
templates, in addition, to publish this semi-weekly in another place.
. . . The more the merrier!"

But the announcement was a little askew, for The Enterprise continued long after the birth of The Square Dealer. The Deseret News of March 10, 1877, says: "Acknowledging The Corn. The Beaver Enterprise of March 6 appears in mourning with rules reversed, stripe and stars upside down, and the spread-eagle also. The day previous the editor, in pursuance of a bet or agreement with Chas. M. Howard, on condition that Hayes became president, carried the U. S. Flag at half-mast, reversed and heavily creped, from The Sentinel office to the court house to a Dead March accompaniment, beaten by two office boys on snare drums." The Salt Lake Tribune of March 11, 1877 puts it: "From the appearance of the last number of the Beaver Enterprise, we should judge the fool-killer missed the editor of that sheet on his last trip south."

The Ogden Junction opines September 6, 1879: "The Beaver Enterprise wants to know when they are going to have 'some more theatrickles.' The only chance for the Beaverites to get their tric(k)les is to wait until it rains, and then stand under the eaves of their houses." It is possible The Enterprise was suspended during much of 1880, if not for a longer period; for we do not hear of it, and the Deseret News of August 7, 1880, begins the obituary notice of another paper, the Beaver Watchman, by saying: "Beaver City is now without a newspaper."

The Ogden Daily Herald, June 22, 1881, informs us: "No. 1 of Volume 10, of the Beaver Enterprise, published and edited by Mr. S. A. Kenner, has reached our table bearing the date of June 18. It is to be a semi-weekly publication, its tone and tendency being indicated in the following words of the publisher: 'The Enterprise is independent on all subjects, but is not prone to be neutral on any. It seeks no quarrels and shrinks from none. It is the organ of its editor but of no other man or class of men. It is sent to paid-up subscribers only.'" And on July 12, 1881, the Deseret News says: "The Beaver Enterprise is the neatest and spiciest paper in southern Utah." The News further says, July 21, 1881: "The Beaver Enterprise refers to the inhabitants of Greenville as Green villians!"; and August 18, 1881, the News says: "The Beaver Enterprise solicits notices of births, deaths and earthquakes!"

"Mr. Joseph Field has assumed the business management of the Beaver Enterprise," says the Ogden Daily Herald, December 14, 1881. And December 19th the Herald says: "Mr. Joseph Field of The Beaver Enterprise wants two girls to learn the noble art of typesetting." The Deseret News, January 30, 1882, says: "Mr. S. A. Kenner, editor of the Beaver Enterprise is in town;" and March 11: "The Beaver Enterprise reaches us very much reduced in size, looking as if its financial status was in a similar situation. We are sorry to see it so dreadfully attenuated." And March 13, 1882: "The Beaver Enterprise is now issued as a daily, which is the reason for the diminution of its proportions." That same date the Ogden Daily Herald says: "The Beaver Enterprise

ELI B. KELSEY
Born October 27, 1819
Died March 27, 1885

E. L. T. HARRISON
Born March 27, 1830
Buried May 23, 1900

Third home of Deseret News (upstairs). From 1862-1902 (site of Hotel Utah).

Courtesy L. D. S. Bureau of Information

having expired in a semi-comatose, we mean semi-weekly condition, it is resuscitated as a daily. 'Essay Caigh' is irrepressible." (Essay Caigh was Scipio Africanus Kenner's pen name.) March 21, 1882, the Herald adds: "Says the Beaver Enterprise: 'Abbreviation is our motto.' Maybe; but spelling would be a better one to begin with."

John F. Tolton's History of Beaver says that Uncle Joe Field, the village boot, shoe and harness maker, also merchant and public hall owner, ran his newspapers in his spare time. Tolton says of Field's "Enterprise": "At first its tone was modest and appealing, but it soon became famous because of its ability to tickle the fancy of both Mormon and Gentile factions; and then it donned its garments of notoriety through its system of divorce proceedings. In this latter respect it outstripped the now famous city of Reno, Nevada. Through its medium, hundreds of divorces were procured by non-residents of the Territory, by the parties to the actions declaring it to be 'their intention of becoming residents of Utah' in conformity to Territorial law, and who never even appeared within the borders of the Territory for such purpose." Tolton says traveling troupes of entertainers presented their minstrel plays in Field's Hall. "They usually had some very clever jokes, and often Uncle Joe Field was made the butt of ridicule. His old mules, dirty socks, ink-stained shirt, unkempt hair, and unwashed face, furnished background for this wit." But in the sentences just preceding, we have written the last that is known of the Beaver City Enterprise. Evidently God took it, as He did Enoch; and it was not! No files.

Beaver County Sentinel available history is brief. "We have received the prospectus of the Sentinel, the new Liberal paper, which is soon to make its appearance in Beaver under the editorial and business management of G. W. McLaughlin," says the Salt Lake Tribune, November 10, 1876. "Beaver offers a fine field for an enterprising paper, untrammeled by the Mormon priesthood, and we are assured Mr. McLaughlin will publish such a journal." And on December 22, 1876, the Tribune adds: "We have received the first number of the Beaver County Sentinel published in Beaver City. It is a 6-column sheet, filled with good local reading matter, but has rather a poor array of advertisements." It will be remembered a freak election bet by the Beaver Enterprise editor in March 1877 required a mock funeral procession "from the Sentinel office to the court house," possibly indicating the paper to be in existence; but unfortunately for this history we found no other information, excepting the tradition that Fort Cameron, just east of the city, was headquarters for the earlier anti-Mormon newspapers.

The Square Dealer was well heralded but as we found no copies we have few specifications. The Deseret News, January 29, 1877, ran a story that the Beaver Enterprise was to be transformed into a daily and weekly paper, under the title of The Square Dealer; and says

Joseph Field, proprietor, had bought the plant of the defunct Salt Lake Mail. The Mail had once said a nasty thing about the Enterprise, and the Enterprise had eaten it up! "Beaver is going to try the experiment of another daily paper under the rather unpromising name of Square Dealer," says The Salt Lake Tribune, January 31, 1877, its news source, like that of the Deseret News, obviously being the publisher's prospectus. Then The Provo Enquirer of February 14, 1877, says a new semi-weekly paper for Silver Reef, Leeds Mining District "will be called the Silver Age, and published by Mr. Joseph Field, proprietor and publisher of the Beaver Enterprise . . . . He will publish a Daily at Beaver called the Square Dealer." A daily and a weekly in a town of 1500 people, published under different names by the same man; and presumably in different plants!

A month later, March 18, 1877, we read in the Salt Lake Herald: "The Square Dealer is the name of a new Daily paper hailing from Beaver. It is an outgrowth of The Enterprise, and appears to be possessed of all the elements of success." And next day the Deseret News adds: "The first number of the new Beaver Daily, the Square Dealer, is dated March 13, and looks as if it meant to stay." But the Provo Enquirer, March 21, 1877, has the most to say: "We have received the daily paper just started at Beaver City under the name of The Square Dealer. The third number came to hand. . . . This number is quite spicy, newsy and well got up, and we are glad to see that it has a good and profitable number of advertisements. . . . Though it is creditable to the publisher, Mr. Joseph Field, it is more creditable to the community. Quite a number of newspaper correspondents have found their way to Beaver to witness the execution of John D. Lee on the 23rd of this month."

O. F. Whitney, the Utah historian, in his volume 2, page 804, says The Square Dealer was a non-Mormon paper, and quotes it as saying in May, 1877, "When (Fort) Cameron had four full companies of soldiers the citizens of Beaver had money, and the newspaper business was a flourishing one. If anybody imagines we are opposed to seeing good times come again, they have mistaken us, that's all. Send on your soldiers, Governor Emery, only Cameron will take four companies instead of two." When Fort Cameron was garrisoned, it will be noted, Beaver had three newspapers, all apparently prosperous. Whitney also says, page 825: "The Beaver Square Dealer (non-Mormon) in its issue three days prior to the execution (March 23, 1877), had this to say of (John D.) Lee's last confession which the editor had the privilege of perusing: 'One particular statement he had adhered to from the first. He has at all times declared that Brigham Young and the Church leaders had nothing to do with the (Mountain Meadows) Massacre.' "

By the way, Whitney's statement that the Square Dealer was non-Mormon, is not concurred in by certain contemporaries—which is one of the penalties of being an "Independent" newspaper. The Provo

Enquirer of May 30, 1877, copies from the Ogden Freeman: "The Beaver Square Dealer and the Provo Enquirer, both Mormons." And the Salt Lake Tribune, June 17, 1877, "Rub-a-dub-dub: The Beaver Square Dealer, an orthodox Mormon sheet is indiscreet enough to admit there is drilling (military?) in the South." The Provo Enquirer, August 29, 1877: "The Square Dealer of Beaver says the editor is gone, but doesn't say where to!" Possibly trying to collect money on outstanding bills, for the Salt Lake Tribune, December 5, 1877, quotes this from The Beaver Square Dealer itself: "We find the Square Dealing, Independent business uphill work; and we remind those who appreciate the sentiments which characterize our paper, that it is their duty to sustain it; if the paper cannot be run on an independent basis, its publication will be given up."

Evidently, however, the editor found a way to keep going, for the Deseret News of June 25, 1878, says: "The Beaver Square Dealer comes to us printed on one side of the paper, after an absence of nearly a month. The cause of the temporary suspension and partial issue is comparative impecuniosity. A change is about to be made in the management and conduct of the journal. It will shortly be in the hands of a joint stock company." The Deseret News borrowed a news item from the Square Dealer, with a credit line, on August 28, 1878, the last we hear of the paper. It shortly expired, and from its substance rose the Chronicle.

Beaver Daily Chronicle was started about October 16, 1878. We first hear of it through the Deseret News of October 26, 1878: "The Beaver folks have started a new paper. It is a Daily, and is called the Chronicel—we follow its own orthography. No 5 is the first issue that has reached us. It is made up from the late Enterprise and Square Dealer material; is a 4-column, 4-page paper, 11 x 16 inches in dimensions, and edited by S. A. Wixom, with John Ashworth as superintendent. It is published by a company of which John R. Murdock is president and Josiah Rogerson is secretary." And October 29th, the News has this: "A Local Mystery: 'A bet was made by our "local" and a prominent gentleman of this place who has just been promoted. Our "local" got away with him.'—Beaver Chronicle. If anybody should happen to sit down on the point of this joke, the pain of the accident should be swallowed up in the joy of discovery."

The Beaver Press of March 8, 1929, says: "O. A. Murdock uncovered a copy of the Beaver Daily Chronicle dated December 16, 1878. It was published every day except Sunday, by The Chronicle Publishing Company, at $7.50 a year with Joe Fields as editor (sic). The 'Daily' was about 10 by 15 inches of 4 pages, and printed one page at a time on an Army press. The fifty or sixty subscribers paid their annual subscriptions in wood, feed, vegetables, hides and even ale and whiskey. . . . The copy is Vol. 1, No. 51." On December 21, 1878, the Deseret News says: "Did not do it. 'For the sake of those of our co-temporaries who think they are firing heavy guns at the editor of the Chronicle we beg to say that his business is merely to write editorials, without even reading the proof.'—Beaver Chronicle. We have never accused anybody of reading the proof of the Chronicle."

"The Beaver Chronicle of January 20, (1879), comes to us in its new dress and somewhat enlarged." says the Deseret News of January 23, 1879. "Our well-known correspondent, Daniel Tyler, fills the position of editor." The News of July 18, 1879, brings the next item: "Paradoxical.—The last number of the Beaver Chronicle comes to us a half-sheet. The cause of the new departure is given as follows: 'The public must bear with our shortcomings for a few days. We had paper ordered which started from Salt Lake on the 2d, and it was not shipped from Juab (then the railroad terminus), until the 11th. We expect it every day.' Hence a short-coming may be caused by a long-coming."

"The Beaver Chronicle is no longer a Daily," says the Provo Enquirer, September 10, 1879. "It will appear henceforth a tri-weekly." And The Ogden Junction, September 13, 1879: "The Beaver Chronicle is again changed. This time from a Daily to a Tri-weekly. It says: 'this will make no difference to subscribers. Each will get their full quota of papers.' As a grammatical and typographical production the Chronicle is original if nothing else." And this is from the Junction of October 22, 1879: "They must be having a famine in Beaver, judging by the following from The Chronicle. 'The young man who observed to his fair one last evening, when passing by our devil with a sack on his shoulder: "Well, he's got potatoes at last, I guess!" was mistaken. It was carrots! friend, carrots!' "

And finally, the Junction of October 29, 1879, says: "We learn from the Beaver Chronicle that a new weekly, entitled The Beaver Watchman will be issued there by Joseph Field about the 29th instant, and thereafter every Wednesday. 'It is the purpose of the publisher,' says the Chronicle, 'to furnish the people of Beaver county and southern Utah generally, with a first class, independent newspaper.' We have witnessed so many instances of newspapers commencing Independent and in a short time drifting into the most dependent of all conditions, that the term has become nauseous." Singularly enough the first notice of The Watchman is copied from The Chronicle; yet The Watchman actually succeeded The Chronicle from that very issue, of October 30, 1879. Evidently the exchanges did not see the discontinuance notice, or miss The Chronicle when it died!

Beaver Watchman. "The first number of The Beaver Watchman was to issue yesterday, the 29th instant, under the direction of that literary genius, Joseph Field," says the Beaver Chronicle of October 30, 1879, reported in the Deseret News, October 31, 1879. The Provo Enquirer says more, November 12, 1879: "The Watchman, a new weekly paper has made its appearance in Beaver, displacing The Chronicle. It is near the same size sheet as our own, although not half so good looking (ahem!). Perhaps there is not a place in Utah where journalism has passed through so many vicissitudes as in Beaver, but so far it has survived." And the Ogden Junction still more, November 15, 1879: "Vol. 1, No. 1, of The Beaver Watchman is before us. Joseph Field, a gentleman to fortune and fame well known, is the proprietor. In the Introduction it states that: 'For intruding on the public with an independent newspaper, no apology is decided necessary. Fortunately a free press is guaranteed by the constitution of our country.' . . . We think it will tax the resources of the good people of Beaver County to a considerable extent to sustain two newspapers." (The Enterprise, formerly owned by Field, was still very much in the field!)

"The Watchman is a 7-column weekly with 'patent outsides' and India rubber stuffing; presents a fair appearance and is mailed to subscribers at $4.50 per annum," reports the Ogden Junction, November 15, 1879. The Logan Leader, December 4, 1879, after quoting a paragraph from The Beaver Watchman, says: "The Watchman exhibits the same defects in the matter of proofreading that so signally characterized its defunct predecessor, The Chronicle." The Watchman was a good source of news, judging from the number of times we found news items credited to it. The Ogden Junction on July 28, 1880, says: "The Beaver Watchman seems to consider the libel suit against the Silver Reef Miner a justified proceeding,"—which does not reveal the plaintiff. It may, however, have been The Watchman, for The Junction of August 11, 1880, has this: "Owing to the great depression in business, and consequently of advertising patronage in Beaver City, The Watchman proprietor has resolved to move his office to Milford, from which place the paper will be issued in the future." The Deseret News (August 7th) added "The late editor has gone to Ashley's Fork (Vernal)." The American Newspaper Directory for 1880: "Watchman, Wednesday; 4-page, 24x36; $4.50; established 1872; Jos. Field, editor and publisher." The editor of the Southern Utonian, May 7, 1881, (quoted by The Ogden Herald of May 10, 1881) says: "It is generally understood around town that Mr. Field intends to remove his printing machinery to Beaver once more, and start another paper. Joe is the boss 'undertaker'."

Southern Utonian, first issue, February 19, 1881. "The Southern Utonian is the name of Beaver's latest venture. It is a 7-column weekly, patent outside, published by F. R. Clayton & Co., and starts with great spirit and courage, in a field which is marked with so many journalistic graves," says the Deseret News of March 3, 1881. "The first number of the Southern Utonian has an amusing article from the pen of 'Essay Kaigh' (S. A. Kenner). 'Scip' is a good deal of a humorist." (Kenner took the editorship of the rival Enterprise in June, 1881.) "It is said that the editorial force of the Southern Utonian at Beaver is composed equally of both sexes," said the Deseret News of March 11, 1881.

"There is now a very preceptible improvement in the typographical appearance of the Beaver Southern Utonian," says the Provo En-

THE MOUNTAINEER.

"DO WHAT IS RIGHT, LET THE CONSEQUENCE FOLLOW!"

NO. 1.   GREAT SALT LAKE CITY, SATURDAY, AUGUST 27, 1859.   VOL. I.

THE MOUNTAINEER

IS PUBLISHED
EVERY SATURDAY.

OFFICE.—North-West Corner of Council Block, in the basement Story.

BLAIR, FERGUSON & STOUT,
EDITORS AND PROPRIETORS.

TERMS: $6 per Annum in Advance.

ADVERTISING.

AUNT MAGWIRE'S ACCOUNT OF
THE MISSION TO MUFFLEGE-
GAWNY.

BY THE AUTHOR OF THE "WIDOW BEDOTT" PAPERS

quirer, November 9, 1881. We learn from the Deseret News of April 11, 1882, that "F. R. Clayton, Esq., editor of the Southern Utonian . . . is superintendent of District Schools for Beaver County." The Ogden Herald of February 21, 1882, says: "Saturday's issue of the Southern Utonian closes the first year of that Beaver Journal. In that time it seems to have established itself on a tolerably fair foundation." The Utonian must have been a first class newspaper, as we found it credited with items in other papers in Logan, Ogden, Salt Lake City, Provo, Manti and St. George. It was the Utonian that told the world of the public auction of the government barracks, stores, officers' quarters and other buildings at Fort Cameron to be held April 30, 1883. The American Newspaper Directory for 1883: "Southern Utonian, Friday, 4 pages, 24 x 35, $3."

A new name comes from the Deseret News of October 5, 1883: "This afternoon we received a fraternal call from Mr. Stephen Hales of the Beaver Utonian;" adding October 22nd, "The Utonian wants a history of Beaver county written." We eavesdrop on a little advice given by the St. George Union, in March, 1884. "The Southern Utonian, published at Beaver City, Utah, is before us. It is a 4-page weekly paper, about 16 x 24, and can afford to print one side at home, the other being patent 'outside'. The printer who runs the 'Inside' does not thoroughly understand the process of keeping the rollers in trim, thereby leaving white streaks, instead of all being printed alike." And yet, how they borrowed news from it, on every hand!

The Ogden Daily Herald of August 18, 1884, mentions "Editor Tyler of the Southern Utonian," but without a file we cannot date the change. The Deseret News of October 5, 1885, says: "Brother George Hales of the Southern Utonian is in town," thus paying for cuttings for some time to come! A bit of "spice" comes from the Salt Lake Evening Democrat of August 10, 1885: "One of the editors of the Beaver Utonian, who is in no danger of going to the penitentiary for his religion's sake, is inspired by the spirit of the departed Penrose, and donning the Lion's Skin, brags as follows: 'The general mistake made by the anti-Mormons and people generally, that the conviction and imprisonment of a few is breaking down Mormonism and destroying plural marriage, is a delusion. Our enemies might as well attempt to obliterate the sun and dethrone Jehovah, as to attempt to put down one principle of the religion of Jesus Christ which has been revealed in these last times.' "

The Democrat gives further developments, March 13, 1886: Messrs. R. Maeser and George Hales, proprietors of the (Beaver) Utonian were arrested and placed under $1500 bonds on the charge of libel, it having accused . . . the deputies of stealing or attempting to steal valuables from some of the homes visited," (in the anti-polygamy crusade.) The Logan Journal of March 17, 1886, says the bonds were $800 each, and the arrest made March 12th. The Manti Home Sentinel May 25, 1886, furnishes the verdict: "Packed jury business done effectual work in the Beaver Utonian libel case on Tuesday last, when they convicted manager Hales, just after the editor, Maeser, had been acquitted by a different jury."

The American Newspaper Directory, 1886, shows: "Beaver, Southern Utonian; Friday; Mormon, established 1881; 24 x 36, 4 pages, circulation 550; 10 lines, 1 month, $2.50; Hales and Maeser, editors and publishers." The Manti Home Sentinel of November 5, 1886, quotes "Utonian Utterings"; "We make our debut in court on the 21st instant." We learn from John F. Tolton that he (Tolton) acted as editor of the Utonian from May to September, 1886, while at least one of the editors was in the toils. The Salt Lake Democrat of December 14, 1886, says: "The Southern Utonian has the following notice: 'Wanted, on subscription, twenty bushels of potatoes, 100 pounds of squash, 50 pounds of cabbage.' The potatoes, squash and cabbage are wanted for brain food for the editor of the Utonian, who must live high, no matter what the cost."

The Provo Enquirer of May 31, 1887, says: "We find in the Beaver Utonian on Friday last, the following editorial correspondence, evidently written by R. Maeser, Esq., who is at present visiting his many friends in the city." And the Enquirer of October 28, 1887, says: "The Southern Utonian apologizes for not appearing in its patent clothing as usual. If the Utonian will believe us—its issue of the 21st looks better than if it had the patent." (ready-print.)

The American Newspaper Directory for 1887 gives Geo. Hales, editor and Beaver Publishing Company, publishers. The Manti Sentinel, January 20, 1888, says: "The editor of the Beaver Utonian has again photographed his mean little soul in a scurrilous local aimed at our Christmas Memento. An academic education can do a great deal for a man but it can't build a barrel on a bunghole!" But the Deseret News borrowed and credited too many items from the Utonian to be anything but a close friend. The Provo Enquirer of July 17, 1888, says: "The Utonian has changed its dress, grown in size, and abandoned patent inside. It looks all the better."

A copy of No. 3, volume 9, Thursday, March 7, 1889, in The Bancroft Library, had four pages of 6 columns each. Far-flung political editorials were interspersed with boosts for the job printing plant. Another copy dated November 21, 1889, contained ten pages, but like that of March 7, carried no name in the masthead. Moreover, it carried very little news, but plenty of filler. The Provo Enquirer of January 3rd, says: "The Beaver Utonian comes out with an enterprising Holiday number, a complete reflex of the business houses of that enterprising city." And on March 7, 1890, the Enquirer says, "The plucky little Utonian comes to us now as a semi-weekly. The paper has made many changes during its existence, but invariably for the better." It adds, May 31, 1890, "Editor R. Maeser of the Beaver Utonian is in town," August 15, 1890, the Enquirer continues, "The Southern Utonian reaches us enlarged, and is now a 6-column folio." The Brigham Bugler of August 23, 1890, says, "The Southern Utonian has blossomed out in a neat, new and enlarged dress." On October 18, 1890, The Bugler adds, "The Southern Utonian, one of our best exchanges, has fallen into the hands of F. R. Clayton. This gentleman is a first class newspaper-man, and will likely do much for his new love." (Not exactly a new love, but a love at second sight, since it was Clayton who started the Utonian in 1881.)

The irony of Fate is shown in this from the Provo Enquirer of September 13, 1892: "Sam LeRoy, formerly editor of the Manti Sen-tinel, now defunct, has assumed the manager and editorship of the Beaver Utonian (after calling its editor names in 1888). R. Maeser finds his time wholly occupied with school work. The Utonian has always been a zealous worker for its section of the Territory."

The present Beaver Press has a copy of the Utonian, dated January 13, 1893; Sam LeRoy, no title; one page ready print; 3 pages of home news, heavy with advertising. The Wasatch Wave of June 20, 1893, says briefly, "R. Maeser has again assumed the editorial mantle of the Utonian," without indicating what became of editor LeRoy. The Iron County Record of January 18, 1895, says, "The Beaver Utonian is now getting out its semi-weekly, a neat 5 column folio." And the Iron County Record adds on March 18, 1895: "J. T. Jakeman is now identified with the Beaver Utonian."

The Nephi Blade of May 16, 1896, reports the epitaphical item: "The Beaver Utonian is talking of suspending. The Blade will wager it isn't because the publisher has got enough out of the business to live in luxury the rest of his days." The actual demise was not chronicled in any remaining contemporary files though the Utonian obviously passed out about this time.

Beaver County Record. First issue June 8, 1883, "Messrs. F. R. Clayton and R. Maeser of Beaver have commenced the publication of the Beaver County Record," says a contemporary, June 23, 1883. "It has a bright, neat appearance and the contents show enterprise and editorial ability." "Beaver City reports two weekly newspapers," says the St. George Union, July 31, 1883, "The Beaver County Record and the Southern Utonian." Through the rest of 1883 and 1884 the Record was frequently quoted in exchanges up and down the State. Sloan's 1884 Utah State Gazetteer says: "Beaver City . . . The Beaver Record, F. R. Clayton, editor and proprietor."

The Ogden Daily Herald, May 27, 1884, says: "Beaver County Record for some time past has appeared as a semi-weekly;" and the Logan Journal adds the name, "F. R. Clayton, Esq." But the Record fell back into first gear, according to the Herald, October 13, 1884: "The Beaver County Record will henceforth be issued as a weekly." The Salt Lake Evening Chronicle borrowed news from the Record at times, and then printed its demise, December 29, 1884: "The Beaver County Record has suspended publication. It did not show enough servility to the Church authorities to meet their encouragement."

Beaver Press, first issue, November 25, 1904, D. I. Frazer & Son, publishers and proprietors. Karl S. Carlton purchased the Press about 1916, selling to Timothy Brownhill about 1920—Karl forgets the exact dates, and the files are broken. Brownhill made the Press mighty attractive to Carlton, who repurchased it, probably to give the Mrs. a job, for on September 29, 1922, "Cora E. Carlton, editor" flew from the masthead, with "Karl S. Carlton, proprietor," the lesser half of the team remaining with the Milford News. This double-header arrangement continued till March 4, 1927, when A. C. Saunders and his wife, Jess E., took the paper. They resold to Carlton again June 1, 1933, the son taking charge, as "Walter L. Carlton, publisher."

BINGHAM, Salt Lake County

Population: (Incorporated, 1904) 1910, 2881; 1920, 2676; 1930, 3248.

The Bingham Pioneer first appeared July 5, 1873. The Salt Lake Herald says, "We yesterday received a copy of the first issue of the Bingham Pioneer, a new weekly paper, edited and published by Charles G. Loeber, Esq., every Saturday at Bingham Canyon. The Pioneer is a 24-column paper, and the first number is well filled with reading matter and presents a very neat appearance, both typographically and in general make-up." Other contemporaries also "puffed" it cordially, probably too hard, for soon it was not! The Deseret News of August 23, 1873, says: "The Bingham Pioneer died of a big dose of 'the times' without an obituary." It is easy to infer the editor meant depression or hard times, though the Pioneer's competitor, survivor and successor, was called:

The Bear Gulch Times. According to the Salt Lake Tribune, Friday, July 2, 1875, "The Times is the title of a diminutive paper, hailing from Bingham, and published by E. W. Peirce. It promises to grow as its facilities are increased." They usually did, but maybe a writer on "The Rise and Fall of The Bingham Exaggeration Club," February 14, 1877, had an explanation for their disappearance from the face of the earth. He says in part: "The reputation of Bingham was spread far and wide through the medium of its two newspapers—

The Carr Fork Mirror (we find no other reference to this paper.) and the Bear Gulch Times. (According to them) Mine owners retired wealthy after about six months of work and . . . deeded their mines, mills and machinery to their employees, who, in turn, retired wealthy, giving those who followed full control of the property. Palatial residences sprang into existence with each retiring miner. Schools and churches, banks and brokers, gambling rooms and gorgeous saloons followed in the wake of this universal prosperity."

"It was conceded by all that the Masonic Lodge of Bingham was the largest—in point of architecture the finest—in funds the richest

of any in the U. S. Its members represented more capital than any
society before or since. The same was said of the Odd Fellows, Red
Men, etc. . . . Six days after the subscription list was thrown open, eight
hundred members were enrolled, representing a cash capital of
$23,000,000. The initiation fee was only $2000 and a monthly fee of
$200, a mere trifle . . ."—*Winnamuck.*

We do not find the going out trail of these newspapers, but if
what "Winnamuck" says is true of their Ananias propensities, they
certainly didn't go to heaven! Unless we have missed something, Bingham was without a newspaper thenceforth for nearly fifteen years,
which is probably the way the miners felt about newspapers in general.

Bingham Bulletin. First issue, June 5, 1891; 4 pages, 6 columns.
Ed. K. Watts, editor. "A sprightly young journalistic venture has
reached our sanctum," the Provo Enquirer says of it June 11, 1891.
The American Newspaper Directory for 1892 shows: "Bingham Bulletin, Friday, local, established 1891, 4 pages, 15 x 22, subscription, $3,
circulation 350. Ed. K. Watts, editor, Bulletin Publishing Co." But
it was not noticed again until March 11, 1893, when the Brigham
Bugler says: "The Bingham Bulletin, Ed. K. Watts, editor, loomed
up this week, all home print, and greatly improved in every way."
Again August 19, 1893, the Bugler says: "The Bingham Bulletin came
out on the half shell today." The Wasatch Wave, December 13, 1895,
says, "Ed. K. Watts, editor, has sold his Bingham Bulletin, with which
he has been connected the last four years, to J. B. Graham, and will
retire from the newspaper business on account of ill health."

In the small private newspaper collection of J. R. Jarvis, is a
copy of the Bingham Bulletin, Friday, November 5, 1897, J. B. Graham, publisher, 7 columns, 4 pages, 2 home print. We do not find it
mentioned again until the Park Record, July 16, 1898, credits a news
item to it; and the Utah County Democrat, March 1, 1899, borrows
an item with credit. The Democrat again on May 17, 1899, says:
"Brother Graham of the Bingham Bulletin, forgot," something or other.
And on August 12, 1899, the Park Record says, "Editor Graham, of the
Bingham Bulletin, is enjoying an eastern trip and during his absence,
the editorial and press work will be done by F. M. Pinneo, formerly
of the Coalville Times."

The next dates come from stray copies in the Jarvis collection:
July 13, 1900, J. B. Graham, publisher, 6 columns, 8 pages, 4 home
print. Also June 14, 1901, and March 28, 1902, each having the
same masthead and format. Kenner in "Utah As It Is," 1904, says the
Bingham Bulletin, is a weekly, independent, circulation 450, J. B.
Graham, editor and manager. But the files are gone and the records
are gone; hence this resumé is of a necessity badly disjointed.

Graham himself at a later date wrote: "On the 25th of December,
1895, I published my first number of the Bingham Bulletin, of which
I had the week before become 'Editor, publisher, and sole proprietor,'

E. L. SLOAN
Born November 9, 1830
Died August 2, 1874

SETH M. BLAIR
Born March 15, 1819
Died March 17, 1875

The Deseret News' Home for forty years from 1862. (Site of Hotel Utah)

Courtesy Deseret News

without paying a dollar down and with nowhere to get one . . . . While in a reckless mood, I met the then owner of the Bulletin, who offered to sell it to me on time, as he was ill and wanted a change of climate. . . . City dailies were circulated every morning about 10 o'clock, making the field for a skinny weekly seem bare as a goose pasture. No wonder this young man is feeling unwell, I thought.

"A half-worn dress for a 7-column folio, a fine hand press, an imposing stone, etc., and the good will, whatever that might have been, were to be mine on payment of $800 within two years, a first installment of $200 being due in 90 days. My first number took well and quite a lot of subscriptions at $3 came in. Expenses were met from the jump, but at the end of three months, nothing had been laid by, which didn't look good to me.

"When my esteemed predecessor showed up, he still had a pain. I told him how rough things were coming, but for a bluff, asked what he would take, cash down and call it square. He said, with $500 in hand he could start a small business, and offered to settle for that." (Mr. Graham approached a wealthy Bingham mine owner in Salt Lake City and asked for the $500.) "I made necessary explanations, looking him straight in the eyes. It seemed as if I could read there that a time might come for him when it would be real nice to stand in with newspaper men. At the end of ten minutes he handed me a check for $500 and a note to sign at 7%, payable in two years." (There was no security.)

"But the altitude of Bingham affected me so seriously that my physician advised me to leave the mountains. I sold the Bulletin and removed to Salt Lake."

In the first issue of the paper under the subsequent management was a scarehead sensation reflecting on the U. S. Mining Company . . . "based on private information, stolen from the company's files." (Graham says he was accused, which let his successor out; but Graham never saw the stolen papers, so that let him out, and a lawsuit was narrowly averted.) "The Bulletin had numerous subscribers in Boston and New York, who had learned to respect its mining reports. After that, though out of business, I got a leer from those who met me. There is nothing in language more potent to blast a man's character than that one word 'blackmailer'!" Graham's name appeared last as publisher of the Bulletin in the Newspaper Directory for 1905. From the broken files, and the Directories, we find Frank J. Tierney was publishing the Bulletin in the Judge Building in Salt Lake City in 1908.

Bingham Press was being edited by T. L. Holman in 1908; but on January 19, 1912 (probably earlier) the Press-Bulletin was being published in Bingham Canyon. Charles P. Diehl was editor and manager in 1912, W. E. Traughber in 1915, I. H. Masters 1918 to 1920, and L. E. Kramer in 1922. Phil M. Goldwater, owner from April 1, 1924, sold out April 21, 1927, to Walter C. Adams, who changed the name to **Bingham Bulletin** the next week. Adams announced he had acquired all the "assets" of the paper. Oddly enough, no editor ever assumed he acquired any of the liabilities, jinx, Jonahs, crosses, or ill luck! Adams bowed himself out November 30, 1927, to make way for Howard A. Jarvis, owner, and J. R. Jarvis, editor and manager, who sold to Howard Barrows in 1934. Leland G. Burress, present publisher, bought the paper June 1, 1936.

BLOOMINGTON, Washington County

Population: small village near St. George.

Union, "Monthly, Mormon, established 1868, 11 x 16, 4 pages, circulation 400; 10 lines, one month, $1," says American Newspaper Directory, 1886. **The Union and Village Echo**—what an appropriate title!—sometimes simply the Union, once bore the date line Bloomington, but it was merely carried there in the Editor's hat while he did his haying. The printing plant and the mailing privileges remained at St. George. (q.v.)

BOUNTIFUL, Davis County

Population: 1900, 1442; 1910, 1677; 1920, 2063: 1930, 2571.

The Davis County Clipper, is considered to have appeared without volume or serial number February 1, 1891. Files: fairly complete, unbound, in the University of Utah Library; the Ogden Public Library has a neatly bound nearly continuous file from 1892 to 1898. This newspaper's informal Genesis was somewhat as follows: Lamoni Call, a Bountiful merchant, printed circulars advertising his store, on a printing press drawn through the streets in a Pioneer Day Celebration, July 24, 1890. A similar advertising circular, enlarged to 4 pages, was subsequently published, first at long intervals, and finally every week.

John Stahle was asked to edit the publication for grammatical errors, and on March 4, 1891, they christened their suckling circular "The Clipper." The name grew out of a small ship model, owned and prized by Mr. Call, called the Clipper Ship. This ship had given publisher Call many day-dreams of pleasant travel abroad, presumably just such as the newspaper now proposed to provide for its readers!

The earliest copy preserved is, No. 1, volume 2, March 4, 1892, then but recently renamed **The Little Clipper.** John Stahle was editor, Lamoni Call, manager, published every Friday, 5 columns, 4 pages, practically all home print. A woodcut art heading of unusual depth, drawn and engraved by John Held of Salt Lake City, represented a ship of many masts and sails, yet fitted with wings and standing, not in water, but on the ground, the title being worked into the ship's broadside.

In that issue a Bear River correspondent says, "A few issues of the Little Clipper were sent to me by a friend. . . . I see that the Little Infant meets with some criticism and disapproval. . . ." (Call later, February 24, 1899, started the short-lifed Anti-Mormon, not strictly a newspaper.) On April 29, 1892, the name became **The Davis County Clipper,** 6 columns.

The Clipper at this time began stepping out. "The Davis County Clipper is the name of a bright little sheet that showed up among our exchanges for the first time last week," says the Manti Times-Reporter, December 8, 1892. January 19, 1893, the Salt Lake Beobachter asked the question whether Davis County had recently been visited by an earthquake or whether the editor of the Clipper had been celebrating New Year. . . . "In looking over the number alluded to by the Beobachterman," says editor Stahle, "I find the ads are alright except the cradle ad, which is upside down, thereby spilling the baby. I will just say that we have had no earthquakes or no drunken editors in this locality. I would ask the Beobachterman not to be too severe with me, as I do not think bachelors are expected to know all about babies."

In the issue of March 9, 1893, the editor says, "This completes volume 2 of the Clipper." Lamoni Call had completed one volume under the name of the Little Clipper. Beginning March 15, 1894, it was reduced to 5 columns, 4 pages, all home print. Important item, May 10, 1894: "The Clipper Manager and scribe rolled up to Ogden the other day on bicycles but it required a vast amount of steam to cross the sand ridge."

On June 28, 1894, we read, "The Clipper people have mutually agreed to divide the machinery and other material of the Clipper Plant and from now on the job printing department will be owned and run by Lamoni Call, while the newspaper will be owned and published by John Stahle, Jr." Call's name was accordingly dropped from the masthead. Thenceforth, to the present day, the same John Stahle, Jr., has acted as editor, publisher and proprietor of the Davis County Clipper, more than forty years practically alone, with proper acknowledgment to Mrs. Stahle, a silent partner, who long ago tolled the editor out of bachelordom and taught him the correct use of the cradle. His is the second longest, continuous record as editor in the State, second only to "Dad" Raddon of Park City. Kenner in "Utah as It Is" in 1904, says the Clipper "is not addicted to religious or political advocacy." Editor Stahle has held to that principle for the ensuing 30 years. Usually gathering the news and hand-setting the type himself through the early days, Editor Stahle has made a remarkable record, if not a spectacular one. In 1932 the son, John Stahle, became Vice President and Assistant Manager, continuing to date.

BRIGHAM CITY, Box Elder County

Population: 1890, 2139; 1900, 2859; 1910, 3685; 1920, 5282; 1930, 5093.

Brigham Bugler. Volume 1, No. 1, Saturday, June 14, 1890, 8 columns, 4 pages, half home print, M. L. Snow, editor and Manager, (shortly went into full bloom as Mansfield L. Snow). Files: The Brigham City Library has a treasure in the first 4 bound volumes of the Bugler in excellent condition. "This, our initial number, is the only newspaper publication which first saw the light in Brigham City. It is the only one in Box Elder County," says the editor. Obviously the paper was well received, for it was generously patronized. On the other hand it earned what it received, for it gave an excellent news service, presented in splendid form.

"The Bugler is a paper of no mean circulation. It already has many patrons beyond Utah's limits; they are found in Idaho, Montana, Wyoming, and California. Our initial bow greets more bona fide subscribers than half of the newspaper publications that both Canada and the United States can boast," Snow tells us. "(The Editor) makes the announcement that the paper will not be a religious or political organ and that it will have no particular party. The Bugler will soon get off that note."—Provo Enquirer, June 17, 1890. Of unquestioned gallantry, nevertheless Editor Snow practically re-enacted the stirring story of the Beauty and The Beast, when in 1891 he swept a woman competitor with a mere Herald, out of the way, and they both lived happily ever after. (See Brigham City Herald.)

The editor brags a little on March 8, 1898, "The Bugler is the only paper in general circulation in Box Elder County, and we have more bona fide subscribers in the county than all the other papers put together," which may be an admission of the existence of a contemporary, since Corinne, nearby, was in its newspaper doldrums. Editor Snow's local news was under the caption: "Brief blasts from the Bugler" many of which, if we may judge from the credit lines seen elsewhere, were usually heard throughout the state. On June 18, 1892, the editor observed, "Two years old . . . we began the paper with the ever objectionable "patent inside" printing some 8 columns of local matter. This continued for several months until November 14, 1891, when we abolished the patent inside and blossomed out a clean, bright, all home print, containing nearly 20 columns of local news, which is three to four times more than the ordinary country weekly newspaper contains."

The Millard County Blade of October 28, 1893, says, "The Brigham City Bugler is not surpassed in contents or makeup by any country weekly published in the Territory." Then or now, the present writer agrees; "hats off" to Mansfield L. Snow! The Provo Dispatch, December 16, 1893, says, "The Brigham Bugler seems indeed a sleek, well-fed paper. It is in every way worthy of the splendid patronage it is receiving." Usually the gossip was only complimentary, but, "The

Brigham City Bugler has been sued for libel," says the Iron County Record, March 29, 1895, though his competitors must have had worse trouble than libel suits, for on April 6, 1895, he said: "Once more the Bugler is the only paper published in Box Elder County. Four competitors have gone down in the past five years, averaging nearly one a year." Three of these were probably in Brigham City, since only one is known to have been in Corinne. All "ver senkt"!

"The editor of the Brigham City Bugler is a tireless worker," humorist Howard of the Salina Press informs us October 19, 1895; "and leaves no stone unturned to make his paper one of the newsiest and best in Northern Utah. If there is a dearth of local happenings in Brigham City the editor of the Bugle is never non-plussed. He puts on a pair of overalls and jumper, and makes a trip into the hills in the interest of Science. He generally manages to kill a tarantula, a centipede, a scorpion, and on special occasions, a rattlesnake. The files of the Bugler in this office show that Brother Snow has murdered with his own sanguinary hands 27 centipedes, 8 scorpions, 3 tarantulas, and 11 snakes, 8 of the latter being rattlers. Every time he kills or captures a specimen, a glowing account of the same appears in the Bugler. It is an example which should be emulated by other newspaper men. The people like to read of deeds of daring, and they always believe everything in the newspapers. One of these days the editor of the Press is going to turn himself loose and publish a thrilling account of his many adventures with mountain lions, porcupines and badgers!"

Editor Snow was so prosperous that on May 2, 1896 he ran this "Notice: On May 11, 1896, Nephi Anderson will take charge of the Bugler . . . during my several months' absence in the East . . . During the coming week the old editor of the Bugler, who has nearly six years' growth of editorial moss on his back, expects to go off occasionally to brush up and rest a bit." Snow resumed charge September 12, 1896.

Unfortunately, this excellent file in the Brigham City Library ends with the issue of June 11, 1898. The very existence of these files themselves is a tribute to the frugality and orderliness of the publisher—and the librarian! Mansfield L. Snow and his Brigham Bugler were doubtless no better than Brigham City deserved, though it is a fact they were too good to remain there, and the Utah County Democrat, Provo, April 12, 1899, packs a lot of news in a little paragraph: "The last issue of the Brigham Bugler gives notice of its removal to Ogden, where it will be consolidated with the Bimetallist and Weber County Times, and published under the name of the latter." "The Brigham Bugler has been succeeded by the Weber County Times and is now published at Ogden," says the Wasatch Wave, April 28, 1899. "The first number of the new issue appeared last Tuesday. We wish Brother Snow success."

Herald: Says the Park Record, February 28, 1891: "The Bugler and the Herald of Brigham City are engaged in a life and death struggle

The Pony Dispatch.

GREAT SALT LAKE CITY, THURSDAY, OCTOBER 3, 1861.

The *Pony Express*, from the east, arrived in this city about 10 a.m, to-day, and brought the following dispatches:

LEAVENWORTH, 25th.

General Lane's command surprised a superior force of rebels at Pappinsville, Mo., on the 21st, and after a severe engagement routed them, loosing seventeen killed, and a large number wounded. The rebels lost forty killed one hundred prisoners and all their tents, wagons, and supplies. Lane is reported to be moving on Osceola.

The gang of rebels who recently sacked the town of Humboldt, Kansas, has been defeated by a force from Fort Scott, and their leader Matthews, killed. On his person was found an order from Ben McCulloch, for the enrolment of the Quappau Indians.

Scouts at Fort Scott report McCulloch with fifteen thousand men within thirty miles of Fort Scott, on the night of the 21st instant.

General Lane has issued a proclamation to the citizens of Western Missouri, in which, after saying for what purpose he is there and urging those in arms against Government to disperse and come to him for protection in person and property, he uses the following language:—

"Should you, however, disregard my advice, ste n visitati ns must t em ted ut to rebels and their a ies. I shall then be convinced your arming for protection is a sham, and rest assured, traitors when caught, shall receive traitors doom; the cup of mercy has been exhausted. Treason hereafter will be treated as treason. The massacre of innocent women and children by black hearted traitors, lately burning the bridges on the Hannibal and St. Joseph rail road satisfied us that a traitor will perpetrate crimes which devils would shudder to commit. They shall be blotted from existence and sent to that hell which yawns for their reception. The two roads are open to you. People of Western Missouri choose ye between them. The one leads you to peace and plenty and the other to destruction.

The steamer Majors this morning took to Kansas city six companies of the Kansas militia and five companies of Jennison's regiment.

Col. Cook's command of regulars from Utah passed Fort Kearney on the 20th inst.

WASHINGTON, 22d.

From developments made to-day I am satisfied the statement forwarded last, purporting to come from a man just from Manassas concerning the strength and condition of the rebels, was garbled coming through. A third party to-day has seen him, and his statement is very clear and is confirmed by numerous other statements made by other reliable parties. His position of late at Richmond, Manassas, Winchester, Harper's Ferry, Munson's Hill and Fairfax at various periods, and his extensive acquaintance with men and things, have enabled him to judge well of the condition and movements of the rebels. He says the number of troops from Richmond to the Potomac at Leesburg, and in the direction of Aquia and Mathias Point, may safely be put down at one hundred and seventy-five thousand. Fifty thousand of them were at Richmond three days ago, and another fifty thousand at Manassas, while the remaining seventy-five thousand are scattered along from that point to Munson's Hill, and from the vicinity of Noland's Ferry to Harper's Ferry and on the Potomac and south of Alexandria, from the vicinity of Aquia Creek and Mathias Point. The troops at Leesburg, and the militia, number about eight thousand. There are also about five thousand in the vicinity of Noland's Ferry. The force at Fairfax Court House is quite small. Genls. Beauregard and Johnston made that place their headquarters.

The main battery on Munson's Hill consists of three forty-two pounders; and a little in the rear of this is another battery more secure, containing three guns. The men are generally well clad, but not with woollen clothing, and they are beginning to suffer for the want of it, especially those from the extreme Southern States. Blankets are very much needed at night, and it is considered impossible to supply their wants. The troops have no shoes but those they brought from home, and most of them are about used up, and there is no possible means for supplying the article. They cannot be manufactured, as leather is scarce, and there being no neatsfoot oil to be had hides cannot be cured for the manufacture of leather.

The cotton crop which has been pledged for the Confederate loan, is not to be removed to the seaboard cities until ready for shipment, for fear of seizure.

They have pressed into the Confederate service nearly all the teams of horses in the valley of Virginia. Farmers are thus deprived of the usual advantages for tilling the ground preparatory to sowing their next wheat and corn crops. Forage for horses is being rapidly bought up, showing that a speedy move is about to take place.

Between Aquia Creek and Alexandria, two new batteries, one five and the other ten miles above, have been erected. The work upon these has been done during dark nights. The intention seems to be the further erection of similar defenses along the Potomac, up to a point as near Alexandria as practicable. He says the rebels felt safe in regard to the protection of the Potomac between Aquia Creek and Mathias Point, and that this feeling of security has probably arisen from the fact that contraband goods have, in several instances, been carried across the counties of Charles and St. Mary's into Virginia. On the Maryland side in these two counties, signal lights have been noticed, giving the rebels timely warning of the passage at night of any of our vessels.

My informant learned before leaving Manassas, that the anticipated advance will be made simultaneously at Noland's Ferry, Alexandria, and a point between Aquia Creek and Mathias Point. The movement at Alexandria will probably be a feint. They have made every attempt to induce Major General McClellan to attack their masked batteries, but they are now satisfied that he will not.— My informant was asked if he ever heard of a plan to assassinate Major General McClellan? He said he never did, but he had heard something about assassinating President Lincoln, who they assert to be the head and front of all their troubles.

He says they regret that General McClellan is in command, and express the hope that Gen. Scott will again assume command. He says that Jeff. Davis, although not quite dead, was announced quite feeble when his death was announced, and that his health is declining fast.

A Union woman, residing at Louisville, arrived here to-day. She reports that there are no more than fifteen or twenty thousand at Fairfax. It was their intention to attempt to cross somewhere on the Upper Potomac. They had moved a large portion of their army in that vicinity. They hoped to cross and then by a flank movement cut off Gen. Banks' division. They swear vengeance against him and his gallant army, and seem more anxious for an engagement with him than Gen. McClellan.

FORTRESS MONROE, 22d.

The S.R Spaulding arrived from Hatteras Inlet this morning. On Tuesday last the propeller Fanny ran down to Ocrocoke Inlet with a company of troops and entirely destroyed the fortifications abandoned by the Confederates.

It is said the Confederates are in force at Washington and Newbern, that two thousand of them had landed on Roanoke Island with the intention of destroying the light house and the dwellings of the Unionists.

A detachment of seven hundred men, accompanied by a naval force, were about leaving Hatteras Inlet to prevent the inroad.

The privateers Coffee and Winslow visited Ocrocoke Inlet to carry off the Confederate guns, but left on seeing the Fanny.

The ship Argonalt, from Yarmouth with fish and salt, ran into Hatteras and was secured as a prize.

NEW YORK, 23d.

About 10 o'clock last night the police discovered that large rocks had been placed on the rails of the Hudson River railroad from 102d to 110th streets, a distance of sixteen blocks. At this point there are very high embankments, and as the express train from Albany was due at 11 o'clock, they would have caused a fearful loss of life.

The *Journal of Commerce* says Secretary Chase had prepared an exposition of the law relating both to the confiscation of southern balances and the prohibition of commercial intercourse with the insurgents. It gives positive assurances that money on deposit in banks and elsewhere, in loyal States, will not be disturbed unless there is sufficient reason to believe that it is to be used to aid the rebellion. The matter of fact that it belongs to a resident of the States declared to be in a state of insurrection is not to be considered a reason for its arrest, and it may remain on deposit as undisturbed as if it were owned in this city.

LOUISVILLE, 23d.

A battalion of rebel cavalry, under Mitchell Lapreile, drove in Capt. Gibson's pickets last night at Salt River; four are missing.

A Federal encampment has been established at Harrisburg. It is said they have arrested Ewing and Silvertooth, two prominent secession Representatives.

WASHINGTON, 23d.

A letter from Paris, received to-day, says that the French government has respectfully declined to inform the Mexican minister of the object of the fleet to be sent to Mexico, saying that the goverment of the latter will be duly apprised of it through the French minister. So far as appears from the letter the movement of France and England is not necessarily hostile.

FRANKFORT, 23d.

It is said John C. Breckenridge and Wm. Preston escaped from here thro' Montgomery county on Friday. Gen. Sherman had possession of Muldroughe Hill yesterday. Henry Dent, city marshal, has been appointed provost marshal of this city.

NEW YORK, 23d.

The North Star has arrived from Aspinwall bringing $950,000 in treasure from California. She exchanged signals with the Northern Light on the evening of 18th.

WASHINGTON, 23d.

A special to the Missouri *Democrat* says, Dr. Wilson, surgeon in the U. S. army, and taken prisoner at Bull Run by the rebels, was released on parole and arrived from Richmond to-day. He says there is great distress and dissatisfaction in the rebel capital. All the hotels are filled up as hospitals, and are filled with sick and wounded. There are four hundred men of one of the Florida regiments in the hospitals. Medicines of all kinds are costly; quinine sells at $8 an ounce, and very scarce. All the necessities of life are dear. Small change is very scarce. The Confederate currency was depreciating; the best commanding 15 per cent. premium.

All the physicians of the city agree that there are at least two thousand influential citizens of Richmond opposed to the rebellion. Knowing ones at Richmond do not believe an attack will be made on Washington. Beauregard's headquarters are at Fairfax Court House; Johnston's are near Winchester.

WASHINGTON, 23d.

A special to the N. Y. *Post* says the Treasury department is still actively engaged in the issuing of the Treasury notes. Large amounts have been sent to the Western States where they enter at once into the home circulation and are eagerly taken up. The loyal men of Maryland are doing their share for the support of the government. Two full regiments have already been raised in that State, and a third is forming. Quarter Master General Meigs is in Philadelphia transacting important business relating to contracts for army supplies.

Secretary Cameron will return to the city to-morrow. The War department has no confirmation of the report of the surrender of the Federal forces, under Col. Mulligan, at Lexington. There is no truth in the report that Gen. Fremont is to be removed. The President especially contradicts the rumor.

The rebels burnt Ball's Cross Roads to-day.

ST. JOHNS, N. B., 22d.

The steamer Persia arrived here, reports meeting the Great Eastern putting back to Liverpool in a damaged condition.

The *London Times* editorially ridicules the passport system of the United States, and says: It will not secure the desired end.

The only complaint that England has to make in the matter, is in regard to the discourtesy to Lord Lyons in leaving him to learn of the new arrangement through the newspapers.

Movements were making of troops preparatory to their embarkation for Canada.

Mr. Russell in another letter to the *Times*, on American affairs, says: That General McClellan is rapidly becoming master of the of the situations, and that the movements of the Federalists by water, both on the seaboard and down the Mississippi river, must greatly embarrass the South.

It was stated that the City of New York took fifty-five cases of rifles for the Northern army, but the agents of the line denied all knowledge of any shipment contraband of war.

It is confirmed that our Minister at Brussels has visited Garibaldi, to offer him a command in the Federal army. The *Dictator* regrets that it cannot give a denial to the rumor of the acceptance of the offer by Garibaldi.

The news is confirmed that Spain is to join in the Anglo France expedition to Mexico.

LOUISVILLE, 23d.

It is reported from below that a small detachment of Rosseau's force has advanced fifteen miles southward of Elizabethtown and that Buckner is advancing northward from Bowling Green with a force variously estimated at from four to ten thousand men.

FRANKFORT, Ky., 23d.

House. A bill passed by a vote of 52 to 15, authorizing the military board to borrow $1,000,000 in addition to the $1,000,000 authorized on May 24th, on State bonds, payable in ten years and establishing a tax of five cents on every $100 to pay the bonds of interest, the said sum to be appropriated for the defence of the State.

CAIRO, 23d.

Yesterday, pickets from the Iowa seventh at Elliot's Mill, eight miles above Columbus, met a large body of the enemy's cavalry. The Iowa boys fired on them, bringing down three or four, when the enemy fired one round and traveled for Columbus. We took four prisoners. No one hurt on our side.

Last night our pickets had a skirmish with the rebels near Hunter, Missouri, four miles below Norfolk; three of our men and horses are missing. The enemies loss is not ascertained.

It is reported that the rebels at Columbus are crossing to Belmont.

NEW YORK, 23d.

A distinguished citizen from Missouri has just purchased for that State three thousand muskets and four thousand equipments, to be sent at once to Missouri, by the most expeditious railroad route. The President's Cabinet gave the order on Friday, and the arms will be on their way to-morrow.

PHILADELPHIA, 23.

The ship Mattison, from Sardinia, with a cargo of salt, was seized here, being owned in New Orleans. Three persons were sent to Fort Lafayette, charged with furnishing goods to the rebels.

JEFFERSON CITY, 24th.

A special to the Missouri *Democrat* says:— The utmost activity prevails here in movements of troops up the river. Ammunition, artillery stores and supplies, with mules and horse trains, are moving rapidly towards Lexington. A decisive blow is to be struck before a week. Price is bagged unless he uses the legs instead of the arms of his army. McCulloch is also in great danger. Price and McCulloch are now in the trap. We have full information of the whereabouts of the latter but are not allowed to send it. Arrivals of troops from St. Louis on Friday were very heavy. All so far landed here have been by the Pacific rail road to Sedalia and Syracuse. The forces as near as I can learn are as follows: Steamers Graham and W. S. Ewing, arrived this morning. Colonel Ellis' regiment of cavalry, about eleven hundred strong, arrived with sabres and Sharp's rifles. They left immediately by land for Sedalia, also Benton's cadets and Fremont's body guards. This afternoon the steamers H. D. Bacon and D. G. Taylor arrived with the third and sixth regiments of Missouri volunteers. They, with the twenty-fifth Illinois regiment are now waiting for extra trains to carry them to Sedalia or Syracuse. Look out for a great battle and victory on our side this week.

A man named Tutt, of this county, was arrested to-day as a secessionist but released again on parole of honor. Eldredge, a rebel from Lexington, is under arrest. He was sent down by Price to learn the strength of our forces. He was miserably deceived. Papers found on him, state our forces at St. Louis, at only about four thousand. He will probably be shot to-morrow. General Thomas L. Price is acting with the utmost energy. McCulloch is marching rapidly to form a junction with Price, but in a circuitous route. He is very near Lexington. By late reports his force is twenty-five thousand strong, with a good supply of artillery.

The loss on the rebel side, and Mulligan's loss at Lexington are both greatly exaggerated, not over one hundred and fifty were lost on Mulligan's side, nor more than three hundred on the rebels side. Forces are rapidly arriving and going up the river.

WASHINGTON 24th.

A special to the Missouri *Democrat* says, the Count De Paris and Duc De Chartres have received commissions as captains. Louis Phillippe D'Orleans and Robert D'Orleans have been assigned as aids to General McClellan. They received no compensation.

It is estimated that two hundred slaves belonging to the rebel Virginians have been made free men here, and are now at work on entrenchments or at liberty.

Weldon, of the Farmer's Bank, Mansfield, Ohio, has been appointed assistant paymaster.

Navy official reports give full account of the Ocracoke Inlet expedition, by the steamer Fanny and Launch, under command of Lieut. Maxwell. Fort Ocracoke, situated on the seaward face of Beacon Island, was entirely deserted by the rebels. It is of octagon shape and contained four small rooms, twenty-five feet square. In the center is a large bomb proof one hundred feet square, within which is the magazine. Above the magazine on each side are four large tanks of water, but there is none in the fort, it is all brought from Washington or Newbern. The fort was constructed with great care, with barrels of sand, covered with earth and turf. The inner framing is bomb proof and is constructed of heavy pine timber. The platforms of twenty guns were partially destroyed by fire, the gun carriages were all burned. Four eight-inch navy shell guns and fourteen long eight-inch twelve pounders were in the fort, two of these were removed on Sunday, and the trunnions knocked off by solid shot from sixty-four pounders.

While the rest of the men were so engaged Lieutenant Eastman, with the Launch went to the mouth of the river, where he found three eight-inch heavy shell guns, lying on the beach and one on the carriage all spiked. There was no battery erected, but one would have been built for the coming of the Yankees. The guns were disabled by knocking them off the casebels, and leaving them in the salt water on the beach. There had been a camp for supremacy. The Herald is edited by a lady and she seems to have the best of the argument." A short but complete story.

Brigham City Report was started sometime in the early half of 1892. The earliest mention of it was by the Spanish Fork Sun, July 14, 1892, which needed some of the Report's news. J. B. Jacobson was editor for the Report Publishing Company. It was a fairly good newspaper while it lasted, 8 pages, 15 x 22, $2. Its change in editors formed a goodly share of its own news. "A. N. Rosenbaum, editor of the sprightly Brigham City Report . . .", says the Provo Enquirer, August 20, 1892. Evidently the Report was poorly printed for even under the Spanish Fork Sun it could scarcely be read! "The Brigham City Report ought to put more ink on its paper, as it comes to our sanctum this week unreadable. The devil must carry the spare ink home on his face instead of applying it to the rag." Its other exchanges, however, were able to read it occasionally until May 2, 1893, when according to the Wasatch Wave: "The Brigham City Report is dead, snuffed out. Its last issue reached us last evening, and from its tone, we should judge it died pretty hard."

Box Elder Voice of Brigham City was first uttered on March 1, 1894, by A. B. Thomson, formerly of the Brighton Star, and familiarly known as "Milo Zip." It was really a fine newspaper, a vox populi. Indeed it had to be to appear in company with the Bugler. Musically, it was appropriate and had its place, but actually, well—it was a hummer! The one copy found in the L. D. S. Church Library, dated June 21, 1894, had 4 pages of 6 columns each, with a two page insert, and 12 columns of advertisements.

The Manti Messenger announced it as the "voice of Brigham" a new Republican paper, but Milo Zip was by no means a spokesman for Brigham Young, as might be misinferred from that form of address, whatever its mission and whatever its value. "The Brigham City Voice last week closed its lips without a murmur, gave up the ghost and joined the innumerable caravan," says its contemporary, the Bugler, April 20, 1895. "As a newspaper graveyard, Brigham City is a close second to Ogden." A year later the Bugler adds, June 13, 1896, "A. B. Thomson, the former newspaperman of this city has his picture in the Rocky Mountain Editor . . . published at Denver. It says that Mr. Thomson is corresponding secretary of the Western Editorial Federation."

Box Elder County News was started in April 1894, by J. R. Hunter, editor and publisher. S. C. Wixom, the present editor and manager of the Box Elder News, became the printer's devil on the Brigham Bugler, August 4, 1890, being promoted to the position of foreman in 1893. Edith B. Hunter became associate editor September 12, 1896; but in 1898 the Hunters were succeeded by Charles Pasco and Hyrum Standing, who dropped the "County" from the name. Mr. Wixom bought Pasco's interest in 1900, and Standing sold to S. Norman Lee in December, 1904. Victor E. Madsen became editor April 15, 1909, followed on June 20, 1922, by S. C. Wixom, the present editor and manager. (early 1938)

Box Elder Journal, established January 15, 1909, B. H. Jones and J. E. Mangum, publishers. Royal M. Jeppson became editor and proprietor January 20, 1910. Lawrence Jorgenson became assistant manager in 1912, and John F. Erdman became manager January 7, 1915. Will R. Holmes became editor and manager June 27, 1919, continuing to date. (early 1938)

Box Elder News-Journal is a recently announced coalition of Brigham's two newspapers. S. C. Wixom, business manager; Will R. Holmes, managing editor. (July 1938)

BRIGHTON, Salt Lake County

West Side subdivision of Salt Lake City

The Brighton Record. (1890) 8 pages, 5 columns, Record Publishing Company. $1.50 a year, only two copies preserved in the Bancroft Library, for March 19th and April 30, 1892, consisting largely of "boiler plate" claiming the unique distinction of being "the only paper devoted exclusively to the west side of Salt Lake City." C. H. James, manager, Brighton, Utah, published every Saturday. The editorials and news items read like a real estate promotional circular. It mentions "The first plat of what is now the enterprising and thriving town (of Brighton) which was first filed October 11, 1889. Since then thousands of dollars have been expended in artesian wells, parks, churches, schools, factories, stores, a theatre, pavilion, a newspaper plant, printing establishment, numerous residences costing from $500 to $10,000. ... There is now in the course of construction the Utah Normal College and Conservatory of Music. . . . We are building a beautiful town and making a grand success." It was a kind of dream city, not to say nightmare, of which little recognizable is left today but the ground. (In the vicinity of Poplar Grove.) It was on the old Utah and Nevada Railroad, five miles west or southwest from Salt Lake City business district, having a telegraph, express, and post office.

American Newspaper Directory, on information furnished by the editor, gives the year of establishment as 1890, and maybe it was, for those were the peak real estate boom days. For the "As others see us" section: The Wasatch Wave, June 21, 1892, gives us the first mention of the Record: "Our old friend, 'Milo Zip,' (A. B. Thomson) has assumed the editorship of the Brighton Record, a neat little 5-column paper, published at Brighton, Salt Lake County." But Thomson evidently disliked the paper's name for the Spanish Fork Sun, September 24, 1892, says:

"The Brighton Star appeared in company last week with a new dress, and is greatly improved in every respect," but if J. A. B. will get a new pair of trousers we will recognize the fact he is still in the sanctum." The Provo Enquirer adds this on October 4, 1892: "Milo Zip, (A. B. Thomson) well known throughout Utah County for his rank liberalism, now comes out in support of Frank J. Cannon, with his bright little paper, The Utah Star. "Hitch your chariot to a star." The Utonian mentioned the Brighton Star, January 13, 1893. The Brighton, Utah, Star went to an early setting.

Biographical: "The Tribune has a correspondent down in Payson who takes infinite pride in sailing under the superstitious nom-de-plume of Milo Zip. He is getting his name up already. They say he is a supremely monstrous liar, and a wholesale lady-masher to boot. . . ." —Brigham Bugler, July 4, 1891.

CASTLE DALE, Emery County

Population: 1890, 303; 1900, 559; 1910, 693; 1920, 715; 1930, 713.

"The Castle Valley News will change hands next week," we are informed by the Nephi Blade of November 2, 1895. Since no previous or subsequent references have been found and none of the old timers in Emery County remember the newspaper, we can only assume that this lamp of intelligence was lit in Castle Dale, and that when it changed hands, the new editor returned it to its Maker.

"The Emery County Pioneer, published at Castle Dale, is the latest venture in Utah Journalism," says the Vernal Express of January 20, 1898. "It is a neat, newsy, sheet printed by Lynch & Jamieson, and compares favorably with the best papers of the state." But so far as remaining evidence shows, the Pioneer went the way of all pioneers, and that very shortly, though one of its editors figures in its successor as listed in the 1900 edition of the American Newspaper Directory.

"Emery County Record, Fridays, independent, 4 pages, 17 x 24, subscription, $1.50, established 1899, A. E. Jamieson, editor and publisher." The Gazetteer for 1900 shows " a live weekly newspaper, the Emery County Record, A. E. Jamieson, proprietor and manager. Olof Anderson, editor." But the Record's day was brief, for on September 1, 1900, Crockett Bros., publishers of the Eastern Utah Advocate at Price, printed in their plant the first number of the

Emery County Progress for distribution through the county—especially at Castle Dale, the county seat. 6 columns, 4 pages, 15 x 21. In that paper, dated Saturday, September 15, 1900, was this "Announcement—The Publishers of the Progress have purchased from Mr. C. A. Hyde, presses and plant of the late Emery County Record, and perhaps with our next issue, at any rate not later than the first of October, will print the Progress at Castle Dale. . . . Crockett Bros."

H. T. Haines bought the paper and took possession October 20, 1900, letting a half interest go to George Cluff August 10, 1901. Hector Evans shortly became local editor, and on August 23, 1902, took over Cluff's interest. Haines took sole control on January 12, 1907, writing his "Farewell" March 20, 1909, when the ownership passed to Jesse S. Moffit. J. W. Johnson became lessee April 8, 1911, and David S. Williams took over the lease December 16, 1911, becoming proprietor February 17, 1912. His extraordinary tenure ended by bill of sale to M. B. Roberts, and his sister, Miss Enid M. Roberts, February 15, 1928. When Mr. Roberts passed away in late November, 1933, Miss Roberts took active charge, continuing to date.

CEDAR CITY, Iron County

Population: 1890, 967; 1900, 1425; 1910, 1705; 1920, 2462; 1930, 3615.

"**The Iron County News** is the name of a weekly paper soon to be issued at Cedar City," we learn from the Provo Enquirer of October 3, 1890. According to C. J. Arthur's journal, page 242, in Wm. R. Palmer's library, No. 1 Volume 1 of the News was printed by Reinhard Maeser, November 22d and distributed November 24, 1890. There are no files, no numbers found.

Biographical: Editor Maeser, son of the illustrious educator and founder of what is now Brigham Young University, was an editor more by ambition than achievement, newspaper work being to him more an art than a science, we gather from a manuscript life sketch of him by his mother, also in Mr. Palmer's library. "He was formerly assistant editor of the Provo Enquirer, probably in the late seventies, but went in the summer of 1880 to take charge of the schools in Beaver. He had the newspaper bug in his bonnet, so he set up the (Beaver) Utonian. This managed to eat up most of the salary he earned from teaching. Then he decided to quit teaching and establish a chain of newspapers. He went to Cedar City and started a paper there, but this, like all his former ventures, was a failure and he soon returned home.

"But the bug still buzzed and he decided to move his apparatus to Provo and set up a paper there. This time he took his family along and they remained there for two years. They got so down and out financially that, uninfluenced by the persuasions of his wife, and the lack of opportunities afforded his children—(one of whom remarked 'Well, I guess we'll have to dress in newspapers, or else get Brother Rawlins to whitewash us.')—he was finally induced to give away his presses and other accoutrements of literary warfare, inasmuch as he could not sell them, and to accept an offer made to him, to return to Beaver as a teacher in the Beaver Branch of the Brigham Young Academy."

"**Iron County Record.** Volume 1, No. 1, Friday, December 8, 1893" is in Mr. Palmer's file. It has 4 pages of 5 columns each, all home print; from its masthead flew the name, "Will C. Higgins, Editor and Proprietor." In his salutatory, he says, "The Record is not as large as the New York World, nor as fine in appearance as the Juvenile Instructor. . . . It will be independent in politics and religion. . . . We are here to stay. . . . We are under obligations to Alex Rollo, a member in good standing in the typographical union, who came to our assistance this week and slung up a few galleys of type. Alex is a first class compositor and could hold a set in any office."

The Bingham Bulletin editor notices the "new paper recently established at Cedar City . . . by Judge Will C. Higgins, formerly editor in chief of the Salt Lake Mining Journal." Mr. Palmer has several copies of the paper through 1894 and 1895. The Salina Press in February, 1894, says, "Will C. Higgins of the Iron County Record will be known as the pioneer newspaperman of southern Utah. When times were rocky and tough in Salt Lake City, and printers were being fed by charitable associations and were slowly starving on thin soup, Mr. Higgins rolled up a printing press in a red bandana handkerchief and started for the sunny south. He hit Cedar City just at the time the town was in the throes of a railroad boom. He rolled up his sleeves and joined the procession. Today the Record is more widely quoted than any country paper in Utah," (and remarkably well patronized by paying advertisers!).

An announcement of importance was made in the issue of June 15, 1894: "The record expects to move into its new office upstairs tomorrow. The stout young men of Cedar are cordially invited to come around in the morning and help us elevate our job press." In January, 1895, the Sandy Independent says, "Friend Higgins, of the Iron County Record, is adding glory to the profession, making a record as a foot-racer. That is a noble calling, and one which might come in handy some day. We know of some editors, who might have been better off, had they not neglected this branch of their newspaper education."

From 1894 to 1899 the Record was good pickings, judging from the credit lines in the contemporaries, but little was said about the paper itself or its editor and proprietor, Charles S. Wilkinson, who with Dan E. Matheson, purchased and operated the paper together for about a year in 1896-97. Wilkinson then bought Matheson out and in 1900 formed the Southern Utah Publishing and Printing Company, and enlarged the plant.

In 1901 Wilkinson Brothers were publishers, J. T. Wilkinson, Jr., editor; and in 1905 Charles S. Wilkinson was editor and manager. According to our disconnected and incomplete sources, Alex H. Rollo was lessee in 1908. Came then A. D. McGuire editor and publisher early in 1913 (possibly earlier); though in November 1913, C. S. Wilkinson is editor and manager. On April 1, 1915, The Observer was taken over by the Record, Charles S. Wilkinson editor, A. H. Rollo becoming business manager temporarily. On September 15, 1915, The Iron County Publishing Co., became proprietor, and Charles S.

Wilkinson, lessee, editor and publisher. The Record's subtitle "with which is consolidated The Observer" was dropped June 1, 1917, and the Observer forgotten—in the Record Office. Will Dobson was listed as associate editor in December 1920, followed February 18, 1921, by A. H. Rollo, editor and manager, and Lafe McConnell, advertising manager and treasurer. Joseph V. Whitmer and Mrs. Whitmer bought McConnell out June 17, 1921. Soon, however, January 27, 1922, Rollo & Sons became publishers, continuing to date. Alex H. was only waiting for those sons to grow up!

COALVILLE, Summit County

Population: 1890, 1166; 1900, 909; 1910, 976; 1920, 771; 1930, 939.

Coalville Chronicle, Vol. 1, No. 1, June 11, 1892. "A neat little six column newspaper has been started at Coalville under the management of C. S. Austin and E. E. Newell, the latter listed as editor and publisher," according to The Wasatch Wave of June 21, 1892. It seems to have been under the protectorate, and probably issued from the office of the Park City Miner, according to a vague word in The Provo Enquirer June 14, 1892. Its exchanges found a little news in it now and then but seldom said anything about the paper. No copies were found. The Wasatch Wave of November 8, 1893 says: "The Coalville Chronicle now comes out as a Democratic paper. John Boyden takes charge of the editorial department and E. E. Newell, the former editor and proprietor, will look after the business department." The paper and its editor disappeared, off in the stilly night; but the handpower press, and old-style type, were left for the creditors, who appeared shortly after to view the remains. A new company was organized which paid the bills and engaged F. M. Pinneo to edit and manage the new paper to be called something else in repudiation of its predecessor.

The Coalville Times, was accordingly launched February 16, 1894, F. M. Pinneo, editor and manager, issued Fridays. It promptly became a source of frequent cuttings for its contemporaries. No file copies were found. On January 25, 1895, the Iron County Record says: "The Coalville Times is rapidly becoming one of the best weekly papers published in Utah." F. M. Pinneo was editor through 1896, though the paper was in charge of E. H. Rhead and Frank Evans through part of 1898 and 1899. The Park Record for December 3, 1898, takes the following from the Coalville Times: "Owing to a slip in a cog in one of the wheels of our big press, and in two or three wheels of the editor's head, our issue of last week did not appear. It grieves us, because many of our friends have called, and have been disappointed in not receiving their paper. It pleases us, because many of our admirers (?) —mostly delinquents—who have always condemned our honest efforts, if we have ever made any, are given a chance, backed by a shade of justice, in ripping us up the back." Charles R. Jones and E. H. Rhead were editors and business managers in 1900, but another listing in the 1900 directory is: "Rhead, E. H., Editor The Coalville Times, Justice and County Surveyor." It doesn't say he also worked in the garden to keep the wolf away from the back door! Jones continued with the paper until 1905.

The Gazetteer for 1908 says Peterson & Chester were publishers; but unfortunately the chronology cannot be traced through a preserved file. N. J. Peterson is editor and publisher 1912 to 1918, and Charles Ruble about 1919. Harry E. Webb took it over July 1, 1920, and Mrs. C. B. Wallace in 1923. Promptly Mrs. Wallace held a christening and launched the

Summit County Bee, about October 15, 1923. But there are practically no files and no one remembers! R. E. Hartman sponsored the paper from October 1923 to September 1924, for Mrs. Wallace. Syd D. Pierce was managing editor in October 1925. On December 3, 1925, S. D. and C. K. Perry ran their "Salutatory," though Charles W. Lansberry is editor and publisher in October 1926, presumably for Mrs. Wallace, still part owner. The Perrys became publishers in their own right in January 1927, continuing so to date.

CORINNE, Box Elder County

Population: 1870, 783; 1880, 272; 1890, ...; 1900, 323; 1910, 231; 1920, 394; 1930, 352.

Utah Reporter, Weekly, was begun April 9, 1869 by Adam Aulbach, John Barrett and James H. Beadle, publishers, James H. Beadle, editor, the paper being a continuation of The Salt Lake Reporter. A fairly complete file is in the Bancroft Library at Berkeley, after mid-October 1869. Saturday, October 16, 1869, Volume 1, No. 1, The Utah Semi-Weekly Reporter, 4 pages, 7 columns, published every Wednesday and Saturday by J. H. Beadle and Company; 20 columns of advertisements in the first number, Wells Spicer, editor. Then came Volume 1, No. 1 of the Utah Reporter, tri-weekly, on November 2, 1869, published every Tuesday, Thursday and Saturday by The Printers Publishing Company. Wells Spicer's name as editor was dropped from this issue. The Salutatory reveals nothing to us; but a letter is published, directed to Mr. Beadle, the former editor, who claims in his book (Life in Utah, etc.) to have retired early in September 1869, the office shortly thereafter passing into the hands of Huyck and Merrick.

The first bad blood-letting was reported in the November 2, 1869 issue as follows; "War Declared! A Horrible Outrage! J. H. Beadle was knocked down and brutally beaten in the streets of Brigham City yesterday by Old Judge Smith's son. Mr. Beadle at this writing, 10 p.m., lies in a critical condition. This settles the matter right here! If we have got to have war with these fiendish Mormons, let us have it at once and know what we have to depend upon. Too late for particulars."

It seems well that there was no powder in The Reporter plant lest spontaneous combustion might have set it off! At any rate, the night was cool and immediately subsequent issues did not carry any Beadle material, though Goodness knows why; the Beadle trouncing did not by any means compel the editors to lay off their anti-Mormon campaign. Beadle's version of the "knockout" is in his book: "During my editorial labors I frequently had occasion to discuss the action of Mormon courts and particularly after our removal to Corinne. Our County Judge was the Bishop Smith, already mentioned as the husband of two of his nieces. In an article on county affairs I alluded to that fact with considerable severity, more, perhaps, than strict equity in journalism would allow. Soon after quitting the editorial position I was summoned to attend court at Brigham City, and while passing from the courtroom to the street received a violent blow on the back of the head which prostrated me almost senseless upon the ground.

"Whether more than one took part I do not know; all I distinctly remember is a confused rush and trampling of heavy boots, and when I revived I was being raised by my friends, who were taking stock of my condition generally. My collarbone was broken in two places and my scalp badly torn, besides minor injuries; altogether it was a narrow escape. There were but a half dozen Gentiles present, from whom I learned that the principal assailant was a son of the Judge; but I did not see and could not now identify him. The attack was probably caused by my strictures upon his father and the Probate Courts. There was nothing to be done about it; it was one of those incidents to which newspaper men are liable anywhere, which are of frequent occurence to Gentiles in Utah, and for which there is no remedy there." (If they wrote like Beadle!)

Beadle left the Territory for his health, actually, toward December 1, but we read later: "Returned. Mr. J. H. Beadle, former editor of The Reporter, after an absence of six weeks on the Pacific slope returned Sunday morning, December 31, 1869." There are no names on the masthead May 12, 1870, when Huyck and Wilson sign as publishers. The previous February 4, 1870, Beadle wrote a letter (published) to the editor, whom he salutes as "Friend Huyck." The American Newspaper Directory for 1870 shows, "Corinne Reporter, Tuesday, Thursday and Saturday, and weekly Saturday, 4 pages 22 x 32, $12 and $5, circulation 500 and 800, Printers Publishing Company."

The Daily Utah Reporter, Thursday, June 2, 1870, is published every morning except Sunday by Huyck and Wilson. They say: "With this issue we commence the publication of a daily paper . . ." A heavy advertising patronage was carried. A month later, July 2, 1870, the Reporter was published by O. D. Huyck and Company, and was enthusiastically boosting J. H. Beadle for election to Congress. Instead, however, Beadle was elected to the position of Editor of the Reporter, beginning August 2, 1870!

The Farmer's Oracle.

The hand of Industry makes the Desert to bud, bloom and bear fruit, and rears the proudest structures of Earth.

No. 1.   SPRING LAKE VILLA, UTAH COUNTY, UTAH, FRIDAY, MAY 22, 1863.   VOL. 1:

Chicory.

Chicory, succory, or wild endive, is not indigenous to any part of the United States, but was introduced here from England, about 1812. There it is found wild, as it also is in many portions of the continent. Its culture in England was begun by Arthur Young in 1788, though in Belgium and France it had long been grown as a forage plant. For the purpose of forage, it is sown the same as clover, and at the rate of from eight to thirteen pounds per acre. Mr. Young considered it very valuable, especially for those farmers keeping a large stock of swine. He also recommended it for soiling, and for fattening cattle. It is a perennial plant, lasting from four to six years, and even longer. Indeed, it is stated that the plant is growing in Western New York, where sown in 1814. By many it is objected to as a field crop, on account of the difficulty with which it is eradicated.

Chicory closely resembles the dandelion, and, like that plant, contains a milky juice. The flower is a very pretty blue. In early spring it makes a fine salad, and is grown for that purpose in the vicinity of most of our Eastern cities. The roots of the plant have for many years been used to mix with coffee and as a substitute for it. The present high price of coffee has called attention to the culture of chicory, and it is being sown to take its place in all parts of the North. The seed can generally be obtained at most seed stores. To grow it for this purpose, prepare a bed the same as for carrots; sow it about as thickly and thin out and cultivate the same.

Its preparation for a beverage is very simple. Gather the roots late in the fall and place them in sand in the cellar. Remove a few of them as wanted, wash them, cut in slices and dry and roast them in the coffee-roaster till they become brown: grind the same as coffee. Make it the same as a cup of coffee. A writer in a late number of the Ohio *Farmer* gives the following as the method of preparation in vogue among the Germans in his vicinity:—"Roast it the same as coffee, and when nearly done, add a small ten-cupful of common molasses to a quart of the browned root, and continue stirring it a while and it will soon be ready for use. Mix with this browned chicory and molasses one-fifth as much roasted coffee, then go on with your coffee-making as usual; and those who have the tact to make a good cup of coffee will have it."

There is a difference of opinion in regard to the healthfulness of the chicory as a beverage. Many of the old English physicians approved of its dietetic properties. It undoubtedly excites the nerves, and its immoderate use, like that of pure coffee, is without doubt injurious.—[Prairie Farmer.

Vertigo, or Giddiness in Sheep.

M. Reynal considers vertigo a disease of the nervous system, occasioned by a worm—the *canaries cerebralis*—located in the brain. Lambs, from the age of two months, or from four to twelve months, become the subjects of it; and but rarely ever after the age of eighteen months. The disease is apt to end in atrophy—wasting of the brain and spinal marrow. In the rank of principal causes he places, first, Hereditariness; second, Intercourse between the sexes too prematurely, especially the employment of a ram for tupping, not more than six or eight months old, as is the practice in some parts of the country.

To guard against the disease, put out of the breeding-fold both males and females that have shown any signs of the disorder, and not breed from the ewes under the age of thirty months, nor from rams until they have attained to their second year. And if there be any binding conclusions from the influence of a first foundation or necessary ones, we ought to put away from the flock females who, though in apparent health them selves, have once produced diseased stock.—[Translation from the French, by W. Percivall.

Sugar from Box Elder.

A correspondent of the *Prairie Farmer* says:—

"I have been trying it, and am better satisfied with the quality of the product than with that of Sorgho, although it produces a much less quantity. Although, from a little sourness of sap before boiling, it did not grain in the kettle, it has since grained nicely, and the color and flavor are satisfactory, and not dissimilar to the common Sugar or Rock Maple. The sweetness of the sap is also about the same. The Box Elder is a handsome and very fast growing tree, exceeded only with me by the locust, cottonwood and white willow, and I incline to think equal to the two former of the three, in most situations. I would advise tree planters to plant for its two valuable characteristics, sugar

producing and quick growing, and if the former be no object, the latter certainly is."

How a Pear Tree was made to Fruit.

A correspondent of the *Wool Grower* says.—"I will tell you of an experiment I tried to make a pear tree bear. About 23 years ago I planted a small pear tree of the Virgalieu variety. It is now a very large and elegant tree. Every spring it would be covered with blossoms, and just after the fruit began to form, the stems would all fall off and cover the ground. In the autumn of 1861 I determined to try an experiment that should either kill or cure. The ground was dug away five or six feet around the trunk, and down to the roots. A small wagon load of clay was first put in and made into mortar; on the top of this I put a barrel of iron filings, and then over this a barrel of air-slacked lime, and the dirt was drawn back over the whole. Last year, 1862, the tree blossomed as usual, a few of the weakest stems fell off, but enough remained to load down the tree with abundance of luscious fruit."

Planting and Grafting Grapes.

A correspondent of the Michigan *Farmer* says. "For the supply of the family only, the recommendation would be somewhat varied. There are but too many among us who plant a tree or a vine as they would a post; and, once planted, expect it to take care of itself. Such persons should confine themselves to the Hartford Prolific, Concord and Isabella; as these will best bear such treatment."

To graft upon the wild vine, the simplest and surest process is to remove the earth from the vine down to the roots; then cut the stem square off about two inches above the root, and split the stump with a pruning-knife or grafting chisel. Shape the cutting wedge-wise to fit, and insert it as in ordinary wedge-grafting. Dip a strip of cotton cloth in some warm grafting-wax and immediately wind it around the grafted parts. The earth should then be filled in and pressed around the vine. Recollect to match the bark of one with the other, as in top-grafting the apple or any other tree. Everybody should plant grapes.

☞ If you would be tolerated, be tolerant. If you would hear the truth, tell it. If you would not be troubled, don't be troublesome.

THE FARMERS' ORACLE.

Farmers' Oracle !

Published the first and third Tuesday in each month.

J. E. JOHNSON, EDITOR & PUBLISHER.
W. D. JOHNSON, - - - PROPRIETOR.

SUBSCRIPTION, Per Annum, - - - $2.
ADVERTISEMENTS, 10 cents per line, each insertion. A fair discount to liberal and yearly advertisers. Hymenial and Obituary Notices, and Reports of Agricultural, Manufacturing and Literary Societies, and Fairs published without charge.

All Correspondence must be addressed to the Editor, Spring Lake Villa.

Salutatory.

We are pleased once more to say to our friends, old and new, one and all. how d'ye do? Fate, or some well-meaning power, places us again upon the tripod, and so we submit, with this our best bow and a grand flourish of our feather. As we have eschewed politics, we come now to the aid of a science more pleasant, profitable and successful, and hope our change will not worse our readers. Our interests now will be to raise potatoes instead of armies—to count cabbage instead of votes—to stick our "poll" for beans, instead of members of Congress—our "beets" will be of the scarlet sort—our "clubs" of the gourd species—our "stump" meetings where our cabbage seed grows, and our "great gatherings" in autumn—from the garden.

Such is life—all change—

"Ah, me! what is there in Earth's various range,
Which time and absence may not surely change."

It is our desire to be useful (as well as ornamental), and so if you like to try us once more, come on, and we will promise the best we have. We want to live with you here, and *earn* our way among you, and this last we are determined to do. So here's our hand !

Our Paper.—The Prospect.

WE wish to say to our patrons that we have commenced the publication of the *Oracle* under circumstances rather discouraging to the dollar-and-cent interest of the publisher; situated far away from markets where necessary material can only be obtained, and purchased at great expense, for cash only. Then we are sadly annoyed for want of an exchange that can be easily handled and transported at small expense; then again our little paper is an innovation upon our customs and habits, consequently many will argue that, as they have got along first-rate without such an institution, they can profitably continue without, and will scarce discover their mistake until the progress of improvement has left them far behind.

We earnestly believe that our valleys and adjacent mountains contain the elements for our necessities, and material enough to make comfortable and even enrich its inhabitants; yet it takes science, skill, industry, perseverance and application to bring out the hidden wealth, and develop the many comforts. Few countries ever offered a wider field for the industrious, the energetic or scientific in the various details of home industry. The farmer, through his own and the experience of others, finds room for great improvement in the quantity of his crops with less than former labor His stock may be improved and increased when an interchange of experience is adopted. The pomologist may learn where is to be obtained the best stock of fruits, and teach and learn the best modes of cultivation, propagation, &c. The mechanic falls into the advancing column, and produces, with less labor and expense, the necessaries of life, and soon, by division of labor and union of means and strength, our artizans may stay importations by supplying all our most important wants. With a limited research, discoveries have already been made of fine beds of stone coal, gypsum (plaster of Paris), salt, brimstone, saleratus, copperas, alum, nitre, borax, iron, lead, and some other valuable metals, as well as springs of coal oil, mineral or chalylate waters of rare medicinal virtues; limestone, chalk and colored earths may also be enumerated.

Now with the farmer and stock-grower, producing a surplus of cereals, vegetables, fruits, wool and cotton, and the industry of the mechanic showing itself in rearing of better and more extended machinery; our chymist dissolving, purifying, melting and bringing to perfection our minerals, we only need the aid of science and the blessings of Heaven to lead us on with gigantic strides to an elevated and envious position among the sisterhood of States.

We feel a sort of inspiration to attempt assistance in this great cause that underlies our prosperity, and is the foundation of all social enjoyment, wealth and power.

Those who feel the importance of this subject should enlighten his neighbor, and awaken a thirst for intelligence and knowledge in every branch of domestic economy and industry, and whilst we strive to assist you, let us not faint for want of sustenance. Should life and health be spared, we expect that the *Oracle* will be published one year, whether well or poorly sustained.

What Fruits shall we grow ?

The above subject gives a broad field for comment, and in the present number can only make a contracted prelude to a subject of such importance, but in future issues we purpose making this a prominent feature in the *Oracle*.

Fruit, in proper or extended variety, may constitute much of the material of human existence, and taking all the range of climate in our Territory, we may produce all of the most important varieties cultivated on this continent. Among the most staple of these are the early berries, such as strawberries, currants, gooseberries, raspberries and mulberries; the cherry, apricot, peach, plum, grape, apple, and pear. Of these and many other varieties, experience has proven to be not only quite hardy, but from the abundance of fruit and rich flavor, we find the soil and atmosphere congenial to their growth. Then we may answer the question above in rather a broad sense, and reply, grow every variety of fruit whose tree or shrub may be protected from the frosts of winter. This question settled, our next in order is the easiest, best and cheapest manner of producing the stocks, starting from the seed, and covering the whole interim of their growth. First the nursery, then the soil most proper, time and mode of removing to, and care of, the orchard.

We hope our prominent fruit-growers will communicate the result of their experience in every branch of this subject, for we shall be glad to present the same to our readers. We shall, from time to time, detail our limited observations and experiments. We have introduced into this Territory quite a number of new varieties, and our experience in growing and propagating may be advantageous. We would say to nurserymen that now is the time to order seeds of every sort of fruit, evergreens and ornamental trees and shrubbery.

Setting aside the comfort and convenience of having an abundance of fruit in variety, there is now no crop grown that pays as well as fruit; and in a country

Beadle begins his editorial services to the world with a column-and-a-quarter screed. In it he admits that the new era for the paper should really be a new book of Genesis for Corinne, as well as "all Gentile Utah from Bear Lake to Panaca and from Quakingasp to Nevada." Beadle always wrote fluently and usually wrote well; in fact there was no stopping him on a favorite text, except when the running, rambling editorial piled into a paid advertisement over in the second or third column! He wrote on all subjects, but the home tone of the major key was the Mormons. Only the business office with its really heavy advertising could confine Editor Beadle to his domain, and thus it was not infrequently we found a three column editorial—just one grand masterpiece occupying all the space allotted to the Editor! The paper ran very little Utah State news; and the Salt Lake City correspondence letters were of the keyhole and back fence variety. Nevertheless, the business concerns surely ate it up, and they applauded substantially with their patronage—not for a month or so, but month after month.

The volume three, No. 1 of the Daily Utah Reporter is dated Monday evening, December 5, 1870, and is reduced to five columns. The front page is nearly solid reading matter, but the other three pages are mostly display advertising, much of it apparently of the exchange or trade type, paid for by the wares or services advertised, not in cash. There was the same masthead, same business office domination apparent, yet with the same spread eagle editorial style and the same dearth of local and down state news, until January 19, 1871, when Editor Beadle's name was dropped and "Judge D. J. Toohy, Editor," succeeded. Also, there were shorter and more varied editorials and more reading matter generally.

The American Newspaper Directory for 1871, gives the circulation as 1,000 daily and 2,000 weekly, which was pretty good, considering a Corinne population at the time of 783! The Saturday, May 27, 1871 issue of the **Corinne Reporter** (note the heading change; the Utah Reporter name evidently took in too much territory) was by Adam Aulbach and Company. There were four pages of six columns each, being 95% news or filler with no advertising to speak of. Dennis J. Toohy was Editor. But in the June 17, 1871 number we read: "Personal: Dennis J. Toohy resigned as Editor of the Corinne Reporter;" and June 27, 1871, "Notice! I have disposed of my interest in the office to Dennis J. Toohy, the former Editor of the paper (to June 12, 1871) the sale taking effect today—Adam Aulbach." While in the July 1, 1871 number, we find, "D. J. Toohy, editor and proprietor." Toohy assures us for the Reporter, "The change involves no diversion of its general course."

Nevertheless, "The publication of the Reporter in Corinne," says the Salt Lake Herald, March 30, 1872, "will stop with the issue of this evening, and a new venture will take its place. The proprietors are moving their material to the capital (Salt Lake City)." But on April

3, 1872, the Deseret News prints the sequel, " 'No Gentile Sun. The following was among our last night's dispatches:' Corinne, Utah, April 2:—The business men of the city, in a body, waited upon Judge Toohy, Editor of the Corinne Reporter, yesterday, and offered him a bonus of $5,000, to continue the publication of his paper here, and not publish the Gentile Sun at Salt Lake City. The proposition was accepted, and Toohy and the Reporter appear again today." The Salt Lake Herald follows on April 4, 1872, "Judge Toohy writes us to discontinue the advertisement of the Gentile Sun, as that Sun enterprise has set, the merchants of Corinne, having in mass meeting subscribed a sufficient bonus to have the Reporter continued. Mr. Aulbach, who had bought into the new paper on condition that the office was to be moved to this city . . . retires from the engagement, leaving Judge Toohy sole proprietor and editor of the Reporter as before."

The American Newspaper Directory notice for 1872 says, the Corinne Daily Reporter was $10 a year and that it was: "the Pioneer Gentile paper in Utah, established in 1868, as the successor to the Salt Lake City Daily Vedette, removed to Corinne April 1, 1869; official organ of the United States, for publishing laws of Congress, orders of departments, etc. The only daily paper in Utah, outside of Salt Lake City." The circulation was 1130. A Reporter display advertisement in the Reporter May 6, 1872, and on other dates, calls itself, "The great Anti-Mormon newspaper; the largest and cheapest paper on the Overland Railroad."

Were they already beginning to salt the (newspaper) mine, ready for a sale? Judge Toohy is quoted in that number as saying, "There is no place like Corinne, of whose bright future, when that railroad to Montana is completed, he has most glowing anticipations." We also find this disclaimer: "No barter advertising for pianos, watches, or sewing machines taken! *cash only*, and no notice taken of anything else!" By the way Judge Toohy evidently practiced a little law on the side, as for a short time he ran a lawyer's "card" in the paper. June 16, 1873, the Salt Lake Daily Journal says: "Green Majors from the Editorial staff of the Corinne Reporter . . . called;" about which time the Reporter is presumed to have changed hands or suspended. The Journal on July 21, 1873, says: " 'How much did Brigham pay for the Corinne Reporter?' was the question asked us this morning. We give it up."

Then came the beginning of the end. "The Corinne Reporter is no more," says the Salt Lake Tribune, July 27, 1873. "In Friday's (July 25) issue of that paper Judge Toohy announced its decease, and his intention of coming to this city and starting the Salt Lake Times." The Herald adds: "Judge Toohy, in a kindly and well written valedictory, briefly reviews the history of the paper and the town, and tenders well merited thanks all around." Sorry, the Bancroft file terminates with July 19, 1873!

The Salt Lake Journal says, August 9, 1873: "No paper yet. The good citizens of Corinne are disconsolate. They want a newspaper, so they can abuse Judge Toohy for leaving them in the lurch. Corinne is a floundering little town, contains a great many white people, and promises hearty support to an enterprising newspaper man. Were it not that we are becoming wealthy and saucy, we might be persuaded to move our quarters to the 'Burg on the Bear'."

Comes now the shadow of the grim hand of tragedy in Corinne Reporter history. "We had a call today (September 1, 1873) from Horace W. Myers," says the Deseret News, "who informed us he had purchased the Corinne Daily Reporter from its late proprietor; and that he will commence on Thursday next, (September 4) the republication of that paper, he having met with such encouragement from the citizens of that place as to give him the most flattering hopes of success. Mr. Myers says it is his intention to pursue a different policy with his new venture in the newspaper line, from that sometimes adopted, he having apparently learned that scurrilous abuse will not pay; and he intends to try to make his new paper a decent sheet."

Two weeks later: "Mr. H. W. Myers, Editor and Proprietor of the Corinne Reporter, called in yesterday. He spoke in high terms of the business prospects of Corinne and of the public spiritedness of the citizens of that place, and also seemed well pleased with the prospects of his paper with that region." (The Salt Lake Tribune of September 13, 1873, had quoted from the Reporter, which had already been revived). An additional copy of the Reporter dated October 8, 1873, shows Horace W. Myers, publisher. That issue carried practically solid advertising on the front page, on three-fifths of the second page, on more than half of page three, and on all of page four. If this had been alive and paying matter, Myers would have been on the road to fortune, instead of a suicide's grave. Another copy of the Reporter in the Bancroft file was for October 15, 1873, and may have been Myers' last one.

The former owners of the Reporter ought to have known when to sell. Many Corinne residents were moving to Salt Lake City at that time; the town was being all but evacuated of its older business firms; only the lad Myers, as a newcomer, might not have been aware of this fact. There was little or no news in the paper probably because the news sources were moving away, and it wouldn't have been good for the town to chronicle all the departures. The fact is, the several liquor and hotel advertisements were for Salt Lake and San Francisco houses, and the numerous Corinne cards of drug stores, engineers, grocers, liverymen, painters and bankers, were doubtless largely for parties that were already or soon would be moving away. All of which was a cruel way of leaving young Myers holding the sack.

The tragic end was not long coming, after these serious facts bore down upon the young publisher. It is chronicled in the Salt Lake Tribune, November 26, 1873. "Corinne, Utah, November 25. Horace W.

Myers, editor of the Corinne Daily Reporter, and formerly of the Salt Lake Mining Journal, committed suicide last night by taking laudanum. Pecuniary trouble is supposed to be the cause." (Editorial) "This unfortunate journalist came to Salt Lake from Illinois and associated himself with Oscar G. Sawyer in the publication of the Salt Lake Mining Journal. He put a liberal sum of money into the enterprise ($4,000, we believe) but through deficient business management, the paper died on their hands. He next went to Bingham, where he engaged in journalistic labors for a few weeks; and thence he proceeded to Corinne, where he purchased Judge Toohy's interest in the Reporter. That place is too small to support a daily paper, and our journalist found a load of debt accumulating on his shoulders . . . Horace Myers was but 24 years of age."

This is just an echo: from the Deseret News, January 2, 1874: "A bad plight. Mr. K. S. Myers was staying at the Salt Lake house last night. This morning he found himself in a pretty fix. During the night some individual of thievish proclivities had crept into his room, the result of which was that he found himself, on waking up, minus coat, pants, and boots, and had to remain in bed until a pair of unmentionables, and other articles were brought to him. Mr. Myers was on a brief visit to Utah, having come for the purpose of settling up the affairs of his deceased brother, Horace W. Myers, late editor of the Corinne Reporter." The Bancroft Library's file of the Reporter is fairly complete from October 16, 1869, to July 19, 1873.

Corinne Daily Journal. Volume 1, No. 1, Tuesday morning, May 2, 1871. Six columns, 4 pages; daily, except Monday; Kenyon and Merrick, publishers and proprietors, $10 a year. A fine, full file, securely bound, is in the Bancroft Library. The paper started with excellent news service and a good advertising patronage, though it was not without its adversities, from the start. Indeed, it seems from this perspective, its sponsors rode to town on Baalam's recalcitrant ass. Those frowns of fortune, however, kept the publishers in the neighborhood of the straight and narrow way of first class newspaper journalism, while they lasted, and their tombstone is practically untarnished.

"We have received the prospectus of the Corinne Journal, to be issued daily and weekly by F. Kenyon and associates at $10 per annum for the daily edition and $5 for the weekly," records the Salt Lake Herald, April 5, 1871. "The prospectus says the conductors of the paper 'will be courteous and liberal in their expressions and views and endeavor to deserve the patronage of the public of Utah, and particularly of the people of the section of which Corinne is the center'." The "conductors" of the Journal were not evidently aware of the efforts of the brakemen in the rear, disguised as census takers who accounted for less than a thousand souls in Corinne, even when all the saloons were filled on Saturday night! Nor the existence of the fiery Reporter ahead of them; nor twenty times that population in Salt Lake City behind them. No, they only saw the hand-writing on the sky above that

town: "Corinne is fast growing to be the Metropolis," as their Salutatory proclaims. Metropolis of what? And why? Ask any emigrant
wild duck today! But to our history.

"In the hurry, consequent upon unpacking and arranging our
type . . . Compositors are scarce. Our thanks are tendered to the publishers of the Reporter for numerous favors. Printer wanted!" is the
running commentary of the Editor in the initial number. It wasn't
necessary that the printer be a Republican or a Liberal (anti-Mormon)
though the Journal was both. "We are again indebted to the editor of
the Reporter," says the Journal, May 10, 1871, "this time for the use
of his exchanges."

"We have received the initial number of the Corinne Daily Journal,
published by Kenyon and Merrick, proprietors," says the Salt Lake
Tribune, May 3, 1871 "It is a handsome, spicy, newsy, sheet . . . It is
to be conducted politically as a Republican paper. We have no objection to that, but we think that it is a trifle too early to introduce political
distinctions in this territory . . . ; at present there can be but two parties
here—one the Church and the other, its opponents." The Deseret News
adds this: "the number contains several apologies for its appearance,
for lack of original matter, for the absence of some material which
had not come to hand, etc. But . . . the paper presents a very creditable
appearance. It indulges in high hopes for the future of Corinne."
While it was regarded as anti-Mormon, the Ogden Junction, May 10,
1871, says of the Journal: "Unlike the 'Slander Mill' published in the
same town, it is respectful in its tone and bearing toward it neighbors,
and appears to be issued in a spirit of fairness and moderation." But
evidently at times at least, the Journal was anybody's plaything and
nobody's business. Hear the Ogden Junction of May 24, 1871: "Douglass (O. J. H.) tax collector, newspaper correspondent, Mormon-eater,
etc., is once more in hot water . . . While the editor of the Corinne
Journal was absent, he seized the opportunity to indulge, whereupon
O. J. H. appears in last Sunday's Journal over his full signature, with
a half apology, half defense. The Journal repudiates his first article
in concise and positive terms, and everybody jeers poor 'Douglass' and
throws out squibs about 'Kodphisch Aristocracy'," which may signify
something or other.

No newspaper ever entered upon its career with more kindness
and generosity of attitude toward positively everybody, in the preparation of its news. But even the Journal soon saw itself as a flower born
to blush unseen, wasting its fragrance on the desert air. Thus the
editor may have been sermonizing to himself, rather than "nodding"
before his responsibilities, when on June 21, 1871, he wrote, "A fine
crop of young grasshoppers has made its appearance here on the
prairie near town. It is to be hoped they will there starve to death;
and the chances are not at all bad for it."

The editorial scissors apparently worked best on the exchanges
from beyond Territorial lines, though possibly outside material was all

that was left around the "windows" previously clipped in the columns by the original reader of the exchanges in the Reporter office. At any rate, the Journal's Utah news was rather scarce, but it ran a considerable amount of personal, travel, and western historical news of those who came and went through Corinne. The Editor's "grapevine" was the railroad telegraph and he had frequent exclusive stories from such places as Terrace, Promontory, Kelton, and Blue Creek, mere railroad sidings! But even with such arteries of news sources open to it, the Journal grew anemic. Consequently publisher Kenyon announced in the July 5, 1871, issue, his intention of starting in Salt Lake City, a Liberal Journal. The Journal had reduced its price but not its quality, and still had more space in news fonts than in advertising or display forms. A call for the settlement of all accounts was made, July 26, 1871. The Valedictory appeared July 30, 1871, signed by Frank Kenyon, in which was no word of bitterness, rather of hope, which sprang eternal, even then, and sprang spontaneously and continuously from such as he. This time it was for the Salt Lake City Daily Review, still hiding somewhere in the Corinne Journal's type cases and in the Editor's dreams.

Corinne Daily Mail first number about September 2, 1874; every evening except Sundays. File in Bancroft Library, from September 7, 1874, Volume 1, No. 5, to October 12, 1875, only a few missing. Mail Printing Company, H. H. Watts, S. S. Johnson, W. S. Cooke, and J. W. Pike. Johnson was business manager; four pages, six columns, 80% advertisements at the start, rather meager news service, both local and telegraphic, for the business office hogged all the space. Being published at Corinne is sufficient assurance that its policy was anti-Mormon. The news service gradually improved, and the items were written with a little more definite slant against the Mormons. Usually there were no editorials but when run they were hot.

The earliest contemporaneous reference is from the Salt Lake Tribune, October 8, 1874. "S. S. Johnson, Esq., one of the publishers and business manager of our able contemporary, the Corinne Daily Mail, is in the city . . . (Able because) Johnson writes up Mormonism with a pick handle dipped in asafetida, which the same, is very appropriate." (The Tribune ought to know, for in those days its asafetida came from the same kind of jug.) The Tribune deposes further, December 25, 1874: "H. H. Watts, Esq., one of the enterprising publishers of the Corinne Daily Mail, dropped in . . . We have a hearty welcome ever ready for our sterling contemporary on the Bear. That paper is a loyal advocate of loyalty and law." Watts became business manager, January 25, 1875, but on February 16, 1875, "The Mail Printing Company, heretofore conducting this paper, has been dissolved. The Mail from this on, will be published by Cooke and Johnson. Mr. Watts, the retiring member . . . will leave for Virginia City, Nevada." Being about the same crowd in command, the advertising never ceased to predominate over the news in point of column inches.

But it was a case of too many assets, or a gluttony for advertisements (which did not pay) that got the Mail down. You never could tell from the looks of the sheet in those days whose fancy bicycle the editor was sporting! The advertising contracts were more often good at the bar instead of the bank; and we thought as we scanned that vast area of quaint advertisements, how like sign-boards of history; tombstones, they seem when we read this: "Snuffed out.—The Corinne Mail has not long survived the Indian scare," says the Deseret Evening News, "as will be seen by the following, from its issue of November 3, 1875. 'With this number the publication of the Mail ceases in Corinne. We deem it unnecessary to state the various reasons for its suspension. One proposition is however applicable—that a newspaper (as any other business), to sustain itself, must have an income greater than the expense of conducting it. No one can slander us with the assertion that we have not published a strictly Gentile paper. And, busted or not, we still retain that gratification. To the business men of Corinne, who have given us their patronage, and to our subscribers, we tender our earnest thanks; and we certainly wish each and every one of our patrons may have better success in the several occupations in which they may be engaged, than the proprietors of the Mail have had in theirs.— Cooke and Johnson.' "

The Corinne Record (nee Gazette), Debut, February 16, 1877. Daily, each evening except Sunday, by John W. and Edward Pike. No files or copies found. The prospectus promised the "Gazette," says the Salt Lake Tribune, February 3, 1877. The Virginia City, Nevada Enterprise of February 8, 1877, says: "It is rumored that the Silver City Reporter Office has been purchased by Mr. Pike, who intends removing the material to Corinne, where he will start a newspaper."

Witness the Provo Enquirer, March 17, 1877, "We learn that the Corinne Daily Record has made its appearance and seems well patronized with advertisements and having a nice list of subscribers. The business men, citizens and officials in that Burg on the Bear, can and do appreciate a paper published in their locality." The Tribune adds, "It is a sprightly, five column sheet, well edited, and full of news. We congratulate the Burg on the Bear."

"The Record did not commence publication for the purpose of eating up the entire Mormon community," quotes the Deseret News, March 21, 1877, "Nor is it the intention of its publishers to revile and blackguard those who may happen to differ with us in point of political opinions . . . The interests of Corinne and northern Utah claim the greatest share—all in fact, of our attention."

The American Newspaper Directory for 1877 and 1878, says "Democratic, 4 pages, 19 x 26, subscription, $8, Record Publishing Company, John W. Pike, editor. Circulation estimated at 300. About 70 miles northwest of Salt Lake City, with which it is connected by steamer." Ship ahoy! also, ships that pass in the night! Evidently a Latter-day Saint soon succeeded to the editorship, for the Tribune

T. B. H. STENHOUSE
Born February 21, 1825
Died March 7, 1882

EDWARD W. TULLIDGE
Born September 30, 1829
Died May 21, 1894

Godbe & Co.'s Exchange Building at left (Main at First South—Montgomery Ward corner). Home of Utah Magazine (upstairs) 1867-1869. The low, third building from left was Mrs. T. B. H. Stenhouse's Millinery Emporium.

erupts the following, May 20, 1877: "Ye Record man in the Burg on the Bear, after hurling foul scorn at this journal for sounding the keynote of alarm, thus cantankerously cheweth the leek; 'surrounded by Indians and Mormons, the both of whom hate us as the devil—the result of Priestly teachings—our position is to say the least, a most unenviable one'." And on May 26, 1877, the Tribune says: "Grandmother (Deseret News) takes great delight in copying the silly vaporings of the young Mormon Editor of the Corinne Record."

"The Corinne Record is now issued tri-weekly instead of daily," says the Salt Lake Tribune, July 21, 1877. "The boys found a daily paper rather an expensive luxury." The Deseret News adds this variety: "Less Numerous—The Corinne Record is becoming less numerous. It is changed from a daily to a semi-weekly. Probably the Salt Lake monster swallowed most of the subscribers and advertisers of the Record, they being unable to swallow the monster, even with the aid of Barnes and Company salt!" The end of the Record comes simply, sine die, in the Provo Enquirer, October 10, 1877: "The Corinne Record has suspended publication, and it is surmised, will resume in Salt Lake City."

Corinne Calliope, tuned in about April 1, 1892, with one L missing, Friday, 4 pages, 17 x 24, $2. J. F. Pribyl, Editor and Publisher. No copies found; probably all used to produce steam. Editor Pribyl might readily perform the orthographical feat of spelling his own name correctly, but not that of his newspaper; (or was he merely short of type?); consequently, the Brigham Bugler took him to task April 16, 1892, "If brother Pribyl would put another note in the shape of the letter L in the head of his melodious 'Caliope' we imagine his tunes would sound a little more complete."

The Spanish Fork Sun had another name for it, and sun-tanned the "Organist" as follows, September 24, 1892. "The Corinne Calliopest must be a particular side partner of Sam Leroy, who has recently taken hold of the Beaver Utonian." Nevertheless, while the exchanges played "L" with the paper's name, bars, strains and whole tunes were frequently borrowed from the Calliope's melodies, for we found them quoted far and wide, during a year or more. A Calliope poem about baldheads went the rounds in the summer of 1892, after which the Manti Times-Reporter (November 24, 1892) admitted, "As a newspaper the Corinne Calliope is better than formerly."

Corinne may have been "Surrounded with fertile soil to the horizon," as one claimant phrased it; yet that soil was pretty punk for rearing newspapers, as several casualties bore witness. And the fifteen fallow years since the plowing under of the last one, did not seem to benefit the Calliope, whose weekly wail through 1893 seemed to be calling the coyotes to the repast! Prybil got away to the mountains for a rest and rumination in June, 1893; meanwhile "Editor Sleater of the Corinne Calliope, gave the (Brigham Bugler) sanctum a call," June 17, 1893.

The Bugler of October 7, 1893, sounds this requiem: "Farewell.
—Corinne Calliope, September 29, 1893. Goodbye, Old Pard; you
have made a noble struggle to shake the millstones from your neck and
keep afloat; but the fates were against you and you sank into oblivion
and were swallowed up in the bowels of the Bear. Fame and fortune
alike go down and are absorbed and lost in the great maw of neglect
and unappreciativeness." The Brigham Bugler of October 23, 1893,
caught this echo; "John F. Pribyl of the Logan Nation . . . came down
to lug home the remains of the defunct Corinne Calliope."

Inter Mountain News, published from 1899 to 1905, without a copy
in existence to show for it (so far as we learned) ; and very few references from which to form its story. The Utah County Democrat, June
14, 1899, says: "The Boxelder News reports another newspaper to be
started in Utah. This one at Corinne, to be known as the Inter Mountain
News." The State Gazetteer for 1900: "Corinne; Intermountain News,
Thursday, J. L. Hamilton, publisher and proprietor." Kenner's book—
"Utah As It Is" (1904) says the Inter Mountain News, 7 column, independent, weekly of Corinne, edited by A. A. Johnson "Is the only
paper published under the great Bear River Canal System!" That explains it! Dunked! The 1905 American Newspaper Directory lists the
News, Saturday, 4 to 8 pages, $1.25 a year, circulation claimed 1,012
(population of Corinne 323) Report Paper Co., publishers, C. R.
Christensen, editor." That is the last we hear of it. Could the Bear
have eaten it up, for storying about its circulation?

DESERET, Millard County

Population: 1890, 661; 1900, 506; 1910, 414.

Millard County Blade. Volume 1, Number 1, about June 9, 1893.
Rognon and Scott, proprietors. "The initial number of the Millard
County Blade, of Deseret and Oasis, has come to hand. It is a neat little
eight column, 4-page paper, and has a fine advertising patronage to
commence with. It announces itself strictly independent in politics, and
that its object will be the upbuilding of Millard county." So we read
in the Utah Journal, Logan, June 14, 1893.

"It is keen and bright, being free from all rust," the Brigham
Bugler says of the Blade, June 17, 1893. The sponsors apparently fled
from it as if it were found to be the two-edged variety. "The name of
J. P. Jacobson, once of this city, now appears in the Millard County
Blade, as manager of that paper," we picked up from the Bugler of
June 24, 1893. It is just possible, however, Rognon and Scott found it
hard to manage and were hiring help for that purpose. Whatever the
worry, the Bugler of September 23, 1893 promotes Jacobson, whose
name "appears as Editor and Manager" and says the paper had changed hands.

Josiah F. Gibbs, who got his newspaper start on the Blade, says Charles Goddard of Salt Lake City, appeared on the scene with a dream of a chain of country weeklies. The Blade, says Gibbs, consisted of four pages, two patent and the two local pages well supported with boiler plate. "The sheet was a novelty, and subscriptions soon totaled one hundred fifty," but the proprietor shortly read the writing on the wall—not in the Blade, and unloaded the plant on Josiah F. Gibbs, George Crane, and Henry W. Holley. Soon two more had a bad "Indian Scare" and then there was only Gibbs, who made an arrangement with the printer, "whereby he was to receive the entire income of the Blade, less the bare expense of material and postage. The Editor and Publisher took his emolument in the form of satisfaction in seeing his name and title in upper-case type on Page 4." So says the Gibbs manuscript, written in the third person, which unfortunately does not fix the date. "Indian Scare" by the way was a way of referring to supposed secret but summary exterminations by "Danites" or "Destroying Angels" alias Mormon Vigilantes. Gibbs says the printer feared for his health (from setting Gibbs' anti-Mormon editorials?) and two young women apprentices were employed. Thereupon the man-printer vanished. The paper grew in size and in fearlessness; and its policy of "On earth peace" was discarded, Gibbs says. "Even a weakly weekly required a 'policy' if it hoped to be noticed;" It did! "The new policy was 'free thinking, free utterance, free conduct within the law, and a square deal to all.'"

In due course, however, "J. F. Gibbs, Editor of the Deseret Blade, has had J. M. Viele and L. W. Gaisford, Editor and Proprietor of the Millard County Progress (Fillmore) arrested for criminal libel" says the Park Record of March 23, 1895, continuing: "The suit grew out of a newspaper quarrel in which Gibbs got worsted. The Progress charged him with being a literary pirate."

Gibbs gives a glimpse of another scene: "One day the late (L.D.S.) Apostle, Francis M. Lyman, opened the sanctum door just wide enough to admit his face, and inquired quizzically: 'Is the fighting editor in?' The gist of that interview was: 'Brother Gibbs, you are doing a good work, but don't go too far!'" He didn't! He just went to Nephi, where his Blade appeared with the new date line and the abbreviated title, "The Blade" late in May of 1895! the last number bearing the Deseret address being dated May 22, 1895. It was the end of the Deseret Blade, though not the end of The Blade, and by no means the end of Gibbs, whose writings against conditions and influences on his blacklist, continued until his demise in 1932.

A bound file of the Millard County Blade and its Nephite successor, The Blade, from Wednesday, February 13, 1895 to Saturday, May 30, 1896, is in the possession of Alfred Orme at Nephi, who was associated with Gibbs at Nephi. These papers had eight pages of 6 columns each and show J. F. Gibbs, editor. Oddly enough, the paper was entered as second class mail matter at the Oasis postoffice, a neighboring village to Deseret. The Oasis postmaster was probably one of the few men in the county who was permitted by the militant editor to say the Blade was "second class matter!"

DELTA, Millard County

Population: 1910, 1007; 1920, 939; 1930, 1183.

Millard County Chronicle. Vol. 1, No. 1, Monday, July 4, 1910. Burtner Post Office, Norman B. Dresser, Editor and Proprietor. Railroad station (one block west) Aiken. Paper printed at Salt Lake City. "Take notice" (N. B.) Dresser disliked both of the town's names and launched a newspaper campaign for an appropriate substitute. This was found in "Delta" a year later. Dresser's Chronicle came pretty nearly being a promotional sheet, for he saw more opportunities in Delta than any mother ever saw in a family of twelve. His optimism and his eloquence would inspire any commercial club secretary, if it didn't shame him into self effacement. In earlier years Dresser lost all the fingers of one hand in a job printing press, hence as a country newspaper publisher, the help he had to hire absorbed his profits, and the meniality of some of his duties must have been depressing.

The present editor, Frank Beckwith, says: "Old timers can remember him going around the various communities in a little dog cart, taking the bundles for each town to the postmasters. Dresser wrote poetry and would read it in public gatherings." So it was that even Dresser had his moments of low spirits; and on January 1, 1914 he sold the Chronicle to Homer G. Busenbark of Oklahoma. Some years later Dresser was killed in a Salt Lake City street car accident.

The newspaper covered the county like a blanket, and we don't mean a wet one. In its fifth number it carried as a department: "L. W. Gaisford, Editor, East Side edition, Fillmore, Utah." The new name "Delta" first appeared on the Chronicle July 13, 1911. Editor Busenbark's wagon was obviously hitched to Dresser's star, and while he ran a good newspaper he seemed glad to sell it to Charles O. Davis, of Cokeville, Wyoming, March 11, 1915. Davis did better in point of tenure if not in earnings; carrying on for four years. He then turned the paper over to the Delta State Bank, which had entered the front office for the same reason banks often enter. Frank Beckwith, Sr., Cashier of the Bank, was at this close range, lured from his money bags to become Managing Editor, publisher and printer of the Chronicle, for the Bank, February 20, 1919. He shortly became proprietor. And if we count Mrs. Beckwith and the son, Frank S., whose name is now on the masthead, the ownership has remained the same to this day.

Frank Beckwith, Sr. takes easy place as one of the state's most picturesque publishers. He speaks with authority on fossils, Indians, history, geology, anthropology, paleontology, photography, snakes, boy scouts—everything under the Millard County sun—before banquets and auditorium audiences far and wide, managing his own Chautauqua circuit. He has peopled that region with storied legions, earning immortality for himself as for the unseen hosts of whom he writes. Beckwith also has a philosophy all his own which makes the Chronicle almost a personal organ.

In Beckwith's own chronology of the paper, his last entry is: "Frank Beckwith, 1919 to date, and only one leap ahead of the sheriff in 1936." Beckwith's flirtation with the sheriff is not likely to result in an engagement, as witness these extracts from his recent unique epitome to a certain "Mr. Linotype": "He came to the Chronicle office seventeen years ago. In all that time he has never taken a layoff; every week, faithfully he has delivered his output, never complaining, asking only fair treatment, never causing any trouble, a most efficient workman; never causing any friction in the shop, but like a good watch, silently attending to business, content only to do good work, let the credit for it be taken by others.

"Mr. Linotype has turned out for us in the paper alone, ten columns of matter weekly, averaging more than 884,000 lines, 37,128,000 letters, dropped into line, moulded into type, and unostentatiously placed before our readers. Counting job work, nearly 75,000,000 letters have been dropped into place. In that same length of time, on pleasure only the Editor and his family have spent on automobiles as follows: a new car, $790; a used car, $700; a new one, $660; a little truck, $125; a used car $175; a new car $660; another new one, $450, total $3,550, and little to show for it. One single investment of $2,635 in the linotype is still making that family its living, still earning the wherewithal to buy more cars."

DUCHESNE, Duchesne County

Population: 1910, 929; 1920, 700; 1930, 590.

The Duchesne Record. Vol. 1, No. 1, April 8, 1909. Published every Thursday at Theodore, Wasatch County. (town later called Duchesne, when Duchesne County was organized), Fred L. Watrous, Editor; Herman Bunn, Business Manager. The Record was combined with the Uinta Standard of Roosevelt and the Uintah Chieftain of Myton, and called the Uinta Record, published at Myton, beginning May, 1910, but was moved back to Duchesne July 2, 1915, as the Duchesne Record, J. P. May. publisher. But Fred L. Watrous is again listed as publisher in July, 1915. He was succeeded by George S. Sloan, August 11,1917, who turned it over to R. F. Walsh August 24, 1918.

Markus and Markus became publishers sometime in 1919. Dr. M. Markus, Editor, and Elizabeth Markus, Associate Editor. The Markuses gave up their lease July 15, 1920, and D. L. Whitehurst became Editor for the owning group. But Whitehurst did not last well, throwing in the sponge in favor of Stephen W. Johnson May 13, 1920. Glen C. Gray became business manager December 23, 1920, but was dead from

DAILY UNION VEDETTE.

Bri. B. Young

A champion brave, alert and strong....To aid the right, oppose the wrong.

Vol. 1.]   Camp Douglas, U. T., Thursday Morning, January 28, 1864.   [No. 19.

Daily Union Vedette,

PUBLISHED EVERY MORNING, EXCEPT SUNDAYS,
—AT—
CAMP DOUGLAS, UTAH TERRITORY,
—BY THE—
OFFICERS AND ENLISTED MEN,
—OF THE—
California & Nevada Territory Volunteers

Terms of Subscription:
"One copy one month, ... $1 00
"One copy three months, ... 2 75
"One copy six months, ... 5 00

Rates of Advertising:
Ten lines or less, one insertion, ... $ 50
Ten lines or less, each subsequent insertion, . 1 00
One-fourth column, one month, ... 15 00
One-half column, one month, ... 25 00
One column, one month, ... 45 00
Business Cards, per month, ... 5 00

Job Work,

SUCH AS
MINING CERTIFICATES,
PROGRAMMES, BALL INVITATIONS,
BILL HEADS,
Cards, Circulars, Blank Forms,
— etc., - - etc., - - - etc.,
IN GOOD STYLE AND ON REASONABLE TERMS.

☞ All Orders addressed "To the Publishers of the DAILY VEDETTE, Camp Douglas, Utah Territory," will meet with prompt attention.

☞ All communications must be addressed to the "Editor of the DAILY VEDETTE, Camp Douglas, Utah Territory."

☞ MR. H. PREVINGTON is our authorized Agent for the transaction of business in Salt Lake City. Office in the U. S. Quartermaster's Storehouse, Main Street.

☞ MR. L. W. A. COLE is our Carrier and Soliciting Agent for Great Salt Lake City.

BY OVERLAND TELEGRAPH.

[SPECIAL DISPATCHES TO DAILY VEDETTE.]

A Speech by P. M. Blair.

NEW YORK, Jan. 26th.

A special to the *Post* says: Postmaster-General Blair made a speech at Annapolis, Friday evening, in advocacy of the President's Emancipation and Amnesty Proclamations. The speech gives much satisfaction.

Congressional.

WASHINGTON, Jan. 25th.

HOUSE—To-day Fernando Wood spoke against confiscation and in favor of peace.

The Committee on Conduct of the War meets to-day and will at once take up the cases of all frauds on the Government.

A special to the *Commercial* says: The House Military Committee to-day reduced the Commutation clause of the Senate Enrollment Bill, to $300 and refused to except Quakers and Clergymen.

SENATE—The Finance Committee will consider the Tax bill.

An important bill will soon be reported from the Post-office Committee making the Department responsible for money sent by mail.

HOUSE—The Committee agreed, by nearly a unanimous vote, to the report of the Committee, requesting the President to give notice of the termination of the reciprocity treaty [with Canada we presume.]

HOUSE—The Committee on Elections have reported against the claims of Field, of Louisiana, and Segar, of Virginia, as Representatives from those States.

A resolution instructing the Military Committee to report a bill increasing the pay of soldiers, was referred to a Select Committee of three.

The Military Committee reported the Senate's amendatory enrollment bill, and amendments. The consideration of the bill is postponed until Wednesday.

CHICAGO, Jan. 26th.

SENATE—In Executive Session yesterday, R. L. Perkins was confirmed as Postmaster of San Francisco, vice Parker, removed.

Another amendment, proposed to the Enrollment Bill of the House, yesterday, provides that those physically exempted, but who have an income of twelve hundred dollars, shall pay the regular Commutation of three hundred dollars.

A bill was introduced in the House yesterday authorizing Utah to form a Constitution and State government.

A resolution was also adopted instructing the Judiciary Committee to inquire into the expediency of organizing a Department of Industry to embrace the Agricultural, Colonization, Emigration, Freedmans, and Mineral Lands Bureaus.

Bank Statement---Foreign News.

NEW YORK, Jan. 25th.

Bank statement shows a decrease in loans of three millions; decrease of specie, eight hundred thousand; decrease of deposits one hundred and seventy-five thousand.

The *Commercial* says: Private advices from well informed quarters state positively that the Schleswig-Holstein question is about to be settled peacefully by an agreement between the Great Powers in which Denmark has already promised to acquiesce in and which will be imposed by Austria and Prussia upon the lesser German States by force, if necessary.

A Pernambuco letter, of Dec. 15th, reports both the Alabama and Tuscaloosa at St. Catharines, on Nov. 20th. They were refused supplies and ordered off at the request of the American Consul. As regards the Alabama the letter must be mistaken.

From Canada.

QUEBEC, Canada, Jan. 25th.

Marshal Kane and thirteen Confederates, mostly escaped officers from Johnson Island, left here to-day for Halifax.

From Arkansas.

CAIRO, Jan. 25th.

Little Rock advices to the 16th, state that the Convention which assembled on the 8th, has about completed its labors. The greater portion of the State was represented. An article forever prohibiting slavery was adopted; only one dissenting vote. A Constitution is to be submitted to the people on the second Monday in March, at which time State officers and members of the Legislature are to be elected. The action of the Convention was universally satisfactory to loyal men. The qualification of voters is that prescribed by the President's proclamation. Loyal citizens say they will be able to poll twenty thousand votes for the Constitution.

Exploit of Col. Palmer.

CHICAGO, Jan. 25th.

A Nashville telegram of Saturday, says: A Federal train, with a guard consisting of six companies of the 15th Pensylvania, was captured 28 miles east of Knoxville on the 14th. As soon as the news was received, Col. Palmer, at the head of a brigade of Union cavalry, was sent in pursuit. In a few hours he overtook the enemy and recaptured the wagons and killed and wounded a hundred and fifty rebels. So complete was the rout that anything like a regular pursuit was impossible, as the fugitive rebels fled to the mountains, each man taking care of himself. Upon Palmer's attack, the Federals who were prisoners drew their sabres, of which they had not been relieved, and cut their way through, all escaping. It was in this fight that the rebel Maj.-Gen. Vance, was captured.

Important Order.

LOUISVILLE, Jan. 25th.

Major-Gen. Foster has issued an order prohibiting the distillation of grain within the limits of the Department of Ohio.

Vallandigham's Case.

New York, Jan. 25.

Washington specials say that the point raised by Pugh in Vallandigham's case, in the Supreme Court, is that the military commission has no authority to try a citizen; having no jurisdiction, except over persons of the military and naval service. Holt submitted a written argument in opposition to this view. The court has reserved its decision.

The President's Views of the Condition of Arkansas.

WASHINGTON, 25.

The President's letter of instructions to Gen. Steele, in regard to an election in Arkansas, says: That it is to be assumed at said election, and thenceforth, that the constitution and laws of the State as before rebellion are in full force, except that the constitution is so modified as to declare there shall be neither slavery nor involuntary servitude, except for punishment of crimes. But the General Assembly may make such provisions for the freed people as shall recognize their permanent freedom, and provide for their education, and which may yet be considered a temporary arrangement with their present condition as a laboring, landless and homeless class.

From Rebeldom.

CHICAGO, Jan. 25th.

The Richmond *Examiner* of the 11th, advises the public that general orders have been prepared in the Adj't-Gen's office, and will be issued in a few days, for the immediate conscription of persons who furnished substitutes. They will be put in camps of instruction within ten days.

The Savannah *Republican* of the 13th says: A flutter is created here by this law, the most interesting papers on record, and will cause an extensive stampede to the north and other foreign parts, by gentlemen who have been engaged in trade.

The Richmond correspondent of the Columbia (Ga.) *Sun* has it, from a trustworthy source, that one of the designs in abolishing the exemptions by substitutes, was to get rid of certain editors and obnoxious to the authorities.

The *Examiner* of the 13th says: The Senate, yesterday, passed the House bill putting in the army all who have furnished substitutes. This will curtail the effective working force of the Virginia railroads, whose executive officers can now hardly keep them in good running order, by all the means at their command. All the Virginia railroad iron is nearly worn out and so are the men working them.

The *Enquirer* of the 13th, says: The loss of our beef raising territory of West Mississippi has reduced the supply of this article, and the most vigorous measures are needed to keep the troops in meat. Great economy is necessary in case our supply is cut off.

The *Sentinel* sees alarming signs of trouble in North Carolina. Speaking of the papers of that State, it says those located at Raleigh, rarely fail to publish every gloomy article and intemperate accusation against the Government which appears any where. Their editorials inculcate the same sentiments as their selections. It contains frequent documents against secessionists for bringing on the war for no cause whatever, and indulge in ceaseless accusations that North Carolina is not fairly treated. Coupled with these they have almost daily editorials over the horrors of war, and the poor promise of our affairs.

Kansas.

ST. LOUIS, Jan. 26th.

Resolutions nominating Abraham Lincoln for President, passed the Kansas Legislature, unanimously.

Foreign.

HALIFAX, Jan. 25th.

By the Canada, from Liverpool the 8th, Queenstown the 9th. Her Highness, the Princess of Wales has given birth to a fine boy.

FROGMORE, Jan. 8th.

Judgment will be given in the Alexandria case on the 11th.

Parliament is formally prorogued until Feb. 4th.

The London *Morning Advertiser* states on the best authority, that Garibaldi disavows the recent Proclamation, and that it is a forgery.

a deer hunter's bullet in six months, (June 7, 1921). The same bullet may have carried away the Record after lingering until about mid-September 1921. We found no newspaper obituary material.

Duchesne Courier, Vol. 1, No. 1, Friday, May 26, 1922; 4 pages, 6 columns, 2 home print. C. B. Cook, Editor and Manager, H. T. Howes, Business Manager. L. A. Hollenbeck, George S. Bowers and N. D. Morrison were part owners. On March 2, 1923, Howe's name was dropped, and on April 20, 1923, Cook's name was dropped. On August 31, 1923, this appeared: "L. A. Hollenbeck, Editor, George S. Bowers, Manager." On October 19, 1923: "George S. Bowers and Arnold Reef, owners; George S. Bowers, Editor and Manager; L. A. Hollenbeck, Associate Editor." This group held together until February 6, 1925, when Mr. Bowers became sole owner, continuing until July 31, 1931, when there arose in its stead:

The Uintah Basin Record (Subtitle: Formerly The Duchesne Courier). Vol. 1, August 7, 1931, the plant having been leased by J. P. May, who enlightens us as follows: "For several years the Duchesne Courier, our predecessor, has been printed at Murray and at Myton . . . a serious disadvantage. This week's issue (August 14, 1931) as well as the last week's issue, will be printed at Murray and sent in on the truck to Duchesne." August 28, 1931, the publisher was able to say:

"A home paper printed at home. At last the type-setting material is here." On September 4, 1931 the Editor adds an helpmeet: "Josephine May, Assistant Editor and Manager." But the new team soon sought other fields, and on May 13, 1932 the masthead spread was "George S. Bowers, Manager and Owner; Gilbert L. Nance, Assistant Manager." Nance's name was dropped March 17, 1933. "Thirty" came unexpectedly for Editor Bowers on August 9, 1933, as a result of a severe illness. He had lived just thirty years at Duchesne and had become its leading citizen. Roy A. Schonian is now publisher.

ELSINORE, Sevier County

Population: 1900, 625; 1910, 656; 1920, 843; 1930, 654.

Sevier County Times (1899). No files or copies. The newspaper history of Elsinore is short and, some of it, hot. The Park Record of March 11, 1899, quotes a Salt Lake Herald dispatch of March 5: "In regard to the prosecution of J. T. Camp, Editor of The Times. Camp came to Sevier last October and with one Lisonbee, purchased the Southern Censor, published here (Richfield), and moved it to Elsinore, converting it into the Sevier County Times. He is an all around newspaperman of more than ordinary ability."

On April 8, 1899, the Park Record picks up from the Salina Press: "The Sevier Valley (sic) Times, Elsinore's petty newspaper seems to be in a peck of trouble. The plant is owned by C. W. Snyder, who is neither printer or editor. One Camp, who was sort of an adventurer, has had charge of the paper. He and Snyder had a 'fall out' and Camp decamped. Last week George Crosby did the scribbling act on the Times. This week Mr. Snyder is advertising for an editor."

The 1900 Gazetteer says Charles J. Olson was Editor and C. W. Snyder, Proprietor. The town was soon advertising for a newspaper it seems, for there is no other documentary record or evidence concerning the Times; and older citizens recall it to have been of short life.

EPHRAIM, Sanpete County

Population: 1900, 2,086; 1910, 2,296; 1920, 2,287; 1930, 1,966.

The County Register, Vol. 1, No. 1, Wednesday, June 4, 1890. "It is a 7 column folio and presents a very fair appearance, and enjoys a good run of advertisements; the first issue is certainly a most promising one," the Manti Home Sentinel quoted from the Salt Lake Herald, adding "So say we!" The Register's prospectus had brought forth from the Sentinel another kind of exclamation May 27, 1890: "A new 'Ephrum' paper will sail under the glaring headlines of County Register. We do not know why the first name is used, but suppose it is only a joke on the county." To the Sentinel, located at the County Seat evidently went the honor of being the "County" paper.

James T. Jakeman was the publisher of the Register, according to the Provo Enquirer; "It presents quite a fine typographical appearance and is a credit of Ephraim City." The Home Sentinel of August 12, 1890 mentions "Mr. Dorius of the Register of Ephraim"; and again the next week, August 19, 1890: "Mr. Jakeman of the Ephraim Register has purchased a place in Ephraim and intends moving his family there this week. We congratulate Ephraim on this acquisition and wish Mr. J. success in his new home." This is quite a different story from that complaining about the Register usurping the "County" name; he first endured, then pitied, then embraced!

Nearly a year later we get wind of the Register from the Provo Enquirer of March 5, 1891, which says: "It blooms without a patent inside." Happily for this record the present Enterprise Publisher has numbers 1 to 11, 13 to 18, and 31 to 76 (May 26, 1891) of the Register. The issue for April 21, 1891, shows: "Register Company, publishers. Directors: J. P. Meilstrup, President, J. T. Jakeman, Secretary, Peter Schwalbe, Treasurer, D. P. Madson and Ole Larson." The Register may have "bloomed without patent inside" in March 1891, but ere long it was to go to seed without anything on—leastwise, it passed to its reward sometime that summer.

Ephraim Enterprise. Vol. 1, No. 1, Wednesday, September 16, 1891, Murray and Goddard, publishers, "Takes the place of the Register," said the Provo Enquirer, September 19, 1891. "Its general get-up is certainly creditable," said the Manti Sentinel of September 18, 1891.

The Enterprise Publishers say of themselves, "We wish to announce to our readers in this, the first issue of the Enterprise, that we have leased the old Register plant for a term of years, and that this paper has no connection whatever with the Register.

Exchanges quoted from the Enterprise, and Ephraim businessmen patronized it, breathing into it the breath of life. A year later a new neighbor, the Manti Times-Reporter, September 17, 1892, says: "What we hear—that Ward Stevenson is editing the Ephraim Enterprise." Then the Times-Reporter says, on December 1, 1892: "The Ephraim Enterprise is again under the management of M. F. Murray and Company. Mr. Ward Stevenson has retired and will be heard from soon in another and more important journalistic venture." The Times-Reporter's use of the word "again" may merely mean the paper had again changed hands.

By the Wasatch Wave of June 20, 1893, we are informed: "The Ephraim Enterprise has gone Democratic." And the Brigham Bugler of September 16, 1893: "The Ephraim Enterprise has completed its second volume. . . . It deserves a more liberal support." The American Newspaper Directory for 1894, 1896 and 1898 shows M. F. Murray and Company, Editors and Publishers and says the paper has 4 pages.

M. F. Murray, Editor, continued several years. Fred Jorgenson took charge about 1903, giving way to Nielson and Thorpe about 1908, according to the Directories. From 1912 E. A. Britsch is Editor and Publisher. He is succeeded February 5, 1919 by Nephi Christensen, who lasted until March 6, 1923, when he was succeeded by Curtus Mickelsen. The paper was taken over by Roscoe C. Cox January 20, 1925, who is still in charge.

EUREKA, Juab County

Population: 1890, 1,733; 1900, 3,085; 1910, 3,416; 1920, 3,608; 1930, 3,041.

Newspaper spooks or spirits hover over this mining town in a flock, and are about as readily singled out and identified as if they really were ghosts. The newspapers, like the mines on the mountain sides nearby, were started, flourished for a time with promise, and were then abandoned with little more tangible evidence of their history than a hole and a dump.

"The Eureka Chief dates from October 18, 1889," according to C. F. Spilman in the Tintic Miner, special edition December 19, 1898. (Copy preserved by C. E. Huish.) The American Newspaper Directory for 1890 says: "Eureka Chief, Fridays, Republican, 4 pages, 15 x 22, established 1888 (sic) E. C. Higgins, Editor and Publisher." The **Provo Enquirer** commented September 15, 1890:"The Eureka Chief has emerged into a very creditable 8-page paper."

The Brigham Bugler of September 27, 1890, quotes the Salt Lake Times as saying, "There is an editor at Eureka who is so dry he has to soak himself in whiskey before he can hold an idea." "The scribe who dropped the above is no newspaperman or he would know that an editor's business is to promulgate and not to hold ideas," says the Bugler. We understood it was finally purchased and consolidated with:

The Tintic Miner. Vol. 1, No. 1, May 1, 1891, C. F. and E. H. Rathbone, Publishers. "A newsy, well edited sheet," according to the Salt Lake Times of May 4, 1891, announcing the new paper. The same day the Provo Enquirer says, "Rathbone Brothers have issued the Tintic Miner. It is a 6-column, 4-page paper." The American Newspaper Directory for 1892 lists, "Tintic Miner, Friday, 4-pages, 15 x 22, subscription, $3, circulation, 550, C. F. and E. H. Rathbone, Editors and Publishers."

The Spanish Fork Sun, March 11, 1893, quotes the Brigham City Report, "Newman A. Mix, formerly of the Tooele Times, has assumed charge of the Eureka Miner." We understood by purchase. C. F. Spilman, in his reminiscent editorial in the Tintic Miner of December 19, 1898, says he purchased the Miner from Mix on August 11, 1894. The American Newspaper Directory for 1896 and 1898 shows Fred Nelson, Editor and Publisher. The paper's policy was "Free Silver." The 1900 American Newspaper Directory shows the Tintic Miner had gone Democratic under C. F. Spilman, Editor and Publisher.

It is assumed that ere long it went where all good Democrats go, for that is the last reference to it, except Kenner in "Utah As It Is" (1904) carries C. F. Spilman, Editor and Manager, "Democratic in politics and religion; circulation, not what it should be," Spilman reported. We did not find the date of the demise of the Miner.

The Eureka Democrat was credited with a news item in the Brigham Bugler September 29, 1894. And in the American Newspaper Directory for 1896: "Eureka Democrat, Fridays, 4 pages, 15 x 22, established 1894, Charles P. Diehl, Editor and Publisher, circulation, smallest edition within a year, not less than 400. Advertisers will take notice that this is the only paper in Eureka to which this Directory accords a circulation in actual figures and guarantees the accuracy of the rating by a reward of $100, payable to the first person who successfully assails it." The American Newspaper Directory for 1898 shows: Circulation 600, James N. Lauder, Editor; Charles P. Diehl, Publisher. The Democrat was quoted by the Park Record, July 16, 1898, but no subsequent reference to it has been found. Out of the loins of the Democrat came a well received but short lifed monthly journal:

Utah Editor and Printer, magazine size, twelve 6 x 9-inch pages, launched by Charles P. and Isaac E. Diehl. The Wasatch Wave said of it July 2, 1897: "The Journal contains twelve pages of well edited matter printed on heavy book paper and is a credit to the typographical

profession." The Vernal Express, July 15, 1897 says, "The Utah Editor
and Printer . . . devoted to the interests of western journalists and
printers." It is feared, however, that it did very little, even for the two
journalists and printers who fostered it; for while it invited subscriptions at $1 a year, according to the American Newspaper Directory, it
is not heard of again. An illegitimate successor to the late Eureka
Democrat is listed in the American Newspaper Directory for 1900 in
the name and style of:

"The **Juab County Republican,** Sundays, 8 pages, 18 x 24, subscription, $2.50, established 1894." This is the year the Eureka Demo-
crat was established and the papers are probably one and the same.
"Republican Publishing Company, Editors and Publishers." The Gazetteer for 1900 says Charles S. King is Editor and Wm. C. DeWar,
Manager. Thus politics makes strange bed fellows and many of them!
This was undoubtedly a political sheet, the plant of which was owned
by first one political party and then by another. However, the newspaper must have run more or less continuously until 1900 when its
successor appeared.

Eureka Weekly Reporter, Vol. 1, No. 1 (about November 1, 1900).
The listing in the American Newspaper Directory for the Reporter is,
"Friday, Republican, established 1894," obviously assuming it to be
a continuation of the Democrat and the Republican, "Reporter" being
a term used to attract them all. The earliest number found of the Eureka Weekly Reporter shows: "The Reporter Publishing Company, J. C.
Sullivan, President, P. J. Donnelly, Vice President, Hans J. Hassell,
Treasurer, Charles E. Huish, Secretary." However, the real editor,
publisher, and proprietor, Mr. Huish, only hoisted these names to the
masthead temporarily for political and business prestige. The men
never actually participated in the editorial policies or business management of the newspaper. Beginning with the issue of November 20,
1903, it was called:

The Eureka Reporter. Editor Huish says it was "weakly" enough
without calling attention to the fact. Space was valuable in the Reporter
and the Editor was modest, hence "C. E. Huish, Editor," and "C. E.
Huish, Editor and Manager," were masthead lines the printer lifted to
the breeze only at intervals, though Huish continued in sole charge for
nearly 32 years.

On April 28, 1932 the masthead revealed in print a relationship
that had long existed between the proprietor and his shop and office
foreman: "C. E. Huish, Editor, C. E. Rife, Manager." (Carlos E. Rife,
who had become foreman of the Mechanical Department in 1915, advanced to a partnership in the Reporter concern in 1923.) And then
because of the press of a more lucrative business picked up as a sideline, Huish retired, and on May 5, 1932, the masthead reveals, "C. E.
Rife, J. Vern Rife, Publishers." Publisher Huish's record of longevity

W. C. DUNBAR
Born October 26, 1822
Died June 8, 1905

JAMES FERGUSON
Born February 23, 1828
Died August 30, 1863

Deseret Paper Mill, installed here in 1861; building enlarged in 1879.
Located southeast of Salt Lake City (now the Old Mill Club).

Courtesy Utah Photo Materials Co.

and prosperity is exceptional, for he is yet a relatively young man. And, be it recorded, Editor Huish's sideline, which outgrew his newspaper interests was a string of motion picture theatres.

FILLMORE, Millard County
Population: 1890, 825; 1900, 1,037; 1910, 1,191; 1920, 1,490; 1930, 1,374.

Millard Progress started about February 1, 1894. "The first number of the Millard Progress, J. P. Jacobson, Editor and Manager, has found its way to this sanctum. It is one of the brightest and cleanest country papers in Utah, and its plump advertising columns show that the business men of Fillmore are wide awake and progressive," says the Brigham Bugler, February 3, 1894.

Jacobson had been with the Millard County Blade at Deseret. He went with George C. Viele, according to the latter, to a town almost abandoned on the U. P. railroad west of Ogden, "on an alkali flat resembling Mud Lake, (Corinne?) and bought an old hand press, a job press, and a supply of pretty good type for $500 and shipped it to Fillmore . . . We set it up in the southeast room of the old State-house, and began its publication . . . Mr. Jacobson became the printer, publisher and editor. He did all the work himself. The principal owners were J. S. Giles, James A. Melville, Alma Greenwood, T. C. Callister, Christian Anderson, D. R. Stevenson, George W. Nixon, and myself," writes Viele.

By the first of April, 1894, it was all home print, according to the Manti Messenger. And then we pick up Jacobson's trail leading out of Fillmore. Says the Brigham Bugler, December 22, 1894: "Millard Progress, Mr. J. P. Jacobson, whose name has hitherto appeared as the editor of the Progress, has left for parts unknown." The Iron County Record has this to say about it: "People of Fillmore do not believe in letting an Editor have any fun at all. J. P. Jacobson, editor of the Progress of that place, was recently fined $10, merely because he whipped his wife. He is said to have skipped the burg." His successor saw some tribulation promptly, for according to the Iron County Record of March 29, 1895, he was sued for libel, (by Josiah F. Gibbs of the Millard County Blade). Incidentally, it is the last we hear of him.

The files are incomplete, but Directories show Lorenzo W. and A. F. Gaisford, Editors and Publishers, in 1896-1898, and only the former, in 1900. Late in 1900 or early 1901, the Progress was joined in a form of wedlock to the Clear Lake Review, becoming the Progress-Review. In July, 1901, it was being published at "Fillmore and Clear Lake," C. W. Aldrach, Manager, S. A. Greenwood, Editor, "Miss L. R. Lorenz, Clear Lake, Local Editress." Knapp and Frampton were publishers in 1905, C. W. Frampton, Editor. Christian Anderson was Editor and Publisher in 1908 and 1912, followed early in 1913 by Joseph Smith, who purchased the paper. James H. Mountford bought the paper January 24, 1919, and in turn sold November 20, 1925 to Mr. and Mrs. E. Vance Wilson, the present publishers.

FORT BRIDGER, Uinta County, Wyoming
(Formerly in Utah)

The Sweetwater Mines. An odd name for a newspaper, and an unusual place for one, since Fort Bridger was then a frontier military post of small, permanent population. The printing plant was being moved from Utah to Central Wyoming. The first number of the paper was published at Fort Bridger in February, 1868, while the printing plant was on its way to the Sweetwater Mines region. The Deseret News of February 19, 1868, lifts from it a story of a "desperate shooting," which the Sweetwater Mines editor found far too important to await until his arrival at destination. The Deseret News of April 14, 1868, again quotes from the Sweetwater Mines, "which is still published at Fort Bridger," then in Utah. But on April 23, 1868, the Deseret News says: "The Sweetwater Mines of the 18th announces its departure from Fort Bridger, the roads being in a condition to admit of travel. The next paper will be printed in the Sweetwater country." The Salt Lake Daily Reporter of May 27, 1868, says: "The Sweetwater Mines is on its pegs again. The first number issued at South Pass City dated May 19, was received at this office today."

FRISCO, Beaver County

Population: ("It is essentially a mining camp with the consequent fluctuations in population and prospects," says the 1884 Gazetteer)

"The Southern Utah Times, (Frisco's first and only newspaper) will make its appearance about the 15th of May. The press, type, and other material were shipped yesterday," says the Salt Lake Tribune May 2, 1880. The Territorial Enquirer at Provo, May 26, 1880, says the paper is a weekly and, "is edited by Mr. F. Lockley, formerly of the Tribune." No copies have been found.

The Ogden Junction, June 5, 1880, says, "The present editor of the Southern Utah Times, about whose journalistic ability there is not more doubt than about his political unfairness and sectarian aggressiveness, has come to cooler ideas in the hotter climate of Frisco . . . Of his successor on the editorial tripod of the Salt Lake Tribune, he exporates (sic) as follows: 'Mr. Goodwin has always shown himself a hearty friend to the Gentile cause in Utah.'" Another impression comes from the Beaver Watchman, quoted in the Ogden Junction, June 9, 1880: "The Times Editor has been weeping over the kind things which the Salt Lake Tribune did not say about his newspaper. When he has bought water at 4c a gallon as long as many of his Frisco neighbors have done, he'll be less humid!"

Changes came quickly, we glean from the Territorial Enquirer of July 21, 1880: "Lockley, alias 'Red-head' has vacated the editorial chair of the Southern Utah Times, a weekly Journal published in Frisco. He has returned to Salt Lake in hopes of 'being taken on again by the

Trib Managers.' One Taylor has succeeded him on the Times." In a personal letter written by George F. Prescott on October 23, 1880 to Mr. Fred Lockley of Walla Walla, graciously furnished by Fred Lockley, Jr., we learn: "We have sold the Frisco Times to (Chas. S.) King of Ogden, who took possession this week."

The Anti-Polygamy Standard of Salt Lake City, for January, February and March, 1881, carried the following display advertisement: "Southern Utah Times, By Charles S. King, late of the Ogden Morning Rustler. The Southern Utah Times is a paper of pepper, pickles, pith and point . . . An outspoken Gentile sheet . . . tells the uncalcimined truth . . . 'shows up' with a clean nose every Saturday afternoon . . . is published within a stone's throw of the Horn Silver, the largest mine in the world . . . is read in every ranchman's and miner's cabin, every dugout, and around the campfire of every prospector, and is in fact the recognized Mining Journal of Southern Utah."

The Deseret News gives us a squint June 13, 1881: "The last issue of the Southern Utah Times comes to us in brown paper." On July 9, 1881, the Park Mining Record says: "The Editor of the Southern Utah Times is once more in difficulty. Saturday evening Charles Auchterman attacked him for publishing an item, and each set himself up as a target. King was arrested but gave bonds for his appearance." And again July 30, 1881, from its lofty perch the Park Mining Record says: "Whenever the gentle raindrops visit Frisco the Editor of the Times and other smart boys hunt up the mudholes and take a bath."

The Ogden Herald of September 14, 1881, quoting the Southern Utonian, a Beaver contemporary: "Mr. Charles S. King of the Frisco Times . . . spent four days in town (Beaver) during which time he industriously and artistically (?) painted the name of his paper on nearly all the board fences in Beaver." Unfortunately we must continue to glimpse the Frisco Times only through the files of the few contemporaries still preserved, some of whose editors didn't like the Times. Not even the advertisements on the Beaver fences remain! It is true, however, that Frisco news items were popular, judging from the number lifted, for it was a promising mining camp, whose fortunes were watched with interest. The Ogden Herald November 13, 1882 says: "The Southern Utah Times of the 11th says that C. S. King received his commission on Friday from the President, authorizing him to assume charge of the Frisco post office." The American Newspaper Directory for 1883 shows: "Frisco, Southern Utah Times, Saturday, Republican, anti-Mormon, established 1880, Charles S. King and Company, Editors and Publishers." And the Herald of January 2, 1883, quotes the Southern Utah Times: "Old Tribunes and other blanket sheets for sale at six bits a hundred at the post office."

Too bad for the Times the blanket sheets were not blank, for according to the Ogden Herald of July 7, 1884: "For several weeks past the Southern Utah Times, Chas. S. King, Editor, appears only on the half shell;" and on July 14, 1884 the Herald says: "The Southern

Utah Times has suspended." The Southern Utonian speaks as follows of the demise of the Southern Utah Times just buried by its publisher, C. S. King: "We are sorry that friend King, though so badly misled on some points, should have been so unfortunate in selecting his town. His talents and persevering energy demanded better results, but he has undeniably missed it."

The Utah Journal of Logan writes a different epitaph, July 19, 1884: "The Southern Utah Times, an insignificant and disreputable sheet, has suspended publication." But we learn from the Beaver County Record that, "The Frisco Times will resume publication the first Saturday in September (6th, 1884);" so records the Ogden Herald, August 18, 1884. We found no reference to the resumption of publication, though: "The Southern Utah Times, under the management of Maurice McGrath, presents a decided improvement," says the Salt Lake Chronicle, November 3, 1884, which borrowed news frequently from the Times.

The American Newspaper Directory for 1885 says of it: "Independent, Anti-Mormon, 4-pages, 22 x 30, $5. E. D. Burlingame and Company, editor and publishers." But the reincarnated Times had its difficulties too. The Manti Home Sentinel, November 27, 1885: "The Frisco Times comes out in a half sheet this time on account of the moving of their material to a new building."

The American Newspaper Directory for 1886 says: "Southern Utah Times, Frisco, Charles S. King and Company, publishers, Anti-Mormon, Saturday, 4-pages, 20 x 28, established 1879 (sic); also dated at Silver Reef; (a suburban edition?)." "The Southern Utah Times was received this week in 'half shell' or cut on the bias, but none the less acceptable," the Park Record tells us March 5, 1887.

The identity of the editor is more fully revealed in this wise by the Salt Lake Democrat, June 10, 1887, "The Beaver Utonian pleasantly alludes to the Southern Utah Times as: 'that lying contemptible sheet, printed by devils, edited in Hell, and issued from the Western part of this county.' After Editor King (for publisher McGrath) has recovered his breath, the public will anxiously await his opinion of the Beaver Journalist." The American Newspaper Directory for 1887 says it is "Republican, $5." The frequency and regularity with which the Southern Utah Times was quoted is evidence that it must have been a good newspaper, in some respects, if not editorially.

Then came a darker day for the King. The Deseret News informs us, December 9, 1887: "C. S. King, publisher of the Southern Utah Times, is receiving the attention of Judge Boreman and others for alleged criminal libel." And the Territorial Enquirer of the same date explains: "C. S. King, editor of the Frisco Times, has been arrested for libeling Judge Boreman, the district and county officials, A. J. Campbell and numerous other individuals." Obviously taking on too much territory!

The Deseret News gives us the libel story in installments through its special correspondent at Beaver. December 7, 1887: "News comes of the arrest at Frisco on Wednesday last of Charles S. King, editor of the

Frisco Times, on an indictment having been found by the late Grand Jury, charging him with criminal libel. The alleged libel is said to consist of a series of editorial articles in the defendant's paper reflecting upon the integrity of the judge and prosecuting attorney, in the conduct of the trial of Andrew Calton, the slayer of Mike Cullen. King is the same individual who was tarred and feathered in Ogden some eight or nine years ago, at which time he was conducting a newspaper known as 'The Morning Rustler'."

And on December 23, 1887: "Charles S. King was sentenced to pay a fine of $100 and costs, amounting in all to $179.80 . . . King, when on the stand, was questioned by his own counsel as to what interests his paper was published in. He replied: "In the interests of the various industries of the country, against the Mormon Church, and in the interest of good government." And on that golden text it went "hence"; for save a single quotation in the Park Record, January 28, 1888, that is the last we hear of the Frisco Times.

We hear of King, however, through the Provo Enquirer June 26, 1891, as having become editor of the Inter-Mountain edition of the Irrigation and Mining Age, Wm. E. Smythe, general editor, which periodical was subsequently moved from Denver to Salt Lake City. Incidentally, looking away back, the Salt lake Herald of August 31, 1872: "Auction house.—Messrs. H. A. Read and C. S. King, auctioneers and commission merchants, placed their card in the Herald this morning. They are live, enterprising gentlemen."

GREEN RIVER, Emery County
Population: 1910, 628; 1920, 645; 1930, 474.

Green River Dispatch, Volume 1, Number 1, February 12, 1907, J. W. Thompson, proprietor, B. F. Miller, manager and local editor, was this town's first newspaper. Later, Mr. Miller bought the local job printing shop of Harry Wood, for laying away the weekly Dispatch forms at home; and he was at different times assisted by Harry Wood, H. E. Blake and W. P. Epperson. Miller later purchased a linotype machine and his wife operated it for five years. The population hopes of the editor did not materialize and editor Miller put the paper to bed the last time about July 4, 1917. Miss Helen Spaulding leased the Dispatch from Miller, resuming publication about the last of July, 1917, with Harry Wood as printer. Miss Spaulding gave up the ghost of her newspaper hopes with the issue of July 29, 1920.

GUNNISON, Sanpete County
Population: 1900, 829; 1910, 950; 1920, 1,115; 1930, 1,057.

"Gunnison Gazette, Fridays, 8-pages, 18 x 24, $1.50 per year, N. Gledhill, editor and publisher," we glean partly from the American Newspaper Directory for 1900. The first number was issued about

The Daily Telegraph.

NO. 2. GREAT SALT LAKE CITY, TUESDAY, JULY 5, 1864. VOL. 1.

The Daily Telegraph:

PUBLISHED EVERY MORNING, EXCEPT SUNDAY.

T. B. H. STENHOUSE, Editor.

(Office—Opposite the Theatre.)

TERMS OF SUBSCRIPTION:

One Copy one year,	$10,00
" " six months,	6,00
" " three months,	3,50
" " one month, delivered,	1,25
" " one month, called for at office,	1,00

RATES OF ADVERTISING:

Business Cards (five lines or less) one month,	$ 5,00
One square (ten lines or less) one insertion,	1,50
" " " two insertions,	2,50
" " " three insertions,	3,25
" " " one week,	4,00
" " " one month,	8,00
One-eighth column, one insertion,	3,00
" " one week,	6,00
" " one month,	12,00
One-quarter column, one insertion,	5,00
" " one month,	15,00
One-half column, one insertion,	8,00
" " one month,	25,00
One column, one insertion,	15,00
" " one month,	45,00

BUSINESS CARDS.

BANKERS.

BEN HOLLADAY. W. L. HALSEY.
HOLLADAY & HALSEY,
Bankers.
East Temple Street, G.S.L. City.

D. W. POWERS. H. L. NEWMAN. W. B. FARR.
POWERS, NEWMAN & CO.,
Bankers,
East Temple Street, (Godbe's Old Drug Store,) G.S.L. City,
Dealers in Coin, Gold Dust and Exchange.

AUSTIN M. CLARK. JOHN W. KERR. MILTON E. CLARK.
CLARK & CO.,
Bankers,
East Temple Street, (Salt Lake House,) G.S.L. City.
Exchange Sold on any part of Europe.

WM. JENNINGS,
Banker,
East Temple Street, G.S.L. City.
Coin and Exchange Bought and Sold.

MERCHANTS.

WM. JENNINGS,
East Temple Street, G S.L City,
Wholesale and Retail Dealer in Dry Goods, Groceries, Hardware, Queensware, Boots and Shoes.
Highest Price Paid for GOLD.

WALKER BROTHERS,
East Temple Street, G.S L. City,
Wholesale and Retail Merchants and Importers of General Merchandise.
Constantly Receiving New Goods from East and West.

W. H. HOOPER. H. S. ELDREDGE.
HOOPER & ELDREDGE,
East Temple Street, G S L City,
Wholesale and Retail Dealers in Dry Goods, Groceries, Hardware, Queensware, Boots and Shoes.

J. B. KIMBALL. H. W. LAWRENCE.
KIMBALL & LAWRENCE,
East Temple Street, G S. L City,
Dry Goods and Groceries. A Liberal Discount made for Gold.

GEORGE CRONYN. WM. CLAYTON.
CRONYN & CLAYTON,
West side East Temple Street, G S L City,
Dry Goods Merchants and Dealers in Groceries and General Merchandise.

RANSOHOFF & CO.,
East Temple Street, G. S. L. City,
Dealers in Dry Goods, Ready Made Clothing, Hats, Boots, Shoes, Fancy Groceries, Cutlery, Tobacco, Cigars, etc., etc.

GILBERT & SONS,
East Temple Street, G.S.L. City,
Dealers in General Merchandise, have constantly on hand a choice Stock of Prints, Lawns, Delaines, Broad Cloths, Domestic Goods, Groceries, etc.

BODENBURG & KAHN,
East Temple Street, G. S L City,
Dealers in Dry Goods, Groceries, Clothing, and other General Merchandise.

BOURNE & NEEDHAM,
East Temple Street, G. S. L. City,
(At the late Stand of Wm. Nixon,)
Dealers in Dry Goods, Groceries, Hardware, Clothing, Boots and Shoes. Jewelry and Fancy Articles.

LAVENBERG & AUERBACH,
West side, East Temple Street, G.S.L. City,
Clothing and Furnishing Goods, Dry Goods, Fancy Goods and Toys.

AARON NEWFIELD,
San Francisco Clothing House,
West side, East Temple Street, G.S.L. City,
(Opposite Salt Lake House.)

BUSINESS CARDS.

MEDICAL.

W. F. ANDERSON, M.D.,
Surgeon and Physician,
Office and Residence—Thirteenth Ward.

J. L. DUNYON, M.D.,
Physician and Dispenser of Medicines.
Office—Two Doors North of the Post Office
Residence—Two Blocks East of the Theatre.

W. S. GODBE,
East Temple Street. G S L. City,
Drugs, Medicines and Dye Stuffs. Prescriptions Carefully Prepared.

T. B. PEARCE,
Surgeon and Mechanical Dentist,
East Temple Street, G. S L City,
(Four Doors below Post Office.)

JOHN V. LONG,
Surgeon Dentist,
Office at Residence. 13th Ward,
Great Salt Lake City.

PROFESSIONAL

PATRICK LYNCH,
Attorney and Counselor at Law and Clerk of the U. S. Third Judicial District Court for Utah Territory;
Also, Commissioner of Deeds for the State of California.
Debts Collected and all Legal Documents made out and acknowledged for the Eastern States and California.
TERMS LIBERAL.
OFFICE—East Temple Street, (opposite Godbe's Drug Store) G.S.L. City.

W. I. APPLEBY,
Attorney at Law and Clerk of the U.S. Supreme Court of Utah.
Debts Collected, Deeds, Powers of Attorney, etc., carefully drawn up for the States and Europe. Depositions, Acknowledgments, etc., taken according to Law, for any of the States or Territories. Declarations for Citizenship attended to at the shortest notice and on Liberal Terms.
OFFICE at my residence, Market Street, one and a half blocks west of the Market House, G.S.L. City.

MUSICAL.

DAVID O. CALDER,
Importer of all kinds of Musical Instruments and Musical Merchandise—for sale at the lowest prices. Fresh supplies, regularly received, of the very best quality of Violin and Guitar Strings. Wholesale and retail.

C. J. THOMAS,
Professor of Instrumental Music and Singing.
Residence—Twentieth Ward.
Instructions given in class or privately. Pianos and other Instruments tuned. Music arranged for Choirs and Bands.

HENRY L. RAYMOND,
Teacher of Music and Dealer in Music, Musical Merchandise and Instruments.
Office—4 doors south of the Post Office.
Musical Instruments Tuned and Repaired.

ARTISTS

EDWARD MARTIN,
House, Sign, Carriage and Ornamental Painter,
East Temple Street, west side, G S.L. City.
Paints, etc., sold by retail.

W. V. MORRIS,
Painter,
Rear of A. Daft's Store, East Temple Street,
G. S. L. City.
Graining and Ornamental Painting.

H. DRUCE,
Engraver and Embroider Stamper,
Corner of East and Second South Temple Streets,
G. S. L. City.

WM. J. SILVER,
Civil and Mechanical Engineer and Draftsman.
Patent Office Drawings Prepared.
19th Ward, one block north of Union Square.

WATCHMAKERS.

O. URSENBACH,
Watchmaker,
East Temple Street, G. S. L City.
Jewelry repaired on short notice.

HENRY RISER,
Watchmaker,
East Temple Street, west side, G.S L. City.
Repairing done promptly and satisfactorily.

O. L. ELIASON,
Watch and Clock Maker,
East Temple Street, west side, G.S.L. City,
(at Martin's Paint Shop.)

BOOTS AND SHOES.

G. C. RISER,
Gentlemen's and Ladies' Fashionable Boot and Shoemaker,
East Temple Street, opposite Town Clock,
G. S. L. City.

HARRISON & TULLIDGE,
Manufacturers of Boots and Shoes,
First South Temple Street, G.S.L. City.

BUSINESS CARDS.

E. B. TRIPP,
Manufacturer of Boots and Shoes,
East Temple Street, G S.L. City,
Constantly on hand a large Stock of Gents' and Ladies' Fine and Coarse Boots and Shoes of the best quality.

TINNERS

EDWARD STEVENSON,
Copper, Tin, Sheet Iron and Zincware Manufacturer,
East Temple Street, opposite Telegraph Office, G.S.L. City,
Job Work done to order.

T. HAWKINS,
Manufacturer of Copper, Tin, Sheet Iron and Zincwares,
East Temple Street, opposite Salt Lake House, G.S.L. City,
Custom Work done to order.

ALFRED BEST,
Tin, Copper and Sheet Iron Worker,
East Temple Street, west side, opposite Salt Lake House,
G. S. L. City.

J. M. ALLEN,
Manufacturer of Tin, Sheet Iron, Copper and Zinc Wares.
Opposite Walker Bros., East Temple Street, G.S.L. City.

BLACKSMITHS

BURR FROST,
Blacksmith,
Third South Temple (Emigration) Street, G.S.L. City.

PHILIP DE LA MARE,
Blacksmithing in all its Branches, at Standish's old Stand.

R. B. MARGETTS,
North east corner Union Square, G.S.L. City.
Mill Irons and Machinery Forged to Order. Blacksmithing in all its branches. Horse, Mule and Ox Shoes always on hand.

SAMUEL BRINGHURST,
Wagon and Smith Shop,
Emigration Street, 3 doors east of East Temple Street, G. S. L. City.
All kinds of Farming Implements Manufactured to Order.

P. MARGETTS. [illegible]
Blacksmiths,
Cor. of East and Second South Temple Street, G.S.L. City,
Are always on hand to do all kinds of Blacksmithing.
Horse, Mule and Ox shoeing done on short notice.

TAILORS.

CLAUDE CLIVE,
Merchant Tailor,
East Temple Street, opposite Town Clock, G.S.L. City,
Clothing of every description made to order in the latest Style of Fashion.

BAKERS

KNOWLDEN & GRENIG,
Bakery, Dry Goods, Grocery and Provision Store,
(Two doors below Godbe's,)
East Temple Street, Great Salt Lake City.

DYE & KELSON,
Bakers and Confectioners.
East Temple Street, G.S.L. City, opposite R. Daft's Gunsmith Shop.
Crackers, Bread, Pies, Cakes and Candies always on hand.

CABINETMAKERS.

E. M. CASTE,
Cabinetmaker,
One and a half blocks south of the Theatre, east side Second East Temple Street, G.S.L. City.
Bench and Hand Screws made to order. Lumber wanted.

CAPENER & TAYLOR,
First South Temple Street, 1½ blocks east of the Theatre,
Cabinet Makers and Undertakers,
Office of City Sexton.

LADIES DEPARTMENT.

MRS. COLEBROOK,
East Temple Street, second door south of the Post Office, G.S.L. City,
Has constantly on hand every article in the line of Millinery, of both Straw and Silk and Fancy Trimmings.

MRS. STENHOUSE,
Milliner,
(First House West of Tabernacle, G.S.L. City.)
Ladies' and Misses' Straw and Leghorn Hats, Fancy Straw, Neapolitan and Silk Bonnets. Feathers, Flowers, Ribbons, Laces, Blonds, Ruches, Head Dresses, etc.

MARIAN PRATT,
Milliner,
One block north of northwest corner of Union Square, 19th Ward, G.S.L. City.
A Superb selection of Ladies' Fancy Goods on hand.

HOTELS.

SALT LAKE HOUSE.
F. LITTLE, Proprietor,
East Temple Street, G. S. L. City, Utah.

NATIONAL HOTEL.
F. REICH, Proprietor,
South Temple Street, G. S. L. City.

BUSINESS CARDS.

MANSION HOUSE.
JOSIAH TUFTS, Proprietor,
Corner of Emigration Street and State Road.
Extensive Yards and Stables.

MISCELLANEOUS.

T. D. BROWN,
Express and Exchange Office,
East Temple Street, G. S. L. City, Utah.

H. E. BOWRING,
Harness and Saddlemaker,
East Temple Street, west side, G. S. L. City,

J. H. VAN NATTA,
Manufacturer of Cooperware,
East Temple Street, a few doors below the Post Office, G.S.L. City.

ELIJAH PEARCE,
Basket and Gig Body Worker,
East Temple Street, G.S.L. City, opposite Walker Bro's.

W. H. HOCKING,
Saloon, Confectionary and Eating House,
First South Temple Street, G.S.L. City, opposite Theatre.

CROXALL, CARTWRIGHT & EARDLEY
Manufacturers of Crockeryware,
First South Temple Street, G. S. L. City, (Basement of Moore & Green's old stand.)

F. J. P. PASCOE,
Manufacturer of White Lead and other Colors,
North Temple Street, 17th Ward.
Lime and Vinegar always on hand.

J. SADDLER,
Combmaker,
East Temple Street, four doors below Post Office.

JAMES & BEDSON EARDLEY,
Deseret Pottery, 7th Ward, G.S.L. City,
Liberal Deductions to Dealers.

HUGH FINDLAY,
Manufacturer of Matches, Blacking, etc.
[illegible] Notions,
East Temple Street, G.S.L. City.

LATIMER & TAYLOR,
Sash, Door and Blind Makers,
14th Ward, G.S.L. City,
(Opposite Mr. S. Snider's lumber yard.)
Varieties of Sash always on hand.

RUBY VALLEY, N.T

H. EGAN & SONS,
Travelers' and Emigrants' Depot,
Choice Liquors, Tobacco and Cigars always on hand.

CALIFORNIA.

JAMES LINFORTH,
Commission Merchant,
208 Battery Street, San Francisco, California.
Sight Drafts on Salt Lake City, Utah Territory.
" " Austin, Nevada Territory.
Particular attention given to Purchases for Utah.

L. B. BENCHLEY & CO.,
206 and 208 Battery Street, between California and Sacramento, San Francisco.
Importers and Jobbers of American and Foreign Hardware, Cutlery, Farmers', Mechanics', and Miners' Tools, etc.

REMOVAL.

THE OVERLAND STAGE LINE, and the Banking House of Holladay & Halsey, has been Removed to their New Building, East Temple Street, a few doors above the Salt Lake House.

HAY CONTRACTS!

PARTIES wishing to make Contracts for putting up HAY, on the OVERLAND ROUTE, Eastern Division, will apply at their Office for three days.

W. L. HALSEY, Agent.

COME AND SETTLE.

E M. CASTE hereby requests all persons indebted to him, or to whom he is indebted, to call and settle without delay.

W. BALLAN,

WATCHMAKER,

TAKES this opportunity of returning thanks for the liberal support he has received, and begs to say, that nothing will be wanting on his part to have a continuance of the same.

I am expecting by E. R. YOUNG'S Train, a Stock of Goods, such as,

CLOCKS, WATCHES, AND JEWELRY,

which I will sell reasonable for Cash, to suit the times.

FOR SALE,

A HOUSE and LOT, in the 16th Ward, fronting on North Temple Street, known as the McIntyre place; situate North of Mr. Staines' and East of Bishop Kesler's.

For further particulars, inquire of

NATHAN TANNER, 14th Ward.

Courtesy L. D. S. Church Historian's Office Library

October 20, 1899. Gledhill and Son, were publishers in 1904, N. Gledhill, editor, continuing with little change till its close in 1919 as shown by the files in the Gunnison Valley News office.

The Gunnison Valley News (a continuation of the Gunnison Gazette), Friday, May 2, 1919, says: "Name of paper is changed; after giving the matter thougtful consideration the publisher has decided to change the name of the paper, familiarly known as the Gunnison Gazette, and with this issue and hereafter, the publication will be known as The Gunnison Valley News. Howard W. Cherry, publisher." Mr. Cherry is still in charge.

HEBER, Wasatch County

Population: 1870, 658; 1880, 1,291; 1890, 1,538; 1900, 1,534; 1910, 2,031; 1920, 1,931; 1930, 2,477.

Wasatch Wave. Vol. 1, No. 1, Saturday, March 23, 1889, 4 pages, 7 columns, all home print, an extraordinary news service, which like its dimensions, 17½ x 23½, and its title, has never changed.

William Buys was Editor and Manager for the Wasatch Publishing Company, and W. H. Kenner was city editor. "In wafting the Wasatch Wave we realize it is but a tiny ripple upon the great ocean of journalism," modestly says the editor in his first. According to a professional card in the paper the editor was also: "William Buys, Attorney at Law and Notary Public, City Surveyor, and Civil Engineer."

The.Wasatch Wave is the perfect newspaper in more respects than one, an outstanding achievement being the preservation of its files in new condition from the beginning to the present day. A few other Utah newspaper files are somewhat longer, but none are cleaner, neater, and more nearly perfect. The paper's own history, like that of the prosperous community it represents is an open book for nearly 50 years, without a number cut, marred or missed.

In the issue of March 30, 1889 we find this extraordinary report: "Excitement has run high for several days after it had been announced that we would issue on Saturday morning. People kept thronging the office from morning until night during all the week, and on Friday evening the place was full. We expected to work all night, as a large number of papers were to be struck off and scattered broadcast over the Territory, and we wanted to catch the mail next morning.

"The copy was all finished at about 8 o'clock on that evening and the proof reading, correcting of galleys, and the imposing of forms were gone through in the midst of a curious and expectant crowd. Finally the forms were put on, the press inked up, a sheet of paper placed on them, and an impression taken. The pressman then turned to the assembly and announced that the Wasatch Wave was born.

"Three cheers were given with such vigor that they were heard a block away and a cloud of hats went flying in the air. From that time

until half-past one o'clock Saturday morning we were kept busy printing, folding, and addressing papers, while every available place in the
office was occupied as a seat by the visitors who put in their time reading papers. Everything worked well and the first issue of the Wave
was completed and mailed in good time and to our entire satisfaction."

Kenner's name was dropped as City Editor April 27, 1889. The
editor takes time out for this explanation December 17, 1889: "We
have heard some complaint because The Wave does not take sides one
way or the other in the political fight now waging in the Territory. We
wish to call the attention of these discontents to the fact that we are
not running either a political or religious organ."

Things ran smoothly until December 16, 1890, when we find: "On
account of press of business, I am under the necessity of giving up the
Managership and Editorship of the Wave . . . George Barzee will assume the management of the Wave hereafter. My journalistic career,
though short, has been a very pleasant one to me.—Wm. Buys." Barzee
had the good sense to continue the same kind of newspaper Buys had
been running. In a reminiscent review March 10, 1891, he says: "The
Wasatch Wave . . . is two years old . . . Started as a venture . . . In the
fall of 1888 William Buys, E. D. Clyde, and W. H. Kenner . . . began
canvassing for subscriptions for capital stock. Obtaining subscriptions
between $300 and $400, William Buys . . . agreed to put enough money
into it to see the matter started . . . At a meeting of the stockholders
held last Saturday, it was resolved to erect a suitable building." A
year later a report in the newspaper says: "March 22, 1892.—At a
recent meeting of the board of directors, arrangements were made with
Mr. William Buys to take the general management of the Wave." Accordingly, on April 5, 1892 "William Buys Editor," is at the masthead; but on November 15, 1892, "George Barzee, Editor," appears
without explanation, a clear case of: "After you, my dear Alphonse!"
However, on March 7, 1893 we learn: "A motion was finally put and
carried that the plant be leased to the present manager, George Barzee,
for a period of three years at 5% per annum, payable in subscription,
advertising, or job work," and Barzee carries on!

Here are the original "three little pigs" of literature: "March 20,
1894. We will take twenty bushels of potatoes, a thousand pounds of
flour, two tons of good hay, and three little pigs on subscription; the
first to apply will be given preference. Also as an encouragement to
our subscribers we will take store pay on either of the following stores
for a short time: A. Hatch and Company, Mark Jeffs, Turner and Sons,
or the Charleston Co-op.—George Barzee, Manager Wave."

(June 26, 1894), "The Office Towel . . . It grew thicker and rough-
er and harder and tougher, and daily put on a more inkey hue, until
one windy morning, without any warning it fell to the floor and was
broken in two.—Richfield Advocate." To which the practical Wave
man adds: "By rubbing occasionally with machine oil the towel does

not become so brittle, but partakes of the nature of cardboard. It may then be used for book-covers . . ."

(September 18, 1894). "We have rented two columns of the Wave to the Democratic Party until after the election. The space is bought and paid for by them the same as advertising space. We still have a couple of columns which we will rent to the Republican Party at the same figure." (March 26, 1895). "Libel.—Libel suits are becoming quite fashionable of late. Three prominent journals have just been put through a course of law for libel and two of them got cinched . . . A newspaper has no more right than an individual to slander a person and has just as much right to criticize and if necessary, to condemn."

Barzee's lease expired May 28, 1895: "Our Last.—With this issue we pay our last respects to the readers of the Wave. We have, for over four years had our little say every week . . . C. O. Glanville and Joseph A. Murdock will assume control of the Wave," on June 1, 1895. Glanville was new, we judge from the following on April 2, 1897 "Editor Glanville's Thumping. D. B. Witt administered it over an article in last week's Wave . . . Editor Glanville of the Wave was licked in a livery barn . . . The first licking ever given a Wave editor for publishing the news . . . Wanted:—A fighting editor at this office. One who stands six feet eleven inches in his stocking feet and tips the beam at 197 pounds fighting weight, who can handle his fists, feet, a gun or a club . . ."

Later, July 9, 1897, the editor writes feelingly: "Editor Wilkinson of the Iron County Record, is the latest unlucky wielder of the pencil in this state, to be given a thrashing by some bully who did not happen to agree with the editor's comments. The last newspaperman to get a licking prior to Wilkinson was brother Crosby of the Censor, who was given a thumping he will have occasion to remember for some time, by a would-be lawyer who got his name into print through his own misdeeds."

In this connection the Salina Editor (Howard) comments in part, as reproduced in the Wave: "This thing is becoming awful. Nearly every newspaperman in the state during the past year has received a terrible thrashing at the hands of viciously inclined bulldozers. About the only exceptions are the Metier Brothers of Richfield, Williams of Mount Pleasant, and the Editor of the (Salina) Press. Jack Metier carries a chip on his shoulder, a syringe in his pocket and will be the next victim. Williams is such a giant in stature, and withal so fierce looking that a bully would think twice before attacking him. As for the Press man, he has a Winchester in the office, and his assistant is a young man who would scrap his own shadow if it got too gay. Arm yourselves, brethren; it looks as if remorseless Nemesis is hot on our trail."

The editorial worries, not to say the dangers, finally got Brother Glanville and on June 3, 1898: "With this issue we cease to be publishers. . . . The Wave will be published by Mr. William Buys, the

president of the Wasatch Publishing Company in the future." Signed,
Glanville and Murdock. A news item adds: "The stockholders of
the Wasatch Publishing Company met Tuesday and gave President Buys
permission to make such disposal of the plant and paper as he sees
fit. Mr. Buys already had this power as he controls about two-thirds
of the stock." Accordingly on June 10, 1898, "William Buys, Editor"
again decorates the masthead. Mr. Buys, like his predecessors, faithfully maintained the uniform size of the paper and the arrangement
of its pages, and the game of "Tag, You're It!" continued; consequently on the first of January 1905 the management of The Wave
passed again into the hands of George Barzee! It was not a disagree-
ment, but more a matter of taking a friendly turn at the task. And on
March 17, 1905, Barzee's name was dropped again with this note:
"While the ownership and general management of the Wave have
passed into other hands, we will still hold down the easy chair in the
editorial sanctum.—Wave Publishing Company, William Buys, Editor."
On April 6, 1906, William Buys again became Editor and Manager.

A note of progress appears July 16, 1909: "William Buys, Editor;
Lucinda Buys (daughter), Society Editor." The biggest news the
paper ever carried was that of William Buys' death, at the age of 57,
which occurred November 27, 1909, and was reported in the issue of
December 3, 1909. The December 10, 1909 issue was out on time,
however, "published every Friday by the Wave Publishing Company."
An all powerful leavening influence in the community, much larger
than any single man! In the issue of January 28, 1910, we find "Charles
M. Broadbent, Editor and Manager." As a mark of the extraordinary
stability of everything connected with the Wave, that name has heralded
the weekly coming of the Wave regularly from that day to the present
time.

The Wave's remarkable files are an inexhaustable mine of information relating to Heber and Wasatch County, as well as the State.
In surprising ways they have furnished evidence of great importance
in the settlement of controversies, adjudicating claims, and the hearing
of lawsuits, according to editor Broadbent. Dates of births and deaths
and other occurrences have been established. The lawful legal notices
of corporations have been presented, and personal kinships have been
established for the use of the courts in the settlement of estates.

Through these precious newspaper files a host of essential witnesses
can be summoned from beyond the grave, and given a respectful hearing in any inquiry!

Heber Herald. Vol. 1, No. 1, Monday, June 23, 1890, 4 pages,
2 columns each, 7 x 9 inches, Abram Hatch, Jr., Editor and Manager.
"Junior" most emphatically! Mr. Hatch being the youngest publisher
in the state. He was born September 8, 1879, and was therefore only
10, going on 11, when he began this rather extraordinary venture. A
sister, one and one-half years his junior, assisted at times and the
father was known to read proof on the local news but seldom with

authority to censor. File complete in one bound volume in Editor Hatch's personal library (Salt Lake City).

"Salutatory. This is our first issue of the Heber Herald, which will be issued every Monday and we hope it will be a success. It will come through the post office to every subscriber if they will pay in advance. All who wish to subscribe, come and see us." And "To the Public. The Heber Herald Publishing Company are so well pleased with the success they have had in running a small two-page paper, they have concluded to enlarge it to a four-page genuine news and interesting periodical. With that object in view we have been to the expense of new type and press. It is our intention to continue to grow with our thriving country, and we solicit the patronage of the enterprising public, for we intend to look after the welfare of the public in every respect that is consistent with justice and right."

The original 2-page journal was begun the previous winter each page consisting of one stickful of type, usually two or three news items on one side and a "snack" from a continued Indian story on the other, the whole looking like a mere hand-size scrap of paper. But the suspense in the Indian story was insufferable; and the paper must necessarily be enlarged to accommodate reader demand! The 4-page paper had a full page of local news items, a page of telegraphic news borrowed from the city exchanges, and a page of story material, and later a page of advertisements. The subscription list averaged 300, as a result of the following appeal: "Subscribe for the Heber Herald; it is within reach of all; subscription price, 25c for three months, 50c for six months, and so on!"

Ex-Editor Hatch, reminiscently recalled recently his boyish habit of eavesdropping among the gossipping members of the Whittling Club at the public hitching post in Heber. "When I got both ears full I hurried back across the street and set it in type." In this way the youthful editor heard the news, and the public's reaction to it, before it was published, which often helped in the presentation of the story. The editorial angle was in this way defined, and the customary editorial opinion easily injected into the news story. Editor Hatch's editorial expression was often in the form of a whip-cracker at the tail end, for example:

"Thursday a young lady, while crossing the Lake Creek bridge on the west side of Main street, fell through and narrowly escaped injury. Whose business is it to attend to such matters?" Also, remembering the city drinking water came from the mountains in the irrigation streams, he says: "Tuesday we saw a dead cow being drug through the streets and ditches. It may be called alright. We don't know!" And another: "One drunk, before his honor Justice Duncan, on the 25th, for getting too much celebration on the 24th (of July, Utah's Pioneer Day). Robie Lindsay was found drunk on the street on the 24th and was run in by the Marshal and find (sic) $1 and costs of court and forfited (sic) his whiskey, which was for some Indian, we suppose."

The Council House, (Home of the Deseret News and The Mountaineer, 1850-1862), southwest corner, Main and South Temple Streets.

The Daily Tribune (left center), 22-26 West Second South Street, from 1875 for twelve or thirteen years.

Editor Hatch copied the following from the Salt Lake Herald of July 28, 1890: "While in Heber City last Saturday the Herald correspondent visited the office of the Heber Herald. This paper is a bright little sheet of 4-pages, published weekly by Abram Hatch, son of Mr. Joe Hatch, a boy only eleven years of age. He is Manager, Editor, Compositor and Pressman, and gets out a paper that would be a credit to a much older person. If properly encouraged Abe will sometime make a great newspaperman." Other newsmen complimented the juvenile editor by clipping and crediting news items from his paper through 1890, 1891 and 1892; but the lad evidently was not given the proper "encouragement" for when he quit in a few years, he never again resumed newspaper work. Hence the world will never know how good a newspaperman it missed!

Editor Hatch's grandfather, the first and steadiest advertiser, was the merchant proprietor of A. Hatch and Company's store. In order to place full credit where credit was due (and especially to avoid being credited for something where credit was not due) the grandsire urged upon Editor Hatch the sub-title "Junior". Accordingly, to oblige a frequent and valued guest of the business office, this noble pennant was hoisted October 20, 1890, and continued to the end: "A Hatch, Junior, Editor and Manager."

The reaction was not so good, however, for on October 27, 1890, we read: "The Editor of the Herald has been on the sick-list for two days, but is able to do some work between doses of physic, so the Herald gets out on time!" The next week the story was different (November 3, 1890). "Last week we were under the painful necessity of stating the editor was sick; we are glad to state that the editor of the Herald is right-side up with care and the editor of the Wave is the sick man." More was meant than met the eye in that exultation, for the youthful prodigy had showed frequent minor animosity toward the Wave Editor, chiefly over their different methods of serving up the News, only one of which methods could be right!

On December 15, 1890 the Juvenile Editor discourses on: "An Editor's Troubles.—Maybe you think it is all fun to run a newspaper, but it aint; when you have to get up in the morning and feed the pigs before breakfast and help feed the other things and do chores and go to school and be bossed around by your big brother, you don't have much time to set type and make proof sheets, write editorials and hunt up news, and if you don't have lots of news your subscribers won't pay up and the folks that write pieces for your paper say your paper is no good and if you don't do better they don't want it. I think them kind of people are cranks. When an editor works hard, gets all the news and gets his paper out on time, you ought to be satisfied, and this paper has been out on time every paper. We did think of having a holiday number with pictures and Christmas stories, but can't, cause school keeps up to the day before Christmas, and we can't use plate matter like the other papers do. There will be vacation after Christmas for about ten days; and we will have lots of time to fix up for a boss paper New Years. That will be a good time to subscribe and start with the new story."

But no sooner is the enemy within disposed of than a discursive expression of "policy" on enemies abroad appears January 12, 1891: "The Holidays are past, with all the fun and excitement following Christmas and New Year. Schools have commenced again. The town is quiet as before we thought of Christmas. Now what are you going to do for the New Year? Be good little boys. We would advise the little readers of the Herald to conform to the city ordinance which compels juveniles to be home before 8 o'clock. The curfew law is tough and aint fair. The Constitution of the United States guarantees to everybody life, liberty and the pursuit of happyness, and why in H - -l the City Council of Heber passes an ordinance interfering with the liberty of boys under sixteen we can't understand, but it is a law and has the approval of the Old Folks, so we must put up with it until we are several years older. While we think it is unconstitutional, we don't propose to make a test case but will use all our influence to have it repealed or changed so as to take in everybody and make the Old Folks stay at home too. While we advise obeying the laws, we don't believe in special legislation. When we get old enough to be a councilor we will see to it that all tyrannical laws are abolished and boys have a fair show."

The year was a good one for the Herald and so were the early months of 1892, but three mid-October numbers were missed and explained thus: "NOTICE (in type two inches high!) when the new schoolhouse was finished and school started, we were assigned more studies than we had last term, and find it takes all our time to keep up with our class, consequently the Herald will not be issued regularly, but occasionally during the winter. Next spring we will go on again just as though nothing had happened. When the Holidays come we will have a week off and will give you an extra Holiday number."

December 25, 1892 was celebrated with a special Christmas number; and another appeared March 20, 1893, after which the weekly issue appeared regularly until Vol. 4, No. 7, August 28, 1893, when we read what unwittingly became the Valedictory: "This is the last issue of the Herald this year, but we start up next March," which never came for the Heber Herald; and L. D. S. series picture film printer Hatch today, has the three printing presses among his basement souvenirs: the little 4-inch hand press, the Middle Sized hand press (big enough for one full page of the Herald at a time) and the big Gordon press on which only a 4-time illegitimate political successor to the Herald was printed during the election campaign of 1894, called "Heber Herald."

HELPER, Carbon County

Population: 1910, 816; 1920, 1606; 1930, 2707.

"The irrepressible A. B. Thomson, the Tribune 'Milo Zip', is going to start a newspaper at Helper, a little town on the Rio Grande Western in Central Utah which consists of (as the American Fork Independent has it) five or six section men, a dog, and a prospect for existence;" we learn this at second hand from the Eastern Utah Telegraph, Price, November 20, 1891. Whether that was a threat or a promise, we shall never know, for apparently no such infant was ever born to Helper. So far as known, the earliest newspaper was:

The Helper Times, established in 1911 by I. A. Lee and published every Saturday as a Republican newspaper. Mr. Lee was still the publisher in 1915, and probably as late as 1919. From February 1, 1921 (and possibly earlier) to August 20, 1924, George Grow was the publisher. At that time Mrs. Grace A. Cooper took charge, continuing to February 28, 1927, when C. L. Conner took charge and continued to September 3, 1928. A stray copy dated April 21, 1927, shows C. L. Conner, publisher, Ruth Metz, society editor. An issue dated April 19, 1928, shows Conner and McKnight, publishers, Ruth Metz, editor. June 5, 1930 the masthead carries Wm. T. Igleheart, editor, as did an issue for November 6, 1930. It is understood to have been printed in the Price newspaper office and distributed in Helper. Igleheart's name was dropped from the masthead in the issue of December 3, 1931. Howard A. Jarvis bought the paper December 10, 1931, at sheriff's sale, and sold December 31, 1931, announcing in the:

Helper Journal, dated January 7, 1932, which continues the serial numbers of the Times: "That the plant was purchased by C. Watt Brandon and his son, DeLos E. Brandon, of Sheridan, Wyoming, who changed the name of the Times to the Helper Journal." Masthead: C. Watt Brandon, owner and editor, DeLos E. Brandon, assistant editor and manager. On February 4, 1932, the Senior Brandon's name was dropped, leaving "DeLos E. Brandon, editor and publisher." Brandon sold to George W. Baker, January 12, 1934, who sold October 1, 1934, to William F. MacKnight and Leland Burress. Hal G. Macknight and Val H. Cowles of the Price Sun-Advocate bought the paper July 1, 1937, appointing Clifton N. Memmott as editor-manager.

HUNTSVILLE, Weber County

Population: 1890, 1,158; 1900, 1,022; 1910, 906; 1920, 814; 1930, 765.

Utah Danske Amerikaner. "A family magazine in the Danish language, with the euphonious title of Utah Danske Amerikaner has been started in Huntsville, Weber County," says the Deseret News, Friday, October 23, 1885. The American Newspaper Directory for 1890 shows: "Utah Danske Amerikaner, monthly, Danish, 10-pages,

6 x 9, subscription 80c, established 1886 (sic) Carl C. Ericksen, editor, Danish Publishing Company, publishers." We were told it lasted only a year or so. No copies found.

According to a Huntsville resident, who was postmaster at the time, the paper was usually only 4-pages, one-half the size of an average newspaper page; while printed mostly in Danish, there were always some items in English. Its circulation was 75 to 100 copies per issue. The editor was well educated, and kept aloof from the population, giving the impression he was entitled to a better place in the world. We were told the editor's father was once official coachman to the King of Denmark, and that editor Ericksen, in Huntsville, wore the stovepipe hat and dark, double-breasted coat that coachman Ericksen had worn in a nobler service in Denmark.

Editor Ericksen's mother, Mrs. Lund, was a much better mixer, and as she was so much better known, the local people were prone to call him "Mr. Lund." The publication was well edited and was really worth a better place in the world. "Where is he now?" we asked, and our informant replied: "He died in the poor-house; what did you suppose would become of a man who would start a newspaper in Huntsville?"

HUNTINGTON, Emery County

Population: 1890, 513; 1900, 653; 1910, 800; 1920, 1,285; 1930, 877.

The Huntington Echo faded away soon after its original sound, October 18, 1910. Its sponsors, M. E. Johnson, John E. Munson, and John P. Brockbank, are said to have sunk a thousand dollars each in the enterprise, without printing a single issue—in Huntington. They owned a little Coates Armory flat-bed hand printing press, the kind army officers at frontier military posts carried about on a pack saddle; but the only echoes that ever came from it were the sounds made in printing hand bills. The Huntington Echo, a 5-column, 8-page paper "published every Tuesday at Huntington, Utah, by E. J. Dunn," was printed in its entirety in the Salt Lake office of the Western Newspaper Union. One of its sponsors informed us the paid circulation was only 85 copies. Thus the Echo died for want of listeners.

That newspaper office is now, (1933) the granary in which the venerable proprietor, past eighty years of age, showed us the printing press and dug up a copy of the paper. He was writing his autobiography on a typewriter, and expressed regret that the sketch could not appear in his own newspaper. As indicated in the number seen, "Application for entry as second class matter at Huntington, Utah, post office," is still pending!

HYRUM, Cache County

Population: 1890, 1,423; 1900, 1,652; 1910, 1,833; 1920, 1,858; 1930, 1,869.

The Knowledge Seeker; Young Ladies' Thoughts; The Evening Star. Manuscript newspapers published in Hyrum. The Young Men's and Young Ladies' Mutual Improvement Associations of Hyrum published weekly literary journals largely in the interests and for the entertainment of the members of those organizations during the 1880s. These publications contained many brief news items, pithy preachments, and discussions of the weather. The publications were called by various names, all being prepared with pen and ink, or in manuscript form, consisting of from 6 to 10-pages legal size. "The Knowledge Seeker, volume 4, number 1, October 18, 1884," was issued by the Young Men, the "Young Ladies Thoughts," also "The Evening Star" were issued by the ladies, the latter succeeding the Knowledge Seeker, under a different set of officers. John A. Israelson's bulky file of these interesting quasi-newspapers, runs to 1891.

South Cache Courier was started about November 15, 1908, determined by subtracting dates from the earliest number found. John W. Harry (of the Smithfield Sentinel) in an autobiographical sketch prepared shortly before his death, says he established, and for a number of years ran, the South Cache Courier at Hyrum. He had started the Smithfield Sentinel in December, 1907, and may have produced both newspapers from the Sentinel plant for a time. The State Gazetteer for 1912-13, says Jacob A. Wahlen was proprietor, with C. F. Olsen, editor. Wahlen's connection is indicated to 1925. John A. Israelson, for many years Hyrum's postmaster, has preserved the files from 1915 to date (1934). From this file we discover that, the South Cache Courier was quietly dunked with the issue of December 4, 1925, the next number, December 11, 1925, appearing in Logan, together with the Smithfield Sentinel as the Cache Valley Herald (q.v.). That was the cue for the

South Cache Citizen, volume 1, number 1, which made its appearance January 29, 1926, dated at Hyrum but printed elsewhere. In it the publisher says: "Machinery for the Citizen will arrive sometime next week." There was also this plaintive letter: "Editor, Citizen: for seventeen years we received weekly the South Cache Courier, but . . . its owner saw fit to move elsewhere . . . We asked the people to support our new paper, its owner and general manager, Mr. Clyde F. Settle.— Hyrum Citizens Club." Obviously the appeal of the Citizen's Club to the "Citizen" had the desired effect, as witness:

The South Cache Courier. (II!) October 22, 1926, "Change in name: With this issue the Courier makes its appearance again!" The new paper carried no name at the masthead until sometime in 1928 when "J. A. Wahlen, editor and publisher," appeared. On May 8, 1931

THE PEEP O' DAY.

A SALT LAKE MAGAZINE

OF

SCIENCE, LITERATURE AND ART.

EDITED BY
HARRISON & TULLIDGE.
{ .... }
PUBLISHED IN THE
TWENTIETH WARD.

Vol. I.   GREAT SALT LAKE CITY. U. T., OCTOBER 20, 1864.   No. I.

MIRIAM ALROY

A TALE OF

THE JEWISH CAPTIVITY.

BY B. D'ISRAELI, M. P., P. C.

PART I.

The cornets sounded a final flourish as the prince of the captivity dismounted from his white mule; his train shouted as if they were once more a people, and had it not been for the contemptuous leer which played upon the countenances of the Moslemin bystanders, it might have been taken for a day of triumph rather than of tribute.

"The glory has not departed!" exclaimed the venerable Bostenay, as he entered the hall of his mansion. "It is not as the visit of Sheba unto Solomon; nevertheless the glory has not yet departed. You have done well, faithful Caleb." The old man's courage waxed more vigorous as each step within his own walls the more assured him against the recent causes of his fear—the audible curses and the threatened missils of the unbelieving mob.

"It shall be a day of rejoicing and thanksgiving," continued the prince; "and look, my faithful Caleb, that the trumpeters be well served. That last flourish was bravely done. It was not as the blast before Jericho; nevertheless it told that the Lord of Hosts was—for us. How the accursed Ishmaelites started! Did you mark, Caleb, that tall Turk in green upon my left? By the sceptre of Jacob, he turned pale! O! it shall be a day of rejoicing, and thanksgiving! And spare not the wine, nor the fleshpots for the people. Look you to this, my child, for the people shouted bravely, and with a stout voice. It was not as the great shout in the camp when the ark returned, but, nevertheless, it was boldly done,—and showed that the glory had not yet departed. So spare not the wine, my son, and drink to the desolation of Ishmael in the juice which he dare not quaff."

"It has indeed been a great day for Israel!" exclaimed Caleb, echoing his master's exultation.

"Had the procession been forbidden," continued Bostenay, "had it been reserved for me of all the princes to have dragged the accursed tribute upon foot, without trumpets and without guards, by this sceptre, my good Caleb, I really think, that sluggishly as this old blood now runs, I would——but it is needless now to talk—the God of our fathers hath been our refuge."

"Verily, my lord, we were as David in

the wilderness of Zipe; but now we are as the Lord's anointed in the stronghold of Engedi!"

"The glory truly has not yet *utterly* departed," resumed the prince in a more subdued tone: yet if—I tell you what, Caleb—praise the Lord that you are young."

"My prince may yet live to see the good day."

"Nay my child, you misinterpret me. Your prince has lived to see the evil day. 'Twas not of the coming that I thought when I bid you praise the Lord because you were young—the more my sin. I was thinking, Caleb, that if your hairs were as mine, if you could call back like me the days that are gone by—the days when it needed no bribe to prove we were princes—the glorious days when we led captivity captive—I was thinking, I say, my son, what a gainful heritage it is to be born after the joys that have passed away."

"My father lived at Babylon," said Caleb.

"O! name it not!" exclaimed the old chieftain. "Dark was the day that we lost the second Sion! We were then also slaves to the Egyptian; but verily we ruled over the realm of Pharoah. Why, Caleb, you who know *all*—the days of toil—the nights restless as a love-sick boy's, which it has cost your prince to gain permission to grace our tribute day with the paltry presence of half a dozen guards—you who know all my difficulties, who have witnessed all my mortification, what would you say to the purse of dirhems, surrounded by seven thousand cimeters!"

"Seven thousand cimeters!"

"Not one less; my father flourished one."

"It was indeed a great day for Israel!"

"Nay, that is nothing. When old Alroy was prince—old David Alroy—for thirty years, good Caleb—thirty long years we paid *no* tribute to the caliph."

"No tribute! no tribute for thirty years! What marvel then, my prince, that the Philistines have of late exacted interest!"

"Nay, that is nothing," continued old Bostenay, unmindful of his servant's ejaculations. "When Moctador was caliph, he sent to the same prince David, to know why the dirhems were not brought up, and David immediately called to horse, and attended by all the chief people rode to the palace, and told the caliph that tribute was an acknowledgment made from the weak to the strong to insure protection and support, and inasmuch as he and his people had just garrisoned the city for ten years against the Seljuks, he held the caliph in arrear."

"We shall see an ass mount a ladder,"

exclaimed Caleb with uplifted eyes of wonder.

"It is true though," continued the prince; "often have I heard my father tell the tale. He was then a child, and his mother held him up to see the procession return, and all the people shouted, 'The sceptre has not gone out of Jacob!'"

"It was indeed a great day for Israel."

"Nay, that is nothing. I could tell you such things! But we prattle; our business is not yet done. You to the people; the widow and the orphan are waiting. Give freely, good Caleb, give freely; the spoils of the Cananite are no longer ours; nevertheless the Lord is still our God, and after all, even this is a great day for Israel . And Caleb, Caleb, bid my nephew, David Alroy, know that I would speak with him."

"I will do all promptly, good master! We wonder that our honored lord, your nephew, went not up with the donation this day."

"Who bid you wonder? Begone sir! How long are you to be here?—Away!"

"They wonder he went not up with the tribute to-day. Ay! surely—a common talk. This boy will be our ruin: a prudent hand to wield our shattered sceptre! I have observed him from his infancy; he should have lived in Babylon. The old Alroy blood flows in his veins, a stiff-necked race. When I was a youth his grandsire was my friend; I had some fancies then myself. Dreams, dreams! We have fallen on evil days, and yet we prosper. I have lived long enough to feed a rich caravan, laden with the rich shawls of India, and the stuffs of Sumarcand, if not exactly like dancing before the ark, is still a goodly sight. And our hard-hearted rulers, with all their pride, can they subsist without us? Still we wax rich. I have lived to see the haughty caliph sink into a slave, viewing far than Israel. And the victorious and voluptuous Seljuks, even now they tremble at the dim mention of the distant name of Arslan. Yet I, Bostenay, and the frail remnant of our scattered tribes, still we exist, and still, thanks to our God, we prosper. But the age of power has passed; it is by prudence now that we must flourish. The jibe, the jest, the curse, perchance the blow, Israel must now bear, and with a calm, or even smiling visage. What then! For every jibe and jest, for every curse, I'll have a dirhem; and every blow—let him look to it who is my creditor, or wills to be so. But see, he comes, my nephew! His grandsire was my friend. Methinks I look upon him now; the same Alroy that was the partner of my boyish hours, And yet that fragile form and girlish face but ill consort with the dark passions we find: "Leslie J. Christensen, Editor and publisher," and that was replaced on June 19, 1931 by "LeRoy Wahlen, publisher, Wendell G. Allen, editor." Wahlen's name was dropped July 10, 1931, but added again July 31, 1931, as "publisher and manager." Accordingly, Allen's name was dropped August 28, 1931.

On December 25, 1931, B. Dale Gibson was Santa Claus' gift to the Courier as publisher. But, while nobody shot Santa Claus, Mrs. J. A. Wahlen, (widow of the founder) became publisher on January 22, 1932, reading from the masthead. A widow's trials are many, however, especially if a newspaper is one of them. E. J. Barrett was manager in 1933, followed shortly by Edward S. Price. Roy Wahlen (the son) became proprietor in 1934, with N. Pratt Smith, manager.

JUNCTION, Piute County

Population: 1890, 125; 1900, 249; 1910, 423; 1920, 389; 1930, 352.

Piute County News, was begun May 23, 1924 by F. A. Jackman, who had bought the primitive plant of The Progress at Marysvale, and moved it to the county seat. The earliest number in the files (all since burned) was dated Friday, December 26, 1924, Vol. 4, No. 52, claiming to be "successor to The Progress." The June 5, 1925 issue shows F. B. Jackman, (son), assistant editor. Mrs. Eva B. Swanson took over the paper by purchase January 1, 1926, and has continued its publication on a primitive Washington hand-press, the only one in use in the state (excepting a few used for proofing). The building and contents were destroyed by fire on August 24, 1933, but the paper was soon going again. A. C. Saunders bought it July 12, 1937, and moved it back to Marysvale, where Chas. M. Giffen has since edited it.

KANAB, Kane County

Population: 1890, 409; 1900, 710; 1910, 733; 1920, 1,102; 1930, 1,195.

Kanab Clipper. This has apparently been a good place to start a newspaper, but a poor place to continue one. The Utah County Democrat of June 24, 1899, first tells us: "J. T. Camp, who has been identified with several newspaper enterprises in Utah, has purchased the 'Loa Advice' plant, and will remove it to Kanab, where he will start a new paper." Camp moved a family, an old style Army Press, about 100 pounds of newspaper type, a few cases of job type, and a can of news ink, in one house, from which the Kanab Clipper was born about January 1, 1900, a 4-page paper, one home print, Camp and Mrs. Camp being the parents.

The Camps kept the paper going three or four months, when they sold to E. Albert Stewart, County Clerk, who shortly sold out to Mr. and Mrs. Heber P. Cram. "The last two issues of the Kanab Clipper," says the Spanish Fork Press, May 1, 1902, "shows signs of its coming down with a bad case of yellow fever, and besides turning yellow, it is only half its usual size. We hope the Clipper pulls through all O. K."

Cram sold out in the spring of 1903 to J. G. Spencer and Will Dobson, two Kanab High School students. These lads not only introduced the innovation of printing all four pages at home, but put in an editorial column and proceeded to use it! The boys were at first doubtful about the wisdom of giving up their chance of an education; but when they tried to make enough to eat and wear out of their newspaper, they found their education was just beginning.

"Finding the type encrusted with old, hardened ink, the accumulation of years," Dobson tells us, "we emptied all the cases, news and display type together, in one hopeless mixture, into a tub of hot lye water. A thorough washing and rinsing made it look almost new. But the job of distribution took three days and nights, and then only to discover that the b's, d's, p's and q's had been cased together, and that there was not enough type for all the boxes. In setting up a sermon I remember, God became 'Gob,' 'Gop,' or 'Goq.' A shortage of l's and s's necessitated the substitution of j's and z's. A worthy subscriber named 'McAllister,' became 'McAjjizter'; and other spellings were equally 'ridicujouz', and got more laughs than the joke column.

"A correspondent was engaged in every town in the county, and at Fredonia and Moccasin, Arizona; and you could tell the size of the town by the length of its news column—the smaller the town, the longer the column. Nothing was ever refused in payment on subscriptions and advertising," Dobson tells us. "Even the rankest of butter offered, was not a total loss; it was made into soap. Dried peaches, apples, pears and plums, home cured raisins, fresh fruits, watermelons, cantaloupes, butter, eggs, flour, grain, hay, firewood, tithing orders, store coupons, and so forth. Most people gave their best. A few found the newspaper a good place to get rid of culls; it is possible they overpaid at that. Figuring out ways to dispose of the produce, developed more brain power than writing the editorials.

"Home town papers are not allowed to print any real news, as it would hurt someone's feelings, and alienate him and all his friends. News tips volunteered by helpful townsmen, often proved to be loaded with dynamite. Seemingly high minded citizens looked upon the newspaper columns as a good medium for taking whacks at their enemies; thus we learned a lot in a short time!"

In 1904 J. G. Spencer sold his interest to Frank Little, who was not a printer, but learned on the job. "It was not long after this that strong opposition developed. The Clipper's editorial page was to blame," Dobson meekly admits. "Finally so much support was withdrawn, that the paper could no longer carry on. The owners were forced to sell. Bowman and Company bought the plant and stored it. This was the end of the Kanab Clipper." But it was not the end of Will Dobson's ambition, and in the spring of 1910 he shipped into Kanab a small job press and some type, and began publication of

The Lone Cedar. The paper consisted of 4 pages, 10 x 15 inches in size, the capacity of the press, only one page being printed at a time.

Its size, and the notable lack of heading and display type attracted attention throughout the State. Some weeks it went out on wrapping paper. Nevertheless it survived until the summer of 1911, when Charles H. Townsend bought it and changed the name to

The Kane County News. Using a larger printing press and several pages of readyprint, Mr. Townsend soon had a prosperous newspaper. There developed however, a strong public opinion in opposition to the News' anti-Mormon editorial policy. This opposition resulted in the organization of a company headed by L. D. S. Stake President and State Senator William W. Seegmiller, which bought the paper and plant.

D. D. Rust was made editor about November 1, 1911, and soon made of it an excellent newspaper, all home print, stressing education, religion and the home. Though it was small—usually 4 pages of only 4 columns each, like its predecessor, it was friendly to everybody and everything including the **Kane County Independent.** Vol. 1 No. 1 March 14, 1912, 8 pages, 4 columns, 2 home print, Charles H. Townsend, publisher. An intense rivalry developed, as the two newspapers divided the populace into two factions, chiefly political. Finally, however, the Independent lost ground, after the election, and the Western Newspaper Union of Denver, sold the Independent plant at public auction to the Kane County News Corporation. D. D. Rust continued as editor of the News for a few years, when he was drawn aside to become a tourist guide. Mr. Seegmiller then engaged Jack Borlase, of Salt Lake City, to take the editorship about August 1, 1914.

Borlase's style was not only ultra modern, but almost radical, for such a community, his editorial horizon being much too wide, and his style sometimes much too vigorous, for even Kanab's lofty isolated position. Borlase and the Kane County News were thus talked about. The following is a sample from the Duchesne Record, April 24, 1915: "The Kane County News, the smallest paper in the state, but which has started one of the largest sensations, by publishing a statement from President Seegmiller of the Kane County Stake of Zion, also Senator in the last legislature, that the reason Governor Spry vetoed the prohibition bill was because he was advised to by President Joseph F. Smith, is still digging in." Borlase's tenure terminated early in 1916, he says, "At the instance of subscribers and advertisers who failed to renew and repeat!"

It was then that Will Dobson, in some respects a fellow disciple of the Borlase school, succeeded Borlase in May, 1916, and ran the newspaper about a year. He dabbled deep in State and National politics, leaving the field of local news so tenderly cultivated by D. D. Rust, to revert to weeds. Dobson is said to have enjoyed the squirms of some of those whom he pilloried,—enjoyed seeing his printed thoughts move a population, whether favorably or unfavorably; but according to this informant, when it came to throwing his cabbages and carrots at polygamy and the Church leaders, a committee of Church authorities waited on him—and a new light led him into a divergent path. Thus the News soon died. J. G. Spencer bought the plant, and moved it to Panguitch, later selling to Will J. Peters, of the Panguitch Progress. George M. Shields was editor in 1923.

KAYSVILLE, Davis County

Population: 1890, 548; 1900, 1,708; 1910, 887; 1920, 809; 1930, 992.

The Kaysville Eagle was started February 16, 1893, by W. E. Smith, editor and publisher. A copy of Vol. 1 No. 17, Thursday, June 8, 1893, in the Ogden City Library, has 6 columns, 8 pages, 2 home print, and shows Eva B. Smith, editor. The next week a line is added: "W. E. Smith, Manager." A display advertisement explains "W. E. Smith, manufacturer of all kinds of whip lashes, harness repairing neatly done on short notice. Satisfaction guaranteed." The Eagle was quoted frequently by exchanges in 1893, and through the summer of 1894, after which it seems to have perished.

The Kaysville Post. In the Park Record of May 9, 1896, we read: "The Kaysville Post is the name of a new paper recently started at Kaysville by John V. Young. It has one local page, while the other three are printed in Salt Lake." The Kaysville Post is also dated at Farmington, according to the 1898 edition of the American Newspaper Directory. In it we find "Saturday, Independent, established 1892, 8 pages, 15 x 22—$2, James MacLaren, editor and publisher;" but neither a whip maker nor a Scotsman could keep a Kaysville newspaper long afloat in those days.

The Weekly Reflex was established in Kaysville in 1904, according to the American Newspaper Directory for 1915. The files are missing prior to 1912. With the issue of April 4, 1912, W. P. Epperson and son, Clyde A. Epperson, leased the Reflex from H. H. Blood and J. R. Gailey, who on April 1, 1912, had purchased the paper and plant from LeRoy Shelby and John S. White. In his Valedictory Editor Shelby says in part: "In our office phrase, the calling of an editor is not usually a 'phat take,' but the 'proof' of his 'make-up' usually justifies itself with enough 'impression' that support is the 'underlay' of his business. The thing that 'kills' is the failure to 'come up' of 'types' of character who should give the moral support that furnishes the 'pi' for strength, and is the method which raises 'the devil' with things, making it not long til the people, 'editor' and all are fit subjects for the 'hell-box'."

The Reflex was entered as second class mailing matter February 15, 1911. For some reason the Gazetteer for 1912-13 says: "Cummings and Nielson publishers, B. F. Cummings, editor and manager, lessees and successor to The Reflex Publishing Company." The Eppersons are shown to be in charge from 1914. W. P. Epperson died suddenly while at a New Year's Eve ball in Ogden, December 31, 1930. The January

2, 1931, number of The Reflex was issued by the staff as a memorial to the Senior Epperson. The paper has since borne the masthead: C. A. Epperson and C. V. K. Saxton (son-in-law—brother-in-law).

LAYTON, Davis County

Population: 1900, 953; 1910, 1,171; 1920, 1,511; 1930, 2,037.

The Weekly News—Express was started October 26, 1925, by Hector T. Evans, who ran it alone to and including the issue of November 9, 1933, when he sold it to John Stahle, Jr., whose name as editor and manager first appeared November 16, 1933. While entered as second class mailing matter at Layton, its dateline showed "Layton, Kaysville, Clearfield, Syracuse, Davis County." This may indicate the publisher's strenuous effort to keep it from going to Limbo! Indeed the paper was printed in Mr. Evans' job printing plant in Ogden during the last year or so of his ownership. Subsequently Mr. Stahle has printed it in his father's Clipper plant at Bountiful, but it is still the Layton News-Express.

LEHI, Utah County

Population: 1890, 1,750; 1900, 2,719; 1910, 2,964; 1920, 3,078; 1930, 2,826.

The Lehi Banner was established May 29, 1891. "It is the official organ of the sugar factory," says the Manti Home Sentinel, June 2, 1891. And November 6, 1891, the Price Telegraph says "Lehi Banner reached our exchange table last week without ink on one side." The American Newspaper Directory for 1892 furnishes these data: "Lehi City, Banner, Friday, established 1891, 4 pages, 18 x 24—$2, circulation 300, Lehi Publishing Company." The Directory for 1894 gives: "Thursdays, 4 pages, 16 x 22—$2, Walter L. Webb, publisher, smallest edition issued within a year 408 copies." The Directory for 1898 shows a circulation of 550.

"The Lehi Banner is 8 years old," says the Brigham City Bugler June 11, 1898; and it must have been a good newspaper, for it was quoted frequently that year. About December 1, 1898, the Banner became a semi-weekly, but "the Lehi Banner is again reaching us as a Weekly, claiming insufficient support for a semi-weekly," says the Vernal Express February 9, 1899. The Directory for 1900 shows, E. S. Carroll, Editor, Lehi Publishing Company, publishers. The 1903-4 Directory gives "George Webb, Editor." It is then a long jump to the 1912-13 Directory, which shows "J. M. Kirkham, Manager." The 1914-15 Directory credits the Banner to the "Alpine Publishing Company." The 1916-17 listing gives "S. W. Ross, Manager." In 1915 the Banner was being published at American Fork, as one of a family of newspapers sponsored by L. W. Gaisford; that is, one paper with different headings for Lehi, American Fork and Pleasant Grove. The Banner

JOSEPH E. JOHNSON
Born April 28, 1817
Died, 1882

FRANKLIN D. RICHARDS
Born April 2, 1821
Died December 9, 1899

GEORGE Q. CANNON
Born January 11, 1827
Died April 12, 1901

JOHN NICHOLSON
Born July 13, 1830
Died January 25, 1909

files do not seem to have been preserved. We were informed that "only Jim Kirkham and God know where they went," and Jim told us he has forgotten. He thought the Church had them; and the L. D. S. Church Librarian wishes they had!

The Rustler. "Lehi now boasts of a semi-weekly paper. The Rustler made its first appearance as such last Friday; Editor Camp . . ." says the Wasatch Wave, April 23, 1897. The American Newspaper Directory for 1898 says, the Rustler was non-partisan, had 4 pages, 17 x 24, Davis and Sleater, editors and publishers. Poor Camp was always de-camping; and the Rustler soon followed in his footsteps, but we don't know when, nor why, nor whither.

The Lehi Sun made its first appearance Wednesday, August 5, 1914, bearing the masthead: "Ole B. Peterson, Editor; Frank Gaisford, Assistant Editor; A. F. Gaisford, Manager, printed and published in Lehi." Editorially, the paper itself says: "The Lehi Sun has risen; new home paper to boost Lehi . . . printed and published in Lehi . . . We trust that it may go on forever in its course and refuse to stand still, even though Joshua of Old commands it to do so." With the issue of May 19, 1915, the masthead presents only "A. F. Gaisford, Manager." On October 3, 1916, publication day was changed from Wednesday to Thursday, "with the idea of giving us more time to gather and prepare the news." The 1916-17 Directory shows "Lehi Sun Publishing Company, Arthur F. Gaisford, Manager." Beginning May 30, 1917, this heading was used "The Lehi Sun, combined with the Lehi Banner. . . We are pleased to announce that we have taken over The Lehi Banner, and in the future its subscribers will receive The Lehi Sun in its stead.

"The combining of the two papers had to come at some time. This was apparent to us, ever since we started . . . and was also known to our competitor. During the life of both papers, a sort of double burden has been placed on the local people . . . Now that there is only one paper, we think that the people will consider the condition, and will see the necessity of the increase of the subscription from $1.00 a year to $1.50; on time, $2.00 a year. Other papers of the State have been receiving these prices for some time. A few of these are: The Vernal Express, $2.00; Garland Globe, $1.50; Emery County Progress, $1.50; Monroe Record, $1.50; Payson Globe-Header $2.00; Springville Independent, $1.50; Millard County Chronicle, $2.00; and Washington County News, $2.00."

The sub-title "combined with Lehi Banner" was omitted from May 2, 1929. A special announcement February 19, 1931, says, "Commencing with next week's issue, J. Nile Washburn, teacher of English in the Lehi High School will take entire charge of the editorial policy of the paper. Local man in charge: George P. Price, an all-around printer and linotype operator with twenty year's experience, is in charge of the office, and will handle the mechanical work along with the management of the office." The Gaisfords still owned it, though only "George P. Price, Manager," appeared on the masthead. Price's name was dropped without explanation November 19, 1931, (probably because he was negotiating for the Free Press q.v.). We read on November 17, 1932 "The Sun . . . is being operated by A. F. Gaisford, Senior, assisted by Mrs. Winzell Gray Swenson, as reporter; and Earl Gaisford as linotype operator."

The Lehi Free Press, "The City's only home owned newspaper," Vol. 1 No. 1, August 25, 1932, George P. Price, Manager (Editor) Thursday." Price says he bought the Myton Free Press plant and the name came with it.

LOGAN, Cache County

Population: 1890, 4,565; 1900, 5,451; 1910, 7,522; 1920, 9,439; 1930, 9,979.

The Northern Light made its first appearance about May 20, 1879. "We have received the fourth number of The Northern Light, printed at Logan, Utah," says the Provo Territorial Enquirer June 11, 1879. "It is a 4-page weekly; could be improved typographically, but it is high-toned." E. W. Tullidge in his History of Northern Utah says: "It was a 5-column folio, one-half printed in Danish, and the other half in the English language. It was very poorly printed, and the press, type and so forth would cost probably $100. A. C. Growe, a watch and clock repairer, was the first owner. He ran it for several months and then sold out to 'Binnie' Pratt, who ran it for a short time, when the Junction Printing Association of Ogden offered to give him $100, providing he would quit the publication of his sheet. Mr. Pratt accepted this offer."

"The last number of the Northern Light has the name of Mr. A. Pratt as proprietor and editor, with L. O. Littlefield, as Assistant Editor. They promise us a better paper in the future," says the Deseret News June 12, 1879. And on July 29: "Northern Light.—The last issue of this paper announces the intention of its publishers to print a semi-weekly the early part of November." From Provo's Territorial Enquirer of August 20, 1879, we learn "The Northern Light, Logan, collapsed on the 15th instant. It will renew again, however, at Oxford, Idaho, under the title of Idaho Banner, with Judge Willard Crawford, as Editor." The Deseret News of August 19, 1879, adds this angle: "The company having been induced to go and set up a journal in Oxford." And on August 25, 1879, we find this further item to aid with that first name: "Mr. Abinidi Pratt, late proprietor of the Northern Light." The Ogden Junction September 13, 1879, makes the wise-crack: "A Salt Lake contemporary says that 'The Idaho Banner is out.' A mistake, friend, it is the Northern Light that went out!"

The Logan Leader. The Junction Printing Association of Ogden, gave Abinidi Pratt $100 to extinguish the Northern Light, says E. W.

Tullidge, who continues the story: "And on the 11th day of September, 1879, the first number of a 7-column folio called the Logan Leader, was issued under the management of the Junction Printing Association. It was what is called a 'patent outside,' and was edited and managed by F. J. Cannon, and was issued weekly. The Leader had no connection with the Northern Light, and did not succeed to either its patronage or plant, such as it was."

Everybody applauded Editor Cannon from the start. "Logan Leader.—The first number of this paper reached us today (September 16, 1879)" says the Deseret News. "It is a neat and attractive sheet, patent outside, and well printed, nearly all of the type used having been obtained from the Deseret News type foundry."

"It does not start out with any sickly talk about probable success. The articles are all bright, crisp, newsy and well prepared," says the Ogden Junction September 17, 1879. It is thus evident that "The Junction" folks (of whom Editor Cannon had been one), were well pleased with their Logan venture. The Junction commented further November 22, 1879: "The Leader is well spoken of by everybody. The only complaint we heard is that it ought to come out oftener, at least twice a week. Mr. Cannon ('our Frank') the Editor, is meeting with gratifying success, professionally and socially." The Territorial Enquirer had another reason for approval: "We like it because it resembles our own paper in style and make-up."

"Our old friend and associate, Frank J. Cannon, is the present editor of the Logan Leader." This kindly reference in the Deseret News September 23, was proudly quoted by the Ogden Junction, September 27, 1879; and other State papers made friendly reference to and clipped freely from Mr. Cannon's Leader, though his leadership was but for a year, 52 numbers, ending with the issue of September 3, 1880.

At that time the Leader "passed into the possession of the Cummings Brothers, Messrs. Benj. F. and Horace G. of this city," says the Deseret News August 13, 1880, quoting the announcement from the Leader itself. B. F. Cummings became the Editor. Here is a quip from the Territorial Enquirer October 20, 1880: "The complaint is made by the Leader that the citizens of Logan do not sufficiently patronize the City Water Works. . . . Go to them, Leader, roast them, make them patronize!"

"The Logan Leader is about to abandon the patent outside arrangement. Next week's issue will be the first issue of the new departure. Right." says the Deseret News August 8, 1881. And on December 24, 1881, the Ogden Herald says: "The Logan Leader is going to have a power press. The press is mighty, and must prevail." On May 17, 1882, the Herald refers to "B. F. Cummings, Junior, Esquire, Publisher and Editor of the Logan Leader."

Cummings Brothers ran the business until August 1, 1882, when they sold out to the founders of the Utah Journal. About 20 numbers of the Logan Leader are preserved in the bound files of the Journal at Logan. Vol. 1, No. 2, Thursday, September 18, 1879, consists of 4 pages of 7 columns each, 10 cents a copy, $3 a year. While the scissors were freely used and there were not many local news items, advertising patronage was generous, including for example: Wellsville Cooperative Mercantile Institution; United Order of Hyrum . . . white and red pine lumber. Beginning in 1882, the size was increased to 8 columns, and the front page was sown solid with reading matter, a formidable acreage of type, but with no money in it.

The Utah Journal. "A company was organized August 1, 1882," says E. W. Tullidge, "with Moses Thatcher, G. W. Thatcher, W. B. Preston, J. T. Caine, Junior, and others, as stockholders, including John P. Smith and E. A. Stratford, who had established a job printing office in Logan in the fall of 1880, and it was desired that the job printing and newspaper business should be consolidated. They turned in their printing office as stock in the new organization. This combination bought out the Leader, and Mr. Cummings became editor and Captain E. B. Burnett, from Nebraska, became Manager. The name of the paper was changed to the Utah Journal, and was published twice a week. A new plant was bought, and the paper greatly improved."

The Journal Editor continued the use of a sharp shears and a format similar to the Leader. The Salt Lake Evening Chronicle February 15, 1883 notices it: "A discovery.—The turnip-fed luminary of Cache County, that weakly shines in the nebulous columns of the Utah Journal . . ." And the Ogden Herald, December 28, 1883, adds this: "The Utah Journal claims to be the best newspaper in the territory, outside of Salt Lake City. Modesty is a jewel of priceless value in Cache County." But the Park Mining Record of February 9, 1884, approves more generously. "The editor of the Utah Journal is a glorious exception to the general run of Mormon journalists." L. O. Littlefield continued as printer, at least through 1884. The Utah Journal says of itself July 9, 1884: "Some time since an eastern house offered a medical advertisement to the Journal, which we could not insert in our columns at any price. The same house subsequently wrote to a business house in Logan asking if there was any other paper published here, and stating that if there was, they would advertise in it; but they would not advertise in the Utah Journal. Sour grapes!"

The Ogden Herald, September 3, 1884, says: "The Utah Journal (Logan) has commenced short sketches on Utah journals and journalists." But unfortunately, the Journal file is missing from July 31, 1884, to May 1, 1885, and none of the sketches were found.

Evidently the partnership was not harmonious, nor the business satisfactorily prosperous, for "Messrs. Smith and Stratford withdrew the job printing plant at about the expiration of a year after it was put in, and resumed business upon their own account," says Tullidge. "Mr. Burnett withdrew in 1884, disposing of his interests to the Thatcher Brothers. Mr. Cummings continued to conduct it until 1885, when the paper having ceased to be self-supporting, was in part at least, on May 1, 1885, turned over to E. A. Stratford, John P. Smith and John E. Carlisle. Carlisle became editor, Stratford manager, and Smith foreman, for the new Utah Journal Company."

The Deseret News May 4, 1885 says: "John E. Carlisle, a well-known and respected man of Logan, succeeds B. F. Cummings, Junior, as editor of the Utah Journal." The Salt Lake Evening Democrat of May 5, 1885 adds: "If we mistake not, this means that the Logan Journal in the future will not dare to question the policy or the authority of the Deseret News. The Logan paper will henceforth take its theology straight." And the Salt Lake Evening Chronicle of May 7, 1885: "The former editor was evidently a man of ability and a certain independence of thought. . . . The first number of the Journal under the new management is before us, and it not only follows the track of its leaders (the News and Herald of Salt Lake), but appears to delight in playing second fiddle to the basest discords of the inharmonious organ."

The following bears on the fellowship existing between the former and the current publishers: "May 13, 1885, Notice.—The Utah Journal having changed hands on the 1st instant . . . Mr. B. F. Cummings, Junior, is not authorized to make collection.—Utah Journal Printing and Publishing Company, M. Thatcher, President."

The Journal editor was fond of second fiddle solo parts. For example, September 23, 1885: "Pat Lannan, the American gentleman who owns and controls the Salt Lake Tribune, and who is by virtue of being chief of that paper the sole controller, governor and high office holder in general, of this Territory, passed through Logan last Sunday on a trip north, and actually ate dinner at a Mormon hotel. It is believed that our city was not demoralized to a very great extent through the occurrence."

The American Newspaper Directory of 1886 says the Journal was issued Wednesdays and Saturdays, 4 pages, circulation 1000. An historical sketch on the 25th anniversary says in part: "In 1889 Mr. R. W. Sloan, a newspaper man of ability and experience, purchased the interest of Messrs. Carlisle and Stratford, and he and Mr. Smith effected considerable improvement in the paper and changed its name to

"The Logan Journal. A year later Mr. Smith withdrew, taking the job plant; but Mr. Sloan continued to publish the best paper Cache County ever had," says the Anniversary Sketch September 17, 1904. But the Brigham Bugler of January 31 reminds us: "The Logan Journal is the most selfish, brassed and radical old billy goat that ever butted the back pants of the unsuspecting." The Wasatch Wave had stated on January 6, 1891: "J. H. Paul, Salt Lake, will assume editorial charge of the Logan Journal on the 15th of the present month, and on the same day J. L. Robinson, of Provo, will become Business Manager." The Manti Home Sentinel had further reported August 14,

MANTI HERALD.
AND SANPETE ADVERTISER.

F.C.ROBINSON
Editor & Publisher.   MANTI, MAY 4th 1867.   No 13, Vol 1.

EDITOR'S CORNER.

THE CITY WALL.

We believe it is an accepted fact, or idea, that Manti is to have a City Wall!

Now when we say "City Wall" we mean one of those substantial rock & mortar Concerns, that will not only inclose, but increase the Value of property immensely and through its solidity and workmanship-like finish, will stand for ages as a monument of credit and intelligent industry, on the part of the builders.

It has been suggested, that the Wall work, be apportioned to each Citizen, according to the amount of property he has to enclose. this Seems to us the best and fairest way; for it is evident that the more property a man gets enclosed and the more he is benefited! it has always been an acknowledged principle of right, that the stronger horse "have the heaviest load.."!

Now if the Wall is to be built on the above plan, and a man finds that he owns more City lots than he can possibly build wall for, he Can sell lots to those without any homestead; and who will be very glad to build wall for them! and thus our City Town lots will find occupants; and the City itself (as it should be) become more compact and City like!

As soon as we ascertain the exact Plan of the Wall, both in extent and manner of building, we shall be glad to Publish particulars. We think, building of a City Wall "a big job" but each one will do a big-ger "job" before he puts the cap stone on the Walls of his "Kingdom"!

BY TELEGRAPH.

Manti May3
Telegraph.
The business of this office has been resumed to day, after a silence of six days. owing to the wire having been cut in two places viz:— Salt Creek Kanyon. and about 2 miles north of Fort Ephraim.

Toqueville May 3rd
President Young is Traveling to day between this place and St George.

St George 4th
President Young & Suite arrived at this City last night party all well.

Scipio 2 of the day
Among a large herd of Stock driven recently through Fillmore by Gentiles about 50 head were recognized as belonging to Citizens and had been stolen thieves were at once arrested and confess to the existence of an or-ganised band of thieves thro' the Territory

LOCAL.

A VISITATION

The recent visitation of Gen.D.H. Wells & Suite, to the various Towns of this County, and the important instructions imparted on the occa-sion, cannot soon be forgot' and the People at large will doubtless unite heartily in responding to the many wise and useful sug-gestions thrown out, of a Military nature, and touching the safety of life and property.

But the Counsels of the wisest men availeth little, it those to whom they apply are slow to hear and act; yet we trust the opposite to this will be the result of the visit alluded to.

MORONI.

We are informed that Moroni is in a thriving condition in business save They have the prospect of having to go to other places, to buy their bread stuffs before next harvest.

Bishop Bradley, we associate were very prompt in proceeding to Salt Creek Kanyon to repair Telegraph Wire that some desparators on the 27th Ult: had cut

VARIETIES.

It is an old saying that in a great future day "every tub must stand on its own bottom" well! what will become of the tubs without bottoms? they'll stand on nothing, and be full of emptiness!

KINDNESS.

Angry looks can do no good,
Most blossoms dealt in blindness;
Words are better understood
If spoken but in kindness!

HAPPINESS.

If solid happiness we prize,
Within our breast the jewel lies,
And they are fools who roam;—
The world has nothing to bestow,
From own selves our joys must flow
And that dear hut — our HOME!

BROTHERHOOD.

"A happy bit hame this auld warld
If men when they're would make shift to agree
And ilk said to his neebor, in cottage an' ha'
Come gie me your hand we are BRETHEREN a'.'

BUSINESS CARDS.

ADMINISTRATOR'S NOTICE

There are still accounts standing unsettled in the Estate of John Lowry Sinr deceased, and we again invite delinquents to come forward with-out delay and settle up.

Administrators
I. Tuttle
A. Lowry
A.M. Lowry

SANPETE
ART GALLERY.

A. LUND Proprietor.

This Establishment is well worthy the patronage of the people, as the Proprietor not only merits support, by his Artistic productions but his untiring efforts to Please deserve commendation.

SEELEY & CO

will still Take good care in their commissions, business.

1891: "R. W. Sloan, Editor of the Journal, has been arrested on the charge of intimidating voters."

The Journal Publishing Company was formed late in 1891 to take over the newspaper, making it a Democratic political organ, of 6 columns, issued semi-weekly. On December 30, 1891, the paper runs this.—"Notice to Journal patrons. On January 1, 1892, the Journal Publishing Company will take charge of this company.—R. W. Sloan, Logan."

The Eastern Utah Telegraph of Price, in its January 8, 1892 number, says: "The Logan Journal has been sold for $6500." The Brigham Bugler January 2, 1892, says: "The retiring editor of the Logan Journal rubbed his fingers across that paper Wednesday, for the last time, it is hoped. From the looks of the sheet, one would imagine he thought he would deal a last deadly irreparable blow to The Nation, his rival contemporary, before delivering over his official robes. About two-thirds of the matter of that paper is devoted to slanderous and malicious attacks upon The Nation and its editor."

"The Journal was the new name adopted for the newspaper. The new company employed G. W. Williams, former city editor of the Salt Lake Times, as editor," says the Anniversary Sketch. "The management of the paper was vested in an executive committee of three, who employed Mr. Charles England as its office representative. Mr. Jesse Earl had charge of the composing room. Mr. Williams found some difficulty in accommodating his work to suit existing local conditions, and resigned in two months, being succeeded by Noble Warrum, Jr., whose name went on the masthead June 25, 1892. He conducted the paper in an able manner until the close of 1896, when, other business requiring his attention, he resigned and was succeeded by . . . Augustus Gordon."

"The various officials being too busy in the conduct of their own affairs to give the questions ever arising the necessary thought and attention, Messrs. Earl and England leased the paper December 12, 1894, and have ever since been in sole control of it." Noble Warrum's name was dropped October 3, 1894, though he continued as vice-president until December 12, 1894. Mr. Earl took charge of the mechanical department, and Mr. England the front office. They promptly changed the paper to a 5-column tri-weekly.

In March, 1896, the Wasatch Wave says: "The Logan Journal is the only newspaper published in Utah that now boasts of being printed by electricity—electric power for running the presses." On April 16, 1896, the lessees added "Noble Warrum, Junior, Editor," to the masthead, but Warrum's name was dropped February 2, 1897, and A. Gordon, Editor, replaced it February 11, 1897. It became Augustus Gordon April 13, 1897.

The Wasatch Wave of July 23, 1897, quotes the Salina Press thus: "There are twelve newspaper liars in Utah, one of them is the editor of the Press, the remaining eleven is the editor of the Logan Journal."

Notwithstanding this facetious send-off, Augustus Gordon distinguished himself and his newspaper in the years that followed, (long after the Salina author of "A Bunch of Carrots" had been gathered to his fathers), in a most extraordinary service of persistent, consistent effort. Mr. Gordon became one of the State's outstanding journalists, and his name was flung from the masthead uninterruptedly, until November 11, 1929, when we read: "Augustus Gordon for thirty-six years editor of the Journal died Sunday morning, November 10, 1929." His name was not replaced, and on August 1, 1931, the Logan Herald (Scripps owned), bought the Journal of Earl and England, and changed the name to **Herald-Journal**, continuing so to date. N. Gunnar Rasmuson is Editor.

Logan Nation, first issue, appeared in April, 1890, Harry E. Baker, editor, Ezra T. Hyde, business manager and local editor. It ran as a daily for about three months, and then became a semi-weekly. The Park Record of August 29, 1891, says: "The Logan Nation has suspended its daily publication, and returned to semi-weekly." The American Newspaper Directory for 1892: "Logan Nation, Tuesday and Friday, Republican, 8 pages, $2.50, H. E. Baker, Editor and Publisher." But about the end of 1892, the Nation was sold to John F. Pribyl and Andy Rosenbaum, who soon transferred it to a Mr. Ricks, according to oral information.

On May 8, 1893, the Provo Enquirer says, "The Logan Nation is now run by Messrs. Rosenbaum and Pribyl, the former being the editor and the latter the 'hired man.' Of course there is an original funny column. Mr. P. couldn't exist without it. The paper is more newsy than ever, and remains true to Republican principles." On September 23, 1893, the Brigham Bugler says "John F. Pribyl of the Logan Nation gave our sanctum a fraternal call on Tuesday (September 17). He came down to lug home the remains of the defunct Corinne Calliope." But Rosenbaum also had burdens to bear it would seem, from the following in the Park Record December 9, 1893: "A. Rosenbaum, editor of the Logan Nation, was assaulted and roughly handled by D. W. Thatcher, of that city."

On May 18, 1894, the Manti Messenger says "Logan Nation will soon be issued as a daily." But it is understood that about that time the paper was sold to Mr. Hyde, Augustus Gordon acting as editor during one political campaign. While Mr. England said the Nation ran until the early 1900's, the precise date of its demise has not been found. On May 25, 1895, the Brigham Bugler refers to "A. N. Rosenbaum, ex-editor of the Logan Nation." On January 8, 1898, the Brigham Bugler says, evidently quoting, "The Logan Nation is seven years old. Congratulations, Friend Hyde!" Kenner, in Utah As It Is, in 1904 says, "Logan Nation, semi-weekly, E. T. Hyde, publisher, Independent, circulation 1200." With such a circulation one wonders why it ceased to exist, about that time.

The Logan Republican. Two newspapers of this name have appeared and disappeared. The first is mentioned in the American Newspaper Directory for 1896, "Fridays, 4 pages, 17 x 22, $2.50, established 1890, Joel Shomaker, editor, Republican Publishing Company. " It must be noted however, that the Logan Nation, a Republican newspaper, established in 1890, was not listed in that directory; but Ayer's Newspaper Annual for 1898 lists "The Nation, semi-weekly," and does not list the Logan Republican.

The Nephi Blade of April 4, 1896, says, "Joel Shomaker has retired from the editorship of the Logan Republican. It is thought E. T. Hyde will take his place." This seems to confirm the suspicion that the Logan Republican may have been just another name given for the Logan Nation. There could hardly have been two Republican newspapers in Logan at that time; though truly it would have taken about six of them to successfully combat the influence and prestige of the Democratic Journal, the Journal was that powerful, both Democratically and financially.

When the Logan Republican, Series 1, departed, or was reabsorbed by the Nation, we did not learn. The Logan Republican, Series 2, Vol. 1. No. 1 appeared Wednesday, September 10, 1902, with "N. Ralph Moore, editor and proprietor," streaming, not to say screaming, from the masthead. Three months later, December 9, Moore's name was dropped, and on January 13, 1903, "Joel Ricks, Manager," was substituted. On January 28, 1903, the Logan Newspaper Company was organized, which bought the Logan Republican. On April 1, 1905, the masthead shows "published by Moore and Turner, lessees, N. Ralph Moore, Editor, Fred Turner, Business Manager." On February 2, 1910, Turner's name was dropped. Oral information is that Moore sold the newspaper to W. W. Maughn and J. A. Hendrickson. Later, Judge Maughn sold to Mr. Turner; and at the expiration of the lease, Mr. Turner held three-fourths and Mr. Hendrickson one-fourth interest.

On January 31, 1910, Mr. Turner sold out to Herschel Bullen, Junior, and Preston Nibley. The 1912-13 Gazetteer shows Bullen and Blood, publishers. The Republican file continues without a name on the masthead until May 6, 1915, when "H. Bullen, President and Editor, J. C. Allen, Junior, Secretary and Manager" appears, continuing until April 13, 1918, when Allen's name was dropped. Bullen bore the burden alone, apparently, until October 28, 1919, when Floyd Rose became Secretary and Manager. It was at this time a tri-weekly issued on Tuesday, Thursday and Saturday. The file is broken, but it appears Rose's name was dropped in 1920 or 1921, and Herschel Bullen again became editor and manager, his name being carried until April 5, 1923, when it was dropped and none substituted.

Publication of the Logan Republican ceased with the issue of April 1, 1924, "After twenty-two years of service to Logan, Cache County, and to the Republican Party." The reason given was the financial condition, it being impossible to publish the paper without a heavy loss to the stockholders. The paper and plant were sold to Earl and England Publishing Company, owners of the Logan Journal, and the subscription lists were combined. A nearly complete file is in the Journal office.

"**Cache Valley Herald.** Vol. 1, No. 1, December 11, 1925 (Courier Vol. 17, No. 3). Hello Friends! We herewith present for your approval, the first issue of the Cache Valley Herald, which is a successor to the South Cache Courier, and is published jointly with the Smithfield Sentinel. . . . We have, to begin with, a fine circulation, using the subscription lists of the Smithfield Sentinel, and the South Cache Courier. . . . We are compelled to print this edition out of town (out of Logan), as our printing plants have not yet been moved here . . . temporary telephone No. 22, Smithfield.—Ralph R. Channell, J. A. Wahlen." The masthead shows that Channell was the editor and manager, and Wahlen publisher and assistant manager. The headings on pages 2 and 7 of the newspaper were "The Smithfield Sentinel, Smithfield, Utah;" and on pages 4, 6 and 8 "The Cache Valley Herald."

With the issue of May 26, 1926, the name and masthead were changed as follows, "The Cache Valley Herald, successor to the South Cache Courier, Tuesdays and Fridays, Channell and Wahlen, publishers, Logan, Utah." Then on July 6, 1926; "Foy & Wahlen, Publishers," followed on September 24, 1926, by "Leslie T. Foy, Editor and Publisher."

The subscribers in Smithfield and Hyrum objected to the arrangement, as will be found by reference to these and other papers printed in those towns; and on July 6, 1927, the Cache Valley Herald carried no mention of the South Cache Courier, and the masthead shows publication days to be Monday, Wednesday and Friday. On February 16, 1928, Leslie T. Foy styles himself "Publisher and Business Manager." The paper was re-named Cache Valley Daily Herald, September 3, 1928. The masthead was "Cache Valley Newspaper Company, E. C. Rodgers, President; Leslie T. Foy, Vice-President and Manager." On February 17, 1929, it became a Scripps-Canfield newspaper; and on September 11, 1929 Rodgers' name was dropped, and N. Gunnar Rasmuson replaced it. On August 1, 1931, Scripps-Canfield bought the Journal, combined it with the Herald, and changed the name to Herald-Journal, continuing so to date.

Laramie (Wyoming) Boomerang, by Bill Nye. "The Boomerang, is the striking and eccentric title of a Daily Paper just started at Laramie, Wyoming Territory," says the Deseret News of March 17, 1881. "It is edited by Bill Nye, who has written himself into fame as an original humorist." The Boomerang must have been on a list of Utah Exchanges, for it was often quoted. The Ogden Herald of November 20, 1882, quotes the following from it: "Yesterday a Laramie Minister put up his stovepipe without swearing! When the Angels sing, On the Beautiful Shore, there will be a name in the song never sung before!" Nye visited Salt Lake City and Ogden in 1883, just about the time the Boomerang, in true form, returned to the forces whence it came.

The Deseret News of September 20, 1883, says " 'Bill Nye', former editor of the Laramie Boomerang, purposes settling in Hudson, Wisconsin. He has tendered his resignation of the Postmastership of Laramie. He told a Denver reporter the other day that he proposed publishing another book to be entitled 'Baled Hay', mostly a compilation of his articles in The Boomerang." And on September 25, 1883 the News adds: "We had a fraternal visit today from Mr. Mark Jennings of the Laramie Boomerang, who with his wife and several members of the Wyoming Press Association, have been spending a few days in this city. Mr. Jennings admits that a suit has been entered against the Boomerang by Bill Nye, its former editor, but thinks it will be easily settled when accounts are compared." But the Ogden Herald of December 13, 1883, says: "The present Laramie Boomerang management is wrangling with Bill Nye, formerly editor of the Laramie luminary, over the alleged dishonesty of Nye!"

MANTI, Sanpete County

Population: 1870, 1,239; 1880, 1,748; 1890, 1,950; 1900, 2,408; 1910, 2,423; 1920, 2,412; 1930, 2,200.

Manti Herald. F. C. Robinson, Editor and Publisher, Vol. 1 No. 1, January 31, 1867. All hand-written. It consisted of one page legal size, divided into three columns, a large art heading being drawn. Besides several display advertisements, there were a number of local news items and a few telegraphic brevities bearing the Salt Lake City date line. It was a real newspaper in spirit and in fact, being the organ or propaganda of no one. Among the earliest of the pen and ink, or manuscript newspapers, it was issued to subscribers only, a goodly edition being run off, in the editor's own right hand. Vol. 1 No. 2, February 10, 1867 contained mostly election, political and other advertisements, local news items being crowded out. A few trite sayings and a few paragraphs under "Odds and Ends" were used as fillers, to balance the page. In this issue F. C. Robinson, Editor, was revealed as the County Clerk.

Vol. 1 No. 6, March 20, 1867, was called "Manti Herald and Sanpete Advertiser." It was legal size, printed on one side. Some advertisements, business cards and local school news appeared. "To our subscribers: (He evidently had them), We feel that an apology is due to our subscribers for the non-appearance of the Herald last week; and by way of explanation, may say that the 'type' we had previously used, proved defective, and we concluded to wait until we could get a fresh supply!" Some humor, since the editor drew each letter with his quill.

"Number 3 (Manti Herald) has come to hand," says Editor Stenhouse of the Salt Lake Daily Telegraph, March 21, 1867. "It is well

JUDGE C. C. GOODWIN
Born April 4, 1832
Died August 25, 1920

A. N. McKAY
Born May 5, 1868
Died Nov. 18, 1924

COL. JOHN Q. CANNON
Born April 19, 1857
Died January 14, 1931

COL. WILLIAM NELSON
Born July 19, 1839
Died October 26, 1913

filled with matter, interesting to the reader. Glad to see the folks want a printing press out there—Hope they get it!"

Vol. 1 No. 7, March 30, 1867, consisted of one legal size page, yet it carried several advertisements, a few Indian news items, and a number of telegraphic dispatches, including this one: "Great Salt Lake City, March 22.—I advise the brethren of Sanpete to keep their cattle where they will be safe, and not be out alone.—B. Young."

Vol. 1 No. 8, April 13, 1867, was devoted largely to local Indian war news. Vol. 1 No. 11, April 20, 1867, had a generous advertising patronage, and a good mess of local news. Vol. 1 No. 13, May 4, 1867; Vol. 1 No. 14, May ...., 1867 and Vol. 1 No. 15, May 18, 1867, (the last containing some Indian and military news), constitute the set of this unique publication, neatly bound and preserved by the Salt Lake Public Library.

Subsequently, the Young Men's and Young Women's organizations of the L. D. S. Church, more especially in the outlying settlements, cemented their common interests by means of periodical journals such as these. They were always hand written, usually with pen and ink. As they developed, they became magazines of many pages, containing sermonettes, short articles for character building, and social uplift. Nevertheless, Society Notes and News paragraphs are said to have done more to popularize these publications than the sermonettes, howsoever good. That is to say, the better they were as newspapers, the greater was the demand for them; and a great many copies were literally worn out in being passed from hand to hand. Other manuscript newspapers were published in Hyrum, Parowan, Mount Pleasant and elsewhere.

The Home Sentinel Vol. 1 No. 1 appeared Friday, April 24, 1885. This was Manti's first mechanically printed newspaper. The files were burned to about 1898, but fortunately, Dr. G. W. Martin and his frugal wife had carefully filed and preserved the papers through those early years, and at his death, they were presented to the publisher. They are now neatly bound and carefully stored in the Sentinel Office, practically complete. The earliest issue preserved, Vol. 1 No. 3, May 8, 1885, shows James T. Jakeman, Manager, D. Harrington, Editor, 6 columns, 4 pages, all home print.

The Deseret News, April 29, 1885 says: "First issue of the Home Sentinel, a weekly paper published at Manti, Sanpete County, is before us; and with the exception of a dearth of advertisements due to the non-arrival of type expected, it presents a fair appearance for a country paper. Editorially, it is quite a creditable sheet." Again on July 13, 1885, the News says: "Editor Harrington of the Home Sentinel, the spicy weekly published in Manti, visited . . ." In the Sentinel itself September 25, 1885: "The Sentinel Office wants a few loads of firewood on subscription. Who will supply it?" It is inferred the editor lived in Mount Pleasant, from the following paragraph found in the Sentinel, quoting the Beaver Utonian, February 5, 1886: "The Home Sentinel is edited in Mount Pleasant it seems, and published in Manti.

'United we stand, divided we fall' should be its motto." This comes in rather bad grace from a paper edited one-half in St. Louis and the other half being so conspicuous for its lack of home news. It might just as well be edited in Pancake."

The American Newspaper Directory for 1886: "Home Sentinel, Fridays, but prints a 4 page supplement on Tuesday, 26 x 40, 8 pages, advertising rate 10 lines, $2.50 one month." D. Harrington's name was dropped after the issue of March 26, 1886. The 1885 and 1886 papers appear to be printed on homemade paper, doubltless purchased from the Deseret News. The Tuesday supplement was issued frequently.

"Mr. Harrington will now take up his residence in our midst, and will devote his entire time to the welfare of the Home Sentinel," is announced April 16, 1886. The issue of April 23, 1886 consisted of 8 pages, 4 home print, not homemade paper. "The first number of the Supplement will appear on Tuesday of next week, and will be issued weekly thereafter." The Territorial Enquirer, Provo, April 27, 1886 says: "The Manti Sentinel comes to us enlarged and otherwise improved." Editor Harrington complained of the Utonian's St. Louis ready-print, and we have heard that the Salt Lake Tribune at one time tried readyprints for the State press. It is interesting to note that the Sentinel issue of May 15, 1886 bore the following readyprint imprint: "W. N. U. Omaha. 315-25."

August 5, 1886: "Low Comedy. 'Dan Harrington has retired from the proprietorship and editorship of the Manti Snide sheet'. The foregoing item of news is taken from that prince of newspapers, the Enquirer . . . Dan Harrington was not proprietor of the Home Sentinel. He has retired from the editorship, and if the Enquirer buffoon, loved the people of Provo more and himself less, he would go and do likewise." The Enquirer August 31, 1886, has this dignified follow-up: "William K. Reid has succeeded Dan Harrington in the editorship of the Home Sentinel, a weekly paper published at Manti."

The winter of 1886-7 brought some rough sledding to the self-appointed Sentinel of the Manti homes, as witness the following from the Salt Lake Democrat, April 25, 1887: "It is said that the Manti Sentinel talks of moving to Nephi. Nephi always was an unlucky town!" The Deseret News May 26, 1887, having borrowed three sizable news items for an adjacent news column, says editorially: "The Manti Sentinel of May 24, is the neatest number of that paper yet issued." And the Salt Lake Democrat has another fling on July 11, 1887: "The Home Sentinel and Nephi Ensign are both published and edited by Jim Jakeman, the first mentioned at Manti, Sanpete County, and the latter at Nephi, Juab County. There is nothing unusual, of course, in the fact that one man publishes two papers, but Jakeman has hit upon a daisy plan to fill the columns of his sheet: the editorials of one are the editorials of the other, and much of the other matter is just the same. For running a newspaper, Jakeman has a Henry Clay head on him, more clay than Henry!"

The Provo Territorial Enquirer, July 29, 1887, refers to "L. A. Wilson, of the Manti Sentinel." Jakeman's habit of running two newspapers with but a single series of thoughts, was noticed by the Territorial Enquirer of Provo, August 9, 1887: "The inside pages of the Home Sentinel published at Manti contain the same subject matter as the Nephi Ensign. We pity those who subscribe to both papers." (What would such a critic say of accepted newspaper practice today, with not only readyprint news features, illustrations and press association dispatches, but often a syndicated editorial service as well?)

September 9, 1887: "Important Notice . . . No person . . . has authority to collect money or receipt bills for the Home Sentinel Publishing Company, except the Business Manager, James T. Jakeman, the Editor, J. M. Sjodahl, or the local agent in the various towns." December 30, 1887 (Editor Sjodahl speaking): "Our article 'Fiat Lux' was recently translated into Swedish, and printed in the Swedish Herald. It is curious to reflect on this: A Swede writes a piece in English, and a Norwegian, (if we are not mistaken), translates it into Swedish. If the piece is not perfect, in point of language, after that, no wonder!"

The story is told by old-timers in Manti, that Manager Jakeman was too busy to cut wood, consequently Mrs. Jakeman dragged a firelog into the house and placed one end of it in the fireplace, and the other end on a chair—Jakeman's easy chair—so the atmosphere would be suitably warm for his homecoming! "October 11, 1887, the Home Sentinel in commemorating its second half of the third volume, will appear in an enlarged form, making six columns instead of five. The Supplement will not appear regularly, and the price of the paper will be reduced from $2.50 to $2.00." January 20, 1888: "Owing to the late isolation of Sanpete, through the severity of the winter, we have not been able to replenish our supply of printing paper this week. The Sentinel therefore appears in a rather diminutive size today . . ."

June 20, 1888. Valedictory. "In leaving the Sentinel . . . J. M. Sjodahl." July 11, 1888: "Mr. J. M. Sjodahl and wife have gone to Salt Lake . . . to superintend the printing of his translation of The Doctrine and Covenants into the Swedish language." October 10, 1888: "On account of the death of one of our young lady compositors, and which caused the withdrawal of others from the office, we are obliged to limit our items this week. There is (sic) many items we are obliged to leave out."

The Provo Enquirer of January 29, 1889, gives this little dig: "The Manti Sentinel now boasts of patent insides. The outside would be all the better for one." The Sentinel publisher gives this notice April 10, 1889: "To Our Patrons: This is the last number of the fourth volume of the Home Sentinel, and contrary to the anticipations of many, the Sentinel still lives and grows . . ." also "Notice: Mr. N. H. Felt of Provo, has become a partner in the Home Sentinel Company. Mr. Felt will have charge of the outside management of the paper. J. T. Jakeman, Manager." On April 17, 1889 accordingly, the name "N. H. Felt, Assistant Manager," was added to the masthead.

The Wasatch Wave editor was both a good editor and a good printer, and probably had a right to say, September 14, 1889: "The Manti Sentinel advertises for a boy to learn the printer's trade. From the blotched and erroneous condition of that sheet, and its lack of news, grammar, punctuation and spelling; and its outlandish makeup, in fact its want of everything that goes to make up a newspaper, save its patent inside, we should think a boy in that office would stand a better chance of learning to be a blacksmith, or how to read and spell incorrectly, than he would of learning the trade of Benjamin Franklin. Printing is an art, and cannot be managed by every ignoramus who takes it into his head to start a newspaper."

On November 11, 1889 Felt's name was dropped from the masthead, and Ellen Jakeman was added; though N. H. Felt was still listed as Assistant Manager, in another column. Then on January 22, 1890, we get the rest of the story from the Provo Enquirer: "Mr. Harry Felt, late of Provo, has sold his interests here, and purchased the entire plant, circulation and accounts, of the Home Sentinel. Hereafter, he will take the management, assisted by his brother, D. P. Felt, and Will Silver, the latter gentlemen to make Manti his permanent home."

"March 4, 1890. Since the Jakemans sold the Home Sentinel, that paper has failed to improve, which is a pretty hard thing to say of it," says the Utah County Gazette, to which the Sentinel editor levels this: "Since the Gazette started, it has grown worse and worse, which would seem to be an impossible thing to say of it truthfully." But good or bad, the Sentinel had a free field, and on May 13, 1890 it calls out: "Subscribe for the Sentinel, the only paper published in Sanpete." "The Manti Sentinel with the patent insides discarded, is a big improvement, and shows enterprise commendable," says the Provo Enquirer August 19, 1890.   A copy for November 21, 1890, in the Bancroft Library at Berkeley, has this masthead: "Ward Stevenson, Managing Editor; H. G. Bradford, Associate Editor, N. H. Felt, Business Manager." And the issue for February 20, 1891: "Ward Stevenson, Editor, H. G. Bradford, Manager." (Apparently printed on hand-made paper). The Sentinel of February 6, 1892, was published by Sam M. LeRoy.

The issue of May 7, 1892 was the last number of that series of the Sentinel. Ayer's Newspaper Annual for 1892 says the Sentinel had four pages, 18 x 24, subscription $2.50, circulation 850, certainly a good support. The Brigham Bugler May 7, 1892, nevertheless, has this story: "On account of lack of patronage of local business men, the Manti Sentinel is thinking seriously of pulling up its stakes and flopping over the hills to drop down in sequestered Gunnison, or unknown Castle Dale, where those one-horse towns of a few business houses each, guarantee double the patronage Manti now offers, says that paper." And the Spanish Fork Sun for May 26, 1892, adds to the obsequies: "The Manti Sentinel has succumbed to the inevitable;" and in its next issue, June 2, 1892, the Sun man side-steps: "The Manti Sentinel is not dead, as was reported, but sleepeth, and will publish again next Saturday." (Not so soon—see Manti Reporter).

The later files at Manti contain (Book 7 Vol. IX), The Sentinel, August 19, 1893, No. 18, Ward Stevenson, Editor, the series continuing to September 9, 1893, four numbers. Then strange to say, a new paper, the Manti Messenger, has this, November 3, 1893: "Ward Stevenson has the press and material for publishing a paper at Manti, and the name will be The Sentinel." And further, on December 8, 1893: "Ward Stevenson has succeeded in producing another issue of The Sentinel," evidently trying to breathe into the dummy the breath of life, and failing in the attempt. The last two numbers were not found by the collators, who bound the file in the Manti Newspaper Office, in which the Sentinel for September 9, 1893, is followed by:

The Manti Messenger, Vol. 1 No. 1, Friday, October 13, 1893. "For the free coinage of silver and protection to home industries. Joel Shomaker, Editor. The Manti Printing and Publishing Company," continuing so to December 29, 1893. But beginning October 20, 1893, L. A. Lauber, was manager. The following appears in the Messenger of October 20, 1893: "The Salt Lake Tribune says of us: 'The Manti Messenger, a new venture edited by Joel Shomaker, is almost the nicest of the rural publications in Utah, if not the very nicest'." And November 3, 1893: "Joel Shomaker . . . lately associate editor of the Irrigation Age, published at Salt Lake City, has started a weekly paper at Manti."

"The Manti Messenger is a well conducted and nice looking journal. It is a credit to the journalistic profession, and one of the foremost country newspapers in the territory . . . Its editor, Joel Shomaker, handles subjects in a manner which plainly shows he is no novice in the business," says the Logan Nation, copied April 27, 1894, in the Manti Messenger. Anyone perusing the files will heartily concur in these compliments. The Manti Messenger was undoubtedly the best weekly newspaper of its time; in fact, there is probably no better country newspaper in the State today, in appearance and in its local news service. The Messenger's ten-point leaded open-faced columns reflect its general attitude of wholesome efficiency.

The issue of November 2, 1894 carries this masthead: "The Manti Messenger, the Manti Printing and Publishing Company, E. Shomaker, President, F. Alder, Vice-President, D. J. Lindsey, Secretary and Treasurer." With the issue of April 5, 1895, L. R. Anderson became Secretary and Treasurer; and on October 11, 1895, Wm. D. Livingston became Manager. Other masthead changes are, January 8, 1897 "The Manti Messenger, Iverson & Livingston, lessees" and on October 23, 1897, "W. D. Livingston, Manager, lessee."

The following is from the Nephi Blade October 12, 1895: "Joel Shomaker has bidden goodbye to the Manti Messenger, and removed to Salt Lake City for rest and recreation. His political brethren in San-

OUR DIXIE TIMES.

Vol. 1.   St. George Utah, Wednesday, January 22, 1868.   No. 1.

SOWING AND REAPING.

[From Moore's Rural New Yorker.]

BY MARY KELSEY.

Long ago upon the hillside,
In the valley, o'er the plain,
From the early morn till even,
Busy hands were sowing grain.
Trusting that the storm and sunshine
Should each tiny leaf unfold,
Till the golden wheat had ripened,
Yielding more than hundred fold.

Harvest comes,'the grain is gathered,
And they place a wealth of sheaves
One by one till all are garnered,
Safe beneath the sheltering eaves.
And with glad and joyous footsteps
Laborers at twilight come,
And with cheerful, happy voices
Shout the golden harvest home.

Often weary in well doing,
We have sown in doubt and fears,
From the morning until even—
Sowing oft with bitter tears.
When the'harvest shall be gathered,
Many tares and withered leaves
Will be bound among the bundles,
With our treasured golden sheaves.

When our sheaves have all been counted
And their value has been told,
When our treasure has been garnered
In our Heavenly Father's fold;
When our happy joyous footsteps
In life's twilight heavenward come,
May we hear sweet angel voices
Welcoming our harvest home.

Trappe, Talbot Co., Md.

HUSBANDS AT HOME.

A RACY SKETCH FOR THE LADIES.

Mrs. Patsey Spangle communicates the following to the Louisville Courier:

SPANGLE AS A LOVER.

I first met Spangle at a country fair. We were introduced to each other about ten o'clock in the morning, and, if you will believe me, I did not get a chance to speak to any other gentleman that day. I never saw a fellow so struck at first sight. I don't think he saw a horse, or in fact anything that was on exhibition that day but me, although there were present many of the most beautiful and accomplished young ladies of that section of the country. As he was extremely good looking, of good family, and of unexceptionable habits and character, I, of course, felt flattered by his marked preference. I had to take him to dinner, and introduce him to pa and ma and the whole family. He made a very good impression. In fact Spangle can shine when he tries. I remember the fact with pride. Well, it is the old story. He became infatuated, and obtained my permission to visit me at my home and spend a day there in just two weeks from the day we met. During these two weeks I received daily long letters from Simon, closely written and cross written. (I wish I had kept them.) At length the day of his visit arrived, and lo! and behold, the servant girl awoke me in the morning with the pleasant information that Spangle was waiting for me in the parlor. Here was a lover for you!

Well, well! As I said before, it was the old story ever recurring,ever sweetly told, and ever listened to by willing ears. Suffice it to say that from that day I saw no peace until I became Mrs. Spangle. Our honeymoon was, I suppose, like all honeymoons, short and delicious. And then come

THE REALITIES OF LIFE.

It is my belief that this is the most trying period of woman's life. However kind and attentive her husband may be, a young wife, when she enters upon the actualities of life, has disclosed to her a state of facts of which she has little or no conception before marriage. When she leaves an atmosphere of romance and adulation, and enters upon the realities of life, it is like stepping out of a garden of summer flowers into the region of perpetual winter, and unless she brings all her good sense and philosophy to her aid, her affections will become chilled, and she will regard herself a disappointed, if not a deceived woman for the rest of her life. It is the hope that our experience may be of benefit to young wives that induces me to reveal some of the domestic incidents and infelicities of twelve years of married life.

After our brief holiday, Spangle—to use his own expression, took a tilt at the world, determined to wrest from it not only a competence but a fortune, that would place me in the most beatific attitude to be obtained by opulence.

The dear fellow did work hard, and if he met with obstacles and difficulties and trials, the world never knew it. He reserved them for his fireside, and, although he did not accuse me as the cause, yet he recounted them in a tone and manner so different from the joyous and buoyant language of courtship, that I could but feel I was some way or other accountable for his troubles. I never seriously doubted his love for me, yet he certainly permitted many excellent opportunities for manifesting it to pass unimproved. Before we were married, he seemed to have a perfect mania for holding my hand, and I used to wonder if he would ever give me an opportunity do any needle work after marriage. Poor foolish me! I was often aggrieved at his apparent coolness, and would ask him twenty times a day if he did not love me. "Why, certainly I do, my dear little puss; I thought you knew it." Yes, he thought I knew it. Perhaps I did. I also knew that we had plenty of flour and bacon in the pantry, but that knowledge did not satisfy my hunger.

THE HONEYMOON IN A PARTIAL ECLIPSE.

It is true that this affection manifested itself spasmodically with all the warmth and ardor of former days, but these ebullitions were the exception. The rule was, "I thought you knew it." Yes, girls, when you get husbands they will expect you to know it; and my advice to you is, that you get all the courting you want before you are married, for after that event what little courting is done in the family will have to be done by the wife.

SPANGLE AS A FATHER.

We have six children, all beautiful and good. Spangle takes great pride in them, loves them, and growls at

them like a dear old bear. You must not think that Spangle regards the "new comers" as burdens. Quite the reverse. He goes into ecstacies over each one; dilates upon its beauties and perfections for five minutes, and then seems to think it ought to be laid away to grow up, and be no further trouble to him till they want to marry. If one of them has the bellyache and cries at night, Spangle thinks that the pain is a special hardship to him, because it keeps him awake a few minutes. The fact is undeniable that the best men are selfish brutes so far as babies are concerned.

SPANGLE AT HOME.

I will say. though, that of all the children I have, Spangle is the biggest baby. 'Tis true he was through most of the ailments I have enumerated, before I got him, but in a thousand other respects he is still is, and always will remain in that chronic state of babyhood which ever attends over-indulged and spoiled husbands. When we were first married, my old baby would almost break his back to pick up my fan, and he would kill a fly in a minute if the fly manifested any disposition to alight on my nose. Now I have to almost literally dress him in the morning. I have to get his boots together, one of which he generally kicks under the bureau, the other under the bed. I always have to find his cravat. If I go to bed first, in the morning I find his clothes scattered over the room as only a man can scatter clothes. He would never put on a clean shirt if it were not spread out on a chair before him. His sleeve buttons are taken out and put in by me, when taken out and put in it at all. I do not believe he has combed his own head since we were married. He can't even wash his own face properly, without being told, like any other child. If I did not wash him, his ears and the back of his neck would be a sight to behold.

SPANGLE ON A SICK BED.

Albeit he has no patience for others who have pains and aches, yet you ought to see him when anything is the matter with him. He tears and groans and grunts over a slight attack of colic in a manner to keep every one awake in the house. At such times he always believes he is going to die, and will not suffer me to leave him for a moment.

Yet with all his faults. I—well, you know the quotation. I believe he is the best man living, and would not give him for a ten acre lot full of men like the scapegrace of a husband which your foolish, credulous correspondent, "Dolly Dash," is so silly about.

A CHEMICAL FREAK.—A platina-crucible is made and maintained red-hot over a large spirit lamp. The acid, though at common temperature one of the most volatile of the known bodies, possesses the singular property of remaining fixed in the red hot crucible, and not a drop of it evaporates; in fact it is not in contact with the crucible, but has an atmosphere of its own interposed. A few drops of water are now added to the sulphurous acid in the red hot crucible. The diluted acid gets into immediate contact with the heated metal, instantly flashes off, and such is the rapidity and energy of the

evaporation that the water remains behind and is frozen into a lump of ice in a hot crucible from which, euring the moment before it again melts, it may again be thrown out before the eyes of the astonished observer. This is indeed "a piece of natural magic" and as much like a miracle as any operation of the force of nature could produce. It is certainly one of the most singularly beautiful experiment imaginable. It was devised by a French savan, to illustrate the repellant power of heat radiating from bodies at a high temperature, and of the rapid abstraction of heat produced by evaporation.

CHINESE TREATMENT OF ANIMALS.—They never punish; hence, a mule that, in the hand of a foreigner, would would be not only useless but dangerous to 'every one about it, becomes in the possession of a Chinaman as quiet as a lamb and as tractable as a dog. We never beheld a runaway, a jibbing, or a vicious mule or pony in a Chinaman's employment; but found the same rattling, cheerful pace maintained over heavy or light ground by means of a furze or cluck k, the beast turning to the right or left, and stopping with but a hint from the reins. This treatment is extended to all the animals they press into their service. Often have I admired the tact exhibited in getting a large drove of frightened sheep through narrow crowded street and alleys, by merely having a little boy to lead one of the quietest of the flock in front; the others steadily followed without aid either from a yelping cur or cruel goad. Cattle, pigs and birds are equally cared for.—Travels on Horseback in Tartary.

FANCY DREAMS.—Some young ladies regard marriage as a fairy land, where violets and roses perpetually blossom, where the cedar tree and the cinnamon tree ever flourish — where the waters of tranquility, and sweetness uninterruptedly flow. Tell them there are briars in their stead; though they do not contradict, yet they do not credit you, for they believe that their love, their devotedness for each/ other, will exempt them from the cares, the vicissitudes and the anxieties pertaining to humanity. All lovers, before marriage, conceive that their destiny will be an exception to the general rule. The future with them will be toujours couleur de rose. Could you give them a sketch in the pages of their future history they would not believe a word of it; they would sit you down as a misanthrope, a painter of gloomy and unnatural scenes, an inimical repressor of the hopes and aspirations of youth. The dark spots that the telescope of your experience might discover, they would regard but as mole-hills in the moon. If they would reflect a little, how much misery they would avoid.

RATHER MIXED.—A tall Eastern girl, named Short, loved a certain big Mr. Little, while Little, little thinking of Short, loved a little lass named Long. To make a long story short, Little proposed to Long, and Short longed to be even with Little's shortcomings. So Short meeting Long, which caused Little in a short time to marry Long. Query—Did tall Short love big Little less, because Little loved Long?

pete nearly worried the life out of Joel by withholding funds that Joel regarded as fair compensation for booming them for office. The Blade has often had occasion to cuff Joel for his unparalleled conceit and bigotry, but for all of that, we have not but kindly feelings for the erstwhile Messenger Man, who has a view of strong manhood in his organization . . ."

The American Newspaper Directory for 1898 lists: "Iverson & Livingston, Publishers and Editors." With the issue of January 8, 1898, P. A. Poulson became Manager and lessee. Poulson apparently continued as editor until the issue of May 17, 1902, reading from the headings of the editorial page, when Christen Axelsen was listed as publisher. With the issue of January 14, 1904, N. P. Nelson became publisher for a year; and on January 12, 1905, J. L. Ewing took over the responsibility, as lessee.

August 5, 1909, a new skipper comes to the helm, M. A. Boyden being listed as lessee, "Strictly a Sanpete man." He held on nine and one-half years, or until the issue of January 17, 1919, when S. Peter Petersen became publisher and owner. Whether as a compliment or as a statement of fact, Mrs. S. Peter Petersen was listed as associate editor. It was a good combination, a good team, for the Petersens held sway until May 31, 1929, when they published this adieu: "The current issue of the Messenger makes the 540th number that has been published under our direction, and incidentally, it is the last one; for our successor, William H. Peterson we bespeak your continued support. He is one of our own boys." With the issue of June 7, 1929 William Henry Peterson became editor and proprietor, and has continued so to the present time.

Manti Times-Reporter began July 16, 1892, E. A. Gregory, editor, 7 columns, 4 pages, all home print. It seems to have been the direct successor to, or a continuation of the Sentinel. On July 23, 1892, N. H. Felt is listed as Business Manager. The Payson-Enterprise Chronicle confirms the names about August 1, while most exchanges call it the Manti Reporter. But the issue of September 17, 1892 is called "The Reporter." It says: "What We Hear: That Ward Stevenson is editing the Ephraim Enterprise."

The Provo Enquirer August 15, 1892, says: "A new exchange bearing the name of The Manti Reporter has been received. It has risen on the ashes of the Sentinel, but has the earmarks of the defunct. Manti must be growing weary of such makeshifts as it has been afflicted with for a few years past." A copy dated December 1, 1892, shows Gregory and Stevenson, Ward Stevenson, editor, N. H. Felt, business manager, continuing so until the end of the series, December 16, 1892.

MARYSVALE, Piute County

Population: 1890, 249; 1900, 435; 1910, 495; 1920, 927; 1930, 647.

The Piute Pioneer. "A neat paper, just commenced publication at Marysvale by J. F. Brunell," says the Nephi Blade, May 9, 1896. The paper was issued on Saturday, had 4 pages, 15 x 22 in size, subscription $2, circulation 500. Unfortunately there are no files and few contemporaneous references. The St. George Union of November 13, 1897, says: "We are sorry to chronicle the death of the editor of the Piute Pioneer of Marysvale, Utah (November 1) . . . Mr. J. F. Brunell . . . arriving in Marysvale two years ago . . . conducting two sessions of the school successfully. At the end of the first session he entered into the newspaper business and founded the Piute Pioneer." The Park Record for November 13, 1897, adds: "He was 24 years of age and was fast building up a reputation."

The next item concerning the Pioneer occurs in the Wasatch Wave January 1, 1898: "With all due respect for ex-editor Brunell of the Piute Pioneer, there has come a great change in that paper since C. A. De Witt (who is a maiden fair, fully equal to the occasion), took hold of the editorial reins. It reminds one of the change a female is competent of making in the appearance of some bachelor's hall after giving it a going over for about ten minutes."

But having cleaned up the shop, Miss De Witt quit; we did not find out why. The Wasatch Wave on June 3, 1898 says: "J. T. Camp, the erstwhile scribe who has figured as chief pencil pusher on several Utah weeklies, has succeeded Miss De Witt on the Piute Pioneer. We hope Brother Camp meets with better success in his new field, than in others he has labored." He evidently did not however, for the Park Record July 16, 1898, quotes from the Southern Censor: "Ed. Camp has severed his connection with the Piute Pioneer. We are sorry, for Camp was a good newspaper man, and was needed in 'Vale'."

Undoubtedly the paper suspended publication, not because Miss De Witt and Mr. Camp departed, but more likely for the want of support in that new mining town. One final attempt was made to revive the Pioneer, according to the San Pete Free Press, July 17, 1901: "John F. Price has taken hold of the Piute Pioneer at Marysvale, as if he intends to make a newspaper out of it." But if he did, posterity does not hear of it!

The Free Lance, Vol. 1, No. 1, Friday, September 15, 1902. Josiah F. Gibbs, proprietor, 4 columns, 4 pages, 10 x 15, all home print, $2 a year. Gibbs was an old time journalist of Nephi and Deseret, born in Nauvoo, Illinois, in 1845. According to the Salina Sun he "drifted to Marysvale, where he has since done not a little, through correspondence and otherwise, to advertise the mining camps of Marysvale." Gibbs declares in his Salutatory, the paper would be: "In politics and religion, absolutely independent." A totally unnecessary declaration, for those who knew him! He continues: "With this issue there will go to every

tax payer in Piute County, and to many old friends and former subscribers of the Millard County Blade, a copy of No. 1 of the Free
Lance."

Also, "This issue of the Free Lance will find its way if possible,
into the home of every family in Piute County, and a large number
in Wayne County. It will be sent to you for a month, and if in the
meantime, you don't want it, just send a postal card, and that one cent
will be all this paper will cost you to October 1." Four columns of
local advertisements were published. The press of the State promptly
acclaimed the new Free Lance: "We are pleased to see that Editor
J. F. Gibbs is once more in the newspaper field . . . He is a good writer,
and somewhat of a free lance himself. We wish friend Gibbs and the
Free Lance abundant success," says the Deseret News September 19,
1902.

In the issue of September 26, 1902, we read: "The Free Lance
is forging ahead by leaps and bounds; 675 copies go out with this,
the fourth number. From Missouri, Pennsylvania, New York, Maryland, Illinois and other states, orders for the Free Lance are being
received from mining men. Congratulations and good wishes are pour-
ing in like a flood. Thus far, but one family in Piute County is not
taking the paper. How is that, for instance?"

Editor Gibbs boosted mining so eloquently, he came to believe
in it himself, and soon turned his own head in the direction of
greater, quicker wealth than was to be had, merely talking about it—
the mines. Consequently, on May 15, 1903, the masthead was changed
to show: "J. F. Gibbs, proprietor, George J. Russell, lessee, editor."
"Leased.—The Free Lance business has been leased to George J. Russell
for a period of six months. In the meantime, the Free Lance is for
sale on easy terms to the right man, subject to the terms of the lease.
Mr. Russell has been with the Free Lance during several months, and
has proved himself honest and efficient.—J. F. Gibbs."

It was not six months, but in nine weeks, July 17, 1903, Gibbs
returned to his old love, and nailed this banner to the masthead: "J.
F. Gibbs, editor. In resuming publication of the Free Lance, no explanation to the public is necessary. An apology is doubtless due Free
Lance readers for permitting the journal 'devoted to the mining industry' to be reduced to the status of a 'Sasiety' sheet; but the apology
is taken under advisement."

On September 18, 1903, we read: "The Free Lance is sold. With
mingled feelings of satisfaction and regret, the editor and proprietor
of the Free Lance bids adieu to Piute County's only newspaper . . .
(the Valedictory is signed one and one-fourth columns farther along!)
J. F. Gibbs." The purchasers: "A. B. Williams, John W. Woodring and
B. S. Young are the fortunate purchasers of the Free Lance. Messrs.
Williams and Woodring are the proprietors and publishers of the Richfield Reaper. . . . They will continue to publish the Free Lance in the
interests of Piute County.—J. F. Gibbs."

But it didn't; the fact is, it suspended publication for a time, and on October 7, 1904, the masthead shows J. F. Gibbs, lessee and editor. Reincarnated, the Free Lance had gone Democratic; there was more money in politics, than in the gold in "them thar" Mount Baldy hills. The Ogden Journal, October 21, 1904, says, "J. F. Gibbs has revived the Marysvale Free Lance and, will of course make of it a splendid Democratic newspaper." Revived for political purposes only, the Free Lance died for good with the issue of November 4, 1904. Editor Gibbs preserved and bound the entire Free Lance series, and presented the volume to his granddaughter, Miss Lois Gibbs, of Marysvale, who kindly gave us access to it.

The Piute Chieftain. Vol. 1, No. 1, Thursday, April 1916, Andrew Jensen, editor and manager. On June 28, 1917, Jensen retired, and Thomas G. Dawson became editor. Then on January 3, 1918, H. W. Cherry succeeded Dawson. But Cherry's faith was not sufficiently contagious, for on March 20, 1919, he writes "Thirty," for the Piute Chieftain, and graciously refrains from saying in his Valedictory all that he thought. He transferred the printing plant to Gunnison. Thank goodness, Editor Cherry loved the paper well enough to keep a full file of it, even if the Piute tribesmen did not think enough of it to take it.

Piute Progress. Late in 1921, according to oral information, Fred E. Eldredge of Panguitch, backed by a group of stockholders, took from Panguitch to Marysvale, a small amount of type and an old Washington hand press, and on January 1, 1922, launched the Piute Progress. The Western Newspaper Union readyprint service record shows the account in Eldredge's name through December, 1923, and in the name of Wallace Johnson from January, 1924, to September 8, 1924, when it ended. F. A. Jackman purchased the plant in 1924, and moved it at once to Junction. (A. C. Saunders brought the Piute County News to Marysvale July 12, 1937; Chas. M. Giffen, editor).

MERCUR (formerly Lewiston) Tooele County
Population: 1893, (Spring) None; (Autumn) 100; 1900, 2,351; about 1903, nearly 5,000; 1910, 1,047; 1913, (Autumn) None.

The Lewiston Mercury. "Do you remember (July) 1893, when C. C. Higgins printed Vol. 1, No. 1, of the Lewiston Mercury, stating that 'The object of the paper is to herald the great richness of the Camp Floyd Mining District . . . and to rake a few chestnuts out of the fire, for our own consumption . . . perchance become a bonanza king— or a mining expert in yellow laced boots!' ", asks the editor of a "Souvenir Memorial Edition of The Mercury, 1935."

Editor Higgins is further quoted: "Eph. Mulliner has found it necessary to discard the old two-horse stage, and replace it with a four-horse coach . . . the stage brought in 11 passengers, Wednesday, and 3 more, who couldn't possibly be squeezed into the stage, came in by other conveyance. . . . Nineteen new frame houses have been erected recently; besides, there are a number of new tent houses, and tents galore. Reminds him of the 'Days of 49' . . . The camp needs a barber . . . Lewiston now has a general store, a weekly paper, an eating house, very few idle men, great expectations and a population of 100 souls. . . . Martin Mahnkin brings fresh meat to the camp every Wednesday, fattened on his own ranch, juicy as a watermelon, and tender as a maiden's first fancy . . . an enterprising, hospitable and moral community . . . a few fights occurred in camp Sunday, but owing to the number of gigantic jags distributed among the combatants, no harm was done."

"Politically this paper will support no party whose chief aim is not the restoration of silver—the old running mate of gold. Neither can trot well in single harness . . . The greatest need of the camp at this time is a post office. A petition numerously signed has been forwarded to Washington, asking for an office at this point, with Captain Tom Gundry as postmaster." (Editor's note—1935.) [The application for a post office was granted with the provision that some other name than Lewiston be chosen, there already being an office in Utah by that name. Accordingly at that time, and for no other reason, was the name of Lewiston changed to that of Mercur.]

Mercur Mercury. (Continuing Lewiston Mercury). Fridays, 4-pages, 11 x 16, $3, established 1893, C. C. Higgins, Editor and Publisher, so says the American Newspaper Directory for 1896. In 1898 the Mercury is credited with 450 circulation, 4-pages, 15 x 22, Independent, by Ayers Newspaper Annual. The Utah County Democrat, March 1, 1899, says: "Brother C. C. Higgins of the Mercur Mercury, has given up the management and editorial charge of that paper to George Ferguson. We regret Brother Higgins' retirement. He founded the Mercury when Mercur was young and when he was obliged to use a tent for a printing office. . . . He is one of the few eminently financially successful newspapermen in Utah." The 1900 Directory gives: "J. N. Louder, publisher." Evidently the Mercury leaked out or entered an amalgam along about this time, for we hear no more about it.

"The Mercur Miner, Thursday, 4-pages, 15 x 22, $2.50, Miner Publishing Company, N. B. Dresser, Editor, established in 1895," says Ayers Newspaper Annual for 1898. It was probably established late in December, 1895, for the Nephi Blade, January 4, 1896, says: "The Mercur Miner, by the Miner Publishing Company, is the latest candidate for public favor. It is a neat, 6 column folio."

The editors of the "Souvenir Memorial Miner, 1935" asked: "Do you remember (November) 1897, when N. B. Dresser published the Illustrated Jubilee edition of the Mercur Miner, recording that: 'Mercur is an incorporated city having . . . a brass band . . . a fire department . . . two teachers . . . one church . . . two newspapers, the Mercury by M. C. Higgins (sic) who is enjoying well earned prosperity . . . the Miner is published by N. B. Dresser, who represented Tooele County last

JAMES DUNN
Born July 10, 1836
Died January 24, 1924

AUGUSTUS GORDON
Born August 13, 1857
Died November 10, 1929

A. HATCH JR.
Born September 8, 1879
Still Living

REINHARD MAESER
Born March 19, 1855
Died September 17, 1926

winter in the Utah Legislature . . . still has to hustle for a living, but he expects to move over to Easy Street in about 18 months . . . Pictures in this issue taken by Joy and Barker.'

"The Opera House Saloon has card and wine rooms and affords the patron of the Opera House a convenient place to go out and 'see a man' between acts or dances . . . Mr. Germo has recently taken over the Boley House . . . It has 26 rooms, but can accommodate twice that number of guests . . . Jerry Anson deals exclusively in 'wet goods' in a town where water sells for a half cent a gallon! . . . The office of the Mercur Cemetery Association is located with The Mercur Furniture Company . . . Mercur is never likely to be a great Metropolis!"

S. A. Kenner in Utah As It Is, 1904, says the Miner, established 1895. 5 columns, quarto, was conducted by J. T. Jakeman, who also issues the Stockton Sentinel, both weekly, the former Independent, the latter Republican, $2.50 per year. Ayers Newspaper Annual for 1905 shows 600 circulation, Jakeman and Gray, publishers. At the same time James T. Jakeman is shown to be the editor of the Stockton Sentinel. The 1908-9 Gazetteer shows: "C. W. Evers, Manager"; and in 1912-13 "W. G. Craft, local editor." The mining camp was abandoned by the closing of the last mine, March 30, 1913. The Mercur mines petered out and the once prosperous camp ceased to exist, but just when the Miner wrote "finis" we did not ascertain. No files or copies were found.

Here is how the death knell of a city sounds: "Mercur, Utah, April 5. 1913, Mr. John Dern, President Consolidated Mercur Gold Mines Company, Dear Sir (and father) . . . The last skip of ore was hoisted at 8:40 A. M. Sunday, March 30, 1913, and the Mercur mine was at an end. . . . As the last skip was being hoisted, the flag was raised on the mill, the whistles were blown for one hour, the fire bell, school bell, and church bell were rung, and the famous old producer passed into history.—G. H. Dern, general manager." (Later Governor of Utah and U. S. Secretary of War.)

MILFORD, Beaver County

Population: 1900, 279; 1910, 1,014; 1920, 1,308; 1930, 1,517.

Milford Sentinel: "Risen again.—The first number of the Milford Sentinel has reached us. It is a semi-weekly, published by Joseph Field, and in fact the Phoenix of the Beaver Chronicle, (sic), recently defunct," says the Deseret News, August 28, 1880. This was Milford's first newspaper, following the railroad into town by a few months.

The Ogden Junction chose to phrase it in this wise: September 1, 1880: "In a new dress. The late Beaver Watchman (sic) has donned a new garb, and comes to us as Milford Sentinel in somewhat reduced size. Still it seems to be keeping good watch, for it has many items from the surroundings of its sentry box. An explanatory notice, however, on its fourth page sounds a little strange. The editor directs attention of readers that 'This issue of August 25 is volume 9, number 1;' and justifies it by saying: 'of course we have not been publishing here for 7 years, but as we have only changed the name and place of publication of our paper, we prefer making the issues consecutive. Hence the ninth volume.' We are unfortunate to fail seeing the sequence from the seventh year to the ninth volume."

The Provo Territorial Enquirer takes still another view, September 4, 1880: "Squelched.—The Beaver people have been ridded of the presence of their Watchman, he having traveled over to Milford, and now appears under the cognomen of the Milford Sentinel. This is about the fifth of these so-called 'Independent Papers' which have been born consumptively, lived and finally died in Beaver. It seems they all have a certain amount of independence, which so to speak is like the tunes of the hand organ. When they get off the last bit, they must either 'scoot' or commence over again."

Its news items were frequently lifted, and in return we find the following in the Deseret News, Wednesday, December 22, 1880: "Brightening up.—The Milford Sentinel is picking up. The last copy comes to us in a much neater shape than any of its predecessors. The printing is better and the whole tone of the paper seems to be improved." Due, it may be, to the advent of an editor more friendly to the News. The change is chronicled in the Deseret News of January 31, 1881: "Mr. Joseph Field, founder of the Milford Sentinel, and other papers in Beaver County, has retired from the Journalistic field. Mr. C. Hughes is his successor." And the News of February 25, 1881, adds: "Mr. C. Hughes, Editor of the Milford Sentinel, has become a husband. The lady is or was Miss W. M. Osborn." An idea of the Sentinel's appearance comes with a paragraph in the Territorial Enquirer of Provo, April 9, 1881: "The Milford Sentinel says: 'a good practical printer wanted at this office.' A glance at the paper would convince anyone that there is truth in the remark."

The Deseret News gives some current gossip on May 17, 1881: "The Milford Sentinel is said to be on its last legs. A feud has sprung up between the Milford Sentinel and the Southern Utonian." That same day the Ogden Herald says: "It Is He.—The Southern Utonian says Joseph Field of the Beaver Enterprise, Square Dealer, Chronicle, Watchman, etc., and latterly the Milford Sentinel, has decided to undertake journalism in his old 'field of failures' once more, and having admitted that he is unpopular, has made another so-called sale of his printing outfit to a certain poetical journalistic lawyer of this town, who really has considerable talents, but unfortunately of the 'hard specie' order."

The Ogden Herald of May 19, 1881 says: "The Milford Sentinel and the Beaver Utonian are at loggerheads." The Deseret News, May 23, 1881: "The Sentinel says dolefully: 'Times are very quiet in Milford at present,'" and on Thursday, June 9, 1881, the Deseret News reports the big fact in a little way: "The Milford Sentinel has suspended." And in another place: "S. A. Kenner, esquire, has leased the entire outfit of the Milford Sentinel and designs starting in Beaver a paper to be called The Enterprise. The first paper Beaver ever had was so called. 'Scip' is able to make the thing boom."

But evidently "Scip" changed his mind about moving to Beaver, for the Deseret News, September 22, 1882, has this: "Admitted to the bar.—The Milford Sentinel says that on Tuesday last (September 14) Mr. S. A. Kenner was admitted to the bar of the Second District. This entitles him to practice law in any Court in Utah, having been admitted to the other Districts and Supreme Court several years ago. Mr. Kenner is now in Ogden, arranging his affairs, previous to his removal south."

And on Monday, October 8, 1882: "We had a call this morning from Mr. W. H. Kenner of the Milford Sentinel, who is in Salt Lake for a few days on business connected with his paper. He is a brother of Mr. S. A. Kenner of Ogden." Was the News mistaken when it said "Scip" took over the Sentinel, or did "Scip" sell it to his brother, or was W. H. running it for "Scip"? Nevertheless, there endeth the available story of Milford's first newspaper. Regrettable it is that not a single copy has been preserved.

"Milford Times, C. T. Harte, publisher, only Republican paper in southern Utah, only newspaper publisher in Beaver County." This we found in the 1903-04 Gazetteer. "Friday, Republican, 8-pages, 11 x 18, $2, circulation 700, established 1902, J. T. Jakeman, editor and publisher," says Ayer's Newspaper Annual for 1905. The 1908-09 Gazetteer tells us: "The Milford Times, only live paper in southern Utah. W. L. Elswick, Manager, Milford Times Company." It appears to have given way about that time to the

Beaver County News. George B. Greenwood was President of the Beaver County News Publishing Company in 1912, but by 1914 we find A. B. Lewis, Editor and Publisher. W. L. Elswick is Editor in 1915. On March 1, 1916, Karl S. Carlton and M. J. Westerfield became the owners, and R. S. Ramsey, Editor. Arthur B. Lewis was the previous proprietor and Editor. Later we read: "With the first of the New Year, 1917, R. S. Ramsey retires, and Mr. D. A. Webster assumes the duties of Editor and Manager." On May 1, 1917, Carlton took active charge, buying Webster's interest about August, 1919.

Carlton sold to Lee C. Brown in February, 1928, who ran the paper about two years, but Karl S. Carlton was responsible from February 7, 1921 to February 8, 1928. Lee C. Brown was Editor and Publisher in 1930, and 1932 Directories show: "A. C. Saunders, Proprietor; Ray A. Williams, Lessee." On March 18, 1933, A. C. Saunders and wife sold the Milford News to David S. Williams, who is still in charge.

MOAB, Grand County

Population: 1910, 615, 1920, 856; 1930, 853.

Grand Valley Times, Volume 1, Number 1, May 30, 1896, Friday, Independent, 8-pages, 15 x 22, $2, circulation 300, J. N. Corbin, Editor and Publisher, says Ayer's Newspaper Annual for 1898. Corbin continued as Editor and Publisher until March 17, 1907. Loren L. Taylor, the present Editor, informs us that on that date Corbin sold to C. A. Robertson, who edited and managed the paper until January 1, 1911. The Grand County Publishing Company was organized, Loren L. Taylor becoming editor and manager at that time.

Mr. Taylor continued as editor and manager until June 5, 1930, when he purchased the paper and plant, and has since been its owner and editor. The files are bound and are complete to date from the founding of the paper. Grand Valley Times from its beginning until 1908 was a 6 column paper, 2 pages home print and from two to four pages ready print. In 1908 it became a 5 column, 8-page paper, 4 pages ready print. In 1917 it was changed to a 6 column, 8-page paper, half ready print. After its consolidation with the Independent, it was an 8-page all home print paper until 1922. Since 1922 the paper has been one half ready print.

The Independent was established in May, 1916. Independent Publishing Company, F. W. Strong, Editor and Manager. It absorbed the San Juan Blade of Monticello on April 4, 1918. In September of 1918 it was itself absorbed by the Grand County Publishing Company, publishers of the Grand Valley Times, when the name was changed to the **Times-Independent,** Loren L. Taylor, publisher.

MONTICELLO, San Juan County

Population: 1890, 115; 1900, 180; 1910, 375; 1920, 768; 1930, 496.

San Juan Record, Volume 1, Number 1, dated September 29, 1915, was manufactured in the plant of the Grand Valley Times at Moab. Oscar W. McConkie was editor and manager for the Grand County Publishing Company, mostly Moab men. On September 12, 1917, H. E. Blake succeeded McConkie as editor and manager, continuing until December 1919, when the Record Publishing Company was formed by Monticello and Blanding men. This company purchased the plant of the Moab Independent and moved it to Monticello, the first paper printed in Monticello being that for December 13, 1919. Leslie T. Foy became editor, Oscar W. McConkie, manager and H. E. Blake, printer in charge of the mechanical department.

Albert R. Lyman succeeded Mr. Foy as Editor on March 10, 1920. The Monticello State Bank became owner of the Record through foreclosure proceedings; and on June 15, 1921, H. E. Blake became editor and manager under a lease from the bank. He purchased the plant within a month.   Blake continued as publisher until April, 1931, when he sold to the Trustees of the Monticello State Bank.

J. L. Oliver became editor April 14, 1931, under a lease, turning the paper back to the bank on December 30, 1932. Wm. T. Igleheart was employed by the bank as editor, the paper being printed in the Times-Independent office at Moab until March 1, 1933. On this day J. P. May of Duchesne, Utah, purchased the newspaper and resumed publication at Monticello. On May 10, 1934, the paper was purchased by Marie M. Ogden, Director, "Home of Truth," a religious society. Since January 1, 1938, C. S. Wilkinson has been editor and manager for Mrs. Ogden.

MORGAN, Morgan County

Population: 1890, 333; 1900, 600; 1910, 756; 920, 995; 1930, 953.

Morgan Mirror seems to have been Morgan's first newspaper. It was started in 1896, but as there are no files we haven't the complete facts. The following is from The Republic, Nephi, August 29, 1896: "Morgan Mirror. With this issue the Mirror takes pleasure in introducing to its patrons and the people of Morgan in general Mr. J. W. Hyde of Logan, Utah, a practical printer and writer of some years experience. Mr. Hyde will be associated with the present proprietor in the publication of the Mirror, and in all probability will move his family here and locate permanently in our midst. (We wish the Mirror success. We can vouch for Mr. Will Hyde, and trust under the combination the paper will prosper.—Editor Republic.)" The earliest description of it is in Ayer's Newspaper Annual for 1898: "Morgan Mirror, Friday, 8-pages, 15 x 22, $1, circulation 365, Matt Edsall, publisher." In 1900 O. W. Covington was editor and publisher. Kenner, in Utah As It Is, 1904, says "Orson W. Covington is publisher." The Gazetteer for 1908-09 shows N. J. Peterson, publisher.

There is no further information concerning the Mirror, as if someone had thrown a rock in it! In the gossip of memories about town, Covington sold to H. B. Fry, F. L. Parkinson and Walter Bramel, Fry soon become sole owner. Fry then sold it (sorry no dates available) to C. H. Ruble. There may have been inheritances of doubtful value to Ruble, for he chose to call his paper

The Morgan County Star, and to report it in Ayer's Newspaper Annual for 1915 as established in 1912. He thus purges himself entirely of the broken Mirror's bad luck. It only goes to show what can be done with the same press and batch of type. The Mirror had become a Star! The 1916-17 and 1918-19 Gazetteers still show Charles H. Ruble, editor, Morgan County Star. But shortly after this the Star fell to earth, we know not where, leaving Morgan without a newspaper for a while. Then with new enthusiasm Brother Ruble gathered up the fragments and launched the

Mineral Cactus

Vol. 1.   St. George, Utah May 2, 1868.   No. 7.

HALLO! HALLO!! HALLO!!!

Everybody & Co.,

Ho for Gold! Ho for silver! Ho for Copper! Go to the tithing office there you will find everybody excited about some secret. Where is I? ask one Up on shirts creek. No it ain't says another it is on the Colorado. You get out I know all about it. Then if you go to the barber shop all the above it is on the Sevier. Then hullo! hullo! hallo! everybody saddle up your calves take your fire shovels and the last bread pan that your wife has got in the house, and go to prospecting in the w ter ditches and if you fail go where it is to be found and scope out the yaller truck by pocket full.

OUR DEVIL.

It seems that our devil can not refrain from making remarks about everybody and everything. He says as it is conference time it is best for everybody to govern themselves accordinzly. If you come to conference and conclude to put up with some to your friends, do not forget to bring your own grub. It any should be so sponging as to not bring their own nourishment, feed them once on lucerne soup, and I am rather of the opinion that they will repent. He also thinks of going into the cattle trade, providing he can find somebody's calf that is not branded. He also says that Chloride of Lime is not used pretty freely this summer, that many will be overtaken with the contagious disease known as Gold fever which is raging among us.

CLAIMS! CLAIMS!! CLAIMS!!!

Come! Come!! Come!!! all you long legged, gander shanked, bowlegged, swaybacked, brushheaded pieces of humanity, and buy what can never be taken from you. viz. A good gold, silver, copper or any o'her kind of a mining claim in Pahreer Virgen Territory, Molasses wanted in exchange. Go in lemons and come out squized.

THEATRE TO NIGHT Co.

Twas on a fine blustery day when I took a walk to Washington, my lady love to see.

Sorghum for sale!

We-a-l I had a fine pair of striped breeches on she tho't they were very nice.

Buy an ax handle?

I said I walked to Washington but I didn't walk back no sir I ran along, the side of

Buy a razor strop?

The vehicle which contained my dear one

NEW BUCKSKIN PANTS!!!!!???

Oh, no guess not.

We wish to announce to the public of this tropical clime, that, we have just received 500, 000, 000, 000, of rings streaked and speckled yellow black humbug grape cuttings.

Everybody & Sons.

They Wave Ropes.—Several of the Brethren, have been up from the muddy as to procure ropes to be stretched as dividing lines, as a recent wind storm had completely submerged their Town Survey.

It is not true that you know who were to curse the night of the 7th inst.

Within the last few days, several of our citizens have given way to the shrine of Bachus, with the excuse that they were merely comparing "Dixie" wines, with those of California. Very good, hey.

I came very near marrying the other day! How near? Why, I asked a young lady to have me and she said she would rather be excused—and I was fool enough to excuse her.

What is the difference between Lieut Gov. Hair Lip and the Empress Eugenia? Hair Lip's lip is natural and the Empress cultivate a Moustache on her lip

Good News.—The wheat heads begin to appear upon Mr. C. Breuse's farm.

Benevolence.—It has been suggested by several, that the committee get up another officer ball, expressly for those who never pay the fiddlers.

J. L. Wishes somebody would 'tespond to his advertisement for a wife.

SNEAKING!!

How sneaking and lowlived it is in a man, and him a saint, to try te sneak into reserved seats at the theatre on fifty cent tickets.

A wheelbarrow maker could do well here now-as teams are poor wheelbarrows are in demand.

Courtesy H. L. Reid

Morgan Independent, the Western Newspaper Union ready print service showing from 500 to 700 copies—a dandy circulation—from October 7, 1920 to October 30, 1924. Just when the Independent began and when it ended we could not learn, possibly not far from the ready print dates mentioned. Mr. and Mrs. C. B. Wallace launched the

Morgan County News and entered it as second class mail matter October 26, 1923. It was run in connection with the Coalville Times. The News was for most of this time a mere visitor in Morgan, not a resident, though Mrs. C. B. Wallace did spend a great deal of her time in Morgan. About December 1, 1925, the Wallaces sold the News to S. D. Perry and Son (C. K. Perry). The father, S. D. Perry, moved to Morgan with a supply of type and began issuing the Morgan County News, the forms being set up in Morgan but transferred and printed in Coalville usually (sometimes in Ogden), continuing so to the date of our investigation. Only a small job printing press was available in the Morgan office.

MOUNT PLEASANT, Sanpete County

Population: 1890, 2,254; 1900, 2,372; 1910, 2,280; 1920, 2,415; 1930, 2,284.

The Sanpitcher. (The following is from the Manti Herald, pen-and-ink manuscript newspaper, March 20, 1867.) "We had much pleasure last mail in receiving Number 1 of the Sanpitcher, David Candland, editor. The paper is published in the flourishing town of Mount Pleasant, and like the Herald is done upon a sheet of writing paper; but instead of being printed with the pen, it is written in common orthography, yet it is a neat concern and highly creditable to friend David, its publisher; and as in duty and friendship bound, we touch our hat! hoping that, like the sling in the hand of the editor's namesake of old, the Sanpitcher will be an instrument in the hands of its talented editor, to assist in slaying the giant of error. We also solicit usual exchanges."

The Deseret News refers to it Wednesday, April 24, 1867: "From Mount Pleasant, Sanpete, with the editor's compliments and good wishes comes Number 5, volume 1 of the Sanpitcher, 'editor and publisher, David Candland,' a neat little news sheet of three columns, with a supplement filled with editorial tidbits and local items. We hear of one or two other interesting little papers of a similar character throughout the territory, illustrative of the taste and the desire for 'news' local and foreign, which keeps growing among the people . . . Friend David has a taste for the 'tripod' and a spicy way of expressing himself."

"This pithy little manuscript effusion is before us again," says the Salt Lake Telegraph, May 21, 1867, of the Sanpitcher. "It has already reached number 9 at date of 11th inst. From its supplemental issue we infer that news making is on the *qui vive*. And how does it pay, Friend David?" Again on June 23, 1867 the Telegraph says of "The Sanpitcher.—Number 13 of this little sheet came to our table yesterday with the Editor's Valedictory. . . . But in a private communication, we are assured of its resumption at the solicitation of its many friends. . . . It is a medium of circulating news, and it is not without its influence."

The Mount Pleasant Pyramid, Volume 1, Number 1, Saturday, December 6, 1890. A. B. Williams, editor and proprietor, 4-pages, 6 columns, 15 x 22, all home print. "Greeting . . . it may be necessary to state that as a citizen we have been a Liberal (non-Mormon). But as the editor of this Journal we propose to lay our prejudices aside and enter into the spirit that desires to make Mount Pleasant the Metropolis of Sanpete County."

The files for the first twenty-three years were destroyed by the flooding of the basement in which they were stored; but we found Number 1. Volume 1, among the treasures of Mrs. Abner Crane of Mount Pleasant. The Provo Enquirer of December 9, 1890, says of it: "And now the Mount Pleasant Pyramid steps into the ring of Utah Journalism. It is another of the Independent kind, and in mechanical make-up, presents a fine appearance."

J. M. Boyden became printer for Williams about June, 1891; shortly M. A. Boyden, a writer on the Salt Lake Times, joined his brother on the Pyramid. Williams departed for Colorado about July 4, 1891. leaving the Boydens as purchasers, if not yet sole owners. Williams returned to Mount Pleasant about 1893, and with George W. Thompson, bought back the Pyramid, so J. M. Boyden informed us. But a few years later J. M. Boyden bought Thompson's interest and was in a little time joined by the brother, M. A., in the part ownership with Williams. On December 13, 1895, the Wasatch Wave says: "Last week the Mount Pleasant Pyramid started on its sixth year of existence, and in it Brother Williams has a healthy kid."

John J. Woodring bought out Williams' interest, and Woodring was a silent partner for some time, before I. E. Jorgensen bought in as a printer-partner, says J. M. Boyden, reading from his book of memories. Incidentally one Will J. Peters, a stage performer, entertainer, and opera house property man, putting on a show in Mount Pleasant, became stranded without a booking, and went to work for J. M. Boyden as printer on the Pyramid. This is the same Peters who with Kramer, later launched the Tooele Bulletin; and still later established himself in Panguitch, as newspaper owner and publisher.

A copy in Mrs. Crane's collection, volume 8, number 6, December 30, 1897, 6 columns, 15 x 24, shows J. M. Boyden, manager. Incidentally an advertisement shows: "J. M. Boyden, secretary of Damascus Lodge, Number 10, F. & A. M." The Utah County Democrat, Provo, November 12, 1898, says A. B. Williams, formerly chief pusher on the Mount Pleasant Pyramid, will go into the field. (He became a very successful newspaper man in Medford, Oregon.) Rowell's American Newspaper Directory for 1900 shows: "Mount Pleasant Pyramid,

Fridays, Independent, 4-pages, 15 x 22, J. M. Boyden, editor, Pyramid Publishing Company, publishers."

"My first experience in the newspaper and printing business was with the Mount Pleasant Pyramid," says C. N. Lund, Jr. "I learned the work there and became a one-third owner for a short time (with J. M. Boyden and I. E. Jorgensen). Later, for a brief period, about 1903. I was the sole owner of the Pyramid. I re-sold the Pyramid to Mr. Boyden, from whom I purchased it." Burke McArthur purchased the paper in March, 1911. Since then the Western Newspaper Union readyprint record shows this to be one of their best accounts. McArthur was the first Mormon proprietor of the Pyramid, and is still in sole control. He has a clear field, but has earned it, by printing a better newspaper than existing or prospective rivals could do; by printing all the news that is handed in, and plenty besides, thereby making the people feel it is really "Our paper". Burke has thus built up a reserve of influence and power sufficient to "lick the best of them" when necessary, in any cause that is just, though usually his beloved Pyramid is not allowed to manifest any of the baser human attributes, no matter how keenly partisan he may feel himself. Once when he declined to let the Pyramid lead in a political crusade, three prominent citizens withdrew their support, menacingly declaring fifty would do the same; but after a visit to the sunny side of the Pyramid, the other forty-seven did not! Consequently Burke resides in one of the finest homes in the city, and has one of the best newspaper businesses in the State—while the departed Shades of opinionated, fighting, crusading editors look enviously down from Elysium!

Mt. Pleasant Call. (New) Volume 1, Number 1; (Old) Volume 13, Number 637, August 24, 1918, entered as second class mail matter at Salina, Utah, as the Sevier Valley Call, June 29, 1906, published every Saturday by C. N. Lund, Jr. The Call had "called" a spade a spade in Salina and got itself escorted to the city limits. Editor Lund gives a little of the story in the first number of his newspaper at Mt. Pleasant as follows: "A case like our own. Margaret E. Sangster's three stanza poem of a home destroyed entitled 'Somewhere in Belgium' is true of 'Somewhere in Utah' too," says Editor Lund. "We take the liberty of applying it to our own case. Efforts are being made to minimize or deny the work of the mob. Just look for the motive in this, please. Let the doubters interview the woman and children who went through the terrible experience. They tell the truth, which certain ones do not want."

"Whether good or bad, Whichever it be, A hot headed mob Raised H— with me; I came from Salina RFD Where they didn't do a thing To a guy like me!" The 1920-21 Gazetteer advertisement says: "The Call is a Journal of American Democracy, forward looking and unafraid." Of course it was not afraid; didn't it return each week to get in the mail at Salina? The paper was suspended in May, 1922, for the want of patronage. The old Mt. Pleasant Pyramid, like those of Egypt, was just that good!

MURRAY, Salt Lake County

Population: 1910, 4,057; 1920, 4,584; 1930, 5,172.

American Eagle. The history of the Murray newspapers was lost in a fire in 1924. The American Eagle for January 23, 1926 carries the statement: established 1891, but the newspaper directories do not mention it until 1898: "Murray, American Eagle, Saturday, 8-pages, 13 x 20, $1.50, established 1896 (sic), M. A. Willumson, editor. (Williamson and Willumson) American Eagle Publishing Company."

The American Newspaper Directory for 1896 had shown: "Murray, American (sic) Saturdays, Republican, 4-pages, 15 x 22, $2, established 1894, W. M. White, editor and publisher." We are thus inclined to believe that Murray's first newspaper was the American, which became the American Eagle with change of management in 1896. At the date of original establishment we find in the Brigham Bugler, July 28, 1894: "A Murray American has reached our table . . ." The form of expression probably indicates a new newspaper.

J. S. Barlow was editor and manager for Eagle Publishing Company in 1908, also in 1915 and 1917, but we do not find the date he took charge. The issue of January 23, 1926 shows P. K. Nielsen, editor and business manager; and it was reported to us that Nielsen had charge from 1924. The issue for January 8, 1927, was titled: **"Murray Eagle and Midvale Journal,** south Salt Lake County's publicity twins." The paper includes a sub-division with a full page head: "The **Draper Journal,** January 7, 1927, volume 1, number 34, John M. Peterson, editor, Jordan Publishing Company, Inc.," and the

Murray Press, published at Midvale and Murray on January 5, 1928. The masthead is: "C. B. Wallace, editor, Mrs. C. B. Wallace, publisher." They have always owned it together.

MYTON, Duchesne County

(Formerly Wasatch County)
Population: 1920, 479; 1930, 395.

The Uintah Chieftain, Volume 1, Number 1, Myton, Wasatch County, Thursday, May 14, 1908. "Today the Uintah Chieftain makes its bow to the settlers of the former Uintah Indian Reservation . . . **The Chieftain Publishing Company."** Presuming to be the grown up Uintah Pappoose, the pioneer Uintah Basin newspaper, started by Kate Jean Boan in Vernal, January 2, 1891, the Chieftain Editor explains that Mrs. Boan had loaned to him copies of the Pappoose, in which she said: "Here I am today!" "And, so it seems, time has told," says the Chieftain, adding: "The Pappoose has returned as Chieftain." He further avers that "The Chieftain has a thoroughly equipped newspaper and job printing establishment. Application made for entry at the post office. Printer wanted at the Chieftain office. A. G. Boan (husband of the pioneer editor?) of the Myton-Duchesne stage has the honor of being the first yearly paid up subscriber. Mr. Boan's teams brought in the Chieftain printing plant from Fort Duchesne."

We were informed Fred L. Watrous was the founder, editor and publisher. On May 13, 1909, he says, "One year ago today the Chieftain began its existence . . . financially the rewards of a newspaper business lie principally in the future. . . . A better day will soon dawn for the Reservation."

Wood cuts of Indians at each end of the title line of the Chieftain, peering at the horizon, were also apparently awaiting that same dawn. A little later the masthead showed Fred L. Watrous, editor, and the last number of the Chieftain appeared April 28, 1910, which was number 51 of volume 2. A week later, May 6, 1910, Fred L. Watrous, editor of the Duchesne Record, says: "Beginning next week the three papers of the Reservation, the Uinta Standard (Roosevelt), the Uintah Chieftain (Myton), and the Duchesne Record will consolidate under the name of **The Uintah Record,** which will be published at Myton. The present editor of the Duchesne Record will serve in the same capacity under the consolidation.

"The amalgamation is brought about for the reason that the owners of the respective publications consider that it is more desirable to have one good paper to represent the Reservation than to have the field so divided that neither can afford, from a business standpoint, to get out the kind of a paper the Uintah Basin is entitled to. Beginning at once The Record will publish a four page, home print publication."

"(As an after consideration, since the above was put in type, and in honor of the mighty stream, which together with its tributaries, furnishes the water for the irrigation of this entire section, it has been decided to retain [the name]

The Duchesne Record.)" Together with Watrous' name on the masthead, May 6, 1910, was "Herman Bunn, business manager," which was dropped from the next issue. Watrous' name continued at the masthead until early 1914, the Record being published at Myton to the end of 1914; but in March, 1914, the masthead showed, "Published every Friday by J. P. May."

Though Watrous' name was on the masthead, we are informed that Wm. H. Smart, Jr., was the proprietor or publisher from sometime in 1913 until Mr. May took charge in 1914. With the issue of December 26, 1914, the paper made its last appearance in Myton, and was moved to Duchesne. We read in the January 30, 1915 issue of the Duchesne Record: "A transaction of much interest to the people of Uintah Basin, and of vital importance to the town of Myton was consummated on Wednesday of this week (January 27) when a company

JOHN C. GRAHAM
Born July 23, 1839
Died March 18, 1906

C. W. PENROSE
Born February 4, 1832
Died May 16, 1925

JOHN T. CAINE
Born January 8, 1829
Died September 20, 1911

JOSEPH T. McEWAN
Born September 1, 1840
Died January 3, 1913

organized by the citizens of Myton, purchased the entire plant of the
Duchesne Record from Mr. Wm. H. Smart . . . incorporated under the
name of the Uintah Basin Publishing Company . . . to publish a
newspaper by the name

Myton Free Press. The first issue will appear in about three weeks.
The new publication will be under the management of C. B. Cook, now
of the Vernal Express." In the Duchesne Record of April 17, 1915,
we read: "The Myton Free Press came out with its first issue last
week. The intial number was a 10-page edition, and under the efficient
management of C. B. Cook." "The Uintah Basin Publishing Company,
purchasers of the Record plant at Myton, have ordered the new equipment necessary for the publication of the Myton Free Press, which will
make its appearance May 1, 1915," says the Duchesne Record, February
13, 1915. Some miscellaneous loose files, a several years' run of the
Myton Free Press, were found (1933) in the vacated newspaper office,
in charge of attorney B. L. Dart. The earliest was number 1 of volume
2, Thursday, April 6, 1916. C. B. Cook's name was at the masthead
until February 5, 1925, when it becomes Uinta Basin Publishing Company; G. E. Philipps, president, W. S. Peatross, editor and manager,
Arnold Reef, business manager."

Also: "C. B. Cook, manager of the Myton Free Press was granted a
leave of absence for six months on account of ill health." In the issue
of April 23, 1925: "C. B. Cook died at Havana April 14, 1925." "W. S.
Peatross, who for 11 years has been with the paper, will act as editor
and manager. Arnold Reef of the Duchesne Courier will act as business
manager . . . Mr. Reef has been in the newspaper business in the basin
for many years," says the Free Press itself, February 5, 1925. The
Myton Free Press was being managed by Arnold Reef when the 1930-31
Gazetteer was compiled. The 1931 Blue Book publishers were informed:
"Myton Free Press, Uinta Basin Publishing Company, established 1915,
Wm. G. Gentry, Vice President, Arnold Reef, Manager." The plant of
the Free Press was sold to George P. Price and moved to Lehi in 1931
or 1932.

Reservation News. Ayer's Newspaper Annual for 1915 lists "Myton, Reservation News, Thursday, Independent, 13 column, 11 x 17,
$1.50, Morton Alexander, editor and publisher, established 1913." The
Eleventh Report of the State Bureau of Statistics, January 1, 1917,
shows: "The Reservation News, Myton, Thursday, F. E. Grant, editor
and publisher."

Aside from these items, little is known of the Reservation News,
which for a time at least was a contemporary of the Myton Free Press.
Neither beginning or ending could be determined. However, C. B.
Cook in an editorial in the Free Press of April 6, 1916, says: "The
Under Dog. On the front page of the Reservation News each week
appears this motto, slogan, or whatever it might be called 'Always
fighting for the plain people and the under dog.' Why not just omit

the word 'for' and be more consistent? A year or so ago the Vernal Express intimated that the News was a 'Scab'; we intimate that 'Scab' was not the proper word. It seems to us that 'Fester' would be better. . . . In 1908, when Alexander's Uintah Chieftain had no competition on the 'Reservation' the price asked for publishing water notices was $12. In 1913 when Alexander's Reservation News had competition, the price asked for publishing water notices was $5." When the Uintah Basin Record moved from Myton to Duchesne, January 1, 1915, the Eastern Utah Advocate of Price observed in part: "This leaves Myton without a paper; that is excepting the Reservation News!"

NEPHI, Juab County

Population: 1890, 2,034; 1900, 2,208; 1910, 2,759; 1920, 2,603; 1930, 2,573.

Nephi Ensign. Volume 1, number 1, 6 columns, 4-pages, weekly, Friday, June 10, 1887, James T. Jakeman, publisher. A couple of prenatal announcements heralded the Ensign. The first was in the Territorial Enquirer, Provo, May 31, 1887: "The irrepressible Jakeman, editor of the Manti Sentinel, contemplating a paper in Nephi, visited Beaver a short time ago for the purpose of obtaining assistance from their typographical line. Mr. D. Martin or J. T. Field became a desirable adjunct to the Nephi office." Then the Deseret News, Monday, June 1, 1887, says: "J. T. Jakeman of the Home Sentinel, was in the city today, and he has everything in readiness for the publication of the Ensign at Nephi, which will appear one week from next Friday."

"We congratulate Nephi on the advent of its Ensign, J. T. Jakeman's new enterprise," says the Territorial Enquirer, June 14, 1887. The Deseret News of June 14, 1887, refers to "The Nephi Ensign . . . Its typographical appearance is much superior to that of the paper issued in Manti by the same gentleman; it is well patronized in the matter of advertising." "But," says the Territorial Enquirer, November 1, 1887, "Five local articles clipped bodily from last Tuesday's issue of the Enquirer, inserted without any credit, in the Nephi Ensign last Friday, is too much of a joke. We don't object to making the Nephi Ensign readable and newsy, but most decidely do insist upon being credited with items."

Maybe that shot brought down its game, for on March 14, 1888, the Enquirer chronicles this colloquy: "The Ensign . . . will hereafter be conducted by John S. Rollo and John T. Field. Perhaps a change of hands was what is needed.—Ogden Standard. Prejudice indicated the above. There is no change in the operating force of the Ensign, only the proprietorship."

The American Newspaper Directory for 1888 says, Fridays, Democratic, 4-pages, 21 x 30, $2, Field and Rollo, editors and publishers. "The Ensign is the only purely Democratic sheet in the territory. They are offering their paper for $2 a year, cash in advance, and will give one half of each subscription to the Democratic campaign fund. (Now is the time for all good men to come to the aid of their party)," says the Manti Sentinel, November 7, 1888.

"Field and Rollo, of the Nephi Ensign have dissolved partnership. Mr. Field retires and Mr. Rollo will continue the business of publishing the Ensign," says the Home Sentinel, September 8, 1889. "James H. Wallis went down to Nephi last night to complete arrangements for the purchase of the Nephi Ensign. Mr. J. T. Field will be associated with Mr. Wallis in the proprietorship," says the Daily Enquirer, January 2, 1890, and adds, January 30, 1890: "Mr. James H. Wallis makes his opening speech in this week's issue of the Ensign. The first issue of the paper under the new management will appear on February 5 as number 1 of the semi-weekly Ensign. Mr. Rollo also delivers his farewell address in this issue." The Manti Home Sentinel, February 21, 1890, adds its mite: "We have not yet congratulated Nephi on their securing the talented James H. Wallis as the purchaser and editor of their city and county paper, the Ensign. We waited 'till we could be heard in the flood of compliments that were poured in." Then came the storm as recorded in Provo's Daily Enquirer, March 22, 1890: "The last issue of the Nephi Ensign is literally boiling over with bitterness and gall towards Provo and the Enquirer. If there is one thing more than another that will hasten the demise of our esteemed contemporary, it is just such a spasm as that with which it attacked on Tuesday last .... That paper will have to be more moderate."

A little gossip was picked up as follows: "James Wallis, the rustling manager of the Nephi Ensign, took in some of the sights, sensations and beverages at the Garden City yesterday. Call again, James." The Provo Daily Enquirer, April 10, 1890. And the Enquirer for April 18, 1890: " 'Nephi is enjoying the first fruits of a tissue paper boom', from the Utonian. May it please the Ensign to copy." Daily Enquirer, April 24, 1890: "Felt and Olson, who had an advertisement in the Nephi 'Insane', says that some time ago, noticing repeated attacks of a scurrilous character in that sheet on this city and its people, notified the editor that they wished their advertisement discontinued. It is still there, however, and they desire to announce through the Enquirer that they are no longer responsible and will not pay for the ad."

Further, from the Daily Enquirer, May 16, 1890: "The Nephi Ensign has put in a Cincinnati cylinder press and has made quite an improvement in the general makeup of the paper. The new type causes matters to appear in a clear light." The Manti Home Sentinel, May 20, 1890, also notices it: "The Nephi Ensign comes to hand in a new dress." But evidently the new type spoke much too freely, for we picked up in the Wasatch Wave of August 19, 1890, this item: "J. H. Wallis, editor of the Nephi Ensign, was arrested for libel about a week ago." The Manti Home Sentinel, August 22, 1890, says: "Editor Wallis of the Ensign has our sympathy. He is being tried for libel and is also 'liable' according to our contemporaries."

In the Bancroft library at Berkeley we found Volume 4, Number 58, of the Ensign, dated Saturday, August 30, 1890. $3, 7 columns,

4-pages, all home print, James H. Wallis, manager. Pro-Mormon. (Co-pies for August 30, 1889 and November 1, 1889, J. S. Rollo, editor and proprietor, were anti-Mormon). The issue for September 3, 1890, in-dicates publication "Wednesday and Saturday," and the issue of Sep-tember 13, 1890 was similar, both being heavily charged with political matter.

"Judge Wallis, prosecuting attorney of Juab County and Editor of the Nephi Ensign, called upon us today," says the Provo Enquirer, October 8, 1890. The Park Record observes, January 17, 1891, "The Nephi Ensign is going to make an addition to its facilities in the shape of a steam engine." And the Home Sentinel of Manti, January 23, 1891, explains why: "The Ensign plant and business lately owned by James Wallis was sold on the 14th day of January to Messrs. John T. Field and W. J. Shimmin."

"The editor of the Nephi Ensign and the postmaster, Whitbeck, had a scrap on the 4th of this month. It would seem by the account given by the Ensign, that Whitbeck wasn't in it at all." The Provo Daily Enquirer, March 21, 1891 says: "The third handed press that was used by the Utah Industrialist has been secured by the Nephi Ensign." A single sheet or dodger dated April 24, 1891 in the files of Alfred Orme, 595 East 1st South Street, Nephi, Utah contains this obituary: "The Ensign is dead. The causes which led to its demise were extravagance, fraud (beer) and the ungrateful acts of an unprincipled rascal . . . A new paper is to be established here by Field and Shimmin to succeed the Ensign."

The Manti Home Sentinel, April 28, 1891, says: "The Nephi En-sign is dead: We understand the plant will be moved to Lehi." "The Nephi Ensign was resurrected Thursday, (August 13)," says the Provo Enquirer, August 15, 1891. "A newcomer named W. Earl Smith, late of Nebraska is the editor and proprietor. The paper will issue once a week." According to Alfred Orme's daily journal, Smith held the En-sign aloft until July 10, 1892. The American Newspaper Directory for 1892: "Nephi, Ensign, Saturday, Independent, established 1884, 4-pages, 15 x 22, $2, circulation 700, W. E. Smith, editor and publisher." A copy for Saturday, August 13, 1892, also August 27, 1892, in the Ban-croft library, have 6 columns, 4-pages, all home print. "An Indepen-dent newspaper," W. Earl Smith, editor.

"S. B. Freed and E. Carroll of this city have purchased the Nephi Ensign plant and will assume charge of the paper on Monday morning next (August 29). Mr. Freed has for more than a year past, been fill-ing the position of foreman in the Enquirer job department and we can recommend the gentleman to the people of Nephi as a very com-petent typo." On September 2, 1892 the Enquirer publishes: "James T. Jakeman is on trial today in Commissioner Dudley's Court on the charge of disposing of a printing plant which he had mortgaged, with-out the knowledge of the mortgagee."

On September 3, 1892 the Enquirer continues the story: "The hearing of J. T. Jakeman on the charge of disposing of mortgaged property without the knowledge of the mortgagee, occupied nearly the whole of yesterday in Commissioner Dudley's Court. Mr. Warner prosecuted and A. G. Sutherland defended. After listening to the testimony, his Honor concluded there was sufficient evidence to warrant the holding of Jakeman to await the action of the Grand Jury. Bonds were fixed at $250." That action, while it did not stop Jakeman dead still, did nevertheless mark the hauling down forever of Nephi's Ensign.

"The Nephi Courier is the name of a new newspaper that found its way to our table last week," we found in the Spanish Fork Sun, September 15, 1892. "It is published by Mr. Carroll and Mr. Freed, both old time printers. The Courier presents an attractive appearance, and is a spicy, newsy sheet. Nephi at last has a paper she may be proud of." It would seem, however, that the Courier had a hard winter, for the Sun further informs us, April 22, 1893: "Last week we received a copy of the Nephi Courier, the first one for over two months." And the further news that: "E. S. Carroll, one of the lessees of the Nephi Courier has shipped to parts unknown, says the Courier of last week."

"The Nephi Courier of June 9th and the Payson Globe of June 10th contain each 13 apparently original editorials, but which were alike, word for word; that is the case of two souls with 13 similar thoughts, or what!" says the Brigham Bugler June 17, 1893. With no files, and the paper not often quoted, we wait until December 16, 1893, for the next item, which also appeared in the Brigham Bugler: "Nephi Courier is launching out into right creditable improvements, and now salutes its patrons twice a week." Maybe it was like Abraham Lincoln's story of the Mississippi River steamboat, the engines of which stopped when the whistle blew, for the want of power. Twice a week may have been too often for the power back of the Courier. We hear no more about it.

Juab County Standard, apparently had its beginning January 21, 1895. A copy of that date is in Alfred Orme's file. But that is all we know about it, except that the Blade cut it down six months later.

"The Nephi Blade has absorbed the Standard, and the publication of the latter has been discontinued," says the Park Record June 29, 1895. The Blade, Vol. 3 No. 1, Nephi City, Saturday, June 15, 1895, says: "Important . . . Down in its former home (Deseret and Oasis), The Blade lived two years . . . and the labor of editing it was done at such times as could be spared from other employment." (With this issue it starts anew at Nephi City). Orme's copy for September 19, 1895, carries only "J. F. Gibbs" at the masthead, which is enough! The Blade itself follows on October 26, 1895: "J. F. Gibbs, of the Nephi Blade, has accepted the editorship of the Provo Dispatch . . . He is a forceful writer, a man of untiring energy, and the Democratic Party of Utah County could not have selected a more able man."

SALT LAKE DAILY REPORTER.

VOL. I.   SALT LAKE CITY, U. T. MONDAY, MAY 11, 1868.   No. 1.

Salt Lake Daily Reporter.

(PUBLISHED EVERY EVENING.)

(SUNDAYS EXCEPTED,)

— BY —

S. S. SAUL.

TERMS:—IN ADVANCE:
| DAILY: | | WEEKLY: | |
Per Annum,........$16.00 | Per Annum,........$8.00 |
Six Months,...... 9.00 | Six Months,...... 5.00 |
Three Months,.... 5.00 | Three Months,.... 3.00 |
Per Month,....... 1.00 | Per Month,....... 1.00 |
Per Week,........ 30 | Per Copy,........ 20 |
Per Copy,........ 20 | |

LEGAL CARDS.

CHAS. H. HEMPSTEAD,
Attorney at Law
and
United States Attorney for Utah,
Office East side of Main Street, two doors above Walker Bros. up Stairs, Salt Lake City.
Office Hours 9 a.m. to 5 p.m.
Residence—North side of 3d South, between 2d and 3d East Temple streets, S. L. City.   1-tf

R. N. BASKIN.   STEPHEN DE WOLFE.

BASKIN & DE WOLFE,
Attorneys at Law.
Office above the Bank Exchange,
Salt Lake City.
1-tf

THOMAS MARSHALL.   JAMES M. CARTER.

MARSHALL & CARTER,
Attorneys at Law,
Salt Lake City, Utah.
1-6m

O. F. STRICKLAND.   R. H. ROBERTSON.

STRICKLAND & ROBERTSON,
Attorneys at Law,
and
Solicitors in Chancery,
Salt Lake City, Utah Territory.
1-tf

J. M. THURMOND,
Attorney at Law,
and
Agent for Buying and selling Mining Claims,
Sweetwater Mines, Dakotah.
1-tf

W. P. SANDERS,
Attorney at Law,
Virginia City, Montana Territory.
1-tf

K. D. HOGE.   E. P. JOHNSON.

HOGE & JOHNSON,
Attorneys at Law,
and
General Collecting Agents,
Office at the Delamatoo Hotel, Salt Lake City, U. T.
1-tf   Up stairs.

MISCELLANEOUS.

I. O. O. F.—Utah Lodge,
No. 1, I. O. O. F., hold their regular meetings in Odd Fellows' Hall, Main Street, on Thursday evening of each week, at 7 o'clock.
Brethren in good standing are invited to attend.
THEODORE AUERBACH, N.G.
W. J. TOOMEY, Secretary.   1-tf

JOSIAH FOGG.   JOHN H. SPARR.

PLANTER'S HOUSE.

FOGG & SPARR,
Proprietors,
SAINT LOUIS, MO.

LUMBER! LUMBER!

SELLING OFF AT REDUCED PRICES.

The undersigned offers for sale cheap,
FOR CASH,
At his place in STOCKTON, the best quality of
WHITE PINE LUMBER.

Stock will be taken in exchange for Lumber.
JAMES FINNERTY.
May, 1868.   1 tf

FORT BRIDGER.

W A. CARTER,

POST TRADER,

FORT BRIDGER, U.T.,

Keeps on hand full supplies of

Dry Goods,

Groceries,

Provisions,

Hardware,

Outfitting Goods,

etc., etc.

Nearest outfitting depot, and directly en route to the Sweetwater Mines from all points west.
1-tf

SPECIAL NOTICES.

HELMBOLD'S FLUID EXTRACT BUCHU

Is a certain cure for diseases of the
Bladder, Kidneys, Gravel, Dropsy, Organic Weakness, Female Complaints, General Debility,
And all diseases of the
Urinary Organs,
Whether existing in
Male or Female,
From whatever cause originating and no matter of HOW LONG STANDING.

Diseases of these organs require the use of a diuretic.
If no treatment is submitted to, Consumption or Insanity may ensue. Our Flesh and Blood are supported from these sources, and the
Health and Happiness,
And that of Posterity, depends upon prompt use of a reliable remedy.
Helmbold's Extract Buchu,
Established upwards of 18 years, prepared by
H. T. HELMBOLD, Druggist,
594 Broadway, New York, and
104 South 10th street, Philadelphia, Pa.
1-tf

For Non-retention or Incontinence of
Urine, Irritation, Inflammation, or ulceration of the bladder, or kidneys, diseases of the prostate glands, stone in the bladder, calculus, gravel or brick dust deposits, and all diseases of the bladder, kidneys and dropsical swellings, Use HELMBOLD'S FLUID EXTRACT BUCHU.
1-tf

Helmbold's Concentrated Extract Buchu
Is the Great Diuretic.
HELMBOLD'S CONCENTRATED EXTRACT SARSAPARILLA
Is the Great Blood Purifier.
Both are prepared according to rules of Pharmacy and Chemistry, and are the most active that can be made.
1-tf

Helmbold's Extract Buchu and Improved Rose Wash cures secret and delicate disorders in all their stages, at little expense, little or no change in diet, no inconvenience and no exposure. It is pleasant in taste and odor, immediate in its action, and free from all injurious properties.
1-tf

Helmbold's Extract Buchu gives health and vigor to the frame and bloom to the pallid cheek. Debility is accompanied by many alarming symptoms, and if no treatment is submitted to, consumption, insanity, or epileptic fits ensue.
1-tf

Enfeebled and Delicate Constitutions,
of both sexes, use HELMBOLD'S EXTRACT BUCHU. It will give brisk and energetic feelings, and enable you to sleep well.
1-tf

Take no More Unpleasant and Unsafe
Remedies for unpleasant and dangerous diseases. Use HELMBOLD'S EXTRACT BUCHU and IMPROVED ROSE WASH.
1-tf

The Glory of Man is Strength—Therefore the nervous and debilitated should immediately use HELMBOLD'S EXTRACT BUCHU.
1-tf

HELMBOLD'S FLUID EXTRACT BUCHU
is pleasant in taste and odor, free from all injurious properties, and immediate in its action.
1-tf

Manhood and Youthful Vigor are regained in HELMBOLD'S EXTRACT BUCHU.
1-tf

Shattered Constitutions Restored by
HELMBOLD'S EXTRACT BUCHU.
1-tf

MONTANA.

E. CREIGHTON,   P. A. LARGEY,
Omaha, Nebraska,   Virginia City.
J. A. CREIGHTON, Virginia City.

E CREIGHTON & Co.,

VIRGINIA CITY, MONTANA,

(Successors to Creighton & Hole,)

WHOLESALE GROCERS,

STORAGE

AND

COMMISSION MERCHANTS.

Prompt attention given to the

PURCHASE, SALE AND STORAGE OF

Produce, Provisions and Merchandise
generally.

Liberal Cash Advances made on Consignments.

EAGLE WORKS MANUFACTURING COMPANY.

Founded over a Quarter of a Century.

P. W. GATES, President.

Manufacture Portable and
Stationary,
Steam Engines and
Boilers,
Sugar Cane Mills,
Evaporators,
Rock Breakers,
Stamp Mills,
Mining Machinery,
Gard's Patent Brick Machines,
Lathes,
Planers,
Drills,
Screw Cutters,
Hay and Cotton Presses,
Saw Mills,
Flour Mills,
Mill Furnishing.

OFFICE, 44, CANAL STREET,

CHICAGO.

SEND FOR CIRCULARS.

THOS. CHALMERS, Supt.   RALPH GATES, Sec. & Treas.
D. R. FRASET, Asst. "   W. L. CHASE, Gen. Agt., N. Y.
and Draughtsman.   Mabbs & Bro. Agents, Lake
        Superior.
1-tf

BENEDICT, HALL & Co.,

WHOLESALE DEALERS
IN

BOOTS AND SHOES,

Nos. 279 and 281 Broadway (opposite A. T. Stewart & Co.,)

NEW YORK CITY.
1-tf

ITEMS.

Tennessee is proud to say that she has imported no corn this year, but has raised more than enough for her wants.

A trial of skill between the girls and boys of West Point, Ga., to settle the mooted question, "Are the mental capacities of females equal to those of males?" resulted in a decided triumph for the girls.

In reference to marriage, a London newspaper announces the discovery that, as a general rule, the proportion of marriages to population is least in England when the prices of wheat are high, and greatest when the prices of wheat are low.

Mrs. Phebe A. Hanaford was lately ordained and installed as pastor of the Universalist church in Hingham, Mass. This is the first instance of the ordination of a woman in the history of the religious denominations of Massachusetts.

Women have a much nicer sense of the beautiful than men. They are by far the safer umpires in all matters of propriety and grace. A mere school girl will be thinking and writing about the beauty of birds and flowers, while her brother is robbing the nests and destroying the flowers.

The Maine Historical Society has a piece of paper taken from the solid wood of a saw log, received for sawing at Augusta some time ago. The paper bears the words "J. B. Dunkirk, with Arnold." Ninety circles in the wood were counted outside of it, the precise number of years since Arnold's expedition up the Kennebec.

A happy woman! Is she not the very sparkle and sunshine of life? A woman who is happy because she cannot help it—whose smile even the coldest sprinkle of misfortune cannot dampen. Men make a terrible mistake when they marry for beauty, for talent, or for style; the sweetest wives are those who possess the magic secret of being contented under any circumstances. Rich or poor, high or low, it makes no difference, the bright little fountain of joy bubbles up just as musically in their hearts.

The ladies have for the past eighteen centuries enjoyed special privileges during leap year. In an ancient Saxon law it is enacted: "Albeit, as often as leape yeare dothe occure, the women holdeth prerogative over the menne in matters of courtship, love and matrimonee, so that when the ladie proposeth it shall not be lawful for the menne to say her nea, but shall receive her proposal in all good courtesie." Girls, this law is still in force.

A little nonsense now and then is a good thing. No sensible person doubts it. If he does he is a sheer nonsensical chap. We all need to unstring the bow occasionally. The face wasn't intended to grow in length merely, but to stretch itself sidewise, which in this case at least a wise side. The heart becomes dull and the circulation languid unless it is stirred by something light and cheerful. Here it is that nonsense comes in and does service. People who don't laugh sometimes—who don't have times for some, if not more, laughter—are to be avoided; in fact severely let alone in a hurry. The men or women who marry such will be likely to live in the shade all the rest of their days and be as miserable as circumstances will possibly allow—and they generally allow a very wide margin. Cultivate nonsense as you would a cardinal virtue. It comes in nice at times, and you can, if you will, have it come in, like your stewed oysters, when you want it.—*Louisville Journal.*

In the issue of November 30, 1895, appears this: "Transferred.—
With this issue of the Blade, the business of publication is transferred
to Messrs. E. H. Pulver and Alfred Orme, and the writer retires from
the editorial and business management. During the last eight years
the above named gentlemen have done nearly all of the literary work,
excepting the editorials, and they have furnished Blade readers with a
bright, newsy paper, and will continue to do so. They are young and
capable, and are practical printers . . . J. F. Gibbs."

The Blade, Saturday, December 7, 1895, shows Orme & Pulver,
publishers. But the next week, December 14, 1895, the partners were
reversed, evidently the other wishing to act as the lady, for the masthead is Pulver & Orme, publishers. And in a few issues, January 11,
1896, it became "Alf. Orme, publisher." The Blade of May 30, 1896,
carried this: "Notice to Our Patrons. For sometime past negotiations
have been pending towards the establishment of another newspaper for
the city of Nephi . . . After deliberating we have decided to transfer the
Blade plant over to the new concern."

"The Republic, for such is its name, will appear one week from
today. All news will be sent addressed to the Republic Publishing
Company, Nephi.—Alf. Orme." A copy of the Republic, August 29,
1896, volume 4, number 13, 5 columns, 8-pages, all home print, issued
Saturday morning, W. L. Roe, editor, $2, the Republic Publishing
Company, H. M. McCune, manager, says: "This is a silver paper," as
if the pictures of W. J. Bryan and long political news items didn't make
that fact obvious!

We are inclined to reprint here a short, short story from that
edition, revealing a warm flirtation of the Gay Nineties, and incidentally
showing (probably) a form of payment on subscription account. "That
was a merry crowd which hung quite familiarly over a box of grapes
at the U. P. Depot by moonlight the other night. In behalf of the
crowd we beg leave to thank the young lady from Provo, Miss B, for
them. They were luscious and the bright and sparkling eye of the donor
must have been wide awake when they were packed, for a more neat
and healthy collection of fruit has not been our lot to see."

The American Newspaper Directory for 1898: Republic, Saturday,
Independent, established 1893, 8-pages, 13 x 20, $2, circulation 700,
W. L. Roe, editor, Republic Publishing Company. On June 11, 1898,
the Brigham Bugler says: "The Nephi Republic has commenced its
third year." And the Utah County Democrat of November 23, 1898,
says: "Brothers Roe and Orme have again resumed editorial charge of
the Nephi Republic, after their election relapse." We found the Nephi
Republic quoted occasionally, as late as December 24, 1898, but it
evidently disappeared about that time.

"The Nephi Times last week admitted that its first editorial *never
seen* a proof reader," is from the Blade, Nephi, Saturday, March 28—
the first we hear of the Times, this being the first paper of that name in

Nephi. The Nephi Republic of August 29, 1896, carries this illuminating paragraph: " 'We are pleased to note that Editor Nelson of the
Miner, repudiates any connection whatever with that pin-hook concern
down at Nephi, classified by courtesy as a newspaper, and known as
the Times'. Friend Adams, we don't know whether you noticed this or
not, but we clipped it from the Eureka Democrat."

The following is from a column-length political editorial in the
Republic August 29, 1896. It is quoted only as it may reveal some
identities: "The editor of the Nephi Times has acknowledged and attempted to answer our editorial, and has—as we believed he would,
miserably failed to come up to our expectations. (A rare Hibernicism!)
. . . We really had great expectations . . . this editor whose mastodon
mind has been brought into play . . . If this man of might and valor
knew as much about grammar as an eight year old school boy . . . by
publishing that, Friend Adams, you have dispelled the idea."

Also in that issue is this borrowed item: "In order to correct any
misunderstanding in regard to the matter, we desire to state that the
editor of the Miner has no connection whatsoever with the Nephi Times.
Our connection with that paper was severed some three or four weeks
ago, and Mr. Henry Adams is sole editor and manager.—Tintic Miner."
Hard Times must have come to the Nephi Times, for we hear no more
about it.

The Juab County Republican was quoted by the Utah County
Democrat April 12, 1899. That is a brief and inadequate history, but
unfortunately, all we found. Those Democrats versus those Republicans!

The Nephi Record, Henry Adams, publisher; so says the Gazetteer
for 1900, but a copy of the Record in Mr. Orme's file for Friday, July
26, 1901, Vol. 12 No. 30 shows "J. T. Pyles, publisher." The Gazetteer
for 1903-4: "The Record, Nephi, J. L. Ewing, W. L. Cook." S. A. Kenner in Utah As It Is, 1904, says: "The Nephi Record was established in
1897. J. T. Pyles is manager and editor. Weekly, 5 column quarto, circulation 780." The Gazetteer for 1908-9 says: "The Record, Record
Publishing Company, T. L. Foote, editor, R. J. Henroid, Manager."
Alfred Orme informed us that E. Carroll and Swen B. Freed changed
the name of the Nephi Ensign to the Nephi Record, as he remembered
it.

Juab County Times. Nephi City, Utah, Vol. 1 No. 1, October 15,
1909, Jacob Coleman, editor and proprietor. Neutral and Independent.
"In taking over the Nephi Record, we wish to express our appreciation
of the splendid jobbing business built up by Mr. R. J. Henroid, as
manager of the Record . . . We are glad to announce that Mr. Henroid
has consented to be with the Times as manager of the printing and jobbing department." It was reported to us that J. M. Christensen purchased a half interest in the Times from Mr. Coleman in May, 1912, and
became editor. In 1913 A. B. Gibson (who had since 1909 at the age of
15 worked as printer), purchased Coleman's remaining half interest,

and became the paper's manager. The two operated it until April 1, 1917, when the paper was consolidated with

Nephi City News (which from meagre data available had been started May 1, 1916, by Dennis Wood and R. J. Henroid). The new paper was called

Times-News. Wood and Gibson were editor and manager, respectively, until January 1, 1926, when Gibson leased Wood's half interest, and became editor and publisher. On March 15, 1928, Gibson bought Wood out, becoming sole proprietor. He changed the paper to a 7 column sheet on January 1, 1930. Roy E. Gibson, A. B.'s younger brother, was associate editor from October 22, 1931; and on June 17, 1933, became editor, at the age of 21, being the youngest editor in the state. The Gibsons have continued in charge.

OGDEN, Weber County

Population: 1850, about 1,000; 1860, about 3,500; 1870, about 5,500; 1880, about 7,000; 1890, 14,889; 1900, 16,313; 1910, 25,580; 1920, 32,804; 1930, 40,272.

The (Salt Lake) Telegraph and Commercial Advertiser. First issue (in Ogden) May 11, 1869, T. B. H. Stenhouse, publisher. Daily and semi-weekly. Plant moved from Salt Lake City to Ogden Saturday, April 24, 1869. E. W. Tullidge in his History of Northern Utah, gives the story: "Brigham Young . . . had Mr. T. B. H. Stenhouse go to Ogden to publish his Daily Telegraph . . . Stenhouse . . . imagined that Brigham Young with a ruthless absolutism of will, designed to sequester him and his paper from Salt Lake City to Ogden, to leave the entire journalistic field to the Deseret News and George Q. Cannon, its editor. Such was the charge of both Mr. Stenhouse and his wife against President Young; but the reasons that Brigham gave our lamented friend, the journalist, at the time he gave him a journalistic mission to Ogden, was that Ogden was destined to be a great city in the future . . ."

"Stenhouse, having resolved to move to Ogden, yet not to resign his hold on Salt Lake journalism, decided that the first number of the Ogden Daily Telegraph should be published the morning after the laying of the last rail on the Promontory, and that it should contain a full account of the proceedings. Stenhouse shipped the presses and type by wagon. T. G. Odell, a printer of first class repute, who had worked on the London Times, was engaged as foreman, and he arranged the type and fixed up things, preparing for the arrival of the managers. The building in which the Ogden Telegraph was to be published, was the old Seventies' Hall.

"On the morning of the 8th, Webber, Jacques and Stenhouse went up to Ogden from Salt Lake City, in the stage. On the day of the laying of the last rail on the Promontory, Stenhouse was there to greet, at the celebration of the grand meeting of the Union Pacific and Central

Pacific Railroads, his brother correspondents, from the east and west. . . . Meantime, Webber and Jacques got the outside of the first number of the Ogden Telegraph up, and everything was waiting for the return of Stenhouse from Promontory, with his editorial notes on the laying of the last rail. The senior editor came in late at night; he was worn out with the events and bustle of the day."

A bound file of The Telegraph running from January 2, 1868 to July 3, 1869 is in the Salt Lake Tribune-Telegram Library. The May 11, 1869 number, first one with the Ogden date line, contained several stories occupying 6 columns, on the Golden Spike Celebration; no wonder Stenhouse was exhausted! In a report of the local celebration in Ogden, among the toasts given, we noticed "The two greatest events of the day,—the uniting of the Union Pacific and Central Pacific Railroads at the Promontory, and the issuing of the Salt Lake Telegraph at Ogden!"

Nevertheless, while there were two full pages of display advertising, from Chicago, San Francisco and Salt Lake City firms, there was not a single advertisement from Ogden. Thus Stenhouse, with obvious misgivings, addresses a statement: "To the Citizens of Ogden. We have brought the entire Telegraph newspaper establishment to this city. As in the past, so in the future, our efforts will be for the advancement of the best interests of the people of this Territory. This issue will be circulated everywhere throughout Ogden, and we trust that the inhabitants of this city and vicinity will accord us a generous support in our present enterprise. With a liberal subscription list we shall be successful in publishing a daily paper that will be a credit to the city and the Territory, but with a scant array of subscribers, it will be impossible for us to publish such a paper as the Telegraph aims to be."

May 13, 1869. "Main Street was alive yesterday. The Daily Telegraph, which for a few days previous had been eagerly expected, was scattered broadcast at an early hour, and its contents were hungrily devoured by its numerous admirers." Also "Greetings! Thanks to everybody who has given us a cheery word,—and that name is legion. Even from the City of the Saints we have already kind words of encouragement. The big-hearted 'John T.' sends us over the wire: 'The Telegraph from Ogden has arrived, brim-full of interesting news. Success to you, my boy!' We have heaps of others in the same vein, and rich in encouragement. Gentlemen, we thank you!"

When Brigham Young and his entourage paid a visit to Ogden, it was good for a laudatory editorial. Stenhouse had gone to pay his respects to the Mormon President, and had only words of praise and inspiration for the visit. We looked in vain through the Ogden series for a complaint, but Stenhouse did not squeal,—not once! On the contrary he evidently tried sincerely to make a "go" of the paper in Ogden, filling it with local news, and booming Ogden and the railroad incessantly. Echoes of the Golden Spike Celebration were published for several weeks, and the railroads always, every day, came in for the Lion's share of space.

On June 13, 1869, the readers were notified that Joseph Hall was going out into northern Utah settlements in quest of subscriptions, and asking that he be given a kind reception. But it was no good, apparently, for the issue of July 29, 1869, announced that, as the last number, to be published at Ogden, with a view of removing the establishment back to Salt Lake City, and re-commencing publication there as a morning newspaper. Tullidge later adds: "After the suspension of the publication in Ogden of the Salt Lake Daily Telegraph, which had given offense to the Ogden people in consequence of its not having changed its name, identifying it with the junction city, Weber County was again without a newspaper."

The Ogden Times planned, but never published. This paper might have antedated the Telegraph, we learn from the Salt Lake Telegraph, March 31, 1869. "We are glad to learn this morning from S. D. Megeath, Esquire, that the material for the Ogden Times, reported to have been dumped somewhere in Weber Canyon and there left, has been loaded up and by this time is probably at the switch near Taylor's Mill, in the vicinity of Ogden. Mr. Megeath told us that the material was unloaded because the car in which it was stowed ran off the track and tumbled down the bank. Another car was immediately telegraphed for, which duly arrived, within a few hours after the accident, and the material was again loaded up and sent on to destination.

"With the necessary material at Ogden and the arrival of the editor and proprietor of the Times from the East, which is daily expected, the good people of Ogden and residents of the nothern county generally, will soon have a live, wide-awake daily paper in full operation."

This does not square exactly with a history of the Ogden Press in the Ogden City Directory of 1883, by Frank J. Cannon and Leo Haefeli, which says: "It was with unfeigned pleasure that in the winter of 1868 our citizens heard that Mr. T. B. H. Stenhouse was intending to publish a newspaper in Ogden. But it was not his intention at that time to move to the city and publish the Daily and Semi-Weekly and Weekly Telegraph. It was the design of Mr. Stenhouse to issue a weekly journal to be called The Ogden Times. For this purpose he purchased press and material in the East, and when the temporary depot, or way-station was located at 'Taylor's Switch', Mr. Joseph Hall was dispatched to Wasatch to hunt up the freight car containing the material for The Times. But fate willed that the journal under that name should not receive birth in the Junction City. Mr. Hall succeeded in finding the freight and getting it released;—no easy task at that period of railroad rustlings. Delays however were frequent and lengthy. The winter rolled away. Spring set in, and the program of the Ogden Pioneer Press was changed."

On July 30, 1869, the day after the last issue of the Ogden imprint of The Salt Lake Telegraph, a correspondent of the Deseret News writes: "Although Ogden has lost The Daily Telegraph, that flourishing city

FREDERIC LOCKLEY
Born December 31, 1824
Died December 19, 1904

JOSIAH F. GIBBS
Born August 27, 1845
Died August 5, 1932

BYRON GROO
Born August 11, 1849
Died April 13, 1915

JAMES T. JAKEMAN
Born August 28, 1853
Died May 14, 1921

will immediately rejoice in a broad sheet of its own, to be owned and conducted by gentlemen of that city, and probably to bear the formerly talked of title: 'The Ogden Times'." Signed "Ursa."

Ogden Junction. Vol. 1 No. 1, January 1, 1870, Wednesday and Saturday, Ogden Junction Publishing Company, F. D. Richards, editor, C. W. Penrose, associate editor, Joseph Hall, city editor, James McGaw, business manager, with many of the other workers formerly employed on The Telegraph. File in L. D. S. Church Library, bound, Vol. 2, 1871. Ogden Standard Examiner Library, Vol. 10, 1879, Vol. 11, 1880 and Vol. 12, 1881. Bancroft Library, Vol. 8, June 6, 1877 to October 26, 1878.

The Salt Lake Herald had frequent occasion to quote or credit news items to the Junction; and on June 12, 1870 made partial payment thus: "The Junction is a spicy, readable, well-edited paper." Tullidge says that Penrose soon followed Richards as editor; and in the Salt Lake Herald, April 7, 1871, we find: "By the Ogden Junction of Wednesday, we note that Charles W. Penrose, Esquire, its editor, has also assumed the duties of business manager." The American Newspaper Directory for 1872 (data compiled in 1871), gives "Ogden Junction, semi-weekly, Wednesdays and Saturdays, 4 pages, size 21 x 28, subscription $5, established 1870, Charles W. Penrose, editor, Ogden Publishing Company, publishers, circulation 1100, the only paper published in Ogden."

The first battle is reported in the Salt Lake Herald, Sunday morning, July 28, 1872: "Yesterday afternoon, as C. W. Penrose, Esquire, editor of the Ogden Junction was proceeding down East Temple Street, he was hailed by some person walking behind him; and upon halting, was accosted by a pettifogging lawyer, named W. R. Keithly, who grabbed him by the coat collar and muttered with an oath, something about taking something back. Mr. Penrose, whose left hand was encumbered with a small box, demanded Keithly to take away his hand, at the same time disengaging himself from him. Keithly then drew back and struck Penrose a heavy blow with a can he carried, the blow taking effect on the cords of his neck behind the left ear, the force breaking off the head of the cane. This stunned Penrose, and rendered him measurably helpless. But the brute, not satisfied, struck him another heavy blow with the stick, across the left temple, this time breaking it in two, and leaving a rather ugly gash. . . . We understand that Keithly took umbrage at an article recently published in the Junction supposed to reflect on him." August 2, "Judge Clinton, after consultation, fined Keithly $100, who filed notice of an appeal."

The Herald goes on, with our available history, September 24, 1872: "The Ogden Junction daily is to hand. It is an evening paper . . . The Junction will now appear daily and semi-weekly." According to the Deseret News, the Junction editor was not only capable, but July 3, 1875, we are told: "C. W. Penrose, Esquire, the handsome editor of the Ogden Junction, showed his pleasant countenance in this office yesterday."

The American Newspaper Directory for 1875 says: "Ogden Junction, every morning, except Sunday, and semi-weekly Wednesdays and Saturdays, 8 pages, size daily 21 x 28, semi-weekly 24 x 36 inches, subscription, daily $8, semi-weekly $4, established 1870, Charles W. Penrose, editor, Ogden Publishing Company, publishers, circulation daily 717, semi-weekly 1572; only paper published at the junction of the U. P., C. P., U. C. and U. N. Railroads; largest circulation of any paper in northern Utah."

"Elder Penrose having returned from California, Bishop Johnson retires in good order from the editorial management of the Ogden Junction," says the Salt Lake Tribune, December 7, 1876. "The Ogden Junction has changed hands," says the Provo Enquirer, May 23, 1877; "Richard Ballantyne, Esquire, has purchased the material and interest." "The new hand at the bellows of the Ogden Junction is said to be Scipio A. Kenner, a former employee of the Tribune, but who has now returned to his first love," says the Tribune, June 7, 1877. And again June 15, 1877: "Scipio Africanus Kenner, of the little priesthood organ on the Weber. had no reply to make to the soft impeachment in yesterday's Tribune." (which was not seen).

"Africanus, of the Junction, one of Brigham's greatest and smoothest liars" . . . says the Tribune editor July 6, 1877; (The Tribune had said another thing, five years before, March 20, 1872: "One of Salt Lake's best read and enterprising young men left yesterday for Pioche, to take charge of the telegraph office at that place. In addition to being a telegraphist, Mr. Kenner is a first class printer.")

The masthead, semi-weekly, June 6, 1877: "Richard Ballantyne, manager and proprietor, C. W. Penrose, Editor." The paper was 5 columns, 8 pages, good news service and good advertising patronage, consisting of 12 columns out of 40. Contents largely lifted from the Daily. The Tribune says September 7, 1877: " 'If anybody wants to pay for the Junction in wood,' says Scipio, the renegade, 'now is the time for him to do so. Only a limited quantity is wanted.' The poor fellow wants enough to make himself a new head."

The Deseret News notes a visit from "Mr. S. A. Kenner, of the Ogden Junction," February 23, 1878; and a visit from "Richard Ballantyne, Esquire, publisher of the Ogden Junction," March 14, 1878. On August 16, 1878, the News says: "About To Move.—The Ogden Junction, which for some time has occupied a building on land belonging to the city, contemplates moving next Saturday into its own new building on Fourth Street. We wish our sprightly co-tem a pleasant sojourn in its new quarters." September 25, 1878, the News says: "The Ogden Junction has entered upon its 7th volume as a daily," and November 9, 1878, "Mr. Joseph A. West, of the Junction Printing Association, visited"; adding December 4, 1878, "The Ogden Junction with its new dress and 28 columns, makes its bow to the public this morning."

Sometime in 1878, the Junction tried a morning issue for only a few weeks, returning shortly to an evening paper. The Deseret News December 16, 1878, says: "We had a pleasant call this morning from Mr. S. A. Kenner, the efficient editor of the Ogden Junction." And December 23, 1878: "We were right glad this morning to shake the hand of Mr. Frank J. Cannon, our sometime co-laborer on the News, but since the advent of the Ogden Junction as a morning issue, one of the editors of that paper. Fatted calf we had none, but such as we had we gave a hearty welcome."

The American Newspaper Directory for 1878 says of the Junction: "Every evening except Sunday, and semi-weekly; daily 4 pages, semi-weekly 8 pages . . . Charles W. Penrose, editor, Ogden Publishing Company, publishers, circulation, daily 800, semi-weekly 1500 estimated." "The Ogden Junction, semi-weekly, is greatly enlarged and improved, and now makes a handsome folio," says the News January 18, 1879; and May 15, 1879: "Mr. S. A. Kenner, of the Junction . . . goes to Provo tomorrow, to report the Wilkerson execution, for his paper. Verily, where excitement is, there will the reporters be gathered together!"

From the News, August 9, 1879, **"Town and Stage.**—No. 9, Vol. 1 of this paper, and the first one bearing the double caption, came smiling into our sanctum this morning. It is a clearly printed, spicy little sheet, devoted to dramatics and sporting affairs, and from its brisk, lively style, is sure to 'take' and be taken. Its headquarters are at Ogden; its editor is S. A. Kenner, Esquire, of the Junction."

"A new paper.—Mr. Frank J. Cannon, of the Ogden Junction . . . will shortly go to Logan to take charge of the Leader, a weekly to be conducted in that city under the auspices of the Junction Printing Association," says the Deseret News August 21, 1879. The Ogden Directory for 1879 and 1880 says the Junction was being published by Richard Ballantyne, S. A. Kenner, editor, F. J. Cannon, assistant editor. An advertisement in the 1879-80 Gazetteer says the "Junction is Independent but not neutral; bold but not abusive; conservative but not timid; nobody's organ, but everybody's exponent." Sounds like Kenner.

"The beautiful but difficult drama of The Marble Heart is to be produced in Ogden next week, with Mr. S. A. Kenner, of the Junction, in the dual role of Phidias and Raphael," says the Deseret News January 15, 1880. In March, 1880, Mr. Leo Haefeli became editor, and George G. Taylor, city editor, continuing until the paper suspended. "We had the pleasure of meeting this morning, Leo Haefeli, Esquire, editor-in-chief of our esteemed co-temporary, the Ogden Junction," says the News, October 6, 1880. "He is accompanied by Mr. E. H. Anderson, also of the Junction." Of Mr. Haefeli, the Junction had said October 22, 1879, "The articles referred to (in the New York Staats Zeitung) are translations by Mr. L. Haefeli, a German scholar of considerable ability."

Looking back through the files, the Junction, under Editor and Business Manager Charles W. Penrose, was a splendid newspaper, running about 9 or 10 columns of advertisements out of 24. There were excellent editorials on a horizon-wide range of subjects, as well as an excellent local and state news service. The arrangement of the matter was neat and orderly, and a lively kaleidoscopy ran through its advertising columns. There was plenty of defense of the Church, its people and its tenets. It is no wonder Mr. Penrose was finally annexed to the Deseret News, for he was not only a loyal, intelligent church man, but a practical newspaper man as well, with the initiative and courage of a born leader. Long one, two and three-column letters from up and down state, entitled Editorial Correspondence and signed "C. W. P." indicate the editor and business manager was also country correspondent, much of the time.

The leading editorial January 11, 1879 entitled, "Enlarged and Improved" explains that the extra space will be filled with the choicest reading matter. "It is our intention to devote more space to the religious interests of our readers." On February 15, 1879, the Junction quotes and says: " 'Why pay $8, $10 and $12 for a daily paper,' says the Ogden Dispatch; that's what we say, $30 is too much these times." Also, March 29, 1879, " 'The first extra ever printed in the Territory, was issued by the Dispatch'; extras were issued in this Territory before the Dispatch man was born." This is from the Junction, July 9, 1879: " 'We always understood that S. A. was on the Junction. Are we misinformed?—or has he lost his grip, that he allows the Dispatch to come so boldly and declare themselves to be the only live, newsy, readable paper in Ogden.'—Beaver Chronicle. And now, if the B. C. (don't construe the abbreviation literally), will inform us what the above paragraph means, we will try to answer."

In the Valedictory, Wednesday, February 16, 1881, we read: "This number is the last issue of the Ogden Junction. This paper has run a fitful career for more than a decade, and for two years and a quarter the present company have endeavored to furnish the public of Ogden City and Weber County with an organ worthy of their appreciation and approbation. . . . It seems the dulness of the times paralyzed our friends in their efforts to help us to carry on the heavy load with which we were burdened. As we were willing to take work for glory, but unable to take glory for our sole pay, we have been compelled by the stagnation of business to retire from a field so unfruitful. . . . We hope that our friends will be able to lend their assistance to our prospective successor, the Weber County Herald, which we herewith recommend to the friendship of our patrons. The W. C. H. will be issued in about a month or six weeks. . . . Junction Printing Association." (The successor became instead, the Ogden Daily Herald.)

THE RIO VIRGEN TIMES

IS PUBLISHED, by

J. E. JOHNSON,

ST. GEORGE UTAH.

Wednesday September 2 1868,

TERMS:

Per Year,	$5.00	3 Months,	$2.00
6 Months,	3.00	Single copies,	25

Rates of Advertising:

A "square" is the space that 10 lines of type, this size, will occupy.

1 quare or less, one insertion,	$200
Each subsequuent insertion,	1.00

Fruit Growers Convention.

St George Gardeners Club Hall.

10 o clock A. M. Sat. Aug, 29 1868.

According to notic delegates from various towus and settlements met at the Hall, with fine spread of fruit covering the table

On motion, L. S Hemmenway was called to the chair—W. H. Branch elected secretary and Henry Eyring chaplain.

Convention opened by prayer.

J. E. Johnson briefly stated the object of the convention, to be for the advancement of fruit growing, to compare fruits, and experience, and organize a Rocky Mountain fruit growers Society.

On motion of J. E. Johnson.

Resolved, we organize such a Society—whereupon J. E. Johnson, W. H. Branch, J. W. Oakley, W, E, Dodge and A. Jackson were appointed a committee to report [illegible] ment of such association.

W. H. Crawford, John Moody, Joseph Birch, were appointed a committee to report permanent officers for this convention.

Fruit was then examined and discussed—Recess untill 2 o clock.

Afternoon session.

2 o clock P. M.

Committee on organization reported—President J. E. Johnson, vice President W E. Dodge, secretary W. H. Branch, Chaplain H. Eyring.

Report accepted and approved.

Committee on constitution and by laws reported the following.

Constitution.

1st. This Soceity shall be known as the Rocky Mountain Pomologial Society. whose aim shall be, advancement and improvement, in introducing, propagating and producing, all the most choice and useful fruits.

2nd The officers of said Society shall consist of a President Secretary, and Treasurer, and as many vice Presidents Assistant Secretaries and corresponding Secretaries as the Socsety may decide to elect.

3d It shall be the duty of the President to preside at all meetings of the Society, and in his absence, one of the vice Presidents shall take his place, the Secretary shall keep record of all proceedings and dicussions of the Society, the Treasurer shall collect and disburse the funds of the association, according to vote of the Society

4th By affirmation vote of a majority at any meeting any Citizen of this Territory or States and Tetritories adjoining, may become a member of this Society by paying the regular membership fee, and otherwise conformning to the rules and regulations of this Society, but no member shall be entitled to any advantages arising from membership, until the annual fee is paid.

5th The Society shall meet at such time and place as may be decided upon, at the last, previous, meeting, and the President or vice President, of the place indicated, shall make provisions for said meeting.

6th An annual convention shall be held at time and place agreed upon at the last previous convention, at which, the officers of the Society shall be elected exhibition of fruits made, and discussed, and new fruits named.

By Laws.

1 A member may be expelled for lack of intrest in the subject of Pomology.

2 Membership fees shall be used for incidental expenses

3 Assessments may be made for importations of rare or valuable trees vines and cuttings.

4 The Society shall procure a good Pomological library at the earliest practical period.

5 New fruits and those of doubtful identity to be brought forward to the meetings, that their merits may be discussed.

6 The corresponding Secretary shall open correspondence with the various prominent pomological associations on this continent, asking reciprocal favors, and journals of discussions &c.,

7 Annually membership fee $1,00. Life membership fee $10,00.

which was reread, ammended, and passed by articles and sections—and passed unammously.

Thirty names were then given for membership—It was then resolved that we proceed to the elections of officers by ballot, which was carried into effect, and resulted in the election of

J. E. Johnson President.
L S. Hemenway vice President.
W. H. Branch Secretary.
Henry Eyring Treasurer.
W. H. Crawford Cor Secretary,

and the following vice Presidents for the various towns and cities were elected viva voce—

For st. Thomas,	James Leathhead·
St. Joseph,	Thos. Day·
Santa Clara,	E. Bunker·
Washington,	Geo. Averatt·
Harrisburgh,	E. K. Fuller·
Toquerville,	John Nebeker.
Virgen City,	Nephi Johnson.
Rockville,	A. P. Winser.
Springdale,	A. L. Siler.
Duncans Retreat,	Wm. Martindale.
Kanara,	Bp. Roundy.
Bellview,	J. H. Johnson.
Harmony,	W. D. Pace.
Cedar City,	J. M. Higbee.
Parowan,	C. C. Pendleton:
Paragoonah,	Silas Smith.
Beaver,	J. Murdock:
Corn Creek,	C. King:
Minersville,	H. Rollins:
Meadow Creek,	Bro. Scott:
Fillmore,	J. Robertson jun:
Cedar Springs,	Bp Stevens:
Nephi,	Bro. Baxter:
[illegible]	[illegible]
Santaquin,	John Holliday:
Spring Lake Villa,	B. F. Johnson:
Payson,	J. Finlayson:
Spanish Fork,	Sam'l Cornaby:
Springville,	E. Whiting:
Provo,	Peter Stubbs:
Battle Creek,	H. Walker:
American Fork,	Bp Harrington:
Lehi,	Bp Evans:
Willow Creek,	J. Rollins:
Cottonwood,	S. Richards:
Salt Lake City,	Geo: B: Wallace.

Other cities and towns wishing vice Presidents, are requested to report to next convention·

Resolved that first local Meeting be held at this Hall on Sat 12 Sept Prox·

Resolved, that the Deseret News, and Salt Lake Telegraph be requested to published these proceedings.

Resolved that the thanks of his convention be tendered to the Gardeners Club, for the use of their comfortable Hall.

Fruits were now more thoroughly examined, tested and discussed—The show was very creditable and extensive and will be discribed elsewhere.

At 6 o clock.

On motion, Resolved to adjourn to meet at this place on the first Sat. in Sept 1869. at 10 o clock A. M.

J. E. Johnson Prest,
W· H. Branch Sec.

NOTICE !

The St. Geo. Gardeners club will hold their annual fair in their Hall, on Sat. the 12 Sep'ember.

Clubs from the various Settlements are invited to join in the exhibition, of fruits &c.

An exhibition of fruits and produce from Santa Clara is also solicited.

W. H. Branch·
Sec.

A-Peep At The Fruit Tables At The Fruit Growers Convention.

Tables through the center, the whole length of the Hall, were crowded with fruit, mingling in great variety Apples, Peaches, Plums, Pears, Figs, Grapes, Strawberries &c., it being too late in the season for all other berries Apricots Cherries, Nectarines &c., Apples—some specimens of Porter—20 oz—Gloria Mundi, Woodburys cluster, Seedlings &c, were large and fine.

PEACHES. Late Crawfords—Wards late free—Carrington, and several seedlings led in size, beauty, and flavor.

PLUMS.— The red Victoria, Green Gage, Magnum bonum, and a few late seedlings were all we had left, the crop being ripened and gone.

PEARS.--Rather early for pears--The Redfield, White Doyene, were among the finest specimens.

FIGS.—Several dishes of well ripened brown figs were on the table but a plate from the garden of Thos, Jeffreys, were very large, fine, and beyond competition. Crop of white figs all gone.

GRAPES,--There were over 30 varieties on exhibition--From the garden of J. E. Johnson over 20 sorts were represented, viz Black Hamburg, Old Mission, Israella, Isabella, White Muscatel, White Chasselas White Malga, Maxatawney, Concord, Canada Cheif, Black Cluster. White Raisin, Anna. Bow-wood Muscat, Muscat Hamburg, Royal Muscadine, Clinton, Royal Chasselas, Rio Virgen, (new) Jarvis, (new) large white grape (name unknown) and several interesting seedlings

L. S. Hemenway exhibited. golden and Red Chasselas—Chasselas mosque—Royal muscadine—Catawba, —Canada Cheif and Black Cluster.

One specimen of old Mission grown by B. F. Pendleton, was of very large size, several rare specimens by W. E. Dodge; very fine cluster of old mission by Jas. Keate. a splendid dish of late Crawford peaches from Bro Jeffreys and an assortment of fine fruits from Washington.

It is a matter of pride to us. that such a variety of choice, fine grown fruit, can be exaibited in a settlement the age of ours.. The tables were garnished with flowers and the walls festooned with fruit-laden vines and boughs of trees.

The meeting althegether was one of much interest

Great Fire!!

19 HOUSES BURNT DOWN

GREAT LOSS OF PROPERTY.

St. Joseph A. T.
Aug, 19th 1868.

Bro. E. Snow and J. W. Young

Yesterday between one and two o clock, P. M. a fire broke out in our place doing great damage burning up 19 houses and nearly all of the contents. It commenced on the east side of the Fort, at Bro O. P. Miles and Wm Streepers destroying every thing of theirs in their houses, also one wagon of Bro Streepers loaded with clothing flour &c., they saved nothing but what they had on. Bro Thomas and Billingsby lost all with the exceptions of their beds. Bro Farmer saved some little of his clothing, Bro Day lost house and some little of his things, he is absent on a trip to St. George, this is the number on the east side that sustained any loss. The meeting house is burned down. On the west line. Bros, Chaffin, Gibson Watt Cahoon, Ferguson and Moys are the losers, Bros, Chaffin Gibson Watt and Cahoon are left nearly entirely destitute, clothing flour, dishes and in fact everything with the exception of what they had on their backs, was consumed by the flames, Ferguson saved the most of his things, Moys lost nothing but his house. The amount of damage is great; several thousand dollars. Those who were in the best circumstances, are the greatest losers. The wind blew a stiff gale from the N. E. and every thing being dry it made quick work: only lasting about 30 or 35 minutes, All the men with the exception of two were out at work, consequently, could not render any assistance. Fortunately no lives were lost, it has left us in a critical condition some are moving out on their City lots, several of the brethern who are on visits north are heavy losers, Bros. Wiler, Pratt, Clayton, Rydalch and others have lost every thing. Cause of fire some small boys went out to make a fire to roast potatoes back of Bro Miles and Streepers houses.

Signed Alma H. Bennett.

News Sumary.

Immense monsters of great length and rapidity of motion have been seen in Bear Lake. An energetic fellow of inquiring mind has been purchasing ropes and tackle in Salt Lake City, to capture the *Sarpints. So says the Telegraph.*

A snake about 20 feet long and over 30 inches in circumference, with a head 20 inches broad, was captured and killed in Tennessee the other day.

It is said that monsters of the lizard spicies inhabit Lake Como, on the U. P. R. R,

The "Press on wheels" the office of the Frontier Index, has moved up to Green River, and issued first number in new locality. The Freeman boys keep moving to the tune of the whistling engine—keep rolling Legh, never mind the moss·

Hon W. H. Hooper has arrived at home in health and good spirits.

On the 16 inst, David Fisher was crushed to-death, by sliding of the earth in Weber Kanyon, while excava ing on the R. R.

Thirty seven deaths by measles among the Danish saints, on board the "Emerald Isle," occured on its passage.

Bishop Murdock was to arrive in the City with *his* Company on the 20th.

At the late election in Montana, the Democratic party was entirely successful carrying their ticket throughout.

Much intrest in silk growing, in California is being manifest. The movement the present season has been very active and entirely successful.

We have a climate equal to California and a soil that makes growth of the Italian mulberry very wonderful, and swarms of boys and girls just suited to a silk business—what shall hinder us from takeing hold of this business at once.

General G. M. Dodge, chief engineer of the U. P· R. R· with family and suit arrived in Salt Lake City a few days since.

Success to the General. we were old frontier neighbors and co-laborers for the great work of which he is engireer, years agone.

Local News.

THE GRASSHOPPERS after stopping with us 4 or 5 days, eating up our lucerne, carrot tops, leaves from our apple, and other trees, hoistd sail and bid us good bye—but a few remain. Some corn and cotton crops were slightly injured along the Clara. We wish them a very long and successful journey.

GONE WEST.—Prest· Snow, accompanied by engineer Burgon, started for the western settelments on friday last, to locate and survey some of the town *sites*, for settlers in that region.

LARGE PEACH—We picked a "Wards late free Peach" the other day that measured 11 inches in circumference and weighed ¾ of a lb—We should like to hear from any one in the Territory (or out) that can beat it.

GONE NORTH.—Bros. Joseph W. Young and R. Bentley started for the City a week ago last monday.

Bro. Calking is raising a nice frame building on Main Street.

RICE—We have a patch of rice now ripening, that is seeded *heavy*, and looks fine.

GRAPES,—The crop here is heavy, very good, and is now ripeuing off, The crop will be at least double that of last year.

WE WANT SOME WHEAT.—Will those of our Subscribers, who are in arrears, and who raised, and have thrashed their wheat have regard for our little ones, and bring us in some wheat—now—right off,—come now,—dont wait for us to call around for it

SUBSCRIBE NOW—Many of those who ought to support the Dixie Press, have excused themselves because they had nothing to pay. A rich harvest has blessed our

Courtesy H. L. Reid

whole region, and few can now longer make this excuse. We are publishing at present without any prospect of receiving one half of our current expenses—we must have a better support, or the denizens of our Dixie will be minus a local paper after the first volume is issued. If we publish longer it will be *for the pay*—It is disgraceful, to a community of this size, to allow an enterprise of this character to fail for want of necessary aid—The Times is the only paper printed within 350 miles and properly the local paper for five counties—via a Washington—Kane—Iron Beaver, and Pah Ute in Arazonia.

Valuable Recipe·

The Ohio Cultivator says the following recipet is worth $1,000 to every housekeeper:

Take one pound of sal soda, and half a pound of unslacked lime, put them in a galon of water and boil twenty minutes, let it stand till cool, then drain off and put in a small jar or jug. Soak your dirty cloths over night, or untill they are wet through, theu wring them out and rub on plenty of soap, and in one boiler of the clothes well covered with water add one teacup full of the washing fluid; boil half an hour briskly, then wash them thoroughly with one suds, rinse, and your cloths will look better than by the old way of washing twice before boiling. This is an invaluable recipet, and every poor tired woman should try it.

Wine Mill Coming.

A complete Wine Mill of large capacity was shipped to our care for St. George, via. U. P. R. R. on the 27.h of july—We are looking for it soon—on its arrival those who are ready may have their grapes changed to gushing—sparkling wine.

Young Folks' Corner

ENIGMA—No. 24.

I am composed of 7 letters.
My 1, 4, 6, 5, is an animal.
· 1, 5, 6, 3. 3, is a covering.
· 2, 5, 5, is to do wrong.
· 3, 4, 6, 1, valuable vegetation.
· 2, 6, 5, 4, is to burn.
· 4, 2, 2, is before,
· 5, 2, 4, 1, is used by weavers.
· 5, 6, 1, is a color.
· 5, 6, 3, 7, is agreeable.
· 6, 3, is a nickname.
· 7, 5, 4, 2, is a vegetable.
My whole is the name of a state in per spective.

SCRATCH

PRINTERS RABUS

WHAT C. O.

How did Adam get out of the garden of Eden? He was *snaked* out.

When war beef the highest?—When the cow jumped over the moon.

A conundrum which we all give up—LIFE.

Estray Notice.

131 Light red ox star in forehead hole in each ear appears to be torn or cut· cut also a slit in each ear S on right ribs little white under belly about 6 years old.

141 Red cow ox yoke and W. on left thigh appears to be G P slit in right ear upper bit left ear left horn broke off calf with her.

142 Red and white cow two white spots in forehead white on both shoulders hips and under belly tail mixed with white about 6 year old branded one left hip W. S.

153 Brindle heifer 18 months old, crop off right under bit left ear.

The owners are requested to prove property pay charges and take them away or they will be sold at the St. George estray pound on the 31th day of August 1868 at the St. George estray pound at 11.

131 Large red ox about 6 or 7 year old, swallow fork in right. crop of left ear, horn turns up, little white under belly

The owners are requested to prove property pay charges and take them away or they will be sold at the St. George estray pound on September 10. 1868.

John Pymm. Co. P. K.

ESTRAY NOTICE

1 Large red cow 6 or 7 years old, high horse; branded ⌒⌒ on left ribs, crop and slit in left, under bit right ears galf with her.

2 Roan stag, 18 months old.

3 Brown stag 18 months old, white belly and hunh of tail, little white on root of tail and on top of shoulders feet all white.

4 Brindle cow 4 years old, crop and slit in each ear, calf with her.

The owners are requested to prove property pay charges and take them away or they will be sold at the St. George estray pound on September 5th. 1868.

John Pymm Co. P. K.

Estray Notice.

5 Red cow about 5 years old, white in forehead and belly, spot on rump, brand supposed to be J.P. Crine on left horn.

6 Red cow, about 5 years old, brockle face, white belly some half tail white under half crop left ear calf with her.

7 Pale red cow about 5 years old, line back, white belly, q on left ribs under half crop left ear, crop and slit right ear, calf with her.

10 Red heifer, 2 years old, white on forehead some half tail white, white under belley, crop and slit right ear T on left shoulder·

11 Brindle bull, 3 year old, crop off right under bit in each ear.

12 Red yearling heifer, large swallow fork in right ear, due lap, calf with her.

13 Red steer 2 year old, crop off each ear. under bit in right, S on left thigh.

14 Red steer· white on both flanks, white spot on right and left shoulder, brockle face, white under belly, bush tail white, forehead on left hip, supposed to be W up-side-down, under half crop right ear swallow fork left.

The above stock if not claimed and damages paid, will be sold at the St. George Estray pound, on the 10th day of September. 1868

John Pymm. Co P. K.

Farm for Sale.

The undersigned have for sale 24 acre. of most excellent tillable land at Eaglesville suitable for any sort of grain an vegetables with house and in crop.

Also

Two houses with two rooms each, on go d lots in town, with Keasls, Yards, and Stables.

ALSO

Twelve acres of Hay land near by—are to be sold together or in parcels to suit purchasers.

Apply to the undersigned at Eagle-Ville. or to J. E. Johnson St, Center,
                  Joe Beecroft,
July 30 1868   C. Beecroft

Home Manufacture?

Let us use the Medicines that grow mid the Mountains and stop importation

I have a well fitted Laboratory for distilling Essentail oils and preparing extracts and invite all who have

MEDICINAL HERBS,

or roots, and those who discover new oilproducing, or otherwise valuable specimens

Of Botany,

to bring them to me and they shall be sat isfactorily rewarded.
                  J. E. Johnson.
St. Geo June 23, 1868.

Can Your Fruit.

Cans For Sale.

A few ince cans for sale. Inquire at the Times Office
St: George August 1868.

Lost Stock.

I have Stock scattered on the range between Cedar City and settlements on the Muddy; cows, heifers, steers and work oxen; all that is over 3 year old has a 5 inch circle brand on left shoulder with J inside, or branded on the horn J. E. J.—or G. W. J. or they may have both flesh and horn brands, and several are branded on the ribs, B. F. J.

Persons hunting cattle are requested to observe and report, any stock bearing such brands, or bring them in, they shall recive pay for their trouble   J. E. Johnson.

St· George May the 20th ,68.

Courtesy H. L. Reid

Ogden Daily Herald. Vol. 1, No. 1, May 2, 1881, evening issue, files, complete in Standard-Examiner Office. John Nicholson, Editor, Leo Haefeli, City Editor, Joseph Hall, Agent and Traveling Correspondent, E. H. Anderson, Business Manager, and Alma D. Chambers, Foreman.

The Herald says in its "Salutatory.—Ogden has for some time been without a newspaper of character, force, vigor and fairness . . . (and so forth, a column!)." "The Ogden Herald is out," says the Provo Enquirer May 7, 1881; "It is a good lively family newspaper— a 7 column Daily, the size of the late Junction, printed in clear, new type." Evidently called a "Daily," but the Deseret News August 20, 1881 says: "The Ogden *Daily* Herald comes regularly to hand three times a week at noon." Editor Nicholson's personal Valedictory appeared October 4, 1881, and his name was dropped from the masthead, with the next issue. The Standard Examiner file of the Herald is for the Daily only; but a copy in the Ogden Public Library for Wednesday, October 3, 1883, was: "Issued Wednesday and Saturday."—the usual semi-weekly accompaniment of a Daily.

The Nicholson-Anderson combination got on well. Those were good names for Ogden, but their successors, well; The Deseret News of March 29, 1884 tells us: "Leo Haefeli, Esquire, Editor of the Ogden Herald, was assaulted by A. R. Heyward, who struck the editor in the face, the alleged provocation being the parodising of Mr. Heyward's name into 'Heydude' in an item in the paper."

On March 22, 1885, Charles W. Hemenway, transferred to Ogden from the Provo Enquirer, becoming editor in chief of the Herald. This 24-year-old non-Mormon, fighting on the side of the Mormons, says in his book Memoirs of My Day, that within five months "the anti-Mormons of Ogden were somewhat demoralized, and did not hesitate to threaten his life (Hemenway writes in the third person), and even attempt to assault him at his place of residence and upon the highways." Hemenway's book was written during his year in jail "on the first floor, northwest corner, of the Ogden Court House." He explains that his enemies carried out the scheme of securing his conviction by an anti-Mormon jury composed of his deadly foes.

Mr. Hemenway records in touching language and tender spirit his abiding love for Miss Ireta Dixon of Payson, and of his brilliant marriage to his Mormon sweetheart on September 29, 1885, only five months before "a Federal Judge tore him from her and threw him in prison for a year!" It is not surprising, under the circumstances, that a chapter in the book is devoted to Miss Dixon, that the book is ever-so-affectionately dedicated to her, and that its only illustration is a picture of 'Ireta', as frontispiece.

Of his libel suits, Hemenway says he defended himself, while Joseph L. Rawlins prosecuted for the people. The first case grew out of "an editorial in which the opinion was expressed that U. S. Prosecuting Attorney, W. H. Dickson, U. S. Commissioner Wm. McKay, and other

Federal officers were pooling their fees. The second case was a suit against Hemenway and the Herald for $20,000 by Gen. Nathan Kimball, who happened to be foreman of the Federal Grand Jury, for an editorial statement "that the impecuniosity of the prosecuting witness, Gen. Kimball, rendered him susceptible to corruption,—a hasty statement . . . which no one regretted more than the defendant himself!"

In the final case Hemenway was accused of libel for charging that Chief Justice C. S. Zane had rendered "a crooked decision," in the case leading to the imprisonment of B. Y. Hampton. Hemenway's plea that "His Honor had rendered a crooked decision in accord with a crooked law" did not excuse the defendant, and was only one more evidence that he was a talented writer, but lacking the seasoning of age, some of which he slowly acquired in the genial company of Sheriff Belnap!

Hemenway's fine and costs, he says, were paid by "public contributions ranging from ten cents to ten dollars, and coming from all classes of people . . . who looked upon the editor as the innocent victim of circumstances." The prison sentence was at first suspended, and Hemenway continued to have the freedom of the Herald Editorial page, —until Ogden Hiles, presumably for cause, reopened the matter and on July 29, 1886, had young Hemenway put out-of-the-way—temporarily!

Hemenway's plight was reported at length in all the papers in the State, mostly with a friendly or sympathetic feeling; though a few anti-Mormon editors thought he got his just desserts.

The Herald said, July 16, 1887: "Next Monday evening, the Ogden Herald will not be issued, but on Tuesday, (July 19), this paper will make its first appearance as a Daily Morning Journal." The Ogden Morning Herald consisted of four 8-column pages. This note is from the Herald of September 25, 1887: "Frank A. Wilcox has been appointed Business Manager of the Ogden Herald Publishing Company". . . "To the Public.—Having accepted a place in the Editorial Department, I retire this day (September 15) from the business management of the Ogden Herald, a position which I have filled for more than six years since the organization of the Ogden Herald Publishing Company in May, 1881.—Edward H. Anderson."

But the jinx persisted and in the Herald Saturday, December 31, 1887, Frank J. Cannon, Editor, headlines "Farewell! With this issue, the Ogden Morning Herald suspends publication. The paper dies with the year; like the year which ends today, and that passes away where countless thousands have already gone, the paper will have a successor, whose life will begin with the dawning of 1888. The name of that successor to the Morning Herald, will be The Standard, to be issued by the Standard Publishing Company, which has purchased the business, all the stock, and good will, advertising patronage and circulation of this paper, and the Herald Publishing Company . . . To the public now, with its dying breath, the Morning Herald commends its only heir, the Standard, at the same time wishing its friends, its foes and all the world, Farewell!"

Tullidge tells us (History of Northern Utah): "No sooner had Frank J. Cannon taken editorial charge of the Ogden Herald (succeeding Hemenway) than both sides were made to comprehend that a Journalist had 'risen in Israel'. . . Like your true Journalist, Frank J. Cannon took the editorial sceptre which belonged to him, and shaped a policy and created a typical character for his paper. The very character of such a paper required a new and typical name; so 'the boy', evidently remembering his great father, as the founder of the Western Standard, (San Francisco) prevailed upon his company to change the name of The Ogden Herald to The Ogden Standard."

The Standard. Daily, Vol. 1, No. 1, January 1, 1888. Files complete in Standard-Examiner Offices. Beginning January 1, 1889, Frank J. Cannon, Editor. "The Ogden Standard reached us Tuesday in a changed form, enlarged from 4 to 8 pages," says the Eastern Utah Telegraph, Price, December 11, 1891. The 1892 Directories indicate the Daily was "8 pages, 15 x 24, $8, circulation 1500; Semi-Weekly Wednesday and Saturday $2.50, circulation 2000, Frank J. Cannon, Editor." But September 8, 1892 a masthead note says: "The editorial management of the Standard during the campaign will be in the hands of Mayor E. A. Littlefield. Frank J. Cannon, the founder, and for a long time the editor of the Standard, having received the nomination for Delegate in Congress at the hands of the Republican Party in Utah, has severed his connection with said paper, and with this issue I assume entire editorial control of its columns.—E. A. Littlefield." (But Littlefield's name did not go on the masthead, and on November 27, 1892, Frank J. Cannon's name was restored to the masthead).

"The Ogden Standard has made a new departure in journalism, and announces that they are agents for the anti-rust tinware, which they say is cheap at any price," according to the Manti Times-Reporter December 8, 1892. "Had they opened a brass foundry, there would have been nothing particularly surprising in the matter: but a tinware establishment is something new!'"

Gooseflesh crept over the Standard in the panic of '93, according to the Brigham Bugler February 25, 1893: "Ogden, the Graveyard of Western Journalism, permitted the light of its chief paper to go out Sunday. The Standard 'went busted'. The stingy patronage of the businessmen of that place, coupled with the tyrannical rule of a selfish, merciless Printer's Union did the work. The Standard was running behind a thousand dollars each month, yet the Union refused to reduce their prices for work, and thus help the paper out of the hole . . . Since the foregoing was written, the Standard came to life again; non-union printers pulled her out of the grave."

On November 26, 1893 comes this: "Farewell.—The undersigned has tendered his resignation as editor of the Standard to the Board of Directors. The reasons for this action are many, but none of them implies any lack of hope in the Standard's future (He had been elected to the U. S. Congress) . . . While this Farewell is voluntary and cheerfully uttered . . . Frank J. Cannon." No name is substituted, until November 9, 1894, when William Glasmann becomes editor and manager.

On April 13, 1896, the Standard runs this: "Evening Edition, William Glasmann, Editor and Publisher. With this issue the Standard will appear at least twice a day, and probably will, when occasion demands it, run off extra editions. In publishing the evening edition of the Standard, we have but one object in view; namely to maintain the Morning Standard . . . It is necessary, in order to take the full telegraphic dispatches." After William Glasmann's death, May 16, 1916, no name appeared on the masthead. The paper was combined with the Examiner, April 1, 1920 as the Standard-Examiner. (q. v.)

Ogden Freeman published by Legh R. and Mrs. Freeman. A reincarnation of the

Frontier Index, "the newspaper on wheels"; that is, on the construction trains and in temporary quarters at the moving terminus of the Union Pacific Railroad under construction in 1868-9. The story is probably best reviewed by Freeman himself, in the Ogden Freeman June 19, 1877. "Today the Freeman enters upon its third year in this place. Twenty-seven years ago the Mormon emigration left a portion of a printing office on Wood River in the then savage plains of Nebraska. This fell into our hands, and by some necessary additions made by the whittling process of jacknife, we began the publication of The Frontier Index in the Fort Kearney Garrison. After the U. P. railroad came along, our print became the advertising medium which built up ten of the terminal towns of that national artery of commerce. When we concluded to move from North Platte to Julesburg, our first side was set up dated Julesburg; we then packed and traveled by cars the hundred miles, stretched our tarpaulins on the greensward, and issued with local items of both towns, given in a sheet one side of which was printed in the forenoon, 100 miles from where the other side had been struck off in the evening.

"We issued in that garrison all winter (near Laramie), and when the townsite of Laramie was laid out, the Frontier Index Office and Frontier Hotel was the first building erected in the city. Up to the time of our removal from Laramie, we had worked harmoniously with the Town Lot Department of the Credit Mobilier, but in the three successive terminii (of the railroad) at the crossings of the Upper North Platte, Green River and Bear River, east, (near Evanston), the mountain people induced us to side with them in building independent towns. And to such an extent did they rally around our press, that the Credit Mobilier built no more towns until Corinne was reached. And it is generally conceded that had we moved into Ogden at the time the golden spike was driven in 1869, the population of Evanston and Corinne would have followed the infatuation diffused by their press.

"The fates however, destined otherwise, the statement of General Williamson, the Credit Mobilier Town Lot Agent, made in the Fort

Bridger Garrison November 19, 1868, to the effect that our paper would cease to exercise its magnetic influence in building rival towns, in less than twenty-four hours, was put into execution. The next morning at break of day, when several thousand graders, headed by the most villainous desperadoes, besieged the office, gutted and sacked it, and threatened to burn us in it, and would undoubtedly have left nothing but a greasespot of our mortal remains, had not a milk-white steed conveyed us to Fort Bridger, where we obtained troops, who arrested the leaders and held the town under martial law until the large gangs of men passed westward to the grading camps of Echo and Weber Canyon.

"Fifteen thousand dollars was the price paid to the leaders to do the deed. Forty-odd rioters are buried around the office. The only citizen killed in the melee was Steve Stokes, the husband of the woman that Affidavit Gilman afterward married. The last of the cutthroats has died with his boots on, and the ringleader had his head chopped off with an ax after he was dead. There is not today even a depot at the Credit Mobilier's town of Benton, while Fort Steele graces our river crossing at Brownsville (on North Platte River); Bryan named for our General Superintendent, Webster Snyder's son, is as good as abandoned, and the Division Shops moved to our old Green River City.

"And although Evanston lives, it breathes not half so easily or thriftily, as it would if her population and that of Hilliard were concentrated at the intermediate spot where repose the ashes of the Frontier Index. Not a lot was sold in Evanston, the entire winter of 1868-69, although some were given to some gangsters who moved back to our town . . . On this, the 27th birthday of our paper, we greet in the streets of Ogden, Jay Gould, Sidney Dillon, S. H. H. Clark and A. N. Towne, representatives of the reconstructed U. P. railroad . . . The Freeman hails the ascendant start of the white man, as the crescent of our enemy is on the wane."

It is necessary to go back, in order to fill in several useful paragraphs of contemporaneous history. Mrs. Freeman looked after the Index very largely, while her husband had a roving commission to go and do as he pleased. Strange as it may seem, after picking the sites for several present day Wyoming towns and even naming the State itself, Freeman chose to pick the "head of navigation" on the Colorado River, not far from the present Boulder Dam, for a new metropolis and shipping center. Consequently before the Pacific Railroad passed Cheyenne coming west, the Deseret News borrowed long dispatches from the Index written at St. Thomas, Arizona Territory, January 27, 1868 and one dated at "Freemansburg" Arizona, January 30, 1868.

"Today," one of them said, "We lay out and christen the town of Freemansburg, at the head of navigation on the Colorado River." This correspondence was signed "Legh," indicating the "lesser half" was there personally. Our Dixie Times, April 15, 1868, says: "The new power press for the Freemansburg paper has been ordered, and will

J. M. SJODAHL
Born November 29, 1853
Still Living

ANDREW JENSON
Born December 11, 1850
Still Living

The Mormon Tribune Building (1870), previously occupied by The Telegraph (1864-69), and afterward by The Review (1872). (Located about 33 W. First South Street.)

Courtesy John F. Bennett

soon be on the road to Arizona. It will be one of the most complete printing offices between Chicago and San Francisco.—Frontier Index."

June 8, 1868, the Desert News says: "Called.—Legh R. Freeman . . . Legh can lay claim to advancing the most sensible idea on states-manship that we have seen for some time, in raising the name of President Young as candidacy for the Presidency of the United States." According to the News, the Frontier Index for July 7th and August 4th were published at Laramie. The Daily Telegraph for July 20, 1868 quotes the Frontier Index of the 14th: "Today the passenger and the freight trains will run through to Brownsville, 100 miles west of Laramie, and Wells Fargo and Company stages will connect with them there." Referring again to the Frontier Index, the Salt Lake Telegraph, on August 31, 1868 says: "That spicy and vigorous sheet . . . will be at Green River City at an early date, when it will be issued daily."

The disappointment of the Salt Lake Daily Reporter is expressed September 12, 1868: "The Frontier Index says it is the mouthpiece of Wyoming Democracy. We were mistaken, badly mistaken, as everyone is likely to be occasionally. We had come to the conclusion that the Index was the entire butt end of the Democracy of Wyoming!"

From the Rio Virgin Times September 21, 1868: "The press on wheels, the office of the Frontier Index, has moved up to Green River and issued the first number in the new locality. The Freeman boys keep moving to the tune of the whistling engine. Keep rolling, Legh—Never mind the moss!"

The following item is from the Salt Lake Telegraph November 2, 1868: "Bear River City.—The Frontier Index of the 30th ult. was issued at Bear River City, about 85 miles east of this place (Salt Lake City). The editor speaks of the new city with the utmost enthusiasm, and says that 5000 persons already obtain their mail from the Bear River Post Office. . ."

"The cars are expected to run to Bear River before Christmas." Obviously the Index preceded the rails by wagon. The News of November 4, 1868, puts it: "The Frontier Index is at Bear River, and reaches us dated October 30. The new city at Bear River must be a lively place . . . We learn from A. W. Street, Esquire, our Postmaster, that Mr. Freeman, of the Frontier Index, has been appointed Postmaster of the Gilmer Post Office at Bear River East."

"Hanging.—By Western Union Telegraph Line. Bear River City, via Gilmer, November 12, 1868! Startling from Bear River!" screams the Salt Lake Daily Telegraph November 20, 1868.—"The telegraph informs us that a terrible state of affairs exists at the magic city of Bear River. Some 200 rioters have possession of the city; they have burnt down the offices of the Frontier Index and fears are entertained that the whole city will be destroyed. The muss arose from the action taken by the Vigilante Committee in hanging the three men on the 11th instant, and it is stated that the citizens have fired upon the rioters, killing 25 and wounding 60."

"A riot at Bear River. Salt Lake City, November 23, 1868, editor Salt Lake Telegraph . . . Mr. Freeman, the editor of the Index, was captured by the 'mob' composed entirely of Chesebrough and McGee's men, and threatened with instant death if he did not reveal the names of the Vigilantes who hung the 'friends' of the rioters. Mr. Freeman at once drew his 'iron', but found a dozen at his head and breast in a second. 'Hang him! Shoot him! Death to the Chief of the Vigs!' was rung in 'Horatio Vattel's' ears for five minutes. When he got the ear of Tom Smith, one of the leaders, Patsey Marley quieted the crowd, and attracted their attention for a moment, when Mr. Freeman made his escape through a saloon, and came out on Bear River Avenue.

"The mob became incensed at his escape, as also at my own, which occurred a few minutes previous, and at once began the search for us. By the assistance of Mr. Chesebrough, Patsey Marley and a few others, Mr. Freeman and myself were disguised and taken out of town. Mr. Freeman struck for Fort Bridger, and at once got troops dispatched to the number of 80. Altogether 14 men were killed, and 35 wounded . . . The printing office and jail will be rebuilt at once. Mr. Freeman has telegraphed to Chicago for a new press and 'outfit' generally. The Frontier Index will be on wheels again, in three weeks."

"The Frontier Phoenix," says the Salt Lake Telegraph December 9, 1868: "From private correspondence received from L. R. Freeman, proprietor of the late Frontier Index published at Bear River City, we learn that his ardor is unabated, and his pluck increasing. As regards his paper he says, 'the Institution shall rise, Phoenix-like, from her ashes, to still advocate the cause of right and truth, to denounce tricksters and mobocracy, uphold the good and faithful'; Mr. F. proposes locating on the U. P. railroad somewhere. F. K. Freeman is in New York, and has already procured a much larger and better outfit than the old one. As an original and lively journal, containing much valuable information, the Phoenix (late Index), will take its stand among the first of the mountain country. Its banners will be flung to the breeze in two weeks. Mr. Harris, the local editor and financier, will call upon our citizens in a few days for subscriptions and advertisements."

The Telegraph for December 16, 1868. "Bear River City.—Friend Freeman, of the Frontier Index that was, and the Frontier Phoenix that is to be, sends us a spicy letter . . . He particularly thinks that the civil authorities of this Territory should demand of the military at Fort Bridger, the ringleaders of the late riot at Bear River City, on the ground that although Bear River is in Wyoming Territory, it was once in Utah territory, and there is no practicable government in Wyoming." Later, here is the letter, dated December 10, 1868 . . . "We will soon be on wheels again, to rise as Phoenix from the white heat, under the name of the Frontier Phoenix. A few more weeks will find us hotter than red, in the vicinity of Ogden, to advocate the right and annihilate demons in sheep's clothing . . . Legh R. Freeman." Also the News for December 24, 1868: "Tom Smith, the leader of the riot was sent to the

Salt Lake Penitentiary . . . Part of the material of the Frontier Phoenix
is at Bryan City. The passenger trains are running to Evanston. Bear
River City is very quiet, but business is lively, considering the amount
of people moving out."

Freeman came to Fort Kearney just after the Civil War, according
to the statement of M. H. Sydenham, an acquaintance, writing in Root's
Overland Stage to California. "He had been an operator within the Confederate lines, and he and his brother were Democrats of the strongest
secessionist kind," says Sydenham. Regardless of the promise and effort made to raise the Frontier Phoenix on the ashpile of the Frontier
Index, the Phoenix only rose in Freeman's dreams, so far as we have
been able to ascertain. We gather this however, from the Salt Lake
Telegraph files, in the Salt Lake Public Library, dated April 20, 1869:
"In the city. Fred K. Freeman, Esquire, of Laramie City, formerly one
of the editors and proprietors of the Frontier Index. The other Mr. Freeman was 'Horatio Vattel', or 'the Scout of the Rocky Mountains', a
terrible writer and fiery orator, and somewhat immortalized at Bear
River in that outburst of popular indignation against rowdyism. Our
visitor is the other Mr. Freeman, a quiet, retiring gentleman, gathering
his laurels in the path of commerce."

The next we hear of the Freemans is in connection with the

Ogden Freeman. Vol. 1, No. 1, June 18, 1875. "Another paper at
Ogden," headlines the Deseret News June 3, 1875. "This morning we
were called upon by Mrs. A. Freeman, wife of L. R. Freeman . . . who it
will be remembered, was editor and proprietor of the Frontier Index.
Mrs. Freeman proposes publishing a semi-weekly paper in Ogden, to
be known as The Freeman. She will manage and edit it herself, until
the arrival of Mr. Freeman, who is at present residing in Wyoming
territory. She expects to issue the first number about the first of this
month."

The News follows June 19, 1875, with: "The first number of the
Ogden Freeman for June 18th, L. R. Freeman editor, Ada V. Freeman,
local, H. M. Bond, manager of the machine department, has come to
hand. The Freeman has a neat and newsy appearance, and is published
semi-weekly. The present number contains a page description of Ogden." (Tullidge's History of Northern Utah, says H. M. Bond came to
Utah in April, 1874, worked as a compositor on the Ogden Junction,
and in 1875 opened a job printing establishment, subsequently becoming partner with L. R. Freeman, in publishing the Ogden Freeman.)

Mrs. Freeman gets in the Salt Lake Tribune Thursday, July 29,
1875: "The editress of the Ogden Freeman says: 'Be it recorded as a
part of the history of Utah, that a Virginia born and bred lady came
to Utah unacquainted with a single soul, and within a period of six
weeks organized, established and conducted the Ogden Freeman; took
charge of two infant sons, and gave birth to a third, and in that time
was never censured, because her endeavors to assist her husband did
not accord with notions'.—Six weeks is a short time; it must have been

in the air, Sister!" The Tribune gives us another item August 8, 1875: "For its Jack-Mormon proclivities, the Ogden Freeman is slapped in the face by The Junction, and called the 'Bondsman'. Even Mormons are disgusted with their Jacks!"

The Deseret News, Wednesday, September 1, 1875, announces the split: "Ogden Freeman, August 31. The partnership between Messrs. Freeman and Bond, of the Ogden Freeman, is dissolved." The reader may make his own pun! The Utah Evening Mail, January 7, 1876, shakes a forefinger thus: "The superannuated school girl, who wears the ——, who presides in the sanctum of the Freeman, is complimentary to the Mail." And again on March 31, 1876: "On Wednesday night last (29th), Mr. Freeman, of the weekly paper published in his name at Ogden, had a business controversy with one Blyman, in the settlement of which he used a cudgel so freely as to leave some claret stains about the sanctum, and the head of his late traveling agent. Blyman tells a touching story of the rencontre, but when both sides of the dilemma are confronted, the dog may be of quite another color . . . After a partial examination yesterday before Justice Middleton, the case was continued until this morning, Freeman giving bail for $200."

The Ogden Freeman is quoted April 3, 1876: "Incarcerated In A Mormon Bastile.—Martial law needed in Utah. The priestcraft attempt to suppress the free press of Utah. An emissary armed with a deadly weapon assails the editor of the Freeman. Mormon priests commissioned as policemen—rush in and give no chance for a possibility of bail, but drag a man from a bed of protracted sickness at the dead hour of night. Warrant retained by the Mormon sheriff-priest for 18 hours, so as to preclude release on bail. Unmercifully forced through a howling, pelting snowstorm, to the private residence of a Mormon Chief Justice of the Peace, without being allowed a wrapping, a stimulant, or to attend to the wants of nature. A bilk, who has committed the highest crime known to the social laws of the Hebrews. A wife deserter, does the dirty assassin's work for the Mormons. The motive is to check the American influence of the Freeman, and to suppress the Press, which the Federal officials wish to make the organ of the Federal Government in Utah."

The Mail continues the story April 19, 1876: "The wearisome case of Blyman against Freeman, at Ogden . . . terminated yesterday . . . by fining the irresponsible Freeman $25 and costs. One of the principal peculiarities of the affair, was that Freeman, it was made to appear in the evidence for the defense, had for sometime past, coveted death itself; or had wanted to find some person silly enough to at least relieve him of what little brains he possessed by the use of powder and ball upon him; failing in which possibly he sought to be revenged upon Blyman, another poor imbecile like himself."

"Mr. Richards, the Prosecuting Attorney, is reported to have remarked in summing up the testimony, that 'Freeman could not play his insanity dodges on him'. Now we protest that if it was not a clear case of insanity under a legal construction, the defendant is not a bad showman in the maniac business. We think he ought to have been acquitted, and at once adjudged a fit subject for the insane asylum to be located on Antelope Island." The Mail on April 20 gives "An explanation (of the above) . . . And only when the paper goes to press, and the sheet is laid before him, does the supposed responsible (Senior) editor for the first time, see a large portion of the items. Such was the case yesterday, when an item referring to the recent difficulty between the editor of the Ogden Freeman and one of his employees . . . We assure the editor of the Freeman that the uncourteous allusions to him in that item are foreign to the spirit and intention of the Mail, and we regret the oversight and bad taste which placed them there." (and so forth, a half column to keep out of the toils himself!).

The Utah Evening Mail, May 17, 1876 says: "The Ogden Freeman comes to us on the half-shell. The half we failed to receive probably contains the reading matter." Also May 31, 1876: "Mrs. L. Freeman, of the Ogden Freeman, favored us with a visit this morning. This accomplished lady is ever a welcome visitor to the Mail sanctum."

The Evanston Age November 4, 1876 says: "A short time ago, the bilk who runs the Ogden Freeman, went over into the Sweetwater country to get subscribers for that contemptible sheet. By talking the people nearly to death, he succeeded in getting quite a number. At Camp Brown . . . the Post Trader had to order him out of his store . . . We noticed about 20 copies of the Ogden Freeman on the floor of the Post Office, . . . addressed to parties here, but they had seen all they wanted of it . . . not wishing to take a paper that was run by so low and contemptible a bilk as the soulless fraud who runs that dirty sheet."

The American Newspaper Directory for 1878: "Ogden City, Weber County, 6000 population . . . Ogden Freeman, semi-weekly Tuesdays and Fridays, Democratic, 4 pages, 24 x 35, subscription $4, established 1875, Mr. and Mrs. Legh R. Freeman, editors and publishers, circulation 2,650." Similar information appears in the Directories up to 1880 inclusive.

A bound file of the Freeman from September 5, 1876, Vol. 2, No. 23, to June 27, 1879, is in the Bancroft Library. It shows Frontier Index Series, Vol. 26, on Sept. 5, 1876, 7 columns, 4 pages. The paper was a strong Liberal Party organ, and had a fair advertising patronage. Every issue up to July 31, 1877, carries a half-page woodcut map of Wyoming, northeastern Utah and southeastern Idaho, evidently a resource map furnished by the railroad company which undoubtedly sponsored the Freemans up to that time, if not subsequently.

The rest of the paper was publicity matter. If it was unfavorable to the Mormons, it was news to Freeman. (How the Mormons must have herded together against the "wolves" of those days!) There was always an editorial squib on anything the Deseret News said. (The worst thing that could be said among the Gentile Press about one another, was that the other truckled to the Mormons.) Freeman traveled considerably,

SUBSCRIBE FOR THE CACTUS
Weekly and Enlarged.
ONLY $3.00 PER ANNUM !!
Every body should take it !!!
No. 1 of Volume 2 will be issued Saturday September 1st at the *Times* Office
Correspondence should be addressed
CACTUS,
St. George Utah.
SANGIOVANNI & Co.

DRUGS AND MEDICINE, at
JOHNSON'S DRUG STORE,
St. George, Utah, may be found a good Stock of well-assorted
DRUGS, MEDICINES, PERFUMERY, &c., the right kind of Medicines for the People, the Climate, and the Diseases of the Country.
Prescriptions put up with care, by an experienced Druggist.
Two doors above St. George Hall.

LOST HOOD!
PASSIFLORA !!
A few plants of the offine natural variety of this beautiful creeping vine, useful and ornamental—for sale at the propagating Gardens of
J. E. JOHNSON.

THE SATURDAY EVENING POST.
ENLARGED AND BEAUTIFIED.

TERMS.
1 copy, (and the large Premium Engraving) - - - - $2.50
4 copies - - - - - 6.00
8 " - - (and one gratis) - 10.00
8 " - - (and one gratis) - 12.00
One copy and Post and Lady's Friend, and Premium Engraving - - 4.00

Address, H. PETERSON & CO
319 WALNUT street Philadelphia

TO THE SAINTS IN DIXIE

Rome Georgia Nov. 21 '68.
Deseret News, requested to copy.

Wool Carding

Gasson Grimshaw,
Parowan 29 Apl, 1868,

Grain and Feed Store
The undersigned keeps constantly on hand a supply of
GRAIN,
FEED,
FLOUR,
MEAL,
CHOP FEED,
VEGETABLES
and other
Country Produce,
at Lowest Market Rates.
Teamsters and Emigrants supplied in any quantity.
Good Stabling and Krauls.
STOCK BOUGHT AND SOLD.
WM. LANG.
St. George, Jan. 15. 1868. 11f

FLOWERS!
I HAVE a few flowering shrubs, bulbs, and bedding plants for sale, viz.:
ROSES,
LILACS,
SPIREAS,
STOCKS,
VERBENAS,
PETUNIAS,
BLACKBERRY,
JAPAN LILIES,
WALL FLOWERS,
Snap-Dragons, Iris, Tuberoses, and many others; also a choice collection of Chinese Chrysanthemums.
J. E. JOHNSON.

BLANKS !! BLANKS !! BLANKS !!
For sale at the "Times Office" Blank Deeds, Bonds, Mortgages, Deeds of trust, Powers of attorney Bills of sale, Subpoenas, and many convenient and useful business blanks.
Blanks of any style printed to order on short notice.

C. WILKINSON,
WAGON AND CARRIAGE MAKER
A block and a half south of the Public Square, on Main Street. Good timber and work done well and with neatness and despatch.

S. G. HIGGINS,
ECLECTIC PHYSICIAN
Residence in the north part of the City, two blocks west of Clark's Tannery.

JAMES CRAGUN,
Joiner and Cabinet Maker, St. George will execute orders in his line with dispatch. 1f.

J. W NIXON,
Copper, Tin and Sheet Iron Worker, St. George, Utah. 1f

WHIPS AND LARIATS.
JOHN LARSEN,
St. George. All work in braiding, &c., done with dispatch. 1f

Nursery & Garden.
Many choice, and new varieties of grapes, both hardy and tender—New varieties of apples—Roses, & hardy varieties of Scrip.
FLOWERING SHRUBS!
Best varieties of
STRAWBERRIES,
GOOSEBERRIES, and
RASPBERRIES,
Also, at the "Times Office"
St. George Utah, Nov. 30, 1868.

LOANED!
A type line was borrowed some time ago, from my place. Will the person record the injure icns of Scrip iaic, and return before being exposed
J. E. Johnson.

McGEATH & Co.,
RECEIVE and FORWARD
GOODS of EVERY KIND
from the
TERMINUS of the U. P. R. R
To all Points in
COLORADO,
UTAH,
NEW MEXICO,
MONTANA,
AND IDAHO
Back Charges Paid
CHARGES REASONABLE !
REFER TO
BUSINESS MEN GENERALLY OF
DENVER
OMAHA or
SALT LAKE CITY.

RANCHING !
HAVING purchased of Mr. R M
Bair the undivided half of the Rancho known as Hamblin & Blair's, in Rancho Valley, and of Spring Valley, I solicit patronage of Dixie stock growers. Being brought by R Texes. I reach no better Rancho any one owns or ever saw north of Mason & Dixon's line.
3-1m WILLIAM MOODY.

BROOMS!
The Undersigned offers a superior article of double-wound wire fastened Brooms, at wholesale or retail; Grain and Produce received in payment.
ALSO
A CHOICE LOT OF
Fruit Trees,
good size and best varieties; also ornamental Trees and Shrubbery, and other plants.
Also a large lot of HARDY GRAPES, such as stand this northern climate, and fruit abundantly.
B. F. JOHNSON.
Spring Lake Villa, Utah.

DIXIE POTTERY.
I am now prepared to supply the Public with all sorts of
CROCKERY WARE.
I will take Corn, Wheat, Flour, Butter, Cheese, Onions, Cotton Yarn, Stumpey Cash or Lead in exchange. Potter instructed on the street running to Washington
1tf JOHN EARDLEY.

Fruit Trees !!
I have a choice collection of
FRUIT AND ORNAMENTAL
TREES,
of good size for transplanting, to EXCHANGE for GRAIN and other Produce; consisting of—
Apple, Pear Quince, Plum, Apricot, Peach, Cherry, Pomegranate, Almond, Catalpa's, Ailanthus, Honey Locust, Mulberry, &c.
Also some New, Choice, as well as Ordinary,
Native and Foreign Grapes.
Also, Flowering and Fruiting Shrubs, Strawberry Plants, Flowering Plants and Vines, House Plants, &c.
As the above stock is small, those desiring to purchase, should be in season.
J. E. JOHNSON, St George.

Tannery.
Brown and Allen,
Tanners & Curriers. Keep on hand a number one article of
Fine sole leather,
Cow-hide,
Kip, calf, & goat skin,
Harness Leather etc.
Which they offer to exchange for grain and other produce.
Parowan Utah Apl 20 1868.

VALUABLE
Family Medicines
Sold at the St. George Drug Store—
ESSENCE OF LIFE,
For Diarrhea, Cholera Morbus, Cholic, Whooping Cough, Pain in the teeth or face, and as a Soothing Cordi l for infants gives immediate relief.
CANKER SYRUP,
For Canker, Sore Mouth, or Ulcerous Humors.
NERVE AND BONE LINIMENT,
For Rheumatism and all diseases requiring outward application for Man or Beast. The very best Horse Liniment.
EYE SALVE,
For weak, inflamed or troublesome Eye Lids, Sore Eyes, &c.
TONIC PILLS,
Will cure the Ague, Chills and Intermittent Fevers immediately.
ALSO
Worm Medicines, Salves, Ointments for Itch, Piles, &c. Hive Syrup, Composition, Syrup Sarsaparilla, and most other popular Family Medicines.

Fancy Goods !!
W. D. JOHNSON,
South Temple St., Salt Lake City,
Keeps an extensive assortment of Fancy Goods, Toys, Confectionery, Books Medicines, Stationary and Yankee Notions, which he offers at the lowest market figures.
Look in—no charge for showing his Curiosities.

Rags, Rags !
Good clean Cotton and Linen Rags wanted at this office.

MATCHES!
Agency for Findlay's celebrated Matches, wholesale and retail, at
ST. GEORGE DRUG STORE

STRAYED!
Several cows, Oxen, and young Stock 2 years old branded E. J. on the horn and most all with a 8 inch circle with (1) inside on left shoulder—I will reward the finder.
St. George Apt.15 J. E. Johnson.

CRAWFORD HOUSE,
Washington. Utah. Travelers and Boarders accommodated with the best table comforts the market affords.
1 tf W. H. CRAWFORD.

COMPOUND
BONESET PILLS
Will cleanse the Blood, remove Billous Complaints, stimulate the Liver, relieve Dyspepsia, break up Billious and other Fevers, and in Headaches, drive away Flatulency and Loss of Appetite, help a Bad Cold, cure the Jaundice, and more to be the best family Pill in existence.
Sold at ST. GEORGE DRUG STORE
Money refunded when satisfaction is not given.

SOOTHING SYRUP!
A superior Medicine for Whooping Cough, Coughs, Colds, Hives, and all affections of the Throat, or Lungs; gives immediate relief—nothing better can be used.
Sold at St. George Drug Store

RIO
Vol. 1. —St. GEOR

Business Cards.

SEEDS, SEEDS!
For Sale, Seeds fresh and pure of most vegetables needed for the garden, and a choice collection of Flower Seeds
St. George Drug Store.

TO SURVEYORS.
A first-rate set of
SURVEYOR'S & ENGINEER'S INSTRUMENTS FOR SALE.
Inquire at the Times office.

Notary Public.
The undersigned will attend to the execution of Deeds, Bonds, Mortgages, Deeds of Trust, Powers of Attorney, Contracts, and all other Official Business required of a Notary Public.
Office—at "Rio Virgen Times" rooms, St. George.
J. E. JOHNSON, Notary Public.

TONSORIAL.
SHAVING, HAIR DRESSING, AND SHAMPOOING,
IN THE BEST STYLE, AT
C. KINGLEY'S
SHAVING SALOON
USE DOOR SOUTH OF PRINTING OFFICE

J. E. JOHNSON,
Auction and Commission Merchant, St. George, Utah.
Will receive and dispose of, as instructed, Goods, Wares, Merchandise, Grain Stock &c. upon liberal terms.

WHEELWRIGHT!
WAGONS made or repaired, and used Jobbing done on short notice at
1f ELMORE'S.

CANE MILL.
A pair of wrought iron Sorgum rollers for sale, inquire of
J. K. JOHNSON.

HOUSE PLANTS,
St. George Floral Gardens,
A nice collection of bedding & potting plants, for sale. Chrysanthemums Verbenas. Stocks. Pansies. Ice plant, Geraniums. Oleander. Petunias. and many other varieties.
J. E. Johnson.

Home Manufacture!
Let us use the Medicines that grow mid the Mountains and stop importation
I have a well stocked Laboratory for manufacturing Essential oils and preparing extracts and invite all who have
MEDICINAL HERBS,
or roots, and those who discover new oils, or otherwise valuable specimens
Of Botany,
to bring them to us and they shall be satisfactorily rewarded.
St. Geo. June 23, 1868. J. E. Johnson.

CROSBY & CLARK,
Tanners & Curriers
ST. GEORGE, UTAH.
10tf

S. M. BLAIR,
ATTORNEY AT LAW.
St. George, Utah Terr 1tf

Rio Virgen Times, St. George, January 20, 1869, p. 4 and first column from p. 1, February 3, 1869.

Courtesy H. L. Reid

but Mrs. Freeman could be depended on to ring true in the columns of the Freeman. What she didn't know about the Mormons, was unknown to Mrs. Grundy.

"Notice, To Printers: (November 3, 1876) We will sell a quarter, third, or half interest in the Ogden Freeman to a man who is capable of acting as foreman of the office, who is a job printer. The office is established on a healthy, paying basis, and is dependent on no ring, clique or party for support. Everybody reads the paper because it is made so lively, that they cannot help it. We have enough brand new newspaper material to publish a large morning daily . . . The Freeman is now a semi-weekly, circulation: Utah 1100, Wyoming 550, Montana 100, Idaho 175, Nevada 750, Nebraska 100, other territories 350, other states 300, total 2925." The above advertisement was run continuously until December 15, 1876.

Explaining its use of "Vol. 28," January 16, 1877: "We count from the time the Mormon emigration first started the office on Wood River in the Platte Valley, where the present editors came into possession of the paper. . . The defenders of our office at Bear River City, sent 40 ruffians to their doom and scattered them in 9 graveyards! The molten type metal between Hilliard and Evanston remains as a monument of the battles of a free press."

Freeman himself usually had a column or two of correspondence from Cheyenne or Boise,. or intermediate points, chiefly promotional, or railroad publicity. In this issue "Legh R. Freeman, Senior Editor of the Freeman, has gone on his canvassing trip through Idaho, by way of Gilmore & Saulsbury Stage Line." An enlightening paragraph appears April 3, 1877: "The Freeman named Wyoming Territory, published in five places in it, and has a larger circulation in that Territory than any paper published in it. The Freeman is regularly and persistently canvassed for by five routes, and has a larger circulation in Idaho than any paper published in Idaho; total circulation 3895."

The Editor's popularity may be indicated by a two-column news story beginning thus (April 3, 1877) "Attempted Murder—Postmaster N. J. Sharp seeks to assassinate the editor of the Freeman with an iron-shod bludgeon. He does it premeditately, after weeks and months of threatening. Dr. advances opinion that Mr. Freeman is liable to die from his injuries any time. The Mormon police defy the Deputy U. S. Marshal to arrest Sharp (and so forth)." (April 6, 1877) "Assassins Licensed To Attack With Deadly Weapons; No Murder Is Intended, If None Is Committed," and so on, one and one-fourth columns.

The wounded editor made a rapid comeback however, for the issue of April 10, 1877, contains one of Freeman's correspondence articles, dated at Sweetwater, Wyoming, instead of Valhalla, Kingdom Come. The editorials became a little more vitriolic, if possible. The editor slurs the Tribune constantly, as the "Tribilk." He may have envied the Tribune editor his ability to use worse language than he could command!

"August the First, our War Map will be out, (meaning the exploitation map), and we will begin the publication of the Daily Freeman," the editor tells the world May 25, 1877. He continues: "Drop off your surplus publications from other localities, and prepare for a first-class Daily sent out from the railroad center of the Inter-Mountains . . . All persons indebted to this office are requested to settle prior to August 1, as accounts of those still delinquent will be put in the courts for collection."

The publisher issued an occasional two-page 3 column supplement, half advertising. He also pulled down several avalanches on himself, by printing everything he heard, and some things that he only imagined. At that he printed a pretty good newspaper, with plenty of telegraphic and local news, though he was often heavy on the scissors. The editor appears to have turned against the railroad company in November, 1877.

The January 1, 1878 number gave 12 pages of boosting for Ogden, Utah and Nevada. On April 30, 1878 we read: "The Freeman will begin the publication of a Daily, containing the telegrams, as soon as our new fireproof building shall be completed; and it will rely on its own merits for sustenance, without the solicitation of any bonus or subsidy, and we pledge the people we will not beg, borrow or steal." And on July 19, 1878: "The Freeman being aggressive and progressive and Anti-Mormon, Anti-Chinese, Anti-Indian, and the only publication that is especially devoted to the news and the interests of the Inter-Mountains, has an established circulation among two millions of liberal spending Westerners, with whom it is the favorite!" This bombastic "brag" ran repeatedly, as late as September 13, 1878. There was no reference or indication of suspension in the last number in the Bancroft file, Friday, June 27, 1879. It was still a good newspaper, but it had been running weekly, instead of semi-weekly from Nov. 1, 1878; and we found no indication that the Daily was ever actually started.

A copy bound in the back of the volume is entitled "Ogden Daily Freeman, Vol. 1, No. 1, (corrected in lead pencil to No. 15), Saturday, December 9, 1876, (Frontier Index No. 26)." This appears to have been a sample, or a form held in readiness, for the day when the Daily could start. In it however, is the following, typical of Mr. Freeman's writing: "A year after we left Laramie with the Frontier Index, leading the vanguard of civilization westward, the (President U. S.) Grant ring at Washington sent out to Wyoming, Doc Hayford, as Auditor of the Territory . . . He started a paper called 'The Sentinel' . . . In course of time a lottery swindler named J. A. Pattee . . . Set up headquarters in Laramie. His printing patronage was worth, to Slack's & Hayford's offices, about $600 a week . . . Congress passed a law prohibiting the transportation of lottery printed matter through the mails. Then Pattee took a new dodge . . . offered for sale shares in immensely rich mines . . . thus greatly discouraging Wyoming by blighting her mining interests."

"Did Gizzardfoot Hayford, or Theodore Tilton Slack ever write, indite or print a word in defense in behalf of the people? No, never a syllable! With the local presses thus muzzled by the swindler's subsidies, the people appealed to the editor of the Freeman for justice! We rendered it! A series of well directed articles caused Pattee and his whole crew of clerks to pack their bags and baggage to ship to the East to return no more forever!"

A full page advertisement in the Ogden City Directory, 1878, says: The Ogden Freeman, established June, 1850, circulation in Utah, 1765, Nevada 550, New Mexico 150, Colorado 400, Arizona 325, Montana 443, Washington 397, Dakota 200, Wyoming 719, Idaho 981, Nebraska 120, British Columbia 75, Oregon 424, other states 300, total 6950; semi-weekly $4 per year in advance, address Mr. and Mrs. Legh R. Freeman." (They do not say whether the circulation figures are current, or are the accumulated circulation since June, 1850).

A better biographer may have been Frank J. Cannon, who with Leo Haefeli published the Ogden City and Weber County Directory for 1883, and included a chapter on The Press, from which the following is taken: "In the summer of 1875, Mr. Legh R. Freeman and wife arrived here, and commenced the publication of a semi-weekly paper bearing their own name, the Ogden Freeman. The first number was issued by the lady, Mrs. Ada V. Freeman. It was very conservative in tone and character. Indeed, Mrs. Freeman appeared desirous to conciliate the people of Ogden, and gain their good will. She succeeded to some extent, by her non-interference with the religious and social system of the citizens. But when Freeman arrived here, the policy of the paper was soon changed. He was a strong anti-Mormon—in fact was a sort of Wild Ishmaelite. His hand was soon turned against every man that he could not bulldoze, but he sometimes met with severe retaliation.

"Freeman was in continual hot water during the time he remained here, in consequence of his malignity, and abuse of many of the citizens. In 1879 he collapsed, and the same season he started with his family for Montana. While enroute, Mrs. Freeman was shot by the accidental discharge of some firearms. The wounds proved fatal. After severe suffering for a short time, she died."

Following the Freemans, with "hands across the mountains," the Ogden Junction of August 27, 1879 says: "From all indications, the Frontier Index is considered anything but a first class respectable journal, by the leading newspapers of Montana." It is our only evidence of the Freeman's new-old enterprise in Montana. But the Junction adds; September 24, 1879: "The Frontier Index and the Miner.—Two papers of Butte, Montana, complain of a lack of support, and hint of a probable collapse." Howsoever, the Logan Leader quotes from the Frontier Index of Butte City, on December 4, 1879, after which news is about as scarce as if "Freeman" were in bondage!

The Ogden Daily Herald, June 9, 1882 says: "Judge Galbraith has refused the order asking for restraining Legh R. Freeman from publishing a paper in Butte, under the name of 'Intermountain'. This puts Legh on his legs again." The Deseret News of August 14, 1882 says: "The Intermountain Publishing Company of Butte, Montana publish L. R. Freeman, formerly of Ogden, as a fraud, unworthy of being trusted." And the Logan Journal April 9, 1884 gives what must serve as an obituary, though it probably was not! "Two eminent journalists engaged in a knock-down . . . Col. Platt Burr . . . and Legh R. Freeman, of Butte."

A post script is added by the Salt Lake Evening Chornicle, Wednesday, April 16, 1884.—"That irrepressible rustler, Legh R. Freeman, has consolidated the Chronicle, Herald, Ogden Freeman, Inter-Mountain, Daily Labor Union, Atlantic and Union Freeman in one huge ten page journal called The Frontier Index, and finally stopped his 'press on wheels' at Thompson's Falls, a 'magic city' in the pine woods on the N. P. railway near the Coeur d'Alene mines . . ."

The Amateur, Organ of Mutual Improvement Association of Weber County, devoted to religious, literary and local intelligence; 4 columns, 8 pages. Joseph A. West, Managing Editor; R. A. Ballantyne, Business Manager. File, L. D. S. Church Library: Monday, July 1, 1878, Vol. 2, No. 3, published every Monday; file ends May 15, 1879. Vol. 2, No. 24, publication interval changed beginning July 1, 1878, to the 1st and 15th of every month. There were one or two pages of local and State news. It was no less a newspaper, and no more a religious periodical, than the Salt Lake City Deseret News; yet the glossy white paper and fine quality of printing make it much more a magazine than a newspaper.

On December 2, 1878, Joseph A. West resigns, and December 16, 1878, Austin C. Brown writes his Salutatory as Managing Editor: "It is with a degree of diffidence that I again appear before the public as editor of the Amateur . . . Not through choice, but because (the editorial duties) have been placed upon me." John L. Wilson became Business Manager January 1, 1879, and on May 15, 1879 Austin C. Brown writes this "Farewell! With this number the Amateur bids farewell for a season, to its readers and patrons, and the undersigned echoes the word as its editor . . ."

The same number carries this "Temporary Suspension.—The second volume of the Amateur closes with this number. We understand that the publication of a monthly magazine under the auspices of the Central Committee at Salt Lake City, is under contemplation. In view of this, it has been thought proper to suspend the publication of our paper, at least for the present, or until we ascertain definitely whether or not such a move will be made." See The Contributor, Salt Lake City.

Evening Dispatch, Daily except Sunday, Vol. 1, No. 1, January 1, 1879, Dispatch Publishing Company, F. B. Millard, Editor; Charles S. King, City Editor. "It was," according to Frank J. Cannon and Leo Haefeli in their Directory of 1883, "an Anti-Mormon sheet, and was of course opposed to the religion, politics and general policy of the Mormon leaders and community. In November of the same year, the Dispatch was sold to another company, consisting of Messrs. Bradford and Crowell. They engaged Honorable Marshall M. Brewster as Editor. After the journal changed hands, it did not live long, although it was more conservative than it had been, under the former management. It collapsed for lack of support."

The Deseret News, October 20, 1879, says: "The Ogden Walk.— The match closed on Saturday evening at 8 o'clock . . . In the young men's match . . . the cup was awarded to Mr. C. S. King, of the Dispatch, he having covered the greatest distance . . . 38 miles and 7 laps." And on December 16, 1879, "As promised, the Ogden Dispatch came out last evening greatly enlarged. It is now about the same size as the Junction."

Another item appears in the News December 22, 1879: "Editor Wanted.—The Ogden Dispatch wants a local editor. Now, where is that man who is always telling what he'd do if he was running a paper? Here's a chance for him to leave some high fingermarks on the walls of journalism!" Forthwith, the man rises up, according to the News of December 24, 1879: "Mr. M. C. Burke . . . assumes the post of local editor of the Dispatch." "Judge M. M. Brewster, editor of the Ogden Dispatch," called at the Deseret News Office January 17, 1880.

The Tribune sings the swan song for the Dispatch February 1, 1880: "The Ogden Dispatch, after a brief career in Zion, has ceased to exist, claiming that its enterprise was hardly appreciated by the citizens of the Junction City. The fact has been apparent to old newspaper men that the business was rather overdone in Ogden. We regret, however, that the field was not large enough to sustain the Dispatch."

"Weber County Chronicle," says the Ogden Junction, September 10, 1879, "Announces that it has been found necessary to change that journal from a daily to a semi-weekly." No files; no other references, probably too busy keeping the ragman from the door, to get itself quoted. Happy landing!

Morning Rustler. No. 1, January 1, 1880, no files. Frank J. Cannon and Leo Haefeli in their 1883 Directory tell us: "A small sheet . . . commenced . . . by the same editors who had published the defunct Dispatch. The local editor of that sheet, Mr. Charles King, was himself a 'rustler'. He was full of zeal, energy and vim. He was severe on immoral institutions, and gave such vivid pen pictures of several parties who it was charged, visited and supported houses of ill repute, that he incurred their wrath and the vengeance of some of them."

"The Rustler was a morning paper, and about midnight on the 22d of February, a party of masked ruffians entered the office, abused Mr. King, dragged him out into the darkness, tarred and feathered him,

SCIPIO A. KENNER
Born May 14, 1852
Died March 15, 1913

FRANK J. CANNON
Born January 25, 1859
Died July 26, 1933

MANSFIELD L. SNOW
Born September 8, 1866
Died October 27, 1923

DAN H. HILLMAN
Born May 29, 1867
Still Living

and then decamped. The parties who committed the dastardly deeds were known, although the misdemeanor could not be proved against them; but Charlie was not only a King but a hero and a martyr. The sympathies of all peaceable and law abiding people were with him. On March 15, 1880, the editors published their Valedictory. The Rustler rushed out of existence, and was seen no more."

The Tribune February 4, 1880, says: "The Ogden Rustler appears as an *evening* paper, since the death of the Dispatch." And February 7th: "Charlie King, of the Ogden Rustler, was in Zion yesterday. He inspected the new tar walk on Tribune Avenue, with considerable interest." Again March 16, 1880, the Tribune tells us: "The Ogden Rustler, after a brief and somewhat brilliant career, dipped its glim yesterday, making the third newspaper failure in that city in the past year." The Ogden Junction puts it, March 17, 1880: "Requiescat: The Rustler made its last appearance today. Its going down hill will not in all probability create such a vortex as will swamp its neighbors, though the event is rather on the sudden order. We have had no occasion to regret the Rustler's existence, and cannot either grieve or rejoice over its downfall. It was a type of journalism which fortunately is confined to the patronage of a few, and those few are anything but the best classes of people anywhere. Personally, we have no grievance with the publishers, and hope they will do better in all respects, hereafter."

The Tribune of May 28, 1880, says: "Mr. King, formerly a rustler on the late Ogden Rustler, came down last evening to take a foot in the walking match. His record is good, and he aspires to the championship." And the Ogden Junction of July 7, 1880, quotes the Logan Leader of July 2, 1880: "Mr. C. S. King paid the Leader Office a pleasant visit on Saturday. Mr. King, who was the hero of the 'tar and feather scrape' at the late Rustler Office in Ogden, is now on the U. & N. as a Route Agent, in the Mail Service."

Daily Pilot, March, 1881. According to Frank J. Cannon and Leo Haefeli's 1883 Directory: "Its initial number was issued early in March, 1881, by E. A. Littlefield, formerly editor and proprietor of the Post, Elko, Nevada. Quite a number of the leading firms in Ogden gave to the enterprise considerable subscription and advertising patronage, with the understanding that the policy of the journal would be non-interference. But the first number contained a vigorous and pronounced attack on the religious tenets of the majority of the citizens, so that they withdrew their patronage, and of course the institution suffered in consequence. Subsequently, Mr. Littlefield sold out to a company, he continuing to act as Business Manager. Instead of improving however, the tone of the paper continued to grow more abusive. Its own friends became disgusted, and the sheet was threatened with collapse. Recently the Pilot changed hands, and with the change, came also a change of temper. Its tone under the new regime is courteous and conciliatory. Mr. William N. Thompson is the Business Manager."

A leading editorial in the Ogden Herald July 13, 1881, starts out: "Scribbling Scavengers.—We have an apology to make to our numerous readers. Hitherto, we have entirely refrained from making the slightest allusion to the sickly sheet misnamed the Pilot, and which the Salt Lake Herald justly characterized as an abortion." (a column and a half more!) The Herald again, September 3, 1881, "The 'Local' of the Ogden Pilot has gone to Montana. It will be a good thing for the paper, if he would remain there.—Beaver Enterprise." The Provo Enquirer March 16, 1881, says: "A contraband sheet known as the 'Pirate' published in Ogden, steals items from this paper. It is a good exponent for the piratical gang that it is supposed to represent."

"We understand that Mr. E. A. Littlefield, of the Pilot, has been appointed Postmaster at Ogden City," says the Ogden Herald January 24, 1883. The leading editorial in the Deseret News January 29, 1883, is entitled: "A Simple Error vs. Willful Falsehood.—A few days ago, we departed from our usual course and noticed an attack upon one of the leading men of the Mormon Church made by an obscure anti-Mormon journal, which is lingering out a miserable existence at Ogden, under the name of the 'Pilot.' In order to acknowledge this, and set the matter right, it becomes necessary to pay a little more attention to the ribald and mendacious little Ogden Pirate . . ." (And he gives more than a column of his Cat-O'-Nine-Tails, displaying plenty of ability at a comeback in language that a pirate could understand!)

The Ogden Herald May 10, 1883, touches the subject again: "The Pilot is still sick from the sound spanking it got from its Aunt, the Salt Lake Tribune. Its 'seating capacity' is seriously affected." And October 23, 1883 the Herald follows with "Before Alderman Stratford appeared today, the Pilot Publishing Company, sued by A. P. Sharpstein, late editor of that paper, for wages, etc. Owing to a fatal flaw in the Constable's returns, the summons was quashed." Then on October 28: "The Justice's Court was occupied nearly all day with the case of A. P. Sharpstein versus Ogden Pilot, for balance due for wages, etc." The Herald informs us November 9, 1883, that: "Mr. J. W. Kinsley is the new editor of the Pilot. He has been in Ogden but a short time." Then January 3, 1884: "The management of the Pilot has changed hands, J. W. Kinsley succeeding William N. Thompson, resigned."

The Salt Lake Evening Chronicle of March 31, 1884 says: "It is rumored that the Ogden Pilot will change hands again in a few days." On April 12, 1884 the Deseret News says: "Saturday, the Ogden Pirate comes to hand with a 13 inch advertisement spread over its face looking for all the world like a circus poster. We ask the veracious circus poster's pardon for the comparison!"

The Utah exchanges left the Pilot so severely alone, we missed the most important item of all, until we picked it up December 1, 1884 in the Millennial Star: "The Ogden Pilot, a rank anti-Mormon paper, has collapsed."

Ogden News. "The Ogden Daily News, and Ogden Weekly News and Stock Journal, two new publications, are advertised to make their appearance very soon, by the News Printing & Publishing Association, the Daily to begin about February 23rd, and the Weekly and Stock Journal about March 7 . . . E. A. Littlefield, General Manager," says the Ogden Daily Herald February 10, 1885. Two days later the Deseret News adds: "We understand the Ogden Daily News will make its appearance the last of the month. It will be an evening paper." There are no files, and very few references were picked up.

The Logan Journal reports December 19, 1885: "The Ogden Daily News, an anti-Mormon paper, has lost from its editorial sanctum the noted Haefeli." And on January 23, 1886 the Park Mining Record speaks of "A. W. Millgate, City Editor, of the Ogden Daily News." The American Newspaper Directory listing 1886 says: "Evening, except Sundays . . . 22 x 31, 4 pages, circulation 400, 10 lines, one month $10." We found quotings from the News as late as October 25, 1886; also a reference to it, as if still running, June 18, 1887, but thenceforth it disappears into space.

Utah Daily Union, Vol. 1, No. 1, May 14, 1888, Marone Skeen, Manager, Union Publishing Company, Inc., according to the City Directory of 1890-91. The Logan Journal had said on May 6, 1888, "The Utah Daily Union is a new paper, which will appear in Ogden . . . with C. S. King as editor. In politics it will be a Liberal."

The Ogden Standard noticed the new paper May 15, 1888: "The Utah Daily Union is the name of a new paper issued in Ogden last night, with Charles S. King as editor. If the public will only do their share, there will be plenty of room in Ogden for an honest, high class, well conducted Evening Journal; and in the hope that the Union is to be such a paper, we bid it welcome to the newspaper field. Charlie is a hustler; he was formerly a 'rustler', but the name may have painful memories for him. He has interred his share of journalistic corpses, and has gained an experience which ought to be of value to himself and to the town."

Twelve copies of the Utah Daily Union between June 11 and June 30, 1888, are in the Bancroft Library; they show Charles S. King, editor, C. J. Pettee, Manager Mechanical Department, W. L. King, Manager Job Department, published by the Utah Daily Union Company. There were two pages of "boiler plate" out of four pages, 6 columns. Anti-Mormon.

Incidentally, the editor picks up the following from the Plattsmouth, Nebraska Herald, and publishes it June 18, 1888: "C. S. King, Editor of the Utah Daily Union, called on us this morning. Mr. King and Mr. C. J. Pettee, formerly of this office and city, are proprietors of the Utah Daily Union and Sunday Utah Times at Ogden. He reports that they are doing nicely. Mr. King is traveling with a handsome car, gotten up in Salt Lake City to advertise that city and Utah. This car is furnished very handsomely both inside and outside, and carries a sample of all the products and manufactured articles of Utah, and Mr. King represents the City of Ogden. He left this morning for Cincinnati."

"The Ogden Daily Union came out on Wednesday in a red dress— our co-tem's joy over the American victory in the Municipal Election," says the Park Record, February 16, 1889.

They say a King can do no wrong, but this one could certainly walk straighter into trouble than most of them. The Standard, December 1, 1889, takes the following from The Union, adding its own comment: "Wrong Record.—Ogden City, November 27, 1889. The article which appeared in the Daily Union of Tuesday Evening, November 26, 1889, under the caption of 'A Family Record', so far as it refers to Edward W. Exum, of Ogden City, or to any member of his family, or to any other person whomsoever, is false, untrue, libelous in every particular, and I hereby retract and regret its publication, and make this apology, for publishing the same. The item in the Daily Union of the above date to the effect that Mr. Exum had welcomed a new arrival to his home and hearthstone, is also false.—C. S. King, Editor."

"In explanation of the above statement, I will say that the absolute denial of the husband, when he refers to Doctors Condon and Powers, the attending physicians, will be accepted as satisfactory authority.—K." The Standard adds: "Exum wrote the retraction and forced King to sign and publish it, but 'the latter part of the statement was considered by the majority of those who read it, to serve the purpose of a repetition of the former article containing the scandal.' Exum met King on the street about 3:30 P. M. Saturday, November 30, 1889, and after a brief colloquy, shot King in the throat, and as King ran, in the leg."

The next morning, December 1, 1889, the Standard said editorially: "An infamy and a crime . . . During the term covered by Mr. King's residence in Ogden, he has been distinguished for the energy he has exerted, in the face of all obstacles, to win success for his newspaper ventures. His labor has been tireless, his hope undaunted, his life self-abnegating. These are good qualities in any man, and lend a dignity to almost any cause, but in King they have been marred by an unholy zeal for sensation, an unconquerable readiness to engage in personalities, and a species of vindictive bravado calculated to estrange his own friends, and render furious those against whom his attacks were directed. Whether from the innate love of fighting, or from credulousness in believing all that the busy tongue of rumor repeated, and lack of judgment in publishing whatever came to his ears—certain it is that as an editor his path has not been a peaceful one, though it has been one of his own choosing . . ."

The beginning of the ending was picked up away down in Manti, in the Home Sentinel December 5, 1889: "They Rend Each Other.— Charles King, Editor of the Daily Union (Gentile, Ogden), was shot

THE CACTUS.

Vol. 4.   St. George, Utah, October 3, 1868.   No. 3.

posed to have been tarnished
by exposure, was overlaid
with a poultice composed of
boiled flour, spread on with
the fingers.

Poppæan unguents sealed
the lips, and the lady was
profusely rubbed with Corona
ointment. In the morning, the
poultice and unguents were
washed off, a bath of asses
milk imparted a delicate
whiteness to the skin, and
the pale face was freshened
and revived with enamel. The
full eyelids, which the Roman
lady still knows so well how
to use, now suddenly raising
them to reveal a glance of
surprise or of melting tender-
ness, now letting them droop
like a veil over the lustrous
eyes,—the full rounded eyelids were coloured within,
and a needle, dipped in jetty
dye, gave length to the eye-
brows. The forehead was en-
circled by a wreath, or fillet,
fastened in the luxuriant hair,
which rose in front in a pyr-
amidal pile, formed of successive ranges of curls, giving the appearance of more
than ordinary height.

I CAN'T
MAKE UP MY MIND.

O, would I were a married man,
My spouse all full of glee;
A smiling partner by my side,
And children round my knee.
The cause why I'm a bachelor
Not hard it is to find;
The fact is that I really can't—
I can't make up my mind!

There's Juliana Lillywhite,
I know that she would drop
Into my loving arms; if I
Would the question "pop,"
With Carry Cowslip, too, I
should
No difficulty find;
She always looks so very kind,
But I—I can't make up my mind!

There's Angelina Marigold,
Who would with me elope,
If to her window I would fix
A ladder made of rope!
She's gentle and she's beautiful,
Her purse is richly lined;
And she'd have me in spite of
'pa, but I—
I can't make up my mind!
Now, when I walk along the
street,
Girls, roguish looks I catch,
As with a sneer they say "There
goes
A rusty fusty-fusty bach!'
Well I'll resolve this very day
Some sort of wife to find—
I'd wed—I think I will—O dear,
I can't make up my mind!

Tithing Office Cat.

If you were ever at the
Tithing Office, perhaps a
small, scrawny, black and
white spotted cat might have
drawn your attention by its
mewing in a very pitiful
manner, as much as to say,
have you anything besides
green peaches for a starving
creature like me, that has
been feasting on the prospects
of what may be brought in at
some future time?

A pulpit has lately been
invented by an ingenious Yankee down east; in such a
manner that when a preacher
becomes tedious, any person
in the congregation can touch
a spring, which is attached to
the seat, and let him down
into a cellar. Very good plan
that; we know where one is
needed.

Our readers will, not doubt
be pleased to learn that the
Cactus, like our soil, has
succeeded in ridding itself
of the Miasma, which has
heretofore, been such a drawback on the new comer.

MY NEIGHBOR'S WIFE.

We are taught to love, from
childhood's years,
'Twas stamped upon my mind;
My earliest article of faith
Was love for human kind;
To love my neighbor as myself,
I Christian like they say,
And if I love my neighbor's wife,
How can I help it, pray?

The Golden rule I strive to heed
Wherever I may be,
And do to others as I would
That they should do to me;
And so one day I tho't 'twere
well
If I this precept tried,
And, filled with generous
thought, I took
My neighbor's wife to ride.

But ah! this kind and simple act
Gave rise to slanders high;
A host of furious tongues as-
sailed
My neighbor's wife and I.
We're taught to share with
liberal hearts
The blessings that we prize—
To smile with others when they
smile,
And dry the mourner's eyes.

And when one day I chanced
to find
My neighbor's wife in tears,
I whispered words of sympathy
Within her listening ear,
I drew her trembling form to
mine
And kissed her tears away;
The act was seen: and lo! there
was
The very deuce to pay.

Alas! alas! 'tis passing strange—
I'm sure I can't see through
it,
I'm told to love with all my
heart,
And blamed because I do it;
The precept that I learned in
youth,
Will cling to me through life;
I try to love my neighbor, and
I'm sure I love his wife.

BULLY FOR HER.—The fol-
lowing is from the Georgetown "Miner. It is too good to
be lost.

Noise! Frank S. Butler advertises me as having left his
bed and board; this is a mistake, as I own the bed and
took it with me.

Melvina Butler

Our Devil having heard
that Messrs Carpenter and
Packer were nightly astonish-
ing the youth of this city, with
the wonders of their magic
lantern, concluded to pay
them a visit on Friday evening the 25th ult., but some
misunderstanding between the
proprietors prevented the
"show" from coming off, and
promoted "Our Devil" from
a spectator to a partner; and
now the "shebang" is run by
"Our Imp" and Carpenter,
Packer having withdrawn.

"Our Devil" informs us
confidentially that it is their
intention to give one or more
entertainments next week,
provided the big boys don't
interfere.

Hunkydunk vs. Calfalbite.

Much has been said and written about "Kanites" but whoever heard of the Canbites?
Yet Calfalbites are numerous.
They are a different "species"
but the same "Genus" of the
Hunkies: what the Hunkies
are to the country, the Calfalbites are to the Town: who
are they? what are they? Have
you a neighbor who insists on
raising a calf (or calves) to
coax his cow (or cows) home
to save the expense of a
herd bill (or bills) and keeps
that calf (or calves) fat on
a drop (or drops) of milk and
the produce of his neighbor's
garden? Well that is a
"Calfalbite." These juvenile
Bovines, when the maternal
progenitor is carefully driven
off to a distant range (of
garden) are turned loose into the Street with the in-
junction to "steal or starve"
and having a decided ob-
jection to the latter they
kindly take to the stealing. A
gate ajar, a bar accidentally
down, a small opening in
some unobserved part of the
fence, affords the opportunity quickly improved by the
intruder, and the young
thieves improve by training,
so these soon learn to enter-
pen gates and let down bars,
creep under and squeeze
through fences, and the 'Calfalbite diurnally rejoice at
their calf (or calves) some nigh-
ly home filled, stuffed, and
groaning from his neighbor's
"truck" patch. Which is he
worst, the Hunly or the
Calphalbites? Echo answers,
which!

THE CACTUS

When we commenced this volume we did not intend publishing the Telegram but as they are new offered to us at liberal rates, we take it upon ourselves to publish them. A few of our friends have already contributed toward helping us in this enterprise and if some more will give their names, we will promise to give them Telegraphic dispatches weekly, making the Cactus eight days ahead of Salt Lake papers.

Description Of St. George.

St. George is a flourishing little town with a population of two thousand, situated about one mile and a half north of the junction of the Rio Virgen and Santa Clara rivers, bounded on east and west by a table-top mountains composed of volcanic matter; on the back ground may be seen a mountain of red sand-stone in a state of decomposition. The city lies at our feet of an acre in size, generally adorned with fine gardens, and are watered by a small spring-creek which takes its rise at the base of the sand-stone mountain.

Naturally, this country is a desert, with only here and there a patch of grass where a few head of stock may be grazed. The Cactus plant is

found in all its variations together with the Masquit and other shrubbery. The soil is of a sandy loam of various hues, from red to black, and more or less impregnated with salts and alkali.

The climate is one of the most beautiful and salubrious, winters are light with but very little snow.

With much labor, the grape, fig, pomegranate, nectarine, peach, apple, plum and other varieties have been grown to perfection and in abundance. Wheat, corn and cotton may be reckoned a sure crop.

News Items.

It is all "gathe" likely that the "Iron house" will be heard snoring at the mouth of Echo Canyon the present winter.

EAST RIVER CITY.—The Provo Index of the 5th proximo, was issued at Bear River City, about 85 miles east of Salt Lake City.

The Deseret University reports that 10,000 each of the 1st and 2nd Readers, the 1st and 2nd Alphabet have been received.

INDIANS STEALING.

A short time ago the Indians made a raid on the ranch of Mr. Allen at the Elk Horn springs between Parowan and Beaver, ran off five head of horses. The next day Mr. Allen and a few men followed them alone to the head of Cottonwood Pass where he came up to them, two in number, captured, killed one of them, captured his horses and returned in safety.

LOCAL.

GENERAL DRILL.

1st Day. From 1 p.m. until evening the Brigade was busy making camp on the hill above St. George. Captain Copan's company of cavalry was the first on the ground. The Stars and Stripes were soon hoisted at the different camps.

Captain Staheli's Brass Band made the mountains "ring" with their music. The camp has been named Camp Bentley.

2nd. Day. The forenoon was occupied in drilling both Cavalry and Infantry and Capt. D. Milne's company of artillery, just organized, which made a fine appearance. In the afternoon a review and inspection of arms took place. We believe that the whole command was generally in fine condition.

3rd. Day. The most part of the forenoon was occupied by a Cavalry skirmish, their evolutions being very creditable to both officers and men. The Brigade formed into a hollow square when a speech was delivered by Gen. E. Snow; in the mean time they were dismissed by Gen. ..., struck and all returned to St. George to attend Conference.

We will here observe that Captain Copan deserves great praise for the good military discipline he displayed in breaking camp, keeping all

company together. Several wagons in their place, and escort, or ing Capt. Milne's Company of artillery to the Public Square.

Prest. E. Snow returned from up the river last monday evening.

Our Semi-annual Conference commenced yesterday at 2 p.m.

A nice gentle shower of rain fell early this morning.

Arrived.

Bros. Aroe. Hale, John Gillespie, A. W. Sabin, D. H. Lenard, and Wm Rydalch of Tooele County, arrived on the 17th inst, all in fine spirits and teams looking well.

They are among the advance guard of the aristocratic class traveled to go to the muddy.

FÜR DIE SCHWEIZER.

Am 18ten. sagen von allen seiten die Miliz in das Lager von St. George worunter die Schweizer auch nicht fehlen. Im Lager selbst wohte die Amerikanische Flagge stolz empor, alles schien lebhaft und munter die neue kriegerische Experiment zu betreiben.

Den 19ten wurde ziemlich streng exerziert und viele neue Einteilungen getroffen, nebst im Betrupp an von O. ... mor, nach die Schweizer Liederkreis, Musik von Louis Clark wurde der Stabe Musik bestimmt, Georg Staheli als ihren Cantain und zugleich Direktor der Musik und der gute sein soll es gefreht verde um man noil ...

Nach auf haben die Lagers bewegten sich Militärischen Truppen in die Stadt zu die Conference seinen Anfang nahm.

We regret not being able to furnish our readers with the Telegraphic news as we anticipated, and offer the following

as an excuse;—

St. George November 20 1868
8 20 p.m.

Editor Cactus,
The Telegraph line being out of repair between here and Salt Lake City this evening we are unable to furnish you the news as per arrangment.
Operator.

While walking down main street we noticed the side-walk between the St. George Hill and the Tithing Office very much out of repair. Perhaps another wheelbarrow load of "old barrels and adobies" would unmake it possible.

Are we to become like the roving red man of the desert and resort to hunting the deer for the purpose of obtaining buckskins wherewith to make moccasins? or are we to stir ourselves and establish more tanneries and invite some shoe-makers to come and start business, that we may not have to wait until our feet are worn off up to our knees before we can get a pair of boots. There is work enough in St. George to support one dozen shoemakers.

Can there not be a move made to comfort our propellers?

Our Devil being of a queer turn of mind lumbered his gloria by walking up to the Militia encampment. While there he noticed a gentleman (quite a nobleman) invite our former Editor to go into the Public Square for the purpose of giving him a nice whipping, but the Editor was to cutting, but he advised me to keep the editors know it.

AN IMPORTANT QUESTION!

Who built Bassett & Roberts' Store!

TO QUICK FOR HIM.

A young New England Clergyman riding in the cars between Springfield and Pitts-

Bed, sat opposite a spiritualist, who was holding a noisy discussion with his neighbor in the same seat. On the subject of miracles. The spiritualist conceded that the universe was governed by a fixed, unalterable law, and miracles were therefore impossible. After listening some time, the clergyman replied, that a law could not execute itself, and that Deity heretofore continually acted; and he expressed the opinion that the spiritualist knew but very little about what he was discussing. The latter replied.

"Do you think you can make a fool of me." "Oh no," replied the minister, "I am afraid the Lord has been to quick for me." "There were no further manifestations."

Two young ladies, both of whom lay claim affection to the same young man, have consented to settle the dispute in a novel way, which mode might be adopted by the strong-er sex, when they feel inclined to meet each other in "mortal combat." Six cord of dry hickory wood have been piled in two separate piles, which is to be sawed; split and corded by the young ladies. The one performing the task first is to have the young man, he being chosen umpire in the matter.

Girls, when another cares like the above comes to light, come to Utah.

by Ex-Deputy Exum about whose wife King had published an article . . . King is a man of 30. King . . . became connected with the Rustler and gave such offense that they treated him to a coat of tar and feathers. He maintained his position however, and received much applause for his bravery. He afterward brought out the Frisco Times, and published a paper so intensely *'mining camp'* that many of the best families would not receive it in their homes. It is possible he will now wind up what might have been a noble career."

The final days of the King and his Union are like Eliza on the ice floes—disconnected, but exciting at that. The Provo Enquirer May 12, 1890 says: "Editor C. S. King, of the Ogden Daily Union, gave us a pleasant call." But the next spring, March 10, 1891 the Enquirer says: "How glorious was the death of the Ogden Union, may be seen from the following item in the Ogden Standard: 'Last evening an attachment was filed by the Ogden Liquor Company on the presses and property of the Daily Union, to satisfy a claim of $45. The liquor company took charge of the articles.' " The last item from the Wasatch Wave, March 24, 1891 is a bit enigmatical; it says: "The Ogden Daily Union has been resurrected, and comes out as a full fledged Republican paper, under the management of W. W. Wallace." We never hear of it again!

The Ogden Argus, Vol. 1, No. 1, May 20, 1888. The Ogden Standard May 21, 1888 says: "Its editors are Leo Haefeli, and P. J. Barrett, who declare in their Salutatory that the business of their little sheet is 'not to keep awake the fires of political or religious contentions, but to unite the interests of Ogden's citizens in bringing about increased prosperity'. It has a neat and newsy appearance, and shows signs of much enterprise. Whatever agency helps to bring prosperity to Ogden ought to be and will be a sharer in that prosperity itself."

There are no files. Percival J. Barrett was editor and proprietor; Mr. Haefeli only helped—on the semi-weekly. Unfortunately we did not hear much of the Argus, but on March 5, 1889, the Standard observes: "The Argus is getting a notoriety it never before enjoyed . . ." It didn't say why; but even at the time, it may have been on the way out.

Going forward for a look backward, we read in the Standard New Year's Eve 1889 an item with a whipcracker reference to the Argus: "Another paper has started publication at the Capital. This last one is the **Great Salt Laker,** issued monthly under the management of Frank B. Beslin. The number before us is a neatly printed 4 column magazine of 16 pages. The work shows the touch of an experienced hand in the business . . . The editor exhibits the ambition to be abreast with the times on one point at least . . . For a paper so young in the Wars, to launch into a competition with the Tribune in lying about the Mormons, while it may be brave, is not very sensible! It is too much like the Argus, of sainted memory!"

The Examiner Editor had previously on July 26, 1889, published the obituary: "Such candor as actuates the 'editor and prop'r' of the Ogden Argus in bowing his journalistic goodbye to the public, deserves the admiration and applause of all truth-loving people. Observe the pathos and veracity of the following. . : 'Unlike many of its predecessors in the journalistic field of Ogden, it, the Argus, is stopped at a period when its prospects were never brighter, and subscribers more numerous. It has no canker worm in the shape of lack of patronage to eat its budding youth, but has paid all connected with it, and has been a successful venture, fully sustaining the opinion of its proprietor that a newspaper in Ogden *ought* to pay, and will do so under proper management. The reason of this action is that the proprietor finds it impossible to run the journal and at the same time attend to his law practice, unless he makes himself a slave to duty and deprives himself of the necessary relaxation, which Nature requires!' "

Ogden Commercial, Daily, Sunday and weekly, 8 pages, 48 columns, Commercial Publishing Company, A. B. Johnson, Editor, A. C. Bishop, Business Manager, O. A. Kennedy, City Editor, says the City Directory for 1890-91. Vol. 1, No. 1, April 4, 1889, Liberal, strong anti-Mormon. Three copies are in the Bancroft Library, Friday morning, October 24, 1890, Volume 4, No. 20, (also 25th and 28th), 6 columns, 8 pages. E. M. Correll, Editor; published every morning except Monday, by the Commercial Publishing Company. It was boosting C. C. Goodwin for Congress.

Before the first volume was completed, the visible trail fades in the slough of despond. "X" in the Standard, December 2, 1891, marks the spot where, and so forth: "Pursuant with former advertisement, Deputy U. S. Marshal Butcher proceeded to sell the property of the Commercial Publishing Company yesterday morning at 10:00 o'clock. The sale was the result of the foreclosure of two chattel mortgages taken as additional security on a couple of notes amounting to between $8000 and $9000. The sale took place at the front door of the Business Office of the company, and was sold to the plaintiffs for $7500,—the Certificate of Sale to be made out to Theodore Robinson." There is no further word, or information about the Commercial.

The Utah Democrat. The Provo Enquirer March 7, 1891, introduces this paper, but fails to give it a habitation; we are only guessing it was published in Ogden, where we later hear of a paper of the same name. "The full fledged Utah Democrat concerning which we have heard so little in its embryonic state, has reached our sanctum," says the Enquirer. "The original 'Essay Kaigh' pronounced by some 'Essay Calf' is the quill driver, so there is no questioning the fact that he will steer the young organ aright. J. H. Parry is manager."

The Ogden Directory for 1895-6 shows: The Utah Democrat, S. S. Smith, editor and proprietor, Tuesday and Friday. No files; no gossip. Was this a "Charlie McCarthy" which spoke only when the

Democratic Party spoke through it? It does not seem to have been a year-long, year after year, honest-to-goodness regular newspaper!

Ogden Post. Daily and semi-weekly. Established May 3, 1892; politics Democratic, 7 columns, 6 pages, $8, the Post Publishing Company, publishers and proprietors. Le dru R. Rhodes, manager; James H. Wallis, editor. Only that, and nothing more, found in a Directory. Later, from the Beaver Utonian January 13, 1893: "The Ogden Post is dead."—Dead as a post!

"Leader, Sunday, Liberal, established 1892, 4 pages, 15 x 22, Rowe & Barber, Editors and Publishers," says the American Newspaper Directory for 1892. Following the Leader was not much of a game, in this case, for only one further reference was found, in the Brigham Bugler August 27, 1892: "The Ogden Leader has changed hands, and now struts out as a Semi-Weekly. It still clings to the crumbling old Liberal Tree, and waxes the Mormons for not spending their dollars with the Gentiles!"

The Evening Sun.—Began October 5, 1893, with a fancy art-heading—the sun setting among the mountainous islands of Great Salt Lake. File: Ogden Public Library has one number for Wednesday, October 18, 1893, 5 columns, 4 pages, all home print, plenty of Democratic politics; every evening except Sunday, W. W. Browning and Company. In that number, the editor reproduces a few comments about his own paper, the first from the Payson Globe—"Ogden has a new paper called the Evening Sun, which began to shed its rays over that city on the 5th. It is Democratic in politics, and will be a thorn in the flesh to the Standard. The proprietors are the well known firm of W. W. Browning & Co., who have the means and courage to make it a success."

"The Globe is right and wrong . . . wrong that it will be a thorn in the flesh of the Standard. They (the Brownings) are great inventors, and we are anxious to see if they can invent a method of making a newspaper pay in Ogden.—Ogden Standard." (a morning competitor). To which the Sun adds: "Since the Sun rose in the journalistic firmament . . . the Standard has improved 50% . . . Competition is the life of trade . . . The Sun was placed in the heavens of newspaperdom to occupy one of the places as a fixed planet, and hopes to fill the requirements . . . Since there is both room and necessity for two daily papers in Ogden." After that—what? The archives answer not!

Utah State Journal. Published daily by the Ogden Typographical Union, says the Ogden City Directory for 1892-3; but we neither saw nor heard anything more of it, until the Directory of 1897-8, which says E. A. Littlefield is lessee and manager. Files, in the Standard-Examiner Office, from November 9, 1903 to December, 1908, inclusive —none other! The paper bears the claim: "Entered as second-class matter November 10, 1903," although it also claims to have been "founded by E. A. Littlefield, A. D. 1896; published every evening except Sunday, Utah State Journal Company, publishers, Frank J. Cannon, President, W. W. Browning, Vice-President, E. A. Littlefield, Secretary and Treasurer."

Frank J. Cannon is editor November 9, 1903, when this notice appears: "With this, the first daily issue of the Utah State Journal, the paper enters upon its eighth volume." Cannon's name was dropped from the issue September 30, 1904, and none was substituted until October 12, 1905, when C. M. Jackson became editor. Jackson's name was dropped April 5, 1907, and none substituted until March 19, 1908, when this notice was run: "M. F. Cunningham, who for the past eight years was connected with daily papers of Salt Lake City, becomes managing editor of the Utah State Journal." Cunningham's name was dropped November 9, 1908, and as the political season was closed, so it appears the record closed for the Utah State Journal.

The Sun. "We are pleased to add the name of the Daily Sun to our exchange list . . . published in Ogden, in the interests of Democracy. It made its bow October 2, under the management of W. W. Browning and Company," says the Wasatch Wave, October 10, 1893. The Wave gives us our next item December 26, 1893: "W. W. Browning, Manager of the Ogden Sun, has brought suit against the Ogden Standard for $10,000 damages for defamation of character." Tarnishing the Sun! The Brigham Bugler quoted The Sun February 17 and March 10, 1894, and then tells us May 26, 1894, "The Ogden Sun has wheeled off into everlasting darkness. This is the 57th burial in the Ogden Newspaper Cemetery."

If everything is working right, the Sun will usually rise again however, and the Gazetteer for 1903-04 gives **The Sun**, Weekly, William Glasmann, Editor and Proprietor. Kenner, in Utah As It Is, 1904, says the Weekly Sun is published in the Standard plant, a satellite, not a real sun!

"Ogden Times, a Woman Suffrage paper, lies on our table," says the Vernal Express, March 19, 1896. "It is edited by Kate S. Hillard, and the sub-head on the second page reads: 'The Morgan Mirror.' Probably the Times woman, like most of her sex, can't get along without a Mirror!" We did not see it, not even in the Mirror!

The Morning Examiner. Vol. 1 No. 1, January 1, 1904. "Published every day in the year by the Union Printing Company. Frank Francis, editor and manager . . . The Examiner will not be a party organ, nor the organ of any clique." On April 30th, 1904, there were stories under these headings: "New Ownership" and "The Examiner Sold." "In surrendering the Examiner to the Standard Publishing Company, we do so not as a matter of choice, but because we could not maintain its present excellent and complete form . . . No paper ever established in Ogden secured a greater number of paying subscribers in so short a time . . . We wish to emphatically deny the rumors that the Standard or Mr. Glasmann held any interest in the Examiner until today.—Frank Francis."

"The New Management.—In assuming control and ownership of the Morning Examiner, the Standard wishes it understood that it does so only because it believes it is necessary, in order to keep a morning newspaper in Ogden. Should the Morning Examiner surrender its Associated Press franchise, the Standard believes the Salt Lake morning papers will be powerful enough to prevent the press franchise from being granted to Ogden parties again . . . Hereafter we shall deliver the Sunday Morning Examiner to the subscribers of the Evening Standard . . . And make it the big paper in Ogden.—Wm. Glasmann." Files complete in Standard-Examiner Office.

The papers were combined in an evening edition April 1, 1920, continuing to date as the **Standard-Examiner.** The masthead was "J. U. Eldredge, Jr. and A. L. Glasmann, Publishers," from March 12, 1923 to Eldredge's death January 20, 1933, when (January 25, 1933) A. L. Glasmann became editor and publisher, continuing to date.

PANGUITCH, Garfield County

Population: 1890, 885; 1900, 883; 1910, 1,338; 1920, 1,473; 1930, 1,541.

The Cactus. (?)   John M. Dunning started the first newspaper in Panguitch about 1878 or 1879, if we may trust the memory of an unidentified informant.   It is possible that reference was made to the **Panguitch Register,** which the Manti Home Sentinel mentions March 26, 1886 as being: "among our latest exchanges;" though the exchange practice was so universal it is more than likely the Register was just beginning when it received this notice.

Mrs. Lucy Hatch of the Panguitch Daughters of the Utah Pioneers, read a paper December 29, 1932 entitled: "Reading Material of the Pioneers," in which she says John M. Dunning published the first newspaper in Panguitch, and that for two years James T. Daly, Sr., was correspondent or writer.   The paper was first called the Cactus, but later the name was changed, some say to the Garfield County News, others say The Recorder, and some say it became the Register.   "It was published from about 1880 to 1884."   After its name was changed, the Cactus page was about 8 x 10 inches in size, 4-pages.   It was not issued regularly, but appeared on the Quaker order, when the spirit moved.   Mr. Dunning was said to have been a humorist and prepared his own jokes for fillers.   He was also a poet of the second order, according to Mrs. Hatch, and many of his poems and other writings appeared in the Cactus.   But neither poetry nor prose paid, and the paper perished. It may have been a manuscript, pen-and-ink newspaper.

Panguitch Progress, established 1898, weekly, Republican, Mormon, E. S. Worthen, editor and manager, so says Kenner in Utah As It Is, 1904.   And that is a pretty brief history for a real newspaper; but

JESSE EARL
Born October 30, 1870
Died May 7, 1936

CHARLES ENGLAND
Born October 6, 1863
Still Living

JOHN R. WALLIS
Born April 13, 1859
Still Living

S. L. RADDON
Born May 13, 1858
Still Living

like its predecessor it was without progeny or files. Several years later, 1903 and 1904, the State Gazetteer gives Elizabeth S. Worthen as editor and publisher, after which it seems to have disappeared for a few years only. Then the Gazetteer for 1908-09 gives Miss Gladys DeLong, editor and publisher of the Panguitch Progress; and in 1912-13 Fred E. Eldredge appears as editor and publisher and is so credited until 1921.

Mrs. Hatch says Eldredge finally sold to Mahonri M. Steele, Jr., Dr. J. J. Steiner, George Haycock and some others. Steele was the manager. But something happened to the Progress, and J. G. Spencer moved the Kane County News plant from Kanab to Panguitch, and shortly sold it to Will J. Peters, who owned the old Progress plant. Peters was manager of a traveling show, who quit the "boards" at Panguitch Lake, according to Mrs. Hatch. He ran the paper about a year and then left, and Miss Elizabeth Worthen, a feminine Printer's Devil, became editor and publisher. According to Mrs. Hatch's manuscript: "Next came Fred M. Gavin, who showed us what a newspaper should look like and what it should mean to a community—for a time. Finally came the Misses Gladys and Winnie DeLong, who made a desperate struggle to pump life into a dying publication."

Fred E. Eldredge returned to Panguitch about 1909, and repurchased the Progress Plant and a new home for it, beginning the Progress all over again in a big way. Mr. Eldredge continued the Progress until sometime in 1921, when he moved to Marysvale and took the printing plant with him.

Garfield County News, Vol. 1, No. 1, April 16, 1920, 5 columns, Will J. Peters, publisher and proprietor, Elnora Mae Peters, associate editor. Mr. Peters died November 11, 1929, since which time Mrs. Peters has continued the publication. Peters formerly travelled with various theatrical troupes. He was for many years a member of the Kirkoff Company and was later at the head of his own company called Peters Peerless Players. He sang, danced and performed in vaudeville acts at times, but usually played heavy parts—an unusual background for a newspaperman.

PARK CITY, Summit County

Population: 1880, 1,542; 1890, 2,850; 1900, 3,759; 1910, 3,439; 1920, 3,393; 1930, 4,281.

Park Mining Record, Vol. 1, No. 1, Sunday morning, February 8, 1880, according to the Salt Lake Tribune, Tuesday, February 10, 1880. But "The Park Mining Record is a new journal that made its first appearance on Saturday last. Mr. Schupbach is publisher," says the Provo Enquirer February 14, 1880. Saturday was probably publication date, and the first number was delayed until Sunday, thus making both the above reports correct.

Many of the early files were lost in the city-wide fire of 1898, but were very largely replaced from the private collection of a Park City mining company official. Thus the files are nearly complete from the beginning, in the Record office. The earliest number in the file, Vol. 1, No. 18, Saturday, June 5, 1880, has 7 columns, 4 pages, and shows James R. Schupbach, publisher. The column of local news items was called "Park Float"—"float" being a miner's term for ore out of place, or loose on the surface.

With June 18, 1881, the masthead shows H. L. White, publisher; and in the Park Float for July 16, 1881, we read: "J. R. Schupbach and family departed . . . for his new field . . . Butte, Montana." And July 30, 1881, "Mr. Samuel L. P. Raddon of the Salt Lake Tribune was in the Park the greater part of the week visiting his many friends, and viewing the improvements in our camp, which have been made since he was here a year ago."

Numerous Salt Lake City advertisements appeared in the Record as early as August 13, 1881. This news item about the editor himself, was of course perpetrated by the "Devil" in temporary charge, November 12, 1881. "Ye Publisher has vamoosed the ranch and turned his attention Zionward. He will probably be absent a week or more, during which time the chicken and taffy market will be livelier than usual, down there."

The State Directories listed Schupbach's successor "White"; but the Salt Lake Evening Chronicle of January 23, 1883, says, "The red raspberry phiz of Harry White, Editor of the Park City Record, illuminated the Chronicle Office." According to the Record masthead, the publisher was still "White, H. L.," until November 15, 1884. Some primitive history of the present owners of the Record appears October 6, 1883. "Sam Raddon, one of our ex-typos . . . after leaving the Record something over a year ago. Sam is now a Daddy; Sam Jr., is a cherub."

"J. J. Buser, editor and publisher," makes "Our Bow" as follows, November 2, 1884. "Four years ago last February, we were engaged in the same duty as now . . . We penned our bow . . . A local paper was then a rare piece of literature in Park City . . . So long as we have control of the Record, no one can find space in its columns to assail the character of any of our citizens."

A week later, the paper's name was altered to the **Park Record,** Buser having obviously noticed a few other interests in the Park than "mining." He announces also that "S. L. Raddon, an old typo on the Tribune, will arrive in the Park tomorrow evening, and for the future will grace the 'Alley' in the Record office." And on December 6, 1884, the masthead accordingly shows "Buser & Raddon, editors and publishers."

That was the real beginning of the longest term of continuous service on any newspaper in the State, and probably in the West, if not in the country, for S. L. Raddon is still the general directing head of the concern, after 54 years!

Buser & Raddon continued as editors and publishers until the issue of July 18, 1885, when we note the following "Adieu. Kind Reader, after 8 months of mistakes and blunders, caused by defective auditory nerves brought about by severe illness in 1881, I bid you Adieu! . . . My successer is well known in Park City, having come with Mr. Schupbach and myself to establish the Record here, viz., Mr. L. E. Camomile. He and my associate, Mr. Raddon, will be the shining lights in the future. . . . J. J. Buser." Consequently, on July 25, 1885, the masthead shows Raddon & Camomile, publishers. There was no change noticeable in the paper itself. The Raddon-Camomile team got many exchange notices, but only a few like this one, from the Provo Territorial Enquirer, November 1, 1887: "Please knock it on the head. The Park Record has got the Mormon rabies bad, and is proving itself to be a consummate ass. Poor thing, it is a financial fizzle as a newspaper, and thinks it may get a living by catering to the taste of anti-Mormons. Will the Call please knock it on the head, and end its miserable existence!"

Shortly after that, company came to the Record, as shown by this masthead, August 11, 1888: "Raddon, Camomile & Company, publishers and proprietors. The week before, August 4, 1888, appeared this "Publishers' Announcement . . . Alf C. Reese, who has been connected with the paper for over two years, has bought out the entire plant with which the late Park City Call was printed, and the material will be moved down to this office . . . dating from August 1, under the firm name of Raddon, Camomile & Company, Mr. Reese being a member of the new firm."

The wonder is: Did the Call undertake to do to the Record what the Enquirer asked it to do! In any event, the Record became big enough to swallow up all competitors. Naturally enough as a consequence, its own waitsline grew, and on October 20, 1888, it went to 8 columns, 4 pages, all home print. As showing the metropolitan spirit of the Record, we note the following, from the issue of April 30, 1892: "The Record, with its usual enterprise, got out an Extra early Sunday evening, giving full particulars of the Trotman shooting. Over 1000 copies were issued and distributed free. They were quickly devoured by the multitude."

The Hard Times of 1893 broke some "records," but it only bent the Park Record, as shown by this note in the issue of October 14, 1893, taken from a full length advertisement-editorial: "The Park Record established February 8, 1880, is now nearly 14 years old. Hard Times are tough on everybody, and during such times everybody should help one another. Business is slack; Advertise! Subscribe to the Park Record now!" The appeal bore fruit, and the paper came back. Thus the history of the Park City Record is almost a history of the city, since it began so early in the life of the city.

A general fire in Park City destroyed the Record plant Sunday, June 19, 1898. Some echoes and reflections of the fire appear in the following, from the proprietors, in a Souvenir Booklet issued in 1902 by the Record: "In 1898, shortly after the Record had completed a new home and received new equipment, it was wiped out by the big fire. It was a bad blow. When the ashes had cooled, the proprietors stood dazed, but only for a moment. In a few short hours after the fire, a tent was pitched, and for several weeks, the paper was issued from the tent office, pictured on this page, (of the Souvenir Booklet)."

The following note is from the June 25, 1898 number: " 'Notwithstanding the destruction of the Park City Record plant in the recent fire, the paper has gone along with regular issues, save one exception, we believe. The publishers are enterprising.—Payson Header'. No neighbor, not an issue was missed. The mail list was burned, however, and some of our exchanges were consequently overlooked." Also the following, "Many thanks are due the Salt Lake Tribune for the use in this issue of some of its cuts of the Park City fire. The Record is under deep obligation to the Salt Lake Herald for the appearance this week as usual, of our paper. Our own plant being completely annihilated, the kind offer of Manager McDaniel of the Herald, to print the paper at his establishment, was most gladly accepted. The free use of any and all departments of this mammoth daily, was placed at our disposal."

The masthead for many years was the same, but April 23, 1910, this form: The Park Record Company, publishers, S. L. Raddon, President, W. A. Raddon, Secretary, was used for the last time, and on April 30, 1910, this appeared: The Park Record, S. L. Raddon, publisher, and was run for 14 years, when the following shakeup appeared —but it was still all in the family: September 12, 1924, "After a continuous connection with the Park Record for more than 38 years, W. A. Raddon this week disposed of his half interest in the business to LePage H. Raddon, having decided to forsake Utah as a place of residence, and locate in Los Angeles, California . . . The ownership of the Record will continue in the family . . . LePage Raddon has been connected with the Record since his school days."

Neither the sun, moon nor stars ever ran more smoothly than the Park Record seems to have run under the Raddons' management, and even a minor change was unusual, such as the following: "The day of publication hereafter for the Record, will be Fridays. The change is made with a view to giving better service to our patrons—and we hope our efforts will be approved and appreciated." (Advertisers had requested the change.)

The Blue Book for 1931 says LePage H. Raddon is Manager, and S. L. Raddon, President. They have continued so to date.

Park City Call. Vol. 1, No. 1, Thursday, January 13, 1887. Editor Buchanan got some free advertising from his contemporary, the Park Record, January 8, 1887, as being "the gentleman who is preparing to commence the publication of a weekly newspaper here. The name of the new paper is to be the Park City Call . . . The first issue . . . will appear next Wednesday (January 12, 1887)." A further notice appeared in the Park Record of January 15, 1887: "Friend Buchanan's first paper put in an appearance Thursday, (Janaury 13). If the proprietor keeps a stiff upper lip, and knows what and how . . . ultimate success will reward our contemporary's efforts."

The Salt Lake Democrat of January 14, 1887, gives it this send-off: "The first number of the Park City Call, a new weekly devoted to the interests of the great mining camp is out. It is well filled with interesting news, and promises to be a success." And the Deseret News January 15, 1887, more clearly identifies this sheet: "The Park City Call is the title of a new anti-Mormon Weekly. The editor is E. H. Buchanan."

The Territorial Enquirer, Provo, apparently did not notice the newcomer formally, but paid it an equally sincere compliment by borrowing many news item from it, with credit, (May 3, August 16 and October 25, 1887), speaking once of "Friend Buchanan." Also the Deseret News evidently liked the Call's "anti-Mormon" way of dishing up the news, copying frequently through 1887. Only one copy of the Call was seen, which the Raddons had frugally bound in with the Park Record for the years 1887-88. It is No. 15 of Vol. 2, dated Thursday, April 19, 1888, E. H. Buchanan, proprietor, 8 pages, 7 columns, all home print.

The Park Record of March 31, 1888 makes a reference: "The originators of the excitement (over gold), Buchanan and White, of the Call." But the real piece of news was deferred until July 14, 1888. Says the Record: "Yesterday, E. H. Buchanan, publisher and proprietor of the Park City Call, made an assignment to J. A. Williams for the benefit of his creditors . . . The liabilities will foot up to about $1000, and the assets will probably cover the liabilities. Our contemporary has been in existence here just a year and a half." The last cry of the Call appears under the date of August 4, 1888, under the Park Mining Record q. v. (Alf C. Reese bought the Park City Call plant and amalgamated it with the Park Record.)

Park City Miner. No files. Two prenatal announcements were as follows: September 2, 1890, in the Wasatch Wave, "The Park City Miner . . . is expected to make its debut . . . about the twelfth of this month, Mr. C. S. Austin, proprietor, editor and manager." Also the Park Record, September 6, 1890: "The material for the new paper, the Park City Miner, was brought up from the depot yesterday, and it is understood the first issue will be out some time next week."

The first notice seen is from the Wasatch Wave, September 23, 1890: "The Park City Miner made its appearance this week . . . containing eight 5-column pages. Austin and Hancock are the publishers, C. S. Austin, editor and manager . . . It is well supplied with first class reading matter . . . Its advertising patronage not what it should be."

A hearty welcome is in the Brigham Bugler of Saturday, September 27, 1890: "The initial number of the Park City Miner strutted up and

Weekly Telegraph.

THE
Salt Lake Daily Telegraph.

At Pioneer Daily Paper in the Territory, Devoted to News and the Religious and Civil and Head Rights of the People

TERMS—IN ADVANCE.
(Delivered at residence in the City.)
Per Annum, $13.00   Six Months, 7.50
Three Months

[Mailed—Cash in Advance.]
Annum, $10.00   Six months, $6.00
Three months, $3.50

THE
Semi-Weekly Telegraph.

A First class Family paper, circulating in every Settlement of the Territory.

PUBLISHED MONDAY & THURSDAY

TERMS—IN ADVANCE.
Per Annum, $8.00
Three months, $2.50

[MAILED—CASH IN ADVANCE.]
Per Annum $7.00   Six months, $4.00
Three months, $2.00

NO. 1.   SALT LAKE CITY, THURSDAY, JANUARY 7, 1869.   VOL. I.

DISAPPEARANCES.

The sudden disappearance of individuals from the midst of society in almost every instance mental or physical. ...

THE MAIL GUARD'S STORY.

Reader, have you ever been obliged to wait at a small country railway station for an early train? ...

gave us a hearty handshake Monday. It is a live, clean, 5-column quarto, published weekly by C. S. Austin and George R. Hancock. The gist of news it contains betokens keen reportorial sense, backed by sinewy legs. Put 'er there boys, Put 'er there!"

But a new odor comes through the Park Record of December 12, 1891: "The Record has known that a suit for libel was to be filed against the Park City Daily Miner . . . The particular obnoxious publication occurs in the Miner on December 1, 1891 . . . Mr. Treweek asks for damages in the modest sum of $25,000."

The American Newspaper Directory for 1892: "Park City Miner, Evenings, except Sunday, Independent, established in 1891, 4 pages, 15 x 22, subscription $9. Sunday only, Independent, Established 1890, 8 pages, 13 x 20, subscription $3. C. S. Austin, Editor, Daily Miner Publishing Company." But a Daily came too frequently at that altitude. There wasn't enough oxygen. The Park Record informs us August 6. 1892: "The Record has been informed that an offer has been made for the Daily Miner plant, and if accepted, it will be moved to another location . . . For the present, the paper will be issued as a Weekly."

And the Wasatch Wave, August 9, 1892, gives an obituary bit: "The Park City Daily Miner is no more, but the company will continue to issue a weekly paper on Wednesday." Reincarnated ten or twelve years later, the Gazetteer for 1903-4 says: Park City Miner, N. B. Dresser, Editor and Proprietor. And Kenner's Utah As It Is in 1904 adds: Park City Miner, Weekly, conducted by N. B. Dresser. But nobody else succeeded in preserving any further record of the Miner (the second), not even Mr. Dresser!

Utah Patriot. "Vol. 1, No. 1, of the Utah Patriot came over the summit from Park City last week," says the Wasatch Wave July 26, 1895. There are no files, and we saw no copies. "The Utah Patriot is the name of a new paper just started at Park City by J. J. Flahiff. It is a neat 5-column quarto, well gotten up and ably edited."

Evidently what the Patriot made up in patriotism, it lacked in news, for it was not frequently quoted or referred to by contemporaries. Even patriotism can be carried too far it would seem, from the following taken out of the Silver City Star by the Park Record of September 4, 1897: "The job of 'licking editors' has recently become fashionable in Utah, the last case to come to our notice was in Park City a few days ago, when Editor Flahiff of the Utah Patriot, and Matt Connelly, of the Ontario Mine, came forcibly together. We would suggest that editors who live in a belligerent community make a breast plate of old plate-matter, and wear it under their shirts."

The episode was undoubtedly reason for a change of some kind, which the Wasatch Wave reports as follows, December 3, 1897: "Again the Utah Patriot at Park City has changed hands. Last Saturday it made its appearance under the management of Messrs. Sarvis and Hunt. J. J. Flahiff, the fat man from Arkansas, has gone north to the Klondike." The American Newspaper Directory for 1898, probably from data gathered in 1897 says: "Utah Patriot, Thursday, Independent, Established 1895, 8 pages, 13 x 20, $2, Circulation 875, J. J. Flahiff, Editor and Publisher."

Then it got to running wild, according to the Wasatch Wave of August 8, 1897: "Wonders will never cease. The Utah Patriot, published at Park City, changed hands on the first, Editor Flahiff retiring, and J. T. Camp, formerly of the defunct Lehi Rustler, resuming its publication . . . The surprise to us is that the Patriot is now a Daily, instead of a Weekly, and this in the midst of the great depression." As the Wave intimates, that was obviously too fast a rate for the machinery, and its bearings wore out, or it lost its bearings; for after that, it was no more.

PAROWAN, Iron County
Population: 1890, 937; 1900, 1,039; 1910, 1,156; 1920, 1,640; 1930, 1,474.

The Intelligencer, a pen-and-ink manuscript newspaper comes to life for a single glance through a reference by Editor Stenhouse of the Salt Lake Daily Telegraph, Saturday morning, April 16, 1865. "Our Southern co-temporary, that unpretending sheet, The Intelligencer, published by the Young Men of Parowan, comes to our table as regularly as the Southern Mail will admit. It contains articles upon education and other matters worthy of perusal."

Parowan Times. Volume 1, Number 1, October 27, 1915, Alexander H. Rollo, editor and manager. The directors of the Parowan Printing and Publishing Company had offered a cash prize of $2.50 to the Parowan school student submitting the most appropriate name for the newspaper. The money was divided between Wilma Lowe and Ross Benson, both of whom suggested "Parowan Times."

The Parowan Times printing plant was partly that formerly used by Editor Rollo on the Observer at Cedar City. The Gazetteer for 1916-17 advertisement says the Parowan Times is "Progressive and aggressive." Herman D. Bayles, president, George A. Mitchell, vice-president, Silas J. Ward, secretary and treasurer, Alexander H. Rollo, manager. Those officers, and James A. Robinson, Junior, constituted the Board of Directors.

The issue of September 28, 1920, appeared without Rollo's name at the masthead; but on October 27, 1920, he made the usual publisher's declaration that he was still the editor. However, beginning with the issue of March 30, 1921, W. W. Mitchell took a lease on the Times. On that date we read, "This issue of the Times will be the last that the present lessees will get out as they have a business deal whereby their entire time and attention will be needed in the Iron County Record office. The Board of Directors has leased the plant to W. Warner Mitchell, who will take charge April 1, 1921. The past three issues of the Times have been issued in the Record Office," of Cedar City. It had been Rollo's intention to run both newspapers from the one printing plant, but the large Parowan directorate of the Times objected. Mitchell is still publisher, and is now principal stockholder.

PAYSON, Utah County

Population: 1890, 2,135; 1900, 2,636; 1910, 2,397; 1920, 3,031; 1930, 3,045.

"The Payson Advocate and The Intelligencer. Manuscript newspapers, 8 pages each, judging from letters, and No. 6 of the Advocate, are proving interesting and beneficial to both writers and readers—a very commendable mode of using a portion of leisure time," says the Deseret News, March 29, 1865. So sorry we found none.

Utah Enterprise. There are no files, and contemporaries have furnished most of our notes. "We have received the eighth number of the Business Enterprise, published in Payson," says the Provo Daily Enquirer, March 17, 1890.

" 'In trouble again. Payson is in need of a good weekly newspaper. Several of the business men have expressed their readiness to assist in the establishment of such an enterprise', says Milo Zip's correspondence in the Tribune, June 7, 1890. Payson is not in need of a correspondent, who stretches a mole-hill to a mountain . . . In the eyes of some people, Payson may need a weekly paper, but these people are the ones, when canvassed for a paper already in existence, and running solely on its merits, can't afford to pay a half subscription of six bits a year, to help the good work along, but wish it success nevertheless, and borrow the paper every week from their neighbors."— Payson Enterprise. Copied in the Provo Daily Enquirer May 31, 1890.

"The Payson Enterprise excursion to Garfield yesterday was an immense affair. Hundreds from Utah County went," says the Provo Enquirer August 23, 1890. And on August 26, 1890, the Enquirer says, "Payson is soon to have a semi-weekly paper. The Enterprise, published in that city, expects soon to make that improvement. Besides this publication, we have learned that a Liberal paper is soon to be published in the same place."

Continuing the story, the Enquirer October 14, 1890, says: "A worthy contemporary is the Payson Enterprise. Eighteen months ago it started as a small, and may we add, insignificant advertising sheet. Now it has blossomed into a fine weekly, that does credit to Payson." The Brigham Bugler October 18, 1890, adds this compliment: "The new dress of the Payson Enterprise is a daisy. Brother Pickering must have pilfered the wardrobe of one of the countless pretty girls of that lovely city, from which to cut his pattern." The Wasatch Wave December 2, 1890, says: "The Payson Enterprise of November 25th tells us that they have received a new subscriber. Good!"

"The Payson Enterprise came out last week on its fourth birthday, in the form of a 7 column folio paper," says the Eastern Utah Telegraph of October 9, 1891. The Corinne Calliope, as quoted in the Manti Home Sentinel April 16, 1892, puts it: "The Utah Enterprise, published at Payson, has done away with its patent insides, and now appears as a 6 column folio." The American Newspaper Directory for 1892 gives this obituary: "Payson, Utah Enterprise, Saturday, local, established 1888, 4 pages, 16 x 22, $2, J. Frank Pickering, Editor and Publisher." Obituary, because the Enterprise had met its match, if not its Waterloo, in April, 1891, when it refers to "Our Failure." (see Leader.)

Payson Leader. "E. R. Powell, Editor of the Payson Leader, gave us a pleasant call last evening. By the way, the Leader is becoming quite a readable paper, and if the publisher will continue to deal fairly with the public without regard to politics and religion, in particular, there is no reason why it cannot command good support," is the fatherly (or Dutch Uncle) advice of the Provo Enquirer, January 29, 1891.

But advice was not what the Leader wanted, and exchanges, including the Brigham Bugler and others, of April 11, 1891, report the suspension of the Payson Leader. "It flunked out," one of them puts it. The Utah Enterprise, quoted in the Eastern Utah Telegraph April 20, 1891, says "Our failure, like that of the paper which has flunked out here, does the town more harm than most people suppose, as capitalists and people outside lose confidence in the city, when they hear of such news."

Daily Hummer. "The latest venture in Utah Journalism, is the Daily Hummer, fathered by J. Frank Pickering, of Payson Enterprise fame. The Hummer is a 3 column folio," thanks to the Eastern Utah Telegraph, Price, January 8, 1892. Sorry none of the remaining exchanges told why nor when the Hummer began using a Harp!

Payson Chronicle. "The Payson Chronicle made its appearance in our office last Saturday."—Spanish Fork Sun, July 21, 1892. This constitutes the entire known history of the Chronicle, except the hyphenated reference, which follows.

Enterprise-Chronicle. The Spanish Fork Sun, August 4, 1892, says, "E. H. Pulver, Editor of the Payson Enterprise-Chronicle, gave us a pleasant call Tuesday evening." That's all there is; there isn't any more. It reminds us of the deadly swallowing battles often occurring between a rattlesnake and a King snake; but they seldom swallow each other and both die, as seems to have been the case of the Enterprise and the Chronicle.

Payson Globe. "Payson now boasts of a weekly paper. The Payson Globe has been launched on the sea of journalism with E. G. Rognon and E. H. Scott at the helm. The Globe is a 4 page, 6 column sheet," records the Wasatch Wave, February 21, 1893. "We have received the second issue of the Payson Globe, a new venture in the field . . ; and one of Cache County's papers says Mr. Goddard, its editor, will show the people of Utah County how a good newspaper is run." That from the Spanish Fork Sun, February 25, 1893.

In March the Globe got itself quoted a few times, even if "It is hard to tell whether the Payson Globe is set up in Italics or Roman," according to the Spanish Fork Sun April 1, 1893. The Western Newspaper Union of Denver, ready-printer, says "The Globe looks neat and clean. and has more patronage than we predicted Payson would give ready-prints."

The neighbors continued to lift news items from the Globe in November, 1893, and April, September and November, 1894; but we lose track of it in 1895. The Nephi Blade borrowed from it in January, 1896, and the Brigham Bugler in April, 1897, also April, 1898. The American Newspaper Directory for 1898, copy for which was probably prepared in 1897, shows "Payson Globe, Saturday, established 1893, 4 pages, 16 x 22, $1.50, circulation 510, C. E. Jackson, Editor, Rognon-Scott Publishing Company." In spite of that generous circulation, this is the last reference we found to the Globe itself. It bobs up later however, with a hyphenated better-half.

"The Header, Payson, is the latest thing in Utah journalism. It doesn't look as if it had tumbled off a bicycle either, as it is chuck full of interesting reading matter," chronicles the Brigham Bugler, April 18, 1896. "A newspaper recently started at Payson has reached the Blade sanctum: The Header presents a good appearance, and is well stocked with 'ads', which means success for it. The publishers are F. A. Huish and T. E. Hinshaw," says the Nephi Blade April 25, 1896. The American Newspaper Directory for 1898 gives: "Header, Saturday, Independent, established 1896, 8 pages, 13 x 20, subscription $1.25."

Globe-Header. Married! But the ceremony is not mentioned in any of the exchanges reviewed and must have been "private." The Utah County Democrat of October 19, 1898, mentions the "Payson Globe-Header," and thus starts us off with the double header. Since the Globe-Header files are missing in their entirety, we only know what the Utah State Gazetteer tells us: In 1903-4 it credits Eugene Pulver as being editor and proprietor; in 1908-9 J. Albert McClellan was publisher; but for some good and sufficient reason, E. H. Pulver was the publisher in the 1912-13 and 1914-15 Gazetteers. R. A. Porter is listed as publisher in 1916-17, when something else happened, and the Globe-Header was no more.

The Paysonian. "Issued every Thursday, by the Paysonian Publishing Company, Lawrence Jorgenson, Editor." The State Gazetteer for 1918-19 says T. F. Tolhurst was president, Lawrence Jorgenson vice-president and general manager, and E. H. Pulver secretary-treasurer of the Paysonian Publishing Company. The Gazetteer for 1920-21 shows Jorgenson still manager.

A copy of the Paysonian for November 1, 1917, which was No. 8 of Vol. 30, shows: "The Paysonian, with which is consolidated the Globe-Header." In that same issue we read: "The directors of the

"LET EVERY STEP BE AN ADVANCE."

Vol. 1.   **Ogden, Utah, May 28, 1870.**   **No. 4.**

The Trans-Continental.

Published Daily on the Pullman Hotel-Express,
Between
Boston and San Francisco.

W. R. STEELE, *Editor.*

CHEYENNE TO OGDEN.

From Cheyenne to Ogden, the western terminus of the Union Pacific Railroad, the distance is 516 miles, the same as from Omaha to Cheyenne. There are but few settlements or towns of importance, but much of the scenery is grand, and several of the points full of interest to the tourist. We again draw upon the *Trans-Continental Railroad Guide* for a few facts and figures:

Sherman, 33 miles from Cheyenne, is 8,235 feet above the sea. It is named in honor of General Sherman, the tallest general in the service. This station is 549 miles from Omaha and 1,225 miles from Sacramento. The maximum grade from Cheyenne to Sherman is 88.176 per mile. Seventy-five miles to the southwest is Long's Peak. To the south, 165 miles away, is Pike's Peak, both plainly visible. To the northwest, about 100 miles distant, is Elk Mountain, another noted landmark.

Dale Creek Bridge is a structure 650 feet long, and 126 feet high, spanning Dale creek from bluff to bluff. The bridge is the grandest feature of the road.

Fort Saunders is located 54 miles from Cheyenne. The fort is beautifully situated on the east of the road, about three miles from Laramie City, close along side of the track, and in full view from the cars for some miles, when approaching or leaving the post.

Laramie City is 56 miles from Cheyenne. Directly to the east of this place can be seen the old Cheyenne Pass wagon road—the old emigrant route—which crosses the plain and river about half a mile below the city, running thence northwest to the base of the mountains, parallel with the railroad. The Laramie plains here are 20 miles wide by 60 long.

Creston is the next place. It is 222 miles from Cheyenne. This is the summit of the great "backbone" of the continent, the Rocky Mountains. According to General Dodge, it is 7,000 feet above the level of the sea.

Point of Rocks is a telegraph station 68 miles farther on. Here is where all who go to the Sweet Water mines stop, and stages leave regularly for the mines—distant 75 miles.

Bryan comes next. It is not a very important station. The country around is barren and uninviting.

Carter's station is 45 miles further west. Here all freight is received for Virginia City, Helena and Bannock City, Montana.

Wahsatch, 452 miles from Cheyenne, is a little town of some 200 people.

Echo City is next. It contains about 700 inhabitants. The railroad company have shops here for repairs, &c. There is no game beyond here till the Humboldt is reached. Coal and iron ore are said to be abundant in this section.

Ogden, the western terminus of the Union Pacific railroad, is 39 miles west of Echo City. It is situated at the mouth of Ogden canyon, one of the gorges which pierce the Wahsatch range, and between the Weber and Ogden rivers. It has a population of about 5,500. *The Salt Lake Telegraph,* a daily, semi-weekly, and weekly paper, is published here by T. B. H. Stenhouse. The town is strictly Mormon, there being no schools or churches excepting those which are under the control of the church of the Latter Day Saints. It is the county seat of Weber county, and will, in time, become a place of considerable importance. The town presents the usual appearance of Mormon towns, the houses being widely scattered, with fine gardens and orchards filling up the intervening spaces.

CHEYENNE.

This is the largest town between Omaha and Corinne. The elevation is 5,931 feet. Distance from Omaha, 516 miles; from Sacramento 1,259 miles; from Denver City, 110 miles. Cheyenne is situated, properly speaking, on a broad, open plain, the Crow creek, a small stream, winding around two sides of the town. The streets are broad, and laid out at right angles with the railroad. Cheyenne contains 3,000 inhabitants. The streets present a lively business appearance, and the traveler feels that he has arrived at a town of more than ordinary business importance and energy.

On the fourth day of July, 1867, there was *one house* in Cheyenne, no more. At one period there were 6,000 inhabitants in the place and about the vicinity; but as the road extended westward, the floating, tide-serving portion followed the road, leaving a permanent and energetic people behind them, who have put up substantial buildings of brick and stone, wherein they are carrying on all branches of trade which mark a thriving and steadily growing city. Its permanency now is fully established, and henceforth the growth of the place will be steady and secure.

Cheyenne is the great central distributing point and depot for the freight and travel destined for Colorado and New Mexico, and the vast country of the Cheyenne plains.

There are two daily papers here, the *Leader,* published by N. A. Baker, Esq. and the *Argus,* published by Dr. Bedell and edited by H. Garbanetti. Both are live, go-ahead sheets.

Paysonian Publishing Company, which was recently organized in this city, met last Monday and completed the details connected with the beginning of operations . . . The new corporation comprises most of Payson's business and professional men . . . The equipment comprises Lawrence Jorgenson's plant from Brigham, consolidated with E. H. Pulver's equipment." Lawrence Jorgenson, editor and manager. The masthead for 1921 shows W. E. Ellsworth, editor and general manager, but the broken file in the Chronicle office does not show the date of his beginning, nor when the paper perished—probably about that time.

Payson Chronicle. This was not a reincarnation of the Chronicle of 1892. The files are on hand from January 4, 1929, to date; but the precise date of beginning of the modern Chronicle was not determined. The masthead to 1931 shows J. H. Mountford, publisher. We were informed orally, the present Chronicle is the direct successor of the Paysonian, from about 1921.

The Western Newspaper Union's ledger, on August 1, 1923, shows L. E. Stephenson, Payson Chronicle. The account was in the name of Warner Brothers after February 20, 1924, A. B. Kennedy, after April 16, 1924, and James H. Mountford, after February 10, 1926, continuing to November 25, 1930. The Blue Book for 1933 gives J. Harold Mountford, proprietor. Sounds like a name taken by a young man! The last note we picked up is: "The Payson Chronicle with the issue of January 5, 1933, began its fortieth year," thus claiming an ancestry under several different names in the past!

PRICE, Carbon County (Formerly Emery County)

Population: 1890, 209; 1900, 539; 1910, 1,021; 1920, 2,364; 1930, 4,084.

Eastern Utah Telegraph, Volume 1, number 1, January 15, 1891. "The Telegraph is a new enterprise in Utah Journalism . . . It is intended to be a paper for the people, and not for any class of individuals and all will be treated alike—fairly," says the Salutatory, Five columns, 8-pages, 4 home print, S. K. King, Managing Editor. An advertising card shows: "S. K. King, attorney and counsellor at law." Two-page, 3 column supplements appeared with the issues of January 22 and 29, 1891. The files in the vault of the Sun-Advocate, volume 1 are nearly complete, volume 2, several numbers, and volume 5 complete. An item published March 19, 1891 intimates that S. K. King, attorney, recently came from Burlington, Colorado.

In the issue of May 22, 1891 is this: "Notice—the Telegraph will hereafter be published on Friday of each week instead of Thursday;" and on June 19, 1891 the paper was increased to 7-columns, all home print. On September 11, 1891 the Editor said: "On account of being engaged for several days on a lawsuit in Salt Lake City this week the Telegraph is delayed in coming out until Saturday of this week."

But Editor-lawyer King soon fixed that, and on September 25, 1891 we read: "This week J. H. Sarvis, one of the Editor's Colorado friends, in company with another Colorado man, has purchased a half interest in the Telegraph. The other member of the firm is S. I. Paradice, of Plattville, Colorado. The new company is divided, part being Democrats and part Republicans, and the Telegraph will in the future be and remain neutral and independent. Mr. Sarvis will fill the position of associate editor, the management remaining unchanged, but will be placed in charge of Mr. Paradice January 1st, after which time S. K. King will devote his entire time to law practice."

The newspaper as a spiritual lamp to light the way for the people, is not supposed to explode or go out; but on December 18, 1891: "the overturning of a lamp in the Telegraph office last Friday created more excitment than a cash subscriber. Owing to the position of the lamp it was impossible to smother the flames until the oil was mostly consumed, which gave the fire so much of a start that it was thought necessary to give up the fight; but by tossing on comforters, laprobes, overcoats, and a collection of summer pants, the fire was extinguished—while the 'devil', through force of habit, was still yelling at the top of his voice: 'now is the time to subscribe'."

In the issue of January 25, 1895 we find this publisher's notice in: "Eastern Utah Telegraph (and Advocate) (sic). With this issue we cease our connections with the Telegraph Publishing Company. We assume all indebtedness and collect all outstanding accounts."

"On February 7th the initial number of the Eastern Utah Advocate will appear. The Advocate will continue to their maturity all prepaid subscriptions to the Telegraph, and complete advertising accounts." (Advocate Publishing Company, S. H. Brownlee, business manager). That, strangely enough, was the demise of the Telegraph; but its successor, after passing its chrysalis state, nevertheless continued the serial numbers of the Telegraph.

Eastern Utah Advocate, First issue, February 7, 1895. The American Newspaper Directory for 1898 says: 4-pages 17 x 24, $1, circulation 461, Thursday, Independent, Democratic, Advocate Printing Company, Incorporated." The files are practically complete, mostly bound, in the Sun-Advocate vaults. In its initial issue, brother Brownlee, editor and manager, claims a distribution, not to say circulation in excess of a thousand copies. There is nothing to indicate that the paper circulated in Hades, but from certain reports, publisher Brownlee got a good start in that direction himself.

The Park Record of October 5, 1895 has this to say on the subject: "Messrs. Brownlee and (Dexter) Smith, editors and proprietors of the Eastern Utah Advocate, published at Price, are under arrest on the charge of arson. It seems that their cupidity was attracted by the big Democratic campaign fund and they planned to get hold of a snug portion of it, and set their office on fire, which was damaged about $50 worth. The scheme was exploded, and instead of getting a cash assistance, got run in for arson."

The Vernal Express for March 26, 1896, continued the interesting story: "S. H. Brownlee, editor of the Eastern Utah Advocate, published at Price, has come up missing, and it is believed that he has skipped for 'greener fields and pastures new' and left his bondsmen in the lurch. It will be remembered that Mr. Brownlee was arrested for criminal libel, found guilty, and sentenced to six months in the county jail. Through the plea of his attorney he was granted 30 days in which to file a demurrer. His bondsmen are now in a dilemma, and are wondering 'where, oh where can he be'."

But Brownlee went to jail, where things were evidently not to his liking, for the Vernal Express gives us this echo April 23, 1896, "S. H. Brownlee, the Price editor, broke jail and skipped to Colorado a few days ago." John A. Crockett says Brownlee "escaped by making a key from a nonpariel slug and making his getaway; he left the country for good."

The files for 1896 are missing, and we found contemporary references enough to suggest that the newspaper may have suspended, at least from the time Brownlee went to jail, until the issue of January 28, 1897 (7 columns, 4-pages, all home print) when "J. D. Smith, lessee" was flung from the masthead. Then on June 16, 1898 the masthead was changed to "Clarence Marsh, publisher," who says "To the Public—This is not a Salutatory; we don't believe in Salutatories." (He then proceeds to write a quarter column Salutatory; a very good one, too!) But his hopes and promises were short lived, for in the issue of July 14, 1898 the masthead shows Clarence Marsh, lessee, P. Lochrie, editor and manager. Then on August 4, 1898, Lochrie's name was dropped, and August 11, 1898 Marsh's name was dropped, due to a mysterious hidden power which kept the paper heavily patronized and swarming with good news items.

The 1898 Newspaper Directory gives "Eastern Utah Advocate, Thursday, Independent, Democratic, established 1895, 4-pages, 17 x 24, subscription $1, circulation 461, Advocate Printing Company, Inc." Came then on August 18, 1898 the new masthead which was to remain for many years: "R. W. Crockett." To be more exact the masthead of March 22, 1900 shows: "Crockett Brothers," for J. A. Crockett had been associated from the beginning.

A new masthead appeared in the issue of July 3, 1913: "Fred L. Watrous, manager . . . the old company having sold its entire interest to Fred L. Watrous of Myton . . . The corporation, the Advocate Publishing Company . . . Fred L. Watrous, president and manager, Meda G. Watrous, Vice President, L. A. Lauber, Secretary."

"Au revoir, but not goodbye . . . The issue of last Thursday, June 26th (1915) was the last . . . With this issue the writer has put in fifteen years in Price and nearly thirty six years in the newspaper profession." Signed R. W. Crockett. July 2, 1915: "This is the last issue of the Eastern Utah Advocate under its present name and management. The Advocate will be consolidated with the Carbon County News, and issued under the name and title of News-Advocate, the same parties having purchased the News as well . . . W. C. Benfer, the present publisher of the Carbon County News will publish the new paper."

Castle Valley News. The Nephi Blade, July 27, 1895 says: "Volume 1, number 1, Castle Valley News, published at Price, Carbon County, is on our table, 'Ex' in blue pencil thereon. Certainly, Mr. M. Graham." The American Newspaper Directory for 1898 shows: "Price, Castle Valley News, Friday, Republican, established 1895, 4-pages, 18 x 24, $1.50. circulation 420, John V. Long, editor and publisher." But if anybody kept a file of the Castle Valley News, we failed to find it.

Carbon County News, Vol. 1, No. 1, April 26, 1907, Carbon County Publishing Company, Inc., J. H. Nelson, manager, published every Friday . . ." On July 5, 1907 a new masthead appeared, "J. H. Nelson, manager, Carl R. Williams, editor." Nelson's name was dropped from the issue of August 16, 1907, and Williams' name was dropped November 29, 1907. In the issue of May 15, 1908 the masthead shows "B. R. McDonald, J. B. Middleton, editors and managers;" but on September 4, 1908 Hector T. Evans becomes editor and manager temporarily. On January 1, 1909: "E. A. Phillips, editor, C. H. Keith, manager," make their bow. "Mr. Keith, until he came to the News, something over six months ago, served on the Inter-Mountain Republican at Salt Lake City; and Mr. Phillips, a couple of weeks since, resigned the position of telegraph editor on the Salt Lake Evening Telegram."

On March 6, 1909, Keith's name was dropped, and on March 13, 1909, Phillips name was dropped. On April 15, 1909, the masthead shows: "J. David Larson, editor, Sid J. Whitehead, manager." Whitehead's name was dropped May 6, 1909, and on July 9, 1909 another masthead shows: "H. C. Smith, manager, and E. J. Dunn, editor." Also this: "No issue of the Carbon County News has been published since the 3rd of last month, and the present number published by the new proprietors is distributed with an apology for the republication of dead advertisements and miscellanium."

August 4, 1911. "We have purchased the Carbon County News." signed W. C. Benfer. The News for December 29, 1911 is "Issued every Friday by W. C. Benfer and Company, J. Holland Starbuck, editor." With the issue of April 26, 1912 "W. C. Benfer becomes sole publisher, issuing every Thursday." The News was consolidated with the Advocate July 9, 1915 as the News-Advocate.

The Sun. Volume 1, number 1. Friday, June 4, 1915. "Politically Republican. The Sun is being sent to subscribers of the Eastern Utah Advocate for the full time for which the subscribers have paid for the Advocate. The manager of the Sun considers this an obligation and his duty, inasmuch as Judge Albert H. Christensen of the District Court has decided that the subscription lists and books of the Eastern Utah Advocate are the property of C. R. Marcussen, Receiver," R. W. Crockett, manager.

The Gazetteers for 1916-17 and 1918-19 give "R. W. Crockett, manager, J. A. Crockett, assistant manager." The latter name was omitted from the Gazetteer of 1920-21. In the Sun of February 27, 1930 we read: "Robert William Crockett, editor and manager of the Sun, and a resident of Price for 33 years, died (February 22, 1930). He came to Price in 1897." (He had previously been employed on the Salt Lake Herald and the Salt Lake Tribune).

In a reminiscent editorial entitled "Looking Backward," about 1932, John A. Crockett says that when he and his brother leased the Eastern Utah Advocate to Fred L. Watrous, with an option to buy the plant, "The name of the Eastern Utah Advocate was in some way omitted, and Watrous retained the same, later selling it to the Carbon County News, that paper taking the name, News-Advocate." Thus the Crockett Brothers, having the old Advocate plant on hand, and a life-long experience in the newspaper business, established the Sun.

While we have only one side of the story, and that from Mr. W. C. Benfer in his Carbon County News, who and which were open enemies of the Crocketts and their new Sun, the story may be recalled with interest by many, taken as follows from the Carbon County News of July 2, 1915. "Indignant Citizen Wallops Editor. Driven to exasperation by the continual jibes directed at himself and members of his family by the Price Sun, County Treasurer Alpha Ballinger last Sunday afternoon seized the editor, R. W. Crockett, threw him to the ground and gave him a sound thrashing. Crockett later stuck a knife blade into Ballinger's abdomen and that gentleman has been confined to his bed on order of a physician since the cutting . . . (and so on for a column)."

The News-Advocate. First issue July 9, 1915, "Being a consolidation of the Carbon County News and the Eastern Utah Advocate, W. C. Benfer, manager." But some of the history must be read between the lines. For example the following paragraph appeared December 24, 1915:

"Ex-editor Benfer was bemoaning the fact a few days ago on Main Street to one of his kind, in a very hostile manner, that the News-Advocate was turned over to a man who was not a newspaper man, business man, or anything else. Never mind, Bennie, there are two westbound trains, each day of the week which you can catch on your way to Oregon, and you will have to think over one certain Dakota judgment, instead of worrying about the News-Advocate."

The new masthead appeared December 31, 1915: "H. W. Cooper, editor and manager. Howdy do, folks! A new name is found . . ." In a friendly, efficient manner Editor Cooper carried on to the advantage of his townsmen and himself for many a happy year until one sad day in August, 1923. The issue of August 16 carried black borders on a 4-column story headed: "H. W. Cooper dead. Age 45 years." A fine

SALT LAKE TRIBUNE.

ORGAN OF THE LIBERAL CAUSE IN UTAH

DEVOTED TO

MENTAL LIBERTY, SOCIAL DEVELOPMENT, SPIRITUAL PROGRESS.

VOL. II. SALT LAKE CITY, UTAH, AUG. 27, 1870. NO. 35

SALT LAKE TRIBUNE.

PUBLISHED EVERY SATURDAY, SALT LAKE CITY, UTAH.

Price $5.00 per year (currency); $3.00 per half year; single copies 15 cents; clubs, 5 copies, $20.00 (invariably in advance.)

GODBE & HARRISON, PUBLISHERS.

F. T. PERRIS, - General Advertising and Business Agent.

ADVERTISING AGENT.—L. P. Fisher, Rooms 20, and 21, Merchant's Exchange, California St. San Francisco, Cal.

GENERAL AGENTS.—H. Snow, 319 Kearney St., San Francisco, A. S. Hopkins, 70 J. St., Sacramento, Cal. B. F. Brooks, Elko, Nevada.

NOTICE TO FRIENDS AND SUBSCRIBERS.—Friends to the principles advocated in this paper will be helping the cause by obtaining for us all the pre-paid subscriptions in their power. All kinds of produce received in this city at highest market rates. Clubs will have additional copies furnished at club-rates

TO CORRESPONDENTS.—All business letters should be addressed "Business Manager, SALT LAKE TRIBUNE," and communications for the Editorial department, "Editors SALT LAKE TRIBUNE." Correspondence is invited on the subject of the Movement. No Correspondence will be published over a *nom de plume*, unless the name of the writer is furnished us. The Editors are not responsible for all the views of contributors and correspondents.

SUMMARY OF NEWS.

LOCAL.

REVISED.—Our thanks are due to Elder Orson Pratt for a revised copy of his Argument in the Polygamic Discussion.

FROM CALIFORNIA.—A minister of the M. E. Church, writes to us from California as follows:

"I received two copies of your paper and read them with great interest, and shall be happy to read them at any time. Though there are points of difference between us in our belief—as I could see by the very excellent articles in the two papers referred to—still there was so much in them that I could most heartily approve that I almost forgot to object to anything. May God bless your efforts in battling for the Truth. Men will read your leaders and be influenced by them. We wish you and your paper great success among your people. You are aiming at a great and good reform and will have the sympathy and well-wishes of all good people throughout the whole country."

PROF. CHADBOURNE.—By letter just received from this gentleman, we learn of his safe arrival at Madison, Wisconsin, but regret that he found Mrs. C. too indisposed to allow them to proceed immediately to the east. Mr. Chadbourne writes very encouragingly in regard to the mining interests of Utah, and we trust to have the pleasure of seeing himself and lady in our city before many months—if not to make it their permanent home at least to spend a portion of their time with us. We earnestly trust that many of the intelligent and refined will yet make their homes in Utah.

THEOLOGY AND MINERALOGY.—Our esteemed friend and co-laborer in the work of reform, Eli B. Kelsey, late Business Manager of the TRIBUNE, leaves on Monday, 29th inst., for the Eastern States on business connected with the mineral development of this Territory. Mr. Kelsey intends lecturing in the prominent eastern cities on the Theology and Mineralogy of Utah, subjects which his long experience and varied ability well qualify him to expound. On behalf of our Utah miners, Mr. Kelsey will represent over three hundred thousand feet in the best ledges of the Cottonwood, East Kanyon, Bingham and Tintic mines, to which he is authorized to draw the attention of capitalists east; not for the purpose of getting them to purchase or speculate, but to induce them to send on their agents, and purchase after sufficient examination on the spot. Mr. Kelsey takes with him a large number of specimens collected under his own supervision, which he will distribute among such persons as may be sufficiently interested in mineral investments in this Territory to get assays made of them for themselves.

Mr. Kelsey has a fruitful theme in the united subjects of theology and mineralogy upon which he proposes to lecture. No man knows better than he does the theological condition of this country, and how far its mineral development will tend to solve that problem. Having for some months been a practical worker in our mines, he can speak with authority respecting them; while his eloquence, force and point as a speaker, are sure to command him a respectful hearing wherever he may go.

We heartily recommend Mr. Kelsey to all seeking to learn the facts concerning our mineral development, as well as our theological status—he is equally versed in both. Our mineral prospects can scarcely be overstated. Utah is one vast mine from one end to the other. Developments are taking place which show that capital, judiciously invested, will yield no richer results in any part of the world than in Utah.

THAT "PRIVATE PIQUE."—With reference to the recent outrage on Mr. and Mrs. Stenhouse as well as that previously on Mr. Gill, we understand there is good reason to believe that two or three of the men will yet be traced. Both Mr. Stenhouse and Mr. Gill believe they recognized some of the men. It is also stated that a connecting link has been obtained by which the men who manufactured the syringes will probably be identified. The propagators of the ridiculous statement that the act was simply the result of *a private pique* had better not rely too much upon the shallow pretense. We know as well as any one can that the Mormon people, as a people, do not sustain these villainous outrages; but we also know, as do the very persons who are trying to cover up and silence this affair, that religious fanaticism was at the bottom of the whole transaction. Men don't utter such phrases as the sanctimonious, "Do your duty brethren" in relation to matters of private pique or personal animosity.

As members of this Movement we have long known that men have been detailed to visit our meetings and follow our members home. Persons so acting have confessed to others unconnected with the Movement that they were especially set for that purpose. We have plenty of evidence on the subject. We have never referred to the subject, and should not now but to explode this subterfuge about "private pique."

We trust, for the sake of our many orthodox friends who are opposed to all such acts of violence, as well as for the security of the unorthodox, that this matter will not be allowed to rest until the guilty parties are ferreted out and the blame be fastened where it properly belongs.

AFTER THEM.—We understand that the principle attorneys of this city have offered their services free of cost, to prosecute any or all of the miscreants engaged in the late assault on Mrs. and Mr. Stenhouse.

THE *Phrenological Journal and Packard's Monthly* for September, comes to hand containing its usual amount of solid and instructive reading. This Magazine should be read by every family in Utah. The articles on John Sartain, the American engraver; Objections to Phrenology Considered; Men as Lovers; Gen. J. E. Johnston; Scripture names, and in fact the whole of its contents are worthy of perusal. Price, $3,00 per year, single numbers 30 cents.

SPECIAL INDUCEMENTS are being offered by Chislett & Co., Echo City, who are determined to sell out their immense stock at astonishingly low prices, and the residents of Wasatch and Summit Co's. will do well to give them a call.

THANKS.—A friend of Typos, in the 19th Ward, will please accept the thanks of our compositors for those luscious peaches. Printers appreciate such things.

CALLING NAMES.—"To call names is bad enough, and some epithets are scarcely justifiable under any circumstances, and deserve severe chastisement."—*Des. News*, Aug. 22, 1870.

If you really mean what you say, Editor Cannon, we shall expect you and your brother Apostles to stop calling names from this out. But we are free to leave your own awakened consciences to chastise you for the use of epithets undeserved and therefore harmless. It is small business for Apostles to go about the country vilifying good men who have taken the liberty to differ from them. "Apostacy," where is thy sting! Fanaticism, where is thy victory!

CHURCH OF ZION MEETING HOUSE.

AMOUNTS CONTINUED.

From profits of Tea-party and Festival, July 27, $155,60

"GRATITUDE."

EDITORS TRIBUNE,

The editor of the *Herald* doubtless thinks he has good reason for designating, in this morning's paper, a corner drug-store as a grocery or bar. I well remember, on a certain winter night not more than fifty years ago, when the said editor came to that corner drug-store in a most pitiful condition—having imbibed so much and so often at some other *corner* store, that he was, for the time being, hypochondriac, or was strongly moved for the weaknesses of humanity, sobbed and cried bitterly. I called Mr. Godbe down from his office to the store, when he saw the editor and requested me to get a buggy to take him home. I waded through the snow and slush to Faust and Houtz's stables, from there to Mr. Faust's house in the 14th Ward, thence to the house of Mr Houtz in the 13th Ward, and back to the stables before I could obtain the buggy. It was after midnight—I contracted a severe cold thereby, which afflicted me all winter. Mr. Godbe stopped in the drug-store till I returned with the buggy, and he requested me to give the editor some morphine and brandy, and then Mr. Godbe drove him home to the 20th Ward, returned to the store, paid for the buggy and walked to his own house about two o'clock in the morning.

For all this the editor now considers himself under obligation to make a kind return—and he does it. As this was not the only favor by a great many to the editor, we shall expect to be visited with a great many tokens of *his* gratitude. His scandalous charge, however, is utterly false.

W. H. PITTS.

S. L. CITY, Aug. 26th.

FIVE HUNDRED DOLLARS REWARD!

The above sum will be paid to any person or persons who will furnish such evidence as will lead to the conviction of the four men who attacked Mr. and Mrs. Stenhouse, on Saturday night last.

I hereby certify that the above amount has been subscribed and will be paid over to any person or persons procuring such conviction as above.

ANTHONY GODBE, Cashier,
First National Bank of Utah.

A STATEMENT OF THE FACTS.

As Mrs. Stenhouse and I were walking home on last Saturday night, about half past ten o'clock, when we had reached nearly opposite to, the dwelling of Mrs.— Kimball, about 60 yards north of the creek, four men came from the trees on the edge of the side-walk. The night was dark and we did not perceive them till we were only a short distance from them. They were talking loud enough so that we heard and saw them about the same instant; their language and forms were both indistinct. I had no suspicion of any intended wrong; and on nearing us, two of them passed over to my side and roughly jostled against me; I thought at the time that it was only their awkwardness in separating to let a lady keep the center of the road and pass by. As the first one jostled against me, we halted to avoid the second, and I expected nothing else than that they would pass and drop a word of apology. As soon as the four got past us, one of the two on the left seized me by the arm near the shoulder—as Mrs. Stenhouse's arm was still in mine, and the first miscreant on the right seized me by the right arm[illegible] that there was mischief intended. [illegible] at the one on the left who held me, and saw that he was masked, and the two on the right were the same; the one behind me to the left I only saw in form. I did not even then think that a personal assault was intended; I thought it was a robbery, and quickly concluded our watches would go, the four would pass on, and that was new experience in life.

When I was seized, Mrs. S. grabbed the man by the collar who held me on the right and exclaimed, "You villains, what do you want to do?" He struck her and forced her to let go her hold and pushed her back. The two men who had the "squirts," as they are called, stood apart from the two who held me, the one on the right front faced Mrs. Stenhouse who still held my arm, and the one on the left behind her had a fair show for the left side of my head. As I hope it was expected that I would be alone, their plan of operation was doubtless based upon that conclusion, and each with his assigned "duty," no talk would be required. With Mrs. Stenhouse being present, I will do the two ruffians the honor of believing that their momentary hesitation to act was a feeling of manliness. Her presence spoils the programme, the villain that held me by the left giving the order: "Brethren, do your duty?" I thought then that we were doomed to assassination,—thought travels quick in such experience,—I concluded that in an instant more a report would be heard, a bullet would strike my head, down I would go, and in a few moments more all would be over. I then believed that the doom of Mrs. S. would be the same. I could do nothing and, accepting the situation, said not a word. When I saw the body of the ruffian by my side in motion, as if he was drawing a short gun upon me, I instinctively ducked my head and the beastly filth intended for the left side of my face passed over between the back of my head and shoulder and dashed against the fence; a very small quantity reached my clothes. While my head was ducked down, the ruffian in front, not being able to reach me, for Mrs. S. was in front of me, deliberately launched the whole of his squirt directly in her face, which covered her from her hat to the skirt of her dress.

Their "duty" thus fulfilled, they ran towards the northwest corner of the Temple block (where, I was satisfied then and have been since, they had an accomplice.) I ran after them, calling out, "I know who you are." I wheeled to see where Mrs. Stenhouse was; and as I turned on the right, she ran past me on the left, frantic with the insult, screaming and calling after them to stop, that they were cowardly villains. Her wild screams and frantic language brought some persons from those widely separated houses, and from those we learned that the ruffians ran down the north side of Temple block.

We hastened to the City Hall, whither I was accompanied by a gentleman—a relative, and there I related to the Captain of Police what had occurred. The voice that gave the order "Brethren, do your duty," was to me the voice of one of the police, with whom I was personally well acquainted. I asked the Captain where he was and learned that "he was out on the street and it could not possibly have been him." In course of time we returned home; I threw off my soiled clothes, took a bath, put on other clothes, got my rifle and with my son came down into the city. Another gentleman accompanied me to the City Hall between 1 and 2 o'clock, and nothing had been heard of the ruffians. On the street we met two of the police and the one I was seeking. He deliberately said there that it was not him; I told him that I would not swear to a masked man, and take oath that it was him; but it was his height, form and voice, and that I was pleased to learn it was not him.

No man can swear to the identity of persons masked, that difficulty removed, I am as satisfied of knowing three out of the four ruffians as the case admits of. It was their heights, their forms and they were three persons whom I had seen together before, time and again.

The narrative that I here give carries with it the conclusion that I anticipated no personal assault, and least of all, that I could expect any. I was unarmed. I have not carried arms for some years, except probably three or four times when I knew that I would be detained late in the city; and the possibility of attack on these occasions was always apprehended through the party that I think engineered it on this occasion.

The three ruffians whom I think I recognized were not persons with whom I had ever been on any terms of intimacy, nor with whom I had ever intercourse or business, and their action on this occasion is only explained by the chief's instruction—"Brethren, do your duty!"

When an outrage has been committed in this community, it has always been observed that some persons have industriously circulated discordant and improbable rumors. In half an hour after the outrage had been committed on Saturday night, I am told that a personage, whose duty it was to have searched for the ruffians, quietly remarked to those who had been attracted to the place, and who expected that he would interest himself, that it was "probably a quarrel between Stenhouse and his wife and he did not want to interfere!" That was an excellent beginning. The next report I heard was that "the New Movement folks had done it to bring him over to their side!" "The Gentiles had done it in order to charge the Mormons with persecution!" It finally reaches point as a family quarrel or some personal pique! I am pleased to acknowledge that the *Deseret News* has no editorial pen yet [illegible]

I am gratified at being able to state that hundreds of the best people in the city have [illegible] and have not only expressed their detestation of the outrage, but very many of them have volunteered me every aid they could to assist in reaching the ruffians. The Bishop but expresed the general impression when he uttered "Wrong thing, wrong thing; shouldn't have been done; do him no harm; hurts you and me; hurts everybody." Exonerating thus the community, it is due to myself as well to say that I have neither had personal nor family quarrels. No one has said an angry or unpleasant word to me, nor have I done so to any man or woman. I know of no person in the community with whom I have not been on speaking terms, save the person alluded to who first expressed the idea of a family quarrel and the writer who gave it to the world.

In seeking for an explanation of the dastardly outrage upon myself and wife, my impression was that the notice, in Saturday's TRIBUNE, of the same character of outrage upon Mr. Gill on the Thursday night preceding, was probably attributed to my pen, and that this filthy organization of "brethren" thought to strike terror into the writers who dare to classify them as ruffians. I knew nothing of the outrage till I saw it published. I, however, endorse every word of the writer's denunciation.

It is the duty of every law-abiding citizen who wishes well the city and the people, to volunteer whatever information may, in any way, lead to the detection of the offenders. Though I cannot swear to masked faces, I feel morally certain of knowing three out of the four, and I promise that I shall never cease to track them till they are brought to justice.

As an editor and as a citizen I have never failed to denounce midnight ruffianism, and to any retaliation now or at any time I shall not lend my countenance. No man is a friend to this people who does not firmly protest against unlawfulness on any side. There is a glorious future before Utah, and it should not be periled; but it is very desirable that the civil authorities should be able at an early day to cope with this ruffianly element that injures the name of the city. Things cannot remain as they are. Citizens will not be intimidated nor held in terror by a clique of midnight desperadoes.

T. B. H. STENHOUSE.

In the Third District Court of Utah Territory.

ELINOR HYDE, Plaintiff,

versus.

RICHARD HYDE, Defendant.

Richard Hyde, the Defendant herein, will take notice that the aforesaid Elinor Hyde did on the 18th day of August A. D. 1870 file her complaint against the said Richard Hyde in the Third Judicial District Court of said Territory, praying for, a decree of Divorce, and for alimony, and the said Richard Hyde is hereby notified that he is required to appear in said Court and answer said Complaint on or before the 29th day of September A. D. 1870—and that if he fail to appear and answer the said complaint as above required the said Plaintiff will apply to the Court for the relief demanded in said complaint.

WM. S. WALKER,
Clerk of Third District Court.

R. H. ROBERTSON,
Plaintiff's Attorney.

Courtesy Salt Lake Tribune-Telegram Library

appreciative editorial, unsigned, was run under the cryptic title "30," and there was no name on the masthead; they were all at the funeral!

Then on June 21. 1925 (the 1924 file was missing) we found the masculine appearing "G. A. Cooper, managing editor; John M. Sharp, city editor." Sharp's name was omitted from the issue of May 25, 1926, and in the issue of August 12, 1926, the masthead banner is: "Grace A. Cooper, managing editor."

Mrs. Cooper and her assistants carried bravely on against great odds until May 24, 1929, when she surrendered in a most touching valedictory. "In retrospect . . . through the thirteen years we have lived in Price . . . we have believed in Price, its present and the future. We have loved its people, they have been kind to us . . . In the next part to be written, we are glad to introduce a new character, one who has been reared in newspaper work and loves it above all else, one who will make a good citizen and a good friend. To him be not only kind, be generous. And so we say au revoir."

In the next issue, May 31, 1929, we read: "A New Deal by William T. Igleheart, editor and manager. The News-Advocate today enters upon a new era of service to southeastern Utah. The new management takes over the publication and dedicates it to the upbuilding of this rich part of Utah." But, sad to say, the issue of July 2, 1930 shows a new masthead: "P. K. Nielsen, Manager; William T. Igleheart, managing editor." And thus it ran more or less smoothly until the issue of December 8, 1932, when the paper adopted the new hybrid title:

"The Sun-Advocate. An independent newspaper, Joseph L. Asbury, publisher." "Beginning with this issue the Price Sun and News-Advocate are merged and will appear regularly under the heading the Sun Advocate. . . Mr. Nielsen, fortunately, will remain with us as superintendent of the mechanical department."

In his farewell R. W. Crockett, Jr. says in part: . . ."The people of Price have been kind, lovable, tolerant. During the life of the Sun the history of Price has been chronicled . . . Each week we have talked over the back fence with our neighbors, so to speak. Our columns have announced the birth of many of our prominent citizens. We have mourned the death of many. We have enjoyed our growth, achievements, and happiness together. We have suffered our reverses, heartbreaks, and sadness together. I am saying farewell. How fleeting are the misunderstandings and unhappiness. How sweet the sobered memory. 'I went mourning without the Sun; I stood and cried in the congregation. Job 30, 28'. There are tears in dusty memory and a lump in our throats as we take (our name) from the masthead. 'fare-thee well; the elements be kind to thee and make thy spirits all of comfort'. Thirty."

The issue of January 24, 1935 carries this announcement: "During the past week negotiations have been completed whereby all interests owned by Joseph L. Asbury have been purchased by Hal G. MacKnight and Val. H. Cowles," former associates of Mr. Asbury, who have continued in charge.

PROVO, Utah County

Population: 1850, about 2,000; 1860, about 2,500; 1870, about 3,000; 1880, about 4,000; 1890, 5,159; 1900, 6,185; 1910, 8,925; 1920, 10,303; 1930, 14,766.

Provo Daily Times, Volume 1, No. 1, Friday, August 1, 1873. Files: From Volume 1, No. 123, December 26, 1873 to April 27, 1875, in the Bancroft Library. Also a copy bound in with the Enquirer at Provo Public Library, Volume 1, No. 1, the Provo Daily Times August 1, 1873. Four pages, 6 narrow columns, heavily loaded with advertisements. Masthead: Robert T. McEwan, Oscar F. Lyons, Robert G. Sleater, Joseph T. McEwan, Editors and Proprietors. "Salutatory: This is our beginning in newspaper publishing, and it is a beginning for the citizens of Utah County in having a newspaper that they may call their own . . . We will take a bold and independent stand on matters of politics, law and religion." There is nearly a page of local news.

E. W. Tullidge, in his Quarterly, Salt Lake City, for July, 1884 says this is the way it came about: "In the winter of 1872-3, John C. Graham had been conferring with several of the leading men of Provo, looking to the establishment of a printing office and the publication of a newspaper in Provo. The matter was submitted to President Brigham Young, who expressed his approval of it, though he witheld his consent to Mr. Graham personally engaging in the enterprise, inasmuch as at the time that gentleman was associated with the management of the Salt Lake Theater, and engaged as a prominent member of the dramatic company . . . (later) Mr. Graham's health became impaired and a mission was assigned him to England. On receiving this appointment, he advised Mr. R. G. Sleater . . . to obtain the cooperation of others . . . The advice was followed and R. G. Sleater, Robert T. McEwan, Oscar F. Lyons and Joseph T. McEwan formed themselves into a company, purchased the necessary material and on the first day of August, 1873, issued . . . The Provo Daily Times."

The Salt Lake Herald observes, August 9, 1873: "The many editors of the Provo Times are going on a fishing excursion. Their physician advises a change of diet from squash to trout." The Times' Editor ran an editorial on April 4, 1874, says J. Marinus Jensen in his History of Provo, saying in part: "We think the change (from a daily to a tri-weekly) will be an improvement; and it seems highly satisfactory to all, until times are better and the money is more flush." This "spicy" paragraph appeared in the Salt Lake Tribune, July 13, 1875: " 'On Thursday Evening an officer appeared in our office with warrants for the arrest of Messrs. Sleater and McEwan, charging them with being drunk and endangering the lives of the community. McEwan was fined $5, and the eye of the Court beamed mildly'. So writes the editors of the Provo Times, concerning themselves."

From the Utah Evening Mail, January 3, 1876, we learn: "The Utah County Times, Provo City, has ceased publication. Lack of support of the City Council, and the failure of citizens to live up to their agreements, is the cause." The Tribune adds its mite January 14, 1876: "The Utah County Times, an obscure little Mormon sheet, lately published in Provo, flickered out with the close of the year. The editor, writing its obituary, complained of the failure of help 'from the source referred to', which doubtless means the City Council. The world sustains but slight loss in the journalistic demise. During its brief and inglorious existence, it has been the born thrall of the Church. It has been edited without ability, and its virulent abuse of the Tribune and Methodism in Utah has, among other sins, rendered it obnoxious to its own supporters."

Of a posthumous publication the Tribune, April 20, 1877, remarks: "Governor Emery has a warm supporter in the Provo Times, a dirty little Mormon sheet, published by a 2-ply polygamist and slave of Brigham Young." And again, September 6, 1877: "Robert G. Sleater has retired from the Utah County Times, and is succeeded by John C. Graham of Salt Lake."

Utah County Advertiser, established January 13, 1876, says Bancroft in 1884. Successor to the Utah County Times. "It was issued twice a week, the expense being met solely by advertising patronage," says E. W. Tullidge in his History of Provo. "This little sheet was succeeded on July 4, 1876 by the Utah County Enquirer."

Utah County Enquirer, Volume 1, No. 1, July 4, 1876. Semi-Weekly, 24 x 36, successor to The Advertiser. Some excellent files in the Provo Public Library. First six months missing. The semi-weekly, 4-pages, 6 columns, all home print, "Published every Wednesday and Saturday by Sleater and McEwan, in time for the southern mail."

On March 28, 1877 we find in it: "Our paper. We are much flattered with the many letters of appreciation which we receive, stating the esteem in which the Enquirer is held by our readers, its usefulness, and the superior manner in which it is conducted. Several literary gentlemen and newspaper writers have called in our sanctum lately. We are almost ashamed to say it, but we do it in a whisper—they strongly affirm that we ought to be in a larger and more progressive city." We agree, in reviewing the paper after 60 years; for it was a very fine newspaper!

July 7, 1877 it was: "published by Robert G. Sleater and Company in time for the southern mail." But, September 5, 1877: "published by John C. Graham and Company, John C. Graham, Editor." "Valedictory: With this number our management and control of the Utah County Enquirer will cease. . . . Robert G. Sleater." From September 15, 1877 it is "John C. Graham, editor." On October 10, 1877 the name of the paper was changed to

The Territorial Enquirer. "After publishing the Enquirer about a year," says Tullidge, "the managers (of the Times and the Advertiser) who had been reduced to two in number, dissolved partnership, and R.

G. Sleater alone undertook the management of the paper. In two months Mr. Sleater found himself unable to keep the 'wolf from the door', and Mr. Graham who had returned from England, and was carrying on a successful publishing and a general job printing business in Salt Lake City . . . assumed control . . . Mr. Graham was trained in the business and editorial departments of the Millennial Star. When he took control of the Enquirer, only 290 subscribers were transferred to him; now (July, 1884) there are close to 2,000. The Enquirer has continued a semi-weekly and owns and occupies a fine brick building."

"The Utah County Enquirer, semi-weekly, made its appearance at Provo yesterday," says the Salt Lake Herald, Sunday, July 2, 1876. The Tribune of February 4, 1877 says: "We understand the Provo Enquirer, which has become too independent for the Kingdom of Smoot, is soon to be removed to Silver City, Tintic." The American Newspaper Directory for 1878 says: Utah County Enquirer, semi-weekly, Wednesday and Saturday, Independent, 4-pages, 24 x 36, $4, "Owned and edited by John C. Graham, proprietor."

Saturday, December 4, 1880, while John C. Graham is editor we also read: "Go and see J. C. Graham tonight, in his comic character The Kinchin, the Gypsy Thief. Graham will appear this evening as the eccentric and funny Lyttleton Lynx." And January 29, 1881 a rehearsal is called for the members of the Home Dramatic Company, signed by John C. Graham, manager. Also: "Payson Theatricals; on Friday and Saturday evenings next, Mr. J. C. Graham will make his appearance in three of his humorous impersonations in Hancock's new Hall, Payson City." Practically every issue contains some theatrical note, news item, or advertisement about John C. Graham—truly the versatile and indefatigable Dr. Jekyll and Mr. Hyde of Utah journalism! March 19, 1881: "Go and see Graham in his funny character of Nicodemus Nobbs tonight!" Yet the Enquirer carried an excellent news service, regularly and was splendidly patronized by advertisers. Graham surely had a way of making things go!

"The editor of the Territorial Enquirer has been made happy by the gift of a bunch of pie plant from an admiring female reader," says the Ogden Herald, May 13, 1881. On May 14, 1881 the Enquirer says: "J. C. Graham apears tonight in his comic specialty of Si Bloom, played by him several times in the Salt Lake Theater." And, believe it or not, a "Political Notice" was signed by "J. C. Graham, secretary Central Committee!"

The files are missing for 1882 to 1885 inclusive. The Salt Lake Herald, May 8, 1882 says: "Professor Maeser has tackled the editorial tripod of the Territorial Enquirer." The Deseret News of January 26, 1884 says: "Suit for $5,000 damages has been instituted at Provo by R. H. Hines against the Territorial Enquirer. All the Enquirer said was that Hines' Drug Store was a billiard hall, a gaming den, and a den of thieves . . . The thieving gang (meaning plaintiff and his employees) cleaned out an Ashley Fork man, (meaning Sterling Colton) to the tune of $500. Now they clean out another man (meaning Samuel Moore) of his watch, chain and money and almost murder him besides. The defendant is John C. Graham, editor and publisher."

Charles W. Hemenway writes in his book, "Memoirs of My Day," that he reached Provo in February, 1884, and through the friendship of H. H. Cluff and A. O. Smoot "was installed in the office of the Enquirer as an editorial writer. During the next few weeks some original articles made the subscribers . . . open their eyes, we suspect." Continuing, in the third person, he says: "Hemenway was not a Mormon, but the Enquirer belonged to a Mormon, and the new editor took delight in defending a people whom he knew were often shamefully abused and villainously misrepresented." As a result of these editorials, Hemenway says, L. W. Shurtliff, E. H. Anderson, and John Nicholson induced him to go to Ogden to take editorial control of the Herald, on March 22. 1885, Hemenway's twenty-fourth birthday.

The Deseret News of May 23, 1885: "Mr. R. Maeser, who is engaged editorially on the Territorial Enquirer, visited." But we learn from the Manti Home Sentinel, August 28, 1885: "Professor Maeser, who has for some four months past, been connected with the editorial staff of the Provo Enquirer, has again been prevailed upon to resume his labors as principal of The Beaver Central School."

Graham evidently stuck to the "boards," for on February 26, 1886 we find in the Enquirer: "J. C. Graham appears as Augustus tomorrow night." April 9, 1886: "We doff our chapeau: The Ogden Herald, in referring to the theatrical bill of fare announced for the entertainment of our conference guests, made the following flattering comments a few days ago, 'that excellent editor and admirable actor, John C. Graham, whose genius has done much for the development of the Historic (sic) Art in Provo'." June 22, 1886, "John C. Graham, manager," calls a rehearsal for "The Lost Ship"; and "J. C. Graham will appear as Bill Trenant in The Lost Ship Saturday night."

We picked this note up in the Enquirer of March 22, 1887: "The Southern Utonian (Beaver) says: 'A loil licker' of the Provo gang had a roundup with Editor Graham not long ago. From personal acquaintance with the editor's fighting proclivities, (not that we have indulged with him!) we are confident that they got the worst of the bargain. Graham is a powerful antidote for deception, and the 'loil lickers' are all hypocritical." What a repertoire!

As a sign of the times, this is taken from the issue of April 26, 1887: "A Washington hand press for sale cheap; inquire at this office." July 19, 1887: "Rehearsal: In the cast of The Lottery of Life, J. C. Graham, manager." Also, "Political—the members of the County Central Committee of the Peoples Party" (a standing display ad) was signed J. C. Graham. And: "Provo Theater, J. C. Graham, manager." The Deseret News of October 6, 1887 says John C. Graham was arrested for

SALT LAKE DAILY TRIBUNE

AND

UTAH MINING GAZETTE.

VOL. I. SALT LAKE CITY, U. T., SATURDAY MORNING, APRIL 15, 1871. NO. 1.

unlawful cohabitation. The story was given in full detail in Graham's own Enquirer of October 7. The paper was renamed

The Utah Enquirer January 3, 1888, and enlarged to 8 columns, 4-pages, all home print. "Our Greeting" (a column) was signed The Enquirer Company, Inc. . . . A. O. Smoot, president. Harvey H. Cluff, Vice President, W. H. Dusenbury, John C. Graham, S. R. Thurman, George Q. Coray, and Joseph T. McEwan, directors. Upon Mr. John C. Graham devolves the management of the business." February 17, 1888: "Mr. J. C. Graham, in his irrepressible character of 'Dicky Dandelion', tomorrow night at the Theater." The State Gazetteer for 1888-9 gives "J. H. Wallis, associate editor."

The Daily Enquirer, bound volumes in Provo Public Library. Volume 1, No. 1, Saturday, November 30, 1889. "The Enquirer will be delivered at your store, office or residence for 80c a month, $8 a year. The Enquirer presses are run by steam power. Competition is futile. Published every evening, Sundays excepted by the Enquirer Company, H. H. Cluff, president, D. John, vice president, L. A. Wilson, secretary, John C. Graham, manager." Two display advertisements were: "Provo Opera House, J. C. Graham, manager," and "Provo Theater, J. C. Graham, manager." Most of the fillers were theatrical items, instead of the usual scissors jokes.

Announcement was made February 10, 1890: "Mr. James Clove, late of the Salt Lake Herald Editorial Staff, has accepted the position of Associate Editor of the Enquirer." Does the following indicate a change? "Mr. Skelton of the Provo Enquirer has been in town," says the Manti Home Sentinel, March 13, 1891. And the next year, July 30, 1892 the Brigham City Report clips from the Manti Times-Reporter of August 27, 1892: "The Provo Enquirer claims to be the oldest paper in Utah outside of Salt Lake. Judging from the impression of much of the type, no one could doubt the assertion!"

The American Newspaper Directory for 1892 says the semi-weekly edition appears Tuesday and Friday, $2.50, circulation 3,340, John C. Graham, editor. The Enquirer Company, publishers. Daily, every evening except Sunday, $8, circulation 1,225. The Manti Times-Reporter, September 2, 1893 says: "Mr. Clove, editor of the Enquirer, was whipped by Councilman Barney a few days ago for making an attack on that gentleman through the columns of the newspaper."

The Enquirer crowd evidently had its stinger out, for the Park Record of January 13, 1884 informs us: "The Provo Enquirer has been sued by R. R. Irvine, for libel. He estimates the damage of his character to be $25,000. The suit is in connection with the charges against him as Judge of Election at Springville." And, the Manti Messenger of May 25, 1894 says: "John C. Graham, editor of the Provo Enquirer, was tried on the charge of criminal libel in the District Court in Nephi on Monday. (A verdict of no cause for action was returned and the prisoner was set free)." According to the Wasatch Wave, June 21,

1895: "The Provo Enquirer, has another libel suit on its hands. Alex Jennings claims to have been damaged to the tune of $10,000 last December by that paper stating that he was held in the County Jail for counterfeiting."

The Provo Daily Enquirer was a most excellent newspaper, forming a splendid local history, until about 1893, when advertisements began to crowd out the news badly. Thereafter for some years its news service was certainly inexpensive. It must have had a monopoly and was enjoying it. A large percentage of the news items were reading advertisements. The news service improved, however, decidedly in 1897 —the year the file ends in the Provo Public Library. The following change was chronicled January 4, 1896 in the Nephi Blade: "John S. Rollo, former owner of The Dispatch, has accepted a position with the Enquirer and will relieve Mr. Clove of the editorial department." Nevertheless, the Utah County Democrat on January 11, 1899 mentions: "The Enquirer . . . of which James Clove is editor."

The 1900 edition of the State Gazetteer gives: "The Enquirer, Provo, John E. Booth, President; The Enquirer Publishing Company, M. H. Graham, Secretary and Treasurer, John C. Graham, Manager." The Gazetteer for 1903-4 carries the same except: "John C. Graham, editor." S. A. Kenner, in Utah As It Is, 1904, says: "Provo Enquirer, daily and semi-weekly, 8-pages, 13 x 20, Republican, Mormon, circulation, daily 1,050 and semi-weekly 2,800, John C. Graham, Editor." On March 7, 1907, H. C. and N. C. Hicks took over the Enquirer and published it regularly until 1920 when the Post Publishing Company was organized and the Enquirer's name changed to the Provo Post.

Provo Journal. Here is all we know about it: The Park Record quoted from it February 14, 1891; and again, more than six years later, August 28, 1897. Incidentally, **The Journal,** succeeding **Public Opinion** and **Progressive American,** published Wednesday and Saturday mornings, began publication in Provo about December 2, 1936.

Provo American, Volume 1, No. 1, April, 1887, no files; first came this notice: "The advent of the anti-Mormon and pro-Loyal League sheet to be known as The Utah American, now seems very questionable," in The Territorial Enquirer April 5, 1887. On April 15th the Enquirer says: "The L. L. American will make its appearance in this city sometime next week. The editors say it will be conservative. We'll see." And again April 22 the Enquirer says: "It calls itself 'The only American paper published between Salt Lake and Frisco'. We have no desire to dispute the contention if it means the Tribune at one end and the Frisco Times at the other. The fewer there are of such 'American papers' the better for the country. We are told that one or two out of the half dozen Mormons who have been inveigled into subscribing for and advertising in the new paper, or as it has perhaps appropriately been called 'The Provo Edition of the Rocky Mountain Christian Advocate' felt somewhat cheap after looking over the editorial page of the first issue. One remarked 'Well, well. After all their taffy about letting religion alone, to think that I have been such a fool!' "

"We have received the first issue of the Provo American published by the Abbott Bros.," says the Park Record, April 23, 1887. On April 26, 1887 the Enquirer says: "Old-Man-Not-Afraid-Of-The-League may expect to catch thunder in 'Rev.' Lincoln's Provo edition of the Rocky Mountain Christian Advocate day after tomorrow! . . . It is said the Reverend Lincoln's Sunday evening congregations are mainly composed of youthful Mormons in couples who don't believe a word he preaches. They go there, so a wag says, to 'spark'." "The Enquirer, has, since Thursday last, published two lively and newsy issues from which the Rocky Mountain Christian Advocate of Provo can obtain its weekly quota of news for Thursday next."

The Enquirer of May 31, 1887, says: "Provo now has two papers. The one essentially Mormon, and the other bitterly anti-Mormon. The latter embellishes its front page with the euphonious title of The American, and is published weekly." The Beaver Utonian is quoted in the Provo Enquirer October 28, 1887 as saying: "The Provo American, which was ratherly liberally subscribed for by outsiders here, is being set down as rather a wishy-washy puerile, sickly affair." On June 3, 1887 is this in the Enquirer: "A number of our newsy locals were clipped bodily from Tuesday's Enquirer by the 'Weakly' outfit down the street yesterday. We have a few more in our issue of today that it will also do the outfit good to clip."

A new management was obviously due, of which the Deseret News of June 29, 1888 says: "H. A. Noon, Esq. of the Provo American visited." But it was past noon for this editor, and sunset came for Mr. Noon on January 2, 1889. He was only 30 when he died of pneumonia. Just "Thirty"! Previously, however: "The Provo American has been changed from a Liberal to a Radical Democratic sheet, with Mr. Ed Pike as editor," says the Manti Home Sentinel, November 7, 1888. But we read in the Millennial Star for May 13, 1889: "The Provo American suffered martyrdom recently to make room for the Utah Valley Gazette." The Gazetteer for 1888-9 shows: "Provo American, Noon and Goodwin."

Utah Valley Gazette. First number April 12, 1889. Doctor Wm. J. Snow, Brigham Young University, has a copy, volume 3, number 3, Friday, April 26, 1889, 7 column folio, 4-pages, all home print, no name on masthead. Published every Friday by the Dixon Publishing Company, Inc. "Special: The Utah Valley Gazette will for the present be published weekly at $2 per annum. The Dixon Publishing Company." The Bancroft Library in Berkeley also has a few copies.

The earliest copy of the Gazette preserved in the Bancroft Library is dated June 28, 1889, being 4-pages, 7 columns, about 25% advertising, fairly good news and editorials. Published every Friday, $2 ($1.50 if paid in advance!), The Dixon Publishing Company, Inc.,

Ireta Dixon, Editor. Apparently neutral in politics and religion—impossible of course—but she was trying.

An issue dated August 30, 1889, carries this: "When the Utah Valley Gazette was first launched upon the uncertain sea of journalism, it announced itself as an independent bark determined to carry to the people honest news and candid views . . . We said moreover that we proposed to conduct this paper in harmony with the views and deference to the feelings and convictions of the people of Utah valley . . . During our very satisfactory experience of 5 months or thereabouts . . . we have discovered several trusted friends, professing the utmost friendship at our face . . . and working us a malicious injury behind our back. We have been falsely accused of cherishing frank and anti-Mormon sentiments . . . Courtesies usually accorded the press, such as complimentary tickets by the Opera House Company, have been studiously withheld . . . We are striving for an honest livelihood."

And September 8, 1889, she adds: "The Utah Valley Gazette has a larger circulation in Utah County than any other paper . . . In the face of the evil prophesies of disaster, in spite of unscrupulous underhanded and shameful opposition, the people have sustained the honest, fearless and independent course of The Utah Valley Gazette. It is going onward and upward, because it started out right . . . In the near future the weekly Gazette will be permanently enlarged." On January 3, 1890, Ireta continues about the paper: "The Gazette will be published on each and every Monday, Wednesday and Friday morning, on and after March 3, 1890, as a prelude to a morning daily . . . The weekly will not be discontinued, but will be enlarged and published every Saturday." All this in large, frank, open face type. The Bancroft collection ends with a copy for January 10, 1890.

The Provo Enquirer borrows this from the Salt Lake Tribune of May 31, 1890: "Hemenway of the Provo Gazette, says Mayor Booth is troubled about its orthography. Booth needs to be; Hemenway hasn't got any!" And the Enquirer adds, July 22, 1890: "The Utah Valley Gazette had no representative at the People's Party Convention, but he was there at the Liberal Convention alright enough." March 22, 1890, the Enquirer correspondent, Ida Coombs, writing from Payson, says: "Hemenway, the pimp of the sheet called the Gazette, allowed the publication of a very unsavory attack on Bishop Tanner in a recent issue."

The Enquirer of March 5, 1890 has this: "The following is from a Paysonite: 'Please send me the Enquirer semi-weekly. I am dying for Provo news, and the Gazette seldom has an item of interest for me, or the right kind of sentiment for ladies, although a lady's name is printed as editor.'"

August 8, 1890 the Enquirer says, "And now comes Hemenway and wants to be heard regarding the great circulation of his paper. He is booming the business in order to get it off his hands. If he would advertise in the Enquirer he could soon find someone to lease his shanty for a few months. It would at least do much more towards it than his own boasting, because so few read the 'Guzzle'."

Then on August 12, 1890, the Enquirer runs this: "The Provo Gazette has hired a man who is willing to swear that the circulation of that paper is larger than that of all the other papers in Utah County combined.—The Salt Lake Times." And August 18, 1890: "The Provo Mugwump paper, The Gazette, has not yet found out which leg is safe to stand on. Poor thing wiggles from one side to the other in perfect desperation.—The Southern Utonian." How hard it was in those days to be "Independent!"

Further, September 5, 1890, the Enquirer gladly copies: "Hemenway's organ, the Provo Gazette, waxed virtuous in its observations on libelous newspapers. The only man in Utah who ever went to jail for libel ought to know something about it."—Ogden Standard. The Enquirer followed with this October 20, 1890: "It is said that a trade is pending between some Colorado parties and the tramp of the board shanty. The former are to purchase the 'Guzzler' plant at 40c on the dollar, so rumor has it. The Colorado men propose running a red hot Liberal sheet."

And October 22, 1890: "The Gazette has been sold and will soon blossom out as a Liberal paper." Clearly some people didn't like the Gazette, and soon we read from its local contemporary, the Enquirer, January 8, 1891: "At last the sale of the Gazette has been consummated, and soon James H. Wallis of the Nephi Ensign will assume control. It is thought that Mr. Probert is a silent partner in the purchase. The consideration of the sale is $2,700, $200 to be paid down, and the balance in installments in five years." The Wasatch Wave of January 13, 1891 puts it this way: "The Utah Valley Gazette has again changed hands. This time James H. Wallis of the Nephi Ensign takes the wheel and compass and will henceforth guide this vessel over the troubled waters of journalism." And finally, January 19, 1891, the Enquirer says: "The Dispatch is the name of a semiweekly that has arisen on the ash pile of the defunct Gazette."

Provo City Press. Volume 1, No. 1, January, 1891, semi-weekly, no files and only these contemporaneous references, which we are inferring refer to the same: "Provo will have a new Gentile paper before many weeks. It will be started by Rathbone Bros., late of Nebraska," says the Park Record, January 10, 1891. And on January 29, 1891, the Eastern Utah Telegraph announces: "We are in receipt of a copy of the Provo City Press, a new paper started at Provo. It is published semi-weekly."

The Enquirer may have chronicled its demise February 28, 1891: "The Press failed to put in an appearance Wednesday. It is understood that hereafter it will issue only once a week; twice in one week is more than it can accomplish, and perhaps as much as its readers can stand." The Enquirer of August 21, 1891, concludes the record: "The Provo City Press has pulled up stakes and gone to Eureka, and will change its title to The Miner.

UTAH EVENING MAIL.

VOL. I. SALT LAKE CITY, MONDAY, DECEMBER 20, 1875. **NO. 1.**

By Telegraph.

Proceedings in the House and Senate.

Hanging of Three Negroes in New York.

A Horrible Scene on the Scaffold.

Geo. F. Seward, Minister to China.

Another Dynamite Explosion Predicted.

CONGRESSIONAL.

SENATE.

WASHINGTON, Dec. 17.—Sargent introduced a bill for the reinstatement of the interests of the United States on the city lands in the city and county of San Francisco, California; referred to the committee on military affairs.

HOUSE.

WASHINGTON, Dec. 17.—Kasson introduced a resolution...

EASTERN DISPATCHES.

Execution of Three Colored Men.

NEW YORK, Dec. 17.—Wesley, Ellis and Thompson, colored men, were hanged in the Tombs prison, at 9:50 this morning, for the murder of Abram Weinberg...

WESTERN DISPATCHES.

Lynched.

SAN FRANCISCO, Dec. 17.—A dispatch from Carson says a gang named Thomas Burt was hung by vigilance last night, and was found this morning hanging to the gate of the cemetery.

FOREIGN DISPATCHES.

Probably a Sensation.

LONDON, Dec. 17, 6 a. m.—The Bremerhaven Zeitung asserts that in spite of all contradictions, according to Pheum-assen's confession, there is another explosive perhaps on board the steamer Seller...

BRIEF TELEGRAMS.

The Empire of Germany has started an association in Berlin for the relief of the Bremerhaven sufferers.

The Cuban insurgents recently destroyed a Spanish gunboat, which was landing men to attack a town near Las Cruces.

Provo City Dispatch. Volume 1, No. 1, January, 1891. This is from the Enquirer: "The Dispatch is the name of a semi-weekly that has arisen on the ashpile of the defunct Gazette. In its opening editorial it says: 'We are going to give credit where credit is due. We care not whether it be Mormon or Gentile, Liberal or Peoples party man, Republican or Democrat.' "

The L. D. S. Millennial Star for February 9, 1891, says: "Provo has two newspapers, the Dispatch and the City Press. The former is edited by J. H. Wallis." On February 21, 1891, the Enquirer man says: "We are informed that the Dispatch is to be the organ of the new Democratic Club started in Provo."

The Enquirer of August 6, 1891, says: "True to our predictions, the Dispatch is proving nothing more than a Democratic makeshift, used to help win the election. Their associated press service has been discontinued and their telegrams are now made up of clippings from other papers." The Manti Home Sentinel tells us, September 15, 1891: "Mr. John S. Rollo of the Dispatch is paying San Pete a visit."

The Provo Enquirer says, September 16, 1891: "The Dispatch advertises this morning for an editor who can live on wind. It may be hard to find a man to accept the position if they propose to pay him in wind. But they are able to pay a high salary!" The Enquirer evidently thought it was penning an obituary July 22, 1892: "The Dispatch has gone where the woodbine twineth." The Wasatch Wave of August 2, 1892, contributes this: "The Provo Dispatch is no longer a daily paper, but appears twice a week."

Its neighbor, Enquirer of August 4, 1892, echoes another note: "Milo Zip's paper, the Brighton Record, says the Provo Dispatch is dead. It was a dirty rag at best and its demise was all too long delayed. The cause which dispatched the Dispatch was too much amateur politics." The echo, above sounded, however, seems not to have been from the Great Beyond; the Dispatch was only changing from a daily to a semi-weekly, reducing its tempo and increasing its power.

The American Newspaper Directory for 1892 gives additional data, some of which must have been gathered, and was true only, early in 1891. "The semi-weekly edition of the Morning Dispatch, issued Wednesday and Saturday, Democratic, 4-pages, 20 x 26, $2.50, circulation 2780; The same, issued every morning except Monday, 4-pages, 18 x 24, $9. Dispatch Publishing Company, James H. Wallis, Editor."

In the absence of files we must have missed a link, depending on contemporary gossip for our news, for the Wasatch Wave of October 10, 1893 says: "The Provo Dispatch has changed management, Mr. John B. Miller retiring and Col. John L. Bartow assuming charge. Mr. Miller has held the position for a little over a year." The next stride forward is a long one, from the Park Record, August 10, 1895: "J. L. Bartow of the Provo Dispatch has turned the plant over to its owner. The plant has a $3000 mortgage against it, and unless it is soon taken up, the plant will be closed down."

We got this from the Provo Enquirer which clipped it from the Richfield Advocate, which quoted it from the Nephi Blade of November 23, 1895: "J. F. Gibbs has vacated the editorial chair of the Provo Dispatch." And here's how easy it was to die: Says the Nephi Blade December 2, 1895: "The Dispatch Plant was purchased by the Enquirer Company!" And another note in the same paper adds: "The Provo Dispatch Plant was sold yesterday for $600 to John R. Twelves at Sheriff's sale."

The Utonian. First number in Provo, May 23, 1896. Files, apparently complete in two bound volumes in the L. D. S. Church Library, Salt Lake City. "Independent, progressive," 6 columns, 4-pages, 3 home print. "Explanatory. (May 23, 1896). The Utonian plant arrived in the city on Monday evening last, several days later than expected. There was the work of placing it, putting up machinery, etc., setting up all the advertising, etc., etc., in addition to the regular work. R. Maeser, Proprietor and Editor, was on Thursday evening called to Beaver as a witness in an important lawsuit, thus depriving us of his services for two days. Really, the first issue of the Utonian, published in Provo, under the circumstances, should have been delayed until next week. But the announcement was made that the first issue would appear today, and here it is, half size only. Hereafter, it will be an eight page paper."

An editorial announcement to the Public ran about a column, explaining and promising: "Financially, we are broke. We start at the foot of the ladder, with every possibility before us.—The Editor." Also this: "The Utonian is not a new venture in the newspaper field. The plant has been moved from its former location at Beaver to Provo. The Utonian has passed through many trials during the 16 years of its existence. During the greater part of the life of the paper the present editor has had personal supervision of its columns . . ." The masthead says it was published every Saturday by R. Maeser; printed by Skelton and Company. "The Utonian informs its readers that just as soon (as a profit is available) we shall begin . . . publishing a daily. Our judgment is that at present Provo cannot, in justice to itself, support a thoroughly live, wide awake, up to date newspaper. Such a paper is indeed a very expensive luxury."

The Utonian was a very fine newspaper—too much news in fact, for the amount of advertising patronage, if that is possible. The masthead for October 6, 1896 is changed to show: "Published thrice a week, on Tuesday, Thursday and Saturday; four pages, 2 home print." "The Utonian will hereafter appear three times a week . . . and will work for the success of the Democratic ticket. The weekly edition of the Utonian will continue to be published as formerly."

The February 5th (1898) number says: "The Utonian comes before the people with this issue in a new form. The editorial staff comprises men who are recognized as writers of ability." There was no name on the masthead, but a lengthy editorial was signed by S. A. Kenner.

On December 16, 1897 a change in the masthead appears, also this: "The Utonian . . . hereafter the paper will be under the exclusive management of the Utonian Publishing Company. Under amicable arrangements with the former firm of Skelton, Maeser and Company, this has been made possible for the present. Mr. R. Maeser will be manager and Mr. Emil Maeser will attend to the editorial work and advertising. After our brief experience in Utah County, we have concluded to arraign ourselves politically on the Democratic side."

Then on December 18, 1897: "The Utonian printing business will be conducted by the Utonian Printing Company," indicating a complete divorce, or at least 'separate maintenance' from the Skelton Publishing Company. The following appeared in the Utonian for February 19, 1898: "From the Roundup: 'The Utonian is now very interesting reading, with such men as 'Scip Kenner, Professor Nelson, Emil Maeser and W. M. Wolfe on its editorial staff'." The April 2, 1898 number was apparently the last issue of the special political series, the original Utonian having expired January 29, 1898.

Utah County Democrat. Volume 1, No. 1, Provo City, Wednesday, August 31, 1898. Files, bound in Provo Herald office, Fred Nelson, editor and publisher. "Our Venture: The Utah County Democrat is not a campaign venture, but is designed to be a permanent institution." The last issue in the bound volume is for August 26, 1899. The next numbers found, also bound, begin with May 5, 1908. "The Democrat Publishing Company, W. M. Roylance and George A. Storrs, Proprietors. J. David Larson, Editor." Roylance's and Storr's names were dropped May 19, 1908. The file ends with February 13, 1909.

Running through the State Gazetteers we find concerning the Democrat: 1900, $2, Fred Nelson, editor and publisher; 1903-4, W. R. McBride, editor and manager; Wells R. McBride, C. W. Barnes, R. W. Hooper, publishers. 1908-9 **Provo Democrat,** J. D. Larson, Manager. A copy for July 24, 1901 shows McBride and Barnes, publishers.

Provo Post. Volume 1, No. 1, March 7, 1907, issued Tuesday and Friday by the Post Publishing Company. In 1912 it was published Tuesday, Thursday and Saturday. H. C. Hicks, editor, N. C. Hicks, manager, in all the files seen. It claims to have been "successor to the Enquirer." The Utah State Gazetteers, 1912 to 1921 list it with Heber C. Hicks, Editor, and Nephi C. Hicks, Manager, but the Gazetteer for 1922-23 puts N. C. Hicks on both horses as—"Editor and Manager." "The last issue of the Post was published May 9, 1924, E. C. Rodgers, publisher of the Provo Herald, having purchased the paper and merged it into the Evening Herald," says J. Marinus Jensen's History of Provo.

Provo Herald. The earliest file is Thursday, March 4, 1909, issued Tuesday, Thursday and Saturday. Masthead, J. David Larson, who had changed the paper's name from the Democrat. On January 17, 1911, we read "Consolidation of Provo Herald, daily and Intermountain Herald, weekly, to be issued semi-weekly." A masthead appears February 21, 1911: "O. C. Soots, editor, E. F. Stacks, business manager." And this announcement: "Entered at the post office at Provo as second class matter January 4, 1911."

All was not peaceful, however, we gather from this: "Announcement (May 2, 1911): By adjudication of the District Court the Herald has been sold to Lester G. Baker and O. C. Soots, after having been in the hands of W. F. Giles, Assignee, since October last, during which time various individuals of different political views, creeds and attitudes have figured in its editing and management." Signed, Lester G. Baker, editor. The masthead became, May 5, 1911, "Lester G. Baker, Editor and Manager," and June 2, 1911, "Baker and Larson, owners," J. David Larson, Editor. On February 10, 1912 came this announcement: "Herald Publishing Company . . . has been purchased by I. H. Masters of the Press-Bulletin, Bingham, and S. H. Wood of the Uintah Land Company of this city, Lester G. Baker and J. David Larson retiring."

The new masthead: "I. H. Masters, manager, Sam H. Wood, editor." But Wood couldn't take it, evidently, and with an editorial, February 26, 1912, Sam H. Wood resigns as editor, leaving "I. H. Masters, managing editor." Masters was complete master, as the paper was all home print. Thus he continued through 1917 and possibly awhile afterward. The 1920 files show no masthead, but I. H. Masters signs the editorials.

The next evidence of proprietorship appears in the issue of April 4, 1921: "Provo Herald to be published tri-weekly, beginning Monday, April 11, 1921 . . . E. C. Rodgers, editor and publisher . . . The Provo Herald passes to a new management." The Daily Herald, first appeared April 17, 1922. And by way of appreciative reminiscence it carried a photograph of the first issue of the Daily Enquirer, along with an article by J. Marinus Jensen on early newspapers in Provo. This addition to the masthead was made November 22, 1922: "E. C. Rodgers, editor and publisher, J. A. Owens, business manager, N. Gunnar Rasmuson, city editor."

The July 1, 1924 number carries this: "The Herald now goes to all former subscribers of the Provo Post," and thereafter, "With which is combined the Provo Post." Came then on October 17, 1924: "With this issue of the Provo Daily Herald the ownership and the management are transferred to W. H. Hornibrook." The new masthead is: "Wm. H. Hornibrook, publisher; N. Gunnar Rasmuson, editor." In 1925 it became "Hornibrook and Rasmuson."

On September 14, 1926. "The Evening Herald and its sister paper, the Springville Herald, were sold today by their editor and publisher, W. H. Hornibrook, to the James G. Scripps Newspaper Interests,

(Scripps-Canfield Newspapers), and Herald Corporation will operate the newspapers." N. Gunnar Rasmuson, editor to July 31, 1931; The Herald Corporation publishers to date.

RANDOLPH, Rich County

Population: 1890, 400; 1900, 700; 1910, 533; 1920, 586; 1930, 447.

The Round-up, Vol. 1, No. 1, May 29, 1896, 6 columns, 4-pages, 2 home print, John R. Wallis, editor and proprietor. Files complete in one volume, presented by Mr. Wallis to the Utah State Historical Society. That was Rich County's first newspaper. The Round-up has the distinction of being the first Utah newspaper to be printed on wheels and away from home. Number 9 of volume 2, dated July 24, 1897, a regular weekly issue, was printed on its own printing press on a Rich County float in the Pioneer Day parade in the streets of Salt Lake City. Nattily dressed milkmaids from Rich County distributed the paper free, throwing them into the crowds on the sidewalk from the float as they were printed!

The American Newspaper Directory for 1898 says the subscription was $1.50, circulation 321, published Friday, non-political. The ready-print in those days came from Portland and San Francisco. The April 9, 1898 number carried the Valedictory: "With this issue of the Round-up our labors as editor and proprietor cease . . . due to a regard for the health of our partner in life, who suffers from this high and severe altitude . . . Our successor, Mr. W. J. McLaughlin, is an excellent newspaper man." There is no further news of the Round-up. Mr. Wallis understood McLaughlin soon quit and junked the equipment.

Rich County News. The Gazetteer for 1903-04 shows Benzley and Robinson publishers; for 1908-09 LeRay Shelly, publisher; (sounds like a girl). In 1912-13 J. M. Peart was publisher, and in 1914-15 Le-Roy Shelby was publisher; for 1916-17 F. R. Morgan, publisher, and for 1918-19 Arthur McKinnon publisher. The Western Newspaper Union ready-print record shows 300 copies were being sent February 1, 1921 to A. L. Larson; the firm became Nicholls & Larson after September, 1924, and continued so until September 14, 1928, when the entries, and possibly the News, ended. It is singular that none of these names agree with those given in the Gazetteers; but such are the adventures of a would-be historian!

Rich County Reaper. It is suspected this was but a new name for a new effort in the old plant of ill-fated predecessors. Oldtimers on Main Street told us that the Bank let the paper to Ruby Larson, editor, and Mabel Nicholl, compositor, who ran it with some success for about two years. Then Bernard H. Ewer took the plant and the paper, giving it the name Rich County Reaper, allegedly to avoid hangovers from previous obligations. It was entered as second class matter at Randolph February 8, 1929. Wm E. Marshall became editor and proprietor January 3, 1930, and has continued as publisher to date.

THE SALT LAKE DAILY HERALD.

VOL. VI.—NO. 237.   SALT LAKE CITY TUESDAY MORNING, MARCH 14, 1876.   PRICE FIVE CENTS.

RICHFIELD, Sevier County

Population: 1870, 4; 1880, 1,179; 1890, 1,531; 1900, 1,969; 1910, 2,559; 1920, 3,262; 1930, 3,067.

The first printing press in Sevier County was bought from a mail-order house by H. P. Miller, and used to catalog his personal library. The press was later sold to Joseph and Albert Thompson, who printed thereon a small sheet chronicling the news of the day. So we learn from a manuscript prepared by the late Dr. M. Markus, and read before the Richfield Daughters of Utah Pioneers.

The Thompsons also sold drugs, some of which were intoxicating, and got the Thompsons into trouble. The authorities made a raid on the drug store. The proprietors were indicted and fined so heavily, they were forced to dispose of the printing press, which was purchased by a Soldier of Fortune named Agra Monte. Monte continued printing the small sheet started by the Thompsons, which indicates there must have been a little money in it; but Agra soon went to Mexico, and took the printing plant with him. No one could recall just when those events occurred, so we have no dates. There are no files.

Sevier Valley Echo Vol. 1, No. 1, August 15, 1884, James T. Jakeman, publisher. It was an echo of the Thompson-Monte paper, and of the activities of the people of the Valley. "A new paper is about to be published in Richfield, Sevier County, with the name of the 'Sevier Valley Echo'," says the Deseret News July 14, 1884. The News follows up the story six months later, December 13, 1884: "The already immense number of newspapers in the Territory is increasing; the last budded number is the Sevier Valley Echo . . . It may have a Sevier time of existence." And it did, for "The publisher of the Sevier Valley Echo announces to its patrons that it will take a change of base from Richfield to Manti. Poor Manti!" we learn from the Salt Lake Evening Democrat, April 7, 1885. Jakeman published the Echo until May 1, 1885, when it was superseded in Richfield by the Manti Home Sentinel, which had a good circulation there, and deserved it!

Richfield Advocate, 4 pages, $1.50 a year; later $2. "It is reported that George Hales, formerly of the Beaver Utonian, is about to begin the publication of a newspaper at Richfield," says the Deseret News August 30, 1887. The Territorial Enquirer, of Provo, October 28, 1887, reports "The Sevier Advocate is the name of a paper to be started at Richfield;" and on November 18, 1887, the Enquirer adds: "We have received the initiatory number of the Richfield Advocate."

The Home Sentinel, February 1, 1888, has this jibe: "The Richfield Advocate tells its readers that he is not much on poetry. Why, that need not be told! Everybody knows that, and also that donkeys do not like music." Then the Sentinel quoted from the Advocate of that date, to show its friendliness. On March 14, 1888, the Sentinel says: "The Advocate is bent on having a railroad from Thistle to Marsyvale.

Well, we hope you get it." The Sentinel of August 15, 1888, says: "Mr. William Cowley, late of the Advocate, Richfield, was in town last week."

According to the Markus manuscript, Cowley was editor, and Hales manager. Tilda Nielson, Annie Peterson, and Merta Hansen, were the compositors, and often the reporters. Their news notes were sufficiently interesting to be borrowed by the exchanges, as we found frequently, though unfortunately, few files of the paper are available. We found a dozen copies in the Bancroft Library, the earliest, Vol. 2, No. 35, July 3, 1889, published every Wednesday by George Hales; 7 columns, 4 large pages, 2 home print. The latest number was dated August 27, 1890. It carries this note: "The Advocate Office is crowded with job work at present. It has turned out some of the finest work lately, that has been done anywhere south of Salt Lake City, and as cheap."

"Mr. George Hales, proprietor of the Richfield Advocate, was arrested on April 29, on a charge of adultery, and went before Commissioner Leonard, of Salina," says the candid Home Sentinel, Manti, May 6, 1890. But the Advocate (whatever it advocated), carried on, and "Mr. George Hales, of the Richfield Advocate, made us a fraternal call," says the Home Sentinel, November 14, 1890. Though evidently not in jail, Hales was nevertheless on his way out of the newspaper business in Richfield, for the Eastern Utah Telegraph, June 19, 1891, refers to "Sol Sprague, Assistant Editor of the Richfield Advocate;" mentioning him again July 17, 1891.

Then on April 22, 1892, the Provo Enquirer informs us: "Editor Sol Sprague, of the Richfield Advocate, is in the city on legal business. He is also attorney for Richfield City." The American Newspaper Directory for 1892 says, "Richfield Advocate, Wednesday, Mormon, established 1887, 4 pages, 18 x 24, subscription $2, circulation 500, Hales and Sprague, editors and publishers."

The Markus manuscript indicates that Sprague became sole proprietor in 1893, and in 1894 sold to the Meteer Brothers. About then, George Hansen joined the force. A tribute comes from the St. George Union, March 18, 1897: "Richfield's two papers are engaged in the highly edifying occupation of saying mean things about each other. The Advocate can say the meanest things, but the Censor shows the greater capacity for taking punishment." The Brigham Bugler of December 4, 1897, says, "The Richfield Advocate is the fiercest Mormon-eating paper published in Utah today."

Retribution got in its work however, and on October 17, 1898, the Richfield Advocate Office was burned to the ground. The Utah County Democrat, November 16, 1898, informs us, "In a few days, it is announced, the Richfield Advocate will be revived by A. B. Williams, formerly of the Mt. Pleasant Pyramid." Information furnished by Dr. Markus is that Williams purchased what could be salvaged from the plant, and also purchased some new type and machinery. The Advocate had advocated so many unpopular movements, the resurrected newspaper was christened with a new name. But before we consider the direct lineal descendent of the Advocate, we must insert: (for chronological sequence.)

Southern Censor. Vol. 1, No. 1, April 25, 1896. George H. Crosby, Junior, editor and owner; Wm. Cowley, printer from the Deseret News, Lura A. Miller, Clara Nielson, and Ada Ramsey on the force. The Nephi Blade, April 18, 1896, says, "The Blade's belief is that Richfield cannot support two newspapers, but we may be mistaken . . . " The Wasatch Wave, May 15, 1896, puts it: "Richfield has another paper called the Southern Censor . . . We will guarantee it to be more deserving if the editor-proof-reader and compositor would take a few lessons in art."

The Brigham Bugler of April 30, 1898, says: "The Southern Censor has passed into Vol. 3." Indeed, the Censor passed on completely, about that time. Mr. Crosby is reported to have sold the plant to J. T. Camp and Lorenzo Lisonbee in November, 1898. These men moved the outfit to Elsinore, where it was later destroyed by fire. Certain references to this newspaper have called it the "Censer," but as there are no files, we are not certain whether the "Censer" was extinguished, or the "Censor" merely passed on to that realm where censors are often told to go!

Richfield Reaper was the physical successor to the Advocate, but it was presumably not an advocate of the Advocate's principles. A. B. Williams was editor and owner. The first mention of the new paper is by the Utah County Democrat, March 22, 1899, which is as near as we can come to its Genesis. Mr. Crosby purchased a half-interest July 16, 1901, becoming editor. The State Gazetteer for 1903-4 gives Williams & (J. J.) Woodring, publishers. The Gazetteer for 1908-9 says Hanway & Woodring were publishers. The 1912-13 Gazetteer says Willis Johnson was lessee and manager. The masthead January 1913 was: N. C. Poulson, lessee, F. V. Fitzgerald, manager. Fitzgerald's name was dropped February 13, 1913. The masthead June 12, 1913: George M. Jones, editor. J. L. Ewing became editor January 7, 1915, succeeding Willard Bean, editor and business manager. P. V. Peterson was associated with Mr. Ewing in the mechanical department. The masthead on January 3, 1916 shows J. L. Ewing, publisher, A. E. Howard and J. L. Ewing, editors.

C. E. Hanway was the publisher of the paper from 1908 to 1910, made himself very unpopular, says Markus, by vigorous attacks on the dominant Utah Church; consequently, the impersonal Richfield Publishing Company was organized, and took over the paper in 1910. The paper was then run for five years, under various managers, says Dr. Markus, including Willard Bean, A. J. Bird, George M. Jones, John Hord and Neils C. Poulson. Finally, the indebtedness of the company led to the sale of the Reaper to James M. Peterson, who let the paper to J. L. Ewing in 1915.

The Reaper and its competitor, The Sun, merged January 3, 1916. "Any former patron of The Sun who is sulking in his tent with a griev-

ance, is requested to call up the Reaper office and register any complaint
he has to make." (Humorist Howard came with The Sun.) In January, 1920, Dr. M. Markus became associated as editor, with Ewing,
purchasing Ewing's interest in September, 1920. The wife, a talented
writer, always shared the masthead: "Mrs. Elizabeth Markus, Assistant
Editor," until her passing, September 13, 1924. Dr. Markus' successful tenure was longer than that of any other editor. He sold the Reaper
to Joseph L. Asbury in March, 1930, going to California where he died
in August, 1933. Dr. Markus received the Doctor of Philosophy degree
from the University of Vienna, where he also had studied law and
medicine. In America he first edited an immigrant paper printed in
fourteen languages, seven of which were handled by Dr. Markus himself. Subsequently affiliated with German language newspapers, he
dropped them all at the beginning of the World War, to become Utah's
most talented and distinguished country editor. Richfield business houses
closed for his funeral, and leading citizens spoke eulogies on a man
they loved, but who was not of their faith.

Asbury's Salutatory contains this, March 27, 1930: "Of course I
need the support of the people . . . You know the story of the Athenians
of old, who, when oppressed by war, applied to the Lacedaemonians
for help, and the Lacedaemonians sent a hunchback singer by the name
of Tirtaeus to help them. The people of Athens were disappointed, but
when they went to battle, Tirtaeus, through his songs, filled their hearts
with such enthusiasm that they conquered their enemies. I want to be
a Tirtaeus to the people of Sevier County."—Joseph L. Asbury. He
came pretty nearly doing just that—but sold the Richfield Reaper
March 1, 1934, to Mr. Joseph J. Fuellenbach. Mr. Fuellenbach died
December 27, 1935, the mantle of publisher falling on the widow, Rula
J. Fuellenbach. Her "Girl Friday", Thelma Jackson, was also secretary
to publishers Asbury and Markus, through the Reaper's best years.

The Sevier Sun, referred to as Richfield's Sun, appears in the Gazetteer for 1908-9, with Arthur E. Howard, publisher. "It shines for Sevier
County, Republican in politics." The Gazetteers for 1912 to 1915 says
that F. W. Tilney was manager; but the Gazetteer for 1916-17 credits
O. W. (sic) Howard with the management. The Sun finally set January
13, 1916, when it was merged with the Reaper.

Arthur E. Howard died March 24, 1917. He came to Utah in the
early 1890s, and began his printing experience as a compositor on an
Ogden newspaper. He founded the Salina Press in 1904, but later
moved his printing plant from Salina to Richfield and established
the Sevier Sun. "A bunch of Carrots" was a book made up largely of
cuttings from Howard's Salina Press, and was a noteworthy record of
life in a Utah country town.

ROOSEVELT, Wasatch County

Population: 1920, 1,054; 1930, 1,051.

The Uintah Standard, Volume 1, Number 1, January 29, 1909, only 4 abbreviated columns of type on the front page, the other 3 pages being blank. It said: "The Uintah Standard, a weekly newspaper, herewith presents itself for favorable consideration . . . The publisher, E. T. Hyde, has had considerable experience in this line . . . Through the kindness of Mr. C. C. Larsen, the popular merchant, the Standard is located in the north front of his building."

Another imprint—Volume 1, Number 1, January 29, 1909—believe it or not—omits all material shown in the above issue, and gives two columns of news and 4 columns of advertisements on the front page. There are 3 ready print pages and 1 inserted sheet. Possibly the first above was run off before the ready prints arrived! Hyde's name was omitted from the title line March 5, 1909. As far as we were able to determine the Uintah Standard thus fell, about mid-March 1909.

The Roosevelt Standard, Volume 1, Number 1, August 29, 1914, published every Saturday at Roosevelt, J. P. May, publisher, Arnold Reef, editor. "The Standard is born again, unfurled this time to remain!" Evidently the reference is to the Uintah Standard, above. In the issue of February 1, 1915, a news item says J. P. May, who was editor of the Duchesne Record and manager of the Roosevelt Standard, had severed his connections with those papers and moved to Salt Lake City.

"The past week the Roosevelt Standard Company was incorporated," says the Duchesne Record February 15, 1915. Arnold Reef was manager and editor from June 21, 1916, to August 23, 1922. In the issue of August 30, 1922, Arnold Reef signs this: "Eight years ago the writer came among you and started the Roosevelt Standard . . . This town is too large for a one-man newspaper . . . I trust that my friends will give the Standard their heartiest support and cooperation."

The issue of September 6, 1922, carries the new masthead: James H. Wallis, editor and publisher, William B. Wallis, manager. (Father and brother respectively of Mrs. Violet Harrison, wife of George H. Harrison.) The Western Newspaper Union ready print account from October 12, 1923 to date is in the name of Mrs. Violet Harrison. Beginning August 27, 1924 the masthead shows George H. Harrison, editor and publisher; Violet Harrison, business manager.

The Myton Free Press, February 5, 1925, refers to the Roosevelt Standard as "The Andy Gump of Utah Journalism!" But the Free Press is gone and the Standard is stronger than ever, after many years! Harrison & Harrison to date. Would this be Mrs. Harrison's beginning? From the Provo, Daily Territorial Enquirer, December 16, 1889: "Another Evidence of a Boom: It has been customary for our Mr. James H. Wallis to come up to the Enquirer Office on a Sunday morning

The Ogden Junction.

$4.00 PER YEAR. PUBLISHED SEMI-WEEKLY, (WEDNESDAY and SATURDAY.) $1.00 PER QR.

No. 45. OGDEN, UTAH, WEDNESDAY, JUNE 6, 1877. VOL. VIII

OGDEN DIRECTORY.

Ogden Post Office:

ARRIVAL AND CLOSING OF MAILS.

ARRIVALS.

Salt Lake City, double daily, 7.50 a.m. 5.45 p.m
West, Through Mail daily - - 7.40 a.m
East, Through Mail daily - - 5.40 p.m

DEPARTURE.

Salt Lake City, double daily 8.40 a.m. 6.30 p.m
West, Through Mail daily - - 6.20 p.m
East, Through Mail daily - - 8.40 a.m

CLOSING.

For Salt Lake and the East - 7.00 a.m.
For Salt Lake and the West - - 5.00 p.m.
The Rich County, Bear Lake County and Soda Springs mails go via Evanston, Wyoming, and leave the latter place Mondays Wednesday's and Fridays at - - - - ; 7a.m
Oncne County, daily - - - - 7 a.m
North Ogden and Harrisville, Wednesdays and Saturdays, 2.00 p.m.
Huntsville, Wednesdays and Saturdays - - - 7.00 a.m.
Lynne, Plain City and Slatersville, Mondays and Thursdays - 2.00 p.m.
Hooper and Alma, Wednesdays and Saturdays - - 7.00 a.m.

OFFICE HOURS.

General Delivery, - 8.15 a.m. - 6.15 p.m.
Sunday, 5 p.m. to 6.30 p.m.

REGISTRY DEPARTMENT
Open from 9 a.m. to 3 p.m.

MONEY OFFICE DEPARTMEMT.
Open from 9 a.m. to 3 p.m.
Outside Door open from 6 a.m. to 8 p.m.

L. B. STEPHENS, Postmaster.

Trains

C. P. train arrives - - -	8.40 a.m.
U. P. " " - - - -	5.40 p.m.
C. P. " leaves - - -	6.20 p.m.
U. P. " " - - - -	8.50 a.m.
U. C. train arrives - - -	9.00 a.m.
" " and - - -	5.40 p.m.
" " leaves - - -	9.40 a.m.
" " and - - -	6.20 p.m.
U. N. train arrives -	4.00 p.m.
leaves -	9.20 a.m.

Religious Services

Every Sunday, in the Tabernacle, at 11 a.m., and in the First, Second and Third Ward School-houses at 7 p.m.
Episcopal Church at 11 a.m. and 7 p.m.
Methodist Church at 11 a.m. and 7 p.m.
Spiritualist Lectures, Liberal Hall, at 7.30 p.m.

Ogden City Library

At 'Geo. W. Turners' News Depot. Open every day, Sundays excepted.

CHAS. H. BENEDICT,
ATTORNEY-AT-LAW.
[Assistant United States Attorney]
Office: Main Street, opposite Driver's Hall, Ogden, Utah. d15-3m

F. S. RICHARDS,
COUNSELOR-AT-LAW
And
NOTARY PUBLIC.
Office at Court House, Ogden, Utah.
Special attention given to cases before the Supreme and District Courts. Conveyancing and Notarial Business done with accuracy and dispatch. a86

N. TANNER Jr.,
ATTORNEY AT LAW.
AND
NOTARY PUBLIC.
Office opposite Driver's Drug Store, Main st., Ogden
Special attention given to collections. Remittances promptly made. Conveyancing and Notarial business carefully attended to. a18

UTAH NORTHERN RAILROAD.

SPECIAL NOTICE IS HEREBY GIVEN TO ALL parties holding the Utah Northern Railroad Company's vouchers, payable in capital stock of the same, that on and after January 10th, 1877, and until otherwise ordered the stock books of the Company will be opened at the Company's office in Logan City, Utah, for the express and only purpose of allowing such voucher holders to subscribe for and take up the stock due them respectively.
MOSES THATCHER,
Secretary of the Company.
Logan, January 4th, 1877. d94-2 s3-tf

R. J. TRUMBULL,
Grower, Importer, Wholesale and Retail Dealer in
Seeds, Bulbs,
Plants, Trees,
ETC., ETC.
The most complete stock to be found on the Pacific Coast.
Seeds and Plants by Mail
A SPECIALTY.
New Illustrated "Guide to the Garden" will be out shortly, and will be sent free to all customers or persons intending to become customers. Also Catalogue of Bedding Plants.
R. J. TRUMBULL,
419 & 421 Sansome St.
SAN FRANCISCO. a16d.1m

BY TELEGRAPH.

AMERICAN.

New York, 21.

A panic took place in a Catholic Church of Stanton county, this morning. A large congregation was gathered to witness the administration of the holy communion to a number of Sunday school children. These latter all wore gossamer veils, one of which took fire from a candelbra. The cry of fire was raised, and the greater part of the congregation rushed for the doors, but the efforts of the priests and ushers, who kept the doors closed, prevented a terrible calamity. The fire having been extinguished, and the congregation reassured, the services proceeded without further interruption. Some parties received severe bruises during the stampede.

A Montreal special says the loss by fire yesterday will reach half a million dollars.

Washington, 31.

It is said that some one has taken away the petitions numerously signed asking for the removal of Fred Douglass as United States Marshal, and has failed to return them, consequently they will probably never be presented to the President, as was the original intention.

Memphis, 31.

Horace T. Smith, general freight agent of the Louisville and Nashville Railway, was drowned in the river opposite here last night.

Hartford, 31.

Monsieur L'Al Vergnat, an instructor of French in the Hartford schools, who was bitten by a dog on April 30th, died this morning of hydrophobia.

Denver, 31.

This morning when the day force went to work in the silver ore tunnel, near the Terrible mine, Georgetown, they found the corpses of John Gregory, Harry Walters and a companion, named Pope, all of whom had been mangled and killed by an explosion of powder. There are no survivors to account for the cause.

Springfield, 31.

Governor Cullom to day vetoed the bill to make silver coin a legal tender in this State, giving as his reasons that he does not believe it a wise measure in its financial aspect, or constitutional.

FOREIGN.

Portland, Ont., 31.

The house of Alexander Synder was destroyed by fire last night. Two children were burned to death.

Rome, 31.

The Italian Republicans have placarded the streets of Rome with notices of a great demonstration at the Apollo Theatre on the 30th inst., to declare that Rome can never again become the Rome of the Popes.

London, 31.

The News Alexandria dispatch says the Egyptian transport steamers have not yet started with the Egyptian contingent troops for Turkey. The strike of the English engineers, which at first delayed their departure, has been settled, but a Russian man-of-war at Petropaulovski, carrying twenty-nine half ton guns, is waiting for them in the Mediterranean.

A special from Paris to the Times says Turkish iron-clads are expected at Alexandria on the 4th of June.

A Blind Kentuckian Sees Again.

Mrs. Betsy McKay, mother of A. H. McKay of this place has been blind for years, until a few days ago she had the cataracts removed from her eyes, enabling her to see as well as when she was young. Mr. Ludd McKay, her son, called in Louisville to see her soon after she regained her sight, and she did not know him, having been blind so long. Mrs. McKay is 90 years of age.—Spencer Courier.

A singular suicide recently took place in Drowana, Australia. A Greek who had become insane by reason of poverty and misfortune, poured a quantity of molten lead down his throat. He died in agony, and after death a lump of lead nearly half a pound in weight was taken from his stomach.

FLOOD AND FIRE!

The Ocean Wave and the Volcano Lava.

San Francisco, 31.

By the arrival of the City of Sidney, we have an account from the Honolulu Advertiser of the great tidal wave of May 10. It appears to have occurred simultaneously all over the group. At Kahului, on the island Maui, the unusual subsidence of the sea was first noticed about a quarter before five in the morning. An observer in this town, who was near the harbor and saw near the harbor and saw the exposed reefs, places the occurrence at the same time. J. J. Porter, of Hilo, Hawaii, fixes the moment of the wave which overwhelmed the Waiakea precisely at the same time, and the statement of Capt. Smithers, of the whaling bark Pacific, which was lying at the time in Hilo bay, corroborates this. The difference between the highes and lowest water mark at various localities we ascertain as follows: Hilo, on the east side of Hawaii, 36 feet; Kealakekua bay, west side of Hawaii, 30 feet; Kawaihae, west side of Hawaii, 6 feet; Kahului, north side of Maui, 22 feet; Lahae, south side of Maui, 22 feet, Lahaina, south side of Maui, 12 feet; Honolulu, south side of Oahu, 4 feet 10 inches; Nawiliwile, southeast side of Kauab, three feet. In some cases the difference in the height of the wave may be accounted for by the configuration of the coast and outlying reefs. The following is an account of the disaster of Hilo from an eyewitness:

Hilo, May 11, 1877.

To W. O. Parke, Esq.:

Dear Sir:—We have had a great disaster at Hilo. Thursday morning, 10th inst., about 4 a. m., the sea in the bay was seen to rise and fall in an unusual manner, and at 5 o'clock it swept in in a mighty wave, washing up into nearly all the stores in front of the town, carrying off a great deal of lumber and all of the stone wall makai, or wharf.

The particular height of the wave, since ascertained by leveling, was twelve feet three inches above the ordinary low water mark at Waiakea. The damage was frightful; every house within a hundred yards of the water was completely swept away. The steamboat wharf and storehouse, Spencer's storehouse, the bridge across the stream, and all of the dwelling houses, were swept away in an instant, and now lie in a mass of ruins far inland. Five lives were lost, and a number were bruised and had their limbs broken. The body of a woman was found by boats off Hoolii. The boats of the American whale ship Pacific, Captain Smithers, lying in harbor, picked up six people who were swimming for their lives in the bay. The Pacific was lying in four fathoms of water, but she grounded when the sea receded, and then would be whirled round and round as the sea came in again. All expected to see her drag ashore. The sea continued to rise and fall all day. I timed one of the tides in the morning about 7 o'clock, and from its lowest ebb to its full flood, was only four minutes. It rose about fourteen feet in perpendicular height in that time. In that afternoon in the space of one hour the sea rose and fell three times, with the height above the half tide of seven, ten and a half and three feet each time. The wave at Waiakea must have had a perpendicular height of sixteen feet to have taken the bridge and wharf where they now lie. The water swept completely over Cocoanut island, and the hospital there has disappeared.

Yours in haste,
L. Severance.

The volcano of Kilauea has been unusually active of late. The steamer arrived at Hilo, Wednesday the 2d inst. As she passed down the coast on the following night the light of the crater was unusually brilliant. Friday, at 2:46 p. m., several pretty severe earthquake shocks were felt, followed a few minutes later by a jet of lava thrown up from the floor of the crater near the east bank through a crack which had evidently been made by earthquake. The lava continued to spout at this place, gradually ascending the steep bluff to its summit, then moving along the isthmus connecting the large crater with the smaller one of Kilaneaiki, down into the pit to which the lava ran. This continued for six hours, the lava being thrown up in numerous jets along the line at different heights, at times reaching one hundred feet. Frequently there would be at least fifty of these jets at once, making a magnificent display. The locality of this eruption and its general characteristics appear to be identically the same as those of 1832, 1840 and 1868. Simultaneously with this, the fires of Old South Lake were suddenly extinguished, and for two days following no fires were seen in Kilaue.

Destructive Tidal Wave.

The Sea Heaving Beyond Its Bounds.

Panama, 31.

The following particulars of a tidal wave on the South Pacific coast has been received. Callao was visited on the morning of the 10th by a species of tidal wave or rather gradual upheaval of the sea, which caused serious damage and great alarm. The docks and piers of Muella Darsena were the principal sufferers, together with some stores along the shore line, which were completely carried away by the water. Vessels made fast and lying alongside the outer walls of the dock were lifted fully eight feet by the upheaval, but were not damaged. The most of the steamers lying at anchor in the bay shipped their cables, fearing further danger. The United States store ship Onward left for anchorage, the officer in command evidently remembering the fate of her predecessor, the Fredonia, in the great tidal wave at Area, in 1868.

The steamer John Elder, which arrived at Callao from Valparaiso on the 13th, reports a destructive tidal wave at Callao and ports to the north thereof. It was known to have extended as far south as the northern boundary of Chili, but how much farther is not known, as communication by cable is interrupted. The John Elder reports the almost complete destruction of Antofagasta, Arica, Inquique, Tanebo, Dealoro, Pabillong, De Pice and Ilo. The destruction of life and property was owing entirely to the frightful upheaval and ingress of the sea.

A gentleman who arrived by the Trujillo, states that the flourishing town of Inquique, the principal port for nitrate shipments, is left as complete a ruin as after the frightful earthquake and inundation in 1868.

At Arica the sea washed over the town to the hill back of the place and destroyed much valuable property.

The wreck of the United States steamer Watteree, which was carried inland two miles by the tidal wave in 1868, was again floated and carried a mile further up the coast.

The lower part of Antofagasta, which is a part of the celebrated Caracoles mining district, in Boliva, is reported completely destroyed. The smelting and other works near the shore were swept ashore.

The shipping at Pobellon, Depica and and the guano deposits suffered severely, and some half dozen fine vessels are reported ashore and are complete wrecks. The sea in some places is said to have risen over sixty feet.

A Cruel Pun.

In these days not even the most solemn subjects are exempt from the attacks of the punster. It would seem that the grave should be gravely treated, and that the scythe of Time should awaken very serious thoughts, but the punster never allows his wit to be limited, and never loses a chance to exercise his gift. A poor fellow who drove himself into a consumption by hard drinking, and drove his old companions crazy by his resounding cough, at last fell a victim to his evil habits. The wit of the coterie looked at him, and while a tear dropped on his cheek, said, sadly:

"Well, I'm sorry for poor John, for that's the worst coffin spell he ever had."

The Pall Mall Gazette, writing of our economic troubles, and speaking of the terrors which the fast increasing tramps inspire, says:

"In a democratic country the action of a couple of millions of unemployed and often starving men, is a force beyond calculation, and justifies alarm."

THE WAR!

RUSSIAN DEFEAT AT BATOUM.

Christian Troops to Fight for the Turks.

ARDAHAN RECAPTURED.

London, 31.

The Telegraph has the following: At Batoum on Wednesday, the Russians attacked the Turkish positions here. Notwithstanding the large force which the Russians brought to the attack and their persistency against the galling fire of the Ottoman artillery and infantry, they were finally repulsed leaving great number of dead and wounded. The engagement lasted ten hours, during which time several close combats took place.

The Russian telegraphic agency reports that according to the latest news from Belgrade, Servia has definitely resolved to maintain strict neutrality.

It is stated in Vienna that three army corps have been unable to take up a strategic position because of the floods. It is announced from Widdin, however, that the Danube is falling.

Berlin advices received from St. Petersburg represent that the Turks recovered Ardahan after the Russians had reduced it to ruins.

A dispatch from Constantinople states the Porte has made levies upon the Christians for 200,000 troops.

The Times' Bucharest dispatch contains the following: The Turkish camps at Nikopolis have been removed behind the hills. This is believed to be a prelude to the bombardment of Turnumagureli. The Roumanians think the Turkish monitors are placing torpedoes along the southern side of the river.

A special to the News from Krajova, commenting on the state of the Roumanian army, says between Kupercent and Cetate there are 30,000 soldiers. They are in excellent physical condition and perfectly equipped and armed and have more than the ordinary proportion of artillery with a definite scheme of action and in complete accord with the Russians.

The Turkish foreign minister has telegraphed the Porte's representatives abroad as follows: Ardahan, which was recently occupied by the Russians, has been recaptured by the Ottoman troops.

A special from Ploiesti says the Danube is so high owing to the melting of snow in the mountains near its source, that an inundation is feared near Oltenitza, which would oblige the Russians to remove their batteries there.

St. Petersburg 31.

An official dispatch from the army of Caucasus, May 29th, says on Monday Gen. Oklobshio, commanding operations against Batoum, ordered his advance guard to the left bank of the heights on the left of the Turkish line. The enterprise was accomplished. Meantime a detachment ascended the Kintrisch, and after great difficulty established a position about four miles from Kalsobani, thus cutting off communication between Batoum and the population of Kabeti-e district. The Russian loss in both enterprises was four killed and thirty wounded.

Vienna, 31.

Tagblatt states that Mukhtar Pasha has been dismissed from command and will be court-martialed for representing that he had equipped an army of 66,000 men, whereas he had only 30,000 at his disposal. The Fremdenblatt denies that any meeting between the Emperor of Austria and the Czar has been projected.

Five thousand Circassians are ready for embarkation. Two thousand men are intended for Alapa. The ships conveying them will take divers to pick up the torpedoes at the entrance of the Sea of Azov.

Mukhtar Pasha has been placed under the control of Djeli Pasha, who was officially sent from Constantinople.

Some Bashi Bazouks crossed the Danube between Kalarach and Jalorinitza. They captured fourteen Roumanian militia men and cut off the calves of their legs.

Paris, 31.

Delegates from Greek provinces of Turkey held a meeting at Athens last night in favor of war. A committee on national defense has been called upon to distribute arms in those provinces.

Courtesy L. D. S. Church Historian's Office Library

and glance over the Exchanges, and so forth. Yesterday his jovial countenance appeared as usual, but we noticed from the first something extraordinary had happened. His face wore a kind of nervous expression. Finally he straightened up, looked us squarely in the face, and burst out with: 'Had a big girl down to our house last night', Saturday, December 14, 1889. The mother and child are progressing nicely. Mr. Wallis is at work today as usual."

ST. GEORGE, Washington County

Population: 1870, 1,142; 1880, 1,332; 1890, 1,377; 1900, 1,600; 1910, 1,737; 1920, 2,215; 1930, 2,434.

(The Deseret Telegraph Company's line was opened to St. George, January 15, 1867.)

Our Dixie Times, Vol. 1, No. 1, January 22, 1868, 4 columns, 15 inches, 4-pages, all home print on homemade paper, J. E. Johnson, editor and proprietor. Terms per year, $5, single copies 25c. There are four columns of advertisements, among which are: "J. E. Johnson, Auction and Commission Merchant," and "Hearty grapevines by mail, J. E. Johnson," "Fruit Trees, J. E. Johnson," and "Notary Public, J. E. Johnson." "Salutatory . . . With press erected, type on end, a clean sheet, and our best bow, we again appear (formerly at Spring Lake Villa) not for applause, but with hopes of gaining your honest approbation."

The next week, January 29, 1868, the editor says: "The New Era. The establishment of a printing press in St. George is the inauguration of a new era . . . to establish the printing press so far inland, and in settlements so new and destitute of means to sustain it has not been small or light . . . there are some in southern Utah who appreciate the labor and risks of a publisher; and we very much regret there are not more of that class . . . with very little help or encouragement from any source we have thus far succeeded in providing an office and starting the press; and should our life and health be spared, we intend to issue our little sheet for one year, but further make no promise.

"We are very well aware that many of the denizens of southern Utah are not oppressed with surplus means, some even finding it hard to get through the twelve months of the year, and supply their families with the necessities of life . . . We hereby instruct our agents to give us the names of those who wish to become subscribers and are *not able to pay,* and we shall make them welcome." In the issue of February 5, 1868 the editor says truthfully: "This is the only paper in the Territory published outside of Salt Lake City."

Files complete (except March 4) to November 24, 1869 in H. L. Reid's library, Dixie College, St. George. The masthead of number 4, February 12, 1868 adds, "S. A. Kenner, printer." In an editorial note the editor asks: "What's The Matter? There are six distinct publications, aside from Dailies, published in Salt Lake City. We have yet to receive the first token of a friendly exchange from the Capital."

February 11, 1868, the Salt Lake Telegraph says: "The Dixie Times reports a pleasant surprise to its editor. On the evening of the first issue of the paper . . . Judge McCullough spoke (among others): 'To me it is a matter of pride that our St. George leads next to Salt Lake City, in this commendable enterprise, the patron of a home paper. Let no home be without it; each subscriber is a weight at the end of a lever, and each copy an exponent and advocate of home enterprise'. St. George will grow. Stick to the Times; keep its editor lively, and he will help you all!"

February 19, 1868, the editor made a strong plea for support, and on March 25, 1868 the editor is "Sorry For It. We are out of paper and cannot make another issue until the arrival of Messrs. Miller, Duncan and Cannon, who have our new supply enroute, which should have been here before this, only for the uncommon amount of rains and mud in California. Keep easy. It will soon be in!"

The ink dried out during the wait for paper, and volume 1, number 11, April 15 (he kept his serial numbers consecutive, if not his publication dates!) was miserably printed. "Be Patient," he coaxes; "Our paper has come, but our foreman (S. A. Kenner) has deserted; yet we have two sons, aged 11 and 15, and who commenced apprenticeship only three months ago; and a daughter of 14 who composed her first stickful on this number, to rely on. Our issues may be a little irregular and perhaps not free from fault, but we will be getting faster and better all the time; so be patient." Kenner's name was dropped from the masthead in that April 15th number. Number 12 was dated April 22, but number 13 was delayed until May 13, 1868, and for good luck was renamed:

The Rio Virgin Times, continuing the serial numbers of Our Dixie Times, as well as the size, form and masthead. "Change Of Name," the editor captions. "We have been induced for several reasons to make a slight change in the title of our paper; first to give the casual observers, and the rest of mankind, an idea of our locality at a glance. Many people at a distance catch the idea of our paper coming from some of the State late in the Rebellion. (Dixie!) We like to have our locality appear marked and distinct."

The paper "is published every Wednesday morning at The Times Building, St. George, Utah Territory." One number was poorly inked and poorly printed. The "Virgin" in the title was spelled with an "e" on May 20, 1868, and thenceforth, at least until November 24, 1869, according to the brief file in the Bancroft Library. All column rules on the editorial page were reversed (printing heavy black lines) on June 16, 1868 in mourning for the passing of Heber C. Kimball of the L. D. S. Church Presidency. But the leading editorial in that number is begging for support. "It is our own fault if we are left without a newspaper. Patronage and material aid is needed," he thunders.

Another editorial is headed, "Broken Down Again," which means his help had left him. "At present our patrons must be content with the best we can serve them, and if we get out a paper only once in two weeks, no use of grumbling. Had we a decent support we could *commend* suitable help." The issue of July 22, 1868, number 19, was also execrably printed, but number 20, dated Wednesday, August 12th (sic) 1868, was neatly and clearly printed though oddly enough the editorial page bore the date "St. George, Saturday, 15th." "Just succeeded after a full week's industrious effort," editor Johnson confesses, "in getting enough of a badly demoralized roller in tolerable order to print this issue."

"The Rio Virgin Times of the 22d ult, says the flies are excessively annoying, making it about as pleasant to stick outdoors and labor as to go indoors and fight the flies," quotes the Salt Lake Daily Telegraph of August 4, 1868, with a "Dixie" date line, continuing: "We might have given further items (taken) from the Times, but the paper is so badly printed that we could not read it. The weather must be hot down there. demoralizing the 'Devil', or his ink roller!"

"Subscribe Now," he pleads, September 2, 1868. "Many of those who ought to support the Dixie press have excused themselves because they had nothing to pay. A rich harvest has blessed our whole region, and few can no longer make this excuse. We are publishing at present without any prospect of receiving one half of our current expenses. We must have better support, or the denizens of our Dixie will be minus a local paper after the first volume is issued. If we publish longer it will be for the *pay*—it is disgraceful to a community of this size to allow an enterprise of this character to fail for want of necessary aid. The Times is the only paper printed within 350 miles, and properly the only paper for five counties, namely Washington, Kane, Iron, Beaver—and Pah Ute in Arizona."

The next three numbers were out on time, with a fine array of intimate news of folks, and little sayings and phrases, expressive of the spirit of the community, making a very fine local history of the people. Number 24 was two weeks in preparation, in which the article "The" was omitted from the title, making it:

Rio Virgen Times in a different font of type. (Note the 'e' in Virgen). Number 25 was also two weeks incubating, as was number 26, October 28, 1868, in which the editor is openly: "Apologetic. The editor is much annoyed that printers and their families can't manage to live without houses, food, and such etceteras. Our printer stoutly maintains he can't, and won't do it, so he has to play carpenter a few days, and pass another issue day without the news . . ."

Number 27 did not appear until December 9, 1868, bearing another pathetic wail: "We have reluctantly been forced to the conclusion that the people of southern Utah are yet quite unprepared to sustain a home newspaper . . . We have very little income from job work or advertising, thus relying upon subscription fees to meet the current, daily expenses. The next ten numbers were spaced at fortnightly intervals, number 37, April 21, 1869 following number 36, by a week and being reduced to three columns, four 7 x 11 pages, and re-christened:

The Rio Virgen Times. "Ensmalleo. Of two dilemmas we have for the present to choose: Close publication of the Times, or bring it into the capacity of the help we have, viz, our children; for all we receive has so far failed to support one man and his wife that he has gone north in hopes of once more enjoying a few good meals, and of eating all he wanted. (We almost envy him!). We shall dispense with such advertisements, while we issue this size, as to give nearly as much reading as formerly. Our patrons must remember that choice goods are usually in small parcels, and see if they don't find it so in this instance."

Thenceforth the paper trotted along on a weekly schedule, of dates at least, until number 49, July 14, 1869 inclusive, which was very largely made up of pomological material, as he called it. Number 50, July 28, 1869, was the last of the miniature, or children's size papers, which, singularly enough had a new masthead: "Job Cornwell and Charlie Johnson, printers," who were mere boys, and who let the paper languish forthwith on their small but willing hands. Number 51 was dated November 24, 1868, its reading matter consisting very largely of the doings of the Pomological Society of the city, and this valedictory, though not even the editor realized it would be such: "To Our Subscribers: One number more finishes the first volume of this paper. Those who are in arrears for subscription or advertising are expected to hand in the money at once. We shall be a little particular, after waiting for over a year; so come along!" But they obviously did not come along, nor come across, for the file ends, and those who know assure us number 52 was never issued.

Could it be the Times' failure was in part due to a miniature, vest pocket sized competitor printed in his own office by his own printers for a local merchant? (See The Mineral Cactus). St. George was without a paper for a few months, when ex-editor Joseph E. Johnson, to give circulation to his special knowledge of fruit and flowers in that land of blossoms, started the:

Utah Pomologist, Volume 1, Number 1, April 1, 1870, 3 columns, 7 x 11, 4-pages, devoted to fruit growing and the garden. $1 a year "strictly in advance" published on the first of each month. "only horticultural paper in the Rocky Mountains." Files, H. L. Reid, Dixie College, has 15 scattered numbers, including the first and volume 3, number 12 for February, 1876. "It is to be hoped that our friend J.E.J. was not joking the public in his choice of first day of issue," came a glad hand across the seas from the editor of the L. D. S. Millennial Star of Liverpool, England. As if to try a little magic, the title was changed to:

"The Utah Pomologist and Gardener devoted to the orchard, vineyard, farm and garden," 8-pages; volume 1, number 1 (of this title) January, 1872, circulation 600, says a Directory listing. But the Directories indicate it had shrunk in 1875 to four pages, circulation 360. Nevertheless Johnson's Pomologist stuck as if it were the marmalade of the village! The Salt Lake Tribune quotes one of its heresies, September 9, 1876: "The St. George Pomologist says there is a good open-

EVENING Telegram.

No. 3. St. George, Utah, Friday Evening, April 18, 1879. Vol. 1.

EVENING TELEGRAM.

Published every evening, (except Sunday,) by
J. W. CARPENTER,

At 50 cents per Month, invariably in advance.

☞ Distribution hours from 6 to 7:30 p. m.

☞ OFFICE UPSTAIRS.☜

☞ Advertising Rates:—75 cents a line per month; 40 cts. per line for 2 weeks. Transient advertisements 5 cts per line each insertion.

BY TELEGRAPH.

Special to the TELEGRAM.

——⸮——

NEW YORK 17.

A loan of $3,000,000 was secured yesterday on six per cent bonds of the Northern Pacific Railroad, for extending the road two hundred miles, from Bismarck to Yellowstone.

The Negro exodus still engages the Tribune's attention, which says; The blacks have unconsciously adopted the Democratic plan of coercion by starvation, and their particular method of withholding supplies is the most effective yet discovered. The Tribune declares that no one can blame them for trying to get out of the States which make life a hell for them during every election campaign, and says of the proposition for the leading planters of Mississippi to meet a committee of blacks to consider the labor problem, that these white gentlemen will probably not bring their rifles with them this time, and it may occur to them that if they had been as temperate in "Joint Discussions" on Political topics, this particular convention would not have been necessary.

Shipping men are jubilant over the recent decission of Judge Choate, in the United States District Court, which virtually exempts vessels engaged in near-by trade from the interference of the United States Shipping Commissioner.

The Times Washington special says; It seems that Fernando Wood, Chairman of the Committee on Ways and Means, is not popular as a leader, with his Democratic associates of the Committee.

LONDON 17.

A dispatch reports that Solovijeff has said that he was appointed by lot to shoot the Czar.

The Daily Telegraph publishes the following private telegram received from Lima 14;

"The entire coast is blocked. A fleet is useless. Peru has accepted favorable terms and negotiations continue. Much depends on the reply forwarded."

It is possible that the above dispatch is intended to influence stock.

OTTOWA 17.

In the House of Commons last night Mr. Bunster, in moving that the petition of Noah Shakespeare and others, be referred to the Committee, to report generally on Chinese labor and immigration, as affecting the dominion, said the question of Chinese labor was the most important affecting the Pacific Coast. The petition stated that in British Columbia there were six thousand Chinese. They work so low as to drive their competitors out of the market. They can afford to work for much less than a white man as they have no wife or families to keep. They seldom marry in this country, and send all their earnings to China. Canada lost two-and-a-half million dollars this way. After much discussion, McDonald said the exclusion of the Chinese from this country might lead to the exclusion of our missionaries from China. It was well known that a variety of nationalities in the country increased its prosperity and for this reason he could not agree

---

ADVERTISEMENTS.

THE
EVENING
TELEGRAM.

Published every evening, (except Sunday,) and distributed at the
POST OFFICE,
AND
OFFICE OF PUBLICATION,
Near Corner of
WASHINGTON & 2d. NORTH STS.
ST. GEORGE, UTAH.

Gives all the Telegraphic and Local News of importance. Try it!
Only 50 cents a month, 15 cents a week! Single copies 3 cents!
BUY IT! READ IT!

---

the cessation. An effort will be made to conclude the debate in the Appropriation Bill under the five minutes rule to-morrow, so that the Senate may commence its discussion of that measure early next week.

CHICAGO 25.
Booth visited Gray in prison to-day, but got no satisfactory reason from him for his late attack. It is not likely that Gray will be prosecuted.

LONDON 25.
In the House of Commons to-day, Sir Stafford Northcote said the Government was considering the advisability of issuing a proclamation of neutrality in the South American war.

WANTED
IMMEDIATELY
A young Lady between the ages of 10 and 15 years to learn the art of Type Setting. Must be Quick and Active, able to read common writing and not Afraid to Work. Steady employment guaranteed when competence is gained.
For particulars apply to
J. W. CARPENTER.

For Sale.
PRICE REDUCED TO 25 CTS.
I have a few pounds of Old Type, suitable for Boxing Metal, which I will dispose of for Cash. Price per pound 25 cents,
J. W. Carpenter.

THE
ST. GEORGE
CO-OPERATIVE MERCANTILE
INSTITUTION
Being desirous to distribute its
CAPITAL STOCK
More extensively among the masses of the people, offers to receive the
CAPITAL STOCK
of the
CANAAN
CO-OPERATIVE STOCK COMPANY
at its Cash Valuation, as
Capital Stock
IN THE
STORE.
Quite small amounts will be received
For particulars, apply to
HENRY EYRING, Sec'y
April 11, 1879.

IN
Probate Court
OF
WASHINGTON CO., U. T.
Letters of Administration having been issued to the undersigned by the Probate Court of this County, upon the Estate of Commodore Perry Liston, deceased, all persons having claims against said Estate are hereby notified to present them, duly authenticated, within four months from date hereof; and all persons owing said Estate are requested to settle their indebtedness forthwith.
Elizabeth R. Liston, } Adm'rs.
Moses F. Farnsworth,
St. George, U. T. Apr. 12, 1879.

Evening Telegram, (pages 2 and 3), St. George, Utah, Saturday, April 26, 1879

ing in Brigham's southern capital for a merchant who knows how to advertise!"

The few copies preserved, chiefly in Reid's Dixie College file, and the L. D. S. Church library in Salt Lake City show it to contain good pomological and kindred articles—if we can judge; also plenty of other good reading matter, save alone, advertising, as hinted by the publisher.

A copy of the Utah Pomologist and Silver Reef Echo, in the L. D. S. Church library, volume 4, number 3, (new) February, 1877, 5 columns, 4 pages, has 13 columns of advertising out of a total of 20 (!) as a result of the new hybrid title the paper was simply *ruined!* That much prosperity was ruin indeed, for the homespun Pomologist, we are to surmise, for that is the last we hear of it.

"Utah, Her Cities, Towns and Resources," 1891-2, devotes one and one half pages to the Valley Tan Laboratory which produced medicines, discovered, invented and manufactured by Joseph E. Johnson, erstwhile newspaper man. No less than 20 proprietaries, cordials, cold cures, eye salve, canker syrup, pills, linament, tonics, corn cure, worm lozenges, elixirs, tinctures, etc. were put out. Of Joseph E. Johnson the article says he was: "Of the Daniel Boone type of pioneers, who set their faces toward the land of the setting sun. Whenever a railroad caught up with him he pulled up stakes and moved forward. In 1848 he emigrated to Nebraska, where he established large supply stores for furnishing and outfitting the overland emigrants to California."

Joseph E. Johnson says of himself June 23, 1882,—"Crossed the Plains to Utah and back in 1850, Established the Council Bluffs Bugle in 1852, destroyed by fire 1853, restored and published until 1856; meanwhile published the Omaha Arrow in 1854, first paper on Nebraska soil. Started the Crescent City Oracle in 1857, published the Council Bluffs Press in 1858 and published the Huntsman's Echo at Wood River, Nebraska, 1859-1861 (See Frontier Index, Ogden). Moved to Utah 1861 . . . Tomorrow, with the blessings of Providence, I shall start for Old Mexico, to open up a place of refuge for the Saints of God. Have three wives and am the father of 26 children, and have 27 grand children." Unfortunately he only got as far as Temple, Arizona, where he died that year.

The Mineral Cactus, Volume 1, Number 1, about February 25, 1868, 2 columns, 4-pages, 4 x 6 inches. Masthead "Published semi-monthly by G. G. R. Sangiovanni & Co. Terms, 6 months, $1, strictly in advance. Printed by S. A. Kenner at Dixie Times office." Our Dixie Times for February 26, 1868 says: "The Mineral Cactus is another miniature newspaper, edited and published by Sangiovanni & Company, St. George . . . It is running over with jokes, funny bits and pleasant railleries. St. George is getting out two newspapers . . . Go in boys; better spend your time in literature than in rum and tobacco."

It was not so much a news sheet as, what today would be called a "house organ." About 35 or 40 numbers are in Professor Reid's file at the Dixie College, probably not, however, all that were issued. Number 4 drops Kenner's name, but the paper goes bravely on, at least for two fortnightly issues. It then lapsed for several numbers. Here are some of the complimentary notices: "The Mineral Cactus is another miniature newspaper . . . We have the first number of a St. George fledgling of the comic order," says the Deseret News, March 5, 1868. Soon, however, the paper became:

The Cactus, with Volume 2, Number 1, September 19, 1868, which was 3 columns of 4 pages, though a little less than 6 x 8 inches in size with this "Salutatory. Once more we come before the public, weekly and enlarged, which we trust will meet with thankful hearts. The Cactus is devoted to sound sense, as well as nonsense. It is calculated to please everybody." In the issue for September 26, 1868: "Our readers will no doubt be pleased to learn that the Cactus, like our own soil, has succeeded in ridding itself of the **Mineral,** which has heretofore been a drawback on the newcomer." The masthead was not changed.

While the Cactus was a joke itself and was filled with jokes, it had a closer following than its adult contemporary, The Times, which really tried to be a newspaper. Thus beginning with the issue for October 31, 1868, a few paragraphs of telegraphic news were published, making it a sure-enough newspaper, though little larger than a label. Even the plodding Times, October 14, 1868, admitted: "The Cactus: This spicy little sheet . . . has now attained its fourth month with fair promise of future progress," evidently sensing the little paper's popularity and importance. A standing advertisement in the Times through 1868 and 1869 was: "Subscribe for the Cactus, weekly and enlarged, only $2.00 per annum; everybody should take it . . . Names taken at the Tithing Office. Correspondence should be addressed: Cactus, St. George, Utah, Sangiovanni & Company."

In the issue of November 14, 1868 (whoever he was, but presumably Sangiovanni himself) admits, "It is our intention to spare no pains in making the Cactus an interesting little paper, and we are sanguine that in time it will not only attain a larger size but a wide reputation in the west. We expect to speak fearless, and defend the rights of those who are struggling daily for liberty. Respecting politics, we stand neutral."

The next week the editor further unfolds his prospectus: "When we commenced this volume we did not intend to publish telegrams, but as they are now offered to us at liberal rates, we take it upon ourselves to publish them . . . making the Cactus eight days ahead of Salt Lake papers." Apologetically on November 28, 1868, a spokesman says: "If our issue this week is not so interesting as usual, we hope our readers will overlook it, from the fact that our senior editor has gone (on a borrowed horse) with Colonel Pearce's command in search of items among the Navajos," an ironical way of saying the editor had enlisted in an attacking party against marauding Indians.

In fact, pronto, the Indian news from the editor in the villages of Washington, Pipe Springs and other points on the telegraph line became abundant and sizzling hot; and the Cactus was equal to the emergency, carrying full reports from the battle fronts. It was consequently read greedily and generally in St. George since most of the able-bodied men-folks were in the party sent to punish the Indian thieves, and recover the stolen livestock.

The issue of December 12, 1868, for example, consists of 6 (tiny) columns of the "Latest from the seat of war" by the absent editor, acting as Indian war correspondent for the greatest little paper in the world—just then! Then, as the war ends as suddenly as an Indian horde can gallop out of sight the publisher gets in a word about himself December 19, 1868: "G. G. R. Sangiovanni's Evening School commences this evening at the basement of the St. George hall. Will the young folks give him a call?" And now, also, we recall the jokes, the humor, and the sketches, (aside from the news) have been aimed at young people, with no particular effort at obtaining subscriptions.

In fact, "Our Devil is running the Cactus his own dear little self, and the way he cries for copy is a caution!" Beginning December 19, 1868, it is announced, "The Cactus is published every Saturday afternoon at The Times office U. T., G. G. R. Sangiovanni & Company, editors. Through January, February, March, April, May and to June 19, 1869 the Cactus was as full of news, jokes and short articles as a Cactus plant is full of spines—a really fine little newspaper, which we are reluctant to dismiss so unceremoniously and with no further word of its existence or its ending. A copy of the Cactus for May 12, 1869, in the Bancroft Library, has 3 columns, 9 x 12 inch page. Other copies there indicate the small size was continued until July 28, 1869, and possibly later, as the last copy in the library is for November, 1870.

Through the Deseret News of April 8, 1869 we pick up the full *sentence* used by the Cactus editor as his name: "Guglielmo Giosue Rosette San Giovanne, Esq., editor of the St. George Cactus, visited our sanctum." We cannot omit in closing to express our wonder at how a man with such a name ever found his way to St. George in that early day, and the still greater wonder at his staying there, fighting Indians, conducting a business college, running one newspaper, and outrunning one or two others! From the Deseret News of December 29, 1868 we learn of an effort of compete with the Cactus, in the publication of:

The St. George Juvenile, "For the benefit and amusement of ourselves, and the young." We hear very little about it. (See the St. George Enterprise which claims to be a continuation of the Juvenile). The following is from the Rio Virgen Times, Wednesday, December 23, 1868: In the Bancroft Library, "The St. George Juvenile is the title of a tiny sheet edited, composed and printed by Joseph Carpenter, a boy of 15 years, who invented and manufactured his composing stick, case, press and fixtures, only troubling the outside world for paper, ink and type; all the rest is the fruit of his own genius. It is issued semi-monthly at 75c for twelve months. That's right! Industry and self culture is better than clanning, loafing and idling with bad company." Unfortunately we hear no more of the Juvenile, though editor Carpenter rides forth to conquer in another coat of mail in a year or so, as we shall see.

The St. George Enterprise. November, 1871, 3 columns, 4-pages, 8 x 11, published monthly by Joseph W. Carpenter, editor and proprietor. Seventy five cents a year. Files, a dozen copies in H. L. Reid's collection, Dixie College. The serial numbering adopted by the publisher, indicates a prenatal existence of about two years, 1872 being volume 3. A clue to this previous existence appears in the Deseret News for Saturday, November 18, 1871. "Now comes the St. George Enterprise, J. Carpenter, editor and proprietor. The Enterprise, formerly the Juvenile, a 4-page, 4 x 3 monthly (we suppose) is bound to make a sensation in the literary world."

Carpenter himself, however, mentions no such reincarnation in the interesting description of "Our Printing Office. There are not many who are aware that our printing office don't contain many imported articles. The press, type cases, chases, and in fact everything but the paper, ink and type, are all our own make. We have made printing ink, and intend soon to make all our own ink. The type we have are most all old type that we have obtained from different persons. Some were obtained at the News office, others at the (late) Telegraph office, and some from The Pomologist, all of which are worn and very bad. We received four fonts of letters, one font of border, thirteen small cuts, and some leads and rules from the California Type Foundry of San Francisco. We hope we shall soon be able to procure new type from the Salt Lake Type Foundry, and then we can print a clean sheet."

We found several numbers of the Enterprise in the Bancroft Library, including volume 3, number 1, April; number 2, May; number 3, July; number 5, November; number 6, December, 1872; and number 10, May, 1873. "Published monthly by Joseph Carpenter, editor and proprietor, terms 75c per annum." Three columns, 4-pages, all home print. In the July, 1872 number, "Our patrons will please excuse us for the non-appearance of the June number, for we were utterly unable to issue The Enterprise without paper to print it on. We will try to be more punctual in the future." Another short-coming is expressed in the November, 1872 number, "All ye who think of winning fame, and would to greatness rise, just hand us six bits and your name and get the Enterprise!" These copies appear to have been presented to Mr. Bancroft by Mr. Carpenter personally, from pencilled notations thereon.

Editor Carpenter publishes this admonition in November, 1872: "Some of our subscribers say they do not receive the Enterprise. We would like Postmasters to be more careful, and forward mail matter as it should be!" In volume 3, number 8, March, 1873 is this, "Apologetic. We are behind again this month . . . We sent for our paper in January but it did not arrive until the 16th of April." Typical of Editor Carpenter's character are these Quaker printer's proverbs, published May, 1873: "Never sendest thou an article for publication without giving the editor thy name, for thy name oftentimes secures publication to worthless articles. Thou shouldst not rap at the door of a printing office, for he that answereth the rap sneereth in his sleeves and loseth time. Neither do thou loaf about, asking questions, or knock down type, or the boys will love thee like they do shade trees—when thou leafeth. Thou shouldst never read the copy on the printer's type case or the sharp and hooked container thereof, or he may knock thee down. Never require thou of the editor the news, for behold at the appointed time he will give it thee without asking. When thou dost enter into his office, take heed unto thyself that thou dost not look at what may be lying open and concerneth thee not, for that is not meet in sight of good breeding. Neither examine thou the proof sheet, for it is not ready to meet thine eye, that thou mayest understand. Prefer thine own newspaper to any other, and subscribe for it immediately. Pay for it in advance; and it shall be well with thee and thine."

There was usually a heavy run of poetry, a full page of poetry appearing in number 10, May, 1873. Thus, like its chimerical, juvenile predecessor, it was not exactly a newspaper. The poetry may have been its undoing, however, for in number 11 which was dated December, 1873 we note: "Home again! Yes, we are home once more, performing our daily labor in the printing office. Last May we abdicated the editorial chair for the purpose of helping to run a lath mill in Pine Valley, but we have had enough of lath mills."

Number 12, January 23, 1874: "To our Patrons. This number completes volume 3 of the Enterprise . . . Our next volume will be 4 columns wide and will be devoted to news (local and general) gossip of the day, telegraphy, agriculture, horticulture, correspondence, etc., etc." A reader-advertisement is: "For anything you want in the drug line, call on J. E. Johnson."

Number 1 of volume 4, February 20, 1874, 4 columns, 8 x 11, was: "Late on account of changing the form of the Enterprise," but he begs politely as follows. "Come young, come old, come rich, come poor, for the paper has come, this time for sure!" Number 2 is March 6, 1874, and number 3, April 3, 1874, this one containing a two page extra or supplement, devoted exclusively to Cotton Planting. Number 4 was dated April 24, 1874 and carried this advertisement: "Read This. The St. George Enterprise (established 1868) devoted to the interest of southern Utah; published every other Friday." But it was a printer's promise! Number 5 was dated May 22, 1874, number 6 was merely "July, 1874," and number 7 August 14, 1874, consisted of but two pages—a single sheet! "We are out of paper, hence we issue the half sheet." And since this is the last copy seen and the last reference to the Enterprise, we are left to presume the rest of the print paper never came! It thus appears St. George was without a paper for a few years,

Salt Lake Evening Chronicle.

VOL. 1.—NO. 29.   SALT LAKE CITY, WEDNESDAY, DECEMBER 6, 1882.   **PRICE, FIVE CENTS.**

LAST NIGHT'S DISPATCHES.
CONDENSED.

Ninderman, in the Jeannette Court, yesterday, continued the narrative of the journey south. He detailed his separation from De Long upon the occasion when he and Noros started in search of a settlement, in a very pathetic manner, and explained how they prepared a boat sole by soaking and burning until they were able to cut it with their willow ten. After this was exhausted they ate their bones.

Carlisle, Randall and Springer are each confident of becoming Speaker of the House.

Senator Windom denies that he recently published a report placing his wealth at $2,000,000. He owns no bank stock and but few buildings, and they are mostly mortgaged. In the West Virginia coal mines he is interested to the extent of $16,000, instead of $1,000,000, as reported.

The House yesterday refused to consider the bill to prevent army officers on the retired list to hold civil offices in the Territories.

The revenue on tobacco in 1882 was nearly $68,000,000. The House committee on ways and means recommend the repeal of the tobacco tax.

Prince Arisugra Nomga, the uncle of the Emperor of Japan, and suite, are expected to arrive in New York from Liverpool on the 12th. The Prince left Japan last summer. He has the highest rank of any Japanese that has ever arrived here.

A resolution was presented in the Senate yesterday, instructing the Judiciary committee to investigate how much money was collected during the recent election in violation of the law against political assessments; how much was spent, and how many persons were dismissed the public service, and how many of them failed to contribute.

A bill was passed in the House yesterday repealing the law for paying three months' extra pay to sailors, and a measure adopted that when discharged at a foreign port, they shall have adequate employment on "another ship or means or return home.

The Adventists, whose headquarters are at Battle Creek, Michigan, are much stirred at predictions from above to the widow of Elder White, that one more prominent in the order are given to worldliness.

The Albany Iron Works, employing several thousand men, have reduced wages ten to twenty-five per cent.

The Grand Jury in St. Louis yesterday, ignored the bill against Cockrill for killing Slayback.

Col. Thos. T. L. Laidley, of the U. S. Army, was placed on the retired list yesterday.

Gen. Geo. C. Thomas, who was a Major-General during the war, and at one time in command of the District of Columbia, is dead.

Butler has been re-elected to the United States Senate from South Carolina.

The Supreme Court has decided that Lee's heirs are entitled to the Arlington estate.

Christine Nilsson drew an immense audience in Chicago. Standing room only could be obtained, and many were turned away. She goes to San Francisco next.

A bill has been introduced in the House to incorporate the Yellowstone Park Railway Company. The road is to run from a point at or near Market Lake, Idaho, through the Teton range of the Rocky Mountains by Roach's Fork, to the foot of Mt. Meridian to Yellowstone Park, thence to the Upper Geyser, Lower Geyser, Upper Falls of Yellowstone River, and Enagmur Gulch in Montana, or to the most available point on the Northern Pacific. The capital stock of the company is to be $6,000,000. The company is to charge for passengers at a rate not to exceed seven cents a mile, and freight not to exceed ten cents a mile.

Philadelphia is excited over the scene of several parties engaged in body-snatching. Four of six bodies in the thievery possession were identified recently. Robert Chew, one of the parties, said he was paid $3 for every body taken from the cemetery. He did not know how many graves had been robbed. He had been in the cemetery eleven years. Body-snatching has been going on nine years. Sometimes wages came, and the drivers said they were short. Coffins were opened in the yard, the corpse "snatched," and the torn or burned parts put in and the box sewed up as empty again after through with next day. The records of burial at the cemetery show no months into the bodies gone. The trial of the prisoners brought a large crowd in the magistrate's office, who became so excited in the testimony elicited that it was necessary to send for a force of a dozen policemen to quell the disturbance.

Washington dispatch: The Utah commission in their report to the secretary of the interior, recommend that a marriage law be enacted for Congress which would have jurisdiction in the suppression of polygamy. The Commission say that, owing to the peculiar state of affairs in Utah, the Territorial law allows no women the right of suffrage on an obstruction to the speedy solution of the question, should be repealed or amended by Congress. The Commission say the law so far has been a decided success in excluding polygamists from the exercise of suffrage. The continued enforcement of the law will place polygamy in a condition of gradual extinction. The Commission notice, in an encouraging sign, that many of the Liberal meetings have been largely attended by Mormons. In conclusion, the report says, after counting the moderation: "If, however, the next session of the Legislative Assembly, elected under the act of Congress, shall fail to respond to the will of the nation, Congress should have no hesitation in using extraordinary measures to compel the people of this Territory to obey the law of the land."

SCISSORS AND PASTE-POT.

W. H. Mills, for the past eight years managing editor of the Sacramento Record-Union, is soon to take the position of Land Agent of the Central Pacific Railroad, as the successor of the late B. B. Redding.

H. F. Nutting fell dead in the streets of Redwood City on Thanksgiving Day. He had filled places of public trust in San Mateo, was editor for three years of the Times and Gazette, and at the time of his death was a teacher in the public schools. Deceased was a member of several benevolent orders.

One of the principal iron mines of Johnstown, Pa., was a two and a-half foot vein. This was followed for two and a-half miles. It took a miner paid in the Allegheny Mountains, may we not expect to see the lands in Montana, which are from ten to forty feet in width, worked some day?

In Leal, California, a few days ago, a little four-year old boy got into a six-inch mesh with his baby sister, and by some means turned the other side. When the father heard of this he seized the little boy and held his legs on the hot stove till he burned the flesh long and deep, leaving a mark the child will carry to his grave.

The increase of the business of the Northern Pacific Railway this year over 1881 is something enormous. During the first week of November the increase was $58,224 over the corresponding period of last year, while during the period from July to November 7, 1882, the increase was $1,199,017 over the same period of 1881.

Whatever may be said of the losses, fraud and uncertainty of mining, the millions of dollars that she shows each year as her precious product and the work she has done and is doing in opening up new fields where other industries live and thrive upon her product, cannot be gainsaid. When this nation shines at the zenith of her glory, and the hum of countless industries strike in one grand paen from sea to sea, the sound of the miner's pick will not be the least honored note in that jubilee of prosperity and power which shall startle the world with its magnitude and grandeur.

A strike that rips the sheep is reported from Red Mountain this week in a new and almost unknown property that is being opened near the Yankee Girl. It is in the Orphan Boy, and is away from the surface 2,900 ounces, very much resembling the Yankee Girl, both in character and formation. Prospectors are coming from all over the San Juan to prospect in this locality, regardless of the show being ten and fifteen inches deep.—Animas Forks Pioneer.

An immense strike is reported in the Iowa-Owena mine, at Sunshine, Boulder county. One chunk weighing about 30 pounds was blown out, which, on being broken up, was discovered to be a mass of free gold and tellurium, which is estimated to be worth over $40 per pound.

The estimated production of lead in the United States this year is about 135,000 tons, of which 100,000 will be made in the Rocky mountains, and nearly 50,000 tons in Leadville and her tributary smelting camps.

In the course of a lecture at New Haven the other evening upon the customs and religions of his race, the Rev. Thomas S. Dutu, an educated Indian, made this singular statement: The Indians never rest anything in the house where they live. They cook outside, and they give as a reason that if they cook inside the steam collects in their clothing and draws the lightning. Whether this is so or not I do not know, but I know that an Indian wigwam is never struck by lightning, and no Indian has been killed by lightning in a hundred years.

Englishmen are fond of allegiance to the "rich incomes" of American railroad management. And yet, when a Pullman sleeping car caught fire in England our matter-days ago, there was no apparatus found to quench the flames, and when the engineer was signaled to stop the train he could not do so because the "printed rules" would not permit him to. One passenger was burned to death, and others dangerously injured.

Mrs. Theodore Tilton desires to give the remainder of her days in her native village at Cranbury, New Jersey, and is negotiating for the purchase of a home in that place.

An Albany man who was worth $100,-000 ten years ago, and who refused the nomination for Mayor, now pays on his case in the street car stables at Peoria, Illinois, at $1 a day.

The first run in the local brought against the luggage smuggler has been decided in New Francisco. The owner of the wrecked trunks was prosecuted in the amount of $412.72. The court held that since a man had received a check for his trunk the railroad had to pay for break-age.

A Philadelphia food fancier says "You can raise a canary inside six hours by depriving it of food for that length of time and then putting your hand filled with seed into the cage. Repeat this at intervals, and the bird will soon become tame enough to fly about the room and come to you when you whistle for it."

Comments.

The Toastors—Nevada—Tibet Record has the following in regard to the old and once famous mining camp: The district, now deserted and inhabited by two or three inhabitants, is still regarded by many as having merits that will sooner or later be developed. The Tibet mines on which machinery has been in operation, the Leopard, Hoay and Panther, have produced a large amount of bullion, the Leopard alone having shipped over $1,000,000. The Hoay, Panther and Companions have been collected, and the assessments are prompt-ly kept up.

though it was in the back of editor Carpenter's head all the time, and it was he who launched:

The Union, Volume 1, Number 1, June 14, 1878, J. W. Carpenter. Three columns, 4-pages, 8 x 11, one page of advertisements, semi-monthly. Files, about 30 numbers in H. L. Reid's collection, Dixie College, St. George. After a break through 1879 and 1880, and about 10 years from 1887, there are several numbers for 1896 and 1898, and practically a full file for 1897 preserved by Professor Reid. The missing numbers were not all published, we may presume, from the editor's gossip about himself and his paper.

In his Salutatory editor-farmer Carpenter says, "A first class newspaper which we hope the Union will be. Heretofore the people of St. George and vicinity have been very negligent in encouraging a home paper. The products of the country will be taken in payment when cash cannot be paid." The paper used for the Union is homemade and was manufactured at Salt Lake City.

Number 2, June 28, 1878 contained an illustrated article on the Yosemite. The Dixieites had not yet been told their own Zion Canyon was a Yosemite done in oils. Believing it pays to advertise the publisher ran a display 'ad' in his own paper, August 23, 1878: "The St. George Union, an Independent, semi-monthly newspaper published at St. George by J. W. Carpenter. Its proprietor will study the interests of people in southern Utah, and ever strive to aid in the development of wealth, honor, and righteousness."

The publication of some of the sermons of the Mormon Prophet, Joseph Smith, exhausted the editions, and increased the subscription list, the editor is glad to say, September 7, 1878; and the sermons were continued in subsequent issues for many weeks. Nevertheless, the sermons were limited, since the Prophet was dead, and two full years elapsed between volume 1, number 11, November 2, 1878 and volume 1, number 12, November 12, 1880. (In this interim Brother Carpenter launched the Daily Evening Telegram, q. v.) In the November 12, 1880 issue of the Union we read: "To Our Patrons. It was with much regret that we were obliged to discontinue the publication of The Union before we had completed the volume . . . at present we can only publish the Union monthly as our other labors are pressing us. We must have food and clothes, and as the publishing business is not lucrative enough to procure the necessities of life and redeem cash expenditures for paper etc. (especially when about half our subscribers do *not pay*) we are obliged to resort to something else . . . Signed The Editor." "Terms, 50c per year," 4-pages, 3 columns, 8 x 11.

Number 13, January, 1881 carried an important "Explanation concerning a change of subscription rate, and expirations of subscriptions,"—if the people cared to know! Number 15, May 12, 1881, "Too Many Printers," announces the editor. "There are too many printers here in St. George, consequently," continues the editor "Bloomington, Washington County, Utah, is to be our future home soon, and we hope to make the Union more interesting in the Sweet Bye and Bye." (There is no known record of any contemporaneous newspaper in St. George at the time). In Bloomington the paper appeared (with the St. George P. O. Box and date line) in June, July, August and October, 1881, number 20 being a combination of the November and December, 1881 issues. It contained six pages. Number 21 came out in February, 1882 with this sad report: "On account of sickness and death hindering us, we concluded not to issue The Union for January." Death hindered! Lucky it didn't leave him in a worse fix! So far as The Union enlightens us, the death referred to may have come to a favorite Ewe!

Number 22 got out in April, 1882 and 23 in May, with a "Prospectus of the St. George Union, volume 2. Patrons and friends. For about 14 years I have been endeavoring to publish at various times a newspaper for the benefit of the people of southern Utah. How far my publications have been a benefit, I leave to the public to judge . . . I now propose publishing a second volume of the St. George Union, issuing it monthly as before."

But how time dragged in the Union office! Number 24, volume 1, dated June, 1882, was brought out long after that date with this explanatory "bull": "Disgusted. For several issues back we have been very much disgusted with the non-appearance of The Union, but we trust that we shall be able to avoid the like in the future!" That number, by the way, bore the hybrid title: **The Union and Village Echo,** Bloomington, Washington County, the village being then as now one of the tiniest communities in the State. Finally, however, volume 2, number 1 appeared Tuesday, December 12, 1882. Number 5, May, 1883 bore also, "St. George, P. O. Box 561," because Bloomington was too small to have a post office.

The paper continued the same general format and advertisements as when it was The St. George Union. The January 31, 1884 issue claimed a circulation of 500 copies, but publication days were very irregular, volume 2, number 8 being dated March, 1884, 8 issues after December 12, 1882! It carried this notice: "Your Attention, Please! We propose enlarging next volume of the Union from three to four columns to the page . . . Our new dress which speaks for itself is the production of the Chicago Type Foundry." Number 9, June, 1884, number 10, August 2, 1884 and number 11, January, 1885, "On account of sickness, and accidentally pi-ing forms, we have not been able to issue as before." Never quite the same after that!

Number 12, March, 1886 was dated at Bloomington, but carried the announcement: "A Change . . . In moving from St. George to Bloomington . . . we lack a post office." Still, Bloomington held him 'til number 13, February, 1887—one issue a year may have been a good accomplishment for that hot climate!—he announces: "Last Number. This number of The Union completes the present volume, and we thank our many patrons and friends for their patronage, and trust we shall have a continuation of the same. We have no pretentions to make in regard to the new volume, but the better the patronage the more able we will be to go ahead . . . The first number will appear about the last of April or middle of May, and we hope to receive a large list of sub-scribers by that time." A sub-title to the masthead: "Official organ of the Farmer's Agricultural Association."

Professor Reid found no more copies of The Union for his preci-ous file; and we are reluctantly led to believe that neither the coveted subscribers nor the "middle of May" ever came to the Union. "United we stand; divided we fall" was run under the title line, on the early numbers; meaning of course, subscribers and editor! P.S. in the news locals: "Owing to breaking our press this (February 1887) number of the Union has been somewhat delayed."

The 1888, 1890, 1892, 1896, 1898 Newspaper Directories do not list a newspaper at St. George. Nevertheless, the following are in Reid's file: Volume 9, number 10, February 15, 1896, 4 columns, 4-pages, 11 x 15; volume 9, number 12, February 29th; volume 9, number 13, March 12, 1896 and January 16, 1897. In The Union for December 5, 1896 the line "United we stand, divided we fall" was replaced by "From the little acorn grows the massive oak." "Entered at the postoffice as second class matter March 27, 1896," possibly indicating a new application for mailing privileges and a resumption of publication after a long lapse. The issue of January 23, 1897 puts a finger on an erstwhile St. George newspaper man as follows:—"Scipio Africanus Kenner, the great cam-paign man, is doing more to earn his per diem than any other member of that composite body, the legislature. He makes more noise than two ordinary men. But then Kenner is a newspaperman. 'Scip' is a hot number!"

Reid's file is practically complete for 1897, editor Carpenter being comparatively thrifty. But a long ardent plea for support is made by the editor March 19, 1898: "Shall we Continue? As some of our sub-scribers are desirous that the Union shall be continued, we have this much to say in regard to the proposition . . . But if you *don't want* any paper, then we will discontinue the Union and go at something that will yield a larger income."

"The St. George Union is still offered for sale," says the Springville Independent. Some enterprising newspaperman who is not afraid of the climate and the natives, should look over the field." (John R. Wallis had already looked it over) and wrote this: "One objection we had to St. George was the bad water there at times, when the drinking water is both food and drink. St. George city water has more kinds of wigglers per quart than a barrel of Springville ditch water. The inhabitants of Dixie make the water palatable by adulterating it with grape juice, turn-ing it into wine, so to speak! Dixie water, when heated sufficiently to kill the wigglers, becomes an elegant consomme!" (Note: Editor Wallis returned to St. George in a short time, and has not only prospered there through these thirty five years, but good health is prolonging his life far beyond even his own expectations!)

The Union editor, Saturday, April 30, 1898 says: "In the past we have had so many avocations to follow we could not do justice to the paper, hence our desire to dispose of our plant . . . But as yet we have been unable to dispose of it to advantage, therefore we have decided to go on until we can make a disposition of the plant in a satisfactory manner . . . John R. Wallis . . . thinks the Union plant too obsolete to purchase, and has ordered a new plant, and intends commencing the publication of . . . the Washington County News."

An editorial in the Union for May 12, 1898 says: "Notwithstanding we are going on with the Union, we don't want anyone to have it who does not want it. (He means subscribers who take it too hard!) If you do not want it, please inform us of the fact immediately." Also: "It appears that the editor of the Iron County Record is giving himself up to prevaricating, according to his notice of the Union and the expected new paper, by saying that: 'The Union will run in opposition, etc.' Now the facts in case are, that the Union has been in the field for years, and unless someone purchases the title, plant, and good will the St. George Union has no intention of throwing up the sponge. We have invested too much to allow it to stand idle."

Volume 11, number 2, May 19, 1898: "Notice To Our Patrons: Knowing full well that to make the Union as interesting as we should, we must spend our entire time and attention to it; and not having been able to rent our farm, we have decided to discontinue the Union for the present, and put a portion of our time on the said farm, until such time as we can arrange otherwise . . . We shall continue to do all kinds of job printing and paper ruling at prices that defy competition . . . Yours fraternally, J. W. Carpenter, editor and proprietor, St. George, Utah."

"Notice To Our Exchanges: As we have decided to discontinue the Union for the present, we respectfully ask our exchanges to discontinue sending us their papers until they shall receive another copy of the Union." Thus the Union publishes its own obituary! The Vernal Express, June 18, 1898 viewed it less seriously: "The publication of the St. George Union has been temporarily suspended, while editor Carpenter cuts his alfalfa. This is a new scheme. However the job press will run on rainy days!"

The Evening Telegram, Volume 1, Number 1, Tuesday, April 8, 1879, two columns, 4-pages, 5 x 8, mostly advertising. Published every evening except Sunday, by J. W. Carpenter at 50c a month, invariably in advance. Files, about 25 numbers through April and May, 1879, preserved by Professor H. L. Reid, Dixie College, St. George. Oddly enough, Volume 1, Number 1 was dated Thursday, April 10 on the front page, Wednesday, April 9, on the editorial page, and Tuesday evening, April 8, on another page. (Joshua's long day!) The Telegraphic News stories are dated April 7th.

"Salutatory: Friends and patrons: We present you the first number of our little Telegram, hoping it will meet with your approval, and that you will use your influence to induce your friends and neighbors to subscribe for it one month, if they have not already done so. Our terms are in advance, and we hope that those who have not paid their subscription, that they will hand it over immediately, so we may be enabled to meet our liabilities. We respectfully invite the business men of the city to step forward with their advertisements and their aid in sustaining The Evening Telegram."

The issue of April 12, 1879 was out of luck in that "The telegraph line being out of repair, we are minus our dispatches for this evening's issue. We are sorry, but cannot help it; yet we trust the like will not happen again." We did not learn when The Telegram itself "went out," but we must salute it as being a most remarkable little newspaper!

The Southern Utah Star, Volume 1, Number 1, July 20, 1895, weekly, 5 columns, 8-pages, 13 x 20, 4 ready print, James T. Jakeman, publisher. Files, none—Professor H. L. Reid has this one copy. "Hitch your chariot to a Star," reads the masthead statement. "Devoted to the interests, and development of the resources of Washington County in particular, and southern Utah in general." The editorial column was dated July 27, 1895, for some reason. The number is heavily patronized by advertisers, and the Salutatory is a graceful one of modest promises. The editor apologizes for bad type, for delays in receiving his paper supply from the railroad at Milford, and failure of the press to perform its proper functions: "Our paper has the merit of having been set by St. George girls, who never set a type before."

The advance advertising solicitor must have been a good one, for this small paragraph nestled in the midst of a large area of white space: "As the medical societies of Utah do not countenance the insertion of professional advertising, a physician in regular practice reserves the space as an expression of sympathy with efforts to establish a local newspaper." It is presumed the sheet was short lifed as only one noncommittal exchange notice was found, in the Iron County Record, August 2, 1895. The Star did not "make" the 1896 or later Directories.

Washington County News, Volume 1, Number 1, June 18, 1898, John R. Wallis, editor and proprietor, $2 a year, 6-columns, 4-pages, all home print (at the start); it soon became half ready-print. File, complete to end of series, July 28, 1900, bound and presented by Mr. Wallis to the Utah Historical Society.

"Notice, We do not wish subscribers to pay for The News for a week or two. We shall run a few issues as an experiment, and if the business houses do not give material support, shall discontinue . . . no country paper can live on its subscription list alone. The editor . . . feels ashamed of the paltry appearance of the advertising columns . . . It is the most starved-to-death looking sheet in Utah." Nevertheless, it is a good newspaper, good locals, good correspondence, neatly printed.

On June 25, 1898 the editor states, "Our Position. Do the people of Washington County want a local newspaper? We . . . put in an entirely new plant, but so far we certainly feel very much discouraged. We were informed that the field had been served by some very scurvy tricks by a man named Jakeman and others; and that some of the people looked with suspicion upon all newspapermen as a consequence.

UINTAH PAPPOOSE.

VOL I.   VERNAL, UINTAH COUNTY, UTAH, JAN. 16.   NO 3.

UINTAH PAPPOOSE.
Published Weekly.

One Copy, One Year . . . $2.00
One Copy, Six Months . . . $1.25
KATE JELM BOAL, Editor and Publisher.

OFFICIAL DIRECTORY

OFFICIAL OFFICERS	
	JOHN NOFF, W. C. ASHTON,
ASSESSOR AND COLLECTOR	E. G. COLTON,
SHERIFF	
COUNTY ATTORNEY	
PROBATE JUDGE	
RECORDER	GEORGE MERKLE,
TREASURER	PHIL STRINGHAM
SCHOOL SUPT.	JOHN CLYDE
SURVEYOR	J. G. DAVIS
CORONER	

COUNTY COMMISSIONERS	
A. B. JOHNSON,	ASHLEY
A. A. HATCH.	VERNAL
H. C. SULLENGER	RIVER DALE
CLERK.	R. G. COLTON

DIED AWAY.

The Birtle—Mears Mercantile Co., are giving away, to their cash customers, finely executed Indic Ink and Crayon Portraits. Call at the store and Jim Mears will explain the scheme and give you a card.

The weather in the Old World is enough to make one think that by some cataclysm the earth had been changed, on its fodline.

Upon learning this we put in our plant so that the people could see and understand . . . and we did not solicit advertising until we were making up for the first issue . . . We then made a canvass of the business houses, and although we made the extremely low rate of 50c an inch per month . . . did not succeed in getting over three inches of space from any of our merchants, except the butcher . . . We realize that it is better for us to quit right now, . . than wait until we are completely broke . . . We will therefore make next week's paper, number 3, the last unless we receive better encouragement.—John R. Wallis."

The editor evidently did some good praying, however, and an editorial, July 2, 1898 is entitled "The News Will Continue." The editorial was a little like the tune one would whistle in the dark as most of the prospects were still in the "promising" stage. It was an excellent newspaper from the start and gradually grew in the graces of the advertisers, and on June 16, 1900 the editor observed: "Our Birthday. The News is two years old and growing stronger every day. Thank you. The News is in a prosperous condition and bids fair to live to a good old age."

With that in view, Wallis' Valedictory came without a premonition of any kind, July 28, 1900. He says: "My sole reason for selling out the news is that I believe my health will be better at some outdoor occupation . . . My successor, Mr. D. U. Cochrane, has had considerable experience in the newspaper field . . . in Oregon." For some reason school teacher-newspaperman Cochrane did not like the paper's name, hence we find:

The Dixie Falcon, successor to Washington County News, Saturday, September 22, 1900, D. U. Cochrane, editor and manager, Falcon Publishing Company. The text was largely political. We conclude the paper ceased publication shortly thereafter, for we find:

The Dixie Advocate, Volume 1, Number 2, Friday, September 13, 1901, Wilkinson Brothers, proprietors, Chas. S. Wilkinson, editor and publisher. The Richfield Reaper says: "Charlie Wilkinson of the Iron County Record has gone to St. George to start a paper called The Dixie Advocate . . . The editor of this paper (The Reaper) was raised with the Wilkinson boys and they are like brothers to him." Of their own prosperity the publishers of the Advocate say, September 13, 1901: "We are not entirely satisfied with the reception that is being tendered to The Advocate thus far. Subscriptions are not rolling in as fast as they should." It may be therefore, that the soubriquet the Dixie "Aggrovate" was coined in the Advocate's own office. It was Will C. Higgins who said in the Salt Lake Mining Review, "Charles S. Wilkinson . . . has purchased the plant of the defunct Falcon at St. George." "With this issue (October 8, 1903) Joseph F. Wilkinson, Jr., who for some months has guided the course of The Advocate, severs his connection, for the winter, having accepted a position as teacher of the Littlefield (Arizona) School. The publisher, Charles S. Wilkinson, will now again assume the responsibilities of the office." Charles hustled in the business, until an occasional three column three page supplement became necessary that winter to carry it all. From October 13, 1905, Leo Prickett is editor. November 6, 1906 the editor's name was omitted. The newspaper plant, name and all were moved to Virgin City. q. v.

The Washington County News (Reincarnation) Volume 1, number 1, June 30, 1908, John R. Wallis, editor and proprietor. Files, bound complete to date in The News office. Neat and orderly, like Wallis himself. "Here we are again! The Washington County News! That was the name of the newspaper which we published here several years ago." It was the beginning of a new era for St. George journalism. Surely we are justified in saying the News was and has been kept equal to the best newspapers in the state.

In the issue of December 8, 1927 we read: "To Our Patrons: With this issue of the Washington County News the business and management passes into other hands, Mr. John F. Stauffer having leased it for a period of two years. It is just on twenty years since I published the initial number of the present Washington County News. Previous to that I published for three years the Washington County News in the old Gardner's Club Hall, so that altogether we have given the people of Dixie nearly 23 years service as a publisher and I want to say right here that I consider these 23 well spent, happy years . . . we are not going to leave Dixie."

On April 1, 1933 The News was bought by Edgar R. Simpson of California, who sought St. George, partly for his health. The new publisher was accompanied to the city and assisted in the negotiations by Dan R. Conway of Great Falls, Montana. Mr. Conway, managing editor, was a man of great energy and ability, with initiative worthy a much larger community. Two issues, by Conway, were outstanding examples of modern journalism, both generously patronized by advertisers, all home print. Even Wallis looked with great interest on the fine spirit of the reborn newspaper. Conway confidently expected St. George to prosper immensely from the building of the Boulder Dam; and at midnight, Saturday, April 15, 1933 he and his linotype operator set out for a day at the Dam. Their car left the road and overturned twenty five miles out of St. George, so seriously injuring Conway he died April 18, 1933. Simpson has continued in charge of the paper to date. (Mr. Conway had loaned to us his office keys and Mrs. Alter and I were working on the files at the time of his accident and death).

SALINA, Sevier County

Population: 1910, 1,082; 1920, 1,451; 1930, 1,383.

Central Utah Press, Volume 1, number 1, November 28, 1891, Saturday, Republican, 4-pages, 17 x 24, $2, no files. "At the masthead is the name of the well known and energetic Ex-Ogdenite, W. W. Wallace," says the Ogden Standard reviewer December 3, 1891, "which is equivalent to saying that the Press is bright and stalwart and an all around hummer." "It is a bright little paper," adds the Wasatch Wave, December 15, 1891.

Quotations from the Press were picked up in the exchanges in February, June and November, 1894 and January and June, 1895. The American Newspaper Directory for 1896 shows: "Saturdays, Independent, 4-pages, 18 x 24, $2, W. W. Wallace, editor and publisher." But about this time A. E. Howard took charge of the paper, of whom we hear in the Wasatch Wave of February 5, 1897: "Editor Howard of the Salina Press has just turned out 'A Bunch of Carrots' in the shape of a neat little booklet, a copy of which has been received at this office with the author's compliments, and for which we are obligated to Utah's Bill Nye. The 160 leaves in 'A Bunch of Carrots' are covered with the comic side of life in southern Utah and are good medicine for a country editor to take. 'A Bunch of Carrots' sells for 76c."

"A Salina Press with Brother Howard hanging gamely to its coattails, has jumped over into its seventh year," says the Brigham Bugler, December 18, 1897. "The Press is funny enough and wicked enough to be published in Salt Lake—Seek broader fields, brother Howard!" Howard was a baseball enthusiast, they told us, and was so good he would go to press on Friday and correctly report the game played next day between teams he had trained!

The American Newspaper Directory for 1898 lists Arthur E. Howard, editor and publisher, circulation 530. A Gazetteer advertisement in 1900 modestly informs us: "The Salina Press, circulation 1,000,000 copies. Published every Friday at the saltiest town in Utah, Salina. Published at $2 per year and payment taken in any old thing that isn't real actual money. Send $2 if you wish a year's treatment for the blues, to the publisher, A. E. Howard."

But the citizenry of Salina couldn't have been in very sore need of that antidote for melancholia, for the Vernal Express, January 12, 1901 says: "A. E. Howard, late editor of the brightest little paper in the state, the Salina Press, has gone into a newspaper undertaking in Lander, Wyoming." However, we saw a stray copy of:

The Salina Sun, Volume 1, Number 17, Friday, July 19, 1901, 7 columns, 4-pages, 2 home print, 7 columns of advertisements, filled with local news. Masthead: "A. E. Howard, Sun-Doctor." Furthermore Kenner in Utah As It Is, 1904, says the Salina Sun was "Established in 1901 by Arthur E. Howard, a journalist of experience and such ability that some people say he hides his light under a bushel, or whatever other measure is handy. He (the gender is proper as to either person or paper) appears weekly and is always a welcome visitor."

A Gazetteer advertisement, 1903-04 says: "The Salina Sun, circulation 1,135,000 copies every week. Read only by wide awake people—people who have at least horse sense. The only newspaper in Utah whose editor never lies. You will never have appendicitis if you read the Salina Sun. Circulates in Denmark, Sweden and the United States.

It goes everywhere. Its publisher has to use common sense or it would go to hell." Possibly the publisher ceased to "use common sense," for the history of the Sun ends without an obituary notice, in any contemporary now extant. Why or when the Sun went into eclipse, we did not ascertain.

Salina Sun (II!). J. L. Ewing, publisher of the Richfield Reaper, established another Salina Sun in 1918. The Western Newspaper Union Ledger account is with Charles Richardson, September 6, 1920 and thereafter; but a directory listing, 1920 to 1921, gives J. C. Jorgensen, editor and publisher—and in 1922-23 "Charles Richardson, editor and publisher." The Western Newspaper Union account is with H. W. Cherry (now of Gunnison) from June 2, 1923 to date. Mrs. Cherry is Chief Nurse for the little Sun!

Salina Call. First issue May 10, 1906, $1.50, C. N. Lund, Jr., publisher. "It went under that name for about 10 years, then the name was changed to the

Sevier Valley Call," writes Mr. Lund. "I was the owner, publisher and manager and it came out regularly for twelve years and six months. I discontinued it July, 1918, and moved it to Mt. Pleasant, where I published it for three and one half years as The Call. It was discontinued in May, 1922."

Editor Lund is reported to have crusaded against modern society a little more forcefully than was acceptable to some citizens of Salina. They made it so unpleasant for him and his family they decided it was best to leave. Hence the transfer of the printing plant to Mt. Pleasant. q. v.

SANDY, Salt Lake County

Population: 1900, 1,030; 1910, 1,037; 1920, 1,208; 1930, 1,436.

The Independent, started December, 1893, 5 columns, 8-pages, 2 home-print, no files. Diehl Brothers (I. E. and Chas. P.) publishers. "It is a brisk and well patronized new venture in the journalistic field," comments the Brigham Bugler, December 16, 1893. "The Sandy Independent has resumed publication after three months rest," reports the Wasatch Wave, August 26, 1898. Mrs. Florence M. Raddon of Sandy showed us a copy of the Independent, number 40 of volume 5, Sunday morning, October 3, 1897. James H. Hayford was editor and publisher, beginning with that issue. In his Salutatory he meekly steps out before his Sandy public: "Those of an observing nature will probably notice that the conspicuous place of honor at the head of the paper until recently showing the name of John E. Hartvikxen, now contains the signomen of your former humble servant, J. H. Hayford." We did not learn anything else about The Independent—which was evidently not independent of support, for it soon passed quietly away.

SILVER REEF, Washington County

Population: 1874, none; 1880, 1,046; 1888, 1,200; 1890, about 500; 1900, about 50; 1903, none.

The Silver Age. "This is the title of a new semi-weekly which Mr. Joseph Field, proprietor of the Beaver Enterprise, purposes commencing to publish at Leeds, southern Utah, on or about March 1, next. The prospectus which is before us, states that it will be chiefly devoted to showing the development of that mining district . . . Mr. Field is a gentleman of great energy," says the Deseret News, February 10, 1877. The Salt Lake Tribune, February 14, 1877 puts it: "The Silver Age is the title of a new weekly paper to be started at Silver Reef City, Leeds Mining District, by Joseph Field of Beaver." But we found no copies and no other references. Possibly it was because of the

Silver Reef Echo (The Utah Pomologist and Silver Reef Echo), the first number of which appeared February 24, 1877, edited and published by Joseph E. Johnson of St. George. What's more, it was a Daily! In it we read: "The Next Move.—It will be noticed that we have slightly changed the character of this periodical. The reason is quickly told. Within the last three months a prosperous mining camp has sprung into existence at Silver Reef, near Leeds, only twenty miles from this place (St. George). In the past our efforts in publishing have not paid us. We like to be paid for our labors, and we think we can see opportunity. . . . We intend to commence at once the issue of a small daily sheet at Silver Reef, in which we will give condensed telegraph reports, stock and market reports, and local news. We shall issue monthly (in St. George?) to fill all advertising contracts, and 'wait for something to turn up', when St. George may be able to sustain a good weekly. This is all, and nothing more!" There are local news aplenty at Silver Reef, under the appropriate head: The Silver Reef Echoes.

The Salt Lake Tribune of March 6, 1877 says: "The Silver Reef Echo is the title of a small daily paper, hailing from the Leeds District. It devotes considerable attention to the mines of that justly celebrated silver-sandstone country, and appears to be well patronized." Here is one reason a daily was launched: "The Deseret Telegraph Company has completed an extension of line from Leeds to Silver Reef, and yesterday (Sunday, March 9, 1877) opened an office in the last named place." It is also of passing interest in a history of news gathering in Utah that on March 23, 1877, "The Deseret Telegraph line was tapped at the Mountain Meadows to report the execution of John D. Lee," says the Deseret News. We picked up from the Provo Enquirer of March 17, 1877, this note: "S. A. Kenner, Esq., attorney and counselor at law, has not settled down at his profession, nor even stuck out his shingle, but is going into the more honest and honorable profession of editing a paper at Leeds . . ."

While Bancroft in 1889 refers to The Silver Reef Echo, semi-weekly, and the Silver Reef Miner, semi-weekly, changed to weekly as if

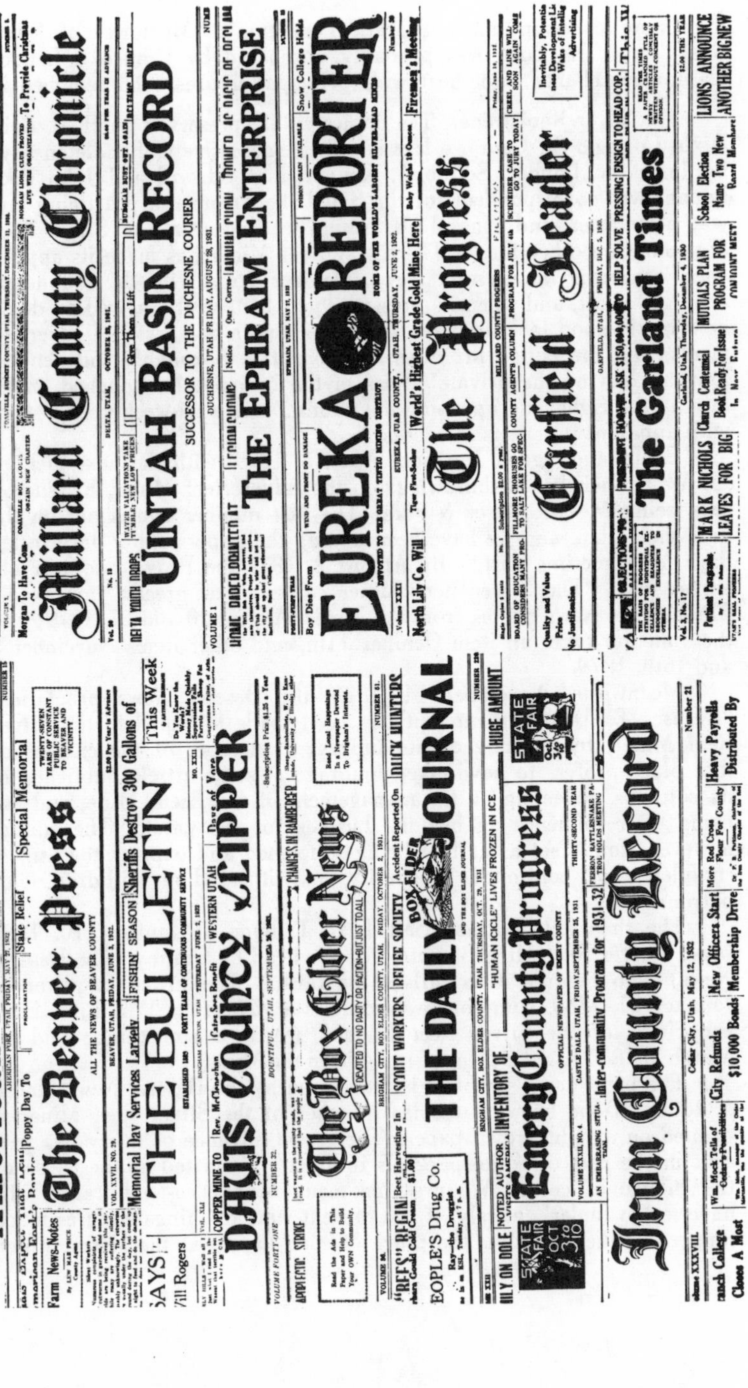

The Summit County Bee

Millard County Chronicle

UINTAH BASIN RECORD
SUCCESSOR TO THE DUCHESNE COURIER

THE EPHRAIM ENTERPRISE

EUREKA REPORTER

The Progress

Garfield Leader

The Garland Times

American Fork Citizen

The Beaver Press

THE BULLETIN

Davis County Clipper

The Box Elder News

THE DAILY JOURNAL

Emery County Progress

Iron County Record

they were contemporaneous, Mark Pendleton's "Memories of Silver Reef" says The Echo was probably purchased by Crouch & Louder, leading merchants, and the town's principal figures, who renamed it:

The Silver Reef Miner. Ten copies, 1882, preserved by H. L. Reid, Dixie College, St. George. It was edited successively, Pendleton says, by James N. Louder, Scipio A. Kenner, and Edward and John Pike. Louder was correspondent for the Salt Lake Tribune, a practicing lawyer, postmaster, and general all around leading citizen of Silver Reef. We found no other files. "The Silver Reef Miner has made its appearance," informs the Deseret News, October 26, 1878. "It is a neatly arranged sheet, and when its pressman gets better rollers, will no doubt be a really good looking newspaper. It shows a fine array of advertisements, and the editor promises to make it a thoroughly independent journal, leaving the private affairs of the individual untouched, maintaining the right, and opposing the wrong. It is a tri-weekly, and starts with apparent prospects of success."

Comes the Ogden Junction, April 5, 1879, with the next pickup: "J. W. Crouch has withdrawn from the Silver Reef Miner, his successors being Messrs. Buser & Pike. The last number comes out on the half shell plan, and we have been getting the papers about once in ten days for sometime past." By August 2, 1879 the Provo Enquirer observes that: "The Silver Reef Miner comes to us greatly improved." The Deseret News quotes from the Miner, August 20 and 27, 1879; and the Junction takes an item October 11th, and other items November 5 and 15th, 1879.

Meanwhile, November 14, 1879, the Deseret News proclaims: "Refuses To Die.—An attempt has been made to 'squelch' the Silver Reef Miner, by shutting off its supply. A number of the citizens of that place profess to have taken umbrage at some article published in its columns, reflecting on the management of the Leeds Mine, and are using their influence against the business of the paper. The editors however, don't feel a bit like being squelched and express the utmost confidence of continued prosperity, notwithstanding withdrawal of patronage."

The then anti-Mormon Salt Lake Tribune of January 10, 1880 says: "Silver Reef Miner is patted on the head by Granny (The Deseret News) who regards it as full in the faith." The Provo Enquirer of January 24, 1880, courteously chronicles a visit from "Mr. Pike, Esq., proprietor of the Silver Reef Miner," which is something; and on March 3, 1880 lifted a piece of news from the Miner.

The print-paper problem is mentioned by the Deseret News March 6, 1880: "Done brown.—the last number of the Silver Reef Miner is printed on a light brown paper. The recent advance of thirty five percent in the cost of white paper is indirectly intimated as the cause of the change of color. We presume many of our co-temporaries will have to 'go under' entirely, if the present state of things endures much longer. In the meantime the pluck of such papers as the Miner, which prefers to lose complexion rather than existence, is certainly commendable."

The business directory and Gazetteer for several western states for 1880 gives: "E. Pike, editor" of the Silver Reef Miner. A better focus on the problems of the Miner comes from the Salt Lake Herald April 8, 1880, under the date line: "Silver Reef, April 5, 1880. At the moment of going to press late on Saturday evening the Pike Brothers, editors of the Silver Reef Miner, were arrested upon a justice warrant at the instance of the secretary of the Christy Mill & Mining Co., upon a charge of libel upon the person of one Henry S. Lubbeck, (Pendleton's spelling) Superintendent of said company. There are but two practicing attorneys in this place; one appeared for the plaintiff and the other has been retained also, and refused to act as counsel for the accused . . ." It was alleged in the complaint the defendants had published certain statements concerning the geological formation "which would have a tendency to defeat the purpose of the plaintiff in negotiating the sale of the company's mines. The company's attempt to thus muzzle the press is generally regarded here as a gross outrage."

Another angle comes from the Deseret News of April 19, 1880, "The Silver Reef Miner, it appears from the latest issue of that paper that has reached us, has been threatened with a general 'cleaning out' by anonymous 'avengers', if it publishes anything more about Captain Lubbeck and the Christy Mine affair. The Miner, however, asserts its right to speak all it wishes upon that subject, and to promise the 'avengers' determined resistance with guns and ammunition and all such things, if they attempt to carry their threats into execution."

"The preliminary examination in the libel suit instituted by the Christy Mining Company of Silver Reef against the editors of the Miner lasted seven days," further deposes the Deseret News, April 21, 1880. "The Miner, notwithstanding the threats made to demolish it . . . is still firing away briskly, and reaffirming its original theory that the Buckeye Reef is a faulted and dislocated portion of the White Reef, which declaration . . . was the cause of the libel suit."

"The last Silver Reef Miner came to us in only half its former size," says the Provo Enquirer, April 21, 1880. "The boys had been evidently too much engaged with their libel suit in Court to find time to write much. Their avengers say: 'Let me tell you that your time is short unless you stop your damn slander'; to which they reply: 'We will permit no man or any number of men to clean out this shebang while a round of ammunition can be procured wherewith to defend it'!'"

"Silver Reef Miner Libel Suit Concluded," headlines the Deseret News, April 24, 1880. "The examination resulted in the Pike Brothers, who edit and publish the Miner, being held to answer to the Grand Jury, in the sum of $2,000 each." The Beaver Watchman says of the matter: "The attack on the Christy Mines was made under the disguise of discussing Professor Rothwell's two-reef theory; but nothing could have been more apparent than the real motive, viz, the defamation of the company's property." Other editors bandied the news about the State in a spirit of: But-for-the-grace-of-God-that's-us; and, I-told-you-so, it-serves-'em-right!

The outcome is unfolded in the Provo Enquirer, July 21, 1880: "The Jury at Beaver righteously decided the press should remain free and not be intimidated by threats of legal prosecution, by dishonest mining speculators. The Silver Reef Miner stock has gone up, while the stock of certain mining companies has gone down. A free press can always defeat the swindling projects of unprincipled speculators."

In this case, lightning struck twice in the same place, as the Ogden Junction repeats, July 28, 1880: "The Pike Brothers, editors of the Silver Reef Miner, have been indicted (again) for libel by the Grand Jury . . . by the Stormont Mining Company . . . whose mining property, it is alleged, has been mis-represented by the paper." The Junction continues: "The Frisco Times and the Beaver Watchman are at logger-heads about the Silver Reef Miner, which the former declares to be petering out, while the latter stands forth as their valiant champion."

"The Pikes of Silver Reef," vouches the Deseret News, August 7, 1880, "intend to sue the Christy Company for damages, as though the prosecution against them for libel, although they were acquitted, the Miner had to be suspended." Meaning temporarily, since the News quoted again from the Miner, September 8, 1880; and the Enquirer records a visit to Provo of "John W. Pike, Esq. editor of the Silver Reef Miner," October 6, 1880. The Deseret News finds rich pickings in the Miner, February 23 and October 25, 1881, and January 25 and May 31, 1882; and there were cuttings noted in the Junction and other papers in the interim.

The Enquirer takes the pains to record an important item, May 11, 1881: "The Silver Reef Miner has changed hands, having passed from its former proprietor and editor, Mr. Edward Pike, into the hands of Messrs. Steele & Louder. Mr. Pike has had charge of the paper for upwards of two years . . . though the Miner in many respects has not and does not agree with our views religiously." "With its issue of last Saturday, the Silver Reef Miner enters upon its fourth volume in improved garb," the Ogden Herald acquaints us August 18, 1881. And "Edwin Pike, who is connected with the Silver Reef Miner," called on the Provo Enquirer, November 23, 1881. The American Newspaper Directory for 1881 records: "Silver Reef Miner, Wednesday and Saturday, anti-Mormon, established 1878, ten lines one month $4." But by February 25, 1882 the Park Record informs us: "The Silver Reef Miner has taken a new departure, and will hereafter appear as a 4-column, tri-weekly." The St. George Union for February, 1882 puts it, "The Silver Reef Miner has been ensmalled, and changed from a weekly to a tri-weekly paper."

The Logan Leader, March 17, 1882 gives this picture: "Silver Reef Miner is not a Mormon paper. In fact it is intensely anti-Mormon, and its cuts and flings at the religion to which Utah owes her existence as a commonwealth today, are often unworthy a respectable journal;

but the Miner man wields a pungent pen with which he prods our statuesque governor . . . Murray!"

The Deseret News of June 27, 1882 says: "Changed Hands.—The Silver Reef Miner is now published by the Miner Publishing Company, with Mr. S. A. Kenner on the editorial tripod." The Ogden Herald, June 27, 1882, gives this additional angle: "Its platform, we understand, is to be strictly independent, or as the editor puts it 'between Scylla and Charybdis', if such a thing is possible." The Park Record wipes a crocodile tear, November 4, 1882: "It must be gratifying to the people of Silver Reef to swallow the Church arguments of that 6 x 9 sheet. The citizens made a fatal mistake when they permitted J. N. Louder to withdraw from the contract control of the Miner."

H. L. Reid of the Dixie College, St. George, has collected and preserved a few precious copies of the Miner. Volume 5, number 13, Silver Reef, Washington County, Utah, Friday, March 17, 1882, 5 columns, 4-pages, 11 x 16, all home print, practically three full pages of advertisements, some telegraphic news, a few locals, published every Monday, Wednesday and Friday, office, Miner Building, lower Main Street, one year $6, delivered by carrier 25c per week, J. N. Louder, publisher. Volume 5, number 32, July 15, 1882, Saturday, Louder's name dropped, Miner Publishing Company, publisher and proprietor. S. A. Kenner, attorney and Counselor at Law, practices in all the Courts of the Territory, Miner Building. The issue for October 28, 1882 advertises "The Silver Reef Miner . . . is the only newspaper published in southern Utah."

Two news notes come from the Park Record, the first March 10, 1883: "Ed Pike came up from Salt Lake Thursday . . . Ed and the writer used to run the Silver Reef Miner when the camp used to dish up a man or two once a week for breakfast. Those were palmy days!" And an echo of the death knell, April 7, 1883: "The Silver Reef Miner has got mired so deep in the sand that the owners could not dig it up again. When the concern got into Mormon hands we felt satisfied it was doomed to death."

SMITHFIELD, Cache County

Population: 1890, 1,080; 1900, 1,494; 1910, 1,865; 1920, 2,421; 1930, 2,353.

Sentinel, Volume 1, number 1, December 13, 1907, J. W. Harry, publisher. Mr. Harry continued to edit and publish the Sentinel until 1924 when he sold it to Ralph R. Channell. Mr. Harry retained the job printing plant. In 1926 Mr. Harry and Joseph W. Peterson purchased the newspaper and published it until Mr. Harry's death, February 8, 1933. The new masthead, May 12, 1933, shows Joseph W. Peterson, editor, and Edwin R. Dowdel, publisher, continuing to date. It speaks well of the Sentinel to say that no other newspaper was ever published in Smithfield.

SPANISH FORK, Utah County

Population: 1890, 2,214; 1900, 2,735; 1910, 3,464; 1920, 4,172; 1930, 4,509.

The Spanish Fork Index, by Mr. and Mrs. J. T. Jakeman. "Saturday, Independent, established 1891 (sic) 4-pages, 15 x 22, $3, James T. Jakeman, editor, Index Company, publishers," says the American Newspaper Directory for 1892. Files: A few numbers in the Spanish Fork Press office. Warner's History of Spanish Fork says the Index suspended that autumn because of "malnutrition." The Provo Enquirer, March 25, 1892 recites: "The temporary suspension of the Spanish Fork Index is over, and the paper appears again, brighter than ever, and all home print." The Wasatch Wave, May 24, 1892 announces:

"The Spanish Fork Sun is to be born, and the Index is to be aroused from its slumbers." And on July 14, 1892 the Spanish Fork Sun mentions the Index, presumably a local contemporary. Stenhouse's Gazetteer for 1892-3 says: "Spanish Fork has two papers, Index and Sun." The Spanish Fork Sun of July 28, 1892 records: "The two devils of the Sun and the Index had quite a squabble last night as to the merits of each others paper; of course the Sun's devil came out victorious!" And again the Sun illumines the Index on August 25, 1892: "Have you seen this week's issue of the Index? She's a Lulu! Bro. Jakeman of the Index excused himself for his half sheet on the plea of sickness. Well, the Index does look sick for a fact, and if all reports are true, or even half of them, he's apt to be sicker. In his issue of May 21st he said the Sun would "go up in smoke!" The Sun still shines, but the Index is getting awfully smoky. Something is going to 'drap'."

Following the Sun spot-light again July 7, 1892 (for the want of an Index file): "A conundrum: 'Spanish Fork, a sa city, will not celebrats Inde pendence day'.—Index Supplement for June 25, 1892. What is an 'a sa city'? and we would like to know what kind of brats 'celebrats' are. As for 'Inde pendence' that must be the apparel worn by the female editor." Mrs. Ellen Jakeman shared editorial responsibilities on the Index.

As late as October 29, 1892, the monitorial Sun was setting the people right with regard to the Index, which had already died but was as yet without a funeral or burial. "On going about town we learn that J. T. Jakeman has visited many business men, urging them to assist him in the incorporation of the defunct Index and make out of it a Republican organ. Our prediction for his success is unbounded, but if we are correctly informed, has hasn't obtained one assistant." And, November 19, 1892: "Mrs. J. T. Jakeman, late of the once-upon-a-time Index, but now of Provo was rusticating on our streets this week."

The Sun gladly preached the funeral November 26, 1892. "Sacred to its memory.—This week we speak in earnest that the Spanish Fork Index is no more. It has not appeared before the public for four or five weeks, and now that one of its proprietors is within the folds of the law, and no show of being redeemed for sometime, the Sun has come to

GUNNISON VALLEY NEWS
Gunnison—"The Sugar Beet and Cauliflower City."
GUNNISON, UTAH, THURSDAY, JUNE 2, 1932

CACHE AMERICAN
A Home Paper for Home People
LOGAN, UTAH, FRIDAY, MAY 27, 1932

The Manti Times

Manti Messenger

MIDVALE JOURNAL
Midvale, Utah, Friday, June 3, 1932

The Milford News
MILFORD, BEAVER COUNTY, UTAH

The Times-Independent
MOAB, GRAND COUNTY, UTAH, MAY 19, 1932

SAN JUAN RECORD
MONTICELLO, SAN JUAN COUNTY, UTAH, THURSDAY, MAY 26, 1932

MORGAN COUNTY NEWS

MT. PLEASANT PYRAMID
Mount Pleasant, Sanpete County, Utah, Friday, Aug 21, 1931

THE WASATCH WAVE

HELPER JOURNAL
HELPER, CARBON COUNTY, UTAH, FRIDAY, JUNE 3, 1932

SOUTH CACHE COURIER

Piute County News
JUNCTION, PIUTE COUNTY, UTAH, OCTOBER, 23 1931

KANE COUNTY STANDARD
KANAB, KANE COUNTY, UTAH, FRIDAY, MAY 27, 1932

The Weekly Reflex
KAYSVILLE, LAYTON AND FARMINGTON, UTAH, THURSDAY, MAY 26, 1932

The Lehi Sun
LEHI, UTAH, SATURDAY, DECEMBER 5, 1930

The Lehi Free Press
The City's Only Home-Owned Newspaper

The Herald-Journal
LOGAN, UTAH, FRIDAY, MAY 27, 1932

the conclusion that the Index has passed beyond . . . Mr. Jakeman, one of the proprietors, forged check after check on various banks of the territory . . . Mr. and Mrs. Jakeman, we predict that you build lofty ruins in some other clime, a foundation of mortal success . . . In closing we will again extend to the Spanish Fork Index a helping hand (to get out of town!)."

Meanwhile, (November 24, 1892) the Manti Times-Reporter uncovers: "James T. Jakeman was captured at Park City on Friday by Captain Donovan and placed in jail on a charge of forgery. Jakeman is in a tight box, having swindled several persons." Which is the end of the Index.

Spanish Fork Sun. Volume 1, number 1, May 19, 1892, 4-pages, 2 home print, 6 columns, no local ads, but space reserved for them! W. H. Kenner and Andrew Jensen. Files, many numbers to 1894 and all from 1903 to date bound in the Spanish Fork Press office. "Our bow.— the Spanish Fork Sun has risen, we hope never to go down . . . We expect to make our Sun shine with such steady brilliance . . . as to merit the patronage of the business men." (Don't they all!) "The proprietors are old time standbys of the Dispatch," is the blessing of the Provo Dispatch. As to the atmosphere of Spanish Fork, we read in the Sun: "Our Position. When we first arrived in this city we were told there was considerable prejudice against starting a home paper, as the people had been disappointed in papers here, two of them having been started and both having suspended, though not from the want of patronage . . . They wanted a paper . . . that would become a fixture of the town before they would offer any encouragement. We then decided that our best policy would be to issue a paper before canvassing for advertising."

The files indicate the advertising was soon forthcoming; but not soon enough for Kenner, who sold out in a few weeks, and on July 7, 1892, the new masthead reads: "Andrew Jensen, manager, Jesse P. Holt, editor," which was still an unstable combination, for September 16, 1892 we find this "Notice.—Mr. Andrew Jensen has this day sold his interest in the Sun to M. L. Scott, and the firm of Scott & Holt will hereafter transact all business of the paper . . ." Jesse Holt became editor and reviews the situation October 1, 1892: "Appreciate. We notice in traveling among and conversing with the people that they are quite prejudiced against home papers, and we do not blame them when we consider how they have been fooled with papers. First the Rocky Mountain Star, which was very rocky indeed. Then the Index, which is and has been a disgrace, especially to the newspaper fraternity surrounding us, as to its typographical appearance—both of which were published by parties not of us, that is whose homes were not here but in neighboring cities."

"In the midst of this newspaper confusion the Sun arose, and has shed its rays in our city now for four months . . . The Sun is the only weekly or semi-weekly newspaper in the territory printed without 'plate' or 'patent inside'."

Milton L. Scott becomes editor and manager with the November 26, 1892 issue, which ironically enough consisted of 4-pages, two of which were boiler plate or ready print! That must have been too humiliating for Holt (or was he deceased?) for on February 11, 1893 M. L. Scott and Company became publishers, and M. L. Scott, editor. "G. P. Holt, Jr. (son and heir?) has sold his entire interest in the Sun to M. L. Scott, for several months past lessee, and has retired from the newspaper business to the school room. Scott proposes to keep the paper alive, hard times or no hard times," opines the Provo Enquirer, February 13, 1893. The Brigham Bugler, February 18, 1893, adds this for the history: "That paper (the Spanish Fork Sun) is in the same flourishing financial condition as the Bugler, which we learn from the following which appeared in the last issue: 'We are Independent, free and fearless, and can now say not a mortgage or anything whatever that may tend to crush it, is visible'."

Scott found good pickings, and occasionally in 1893 issued a 3-column, one page supplement; but he also attended the obsequies of the final setting of the Sun on May 6, 1893. "Scott proved to be unpopular as an editor in Spanish Fork," writes Elisha Warner in his History of Spanish Fork; "and the paper suspended publication after about a year of life." After being without a newspaper a year or two an appropriate name for a new paper was:

Spanish Fork Herald, which we find first quoted January 26, 1895 in the Brigham Bugler. There are no files, and no descriptive references. "Fred Smith, editor of the Spanish Fork Herald, has been arrested on the charge of criminal libel sworn out by R. J. Stewart," deposes the Wasatch Wave, April 16, 1895. The Park Record adds April 20, 1895: "He called one Claude Stewart a 'bum' and the latter had him arrested." Stewart evidently had a lot of influence or editor Smith had too little, for the paper not only changed hands soon thereafter, but the obituary appears in the Nephi Blade November 9, 1895: "The Spanish Fork Herald suspended publication last week. Its editor, Wm. F. Gibson, is now a member of the Springville Independent force."

Spanish Fork Press, Volume 1, Number 1, January 23, 1902. Andrew Jensen, editor and publisher, "Local and long distance printing office," he proclaims. But he owned his plant and it was located in Spanish Fork, a job printing office bought from Heber C. Jex. A hand press was used. "Our bow. The Spanish Fork Press, as we have chosen to name this paper, should have made its first appearance two weeks ago, but on account of the delay of the new press, and other printing material, we ·were compelled to wait."

Jensen found a swarm of local news items and in turn was awarded a generous advertising patronge. The Springville Independent, February 13, 1902, speaks of the situation: "Spanish Fork people have been buncoed so often by unscrupulous newspapermen, that a square deal, long continued is the only thing that will appeal to them. This, Mr.

Jensen will give them." On March 10, 1910, a change of management was announced: "With this issue of the Press the business passes from my hands into the hands of Elisha Warner, who has been connected with the Press office for the last five years . . . He is a Spanish Fork native son.—Andrew Jensen. In the future the policy of this paper will be the same as in the past.—Elisha Warner, publisher."

"In June, 1912," Mr. Warner writes, "George A. Yates purchased a half interest as a silent partner. In February, 1914 Mr. Yates sold his interest to Ezra Warner, and the Warner Brothers have continued the business since that time—Elisha as editor and Ezra as manager." These men and their predecessors have made the Press ultra modern, in that it has been much more a business enterprise, a necessity in the community, than a personal or opinionated mouthpiece; and it has been used by the leading interests of the town as freely as by its own editors.

Considering the previous newspaper wrecks in Spanish Fork, the Press distinctly marks the new era in newspaper journalism, to which practically every newspaper in the State has since adapted itself more or less gradually. Only, in Spanish Fork, the Press from its beginning, January 23, 1902 has been distinctly of the new order, with a very fine sense of discernment of the difference between personal and community promotion. Thus the Press is a respected institution in the community!

SPRING LAKE, Utah County

Population: (A farming community near the present Payson).

The Farmers Oracle. First issue Friday, May 2, 1863, published the first and third Tuesday in each month, J. E. Johnson, editor and publisher, W. D. Johnson, proprietor. Three columns, 8-pages, 8 x 11, all home print, $2. This first country paper in Utah was not exactly a newspaper, for the Johnsons were florists, farmers, and medicine men; but "Hymenial and Obituary notices" etc. were published free, according to the masthead declaration. Two pages of volume 1, number 1, are reproduced herewith through the courtesy of the L. D. S. Church Historian. The Salutatory, and The Prospect, should be read at this time. (p. 52-53) "Whether well or poorly sustained" he would run a year! The only other issue known to be in existence today is Number 9, dated Tuesday, September 22, 1863, in the Bancroft Library at Berkeley.

It was printed on a dark, dank sheet of home made paper from unbleached pulp; three columns, 8-pages, 9 x 12. Front page articles were on Cheese Making, Onion Culture, How To Grow Early Celery, Signs Of A Good Ox, Treatment for Kicking Cows, How to Kill Lice On Calves, and The Sex Of Eggs! The masthead on page 4 was identical with that on number 1. On page 5 appears this editorial statement. "Our Delay, Paper, etc. No doubt some of our readers have been anxious about our delay in issuing, having missed the date of one number. Circumstances over which we had no control have denied us paper, and even the lean supply at present is of indifferent quality. The rains from heaven have descended and we shall doubtless be better provided in the future and shall try and keep the 'masheen' running to time if possible." "Our Position. At the present moment we do not intend to ventilate the above caption, either upon politics or religion, but merely state our position to be desperate unless our patrons 'shell out' some wheat without delay. We promised to be quiet until after harvest. That period is past, and we are getting hungry. Let us have some wheat. We mean no particular one, but everyone that is indebted to this office. (Residents of) Payson and Pondtown deliver at Simons Mill; Spanish Fork deliver to Thomas Day; Springville to W. Mendenhall; Provo to J. McEwan; American Fork to R. Steele; and Lehi to I. Goodwin. All subscribers south of here and this side of the cotton region (Utah's Dixie) are expected to deliver here, or pay over to our agent enough over the two bushels to pay transportation. We have some valuable seed to distribute over the country among our most punctual subscribers."

Several breezy news items appear, including: "Tobacco in this section has produced finely, and is now being harvested. Mr. Ballard of Payson is preparing to do something at manufacturing the article." The paper was remarkably well patronized by advertisers, including the Johnsons, who sold "Family Medicines: At Spring Lake Villa May Be Found A Complete Line Of Family Medicines Which May Be Had For Grain." "Flowering Plants, J. E. Johnson." "Have You Any Sheep . . . Spring Creek, between Payson and Santaquin. One of the best and most extensive sheep ranges in the Territory. The subscriber proposes to take sheep on the shares. Accomodation good and attentive shepherds. Fine mountain and bench range. Bring along your sheep from the bare ranges, damp bottoms and saleratus beds where your wool and lambs may not be lost, and your sheep become victims of the scab. B. F. Johnson, Spring Lake Villa, June 1."

Editor Johnson (Joseph E.) by the way, had in 1852, bought the Bugle at Kanesville (now Council Bluffs) Iowa, and from that office he issued the Omaha Arrow for a time. In the Salt Lake City Deseret News of May 23, 1860, we read: "The Echo.—The first number of the Huntsman's Echo, published by our old friend, J. E. Johnson at Woodriver, Buffalo County, Nebraska, has been received. We wish it success! But the concern is too far off to have the reverberant sounds heard distinctly. Come up higher, Joseph, or blow a little louder!" And October 2, 1861 the News mentions the arrival in Salt Lake City, Friday evening, September 27, 1861 of the last company of emigrants for the season, adding: ". . . among the number J. E. Johnson, late editor of the Huntsman's Echo, . . . who has ventured to come up to the mountains at last."

Miss Anna Marie Moore, teacher, Spring Lake School, wrote a history of Spring Lake in 1931, aided materially by Milas E. Johnson of Huntington, Utah, son of George W. Johnson. From Miss Moore's manuscript we learn that the big Johnson house at Spring Lake, called the Villa, inclosed within an adobe wall, was erected by James Pace and others. It was purchased in 1862 by Joseph E. Johnson. He at once transformed it into quite a mansion, consisting of several indentical two story inter-communicating units, and containing a total of at least 18 and possibly 24 rooms. He renamed it Spring Lake Villa. One room was the printing shop, home of the Oracle. In another room Johnson established a very pretentious drug store, the stock comprising practically every existent patent medicine and known home remedy. The latter were largely prepared and bottled or packaged by J. E. Johnson himself, and bore his name. The remainder of the Villa was occupied by J. E. Johnson's three families; the many children and some hired help assisting with the planting and cultivating of flowers, shrubs, and general crops.

One of the employees writes, January 26, 1864 (Millennial Star March 26, 1864) "The country is hard to begin in . . . The customs being strange and the channels of trade and manufacture so imperfectly filled at the present, a man has to do almost anything and everything, he generally not being able to obtain employment at his particular business . . . After a residence of a short time in Great Salt Lake City, I received an offer to work on the 'Farmer's Oracle', a small agricultural sheet, published in this place, about 71 miles south of the city. I have now a cow, one yearling calf, four sheep, two pigs in the pen, and a fat one on the shelf; enough potatoes or more to last me 'til they come in again; about twenty gallons of molasses, chickens almost out of number; and if I stay in this place (which I have not yet decided on doing) I shall fence in about three acres and plant my orchard in the spring."

"By the mail last evening," says the Salt Lake Daily Telegraph Thursday morning, September 15, 1864, "we received the last number of the first volume of the Farmers' Oracle. Our friend 'Joe' has done his best to give the people a useful little paper, but he has had a 'hard road to travel', and feels weary. Yet he does not seem used up, nor finally squelched.

"He proposes 'to rest—work and earn some bread—recuperate and prepare to go on with the next volume as soon as the people are ready for it, and will sustain it with a good prepaid subscription list'. We hope that 'Joe' will recuperate and go ahead with his pen. He is a genial, agreeable fellow, with the natural instincts of a good editor, and has every capacity to make an agricultural paper interesting—if well supported. In the last three words is the secret of inspiration. If a second volume is tried, the Oracle can count upon our best support."

In a couple of years Johnson moved to St. George, where as a newspaper man we hear of him again. The Oracle was published only two or three years, J. E. taking the printing plant with him to St. George. The brother, B. F. Johnson, succeeded J. E. at the Villa, and in 1868 increased by 100 acres the original tract of 100 acres, and estimated his

crop of cane molasses alone at 2,000 gallons, according to a story in the Salt Lake Daily Telegraph, September 15, 1868.

The Farmer's Oracle literally "passed on" to St. George where we picked up the following from Our Dixie Times, Volume 1, Number 1, January 22, 1868, published by J. E. Johnson. "Farmer's Oracle. There are delinquent subscribers in many settlements in this territory. We ask them this once more to pay up. After giving proper time, we intend publishing a list of the names of those who won't pay!" Sorry we didn't see the list, if it was ever published. Possibly they all paid!

SPRINGVILLE, Utah County

Population: 1890, 2,849; 1900, 3,422; 1910, 3,356; 1920, 3,010; 1930, 3,748.

Springville Independent, Volume 1, Number 1, August 20, 1891. Thursday, 7 columns, folio, Newman A. Mix. (A. G. Johnson recalls that George Sanders was associated with Mix.) There are no files but it was noticed by several contemporaries. It "looks after local interests with its circulation of 600," says Stenhouse's Gazetteer for 1892-3. "Another nice country paper has been added to our exchange list," says the Davis County Clipper, May 30, 1892.

The Spanish Fork Press, June 9, 1892, reports a visit from "George Sanders, manager of the Springville Independent," and exchanges browsed from its columns freely and profitably, the Brigham Bugler repaying thusly, August 20, 1892: "The Springville Independent has overcome the invariable obstacles that pile up on each new paper during its initiatory twelve months, and is now sailing gaily down the smooth path of the second year."

It took on a new skipper about that time, as indicated by the American Newspaper Directory listing for 1892. "Four pages, 17 x 24, subscription $2, D. C. Johnson, editor, Independent Publishing Company." A friendly ear for Mrs. Grundy is indicated by this from the Brigham Bugler for September 16, 1893: "About half the locals in the Springville Independent last week were announcements of new arrivals from babyland." A comment of greater import to editors generally is from the Bugler of October 14, 1893: "The Springville Independent has done away with its patent insides. Editor Johnson is a pusher who deserves a hearty patronage of the neighborhood he represents so well."

The Park Record informs us, April 20, 1895, "D. P. Felt is now the editor and publisher of the Springville Independent, having purchased the paper and assumed control last week." "Editor Felt of the Springville Independent, was disciplined by the Utah County Church officials for his publishing a certain article concerning the 'New Manifesto'," vouches the Wasatch Wave, May 8, 1896. But it obviously did not effect the editor's ecclesiastical standing, for the Brigham Bugler deposes, August 7, 1897: "The editor of the Springville Independent,

D. P. Felt, has gone on a Mission. W. F. Gibson now has charge of that paper." And the St. George Union adds, September 25, 1897: "The Springville Independent has been enlarged and improved and our old friend, Wm. F. Gibson, has been installed as editor and manager."

The new editor was *too* good, in fact, for we have it from the Vernal Express, August 11, 1898: "W. F. Gibson, former editor of the Springville Independent, is making preparations to publish a tri-weekly Democratic paper in Provo, and expects to issue the first number about August 16th." The Democrat got going, and the Independent kept going, for the former quoted from the latter, October 22, 1898, with a credit line. Some further acrobatics are indicated in the Utah County Democrat of November 9, 1898: "The Springville Independent, with its last issue, changed its editorial management, Wm. F. Gibson succeeding Sam L. LeRoy."

The next move is prophesied in the Utah County Democrat of April 12, 1899: "Brother D. P. Felt, formerly editor of the Springville Independent, will return from his Mission in September and resume his newspaper work in Utah." Editor Felt's work, however, consisted only of disposing of his interests in the Independent to D. C. Johnson, with whom he had contracted previously to purchase. Editor Gibson continued at the helm, however, for some time, until Johnson returned from the Spanish-American War.

A 1900 Directory shows Gibson as editor and E. N. Jordan, business manager. "With the last issue of the Springville Independent, Wm. F. Gibson severed his connection with that paper," says the Spanish Fork Press, February 6, 1902. "Mr. Gibson has been with the Independent for about six years, during which time the Independent has been one of the cleanest and newsiest country papers in the State. Mr. Johnson, who succeeds Mr. Gibson, is a prominent lawyer in this county."

Mr. Felt recently recalled Mr. Gibson's coming to his shop as an itinerant with a bedroll, asking for food and lodging. Gibson was not an ordinary tramp, and proved it by making a place for himself in Mr. Felt's newspaper plant, and in the hearts of the people of Springville, taking entire charge of the paper during Mr. Felt's absence on a Mission. A 1904 Directory gives: "D. C. Johnson, editor, A. Gus Johnson, manager." In August 1922, the Johnsons sold to A. F. Gaisford and Son, who continued the Independent under the name:

The Beacon, for about a year. No copies of, or references to the Beacon were found. The Springville field was surrendered to the Provo Herald, which began, according to the 1924-25 Directories as the **Herald-Beacon,** Springville. E. C. Rodgers and Thorn C. Miner, editor, were sponsors. In 1927-28 it was the Springville Herald, N. C. Hicks, editor and manager, continuing the same to date, the ownership remaining with that of the Provo Herald, which is now a Scripps-Canfield publication. Fire destroyed the Springville Independent Publishing Company's plant in June, 1924, destroying practically all the newspaper files.

TOOELE, Tooele County

Population: 1890, 1,000; 1900, 1,200; 1910, 2,753; 1920, 3,602; 1930, 5,135.

Tooele County Times: "Established 1892, Fridays, 4-pages, 16 x 22, $2, Newman A. Mix, editor, H. D. Trenam, publisher," says the American Newspaper Directory for 1894. No files. The Spanish Fork Sun of March 11, 1893 quotes the Brigham City Report: "Newman A. Mix, formerly of the Tooele Times, has assumed charge of the Eureka Miner." The Brigham Bugler, June 10, 1893, says it "is edited by a Gentile and Liberal." The Bugler on September 16, 1893, says: "The Tooele County Times is now printed on the half sheet. It runs 4 columns of solid matter on the last page; that is mighty pleasing stuff to the proprietor, if not so interesting to the subscribers." On March 3, 1894 comes an echo of the erstwhile Tooele Times, which is grouped with the Coalville Chronicle and the Ogden Trade-Review, by the Brigham Bugler as having "lately succumbed to the terrific strokes of Hard Times."

The Tooele Transcript, Volume 1, Number 1, June 29, 1894, 6 column folio, price 10c a copy, $1.50 a year. It was printed in Salt Lake City. "One of the nicest and cleanest county newspapers published in Utah," compliments the observing Brigham Bugler, July 14, 1894, though it was mostly printed in 6 point type. No early files. A little later the Brigham Voice, after admitting the Payson Times should meet an early death, reckons "The Transcript ought to live; it has a good field and is without competition, aside from Salt Lake."

Of itself, in a sort of Salutatory, the Transcript says: "It will be breezily brilliant, winningly witty, curiously clean, satisfactorily sagacious and liberally loquacious, non-partisan in politics, independent in expression. Mining, agriculture, stock raising, fruit growing, general and local news, as well as breezy, pungent departments of absorbing interest, as well as timely editorial talks will constitute the contents of the Transcript. First class job printing; prices beyond cavil."

In volume 1, number 3, July 27, 1894, we learn some other facts (burned since we copied them!). "Owing to unlooked for difficulties in a direction totally unexpected, the Transcript has been compelled to forego the publication of two issues; but another reason, and one which will meet with the satisfaction of the people is that the plant of the Transcript has been moved from Salt Lake City to this place, and the work of publication and concomitant business will hereafter be done at home. The office has been opened in George Atkins' store, opposite the Court House . . . The latch string is outside from now on."

It was not until October 26, 1894, the sponsor's names appeared as publishers, "Beesley & Gabriel," and the note "entered as second class mail matter at the Tooele post office August 14, 1894." We consulted an excellent file of bound volumes, from volume 4, number 21, November 19, 1897 to date in the Transcript office which were since destroyed by fire. F. E. Gabriel was publisher. Six columns, 4-pages, 15 x 22. In the December 31, 1897 number, "Mrs. Margaret Gabriel, publisher" appeared on the ready print page, and on the masthead: Mrs. Maggie Gabriel, manager and publisher; James Dunn, editor. The next change was with volume 5, number 1, July 8, 1898, "James Dunn, editor and manager." Every Friday, 6-pages, 17 x 22.

"In acquiring the Transcript, the down payment was a stumbling block until Thomas Speirs, an enterprising pioneer merchant, offered the loan of the required $10 down, and more if the paper ever made any money, to start James Dunn, then 60, in this doubtful business venture," we read in a biographical sketch of Mr. Dunn. An armory press was used, the type forms being hand inked. James Dunn passed away in 1924, according to the sketch, but the Western Newspaper Union ready print account was in the name of Martha and Alex Dunn as early as July, 1921. The Transcript bought out its minor competitor and it became:

Tooele Transcript-Bulletin, With the issue of December 4, 1923, according to the Western Newspaper Union ready print account. The lamentable fire which destroyed the entire plant and the precious files, occurred Tuesday, October 18, 1932. Alex F. Dunn, son of James Dunn, who lacks a year of being as old as the Transcript, had been editor and publisher for several years; and the Transcript-Bulletin has long been one of the most enterprising and successful country papers in the State.

The Tooele Times. No files. (New series) "Established 1901, Republican, J. W. Sloane & L. E. Kramer, editors, Sloane, Kaul and Kramer, publishers," says the 1915 Directory. We were informed C. T. Stoney joined James T. Jakeman in running the Tooele Times for about one and a half years, after leaving Beaver about 1903. The first Gazetteer to mention the paper is that for 1912-13, "Tooele Times, Tooele County Publishing Company, George W. Kaul, business manager, L. E. Kramer, city editor, J. W. Sloane, managing editor, publishers of the Tooele Times and Grantsville Reflex." On the same presses in Tooele, we were informed by the paper, "We mix brains with ink." The 1914-15 Gazetteer still carried Tooele Times, Tooele County Publishing Company, and in 1916-17 added: "George W. Kaul, manager, L. E. Kramer, editor." No copies and no other facts were found of the re-incarnated Times.

The Daily Bulletin, Volume 1, Number 1, Saturday, November 7, 1914, no files preserved. Alex Dunn gathered the first 31 numbers for preservation, but these were burned in 1932, after we gleaned from them these facts. It was "published every afternoon in connection with the Johnston Theater." In the first issue was this "Announcement. The Bulletin makes it first appearance today, without any apologies to the public. Its columns are open to the public for news, lost and found articles, and especially advertising matter, which will be printed at a reasonable rate. Six hundred copies will be distributed free each day.

As fast as possible we will increase in size until we are full grown. We will enlarge Monday. Watch us grow. Watch the front page each day for matter relative to the Johnstons. The Bulletin is printed at Oquirrh Print Shop, one door east of the Oquirrh Hotel, in one half of the Bollschweiler Tailor Shop. When we are not in, ask Charlie!"

This first number consisted of one page, 7 x 11, 3 columns, two-thirds of the space devoted to advertising. It went to four pages, November 16, 1914, volume 1, number 8. The Gazetteers and Directories for 1915 did not list it, but in 1916-17 Tooele Daily Bulletin was sponsored by H. H. Johnston and W. J. Peters, and in 1918-19 Gazetteers it was simply "The Bulletin, L. E. Kramer, editor, W. J. Peters, business manager" which was the same in 1920-21. In 1922-23 Peters' name was dropped, and subsequent directories do not list it. The paper was absorbed by the Transcript December 4, 1923. (q. v.)

Tooele Daily News, Volume 1, Number 1, February 18, 1924, 3 columns, 4-pages, 8 x 11, distributed free, being supported during its life of about a month by advertising. No sponsors shown on the sheet. Alex F. Dunn had collected numbers 1 to 25 at the Transcript office, but these were burned in 1932.

TREMONTON, Box Elder County

Population: 1910, 303; 1920, 937; 1930, 1,009.

The Tremont Times, Republican, Fred Nyhart, editor, Nyhart & Eveleth, publishers. Entered as second class matter at Tremonton post office April, 1904, the approximate date of establishment of the newspaper. No files; but a few copies are preserved by Louis Brenkman. A little newspaper history is given in the special issue of the Bear River Valley Leader, December 16, 1927, which says, Fred Nihart (sic) named the town and opened a real estate office in which he prepared the copy for a newspaper which he called the Tremont Times, and which was printed in Logan.

Later, postmaster Sherman purchased the paper, and assisted by Miss Rosa Carter (now Mrs. Israel Hunsaker) ran it a year or so, the printing being done at Brigham City. The paper was purchased by W. H. Capwell about 1907, who also became postmaster. Some of these data are given by different authorities, with conflicting dates.

An official publisher's statement in the issue of May 8, 1913 gives: "The editor, managing editor, business manager and owner, Wm. H. Capwell." Capwell advertised land, magazines and subscriptions for sale. A copy of Tremont Times for June 26, 1913 shows V. S. Peet, editor and manager, though we are to learn vaguely that Mr. Peet did not really get a good start, and the town was without a newspaper through the latter part of 1913 and at the beginning of 1914.

The Tremonton Leader, Volume 1, Number 1, March 4, 1914, Alva D. McGuire, publisher. No files or references. The 1915 American Newspaper Directory shows:

Bear River Valley Leader, Thursday, Independent, established 1914, Alva D. McGuire, editor and publisher. Files 1928 to date more or less incomplete. The American Newspaper Directory for ten years later, 1925, shows: "Leader, circulation 542, Alva D. McGuire, editor, A. D. McGuire and Sons, publishers." The other data are the same as in 1915.

With the issue of September 24, 1925, W. E. Settle became editor and publisher, though through what process or transaction we did not learn. The Western Newspaper Union Ledger shows Wm. E. Settle beginning September 22, 1925. He lasted until November 1, 1928, when: "With this issue W. E. Settle, who established the Bear River Valley Leader in 1925, steps down and out and turns the reins of the Leader over to . . . James Walton (who is) new at the publishing game . . . When the Bear River Valley Leader was started, the editor had in mind certain ideas of what he believed a weekly newspaper should be. In order to carry out those ideas it was necessary to incur obligations which . . . were unwise from a financial standpoint . . . Wm. E. Settle."

We note Settle's use of the words: "started" and "established" with ungratified curiosity; they may indicate a hiatus in the newspaper run between the McGuire and the Settle regimes, which we did not determine. An invisible thread of ownership runs through these several transactions, discernible in the line: "Published by the Leader Publishing Company, Incorporated," which remained until the issue of November 14, 1929 when "James Walton, editor and publisher" was substituted, by reason of his having acquired full ownership. He has continued so to date with slight variation. A reference dated September 23, 1933 says Editor Walton had been appointed Postmaster of Tremonton, and that Mrs. Walton had become managing editor. Other current references show Walton to be Bishop of the L. D. S. Tremonton Ward, and Mayor of Tremonton City—assuring himself of plenty of news sources!

VERNAL, Uinta County

Population: 1900, 664; 1910, 836; 1920, 1,309; 1930, 1,744.

The Uintah Papoose, Volume 1, Number 1, January 2, 1891, 4-pages, 3 columns. Mrs. Kate Jean Boan, editor and publisher. Three or four copies preserved in the Vernal Express office. The paper was well received and items were often borrowed by exchanges, we noted. Mrs. Boan's Salutatory says in part: "Here I am today, The Uintah Papoose, young in years and experience, but if 'time will tell' I hope to become a 'heap big chief me'. My 'paper talk' will be limited, but I shall use my eyes and ears and let you all know what is going on from one end of the county to the other. I may wail sometimes, as any papoose will, but a good medicine will be a new subscription."

The newsy little sheet was abundantly patronized by advertisers from the start. Volume 1, number 3, January 16, 1891, confesses: "The Uintah Papoose, so it is said, is growing fast and we hope it will spread;

both far and near to the great and small, and get to be big chief after all!" The Vernal Express Forty-Years-Ago Column, May 2, 1935, quotes the Papoose editor: "La Grippe left our eyes in so bad a state that we decided to rest them by giving ourselves a vacation. The Papoose also took a rest. We felt entitled to four days. We wanted to rest as the editor, as the compositor, as the 'devil', and as the small Epluribusunum,who had the Grippe. We have been told that our action is unusual, that no-one ever heard of stopping a paper at the Editor's sweet will. We do not know of anyone doing it either, but we have established a precedent."

Volume 1, number 33, August 21, 1891 is the same size with the same masthead as at the beginning. A copy dated October 23, 1891 says: "If you want to see the Papoose become a big Brave or Squaw, bring in your ads. You can't run a country paper on wind and promises." There were plenty of advertisements, but they must have been carried gratis or too cheaply, or as Mrs. Boan hints, on promise. "The Uintah Papoose has changed hands," advises the Heber Herald of January 18, 1892. "James Barker (has) bought out Mrs. Boan. The Papoose ought to grow now into a big Injun." It did not, however, for at the end of its first year it became the:

Vernal Express, exact date of beginning not ascertained. Files, 1896 to date, (a few early issues missing, mostly unbound) in the Express office. The Wasatch Wave, February 23, 1892 tells us: "The little Uintah Papoose is no more, but in its place we have the Vernal Express, the initial number of which is on our table at the present time. It is edited by M. W. Schick . . . and is somewhat larger than its predecessor."

"Little Charlie, a Uintah Indian, called at the Vernal Express sanctum last week and informed the pencil pusher that they were going to have a Sun Dance soon. There will be about 60 Indians take part, and they will dance three days and nights without food or water," we picked up from the Park Record, July 7, 1894. ("The Vernal Express of March 17 has enlarged to 8-pages," the Heber Herald had said, March 28, 1892).

The Brigham Bugler, December 29, 1894 says: "It is almost four years ago that the Papoose began its career as a representative of Uintah County . . . Mrs. Boan sold the plant at the end of the first year to the present manager of the Express, who, being an old bachelor did not like to be 'guyed' about his Papoose by the brethren of the Press, changed its name, Vernal Express."

The 1894 Directory listers overlooked Vernal. The earliest copy preserved in the Express office is volume 4, number 44, November 27, 1895, 4-pages, 2 home print, page 1 ready print. Masthead, J. M. Barker and Dan H. Hillman, editors and publishers. "It is just one year since the Express was enlarged from a four to a six column folio," they state. "That it has kept pace with the requirements of Vernal and of Uintah County, everyone of its readers must admit. Yet a great many do not seem to think that it takes money as well as labor to do this, and

are behind with their subscriptions. We have taken and still continue
to take such produce as we can use or dispose of; and those who cannot
pay in money surely have something that will fill the bill."

An illuminating note appears in the January 9, 1896 number: "Dan
H. Hillman, assistant editor of the Express, when he was editor of a
Colorado paper, thought the Mormon editor of the Vernal Express had
queer ways of enlarging his subscription list, by taking chickens in
payment for his paper. Mr. Hillman has now come to the conclusion
that there are 'more ways than one to kill a cat to save its hide and
tallow', and he would have made a splendid picture a few days ago
for a Comic Almanac, trying to set type with a couple of roosters, with
their legs tied together and flopping around his feet, picking up the
quads he dropped on the floor."

Some early numbers in 1897 carry a wood cut of a locomotive and
smoke stream, between the words "Vernal" and "Express" in the display title—a prophesy not yet fulfilled! The issue of March 25, 1897
says: "Dan H. Hillman has severed his connection with the Express . . .
I have nursed the paper from its infancy up to the present standing.—
J. M. Barker, Editor and Proprietor." Occasionally the ready print did
not arrive, and Barker issued a 2-page, all home print paper as for
example, July 8, 1897, in which he says: "Many of the readers of the
Express will blame the editor for not getting out a full paper this
week; but it is not our fault. We get the inside pages printed in Salt
Lake City, and owing either to the carelessness of the Express Company
or the firm furnishing us the paper, it has failed to reach us on time."

This note was picked out of the Express, September 2, 1897:
"Murray Schick, formerly editor of the Craig Pantograph, Colorado,
and editor of the Victor Record, and representative of the Denver Post
. . . was chief pencil pusher for the Express the first few months of its
infancy." Also this from the September 16, 1897 issue: "J. M. Barker
is taking a much needed layoff . . . Dan H. Hillman will manipulate the
pencil for this moral and religious propounder of Truth. Our motto:
'an eye for an eye and a tooth for a tooth'; look out! Don't tread on
the tail of our coat!"

A new Salutatory was printed St. Patrick's Day, 1898, and a new
masthead was run: "J. A. Holdaway, editor and proprietor," and J. M.
Barker signs this: "My Last Howl. With this issue of the Express, J. A.
Holdaway assumes the reins and hoists his name as editor and proprietor, I having sold the entire plant, and subscription list to him . . . After
over six years toil on the Express I now step down and out." The issue
of March 31, 1898 says: "Barker's last prayer was: 'May the blessings
of the Lord, Jesus Christ, follow the delinquent subscribers all the
days of their life, and never overtake them'."

"Chipeta, the Queen of the Tribe, visited the Ouray school the
other day. She is about 40 years of age and is reported to be a very
handsome woman," the new Express man wrote June 7, 1898.

The September 29, 1898 issue gives this news item: "J. M. Barker, ex-editor of the Express, after rusticating two months in the mountains, is again in Vernal. Editor Asbury and wife left Vernal today, enroute to their home in Oregon." Holdaway remains at the masthead, but runs this significant allegory: "An editor who died of starvation, was being escorted to Heaven by an angel who had been sent for that purpose. 'May I look at the other places before I ascend to eternal happiness'? asks the editor. 'Easy'; so they went below and skirmished around, taking in the sights. The angel lost track of the editor and went around Hades to hunt him up. He found him by a big furnace, fanning himself and gazing with rapture upon a lot of people in the fire. There was a sign on the furnace which read: 'Delinquent subscribers'. 'You can go on', said the editor; 'I am not coming; this is heaven enough for me'."

Editor and proprietor Holdaway was so busy with the rest of the paper he did not get his own name on the masthead spelled correctly until it was reset in the March 2, 1899 issue. Previously it was "Hoidaway," and maybe that's what it meant! We find what becomes of ex-editors in the June 8, 1899 issue of the Express. "Wild Grass Pasture, At Old Ashley; horses one dollar and cows seventy five cents a month, strictly cash when stock is taken out," signed Dan H. Hillman.

It must have made editor Holdaway envious, for the next week he says: "The editor is expected to leave his labor among you for labor in another land;" and June 29, 1899: "For Sale!!! The Vernal Express. The proprietor has received a final letter from 'Box B' and must close out the business by the 15th of July." (Box B, be it known, is the return card on the envelopes received from the L. D. S. Church General authorities in Salt Lake City, containing a call to the Mission Field. The call is more or less inexorable and is expected and obeyed by all enterprising L. D. S. Youth). "Anyone desiring a newspaper plant with a ton of type and a good field, apply at once."

July 6, 1899, the paper announces: "J. M. Barker, ex-editor of the Express, is in town." And August 3, 1899, with no preliminary announcement, a new name flies from the masthead: "Bartlett Bros. & Merkley, Proprietors, Charles B. Bartlett, editor, Ward E. Pack, associate editor." Also an editor's perfunctory farewell, signed by Holdaway. The new Salutatory informs us Bartlett is also the business manager, and that "Dan H. Hillman will look after the typographical."

The Salt Lake Herald, August 10, 1899 says the Express "Passed into the possession of a firm of Bee-keepers. Whether they intend to make a hive of the office or to train their bees to sting delinquents is not yet known, but it does seem that bee farming and running a rural newspaper should go well together." The Bee men loaded their paper with local news items, but it was not very well patronized by advertisers. Beginning August 24, 1899 the paper was 4-pages, all home print. On December 30, 1899, in retrospect, the editor says: "Today the Express is celebrating its eighth birthday." (They all persisted in ignoring the tenure of the Papoose, which was in fact the infant from which the Express matured!) "The paper has had a very successful career, since the enterprising Mrs. Kate Jean Boan ventured into the field of journalism with the little Papoose, the first paper ever published in Vernal. Since then the paper has changed hands several times, the present management having been in charge since August 1 of the present year."

Hillman re-entrenched himself on the paper after recuperating on wild grass pasture; and a new banner is flung from the masthead December 22, 1900: "Bartlett and Hillman, Dan H. Hillman, manager," and this "Adios: The entire interest of Bartlett Brothers and Merkley has been transferred to Dan H. Hillman and Ashley Bartlett, who will guide the destiny of the paper from now on. Charles B. Bartlett." And an editorial announcement signed by Dan and Ashley: "The Associated Press dispatches and sensational war articles, you will find in the daily papers!"

Another change in the Express family was announced May 17, 1902: "Once again there is a partial change in the ownership of the Vernal Express. The patronage of the paper has grown wonderfully. Our subscription list has increased one third and is very nearly all paid up," says Dan H. Hillman. "From the above, the readers of the Express are aware that Dan H. Hillman wears both editorial slippers, and wields the ink pointed sceptre alone.—Ashley Bartlett."

And the way Hillman hung on and prospered surprised even himself and was certainly a recommendation for "wild grass pasture," not to say "wild oats" training. Hillman tried six and seven columns several times without ever concluding which was best! He often required 8-pages and went awhile in 1909-10 without the two standard ready print pages. He was beginning to need more wild grass spinach it would seem, however, for this soliloquy was printed editorially April 1, 1910: "Goodbye, Old Towel, goodbye! . . I become a tiller of the soil. A stock company of citizens of Vernal is being formed to take charge of the Vernal Express. Twenty five years in the harness is enough."

The new masthead name appeared April 8, 1910: "Published by the Vernal Express Company." A "Farewell" signed by Dan H. Hillman of the quarter century record says: "The undersigned is quitting the newspaper business for the reason that he is tired of it and wants a change. We have owned and controlled the Vernal Express for over ten years . . ." (nearly a column to make it emphatic!)

But did Hillman quit? You guessed it! An eight page, mostly ready print paper appeared until August 4, 1911, when an additional streamer flew from the masthead: "Ashley Bartlett, managing editor." The new-old masthead, November 8, 1912, is "Dan H. Hillman, manager." "Mr. Dan H. Hillman, for many years editor and proprietor of the Vernal Express, has accepted the position of editor again, and will assume the official duties next Monday. This change follows the resignation of managing editor, Ashley Bartlett, who leaves the printing field for other lines of work."

Another turn of the Express kaleidoscope to August 8, 1913 shows: "Don B. Colton, president, Dan H. Hillman, manager, C. B. Cook, editor," which couldn't last, and November 14, 1913, Dan H. Hillman becomes managing editor and C. B. Cook news editor. A. V. Watkins succeeds Cook April 3, 1914, but Cook succeeds Watkins again July 17, 1914. All names were dropped March 19, 1915, save "Dan H. Hillman, manager," who continues into 1917. May 4, 1917, "Mr. James H. Wallis of Salt Lake City . . . is to take charge of the Vernal Express, having tendered his resignation as state sanitary inspector and clean town judge to Dr. T. B. Beatty." Wallis had evidently given a high award to Vernal City! (We had noticed in the old Utah Journal, Logan, for January 16, 1883, "Mr. James H. Wallis is canvassing for the Journal!")

May 11, 1917 the new masthead name was, "James H. Wallis, manager." The title was variously editor and publisher, but mostly "editor and publisher," to January 28, 1921, probably indicating control, if not full ownership. At that time these names were added: "George H. Harrison, associate editor; Violet Harrison, business manager," the Harrisons being daughter and son-in-law to editor Wallis. June 15, 1923 Wallis' name was dropped, and the other two moved up, "George H. Harrison, editor and publisher, Violet Harrison, business manager," which continued to January 8, 1926 when, the Harrisons having gone to Roosevelt, (q. v.) the masthead became "James H. Wallis, manager and publisher, Wm. B. Wallis, city editor," Wm. B. being the son of James H. Another adjustment became desirable June 18, 1926 when George H. Harrison became editor, Violet Harrison, business manager, and Wm. B. Wallis, city editor. However, young Wm. B. had earned his spurs, and buckled them on, one at a time, November 12, 1926 as "Manager," November 19 as "Editor" and November 26, 1926 as "Editor and Manager," the senior James H. being listed as "Publisher" from November 19, 1926, remaining without significant change to date.

VIRGIN CITY, Washington County

Population: 1890, 213; 1900, 269; 1910, 136; 1920, 212; 1930, 202.

Dixie Advocate, born in St. George (q. v.). Moved to this place about the close of 1907, one copy only preserved in Professor H. L. Reid's collection at Dixie College, St. George, for Thursday, April 2, 1908, volume 7, number 31, dated Virgin City, Utah. "Dixie Advocate, vim, vigor, veracity, vitality." The masthead banner: "Robert Graham, editor and publisher. A weekly newspaper, at present issued every Thursday at Virgin City. Formerly published at St. George, Utah. Office, Main Street, Virgin City. To advertisers and patrons: The Advocate is all home print. This paper is not a member of nor represented by any advertising agency."

Sylvester Earl and James Jepson were financial sureties for the Advocate in Virgin City, where it was published something less than a year. As time went on the Sureties came to feel editor Graham was a little too radical, more especially in his attitude toward the St. George newspaper. Consequently they forced the suspension of the paper, fearing the editor might bring onto the paper a libel suit, so Mr. Earl informed us. This gave rise to

The Virgin Valley Enterprise, started toward the close of 1908, 4-pages, all home print, by a local stock company, including the sponsors of the discontinued Advocate. There are no files, and only a vague memory remains of the tenure or nature of the paper. It probably winked out within the year. The type, presses, and other equipment of the Advocate were used in producing the Enterprise. Miles Earl, son of Sylvester, was the Enterprise devil and junior printer. H. F. Sution became editor, and M. A. Hamilton, printer. It lived during the oil boom at Virgin and had a considerable patronage, yet it never paid its full way. How could it with the population figures given above!

SALT LAKE CITY, Salt Lake County

Population: 1850, about 4,000; 1860, 8,236; 1870, 12,854; 1880, 20,768; 1890, 44,843; 1900, 53,531; 1910, 92,777; 1920, 118,110; 1930, 140,367.

"Utah Christian Advocate is a new paper issued in Salt Lake by Messrs. Edward E. Carr, and Robert T. Smith," says the Provo Enquirer January 19, 1891, adding: "They will be friendly to the Mormon people, but will make war on their religious institutions!" No files; no other references found.

Enoch's Advocate. The Millennial Star November 24, 1874, copies this from the Deseret News: "Enoch's Advocate July 4, 1874. 'Poor mortals like us must throw up the sponge'. Overflowing of the gall supposed to be the primary cause of death." Another reference: "A temporary journal devoted to the interests of the United Order of Wooden Shoes. Sarcastic, ironical, bitterly opposed to the Church, and especially to the Order of Enoch." There were several wood cut illustrations in the five numbers preserved (May, 1874) in the L. D. S. Church Historian's Office Library.

The Argus, is old when it first comes to light, in the Iron County Record, April 19, 1895, which says: "It has entered upon its third year." A single copy is in the personal file of W. D. Kuhre, Sandy, Utah, dated May 16, 1896. Established April 14, 1894. Published every Saturday by James B. Bloor, 65 West Second South Street, 4 pages, 4 columns, 13 x 16.

The Wasatch Wave, September 4, 1896: "The Salt Lake Argus has changed hands, and now Almo D. Katz . . . will pull the editorial string

. . . Mr. Bloor, the past owner, will take a rest for the time being." The next notice was in The Wave of March 26, 1897. "Again a change in the Editorial Department of the Argus . . . Colonel Noble G. Warrum is in charge. The Colonel comes from Logan, where he has ably edited the Journal for years past." And then the semi-final: "The Salt Lake Argus plant was seized by the sheriff Wednesday under a chattel mortgage held by the Bank of Commerce . . ." according to the Wasatch Wave October 1, 1897.

Nevertheless, the Gazetteer for 1908-9 carries the Argus: (another Argus?) "James T. Jakeman, publisher;" while the Gazetteer for 1912-13 gives: "Argus Publishing Company, D. P. Felt, Editor and Manager," a similar reference appearing in the 1914-15 Directory without Felt's name. In 1916-17 Harry A. Wood was manager.

Beobachter (German), established August 9, 1890, 6 pages, 17 x 24, $2.50, Joseph H. Ward, editor and publisher, says Ayer's Newspaper Annual, 1892. It was a continuation of the "Intelligenz-Blatt," of which ten numbers had been issued. Beobachter became the property of the L. D. S. Church when Ward died, July 15, 1905; and Arnold H. Schulthess became editor, succeeded by Herman Grether in April, 1918, and by Willy Wehler in October, 1920. J. M. Sjodahl became editor May 14, 1923. Adam L. Peterson, Reinhold Stoof, Edward Hoffman, and John S. Hansen did editorial work on the paper, before its final suspension about October 1, 1935, along with other foreign language Church papers.

Bikuben Vol. 1, No. 1, August 1, 1876. Danish-Scandinavian language-weekly, Anders W. Winberg, publisher. "A new arrangement has been entered upon for the publication of the Scandinavian paper Bikuben. An association has been formed for the publication of that journal. It will be edited by John A. Bruun, and published by the Bikuben Publishing Company. A. Jenson will act as Business Manager, and A. W. Winberg as Treasurer . . . beginning May 2d," says the Deseret News, April 24, 1878. The Democrat of April 15, 1885 informs us: "The two Danish weekly newspapers which have been issued in this city, recently consolidated (April 1, 1885), and will hereafter be published as the Bikuben (meaning Beehive) with Jenson and Winberg as publishers . . . Mr. P. O. Thomassen, . . . who has of late been defacto editor of the Bikuben, has severed his connection with the new enterprise."

This Scandinavian organ of the L. D. S. Church, says Andrew Jenson, was launched to offset the influence of the apostate periodical "Utah Scandinav." Jenson and Johan A. Bruun were connected with Bikuben for a time. Thomassen died October 28, 1891. On November 17, 1891, Apostle Anthon H. Lund organized the Bikuben Publishing Co. It was taken over by the Deseret News in 1893. Olaf J. Anderson edited it from 1892, retiring in 1895 in favor of J. M. Sjodahl. Andrew Jenson took charge in January, 1898, for the Church. Other editors were Carl V. Anderson, C. C. A. Christensen, Hans J. Christiansen, and Morten A. C. Nicolaysen. Andrew Jenson was again in charge in 1914, and John S. Hansen in 1915. Bikuben suspended October 1, 1935.

The BroadAx, is the gruesome title of a Negro newspaper launched about 1895. No files. A country onlooker observes: "The editors of the BroadAx and the Salt Lake Herald are indulging in the pastime of calling each other such pet names as 'wild-eyed anarchists' on one side, and 'blue-green nigger' on the other." The Wasatch Wave gives us this paragraph February 19, 1897: "The capital city has two weekly papers, edited by colored gentlemen, who have been saying . . . unpleasant things of each other. Here is the last cut of the BroadAx: 'Run home and tell your dear little wife that the editor of the BroadAx has called her sweet little sugar lump an ex-crapshooter, an ex-gambler, a liar, a coward, a scoundrel and a dishonest man in every sense of the word'."

The Brigham Bugler of August 28, 1897 says: "The BroadAx, a Salt Lake paper, has hewn its way into the third year. Brother Taylor keeps his paper always sharp and bright." The Wasatch Wave closes the available history December 2, 1898: "J. F. Taylor, Editor of the BroadAx, made us a pleasant call. He is a bright, intelligent young man,—a credit to his race . . . His paper hews to the line." Sorry, someone seems to have burned all the chips, and thrown the ax in the river!

Salt Lake Evening Chronicle Vol. 1, No. 1, Thursday, November 2, 1882. Complete file bound, Utah Historical Society, 6 columns, 4 pages. Daily, except Sunday. Clearly anti-Mormon; frequent mining, political, anti-polygamy and general editorials; apparently "high-hatting" the Utah country press. Frankly outspoken, usually with dignity, against everything Mormon, including the people! The Herald strikes a spark November 4, 1882: "The sensation monger on the tripod of the Salt Lake Chronicle, starts an editorial with the old threadbare yarn of Lucretia Borgia's poisoned cups; about as true as his remarks on the Mormons."

The first name to appear on the masthead was "J. B. Wilson, Business Manager," October 22, 1883. A news item had been run on September 7, 1883: "J. B. Wilson, of the Tribune, has returned from his northern trip." On Saturday, October 13, 1883, we read in the Chronicle itself, "Withdrawn from The Chronicle.—October 1, Mr. Joseph Lippman severed his connection with the Chronicle Publishing Company, having on that date sold his interest to Messrs. Cook and Buckmaster. Mr. Lippman was one of the founders of the Salt Lake Evening Chronicle, and from its initial number to the first of the present month, acted as editor and general business manager, of the journal. He has not yet fully decided upon his future course, although it is highly probable that he will return to the East, and there pursue his journalistic career."

"Turning Over A New Leaf.—(October 15, 1883). The Chronicle proposes to turn over a new leaf, pleasurable to its new managers, and we trust it may be to its patrons. No newspaper worthy of the name, can or ought to exist in this Territory, without taking cognizance of a system whose ecclesiastical atrocities are only equaled by its political intolerance." . . . "It will be the special ambition of the Chronicle to assist in building up this city." Thus the editor re-dedicates the sheet to the business of opposing Mormon practices, and then proceeds to carry out the policy as if his predecessor had merely "tried."

There were from three to five brief well written editorials, every day, never missing a chance to strike out at the Mormons. Nevertheless, on January 5, 1884, the editor says: "The press on which the Chronicle is usually printed, recently became temporarily disabled, and the Deseret News obligingly helped us out, by printing a few editions of our paper . . . At the same time, the News appeared in a new dress, and now presents a clear and beautiful impression of typographical beauty to its readers. We shall be glad to chronicle a corresponding improvement in the principles and the policy inculcated by the News!" A specimen of crust!

"A gentleman stepped into the Chronicle Office this morning, (February 2, 1884), and asked if a humorous writer could find a place on this paper. Being informed that the humorous places were complete, he went to the News, where it is understood, an engagement will be made." On April 21, 1884, "A. F. Lazier, having severed his connection with the Editorial Department of the Chronicle, intends to go into the law business."

The Logan Journal gives the first intimation of a change: "The Salt Lake Herald printed an article presaging the early establishment of a Democratic newspaper in the capital, and intimating that the Chronicle would die with the year. This has made the Chronicle warm under the garment which it wears next to its skin, and it retaliates by charging that the Herald is $47,000 in debt, and is trying to sell itself to liquidate."

But on May 16, 1885, with 19 columns of display advertising and several reading notices, the editor quits. "Good-bye.—The fifth volume of the Salt Lake Evening Chronicle is completed. For two and a half years . . . We have been cheered by hearty words of approval . . . With very positive opinions upon the vital questions at issue in this Territory . . . We may have resorted to harsh words, weakening alike the argument we used and the cause we advocated. With no time to rewrite and prune, a newspaper writer, local or otherwise, must not be judged too hastily."

"Wherein the Chronicle has offended in respect to matter or manner, pardon may well be asked. It is needless to say to those who are at all familiar with the cost of running a daily paper, no larger even than the Chronicle, that to the half dozen practical men, but by no means plethoric purse bearers who bore the heat and burden of the day, the enterprise, in view of the prevailing depression in business, and in connection with a secret and disreputable transfer of our telegraphic report to other parties (the Associated Press), could not at present be otherwise than a losing one. Whatever losses have been incurred, will fall upon our few stockholders. Our Bills Receivable . . . are amply sufficient to pay every debt of the company, outside of the shareholders . . ." "This will be the last issue of the Chronicle for the present."

From perusing the file, everyone must agree, Mormon and Gentile alike, that it was an exceptionally good newspaper, save only its editorial policy. There were too many people hating it, for that one reason. The Salt Lake Democrat had said May 19, 1885: "The Chronicle was a journal of the present, with ideas of the past, and had it continued in existence for a thousand years, it would always have been fighting over again the issues that were settled forever twenty years ago."

The Commercial had a brief run, but we found little gossip and no files. The Deseret News of December 12, 1878 gives it a "blessing": "The Commercial should change its title. It might with greater propriety be called the O. J. H., the anti-Religionist, the Mormon Hater, the Scandal Spreader, or the State Hash! Either name would be much more appropriate, than The Commercial. Those who scatter the sheet around, should examine its slanderous and illogical contents, before they hand it to others. It is a disgrace to all who take part in its circulation." The Ogden Junction October 15, 1879 says: "The Commercial (so-called), contains a side-swipe at us!" The Junction does not say what it did by way of retaliation; nevertheless, thenceforth, the Commercial was no more!

The Contributor, Volume 1, Number 1, October, 1879, published monthly by Junius F. Wells, in the interests of the Mutual Improvement Associations of the L. D. S. Church, sponsored by the Church. It carried this "Salutation: . . . In Weber County the Officers of the Associations, appreciating the ability so manifested, were encouraged to publish a very interesting semi-monthly magazine, The Amateur (q. v.), which ran through two volumes, and was pronounced a literary success." It became a very fine and important journal, continuing so under Mr. Wells' leadership, until October, 1896, when it gave way to the Improvement Era.

Salt Lake Democrat, Vol. 1, No. 1, March 2, 1885, Salt Lake Democrat Company. Files, Salt Lake Public Library, and L. D. S. Church Library. Daily and semi-weekly, 7 columns, 4 pages, 24 x 36, circulation daily 1000, semi-weekly 500, 10 lines, 1 month, $10. Anti-Mormon. Not until July 17, 1886, do we find a name: "Major John H. Denis, Editor-in-Chief of the Salt Lake Democrat," and May 21, 1887 "John M. Young, Business Manager."

In Vol. 1, No. 1 appears: "As to this paper.—We believe that neither the dominant local Church nor other church or combination; nor the commands of the National Government, should direct the affairs of this Commonwealth; but that rather the people, combining upon the basis of Democratic principles, should bring Utah into line with the age in which we live, even though we may have to disavow associations dear to us, and give up practices we have been taught to believe were in harmony with Divine laws, still for the honor of our country, and the happiness of our children, let us become obedient to law."

"To The Patrons Of The Democrat, (March 7, 1885) The Executive Committee of this paper recognize that it has not been what its friends had a right to suppose it would be. Largely this is caused by the fact that too great a burden was laid upon Mr. Clark, as up to Thursday, he performed all the duties of Business Manager, Editorial Writer and Proof Reader . . . On Thursday, Mr. Charles A. Clark placed his resignation in the hands of this Committee . . . On Monday Mr. Alfales Young will take charge of the Editorial Department." (Signed Ben Sheeks, and Simon Bamberger, of the Committee).

Alfales Young, the new editor, was a son of Brigham Young, but was usually rated a non-Mormon. His name first appears on the masthead March 30, 1885. "The second number of the semi-weekly Democrat . . ." says the publisher March 14, 1885, "Our canvassers say it is the handsomest and most popular newspaper which has yet struck Utah." (If he does say it himself!) An editorial, run March 7, 1885 says: "The Democratic Party of this Territory is, by the Provo Church paper designated as a headless mob, and this newspaper is set down upon in unmeasured terms. Two facts account for Mr. Graham's anger: One is the presence of Deputy Marshal Gilson in Provo, and the other is the eager demand for the Democrat at that point!"

Concerning the editorial policy: These memoranda are from my own notes made when reviewing the files: "Very friendly to the Mormons." "Obviously a Mormon newspaper, determined to see the Gentile viewpoint, more especially of polygamy." Later: "It now has a Gentile viewpoint, but very kindly towards the Mormons." "This issue certainly not Mormon." "This paper is positively non-religious, not anti-Mormon, not pro-Gentile!" "Seems to become more anti-Mormon." "Every issue contains something against the other newspapers, and against the Church." "(March, 1887) Attacked the Tribune because it was Republican, and the News because it was Mormon." Some random editorial headlines: "That Mormon Disgrace," "Insulting Coolness," "Democracy And Mormonism," "The Latest Blasphemy," "The Saints' Crawfish."

Within a month after Alfales Young became editor, we find this: April 3, 1885 "The editor of this paper knows fully as well as the editor of the Tribune, the power of the Mormon Church over its members, and humbly begs to say he is as free from it, as the gentleman who edits the Tribune, and is not so apprehensive about it."

In spite of the fact that the Salt Lake public was at that time served (not to say surfeited) with five daily newspapers (News, Herald,

Tribune, Chronicle, Democrat!) the Democrat had a fine telegraphic and local news service, and an excellent advertising patronage. There was plenty of polygamy-prosecution news, and the editor couldn't refrain from writing an editorial broadside about the way polygamy was working out, with abstract comments on the Divine aspects of polygamy, such as "Enoch and Eunuch," "Polygamy Hot, Polygamy Cold."

Nationwide attention was continually oriented towards Utah, and the Democrat quotes October 3, 1885, from the Omaha Herald: "Salt Lake Journalists.—Some of the strongest editors in the West, are found in Salt Lake City. Among them are Nicholson of the News, Groo of the Herald, Goodwin of the Tribune and Alfales Young of the Democrat, who, although the last mentioned, is one of the brightest and most promising young journalists in this part of the country.

"But for the angry controversies that largely restricts debate to one subject in Utah, these men would make broader marks upon the newspaper life in the West, than was ever made before in any territory. The Democrat engages the Omaha Herald's special sympathy for both personal and political reasons. In contending against Mormon extremists on one hand, and the aggressive radicals on the other, it is difficult for it to find a footing, or secure a hearing on account of the prevailing clangor of hate and unreason."

This Publisher's Announcement was run May 5, 1886: "On and after this date, the business management of the Democrat will be assumed by Mr. John W. Pike . . . Salt Lake Democrat Company." On October 26, 1886, John H. Denis became General Manager. As to the place of its star in the firmament (December 13, 1886) "The success of the Democrat is one of the wonders of Salt Lake City," the editor admits. "Although less than two years old, it has already overhauled its antiquated competitors, and is fast outstripping them in the race for popular favor . . . Today we reach the high watermark of 2,139 copies for city circulation . . . In order to meet the demand . . . The Democrat will hereafter issue a morning edition . . . The Ogden edition, which begins today, is issued in response to the demand for a live newspaper in the Junction City."

The Democrat lifts this February 12, 1886 from the Tribune: "The Democrat thinks the Herald editor should be taken out on the desert and kicked to death by a band of wild asses. If that should be done, how would the Democrat like to be arrested, charged with being an accessory before the fact, to the fratricide?" The Democrat had the lion's share of the U. S. legal notices; and proudly fathered a brood of "four issues a day, namely, the Ogden edition; morning edition, one a. m.; first edition, 3:20 p. m.; second edition, 4:15 p. m. City circulation yesterday (January 3, 1887), 2,278." A "Notice To Patrons" June 1887, is signed "J. M. Young, Manager." It continued grossly anti-Mormon, but usually kept within the libel law. Whether it paid or not, may be judged from the editor's statement March 1, 1887: "With this issue the Democrat enters upon its 5th volume. While it isn't accumulating much wealth, it is gathering lots of honors, and having a heap of fun." The Nevada Silver State is quoted March 5, 1887: "The Salt Lake Democrat, one of the ablest and newest papers between San Francisco and Omaha . . . pours hot-shot continuously into the camp of the Utah polygamists."

The Democrat moved into "its mammoth new quarters in the Wasatch Block" March 14, 1887, and on March 29, 1887: "The publication of the semi-weekly Democrat has been discontinued, and in lieu thereof, will be issued an enlarged weekly edition. The first number of the weekly will be issued tomorrow." In the same issue the editor borrows a paragraph from the Evening Inter-Idaho, concerning the Salt Lake Democrat: "It is by far the best newspaper published in Salt Lake City. The editor, Major Denis, modestly says that his other business requires his absence from the city a considerable portion of the time, and the greatest proportion of praise is due to Mr. G. R. Caldwell, Associate Editor, and the reportorial corps for the Democrat's favorable position in the journalistic field."

Also from the Carson Appeal, reproduced May 10, 1887: "The Salt Lake Democrat, under the editorial management of John Denis, has enlarged to a 32 column paper. The Appeal sadly misses the hot-shot that Denis used to pour into it. Since he has left Nevada, nobody seems to be firing at us." The Southern Utah Times, quoted May 17, 1887: "The Salt Lake Daily Democrat, a live American journal, has distended its dignity to blanket-sheet size." Concerning the same "authority," the Democrat editor goes on: "The Apache Dude, who runs the Local on the Frisco Times says: 'The slab-sided, double-jointed, bow-legged, rattle-brained, wind-galled reporter of the Democrat, has lost something—a chestnut!' It don't matter, we never have any use for them, but if we had, we could shake a bushel or two out of the 'Frisco (Behind The) Times'!"

"The Herald this morning (July 13, 1887) has another of its inexhaustible rumors about the future of the Democrat. One day our Mormon friend has us busted, the next day sold, the next day transported, and so on, to infinity. And still the Democrat is the Democrat, and is likely to continue." That statement however, was densely veiled, and the Herald was apparently right, for that issue was the last seen of the series, and on July 19, 1887, the Provo Enquirer prints the obituary: "The Salt Lake Democrat has succumbed to the inevitable. Pat Lannan, Manager of the Tribune, is said to have purchased the remains, with the purpose of preventing the thing from being resurrected. During the checkered career, the Democrat has been the source of much expense and anxiety to its two or three wealthy backers."

Andrew Jenson's Church Chronology says: "It succumbed for the want of support, after struggling for existence a little over two years." And Orson F. Whitney, in his History of Utah says: "The Salt Lake Democrat, whose hand, if not 'against every man,' certainly dealt blows in all directions—in consequence of which, it made few friends, and many foes—followed by the inevitable collapse."

Deseret News, Volume 1, No. 1, June 15, 1850. W. Richards. G. S. L. City, Deseret. Lat. 40°, 45', 44"; Lon. 111°, 26', 34". Eight pages, three columns, 7¼ x 9¾ inches in size. Files complete in News office, L. D. S. Church Library, and Salt Lake Public Library. The Prospectus, circulated in advance and published in the first three numbers was: "Motto—'Truth and Liberty.' We propose to publish a small weekly sheet, as large as our local circumstances will permit, to be called 'Deseret News,' designed originally to record the passing events of our State, and in connexion, refer to the arts and sciences, embracing general education, medicine, law, divinity, domestic and political economy, and everything that may fall under our observation, which may tend to promote the best interest, welfare, pleasure and amusement of our fellow citizens.

"We hold ourselves responsible to the highest Court of truth for our intentions, and the highest Court of equity for our execution. When we speak, we shall speak freely, without regard to men or party, and when, like other men, we err, let him who has his eyes open, correct us in meekness, and he shall receive a disciple's reward.

"We shall ever take pleasure in communicating foreign news as we have opportunity; in receiving communications from our friends, at home and abroad; and solicit ornaments for the 'News' from our poets and poetesses. The first number may be expected as early in June as subscriptions will warrant—waiting the action of 300 subscribers.

"Terms, 6 months, $2.50, invariably in advance. Single copy, 15 cents. Advertising, $1.50 per square lines, and 50c each succeeding insertion. $1 for half square, or 8 lines. TRAVELLERS AND EMIGRANTS, 25 cents per copy, with the insertion of their names, place of residence, time of arrival and leaving. Companies of 20 and upwards, entered at once, 20 cents each.

"A paper that is worth printing is worth preserving; if worth preserving, it is worth binding; for this purpose we issue in pamphlet form; and if every subscriber shall preserve each copy of the 'News' and bind it at the close of the volume, their children's children may read the doings of their fathers, which otherwise might have been forgotten; ages to come."

At this juncture, the historical sketch entitled "Something of Ourselves" published by the News July 24, 1897, is worth repeating in part: "During the winter of 1846-47 Judge W. W. Phelps was sent from Winter Quarters to Philadelphia . . . to purchase a printing press, type, ink, etcetera . . . and brought to Winter Quarters a small printing plant . . . This printing outfit was conveyed across the plains by the Pioneer Company . . . The press was a small wrought iron affair known as a Ramage Press and the quantity of type was but small.

"In the spring of 1850 the press was set up in a small adobe building which adjoins on the east the present Deseret News buildings . . . (Eastern edge, Hotel Utah). On this press was printed . . . the first number of the Deseret News . . . Horace K. Whitney set the type and Brigham H. Young worked the press for the first issue."

(S. A. Kenner, in Utah As It Is, says the Ramage hand press was but little larger than a clothes wringer; and the first home of the Deseret News was an adobe shack that was as easy to get on top of as into!)

On the editorial page of the first number was this notice: "Deseret News, published every Saturday. Office of Delivery—The News will be delivered at the P. O. Subscribers from distant parts of the valley to order, but for their convenience, we propose to forward packages as we may have opportunity to Anson Call, North Kanyon Ward; Daniel Miller, North Cottonwood; Isaac Cark, Brownsville (Ogden); Joel Johnson, Millcreek; Wm. Crosby, Cottonwood; Isaac Higbee, Utah Valley; Phineas Richards, San Pete Valley; Ezra T. Benson, Tooele Valley; and request them to act as our agents. Subscribers will do well to inform us or the above agents where they will receive their papers.

"City subscribers can have their papers delivered for an additional 50c for the term, provided enough wish it to employ a carrier." "Wanted.—At Our Office: flour, wheat, cornmeal, butter, cheese, tallow and pork in exchange for the News."

The editorial shears were useful, when there were any papers to clip, borrowing both news and features; but correspondence of local news items were given conspicuous places along with sermons, minutes of church meetings, and general epistles of the L. D. S. Church authorities, usually reported verbatim. Advertisers were not lacking; in fact competing blacksmiths and other business men seemed from the start to know what a newspaper was for, and in two months there were two or more pages of advertisements. Unclaimed letters, and emigrant rosters occupied considerable space, and are to this day interesting reading. Beginning October 19, 1850, the News slowed up to "every other Saturday."

"Rags! Rags!! Rags!!!" the editor shouts November 30, 1850. "Save your rags. Everybody in Deseret, save your rags; old wagon covers, tents, quilts, shirts, etc., etc., are wanted for paper. The most efficient measures are in progress to put a paper mill in operation the coming season in this valley and all your rags will be wanted."

"Three numbers more will close the present subscription," the editor announces December 28, 1850. "As we anticipate time sufficient after the close of the present half year, and before the arrival of our large press to issue another quarter of the News in its present form." . . . "News, very scarce at this season of the year. All foreign news frozen. We have recently received a large bundle of scraps, scissored from old news; and if we omit credit for some items, we must be excused, 'til we learn whom to credit."

The seasonal dearth of news was due to the cessation of travel and of outdoor business and operations. It was a good time to fill up the columns on pulpit sermons, as well as the lead pencil variety; but the paper was none the less interesting and readable; because most news stories were short. The stories were unusually well edited and well phrased in correctly spelled words, handled by well educated, discerning writers.

"It has been intimated by a few that the subscription price is too high," explains the editor February 8, 1851. "For the gratification of such who are ignorant of the art of printing and of printer's rules, we would remark, that high as is the price of the Deseret News, it is several hundred percent cheaper in proportion to the actual cost to the publisher than the current news of the States, that when we issued our Prospectus we had no bills before us on which we could predicate our expenses, and that on receipt of such bills, we found that a ream of such paper worth in the States from $3 to $4, would cost our office from $18 to $20. That a pound of ink worth 25c or 30c in the market cost us from $1.25 to $1.50. That the setting of a thousand M's, current in the States generally from 25c to 31c, and in the cities where women and children are employed to a great extent, probably not more than 12½c or 15c, besides, using the same setting for daily, tri-weekly, semi-weekly, weekly and pamphlets, which would make the setting for each not more than 3c or 4c per thousand; it has cost us most of the time $1.20 per thousand . . . No-one who wishes the News need be without, as we will receive other articles where cash cannot be had. A bushel of wheat is very convenient change. We shall send the next number to all old subscribers, and any who do not wish it continued will return their papers immediately, or we shall consider their subscription renewed."

"No admittance, printed on a door, signifies literally 'no permission to enter'," the editor warns February 2, 1851; "and we understand that No Admittance, printed on our printer's door, literally signifies the same as when printed on any other door; and our friends will do themselves a great favor if they will carry out the popular definition of No Admittance in their acts, whereby our printer's files will not be disturbed, and valuable communications will not be mislaid and lost to the readers of the News."

Referring to the scarcity of paper March 22, 1851, the editor says: "Until further receipts we shall be obliged to use economy in relation to the News; and our patrons need not expect the next number until after the 6th of April."

"To Subscribers (May 3, 1851): Many have said to us, we have not the cash to pay for the News; what shall we do? Our reply has been, bring us your wheat, corn, butter, cheese, eggs, etc., or pay the cash as soon as you can; and we are compelled to repeat it. Our printers are in want of eatables; they cannot work without bread, and we wish our friends and patrons who have not done it to bring us of their substance, that we may be able to feed the laborer, and we will continue to print. There is no time to be lost in this matter, without the loss of news! This is no dun; a reciprocity of action on the principle of brotherly love is all that is solicited." After July 26, 1851, the next number was dated August 19, 1851.

In the last number of volume 1, Tuesday, August 19, 1851: "To the patrons of the News. This number closes the volume which we proposed to publish of the News in its present form. It was commenced with very few subscribers, which have since trebled; with very little facility of intelligence from abroad which has since greatly multiplied, and on large type and little matter which has been improved by smaller type and double the matter.

"Our course has been before you . . . How far we have succeeded, judge ye—this consolation we have, that what we have done, we have done gratuitously. Bills for labor, paper and other materials were so much higher than we expected at the issue of the Prospectus that the subscriptions will be exhausted in defraying the mechanical execution of the News, without administering to our necessity.

"Should the News be continued, we anticipate it will be on a a super-royal sheet or twice the size of the present, or a little more than twice the amount of present matter, and re-commence sometime in September; but this will depend on the number of subscribers. If our subscribers will each procure two new subscribers so that we can have a list of 2,000 we anticipate that there will not be any increase in price."

The new "Prospectus of Deseret News continued and enlarged. W. Richards, Ed. and Proprietor," was dated G. S. L. C., October 20, 1851. "To the friends and patrons of the Deseret News, we would say that our new office is nearly completed, our new press, type and stationery have arrived, and if our subscribers increase in proportion to the increase of the size of our paper, we propose to issue our first enlarged sheet, more than twice the size of the former, about the middle of November, and thenceforth semi-monthly on the first and fifteenth of each month at $5.00 per annum, *payable in advance,* together with arrearages . . . We cannot proceed with the News without a large increase of subscribers and *ready pay;* yet all can pay who have grain, beef, pork, cattle, horses and such other articles as may be useful to the laborer, though our friends who can procure cash will please remember we must have cash to pay for stock, and oblige us accordingly.

"Payment will be due at our office on receipt of the first number, and no-one need expect the second number until these terms are complied with, as credit will not create the paper, ink, press or hands to labor. Advertisements inserted at our usual rates and received at the P. O. where all business concerning the News will be transacted."

After three months' time the first number of volume 2 appeared Saturday, November 15, 1851, 6 columns, 4 pages, four times the size of the original pages. Church news is plentiful, including sermons and the life of Joseph Smith. It was a clumsy sheet in comparison to the first volume; though the wide columns and large type are easily read. There was an abundance of state correspondence, all very read-able and interesting. There were sermons galore, besides editorial preachments addressed "To the Saints." The paper was published bi-weekly instead of the first and fifteenth.

The editor had a unique system for delivering his papers: (December 13, 1851) "We suggest that the agents of the different wards in the city take the papers for their ward on Saturday evening and distribute them at their ward meetings on Sunday. This will save much travel and trouble to subscribers. Let the Bishops inquire of their wards if this would not please them."

The newspaper borrower was detested and told so many times, for instance: March 20, 1852 "When your neighbor asks you for your newspaper to read during the night, ask him to lend you his horse to ride through the night, and he will see at once that your request is the most reasonable, inasmuch as he is able to buy a newspaper, and you are not able to buy a horse . . . We hear several complaints of late that our patron's papers are worn out by their neighbors before they have time to read them themselves. Alright, if you are pleased to let your neighbor read your paper instead of reading it yourself, and inviting him to subscribe for himself, that is your job and a bad job too, for yourself, the neighbor and the printer."

Doctor W. Richards, editor, was also postmaster, and on April 3, 1852: "We repeat our notice to our patrons, that the News Office is at the P. O., and we do not wish the Printing Room disturbed with visitors or business." In addition to the new press and type already mentioned the historical note published July 24, 1897 says: "In the same year, 1852, Almon W. Babbitt brought to this city a printing plant which included a press and a quantity of job and body type, with the intention of establishing a publication. But immediately, upon the arrival of the plant, he abandoned his purpose and sold his printing material to the church, and it was also added to the Deseret News plant. Thus before the close of its second year, the News establishment had three presses and a good supply of job and body type."

"All saints, on arrival in the valley, can procure the News with or without the back numbers," announces the editor August 21, 1852. "If you have not the cash, you have other things which will buy the News and do yourselves and the press good. Call at the P. O." Having inside information, the mail service was always good for a paragraph, if not a column! The first Deseret News Extra was issued September 13, 1852, a 48-page pamphlet, "sufficient for a book of 200 pages in popular style, including the full minutes of the late special conference. Business, speeches, sermons and addresses on matrimony; the great 'Revelation given to Joseph Smith, Nauvoo, July 12, 1842' concerning marriage for time and eternity."

"President Young's sermons of August 8th and 15th, and other important items which will not soon be found again, embodied in one work; for sale at the News office. Price 50c cash, and those who do not apply soon will apply in vain—they are fast going."

The owner is identified October 16, 1852: "To the Saints.—The next number of the News closes the second volume; the printing office is your own, the property of the Church; and the loss or profits thereof are your own. We have devoted what time we could be allowed from other duties to give you the news, and not in dunning you. The paper and ink of the office are exhausted, and although a great portion of subscribers have paid promptly, those payments have not been in such articles as would enable us to purchase a new stock . . . We will further state that if the friends of the News wish it continued, they now have the opportunity of renewing their subscription and making payment in cash and such articles as will sustain the office; and if cash is forthcoming without delay, to purchase paper for another volume, it shall be commenced as soon as paper can be had, which will be but a short time. Otherwise 'Deseret' will remain without the 'News'. We are ever ready and willing to do all we can to comfort, bless, edify and instruct and do good to the saints; but we are not sufficiently versed in chemistry to convert *earth* into *gold*.

"We leave this subject with you. The saints can have the News again if they wish by making cash payments in advance with which to purchase paper, or they can let it pass just as they please. Two weeks will decide." Dr. Richards probably did not mean to scare them; he just talked that way; for in that issue more than six out of twenty-four columns were advertisements. Practically every one was in "body" type. Nevertheless, the next issue did not appear until Saturday, November 6, 1852 and the next, November 27th. The July 24, 1897 historical story says that "In the fall of 1852 the plant was removed to the second story of the present main building (site of Union Pacific Ticket Offices, Hotel Utah) where it remained about 18 months."

"Wanted in exchange for the News," advertises the editor December 11, 1852: "A few dozens of beaver, otter, mink, martin, wolf, fox, deer, antelope, sheep and other light skins which may be useful in manufacturing gloves, wash leather, linings, etc., or whose furs may be appropriated to clothing and various domestic purposes; also 25 calves and 50 pigs. Everybody has something with which they can pay for the News."

Mormon Bishops too busy to read, were pointed out as early as February 19, 1853: "Since the first side of this paper containing our list of agents went to press, we have discovered that some eight or ten bishops and agents for the News do not even take the paper themselves and perhaps this may account in part for there being very few papers taken in several wards in the Territory; while in several other wards, almost every family takes it. Like all other men, Bishops are made manifest by their works, and their rewards will be parallel with their works!"

Practically every issue to date contains a leading editorial "To the Saints," about wheat, baptisms, marriage, livestock, housekeeping, farming, highways, etc., but sometimes the church spokesman ran dry or nearly dry, as for instance: May 28, 1853, To the Saints, "As you are or should be always ready for a little or nothing, anything or everything, according to circumstances, we give you a dish of suckertash from the old world, as a kind of editorial, and hope you will be edified and blessed in your meal after a long fast." Then follows the local news column! Nevertheless, in that issue was big news: "The Paper Machine intended for this city is now in St. Louis with a prospect of being brought on the coming season; and the saints will therefore do well to save their rags and other materials to have them in readiness when the machine is in operation."

"The issuing of the News oftener than 3 weeks after this number until the receipt of more paper will depend on news by the mail yet to come. We design to close the volume by the close of the year; if we cannot issue as often as we would at present, we design to issue the oftener on arrival of our paper." And so for some time publication dates were three weeks apart.

Another appeal to pay up was made July 30, 1853: "More than six months have now passed since many of our friends who are indebted to the Tithing Office for the News. Harvest is now on hand; those who wish to pay in wheat, wood, butter, cheese, grain, pigs, beef, pork and white beans will please hand in at harvest . . . Brethren, now is the time, while the valleys are full of good things. The press will not drop new wine without wheat to sustain the laborers! Paper is scarce and paper makers and mills are few in Utah."

The next regular issue was dated October 1, 1853, but a Deseret News Extra, Thursday morning, August 25, 1853, 6:00 A. M., says: "We wish our friends and patrons to be patient with us, as we are with all men, and especially the paper dealers, and let all those which receive this little sheet read it quickly and give it to the next one deserving; or call your neighbors around and read it aloud, for it is an *extra express* for the good of the whole Territory."

"No foreign mails of late; no news from the other world, no spirit rappers in particular, to disturb you. Nothing in particular to prevent you serving God and working righteousness. Take care of yourselves! Read the Governor's Proclamation, Indian difficulties, etc. and follow good counsel and good example . . . Should our carriers having printing paper come in contact with the mail carriage in any safe conveyance, don't fail to send us a few bundles of paper ahead of your train!"

Beginning Saturday, Nov. 12, 1853: "Publication day of the News will hereafter be on Thursdays instead of Saturdays." The editor complains, December 8, 1853: "If the readers of the News would continue to read the News they must hand over some tallow and lard by the light of which we may write, and some wood to keep our fingers warm. *No mistake on this subject* and we wish our agents to *look* at it." And December 22, 1853: "A few gallons of Sugar House molasses wanted immediately at this office for the purpose of making rollers in order to continue printing the News. There is none in the market to be had, or else we would not trouble our patrons. We hope some friend will come forward and administer to our necessities for which we will pay a liberal price in cash."

"A few pieces of sponge wanted immediately at the News office for cleaning type, rollers, etc. There is none in the market, and we wish our friends who may have some of this article would divide and let us have a portion."

"The News has hitherto been published semi-monthly or 26 copies per volume at $5.00 per annum. This to some has appeared to be a great price . . . But is and has been a little below par . . . This number closes the third volume, and the fourth volume of the Deseret News may be expected to commence on Thursday, the 5th day of January, 1854, and issuing weekly. Close with the year at $6.00 per volume if paid within 60 days of its commencement; $8.00 if not paid until after sixty days . . ."

"Many newspapers derive their greatest profits from advertisements, by admitting them into their columns until they are nearly full, and many of them of long standing to the exclusion of almost all reading matter or general news . . . such a course we wish to avoid . . . Hitherto the News has been reasonably supplied with advertisements, but our prices have been so low, the income has been small . . . we propose not to insert in News, Volume 4, any advertisements over three weeks standing, unless it be on special contract. No-one need be without the News. The families of those elders who are abroad on foreign missions can have the News by signifying their wish, paying when they can . . ."

"The News is for all Saints and as many others as please to read it, and all those who desire to know what is going on in our city, who desire to hear the instructions and teachings which are presented in the Tabernacle from Sabbath to Sabbath; and all elders who wish to learn their duty, whether in cultivating the soil or preparing for foreign missions, will need to read it and practice its precepts . . ."

Beginning February 16, 1854: "It is thought wisdom to issue the News every other Thursday for the present, lest some accident may delay our stock of paper that we have sent for to California; which if continued weekly, would leave us without stock, . . . If anything special should transpire, extras may be expected."

The issue of March 16, 1854 had the leads turned throughout the four pages for the "Death of our Beloved Brother, Willard Richards" founder and editor of the News. . . (One and one half column editorial) —signed Orson Spencer. On March 30, 1854 Richards' name was dropped from the Masthead and none substituted. Brigham Young signed the leading editorial.

Another call came May 25, 1854 for "Rags! Rags! Rags! Bring in all your cotton and linen rags to the tithing office as fast as possible, that the paper factory and the News can go on until paper comes from the east." Consequently the June 8th number was a single sheet, 2 pages. The masthead for that number showed "Albert Carrington, Editor. In taking our seat in the chair editorial . . . Our duties having commenced with the 12th number (April 27th) our readers may like to know why our name was not sooner published. It was owing to a lot of material in type, and we did not like to set them aside nor take credit for other labor . . .

"Being very anxious and determined that the News should not stop until every possible effort was made to prevent it, we called at the embryo paper factory of Messrs. Hollis and Howard, and learned that they could furnish the requisite number of half sheets every two weeks, and as soon as they could get larger felting which Mr. Gaunt had then in the web and a few other fixtures and more paper rags, they could supply the number of whole sheets every fortnight . . .

"In advertising for paper rags in our last number, we omitted to mention that it is not necessary to wash or sort them as that will be done at the factory. We also wish the Bishops in the several wards throughout the Territory to urge the people to gather up and send on their cotton and linen rags, colored or uncolored, washed or unwashed, as this is the only chance for getting paper for the News until next fall."

On June 22, 1854 the News was printed on the first sheet of home-made paper. It was a little coarse, a little heavy and a little gray, but nevertheless it was a fine strong sheet, the paper consisting of 2 pages only.

"Take Notice: (June 22, 1854) The Post Office, Editors and Printing Office are moved into the north rooms of the Tithing office in Great Salt Lake City!"

July 6, 1854, only two pages. "To Our Readers: We are compelled to come out again in a half sheet . . . In the first place, notwithstanding two published notices, and all we have said, paper rags come in very slow. (they may have been wearing some of them, if we read the News clearly! J.C.A.) Again our paper makers cannot use the colored rags at present through lack of material for bleaching, and lack of skill to make that material. And still further, Bro. Gaunt does not yet furnish the new felting that was ordered long ago . . ."

August 10, 1854: "Doubtless, the readers of the News perceive that the paper has at last got a rather dark shade and we do not fancy its color any better than you do. This arises from the fact that the rags come in at a slow rate and in small quantities, hence as the makers have as yet no means of bleaching, all colors have to be used except black, thus necessarily causing a very dark gray, but the dark gray is better than no paper, which will soon be the case unless all . . . gather up and bring or send immediately all their paper rags, clean or dirty, white or colored. This request is expected to apply to every person who has either many or few rags throughout all our settlements in Utah, a compliance with which will enable us to furnish you with a whole sheet weekly, until the arrival of the paper ordered from the States, when we will cease to tease you on the subject." The October 25, 1854 number was the last paper with homemade paper.

The editor rejoices October 12, 1854: "White paper. We are happy in being enabled by the arrival of our year's supply in the Church train to again issue the News on white paper, for we think our industrious subscribers will now be able to read their paper by candle light. At the same time we tender our thanks to Messrs. Hollis and Howard for helping us to the best paper their facilities would permit. Until further notice, we are obliged to stop paying *cash* for rags, but they will be taken on subscriptions to the News and on tithing."

The paper beginning March 14, 1855 was reduced to four columns, 8 pages, 10½ x 15 inches. Half size page, but same amount of paper. "Inasmuch as the history of Joseph Smith and the sermons delivered in the Tabernacle first appear in print in the News it has been deemed advisable to alter the form into a better shape for binding . . . For the encouragement of subscribers it may not be amiss to state that all the profits arising from the paper, and from all the work done at the printing office flow in the same channel with the tithing as all the material is owned by and the whole affair is managed for the Church, and is designed to be a benefit for the Saints, and to all who prefer truth to error."

At the bottom of a correspondent's letter the editor says: "We shall be obliged to our correspondents if they will quit writing their communications upon *tissue* paper, for it compels us either to impose upon the compositors, to reject the article, or re-copy it."

Beginning March 14, 1855 the paper is dated Wednesday.

Here is how those old editors recuperated! June 20, 1855: "Hon. Albert Carrington, editor of the News, is absent enjoying a treat at his old profession of civil engineering, in company with Gov. Young; and while determining the heights of mountains, the latitude and longitude of valleys, he cannot be personally responsible for the conduct of the News."

In 1855 we noted the paper was made up mostly of sermons, conference reports, discourses, correspondence, a little local news, still less United States and foreign, and plenty of good reading matter clipped from exchanges including instructive material for farming, livestock raising and housekeeping.

Remy and Brenchley in September, 1855 said of the columns of the Deseret News: "They contain sermons, editorial articles, facts and events occurring throughout the world, historical fragments, biography, poetry, fables, allegories, curious anecdotes, narratives of travelers and missionaries, political and religious correspondence, descriptions of machines and objects, scientific discoveries, sketches of manners, accounts of battles, culinary and other receipts, hints to farmers and gardeners, perplexing enigmas, ambitious anagrams turning most frequently on the names of their leaders, finally advertisements, notices, marriages, as so many savory morsels."

Editor Carrington was a member of the Legislative Assembly which met in Fillmore the winter of 1855-56, and he departed November 28th with Governor Brigham Young and other members leaving Judge Elias Smith in the editorial chair. Smith modestly acknowledged his own material with his initials and seemed to enjoy his duties greately, though admitting he was not posing as a proficient editor. It was a cold winter, and on January 2d there was "Wanted at this office immediately 10 or 15 cords of wood . . ."

Carrington resumed charge of the paper on January 23, 1856. He very shortly—March 5, 1856—told his readers again he was only working for the paper and for the Church.

Looking ahead, the editor makes his plans. March 5, 1856: "It must always be borne in mind that the News is emphatically a church paper, and that its reading matter should be in keeping with its known character and design, and this must continue to be the case until the reading portion of Utah's population are ready and willing to properly sustain the publication of two or more papers. When that time arrives the church paper can be thrown into a still more convenient form for binding, be confined more exclusively to doctrine, history and Elder's correspondence, and the world and its affairs find more ample space in a paper devoted to that kind of matter. As it is now, it must all be mixed up, history, sermons, correspondence, news, biographical, geographical, scientific and other articles etc. etc. . .

"When more than one paper will be published in Utah depends entirely upon the patronage of the reading portion of the community. Should subscriptions much increase and payments be promptly made, another good paper could be sustained, but profit or no profit, a church paper will continue to be printed. It may not be amiss here to remark that all the profits arising from the publication of the News go directly to swell the funds at the control of President Brigham Young . . ."

That must have been a cold, late spring season, for on March 26, 1856: "A few loads of wood are wanted as News subscriptions," and April 30, 1856—the editor's needs were varied: "Wanted forthwith.— about 6 loads of poles, not less than 17½ feet long, also a few loads of wood, for which a good price will be allowed on the News."

The editor became a bit "high hatty" at times, and June 25, 1856: "Pencil Marks.—Two or three advertisements and other writing in lead pencil now in this office can be inserted in the News when rewritten with ink." At the same time he confessed he was in need of "Pigs.—Six or eight small pigs wanted on subscription for the News."

Autumn was a reminder of winter, and on October 6, 1856: "Those who have promised or may wish to pay their dues to this office in wood will do well to bring it in while the weather is good, as some is wanted immediately . . . A few loads of hay are also wanted before Conference." And, November 12, 1856: "Hay and fodder wanted immediately in payment of subscriptions to the News. Who will do as they would be done by?"

In retrospect again, March 4, 1857: "Deseret News closed its 6th volume with a steadily increasing number of subscribers . . . An effort will be made to make the News . . . still more worthy of a list of subscribers that will embrace at least every head of a family in our Territory . . . Our paper is one in which all who love truth and the prosperity of Zion are, or should be, deeply interested for the history of Joseph Smith, and the public counsels, teachings and exhortation of the First Presidency, the Twelve, and others at headquarters first appear therein. In addition to the important facts pertaining to the general welfare and progress of the church, Elders' correspondence, etc. . .

"As you are aware, all profits arising from the economical conduct of the business of the News office are controlled by President Brigham Young for the salvation of Israel and the redemption of Zion, so that each paying subscriber is accomplishing a twofold good by providing himself with the best of reading matter and aiding in the spread of righteousness. It may be queried by some why we do not print two papers, one still more exclusively restricted to Church affairs, and the other devoted to miscellaneous articles, advertisements and the current news of the world. Such a course has for sometime been under advisement and the opportunity waited for, but the time and circumstances have not yet transpired to warrant the undertaking . . .

"The number of subscribers to Volume 7 of the News, together with the time and kinds of payments of subscriptions will tend materially to indicate the progression of our community in favor of right education and to determine the time when a sound policy will dictate the publication of two papers in Utah."

Each volume had a complete index at the end. May 27, 1857: "Explanation. Prof. Carrington has been absent with the Governor during the last five weeks, and the 'News' has been managed by the hands in and about the office who were left in charge, consequently they are responsible and not the editor for what has been done, right or wrong. Next week the editor will be at his post again, and our readers may expect . . . after the arrival of the mails, shortly due, that they will be better supplied than of late."

The News had high ideals and often referred to them. For example on March 3, 1858 the editor refers to "Complaints outside.—There seems to be an impression with many abroad that they cannot, from our paper, learn the real state of affairs and the tone of public feeling in Utah. The impression is the more singular when we take into account that the public teachings by the First Presidency, Twelve, and others are printed in full and embrace the whole range of matters of general interest and importance and actually show forth the aims, feelings and views, political, social and religious of the Latter Day Saints . . .

"The world newspapers are so freely sprinkled with details of crime, aside from the vast amount not made public, that it is not much to be wondered at that they feel a little skeptical when reading so candid and clear a sheet as is published in Utah, but how can we gratify readers by printing the commission of crimes when there are few or no crimes committed. Again, how can we print lengthy columns of heavy commercial operations when we are almost entirely un-influenced both through circumstances and feelings by that mad fury of gain which so unwisely absorbs the majority of mankind, or how can we home-chronicle the corrupt, conflicting and destructive moves and designs of caucuses, conventions and cliques controlled by supremely selfish and rotten professed politicians, when Utah has no such disorganizing classes of far worse than useless population. Our politics are one, and for many years have been widely proclaimed identical with sustaining and extending all the rights wrested from British tyranny by our forefathers.

"Aside from the above facts, we are so busily occupied in fencing, plowing, building and other labors connected with redeeming deserts and mountains, and are so earnestly engaged in teaching and in striving to practice truth in all its ramifications that we really have not the leisure, even if we had the disposition, to study, practice and print the political and social deviltry that is blinding the world and daily undermining their power and robbing them of every really valuable Governmental institution with which they have been blessed."

A lot of history was transpiring in the year 1858 in Utah, but little of it got in the News. The historical article in the News, July 24, 1897, goes on to say why: "On account of the approach of Johnston's army in the spring of 1858 the plant was divided, and one part was conveyed to Fillmore and another part to Parowan, and the paper was printed first by one part in one town, then by the other part in the other town. This was done in part for strategic reasons as it was desired to conceal from the approaching army the exact location of the Church Printing Plant."

The News for April 28, 1858 was the last with the Salt Lake City date line. The issue of May 5, 1858 was dated in Fillmore. It is probable that only two small job presses were taken to Fillmore and Parowan. The paper dated at Fillmore was made up of new or different type faces and a slightly different kind of paper was used. But there was never a word printed other than the date line to indicate that the News had become a "Press on Wheels" nor was there any more local news from Fillmore than usual. The paper still had the statewide horizon—the same solicitude for the L. D. S. people. However, out of those trying times came such editorials as "Truth Will Prevail"—May 12th; "Unfair Treatment of Utah"—June 2d; "What of Utah"—June 9th and "Utah Peace Commissioners"—June 23rd, all printed at Fillmore. The writer of the news items wrote as if he was phrasing them in Salt Lake City and the plans for peace were all inclined toward Salt Lake City. July 14, 1858, Fillmore City: "Returning to their homes.— The First Presidency and a few others left Provo at 6:00 P. M. of June 30, and arrived at their homes in Great Salt Lake City at 3:00 A. M. of July 1. All who wish to return are at liberty to do so."

The News remained at Fillmore, however, until after September 1, 1858. When this number was run off it returned to Salt Lake City in time to publish September 8, 1858, without a word of the trip south. With some feeling, however, on September 15, 1858 the editor raised a crushed head and uttered a strong editorial against the mistreatment of the Mormons. And the next spring on March 2, 1859 he says: "The history of volume 8 of the News, owing to certain events which transpired during its period, is characterized by one rather peculiar feature, the reduction of two thirds of its circulation when subscribers were urging for an increase much above even the highest figure. Our readers are well aware that the force of circumstances beyond our control alone compelled such a reduction, and also the change from a whole to a half sheet, alterations probably much more disagreeable to us than to them. But certain hindrances have, to all appearance, now vanished and volume 9 will commence with a full sheet and a number that will go far towards accomodating all who may wish to peruse its columns . . ."

The editor seemed frequently to have other irons in the fire—other business to attend to—and finally March 9, 1859 we read of a masthead change occurring: "March 9, 1859, Volume 9, No. 1, Elias Smith, Editor & Publisher. To Our Readers: . . . This morning without reflecting much on what we were doing, we took a seat in the Deseret News office . . . A short investigation convinced us that we were in the 'editorial chair'. . . In making this announcement to our readers, we expect they will . . . be taken by surprise as no change in the editorial department has hitherto been communicated to them . . . The late editor, Prof. Carrington . . . now retires from the station . . . to perform other duties . . ."

March 16, 1859: "Circumstances have compelled the adoption of the rule that on an average, at least one third the amount of the yearly subscription must be paid in cash to enable us to pay for the stock . . . (2 columns!). When we commenced penning this article we had no intention of making it so lengthy, but seeing no place to stop we kept writing, and if it does not suit your ideas and taste you need not read it."

September 14, 1859 "Our New Dress" is mentioned. "By the Church train which arrived on the 1st inst., we received from Messrs. LaDeu, Peers and Co. of St. Louis a new and handsome font of Brevier type on which this number is printed . . . The old type heretofore used, some of which has been used for years, will now be laid aside for purposes other than printing the News."

An advertisement was run May 30, 1860: "Save your paper rags. The inhabitants of Utah are requested to gather up and save their worn out wagon covers and every description of cotton and linen rags for paper making and deliver them from time to time to the Bishops of the several wards for the News and Mountaineer offices, or their agents for which when clean they will be allowed five cents a pound. The rags can be sufficiently cleansed in pure water without soap. It is expected that in a few months all who wish can receive paper in exchange for rags." Edward Hunter, Presiding Bishop.

In 1860 the news items and advertising matter were given a more orderly arrangement. The type seemed newer, the paper whiter and the editor was acquiring experience.

February 13, 1861 we read: "The paper mill imported last season by President Young is to be put into operation at the earliest possible date in the Sugar House building . . . The manufacture of paper in these valleys will be another step toward that social independence so much desired. As the paper mill will soon be in operation there will be needed immediately thereafter some ten or fifteen thousand pounds of rags and other material suitable for paper making."

April 17, 1861: "Much has been said from time to time about saving rags and other materials suitable for the manufacture of printing and other kinds of paper, but it seems as a general thing very little attention has been paid to the subject, most of those concerned evidently considering it a small matter and unworthy of their notice . . . The paper mill will soon be completed but there is not much material on hand and unless it can be attained, the amount of paper that can be made will be limited and insufficient to supply the demand for printing purposes that now exist . . . However small this matter may appear to some, it is one of much importance now, as without material the paper which will be shortly needed, cannot be made." The people were confronted with this dilemma: whether to give their shirts to the paper mill or to continue to wear them!

At the beginning of the Civil War the editor rose to the emergency and announced: "Wednesday, May 8, 1861. To Our Patrons: . . . We have now to watch a nation on tiptoe for war. To discharge our present duty . . . we shall have much pleasure in continuing the publication of . . . extras as early as possible after the receipt of dispatches provided our patrons (subscribe for the extras) ; but those who prefer can have them at the office. So soon as enough subscriptions justify it, we shall make a uniform and reduced charge for those delivered."

In the issue of July 3, 1861, "The paper mill imported last season by the Trustee in Trust . . . is nearly or quite in readiness for successful operation. The principal thing now wanted to make the success of the enterprise complete is a sufficiency of material of which to manufacture paper . . . The agents of the News and Mountaineer and every Bishop in the Territory should make it their special business to see that all the linen and cotton rags, old tents, wagon covers, refuse, flax and hemp (etc.) are brought forward . . . for that purpose immediately."

September 11, 1861: "To Our Patrons: The stock of paper on hand at the commencement of the current volume of the Deseret News which was thought sufficient to last until the paper mill, imported by President Young last season, could be put in operation and furnish a supply without further importation from the states, having been used up some two months since and before the mill and all its machinery was fully completed, we were compelled to suspend publishing without being able to inform our subscribers when we should probably resume again . . . There cannot in justice be any fault found . . . All concerned and especially Mr. Howard, the chief manufacturer, have moved as fast as circumstances would permit . . . and the mill is now in working order, and will convert into paper all the material in the country as fast as it can be obtained." "The first paper made after the bleaching material was obtained—that on which this issue is printed—. . . is not as white as will be made . . . On resuming the publication of the News, we have no promises to make other than those heretofore made."

(The Pony Dispatch). The first daily newspaper in Utah, issued by The Deseret News from its own plant. With the advent of the Pony Express in 1860, eastern dispatches increased greatly; and by the early summer of 1861, so great was the volume of dispatches, and the reader interest in Civil War news, a new arrangement had to be made by the Deseret News, for true to its principles, nothing should ever crowd out religious discourses, sermons or remarks by the Church general authorities. Moreover the publication interval of the News, was entirely too long for flash news publication.

As a consequence, early in 1861, The Pony Dispatch, a single sheet newspaper size, was begun, later printed on both sides and carrying a few advertisements. At first it was distributed as a gratuity to News subscribers and friends, but later a subscription fee was charged, largely to cover delivery service. Then the following notice appeared in the News, September 25, 1861:

"A Word About The Extras: The telegraphic dispatches which have been received by pony and published in the form of Extras for some months past, have been attended with considerable expense, which has to be paid in cash; and inasmuch as some of those favored by the operation have not contributed very liberally towards paying the expense thus incurred, the publication in manner and form aforesaid has been suspended, and will not be resumed until there are enough cash subscribers obtained to warrant resumption. If there shall be a sufficient interest manifested by handing over that ready to justify us in obtaining and publishing the Dispatches as heretofore, they will be printed and delivered or sent to those thus subscribing, in the form of Extras only, as soon as practicable after their reception, at the rate of one dime for each Dispatch. Those favoring the plan can manifest it by sending us their names and addresses, accompanied by the cash."

The reverse side of the Pony Dispatch illustrated elsewhere, carries a column of display advertisements, by Livingston, Bell & Co., Staines, Needham & Co., Hooper, Eldredge & Co., Walker Brothers, and "Deseret News: Office in Council House, Corner of South and East Temple Streets," soliciting job printing and subscriptions. The news columns on both sides, were exclusively made up of Civil War dispatches. The Deseret News itself suspended for the want of print paper from October 23, 1861 to December 25, 1861, and it is presumed The Pony Dispatch went out by the same route, its service being incorporated in the Deseret News pages when the paper was resumed. (See July 6, 1864.)

October 23, 1861 the News editor again axplains: "To Our Subscribers: It is not pleasing to be compelled to make as many explanations and excuses for not publishing the News regularly each week. The signs are decidedly more favorable for obtaining the necessary material for the manufacture of paper than they were six weeks ago; but there is still much to be done before a supply for the winter can be produced. That large amount of rags, expected from Ogden, has not been received at the mill, and other promises have not been fulfilled . . . From present appearances, we may not be able to publish another number 'till the first week in November."

The next issue was dated December 18, 1861: "After another delay of some two months the publication of the News is again resumed . . . During the time we have been unable to publish the News our patrons are assured that they have not been forgotten . . . It is believed, however, that it has been generally understood that the suspension was from no other cause than the want of paper, which could not be made without material, the opinion of some to the contrary, notwithstanding . . ."

The issue of March 12, 1862 contained 5 columns of advertisements out of 32. The quality of paper was not uniform from issue to issue in either color or weight, but most of it was fairly good. After the telegraph wires came, the breaks in the line figured conspicuously in the news. April 30, 1862. "Explanatory. Some of our subscribers did not receive their papers last week . . . The same may be said this week. We have very nearly learned how to make something out of nothing, but not quite . . ."

On May 14, 1862, we hear "Paper rags once more.—Notwithstanding all that has been said in relation to gathering rags and other material for the manufacture of paper there has been so little attention given to the matter and so few rags collected that it was with the greatest difficulty that the mill was started and the manufacture of paper commenced . . . With all the exertions that have been made, it has been impossible to do more than just to keep the concern in motion and make a sufficiency of paper to keep the News establishment from closing up . . ."

"As soon as it became apparent . . . there would not be material enough obtained to keep the mill at work more than one day in a month, Mr. George Goddard . . . was employed to visit every town and settlement in this and adjoining counties for the purpose of gathering up whatever might be obtained convertible into printing paper . . . The people generally, deemed the matter of trivial importance, and looked upon rag gathering as the lowest vocation that could be followed . . . Some may think it beneath their dignity to do an act of that kind . . . The machinery was imported and the mill put in operation at a great expense and it should now be kept in motion; otherwise it will be a ruinous concern . . ."

The Church authorities could not forever continue to be responsible for all that was printed in the News, and on January 28, 1863, we find this notice: "To the Public: I hereby inform the public that the Deseret News is not and has not been an organ of mine for, except matter accompanied with my name, I have only occasionally, and that too, sometime ago, known any more of the contents of the News until after it is published than I have of the copy furnished to compositors of the N. Y. Ledger. Brigham Young. Great Salt Lake City, January 28, 1863." (This notice was run each issue until June 17, inclusive.)

More paper trouble came August 5, 1863: "What may be expected. —The creek on which the paper ·mill is located . . . is now but a very small stream . . . consequently the mill has stopped. If . . . the mill can be put in motion again in a few days, we can issue a paper next week; otherwise none may be expected."

The next issue did not appear for three weeks—August 26, 1863, is when we find: "To our Readers.—The excessive drought which has prevailed . . . has so lessened the streams that all the water flowing from the mountains has been needed for irrigating purposes, and particularly the waters of Big Kanyon Creek on which the paper mill is situated. Consequently the mill has been idle most of the time since the middle of July, and only about a dozen reams of paper have been made during the last month. Not having enough on hand for a full issue, after a delay of three weeks, we came to the conclusion reluctantly that half a loaf was better than no bread . . . and so this week issue a half sheet. The watering season is nearly over, and the prospects are that the mill will be moving again in a few days . . ."

A change in the masthead appeared September 23, 1863: "Albert Carrington, Editor. Although my connection with the News has been of long continuance, as it commenced soon after my arrival in the Territory in 1851, it is well known that I had no proprietary interest therein . . . When I was unexpectedly promoted to the Editorial Chair, the finances of the establishment in consequence of the 'crusade' which had paralyzed all business operations throughout Deseret . . . the times were troublous and stormy."

"There is one thing to which duty compels a reference, and that is the editorial columns of the News from the 9th day of March, 1859, to the 16th day of September, 1863 were entirely under my control and for their tone no other person is or has been responsible . . ." E. Smith.

"I am again undertaking the editorial responsibility of the News with the added responsibility of the conduct of its business affairs . . ." Albert Carrington.

"Our Assistant.—It affords us pleasure to announce to our patrons that T. B. H. Stenhouse, Esq., is to assist us in our editorial labors . . ." "Judge Elias Smith succeeded Carrington," says E. W. Tullidge in his History of Northern Utah. "His later retirement was caused by the publication of an editorial in 1863 which seemed to breathe the tone of the Southern cause, and though the article was written by a subordinate, Judge Elias Smith was too much like Joseph the Prophet to shift the responsibility from his own shoulders."

December 16, 1863: "Mill wheel gone again. While locking up this issue we have no hope of being able to issue a paper next week, for we are told that a portion of the valve wheel of the paper mill has gone downstream and left us without paper . . ."

March 2, 1864, No. 23. "To Our Readers.—It would be rank Hibernianism to inform our friends that we have again been furnished with paper to resume the publication of the News. They have that information before them. We have no apology to make for ourselves . . . At all events it is proper to say that as we have had some experience in the silence line we shall try to keep out of that in the future. Our readers will be furnished the full amount of papers for their subscriptions."

The editor brings up a financial problem, March 23, 1864: . . . "We are hampered by the multitude of trifling accounts on our books which, in the aggregate reach the useful sum of $41,000, and an addition of $10,000 against our agents. Readers, do you wonder that at times we feel sore?"

Extras between publication dates were being frequently circulated in the summer of 1864, which led T. B. H. Stenhouse to announce his forthcoming Daily Telegraph in June, 1864, and on June 29th we read in the News: "With the commencement of the Daily Telegraph, Dispatches will be discontinued. The first number of the Daily Telegraph will be issued on Monday morning the 4th of July, 1864, from the temporary office of that paper opposite the Theatre. The Telegraph . . . is altogether a personal enterprise of Mr. Stenhouse and has nothing whatever to do with the News. A power press, engine, large fonts of type, a goodly supply of binding material, etc., have been purchased for the News and are on the way. Upon their arrival the News Office business will be extended . . . provided the paper mill does not disappoint us."

Then, in the first number of the Daily Telegraph, July 6, 1864, we learn that the News issued Utah's first "Daily." "Dispatches.—The few known as the 'Dispatch Club,' wearying of sustaining the monthly payments for Dispatches, and the News Office, as the News is published but once a week, suffering quite a loss through issuing the daily telegraphic slips, the Club and News Office gladly resign the daily printing of telegraphic news to the first number of the Daily Telegraph. At the same time arrangements were made to print in the News each week those portions that may be deemed of general interest to our readers as heretofore."

September 21, 1864: "Captain W. B. Preston's church train which arrived on the 15th inst. brought us large fonts of newspaper, book and job type . . . an abundant supply of the best quality of printers ink . . . As the chief design in publishing the News is to benefit the people, we had thought of delivering their papers to all city subscribers without extra charge. But our city occupies so much ground and the dwellings are so scattered and remote from the sidewalks that this plan would at present prove too burdensome . . . We have concluded to try a plan between that and the old practice of everyone's calling or sending for his paper . . . It is this: To deliver at an early hour all the papers to the stores, offices, officials and other places and persons within a handy distance from the office. It is customary at the close of a volume to stop all papers until further advised by agents and subscribers . . . Any person residing within a News Agency can, if he wishes, subscribe at this office and have his paper sent separately . . ."

The editor tells us October 5, 1864, that "This number of the News is printed throughout upon new type . . . "—mostly eight and ten point instead of the old six and seven point. Incidentally, with new type there was less reading matter than formerly, but it was easily read, and there was plenty of money in the advertising columns—very little local and foreign news.

As a consequence, on November 23, 1864, a News Supplement was issued: "The reading matter and advertising each calling for more room, it has been deemed best to issue a supplement with this paper, free of extra charge . . ." says the editor, "whenever circumstances may require and the paper mill permit." The News' Supplement for November 30th was all advertising, while the News' Supplement for December 7, 1864 consisted of 4 pages, 3 of which were advertisements. "To accommodate advertisers in so large and general a circulation as has the News, advertisements were admitted until they encroached too much upon the reading matter. To obviate this . . . an 8 column supplement was issued . . . Readers will now have 32 columns of reading matter in each number, consisting of sermons by the First Presidency and Twelve, editorials upon a variety of subjects, both local and general. Full minutes of Conferences, mass meetings, etc., . . . the gist of the news by telegraph, original and selected poetry, correspondence from elders . . . useful and amusing selections . . . and news in detail of the important doings of all the world . . . and some 15 columns each week for advertisers."

The reading matter in the supplements was often a continued story, set up and run separately from the regular paper. The supplements were run about every other week in 1865 but the News was then more a magazine than a newspaper. The Semi-Weekly was started on October 8, 1865, coming out on Tuesday and Saturday — while the weekly edition appeared on Wednesday.

September 6, 1866: "Change.—To better meet the schedule times of the marts, the Deseret News will be published Saturday, Tuesday and Wednesday, beginning on Saturday, September 8."

January 2, 1867. "Volume XVI of the Weekly and II of the Semi-Weekly, after suspending publication a short time (since Nov. 28, 1866) to accomplish the object, begins its new volumes as near the 1st of January as its three difficult days of issue each week permit . . . As heretofore the News will contain sermons, telegraphic dispatches, correspondence (which is solicited from all parts of our Territory and from abroad). Details and items of latest news from exchanges, current local items deemed worthy of note, and in short, everything interesting, useful, amusing, instructive and promotive of the great cause of human progress . . . Five dollars for the weekly and eight dollars for the Semi-Weekly. Two dollars a bushel will be allowed for wheat delivered."

"The Paper Mill. (June 12, 1867.) From a report by Bro. George Goddard, courteously furnished to us by the Historian's Office, we learn that the Paper Mill, during the first fifteen months after it was put in operation, consumed 35,021 pounds of rags and produced 28,997 pounds of boards and paper of various quality, the largest portion being printing paper." Also October 9, 1867, "Explanatory. —The News, through the want of paper, was compelled to suspend the regular issue of its 'Semis' (Semi-Weeklys) of September 28 and October 1, and its Weekly of October 2. The arrival of General H. B. Clawson yesterday . . . enables us to give the following information: All the paper, instead of two-thirds, as first reported that he had purchased for the News, was burned by Indians in the forepart of August at the time they ran a freight train off from the track and destroyed its contents in the neighborhood of Plum Creek (Nebraska), Clawson informs us."

A masthead change occurred November 20, 1867, "George Q. Cannon, editor." "Other duties caused my labors to cease," signs off Albert Carrington. The Daily News was started November 21, 1867; and on Wednesday, November 27, 1867 is this "Salutatory.—In entering upon the publication of a daily paper we do so with a consciousness of the responsibility of the position." In this issue were carry-overs from Thursday's Daily, from Friday's Daily, from Saturday's Daily and from Monday's Daily; thus it is evident the Daily began on Thursday, November 21, 1867.

After starting the Daily the News had a good local and telegraphic news service, apparently unwilling to keep strictly to the Church field and to let the Telegraph print all the news. The name of the paper was changed from The Deseret News to Deseret Evening News, November 29, 1867. The size of the page was increased April 6, 1868, and the editor says: "We hope yet to see the various editions of the Deseret News—the Evening, Semi-Weekly and Weekly at least equal in every respect to every paper of their class in the entire country." He may have been intimating a plan in the back of his head to make it more strictly a *news* paper. Incidentally that made the third Daily in the city, the Telegraph and the Vedette being the other two.

By June, 1868, the wire dispatches were coming at such great length as to exclude much editorial and other local matter; and for the first time the Monday Evening paper (June 1, 1868) carried no sermons; that therefore might be considered the beginning of the *news*paper succeeding the church paper. As a result, the editor says on February 8, 1869: "Its circulation has increased of late beyond our most sanguine expectations."

George Q. Cannon carried on with great success until August 20, 1873, when his valedictory appears: "Our position as editor and publisher of the Deseret News has not been so agreeable to us of late . . . The business connected with the Deseret News office has grown to proportions which require the undivided attention of the responsible head. Besides the Daily, Semi-Weekly and Weekly editions of the paper, there are a Book and Job Office, a Book Bindery, a Type Foundry and a Paper Mill connected with the establishment . . . Other duties have claimed our time and engrossed a considerable portion of our thoughts . . . Today the entire business of the Deseret News Office, its editorial, publishing and business management have been transferred to Elder David O. Calder" . . . George Q. Cannon.

Mr. Cannon may have been intimating the duties were too heavy for him, but the fact is he had been elected and went to Washington as a member of Congress. On August 21, 1873, accordingly, David O. Calder became editor and publisher. He first speaks of his paper, November 10, 1874: "Our weekly edition of the News, published every Wednesday, is the largest weekly paper published between the Missouri and the Sacramento. It contains 16 pages or 80 columns, and is filled with the current news of the week, local and distant, editorial articles on interesting topics, sermons by the First Presidency, and the Twelve Apostles, and a variety of other matter interesting and instructive." With all that, in addition to his other duties, Mr. Calder sometimes put the paper to bed without an editorial, which is not surprising.

In due time George Q. Cannon returns, and this masthead change occurs August 1, 1877: "George Q. Cannon, Brigham Young, Jr., Editors and Publishers." It was a two-man job for sure! "All communications, business and otherwise, for the Deseret News will hereafter be addressed to Cannon and Young." It was on August 2, 1879 the names, Cannon and Young, were dropped from the masthead and none substituted. The paper carried this: "Resignation.—Salt Lake City, July 19, 1879, President John Taylor, the Twelve Apostles and Counsellors, Dear Brethren.—In consequence of the frequent absences from home of one of us, and the claims upon the time in other directions of both of us, which prevent us from bestowing that attention to the business of editing the Deseret News which it should receive, we respectfully tender to you our resignation as editors and publishers of the Deseret Evening, Semi-Weekly and Weekly News. Respectfully, Geo. Q. Cannon and Brigham Young." "Salt Lake City, August 2, 1879, editors Deseret News. This resignation should have been forwarded to you for publication before, but owing to a press of business, has been neglected.—John Taylor, on behalf of the Council of the Twelve Apostles."

Through the 1870's the paper on which the News was printed has the appearance of being homemade. The format and general appearance of the paper were almost unchanged through that decade. We hear more about the "Deseret Paper Mill, August 11, 1879. The work of putting in the new steam engine and boiler is progressing rapidly. The Mill will be running the latter part of this week. Heretofore, the machinery has been run by water power, and drought in summer, and freezing in winter, have operated alternately to much disadvantage." And again August 21, 1879, "The Deseret Paper Mill, which has been idle since May on account of repairs, and the introduction of steam power, started up again on Monday, and the first lot of paper reached us yesterday. The Mill will continue in regular operation hereafter." The News was evidently using homemade paper. The editor says, November 21, 1879, in launching "another volume.— We are gratified to know that with each succeeding year this paper is more highly prized by its subscribers who look to it for reliable information upon those subjects and affairs in which they are immediately interested and for the general news of the day, obtained by telegraph, by correspondence, and by other means from the most authentic sources that can be reached.

"The Deseret News does not aim at any distinction as a sensational, or what is commonly called a 'spicy' paper. We have no desire to pander to a depraved public taste . . . We would rather have our paper tame and truthful, than sprightly and misleading. As the Organ of the Church the News is expected to record the minutes of the numerous Conferences which are held periodically in the various Stakes of Zion, and to publish accounts of Missionary labors and the progress of the Latter Day work throughout the world . . .

"In explaining and defending the doctrines and principles of the Church the News has sought to present our faith in plainness and simplicity, as is set forth in the revelations of God, rather than present the opinions and deductions of men . . . And in criticizing the acts and sayings of our opponents to avoid as much as possible, offensive personalities, and to attack measures rather than men . . . When strong language has been used by this paper, it has been rendered necessary by the exigencies of the case, and the course of unprincipled enemies, and has had for its object the vindication of our cause, and not the stirring up of the passion of the people. Our position on what is called the 'Mormon' question is well defined. We have no halfway policy to hamper us in our arguments, or trammel us in our course. We are for the Church of Jesus Christ of Latter Day Saints, its authorized tenets, its recognized leaders, and its fellowshipped members, first, last, and all the time."

On September 6, 1880, comes another change in the masthead: "Printed and published by the Deseret News Company, Charles W. Penrose, editor." About February 4, 1880 the News apparently began the use of news print paper not made in Utah. Also new type, for on that date the editor speaks of the paper's "New Dress.—The Deseret News today dons its new dress. Our new outfit of type, etc., is from our own foundry."

On September 3, 1880, something else happens to the paper: "The Deseret News Company, a joint stock company, was this day organized and incorporated under the title of The Deseret News Company, with a capital stock of $100,000, in one thousand shares of $100 each . . . The objects of the company are the carrying on in this city of the business of printing, publishing, book binding, lithographing, stereotyping, type making, paper making, and all other branches connected with a first class publishing establishment. The stockholders met in the city this morning and elected the following directors, viz.: John Taylor, F. D. Richards, Geo. Q. Cannon, Joseph F. Smith, and Angus M. Cannon. The Directors met this afternoon and elected John Taylor as President and Angus M. Cannon as Vice President of the Company. Arrangements were made by which the whole property of the Latter Day Saints printing and publishing establishment is purchased and transferred to the Deseret News Company, which will in future assume entire control of the business of this office."

Beginning with Penrose's editorship, political editorials appeared frequently, political advertisements were run occasionally and certain political movements and leaders were sponsored, as a result of the strong non-Mormon "Liberal" party movement which grew up about that time. Penrose was a vigorous, tireless writer, always having a fresh, strong editorial with a new viewpoint, or with an old one redriven completely home; yet he obviously had time enough to look after the rest of the paper.

It was about this time the News was occasionally referred to by its contemporaries as "Grandmother" or "Granny" hence the significance of the following from the News of November 10, 1883: "The Herald claims to have given birth to a rumor Friday morning, which was first announced in the News on Thursday night. All right, 'Step-mother!'" The Salt Lake Democrat and other non-Mormon papers also referred to the News as "The Mormon Hand Organ."

The News editorials were usually dignified, and free from vituperation, but if you had thought Editor Penrose couldn't, just note this, on April 12, 1884: "The Butte-Intermountain, much of whose contents is made up from the vicious imagination of one J. B. Read, formerly of Salt Lake, has degenerated into one of the most shameless, lying sheets published in the west."

Penrose was powerful, but he wasn't almighty; and the News was not only a big institution, but had big battles to fight, consequently on July 5, 1884, came this "Announcement.—We are pleased to announce that the able services of John Q. Cannon, Esq., who was formerly on the editorial staff of the Deseret News, have again been secured for this paper."

Shortly after that (Nov. 7, 1884), appears the first Anti-Tribune editorial, entitled "The 'Gentlemen of the Tribune'," and the editor proceeded to delineate their characters! Cannon had other qualifications also, as we learn November 10, 1884: "A Reporter Rawhided.— Encounter between a respectable citizen and a 'Tribune reporter'. A Tribune Reporter named Lippman, noted for his effrontery, mendacity, and the free use in the columns of that disreputable sheet, of the names and personal affairs of decent and respectable citizens, was soundly thrashed on Saturday afternoon, 18th, by Mr. John Q. Cannon."

The Anti-Tribune editorials appeared frequently in the News thereafter! Indeed, the Tribune is excoriated in column after column, in an unrelenting fight back; for be it remembered, the Tribune was doing some excoriating itself! Penrose's name continued at the masthead, and he apparently devoted himself in a scholarly manner editorially to the many angles of the polygamy crusade, on the defensive; while John Q. Cannon attended to the newspaper in general, assisted in all departments by John Nicholson. "The Deseret Paper Mill is now (June 25, 1885) manufacturing various kinds of paper of a superior quality and in quantities sufficient to supply the demands of this region . . . The prices also compete with eastern figures. The grades manufactured are news print, straw and manilla wrapping and book paper."

In the anti-polygamy crusade, editor Penrose was forced to the "Underground" which is indicated by the following Valedictory of his understudy: (Oct. 13, 1885). "By the time this reaches the eye of the Public the writer will be an inmate of the Utah Penitentiary. The power that put me there was also instrumental in placing me during the present year in temporary charge of the editorial columns of this journal. It drove the chief of the staff into exile, and I, being his associate, have endeavored in my humble way with the help of God to fill his place during his enforced absence . . . John Nicholson."

Penrose's name, however, had not been removed from the masthead. Oddly enough, the News' Staff once actually wanted to go to prison! September 4, 1885 the Salt Lake Evening Democrat says: "The Deseret News bewails the fact that its reporters cannot enter the Penitentiary. This reminds us that the Penitentiary is like the Kingdom of Heaven. Marshal Ireland says no liars can enter therein!"

For many years the "State News" was gleaned very largely from the country exchanges; but in 1888 the News began the employment of country correspondents, and instead of quoting other papers, its dispatches were "Special to the News." Charles W. Penrose was editor until September 30, 1892 when this Valedictory appears: "The transfer of the Deseret News and all its affects to a new company brings my connection with the paper to an end. For more than fifteen years I have devoted my energies, influence and what talents I possess to the editorial department of this journal . . . For twelve years I have had editorial charge of the Daily, Semi-Weekly and Weekly Deseret News . . . Of my Associate Editor, Elder John Nicholson, who also retires from this office, I cannot speak but in terms of the highest praise . . ." Charles W. Penrose.

The new masthead, October 1, 1892: "Deseret News Publishing Company, lessees. As To Ourselves . . . Briefly and specifically stated the intention of the present proprietors is to continue the News as the authorized organ of the Church of Jesus Christ of Latter Day Saints, and the friend and advocate of righteousness everywhere; to keep it free from partisan bias and wholly unprejudiced and independent in politics, to conduct it as the people's newspaper, and not in the interest of any party or candidate . . . The Deseret News Publishing Company." (Among whom were Abraham H. and John Q. Cannon.)

The Saturday News averaged about the same size as the other daily issues except for an occasional special number, until about 1891, when four extra pages were put in pretty regularly each Saturday. By the middle 1890's those pages were devoted to features printed in advance of the regular issues. It had four extra pages, making twelve in all. This continued until 1898, when they were running eight extra pages on Saturday—mostly features, some of them "boiler plate." At the close of 1898 the weekly edition was finally discontinued, leaving only the Daily (except Sunday).

On June 16, 1900 the News ran: "Fifty Years of Progress. The News and Its Growth. The first office of the Deseret News was within the stone wall at the eastern end of what is now the (Hotel Utah) used previously in 1849 as a mint . . . The first type were cast in 1854 by J. H. Rumel, about which time the first paper was manufactured on what is now the Temple Block . . ."

Continuing this retrospection (June 16, 1900), and referring to Charles W. Penrose's tenure as editor, he acted "until 1884 when, owing to the Anti-Mormon crusade, he left the city and was absent for some time . . . John Q. Cannon became Editor in Chief (Oct. 11, 1892) acting until July, 1898, when he galloped away with a troup of rough riders (In the Spanish American War). J. M. Sjodahl acted as editor until the Church took back the management of the News, January 1, 1899, when Chas. W. Penrose again became editor."

"Deseret News Publishing Company, Lessees," continued at the masthead until September 20, 1898, when without explanation or substitution it was dropped—when the Church took charge again. On December 31, 1898 was made this "Official Announcement.—The Deseret News, with all its property and appurtenances, has reverted to the Church of Jesus Christ of Latter Day Saints, by which it is now owned and controlled. On and after January 1, 1899 . . . all the reading matter in the columns of the paper will be placed in charge of Elder Chas. W. Penrose; the business management will devolve upon Elder Horace G. Whitney (son of the original type setter on the News in 1850). The Daily will be published every evening except Sundays and holidays; and Semi-Weekly every Tuesday and Friday. The Weekly will be discontinued . . . The Organ of the Church will in a short time obtain universal circulation . . . Lorenzo Snow, Trustee in Trust."

The masthead thereafter was "Deseret Evening News, Organ of the Church of Jesus Christ of Latter Day Saints; Lorenzo Snow, Trustee in Trust; Chas. W. Penrose, Editor; Horace G. Whitney, business manager." Penrose's name was dropped and none substituted February 1st, 1907. Whitney's name was dropped and none substituted April 16, 1920. On June 3, 1920 the First Presidency approved the change from "Deseret Evening News" back to the original "The Deseret News." Elias S. Woodruff succeeded Whitney. Some years later B. F. Grant, a brother of President Heber J. Grant, served as manager a short time; and was succeeded by S. O. Bennion, the present manager.

Abraham H. Cannon was business manager 1892 to 1896, and John A. Evans to 1898, preceding H. G. Whitney. Since the days of the truly illustrious Charles W. Penrose, editor, the editors have been, at various times, John Q. Cannon, at least two terms, Colonel E. Le Roy Bourne, Harold Goff (died October 1928), Joseph J. Cannon, and at present, Mark E. Peterson and James A. Langton, Associate editors, under S. O. Bennion, general manager and editor in chief.

The News was born at what would now be about No. 31, East South Temple Street. It moved about October 31, 1851, to the new Council House, ground floor, on the southwest corner of the intersection of Main and South Temple streets. It moved back, early in 1862, to the opposite corner, with entrances at Nos. 1, 3 and 5 East South Temple Street, the business office long being at No. 1, within 150 feet of its birthplace. Forty years later, in 1902, it moved back again to the southwest corner of the intersection, into its own new red sandstone skyscraper, on the site of the old Council House, where it remains.

Always obliged to reflect, in its news and editorial columns, the exemplary attributes of the Church that owns it, yet almost equally obliged to present all the news satisfactory to Mormons and non-Mormons alike on its delivery routes and in the business office, The Deseret News stands unique among the newspapers of the world today! It is not only the oldest, but is the most influential and esteemed 6-day newspaper in the country. It has never borne a Sunday date line, but the Saturday News is superior to the average Sunday paper for the widely varied purposes and patronage it serves. (Since that was written an "Extra" announced the death of A. W. Ivins, Sunday, September 23, 1934.)

"Salt Lake Mining Gazette, is the title of a new weekly paper devoted to mining and commerce, to be published by Fred Perris & Co. The gentlemen have purchased the press and material of the former Endowment, and propose to issue a journal strictly treating of the industrial resources and progress of the Territory . . . The first number will appear on or about the 30th instant." The Tribune welcomes it September 1, 1873: "The Mining Gazette, an illustrated journal devoted to the mining, commercial and other interests of Utah, No. 1, Vol. 1. This is a new local, weekly journal . . . It is a five column quarto . . . ; the first page contains the history, description and illustration of Alta City." The Tribune follows with another story, Wednesday, October

3, 1873: "We have received the 6th number of the Utah (Sic) Mining Gazette, and are pleased to notice a constant improvement in its columns. The publishers give a wood-cut with every number."

The Deseret News, August 24, 1874, indicates how "uphill" the mining magazine business was in Utah: "Suspended.—The Utah (Sic) Mining Gazette of Saturday (22d) announces its suspension. The same number also closes its first volume. The Gazette failed for the want of the vital force—cash—which has proved disastrous to so many other business enterprises the past year." However, the News thought well of the Gazette, usually publishing the full list of contents of each issue, and occasionally briefing some special article by calling attention to its illustrations.

The 'Great Campaign 1895. No files. It is described by its editor, S. A. Kenner, in his Utah As It Is, 1904: "The Great Campaign, issued during political campaigns, as often as required and circumstances permit. Neat, natty and nice, saying things in a way that no other paper does or wants to. The only exclusively political publication in the State. Price 25 cents per series, and as much more as can be got! It originated the plan of presenting portraits and sketches of candidates for office in 1895 ... Now the woods are full of them, making the grass correspondingly short! S. A. Kenner is editor, proprietor, manager, director, publisher, supervisor, architect and all the rest of it!"

Utah Genealogical and Historical Magazine, published quarterly by the (L. D. S.) Genealogical Society of Utah, from January 1910, to date. Anthony H. Lund was first editor, succeeded in 1921 by Nephi Anderson, (died January 11, 1923), and by William A. Morton to 1924, by Richard Summerhays to 1928, and by Archibald F. Bennett to date.

Svenska Harolden (Swedish), Thursday, Established 1885, 24 x 36. Jenson's L. D. S. Church Chronology, Thursday, June 4, 1885 said: "The first number of Svenska Harolden, a weekly, the first Swedish newspaper in Utah, was issued in Salt Lake City by the Swedish Publishing Company, recently organized." Its principal editors were John C. Sandberg, Eric F. Branting, and Carl A. Carlquist. In 1888 F. S. Fernstrom and Carl V. Anderson became owners, succeeded in 1890 by a company for which J. M. Sjodahl became editor. The paper plant was destroyed by fire in 1892, and the paper died.

Herald, Daily, Vol. 1, No. 1, Sunday, June 5, 1870, files, Salt Lake Public Library, 6 columns, 4 pages, every morning except Monday, $8 a year, 75 cents a month, 25 cents a week. William C. Dunbar, Business Manager, E. L. Sloan, Editor. "Salutatory ... The Herald has been started under unusual difficulties ... Instead of entirely new material, we are compelled for the present, to employ some which has been in use for a time ... We acknowledge favors received from the Deseret News Office, and from many friends." ... "Our Platform Heading.— ... Deeming it better to represent ourselves, than to be misrepresented by others, when the people of Utah, their faith and institutions are aspersed, maligned and unjustly attacked, we shall esteem it a solemn duty to present the truth in reply, when the source is worthy a rejoinder . . . We have lived in this community for years, and hope to live in it for many years to come . . . Add to this a desire to be courteous, gentlemanly and liberal in expressing opinions, and a determination to give the greatest possible amount of news in the space, and our platform is before the people!"

Noble Warrum, in Utah Since Statehood 1919, says the publishers had purchased the type and press of the (Salt Lake City-Ogden) Telegraph. Edward W. Tullidge, in his Quarterly and his history of Salt Lake City, says: "The Salt Lake Daily Telegraph had just been discontinued, leaving the field open for a new paper. Sloan was editor, and Dunbar the business manager of the Telegraph, during the latter part of its career . . . Notwithstanding the Telegraph had been moved to Ogden by counsel, these gentlemen sagaciously saw that a secular newspaper . . . was needed most in Salt Lake City."

Mr. L. S. Hills in a letter to the Millennial Star July 26, 1870 said: "The Daily Herald, published by Dunbar & Sloan over the old Eldredge & Clawson Store, seems to be making a good start." (near present McIntyre Building). There were 14 columns of advertisements out of the 24, in the first number. The western news dispatches were played up conspicuously, especially the mining and smelting columns; and the editorials were pro-Mormon.

On August 17, 1870, we read in the Herald: "The first number of the semi-weekly Herald has been issued . . . It contains over 24 columns of reading matter. It is a larger size paper than our Daily, and is furnished at the unprecedentedly low price of $4 a year." And September 1, 1870: "We take pleasure in announcing that from this date John T. Caine, Esquire, will be interested in and associated with the Salt Lake Herald. Mr. Caine will assume the position of Managing Editor; Mr. Sloan will continue General Editor, and Mr. Dunbar will be general Agent."

Like some other early editors, he loved to call his short telegraphic dispatches "Lightning Flashes!" Those were the days when the "local news" columns began to be infested with 'reader' advertisements; in fact, it often appeared that the column of reading advertisements contained frequent news items! Another quaint system of the time, is this (December 3, 1870) "Subscribers receiving the Herald, daily or semiweekly, in a colored wrapper, will please note that their subscriptions have expired."

On June 4, 1871 we learn "Twice during the past year we have been compelled to enlarge our sheet, caused by the demands made upon our columns by advertising patronage . . ." (and June 6, 1871) "Our subscription books prove that the Herald—daily and semi-weekly— circulate in every Territory, and in 24 States of the Union, while many countries in Europe also appear upon the list."

As to the Herald's success, Tullidge wrote in his Quarterly: "The Daily Telegraph . . . was a subject, and therefore it failed; but the Herald has never been a subject, and it has succeeded! A Journal as a vassal of any power, either ecclesiastical or political, is very impotent in itself . . . The Salt Lake Herald did in fact fulfill the very mission for which the Tribune was started . . . This we, the old editors of the Tribune, were forced to confess while our paper was under the dictation of a Board of Directors, and we in vassalage; the Salt Lake Herald was free!" Also J. Bonwick, in his book The Mormons And The Silver Mines, (1872), had said: "The Salt Lake Daily Herald has greater vitality about it than its venerable companion, though less appreciated of course, in high quarters."

It is worth recording too, that in the first year or two, the Herald editor was too busy making a newspaper, to find fault with his contemporaries—too busy minding his own business! Entering the third year however, the Tribune as a "morning contemporary," was occasionally chided mildly, for its views,—and it was not long until the morning "contemporary" became a "contemptuary." The Herald also gave considerable space to polygamy and other Mormon controversial subjects, taking a broad but somewhat biased stand at times. The editor's especial delight was "sniping" at Eastern contemporaries caught writing unfairly about the Mormons, or incorrectly appraising the Utah political situation, and the editor usually had one or more of them on his hands.

On June 5, 1872, "Our third year . . . The Herald is also presented again in enlarged form, with the present issue. The blockade on the U. P. railroad last winter, compelled a reduction in the size of the sheet, as the paper could not be procured of the size required . . ." (the readers undoubtedly regretted he was ever able to get the unwieldy 9-column paper again! But like all others of his day, he either could not, or would not print more than 4 pages).

The quantity of advertising in the Herald as in most other early papers, was out of all proportion to the needs of the business office. Much of it was either not paid for, or was accepted at rates too low. The suspicion naturally is that many of the advertisements were trade-ins, or complimentary. Some obligations could be paid for by a puff in the news columns, but one is inclined to the belief that patent medicine, stage coaches, railroads, hotels, resorts, sewing machines, pianos and other articles and services were part if not all, to be traded out.

That the early-day editor was on the frontier literally fighting for existence, is indicated by this paragraph from the Tribune, January 2, 1874: "Pugilistic.—On Wednesday Evening (December 31), John L. Burns, of the recently defunct firm of Burns & McChane, of the Delmonico (restaurant) made a fistic attack on Mr. E. L. Sloan of the Herald. The affair is supposed to have arisen from some squibs that appeared in that paper, and which Burns thought reflected on him . . ." The size of the paper went back to 8 columns on January 1, 1874; and on February 21, 1874 all names were dropped from the masthead, and replaced by "The Herald Printing & Publishing Company." E. L. Sloan died August 2, 1874.

A Yuletide Tribune editorial says December 25, 1874: "We regret that this blessed season of Christmas should find our Church contemporary in such a bad humor. The great and manly heart of the Herald editor, and the meek and amiable spirit of our "Grandmother" do not expand with the expectancy and hope of this auspicious morn, but with a green and yellow melancholy gangrening their souls and impairing their digestive organs, this unhappy pair of Church oracles get on their capacious ears and send forth such rasping and inharmonious sounds, that the rude sea grows more uncivil at their vocal utterances!"

One gathers from perusing the files, that the Herald sought honestly and valiantly to be an independent paper; but the Tribune persistently heckled it as the "Mormon Herald," and its publishers as "Elders So-and-So." The Salt Lake Chronicle later acquired a similar habit of calling it "The Organ of the Lesser Priesthood," the News being the organ of the "Superior Polygamous Priesthood." And when these two organs did their duets in unison, the "music" was all the more "reprehensible"—though really it was quite an extraordinary feat, as one reads the files today.

The News of March 6, 1882 says: "Mr. W. C. Dunbar, of the Salt Lake Herald, was out with his bagpipes last night serenading a friend," which is something! The News of March 13, 1884 says: "Mr. S. A. Kenner severed his connection with the editorial staff of the Herald, and associated with Mr. S. W. Darke, will henceforth devote himself to the practice of law." We see how good the law business was, in the Herald January 1, 1885, which runs "Love and Business, Or How He Got There," a romance of the Sixth Ward, being the New Year's prize story, 6 chapters, by "Essay Kaigh."

Dunbar's retirement is reported in the News Monday, April 21, 1884: "The Salt Lake Herald of Sunday morning, (20th) announces editorially that 'Mr. William C. Dunbar has severed his connection with this institution'. The announcement will be received with general regret. Brother Dunbar was one of the founders of the Herald, and has stood by it under circumstances of great difficulty, devoting his lively energies and unfaltering fidelity to its interests . . . Although his health has been feeble for years, the effects of the Saluda explosion of historic memory, (on the Mississippi River), and a subsequent sunstroke having weakened his otherwise vigorous constitution, he has stuck to his post with a persistency that is remarkable and commendable." The News adds August 15, 1884: "There is talk that H. G. Whitney is about to accept a position as one of the regular editorial staff of the Salt Lake Herald." And August 19th: "Whitney, dramatic and lyric editor of the Herald, succeeded James A. McKnight, Monday, (August 18)."

This item is in the Herald through June, 1885: "Notice, May 8, 1885. We have this day leased our job printing and bindery departments to Mr. D. C. Dunbar . . . Herald Printing & Publishing Company."

A controversial item appears in the Democrat, February 5, 1886: "The 'Go-liar' of the Herald, got a stone in his forehead that proved harder than his head." The Democrat delights in calling the Herald "The Church Echo." A new masthead appears May 24, 1891: "The Herald Publishing Company, Directors, R. C. Chambers, President, Heber J. Grant, Vice-President, F. H. Dyer, John R. Winder, E. A. Smith, John T. Caine, J. L. Rawlins, Thomas Marshall, J. W. Judd, R. W. Young, George Cullins, Simon Bamberger, R. C. Whitney, Business Manager." Announcement: "The Herald is a Democratic newspaper."

A news story in this issue says: "A score of Salt Lake's most prominent citizens, Gentile and Mormon, have just united to show that Democracy in Utah henceforth will be as firmly established as in Colorado, New York or Indiana . . . They put up $100,000 to place back of the Utah Democracy such a journal as should dissipate the idea that the Democrats were fooling." The subscribers in addition to the Directors, already named are L. G. Hardy, A. L. Pollock, P. L. Williams, and others. "Byron Groo remains Editor-in-chief, Mr. A. L. Pollock, late editor of the Omaha Herald, takes a place on the editorial staff. Prof. J. H. Paul will continue his connection with the paper, and H. G. Whitney retains the position of Business Manager."

On August 26, 1891, we note in the Semi-Weekly: "B. H. Roberts, Editor, Horace G. Whitney, Business Manager." In addition to being the organ of Utah Democracy, the Herald was something else, according to the country press, picked up from The Utonian, Beaver, January 13, 1893: "The Brigham Report justly enters a protest against a leading Territorial paper: 'The Salt Lake Herald has just got onto the old time scheme of writing the local news from the various parts of the Territory at their office in Salt Lake. This scheme was formerly used by the Ogden Commercial, the Salt Lake Times, and one or two other papers, which are 'up with the angels now'. It would look much better for the Herald and other papers to give the various papers credit for such items, instead of doing so much cribbing."

At the beginning of 1894 all names were dropped from the masthead except R. C. Chambers, President, Heber J. Grant, Vice-President, and Richard W. Young, Manager, with this announcement.—"The resignation of Mr. H. C. Brownlee has been accepted, and Mr. Richard W. Young, who has acquired a financial interest in the company, has been appointed as Manager of all departments of the paper."

The Church & Farm Department of the Salt Lake Herald devoted to the religious, agricultural and domestic interests of the people of the Intermountain Region, edited by Joseph Hyrum Parry, Vol. 1, No. 1, Salt Lake City, Saturday, July 14, 1894, 3 columns, 8 x 11, 16 pages, every other Saturday. These papers were run through 1896, with very few advertisements, and some issues with none.

In the May 1, 1896 issue of the Daily Herald, is this "Announcement.—April 30, 1896, Mr. Richard W. Young having voluntarily tendered his resignation as Business Manager of the Herald, Mr. E. A.

McDaniel is hereby appointed to fill the vacancy . . . Signed R. C. Chambers." Also this—"In consequence of having been appointed by Governor Wells to a place on the Code Commission . . . Mr. Richard W. Young tendered his resignation . . . The Herald has been under the business management of Mr. Young for more than two years."

Another change, not mentioned in the Herald, is announced in the Park Record May 16, 1896: "B. H. Roberts has resigned as editor of the Salt Lake Herald, giving as a reason that the position that paper has taken on the recent Church Manifesto, was apt to place him in a false light." The Herald announces August 9, 1896: "The Salt Lake Herald by an alliance with the United Associated Presses, secured increased telegraphic facilities . . . Hereafter the Overland special wire will be directly connected with the Herald Office."

On October 25, 1898, all names were dropped from the masthead; and other changes are known to have occurred behind the scenes, with no intimations, in the columns of the Herald. The late Senator W. A. Clark and associates of Montana, purchased the paper, at that time, but had absolutely nothing to say about themselves. The following transfer announcement was made Friday, August 13, 1909: "The Herald has been sold to an association of prominent Utah Republicans, and this issue marks its last appearance as a Democratic newspaper . . . Senator W. A. Clark, the owner of the paper, was offered a price which justified acceptance . . . He took the property when it was practically a derelict, and sustained it at a heavy cost until it was on a paying basis. It was consistently Democratic, though not violently partisan, yet in all the years of his ownership, he had no adequate expression of appreciation from the Democratic leaders.

"On the contrary he was not unfrequently arraigned most unjustly, because his conception of what a newspaper should be did not agree with the ideas of men who sought to profit politically by the influence of the Herald . . . In the eleven years under the retiring management, the paper trebled its revenues, nearly trebled its daily circulation, and more than quadrupled its Sunday circulation. It passed from a very heavy annual deficit to the stage where it earned a profit, and the property increased in value, so that its selling value more than realized all that Senator Clark had invested in it . . ."

At a dinner given to the retiring staff of the Herald, August 15, 1909, the news stories inform us "Mr. A. G. Mackenzie presented A. N. McKay, the retiring managing editor, with a pretty watch fob. Mr. McKay was for the past eleven years editor of the Herald." In Mr. McKay's name it may be said that those eleven years marked the beginning of a new era in metropolitan newspaper management in Utah, opposing no one, no church, no political party, nor organization.

The Herald-Republican First issue August 14, 1909, continuing the Inter-Mountain Republican established February 12, 1906, and the Herald established June 5, 1870. "The Herald-Republican this morning prints its first issue. As a consolidation of the Inter-Mountain Republican and the Salt Lake Herald, the Herald-Republican hopes that it will be able to please the readers of both in the same measure that each paper has pleased its patrons in the past."

From the columns of the Herald-Republican, it has not been possible to identify either owners, editors or managers, for no names were carried on the masthead; but from the Salt Lake Tribune of October 1, 1913, we pick up the following: "Fulsome praise of Senator Smoot, which appears almost daily in the Salt Lake Herald-Republican, amuses Mark Sullivan, Associate Editor of Collier's Weekly. Mr. Sullivan . . . adds 'Having read this, turn now to an official list filed with the P. O. Department at Washington, showing the owners of that paper: Reed Smoot, Provo, Utah, D. C. Jackling, Salt Lake City, Utah, H. E. Booth, Salt Lake City, E. H. Callister, Salt Lake City, E. M. Allison, Salt Lake City, E. E. Jenkins, Salt Lake City, James H. Anderson, Salt Lake City, and George Anderson, Salt Lake City'."

It was the beginning of the end, when on January 1, 1918, names of individuals were first hoisted to the masthead: H. E. Booth, President, A. L. Thomas, Vice-President, Ed. E. Jenkins, Treasurer, Adolph Anderson, Secretary, James P. Casey, General Manager. Two months later, February 28, 1918, the white flag of surrender went up, boldly entitled: THIRTY. " 'Thirty' may not mean much to the average reader, but it means a lot to the boys that get out the paper. It is a time honored signal that the deadline on copy has been reached and the forms closed. This very beautiful issue of the Herald-Republican is the last under the present management . . . Good-bye Old Sheet, and may all good luck attend you! James P. Casey."

In a front page box is this "To The Public.—The Herald-Republican Publishing Company makes the announcement that it has leased the Herald-Republican and its property to the Telegram Publishing Company, and that the Telegram Company will on March 1, 1918 and thereafter, issue, publish and deliver the Herald-Republican to each and every subscriber as before." The new paper carried no names, and was practically without an editorial column or page, being more of an advertising medium than a newspaper. The regular issue of March 31, 1918 entitled Herald-Republican-Telegram contains 72 pages, the great bulk of it display advertising.

On July 5, 1918, another change occurred, as if through some higher instruction, and the name was changed by dropping reference to the Telegram, and continuing as the Herald-Republican, but "published by the Salt Lake Telegram Company." On Sunday morning, July 7, 1918, on one of the paper's 56 pages, appeared this bold-face notice: "So The People May Know.—The Telegram Publishing Company with this issue ceases the publication of a Sunday morning edition . . . The change is in accordance with (recommendation of the War Industries Board)—Sunday morning papers have ceased to be real newspapers; they have been built up on comic supplements, magazine sections and other features, with little regard to the news. Signed

George E. Hale, President and General Manager, Telegram Publishing Company."

On January 1, 1920, the new masthead shows A. L. Fish, General Manager, G. B. Heal, Managing Editor. "To The Public.—The control of the Herald is today taken over by me, in behalf of myself and associates . . . A. L. Fish." The Intermountain Republican name had been dropped some time previously. The new owners however, made a good newspaper out of the reborn Herald, until Sunday, July 18, 1920, when we read:

"The Herald Passes.—With today's issue, the Salt Lake Herald suspends publication. Established June 6, 1870, this paper has seen more than 50 years of active service . . . But now a new era in journalism has come; mounting costs of operation, and the trend of advertising toward the evening field, have made it impossible for the Herald to profitably continue publication . . . The Salt Lake Telegram Publishing Company has made arrangements to take over the circulation and serve the subscribers of the Salt Lake Herald, with the evening and Sunday Telegrams."

Improvement Era, published in the interests of the L. D. S. Young Men's Mutual Improvement Association, (and the Young Ladies' Mutual Improvement Association, from November, 1929) Vol. 1, No. 1, November 1897, E. H. Anderson, Editor, who died February 1, 1928, (born October 8, 1858). Hugh J. Cannon succeeded as editor until December, 1931, when Harrison R. Merrill took charge of the enlarged and greatly improved "Voice of the Church." Merrill was succeeded in March, 1936, by the present editor, Richard L. Evans.

The Independent, Daily, Vol. 1, No. 1, January 2, 1878, 7 columns, 4 pages, 25 cents a week, John W. Pike, Managing Editor. File to March 8, 1878—which may have been the end, in the Salt Lake Public Library; also a few numbers in the Bancroft Library. It had the Associated Press service, and there were plenty of advertisements, but little local news. It was avowedly anti-Mormon, anti-Tribune and especially anti-Lockley (Editor of Tribune). Jenson's Church Chronology says the Independent career terminated in about two months.

The Deseret News said of the Independent January 2, 1878: "The material is evidently the same that was used on the Corinne Record, and the former editor of that paper is Managing Editor of the Independent . . . We hope the Independent will maintain its dignity, and uphold its good intentions; if not, we cannot in truthfulness wish it that success which its promoters desire and anticipate." Again January 16, 1878, the News said: "The Independent comes to hand once in three days, and then always one day later than the day of issue." Very shortly it "was not"!

Inter-Mountain Catholic, Vol. 1, No. 1, October 7, 1899, 7 columns, 8 pages, weekly (combined with the "Colorado Catholic" of Denver). Thomas H. Malone in turning over the Colorado Catholic said of the new publication: "It will be the personal organ of no man, nor will it in any way seek the advancement of anything but Catholic principles and the welfare of the Catholic people. It will publish extensively the news of interest . . . and a line of special articles by writers of ability." Bishop Lawrence Scanlan was editor.

For 21 years the Inter-Mountain Catholic was published weekly under the direction of Bishop Scanlan and his successor, Bishop Glass. With the issue of October 16, 1920, the publication was suspended, owing to the World War. In December, 1920, a 32-page 7 x 10 magazine appeared at San Francisco, for this district, with the title "The Catholic Monthly"; but the name was changed in February, 1923, to the "Monthly Bulletin." In September, 1923, the Monthly Bulletin was transferred to Salt Lake City, and its name changed to "The Diocesan Monthly"; and in May, 1926, the right to again use the old title, Inter-Mountain Catholic, was obtained. It appeared as a monthly magazine under that name until February 2, 1927, when it again became an 8 page, 5 column weekly newspaper, under the guidance of Bishop John J. Mitty, who says it was "To proclaim Catholic truth, to warn the faithful against doctrines and practices that endanger faith and morals, to neutralize the misrepresentations in non-Catholic publications, and to build up a sound Catholic opinion upon all questions that deal with the policies of the Church and the spiritual interests of her members." The paper has continued to date.

Inter-Mountain Republican, Vol. 1, No. 1, Monday, February 12, 1906. "Published every morning by Inter-Mountain Republican Company, A. E. Blunck, President and Manager. Blunck's name was dropped May 23, 1906, and none substituted; and the next day this announcement was run: "At a meeting of the Board of Directors of the Inter-Mountain Republican Company yesterday, A. E. Blunck, former President and General Manager of the Company, and Lewis A. Blunck, former Secretary and Treasurer of the Company, resigned their offices. H. E. Booth was elected President of the Company, and William Spry was elected Director and Secretary-Treasurer. The stock of the company formerly held by A. E. Blunck and Lewis A. Blunck, has been bought by Mr. Spry and other members of the Republican Party in Utah . . . Malcom McAllister, of Salt Lake, was elected General Manager of the paper yesterday, and will take charge June 1." Mr. McAllister's name went on the masthead June 5, 1906, and it remained there until January 29, 1908, when it was hauled down, and there was none to take its place. The paper began the use of red ink head lines August 18, 1908, the first two-color work of the kind in the city. Advertisement pickings were none too good, and on Friday, August 13, 1909, this notice was printed:

"To The Republican Patrons.—This is the last issue of the Inter-Mountain Republican in its present form. Tomorrow, patrons will receive the Salt Lake Herald-Republican . . . The property and good will of the Republican have been sold to a company which has also secured the Herald, and in a sense, the paper to be published by the new company will itself be distinctly new." File, Salt Lake Public Library.

Daily, (Utah Mining) Journal, Vol. 1, No. 1, June 26, 1872, 7 columns, 4 pages. File May 22, 1873—August 14, 1873 in Bancroft Library. The Herald, June 25, 1872, says: "The Utah Mining Journal, Messrs. Sawyer & Myers, Proprietors, will be issued tomorrow. The new paper is the successor of The Review, and will be published daily, as an evening journal." And the Tribune follows June 27, 1872: "Last evening, per announcement, the Journal made its first appearance. We hail its birth as quite an acquisition to the newspaper press of Salt Lake. Our readers at a distance will be surprised to learn that this makes our fourth daily! It will supply a want long felt, by our citizens, for good newsy evening reading, and will speedily supplant that relic of old fogy journalism, the News. The first number, which is before us, is replete with lifey and spicy news, local, telegraphic and communicated—just such as everybody likes to read in the cool of a summer evening. With the Tribune in the morning, and the Journal in the evening, everybody throughout the Territory may rely upon getting the very latest news from all quarters of the globe. Messrs. Sawyer & Myers have our best wishes for success in their new enterprise." That same day the Deseret News says:

"The first number of the Utah Mining Journal was issued yesterday evening. It presents a creditable appearance typographically; its locals are spicily written, the Salutatory is brief and non-committal, and the paper starts out with a respectable amount of news judiciously compressed in small space." The Tribune observes August 7, 1872: "Our co-temporary, the 'Junior Partner' of the Utah Mining Journal, seems to be under the control of an adverse planet . . ." And again September 16, 1872: "Mr. Meyers, one of the proprietors of the Utah Mining Journal, left for the east this morning on business connected with his paper."

The issue of May 22, 1873, of the Journal carries—"Dennis J. Toohy, Proprietor," on the masthead, and runs this story: "Change of Title: Our readers will observe that we have adopted the title of The Salt Lake Daily Journal; but notwithstanding the slight change in the name of the paper, the Journal will endeavor to chronicle correctly the mining intelligence of the times. The time of issue will be as heretofore, every afternoon except Sundays."

Another change is noted Saturday, June 14, 1873: "Change of Publisher: I have sold and transferred the Salt Lake Journal to O. G. Sawyer, Esquire . . . to take effect this date. There being no indebtedness outstanding . . . except my thanks to the public for its liberal patronage . . . This occasion is taken to announce that on or about the 7th day of July next, I will commence the publication of a newspaper in this city, to be called the Salt Lake Daily Times."—Dennis

J. Toohy. "I hereby assume complete proprietorship . . . My journalistic career, well known in Utah, is a guarantee of the future."—Oscar G. Sawyer.

After that show of modesty, the editor dares to print this, June 26, 1873: "Greetings," (Commencing second year and reviewing the first year and speaking of other failures) "The Mormon element is ignorant and illiterate, and cannot be regarded as a patron of newspaper literature . . ., Gentile or anti-Mormon newspapers of course, never did enjoy popular patronage . . . General Connor tried the experiment to a sorrowful extent." (His closing statement was supposed to be significant, that "the Americans are now stronger, and the mines are looking up"!)

Some improvement may have been shown as the editor indicates, July 9, 1873: "We shall hereafter publish two regular editions, the first at 2 o'clock, and the second at 4 p. m. The Journal will therefore reach Bingham, Alta, Sandy and other camps before dark." (What! no lights?) Nevertheless, darkness and oblivion overtook the Journal on Thursday, August 14, 1873. "Conclusion. This is the last number of the Journal. It does not close because it has accumulated a large sum of money. On the contrary, it has vigorously wrestled with financial problems that would have paralyzed the brains of a Rothschild, and has fallen; that is in brief, its history . . . It leaves we trust, many friends, who will sincerely regret its demise; but a daily journal has never been very successfully published on regrets alone! It needs money to subsist upon; especially a Gentile paper, in a Mormon and Jack-Mormon community; and that medium of commerce has been as scarce in our office, as it has been in other business establishments in the Territory. So with no more words we say Adieu!" (Incidentally, there isn't money enough among newspaper readers and advertisers in Salt Lake City to support four daily newspapers today!)

Keep-A-Pitchinin, Vol. 1, No. 1, 3 columns, 4 pages, 8 x 11, Wednesday, March 2, 1870. "A small periodical, semi-monthly, devoted to fun and amusement," issued by (Uno Hoo and Ubet Urlife, aliases) George J. Taylor and Joseph C. Rich. File, Salt Lake Public Library. The Mormon Tribune of March 5, 1870: " 'Our hired man' acknowledging with pleasure the receipt of the Keep-A-Pitchinin, the new illustrated paper of the Orthodox party, and compliments them on their 'New Move'."

The L. D. S. Millennial Star makes acknowledgment April 26, 1870: "Numbers 1 and 2 of the Keep-A-Pitchinin have come to hand. They are full of spice, wit, humor, fun and all that sort of thing. The illustrations are wonderful (wood cuts). The Keep-A-Pitchinin is published . . . at $1.50 per annum." The Salt Lake Herald furthers the story July 16, 1870: "We had another dose of Keep-A-Pitchinin yesterday, and find it pretty good to take. The editor only needs a 'sleeping partner' (silent partner?) to make the concern sufficiently lively . . . Keep cool, George . . . What would your multitudinous carriers do for a living, and the lively craft 'Dwyer' do for freight, if anything should happen to your precious headpiece!" The fortnightly publication interval grew longer, much longer, the last one still not ended! The Deseret News' Journalistic Mortuary, September 29, 1874, says of the Keep-A-Pitchinin, "The editor stoutly asserts that it is still a live paper; that the last number has not been issued!" It is probably one of the longest remembered and least important of all Utah papers.

The Leader.—Prospectus: "The Directors of the Tribune Printing and Publishing Company beg to inform their subscribers (Sunday, July 27, 1873) and the public at large that in consequence of arrangements lately effected for the transfer of their weekly paper to the Superintendence of Mr. E. L. T. Harrison, its publication under its present form and title will cease with the present number." (Thereafter the Tribune published daily and Sunday.)

"The next issue of this paper, which will be on Saturday next, will be under the title of The Leader, which will be edited and directed by Mr. Harrison . . . The Leader, a Salt Lake Weekly newspaper, with which will be combined the original Mormon Tribune. The Leader is intended to supersede the present Weekly and to revive the features of the original Weekly (Mormon) Tribune. It will combine the advantages of a weekly newspaper with those of a philosophical and intellectual sheet. Its news department will be made up, as at present, of items and articles selected from the columns of the Daily Tribune.

"But in addition to this it will contain an entirely new department which will be devoted to the free discussion of all intellectual, social and religio-philosophical questions, now agitating the age. The object of the intellectual department of The Leader will be to promote the growth of 'cultured, free thought,' inviting discussion, but avoiding extremes of every kind. It will assail all popular fallacies without the least distinction as to whether they are of Gentile or Mormon origin.

"In local questions The Leader will be an unsparing and impartial reviewer, criticizing newspapers, sermons, speeches, and public men without distinction of party . . . The friends of progress and independent journalism everywhere will confer a favor by canvassing and forwarding subscriptions to E. L. T. Harrison, Salt Lake City." The Leader of September 26, 1873, refers to " 'That half-brother' of ours, The Tribune . . ." Possibly "twin-brother"would have been better; it was all in the family anyway—what appeared in The Leader was locked up in the Daily Tribune, and sometimes vice versa.

Accordingly, Volume 1, No. 1, appeared August 2, 1873. The Salt Lake Daily Journal of that date says: "The first number of E. L. T. Harrison's paper, the Leader, made its appearance this morning." The Tribune comments August 23, 1873: "We have before us the fourth number of the Leader, published this morning. It is full of original, bold and racy matter." Among the leading articles we noticed the following: Moonlight versus Mormon Editor; On Its Last Legs; The Herald's Anti-McKean War; The New Proprietors Of The Theatre;

Going Abroad For Their Education; Got To Stop It; Incomplete Development Of The Maculine; What The Spiritualists Say About The Origin Of The Colored Races; What We Know Something About, In Utah; . . . to which is added the news of the week. Topheaviness may have thus caused its downfall. The only other news we have of the Leader is from the Deseret News' Journalistic Mortuary, September 29, 1874: "An undated Salt Lake Leader.—'This is our closing number; reasons given in full in our preceding number'." Too sad to repeat!

Utah Evening Mail. Volume 1, No. 1, Monday, December 20, 1875. Six columns, 4 small pages, $8.00 a year, 20c a week. File, Salt Lake Public Library. Masthead: "The Utah Evening Mail is published every evening at 4:00 o'clock (Sundays excepted) by the Mail Printing and Publishing Company. Greeting.—As the youngest of a somewhat numerous family, we proffer our infantile hand to our big brothers of the press for a friendly grip or buffet as circumstances may require. Where the crib is narrow and the 'vittals' scarce, a newcomer with an unappeasable appetite and much 'cheek', is not always welcomed with the ringing of bells and a National Salute. But we believe that our jolly big fisted brothers have hearts as big as their fists and will 'lie along' to make room for our 'bantling'.

"If the venerable relation at the Tithing House puts on airs because his matutinal mail is cooked by steam, while ours is done brown by hand, we may be tempted to insert our bodkin under the fifth rib of his conceit by reminding him of his inability to sing anything but *Church music,* while we can practice street, opera or chin music without being rapped over the knuckles by any Church beadle . . ."

"Wanted.—A good smart boy to peddle the Mail every day. Good wages given. Apply to D. Camomile or at this office." "Ford, the Printer.—That very popular professor of 'the art preservative of all arts' can now be found at the office of the Utah Evening Mail, second South Street, next to Walker Bros. Grocery Dept. The Mail Printing and Publishing Company has performed with him the same feat that the whale did with Jonah's corporosity — swallowed him body and britches! Ford has lost his identity and is now a fractional part of said company."

"Salutatory.—And now comes the Evening Mail, owned and conducted by an association of practical printers and journalists, and it comes *to stay* . . . (a column of this). The overshadowing mining interests in Utah justly demand and shall receive at our hands a hearty recognition and honest advocacy." The editor leaps headlong in the first issue at "The Mormon Problem . . . During a residence of more than four years in Utah . . . we have received only kind treatment, and courteous hospitality from the Mormon people . . . But, no independent journal can exist a day in Utah without taking a decided stand against the assumption of priestly power . . . 'These be hard words,' but we use them understandingly . . ."

The paper started with good local news, good telegraphic service, good country correspondence, and plenty of advertising, whether paid for or not! The Ogden Junction observes and hopes: "The Utah Evening Mail . . . appears to be made up of the old material of the defunct Corinne Mail, Reporter, etc., etc., and to be conducted in much the same spirit as those dead-and-gone publications. Smartness, snap and ability are exhibited in its editorials, but it is plainly to be seen that its chief object, next to making money, will be to attack Mormonism and the Mormons, and that when the big Tribune dog barks, the little Mail cur will snarl in chorus . . . If, as we believe, it intends to take the same course as its predecessor at the 'Burg on the Bear,' we hope it will meet with a similar fate."

The Ogden Freeman also has its own opinions, December 24, 1875: "The first issue of The Utah Mail has come to us. Its labors appear to be directed toward the attainment of the same end that ours are, only with the difference in the means to be used. It denounces Mormonism on general principles. We praise Mormonism for its good features, and condemn evil in individual members. The Mail, like the Tribune, seems to expect to convert people by sarcastic abuse."

The editor quotes the Utah County Times: "The Utah Evening Mail . . . is about the same size as the Times. It makes a good appearance typographically and is quite newsy; but for a paper that claims to be independent, we cannot say we admire its leading articles." The first name reaches the masthead December 27, 1875: "S. S. Johnson, manager." And on January 3, 1876: "Owing to the severe indisposition of our manager, S. S. Johnson, Mr. J. McKnight will at present assume the responsibilities." Beginning April 3, 1876, there was a "Monday morning edition," also a "Monday evening edition." By April 28, 1876 he had nearly a page of 'Legals'. Notwithstanding the apparent success—or was it because of this apparent success?—On May 18, 1876, we see this "Special Notice.—To my friends and patrons: I have this day sold my interest in the Mail Printing and Publishing Company to Archie McGowan, Jr. . . . S. S. Johnson."

Johnson may have merely preferred the payroll, or a "space rate" to being the proprietor, for we learn on May 26, 1876: "S. S. Johnson, Esquire, left on Tom Doyle's fast coach line yesterday for the lively camp of Bingham, and will make a trip through the different mining camps in Utah in the interest of the Utah Evening Mail. We want our friends . . . to assist him in the good work." The masthead on May 19, 1876 showed the new name: Archie McGowan, Jr., manager.

The Mail was published every evening except Sunday until March 21, 1876, when it began to be "published Monday mornings, and every evening, Sundays excepted." An explanation is made April 29, 1876 in this "Special Notice.—James McKnight is not in the employ of the Mail Printing and Publishing Company; is not authorized to solicit advertisements or subscriptions or transact any business of any description or nature in behalf of the company." S. S. Johnson, Manager.

That change made, this "Notice" followed on June 19, 1876: "The publication of this paper has changed hands. It is no longer the property of the Mail Printing and Publishing Company of Utah, but is now owned exclusively by an association of practical printers and journalists. For the sake of patronage, however, and to show good faith, we will continue the publication of all prepaid cards and advertisements without charge, and deliver to subscribers who have paid in advance, the papers due them" . . . James McKnight, publisher.

And this on June 20, 1876:—"Notice. This paper *is* published by the Utah Mail Printing and Publishing Company. Any arrangements made with one James McKnight, alias 'Bilk' McKnight, will not be recognized by this company, said coward having climbed over a twelve foot fence late last night and has not been seen since. Any information regarding his whereabouts will be gratefully received at our office."—Archie McGowan, Manager Evening Mail.

Another county is heard from on June 21, 1876: "A Card.—(in other Salt Lake papers). Editors, the Mail: The statement made by late employees of the Mail and published in the city's morning papers, so far as I am concerned is totally and absolutely false."—Charles King.

"That Card.—The morning papers obtained an advertisement and an item in publishing the lying card of James McKnight and his paid retainers. The Mail does not propose to bore the public with details of the disreputable attempts of McKnight to defraud the men who, under the pressure of sickness, entrusted their interests to his hands. In spite of envious rivals and scheming Knaves, the Mail will pursue the even tenor of its ways, satisfied that its readers and patrons will sustain it in the independent course hitherto pursued.

"We ask no favors from our contemporaries of the Daily Press, other than that regard for fair play in journalistic and professional matters which characterizes respectable representatives of the press in other sections. We aver that in the exercise of such ordinary courtesy, no paper could have published so abusive a Card as the one in question, without at least inquiring of its neighbor attacked as to the truth of its statements. In this case courtesy is out of the question. The animus is apparent, and most discreditable."

The Herald tells the story June 20, 1876: "A Change.—James McKnight took possession of the Mail establishment yesterday and last evening's paper came out under his supervision . . . The former conductors of the concern propose to make a legal fight to recover the paper and oust the McKnight party who were still in possession last night. Since the above was in type we learn that at a late hour last night Mr. Archie McGowan, Manager of the Mail Printing and Publishing Company, who has been confined to his room with sickness, proceeded to the Mail establishment and ejecting the McKnight crowd, again took possession, placing his employees in charge . . ."

Wail of the Compositaire, June 21, 1876: "Editors Salt Lake Herald: The statement this morning that Archie McGowan, Manager of the Mail Company, ejected us from our possession—which was right-ful and legal—is unqualifiedly false. In the first place McGowan has no lawful claim as Manager, having obtained it in violation of the articles of incorporation. We were employees of the late Mail Company. We worked faithfully and patiently for the concern until our claims amounted to from $60 to $300 each, and were brought to great necessity through the repeated failure of the concern to pay us, though ever promising to do so. Knowing that Mr. James McKnight also had large claims against the company, we went to him for relief. He kindly supplied our most pressing wants by furnishing us food and money. Resolved not to be imposed upon longer by false promises we unitedly agreed to quit, which would be likely to stop the paper. When this was told to McKnight, he thought something might be done for the paper and proposed to go in and take possession securing our claims against the Mail Company by virtue of his bill of sale. To this we agreed, seeing no other prospect of getting our pay, and knowing that Mr. McKnight had always done as he had promised us.

"On Monday morning Mr. McKnight entered the Mail office without opposition, with all the former hands, excepting two, at the cases and in his employ. Mr. Chas. King, an elderly gentleman, the owner of the premises—and to whom the Mail Company were in arrears for rent nearly $300—as per his own statement, came up with Mr. McKnight to deliver possession of the rooms. As he entered he said, 'Boys, I told you I would protect you in your rights. Now I am going to do it. I want Mr. McKnight to take possession and run the paper. He can do it.' He also referred to the foul treatment he had received from the Mail Company as their landlord. Mr. King then said he would make Mr. McKnight his tenant, the rent to begin from tomorrow morning. We issued the paper as usual; and not suspecting any treachery two or three of us remained in the office 'til a late hour. We had no firearms of any kind about us.

"At midnight some noise was heard at the office door. The assailants who were armed with Henry rifles and revolvers were told they could not come in at that hour. Finally, after considerable going and returning, Mr. King came up to the door and asked to be let in. Supposing him to be a friend, the door was promptly opened and Mr. King entered, bringing also the unscrupulous pauper, McGowan. We saw we had been betrayed by King and not wishing to have any disturbance left the office . . . Alfred C. Owens, Arthur C. Salisbury and Wm. W. Copeland." "I affirm that the above is true . . . Jacob E. Bosch, late Foreman, Mail Office."

The usual "comeback" appears in the Herald June 21, 1876: "John Phoenix outdone. Most newspaper readers recollect the adventures of John Phoenix, who being once left in charge of a California paper by the editor for a few days, proceeded to change its politics and general tone and character, so that its editor, who returned a little earlier than expected, could not recognize his own handiwork.

"The recent remarkable transformations of an evening sheet of this city, during a single day, surpass even the exploits of John Phoenix. The morning issue of Monday was published by one set of proprietors; in the course of the day another set came in uninvited, took possession of the office, and issued the evening edition, in which the public was informed that the old company had been dissolved, and that a new association of practical printers had assumed the management . . .

"The party of the first part were not disposed to aquiesce in the proceedings, and with the assistance of the landlord, again took possession and rescued a free press from its great peril . . . We understand there are several lawsuits pending against the proprietors, brought by the man who played the role of editor in chief for a single day. Further developments in this racy, journalistic squabble are hourly expected."

The Herald on Friday, June 30, 1876, continues the story: "In Hard Luck.—The Evening Mail is having more trouble. After changing proprietors or managers two or three times, the concern fell into the hands of the constable, who has been holding it by attachments for several days, but permitting the Mail Company to strike off its regular evening edition. Three or four days ago the forms were taken to a neighboring printing office, where the paper has since been printed until yesterday. On Wednesday evening the Mail came out on a half sheet and announced that it would take 'a centennial sleep'. However, James McKnight again corraled it yesterday and tried to infuse new life into the concern, but the effort was weak . . . He said: 'How long we will stay is a matter of very little moment to us.' Resigned to fate!

"It is a matter of regret that a newspaper should die, but indications point to the early demise of the Mail. Poor Forbes, when his New Endowment winked out, honestly gave as the cause of its death that he 'didn't bring money enough with him' when he came to Salt Lake to start a newspaper. That has been the disease of which numerous Salt Lake journals have died; but that doesn't seem to have been what has ailed the Mail, as it appears to get along just as well without money as if it had millions!

"Since the above was written, we learn that Mr. McGowan, the manager of the Mail Company, has again come to the front and announced his ability and intention of recapturing the paper . . ."

The Herald continues the story Wednesday, July 12, 1876: "Yesterday the Mail Printing and Publishing Company was adjudged bankrupt, and last evening the Marshal took possession of the company's effects. The McKnight Outfit again being ousted, we understand the Marshal has granted the manager, Mr. Archie McGowan, the privilege of using the material to publish a few issues of the paper, in order to protect the mining advertisements therein, which will expire in about a week, when the Mail will be no more! It has made a desperate struggle for life, has experienced numerous changes of proprietors, and the want of patronage has now terminated its brief career. Mr. McGowan, although ousted two or three times, has stuck to it to the end, and he will now have the farewell swing at the concern."

The Deseret News Thursday, June 29, 1876, says: "Taking a Holiday: The Evening Mail has stopped for the Centennial Holidays. It will probably not resume until the next Centennial, seeing that it came 'to stay'!" The Tribune puts a new kink in the story July 12, 1876: "The Mail, now in bankruptcy, will be issued until the 16th under the auspices of Archie McGowan. At that time the patent notices expire and the Mail will be numbered among the things that were." Accordingly, the Tribune says, July 18, 1876, "The Mail laid it down and died last evening." The story was seconded by the Deseret News that evening: "Defunct.—The Evening Mail, which was born six months ago and came here to 'stay', flickered out and died yesterday." The Tribune closes the obsequies and nails up the box, January 16, 1877: "The old material of the Mail, which was sold last week to a Beaver man for $1000, was packed yesterday and shipped to Beaver!"

The Mountaineer, Volume 1, No. 1, Saturday, August 27, 1859, weekly, file in L. D. S. Church Library. Motto: "Do What Is Right; Let The Consequences Follow." Masthead: Published every Saturday, office, northwest corner of Council House in the basement story. Blair, Ferguson & Stout, editors and proprietors. Terms, $6 per annum in advance. Six wide columns, 4-pages. A fair quality of paper used. The front page consisted mostly of a fiction serial. The column-long Salutatory was a bit rambling as most of them are. Promises to be a crusader for the right as he sees it. There is some local news, some foreign news, and plenty of "scissors" news. On September 14, 1859, the Deseret News tells us, among other things: "The Mountaineer has sprung into existence and the proprietors have rented the hall in which the Court was held, for a printing office."

A masthead change occurred September 17, 1859: Blair and Ferguson, editors and proprietors. The Deseret News holds them up for better view, October 26, 1859: "What next! Our neighbors of the Mountaineer in the room below, are becoming quite sharp and clear sighted of late. Their last issue was a real *Solferino* attack on many things in general, and some things in particular, and 'grape and cannister' was used in profuse abundance. If everything within range of their 'armes de precision' was not demolished, it is certainly a wonder.

"We were well aware that Mountaineers in general were a 'savage set of beings,' were not slow on the 'tramp' and would show signs of 'fight' occasionally if measures were pushed too far; but we did not expect that our legal friends on engaging in the 'chase' would burn powder quite so fast, and not be quite so lynx-eyed on 'promenade'. Their discovery of a 'Danite Band' at this day was quite remarkable, but no more so than some other things which they said during their late 'ermine' hunt."

Another masthead change occurred July 21, 1860: James Ferguson, editor and proprietor. Numerous supplements were issued in 1860. The last number in the first volume, dated Saturday, August 18,

1860, says: "To Our Friends.—This number closes the first volume of the Mountaineer . . . The Mountaineer was started under the most unfavorable auspices, away, far away from sources of materials; it was to all appearances a wild venture, but the citizens called for such a paper, and they would have it.

"At the commencement we were strongly supported by two of the most eminent of the legal profession in our Territory . . . Now they have turned to other occupations . . . It has been our portion of duty to record many a tale of blood and villainy which we would fain have not been called upon to do. When we appear again, we trust the next act in the drama will be less gloomy, but we may be mistaken. It is true that the army and its disgusting appendages have nearly all evaporated. They have been directly or indirectly the source of most of the recent troubles in Utah.

"At present we cannot promise that we will continue our issue without a slight interruption. Our paper, ink, and new type are on the road hither, but it may not arrive before our present supply is exhausted. The delay, however, will not, we think, extend beyond two weeks. In the meantime, good friends, if you have liked volume 1, please help its successor."

Supplement No. 1, distributed gratis, September 1, 1860, consisted of two pages, on one of which is: "To Our Friends.—We anticipated by our arrangement last spring that before the commencement of our second volume we would have been prepared with materials to continue our labors without interruption. A delay of the train, in which our paper is being conveyed, has compelled us to ask the pardon of our friends for a short delay in the commencement of our second volume . . .

"We have had but six who, through pecuniary embarrassments, decline a further subscription; but in their stead we have had scores of new subscribers. Our friends who feel rich will aid us; from our *very poor* friends we ask no pay." The editor also joyously calls attention to some new advertising contracts. Supplement No. 2 appeared September 8, 1860, one of its two pages being solid advertising. Supplement No. 3, September 15, 1860, says: "Through the kindness of our neighbor and friend, the editor of the News, we have so far been enabled to present our readers by way of supplement, a record of current events (instead of full sized papers)."

Supplement No. 4 was distributed gratis, September 22, 1860, one of its two pages remaining all advertisements. In supplement No. 5, September 29, we find: "Materials for volume 2. We feel gratified at being able to inform our readers that paper, ink, etc. for the second volume have arrived, and that we shall commence the issue of a full sized sheet next week." The Mountaineer's display advertisement for Book and Job printing was kept standing; it carries a small wood cut of a Washington hand-press. September 29, 1860 becomes the latest issue bound in volume No. 1.

Volume No. 2, October 6, 1860 to June 29, 1861, No. 39, is all 7 columns, 4-pages. The Deseret News had observed Oct. 12, "Gone to the Mountains.—Our friends of The Mountaineer went to the Mountains yesterday—what for, and how long to stay, we do not know." And November 30, 1859, the News adds: "Our friends of The Mountaineer, after three months hard service, during which time they have taken many a 'tramp', corrected several Officials, elected General Houston to the Presidency, and performed divers valorous acts, the last of which was the annihilation of a 'weakly' paper published in the city of Gotham called The Century, have 'bid adieu for a season to the Mountain heights', and concluded to remain in the city for the winter, and devote their time more or less to the subject of Education . . ."

The News of January 18, 1860, gives: "The Pure Gold.—In The Mountaineer of Saturday last appeared an order, purporting to have been issued at Camp Floyd, the headquarters of the Army in Utah (concerning the Mormon $5 gold coins.)." And on February 8, 1860: "Recovered.—S. M. Blair, Esq., Attorney General, who has been sick and confined to his room most of the winter . . . We presume that his Milesian partner will feel himself materially relieved from the onerous duties that have devolved upon him during the winter, and doubtless articles bearing the impress, or savoring of the spirit of, the 'Lone Star' will occasionally be seen in the columns of The Mountaineer, of which he is the senior editor."

"From a gentleman late from Camp Floyd we learn . . . That Johnston (General Albert Sidney) complains of a great injustice done him in an editorial published in last week's Mountaineer," says the News April 25, 1860. It further records for us, Wednesday, May 9, 1860.—"Among those who have been the sufferers by the thieving propensities of some of the lazy scoundrels that are loafing about by scores, is General Ferguson, one of the Editors of The Mountaineer, who had a fine horse taken from his stable on Sunday night last."

"Retired!" Announces the News Editor July 6, 1860. "By the last number of The Mountaineer, we are informed that Major Blair, the late Senior Editor of that paper, has retired from that establishment with the intention of entering once more upon the scenes of a frontier or border life, which seem congenial to his taste and suited to his constitution. He is preparing to erect a sawmill at Franklin, the most northern settlement in Cache County. The Major's health is not good. He will please accept of our best wishes." The sawmill was finally erected at Providence, near Logan.

A Mountaineer EXATR (Sic) G. S. L. City, Tuesday, January 14, 1861, 8 pm, gives the "Latest By Pony Express," dispatches being published dated Washington, D. C. January 1, 1861; also December 25, 26, and 27th. Four columns were printed on one side of the sheet as long as a "Poster." The Mountaineer Extra of January 22, 1861, 5 pm, contained "Important news from the East, by Telegraphic-Pony." The most recent dates were January 7, 8, and 9, 1861. One was dated Saint Louis, January 11, by way of Fort Kearney, thence by Pony.

The last of the series preserved is No. 42, dated July 20, 1861; it contains this reference to possible discontinuance: "Paper.—we are pleased to learn from our friend, A. C. Pyper, that there is a good prospect for a fresh supply of paper. Much means and labor have been expended in endeavoring to manufacture and introduce into the market this much needed article. We are sorry to say that we will be compelled to suspend operations in our office for a week or two for want of the material. It is to be hoped, however, that before long, we will renew our publication without interruption. Messrs. Howard and Pyper deserve our warmest thanks for their indefatigability. In the meantime our friends will do us the kindness to exercise their patience."

The News, in its Journalistic Mortuary, September 29, 1874, says the Mountaineer died in 1861 of "Episinthic Impecuniosity!" Nevertheless, the Mountaineer ran a pretty good newspaper. He was always interested in Indian news, as well as Eastern news in general. The editor loved to mention names of persons in his paper, undoubtedly attracting much attention thereby. He even ran a foreign nation news department, made up of clippings and correspondence.

He used large type and wide columns, making an inviting paper, whose horizons met at the International Date Line! However he was always glad to give up his editorial column to a decent news dispatch or a local news item of real importance. He found a lot of news, appropriate for his "Mail" and "Pony" columns. His advertising, while changeable enough to be attractive, held up to four or five columns as a rule, although he supplied some of it himself! Of all the long list of causes for newspaper demises, the Mountaineer was the first one to perish for the want of paper!

New Endowment, Vol. 1, No. 1, February 17, 1873, mentioned by the Tribune February 18, 1873: "The New Daily.—Yesterday the first number of the New Endowment made its appearance in our city. The typographical appearance is extremely neat and tasty; in the amount of its news, all that could be desired; and in tone, all that a gentleman can make it. Mr. Forbes, the proprietor, comes with a fine reputation as an able and spicy journalist, and the new paper gives evidence of a personal supervision which shows that its proprietor is master of his business in all its details. The New Endowment will be an American newspaper with independent Republican politics, opposed to the union of Church and State, and devoted to advocating the material prosperity of the Territory. As a whole, we think the New Endowment incomparably superior in every way to many newspapers previously started here, and will undoubtedly do much good in correcting public sentiment and giving a new tone to newspaper literature in this city."

Also the News February 21, 1873, "The New Paper.—This morning we received copies of the New Endowment, the daily paper just started in this city, and of which Mr. W. J. Forbes is the editor. It is a 7 column journal, and is *un*exceptionally neat in point of typography, etc. Its articles so far as we can judge, from a casual perusal, evince considerable ability; as the paper is five days old, this notice may appear somewhat tardy, the cause of which is that for some reason, copies of the paper did not reach us before this morning." No files. The Deseret News' Journalistic Mortuary September 29, 1874 says the New Endowment passed on July 8, 1873, its publisher, W. J. Forbes observing: "I'd like to publish it longer, but the fact is, I didn't bring enough money along!"

Peep O' Day, Vol. 1, No. 1, October 20, 1864, a magazine of science, literature and art, edited by Harrison & Tullidge, published in the Twentieth Ward. Copies in the Salt Lake Public Library, L. D. S. Church Library and Utah Historical Society Library. Three columns, 8 x 12, 16 pages, practically no advertising. $2 per quarter, $7 a year, J. D. Ross, Agent for subscription. The leading editorial is entitled "Mormonism Republican In Its Genius," and ran nearly one and one-half pages, signed "T." Another editorial title is "Man, A Proof Of Diety," by E. W. Tullidge. "Adv.—We intend shortly to issue without any extra cost to the subscribers, a weekly wrapper with this paper, three pages of which will be devoted to advertisements."

Something of the breaking of the Peep O' Day is indicated in "Our Title.—This morning we herald forth to the world the first number of the Peep O' Day, a title by which we by no means refer to any supposed light about to be shed by our individual efforts on a darkened world, but to the dawning of a bright civilization, which will spread its glorifying influence over the earth" . . . (and so on, for almost a page). A lofty preachment showing the world's readiness to 'say with us—Hail To The Peep O' Day' Signed 'H'."

Another editorial heading "Pure Benevolence . . . Some amiable gentlemen of this city with a view of course toward increasing our subscription list, have generously saved us the trouble, and expense of advertising, by going around, unknown to us—under the pretense of being opposed to our paper. Knowing the principle of opposition that dwells in human nature, they have hit upon this expedient as the best method of helping us, fully calculating that human, like pig nature, will always go the contrary way to the one you pull it. In his enthusiasm in our cause, one of these persons went so far as to say some very hard things about our unborn sheet, and did it so naturally too, that it was taken for a real expression of his feelings.

"Now some ignorant people would call this meanness! Nonsense! Nothing of the sort! It was merely an underhanded way of doing good . . . taking this very delicate way of working in our interest . . . Gentlemen we say—our right hand pressed modestly upon our shirt bosom— we admit this method of advertising has increased our subscription list . . . with tearful eyes directed to our subscription list we say—imagine a pair of parental hands about two feet above your heads, trembling to low music from Professor Thomas' fiddles—and consider you have our blessing!"

"A Letter. Great Salt Lake City, August 12, 1864, Messrs. Editors Peep O' Day, Sirs: At the time of my subscribing to your Prospectus . . . I presumed it, as it promised, was to be conducted by Latter Day Saint Elders . . . *But* when it has to resort to a Pandemonium for its publishing place, and its editors so far forget themselves as to resort to an avowed enemy to them . . . I respectfully decline, and wish my name withdrawn from the subscription list.—David Candland."

The editor turns to Mr. Candland: "It is a matter of serious regret with us that we have to present our readers with so lamentable a specimen of bad feeling . . . In reply the Peep O' Day . . . is and will be published in no 'Pandemonium' unless such can be found in the Twentieth Ward of Great Salt Lake City . . . our correspondent has confounded the editing and publishing of a paper . . . with the printing of it . . . For the information of our friends who may be curious, we will say that on first starting of the enterprise, an unreserved offer of the whole of the printing was made, first to the Deseret News, next to the Daily Telegraph, and lastly to the Farmer's Oracle. A lack of materials, or some necessary convenience as stated, prevented them from accepting our offer. Nearly a month was spent unceasingly on these efforts . . .

"Finally we obtained on very generous terms, the use of the press on which this magazine is now printed . . . We intend the Peep O' Day to be an independent paper—independent of, but courteous to one and all. We hold ourselves unbound to endorse the views of any paper in city or camp. No existing paper of any name has anything to do with us, or we with them . . . As to the success of our paper, we expect to stand or fall upon its own merits, and not upon the question where we get our type . . . In conclusion . . . however foolishly individual Mormons may act, Mormonism—such as we have learned from boyhood —is a wide and glorious system that claims all arts, all sciences and all literature as its own, and accords to all who in any way promote them thanks, gratitude and honor, so long as they do it honestly."

In No. 2, the masthead becomes E. L. T. Harrison & E. W. Tullidge, Editors. The editorial writings usually covered two pages presented in two wide open-faced columns. Some titles follow: "Not All Dross" by E. W. Tullidge; "Man's Resemblance to Diety," by E. L. T. Harrison; "Jewels of Thought—A Comprehensive Plan" by Brigham Young; "Selections From Joseph Smith"; "When Will Christ Come?" by Amasa Lyman.

In No. 3, November 4, 1864, the leading editorial covering one and a half pages, is on "Mormon and Gentile," signed "H." There is also an article on "The Mormons and the Development of Western America." While the material was mostly fiction and feature articles of the magazine type, the editor frequently quotes from Brigham Young. His pro-Mormon editorials, his notes by the week and so forth, made the magazine a personal organ of the very type and spirit which a little later became the official organ of the New Movement.

While Harrison occupied the bulk of the space, and probably had the bulge on Tullidge in the use of adjectives, sarcasm and other compelling attributes, Tullidge nevertheless had plenty to say. On November 25, 1864, No. 6, this "Notice To Our Subscribers" was run. —"We learn before going to press, that the paper on which this magazine is to be printed, will have to be raised in future, to about one-half as much again as at present. This may cause a delay of a short time in our issue. The public may, however, rely upon our issuing as soon as the difficulty is disposed of. Our future price to subscribers cannot be less than $3 per quarter . . . We publish a paper without advertisements—the 'first so published in Utah. We give more reading matter for the price, than any other paper, and we intend to struggle through on the same principle. Let every friend to our enterprise procure us half a dozen subscribers, and pay their year's subscription in advance, and the thing is a success."

The Deseret News quoted in the Millennial Star November 24, 1874 says of the Peep O' Day: "It was not more than born, when it died. It peeped, and went out." Tullidge in his History of Salt Lake City, says of the Peep O' Day: "It was the first magazine published west of the Missouri River, and was printed at the Vidette Office, Camp Douglas. The financial backers of the Peep O' Day were the Walker Brothers, John Chislett, and Colonel Kahn; but through inexperience, too large an edition was published and several thousand dollars capital was lost in the inception. This occurred at the time of the paper panic in America; paper in Salt Lake City was worth 60 cents a pound, and the stock of the Vidette was no longer able to supply the issues of the Peep O' Day."

Utah Plain Dealer. A copy in the L. D. S. Church Library dated January 9, 1897 is No. 19 of volume 2. Six columns, 4-pages, two local print, two patent. It carries a fine half tone cut of the Negro editor, W. W. Taylor. "Peace if possible; Justice at any rate. Help the Negro industry." Also "The recognized race journal of Utah." It evidently published the "Salt Lake City and Fort Douglas Blue Book and Directory of colored residents, 60c." The Directories list it in 1903-4 with W. W. Taylor, editor; and in 1908-09 with Mrs. L. A. Taylor, publisher. Kenner, in Utah As It Is, 1904 says it was a weekly, Republican.

Anti-Polygamy Standard, Volume 1, No. 1, April, 1880. Monthly, 8-pages, 4 columns, 12 x 18, file three bound volumes in the Salt Lake Public Library. A crusading organ, "Published in the interests of the Ladies' Anti-Polygamy Society." Ostensibly by women, for women, it was openly and in all ways anti-Mormon. Mrs. B. A. M. Froiseth was editor. Mrs. Ann Eliza Young of Battle Creek, Michigan, Agent.

It was well patronized by advertisers, including an advertisement for Mrs. Froiseth's book "The Women of Mormonism." Mrs. A. G. Paddock was a contributor,—she who authored "In the Toils" and "The Fate of Madam LaTour," anti-Mormon books of that day. Incidentally, Lydia E. Pinkham took space regularly! C. C. Goodwin and Wm. Jarman, Anti-Mormon authors, were also contributors. Jarman published a book, "The Mormon Hell Upon Earth."

Numbers 11 and 12 at the end of volume 3, for March and April, 1883, carried the announcement that the fourth volume would begin soon; but the advertising had become very lean, and a great wail went forth from those issues for aid in starting the next volume. It must have been like a "voice crying in the wilderness," for there are no more files.

The Daily Press, bound volume Salt Lake Public Library, beginning as The Real Estate Circular, 4 columns, 4-pages, more than 11 columns of advertising out of the 16! Volume 1, No. 1, Saturday, August 30, 1873, published by J. C. Young and C. P. Huey. Salutatory: "We will state simply and in short that we publish it because we want to!" In the issue of Monday, November 10, 1873, we find this concerning itself: "The Circular drops the 'Real Estate' part of its name with No. 11 and will hereafter be issued on Mondays. The name of J. D. Riter appears in place of C. P. Huey as one of the publishers, and from this time on Mr. R. will devote his time to the paper and the interests of our advertisers."

The next material in the editorial column was a very out-spoken editorial belittling the Tribune's tirades against Brigham Young, pillorying them "as simply rehashes of the old twaddle published in its columns when Mr. Harrison did the grinding." On Saturday evening, May 16, 1874, the name was changed to The Daily Press, which was called Volume 1, No. 1. The file is complete to August 7, 1874 without change of publisher.

"Salutatory: Today we commence publishing daily. We have changed our name only because we think that of Press is more appropriate for a daily paper. We adopted that of Press in preference to any other because newspapers generally are pressed—for green backs! We can make no promises to our numerous patrons and friends any further than that we shall always endeavor to say just what we please, allowing that everybody else has the same right. Our policy: to hit the head that needs hitting. To join Enoch or his grandfather if it pays. To tell the truth, which telegraph lines avoid, and newspapers omit. To be the only live newspaper in Salt Lake City." It carried ten columns of advertising out of a total of sixteen.

The editor not only dabbled in politics, but bandied the subject of Mormonism now and then; and on July 30, 1874 "A thousand copies free. The Press is the acknowledged organ of the Liberal Mormons and Gentiles of Salt Lake County . . . We ask our friends to assist us in this effort to disseminate Campaign Truths." On August 7, 1874 came this "Valedictory.—Today the Press suspends. The Utah Mining Gazette, which is doing our Press work, has sold out, having been forced to the wall for lack of patronage—be it said to the shame of our mining men—leaves us without any facilities to do our printing.

"We will, however, recommence publishing as soon as we can raise the wind. We owe our deep gratitude to all our patrons, and when we again commence publishing we will look for renewed support. Our subscribers who have overpaid the quarter completed with this issue will have what is due them sent to their respective addresses; and those who are owing us, we ask to give our bills their earliest attention."

The Referee. No files. The whole story as we know it is told in brief paragraphs from the contemporaries, starting with Deseret News, January 13, 1885: "In all human probability, the literature of our city will, in the near future, be augmented by the debut of the Referee. A company of five young men signed the articles of agreement the day before yesterday, and some of the matter of the first issue which will probably make its appearance next Saturday (17th) is in type. It will be an illustrated paper, devoted to fun, fashion and amusement. We understand the editorial department will be conducted by Messrs. Jos. C. Rich and S. A. Kenner . . . John Held, a member of the company, will do the engraving."

The Salt Lake Evening Chronicle says, January 20, 1885: "It is rumored that the much *Herald*-ed Referee made its debut yesterday . . . It is hinted that the editors, like Dr. Holmes, did not dare to be as funny as they could in their first issue."

The Chronicle was first to mention the passing of The Referee February 16, 1885: "It is reported that The Referee is already numbered with the dead. The demand for juvenile literature was not great enough to sustain it!" The Referee was "out," however, for only a few months, while first aid was being administered, after which the contest went on, according to the Deseret News, Monday, July 5, 1885: "The Referee came out on Saturday, August 27. The Referee still lives, notwithstanding assertions to the contrary." The Democrat adds, July 9, 1885: "The Referee was awakened from its slumbers on the 4th and made its second advent in glowing colors. It will be devoted to light literature, sporting events, humor and sarcasm, as set forth by Mr. S. A. Kenner, its versatile editor."

The Democrat carries on the story, August 12, 1885: "Fifth number of The Referee, an 8 x 12 sheet filled with bad grammar, worse wood cuts and horrible burlesques on wit, was imposed upon a long suffering public yesterday . . . The Referee is edited by the Shears, New Jersey whiskey and Essay Kaigh." On August 17, 1885 the Democrat further observed: "The Referee has again dropped into the grave of bankruptcy. Poor thing! It was surrounded by the Herald atmosphere, and the contagion was too much for it. *Requiescat sheol*." (It seems to have been printed at the Herald office).

After that consignment to limbo the Democrat man must have had a horrible nightmare before running the following, September 5, 1885: "The Referee is to appear on Wednesday of each week in place of Saturday as heretofore. The new management say they propose to confine the paper hereafter strictly to the news of the day, regardless of the

existing Church and Government affairs in Utah." And then the end did
come for sure!—So far as we know.

Daily Reporter, Volume 1, No. 1, Monday, May 11, 1868, 4 columns,
4-pages, more than half advertising. Published every evening, Sunday
excepted, by S. S. Saul, file complete in L. D. S. Church Library.
"Salutatory.—We have pleasure this evening of laying before the public
our paper, the Salt Lake Daily Reporter. It is printed on the material
of the Vedette, which was suspended some months since and will not
be again revived.

"While the Reporter is both theoretically and practically a new
paper, and in many respects a new enterprise, we trust that it will
successfully and creditably fill the place of the Vedette. Our greatest
efforts will be to make the Reporter a good general newspaper, and
especially a conveyor of local information to the Non-Mormon public.
It is true there are already two newspapers published here, but the
Reporter will reach and represent a class of readers . . . not within the
range of these papers.

"Finally: We start in, a new man in this community, as well as
with a new paper, and consequently have no old scores to rub out or
to get even on and no favors to cancel." With the issue of August 18,
1868, the name S. S. Saul was dropped, and The Reporter Publishing
Company substituted, though Saul remained at its head.

A reference May 29, 1868 says: "S. S. Saul, formerly editor and
publisher of the Alameda County Gazette." The publisher made a
great deal of news out of Masonic Fraternity activities, and while the
Reporter was avowedly Anti-Mormon, it was certainly a gracious gentlemanly newspaper compared to its predecessor. The editor could be
depended on for at least one well rounded, well written editorial on a
non-controversial subject, specimens herewith: Manufactures in the
West; Education in Utah; A shipment of Ores; Utah, a Summer Resort;
The admission of Territories; Who projected the Pacific Railroad;
The Soil of Utah. He occasionally knocked chips off the shoulders of
the Telegraph and the Deseret News, but his attentions were more
sporty than serious. He probably wore gloves, spats, and a tall hat;
and it is certain that he usually wore a smile. His journal was more
specifically for the Non-Mormons, rather than the Anti-Mormons!

On August 19, 1868, this sentence was run: "A company has been
formed for the publication of The Reporter, and hereafter it will be
issued in the name of the company." Indian Difficulties, Railroad matters, Eastern Mails and the like were always interesting subjects to the
editor; and the incurable habit of the telegraph wires failing, was also
a source of news. September 17, 1868: "No dispatches. A line, which
had been out of order, commenced working this afternoon; and just as
we were going to press, furnished us a few sheets of dispatches."

By the autumn of 1868, our editor, whoever he was or had become,
began to say sharper things about the Mormons and Utah institutions;
his culture and kindness began to wear out! His leading editorial, two

columns in length, on October 8, 1868 is "Are we to have a reign of terror in Utah? Is the freedom of speech to be denied, and a free press demolished?" (In which he compares the Reporter to the Nauvoo Expositor which was burned because of rumored threats against "such a paper as the Reporter").

There was no issue from October 10th to October 20th, 1868, when the paper changed to 5 columns, 4-pages of a little larger size. Other editorial headings in October were: Persecution, What Is Our Offense, A Christian (?) Offer, and A Burly Brighamite. In fact at least a half dozen editorials were written under the head Persecution.

This Valedictory appeared December 16, 1868: "Having severed my connection with the Reporter, it is meet . . . to take formal leave of my friends . . . On the 11th of May last, I issued from the office of the late Vedette, the Daily Reporter. It appeared as a 16 column paper and so continued until the 20th of October last, when I added 4 columns, and now leave it a handsome, sprightly little sheet."

"The plain, unvarnished truth is that pecuniary embarrassment caused by the establishment of the Reporter compelled me to withdraw from it. I shall now return to my home in California . . . I take leave of the press of the country with a full appreciation of the courtesy with which the Reporter has been treated, and I regret I cannot include in this paragraph the Reporter's city co-tems. Adieu. S. S. Saul." Obviously many of his advertisements were either complimentaries or exchanges, for the paper certainly looked prosperous.

Saul's successor knew how to go after the Mormons, and how to write at length and ad libitum on many subjects. His editorials were longer and sprinkled with nastier language. The Mormons got the bulk of his editorial attention when lo, the new name appears on the masthead January 6, 1869: "J. H. Beadle, editor." If he wasn't for something with a vengeance, he was against it with the same pressure. On the front page of that number was this masthead: "Salt Lake Daily Reporter, Aulbach, Beadle & Barrett. Adam Aulbach, J. H. Beadle, John Barrett, Publishers and Proprietors. Published every morning, Mondays excepted." But on April 21, 1869 it was changed to Aulbach & Beadle, Publishers and Proprietors, and the name of the paper was changed to the Utah Daily Reporter, and was dated at Corinne, U. T. (q. v.) although a great many Salt Lake advertisements were still carried.

Mr. Beadle had been traveling correspondent for the Reporter though the early part of 1869, writing long letters for publication from various Utah and Wyoming towns on the new Pacific Railroad. Thus after the golden spike was driven May 10, 1869, and through train service established, Mr. Beadle and many others actually thought Corinne would be a coming Utah Metropolis. He had on February 5, 1869 issued a Prospectus for the Weekly Reporter, which appeared Saturday, February 13, thus giving him time to get his breath between blows! In his first Corinne number, April 9, 1869, he says, "The New Dispensation.—Our advice to persons who contemplate fleeing from the tyranny of the Mormon leaders is to go to the new town of Corinne, where they will find entire freedom, religious and political. The surest way to break up the despotism prevailing in Utah is to build up just such a town as Corinne!"

"The first number of the weekly at Corinne will go forth this morning. It comprises all the valuable reading matter of the Daily during the past week." One has the feeling that Beadle, nevertheless, left his heart in Salt Lake City, along with his general interests; for there was sarcastic correspondence by the column from Salt Lake City regularly. And the quarreling between the Telegraph and the Reporter became correspondingly louder so that each might be heard over the greater distance! Stenhouse versus Beadle—both extraordinary writers, whose books on Utah subsequently were widely read.

In his book, Life In Utah, Beadle says: "Early in 1868 Mr. S. S. Saul arrived from California . . . and purchased the remaining material of the Vedette plant (that the Utah Magazine and the Sweetwater Mines had not bought) and on the 11th of May issued the first number of he Salt Lake Reporter daily only. On the 10th of September, 1868 the writer entered Salt Lake City, and on the 19th of October took editorial charge of the Reporter, in which position he continued for 11 months, until September, 1869. On the first of December he joined with Messrs. Aulbach and John Barrett in the purchase of the entire office, which partnership continued for eight months, with real pleasure to the writer, but with little pecuniary profit. A weekly edition was commenced in February, 1869."

The Reporter, Volume 1, No. 1, November 21, 1890—according to Kenner; while January 30, 1892 the Manti Home Sentinel says of this, or another Reporter: "Volume 1, No. 1 of the Reporter reached our exchange table this week. It is devoted to society, drama and music." It is a long time between drinks, at least between the notices of this paper, if not between its appearances. The next we hear is in the Wasatch Wave, September 16, 1898: "C. O. Glanville, former editor of The Wave, is now chief pencil pusher on the Daily Reporter in Salt Lake City."

The Daily Reporter appears in the Directories from 1900 to 1904, in 1900 Peter Myers, J. T. Harris and W. W. Stoddard, sponsoring it, while in 1903 and 1904 Jay T. Harris is president and manager. Kenner, in Utah As It Is, 1904 says: "The Reporter, a hotel and commercial publication, was commenced November 21, 1890, and has issued uninterruptedly since that time." The publication was discontinued a few years later.

The Review Vol. 1, No. 1, August 9, 1871, 8 columns, 4 pages, 26 x 38, $10; every evening except Sunday, F. Kenyon and W. Fenton. "Independent in all things, neutral in none." Anti-Mormon. File, Bancroft Library. Circulation 1872, 1,100. "We this evening lay the first number of the Review before the citizens of Utah Territory . . . Our intention is to make it a first class daily paper . . . Personalities will be avoided as far as possible, and shall restrict all communications within the bounds of respectability.

"Our Corinne subscribers will receive the Review in lieu of the Journal, lately published at that place. Anyone not receiving a copy that may desire to peruse the Liberal Organ, will please communicate the fact to this office." On August 10th we read: "The wide-awake subscribers to the Evening News will of course at once desert it and take the Review.—Tribune. Yes, when the Devil takes his regular bath in Holy Water, and not till then!"

The Review runs this item August 19, 1871, from the Omaha Herald: "The Salt Lake Daily Review is the name of the resurrected Corinne Journal. It contains more venom than vigor, and will probably live a short and unhappy life." The editor says August 16, 1871: "Our friends throughout the mining camps who do not receive the Review, and are entitled to receive the late Corinne Journal, will please notify us at once. The Review is furnished at the same price, yet contains double the amount of reading matter."

This note is from the Nonpareil, August 27, 1871: "F. Kenyon, the able editor of the Corinne Journal, is the editor of the new paper." Also this paragraph is from the Nevada State Journal: "It is the representative of a rapidly growing party in Utah, and started on its mission regardless of the fate of the Valley Tan, Vedette, and Reporter, which preceded it, and have gone up the flume." October 2, 1871: "The Review office has been moved to First South Street, into the building formerly occupied by the Telegraph and Tribune offices."

The Bancroft Library file ends with February 14, 1872—obviously the "Finis," but it didn't say so—most of us do not know when we are going to die! The Tribune says February 16, 1872: "Our evening cotemporary, the Review, did not come to hand yesterday evening. What's up?" The Tribune adds April 18, 1872: "We observe that F. Kenyon, Esquire, late of the Salt Lake Review, has succeeded to the editorial chair of the Ely Record." The Deseret News ends the tale May 7, 1872: "The bankrupt stock of the defunct Salt Lake Review was sold under the hammer this morning, for $1100. Mr. O. G. Sawyer was the purchaser." The Tribune magnifies the same story with "A young newspaper is to be born of the purchase in two or three weeks." The Herald adds another thought to the same story May 9, 1872: "The material of the defunct organ of 'The Ring'—the Salt Lake Review, has been sold."

Utah Scandinav Vol. 1, No. 1, Thursday, October 22, 1874. "The first number of the Utah Scandinav, an anti-Mormon weekly newspaper, was issued in Salt Lake City, in the Danish-Norwegian language. After about three years run, it ceased publication," says Jenson's L. D. S. Church Chronology. The Tribune welcomes it October 23, 1874: "The Utah Scandinav made its appearance yesterday—a spirited 7 column sheet, looking as bright and clean as a star . . . Upwards of 9 columns of good paying ads, certainly form a good leg to stand upon."

The American Newspaper Directory for 1875 adds these items: "Saturdays, independent, 4 pages, 24 x 34, $3, Utah Scandinav Association editors and publishers; the only Scandinavian newspaper published west of Omaha." The Tribune mentions it again Sunday, July 4, 1875: "The Utah Scandinav makes its regular weekly appearance upon our table, having an exceedingly bright and inviting look. This very useful hebdomadal (quiet, Reader; he only means once in 7 days!) was started about eight months ago . . . The publication has been received with favor, and is now on a paying basis." Paying basis! It probably quit while it still was, and could pay its bills!

The Evening Telegram Vol. 1, No. 1, January 30, 1902. No names, no Salutatory. Issued by the Salt Lake Telegram Publishing Company. It was not mentioned by either one of its three contemporaries! Beginning with May 31, 1904, "Elliott Kelly, President and General Manager"—appropriate from the beginning! Again on January 15, 1906, Judge C. C. Goodwin's daily full page of editorials began. Kelly's name was dropped from the masthead without explanation January 27, 1908. Goodwin's huge editorials terminated with Saturday, January 24, 1914.

A new art heading—a spread-eagle title line appeared Monday evening, March 1, 1915, proclaiming through a banner in the eagle's beak; "Utah's Independent Newspaper." From March 1, 1915, the paper was without an editorial page for a time. On March 2, 1915, the Telegram appeared in two separate sections, the first, or front page of the second section being the Home News page, which had previously covered the back or last page of the paper, as was the custom with other Salt Lake Dailies. This two-section plan "clicked" with the public, and soon the other Salt Lake papers followed suit, though the Tribune's local news remains on the last page.

On February 28, 1918, the Telegram announced: "Beginning tomorrow morning, the Salt Lake Telegram takes over the Herald-Republican on a lease, and the two newspapers will be issued from the office of the Telegram as one continuous newspaper . . . This is the most astounding announcement ever made in newspaper annals in the West! It means that henceforth the people of Salt Lake will be provided with the news of the world every evening and every morning from the greatest news sources in America . . ." (Signed) Telegram Publishing Company, George E. Hale, President and General Manager. The new name was variously—Salt Lake Telegram and Salt Lake Herald-Republican; and Salt Lake Telegram—Herald—Republican.

On July 1, 1918, the Herald-Republican name was dropped, and the spread-eagle art heading was restored, without an editorial page, but running an occasional "So The People May Know." On July 21, 1920, came this change: "A. L. Fish, General Manager, Fred Goodcell, Editor;" and on Sunday, July 25, 1920, the first Sunday Telegram appeared. Goodcell's name went off September 13, 1921. The Tribune took over the Telegram September 27, 1930; and on December 7, 1930, the last Sunday Telegram appeared. On January 5, 1931, the Telegram address was changed from 252 Main Street, to 145 Main Street—the Tribune number, continuing to date, A. L. Fish, General Manager. P.S. The Tribune-Telegram moved to 143 South Main Street on July 1, 1938.

  G. B. (Bert) Heal went to the Telegram in July, 1920, as Associate Editor, becoming Editor September 13, 1921. He was taken over by The Tribune February 1, 1927. He was succeeded as Editor of The Telegram by Robert Elliot, and he by Burl Armstrong. Colonel E. Le Roy Bourne succeeded Armstrong in February, 1930, continuing to date, unlisted at the masthead, as have been his predecessors since Goodcell's departure.

  Daily Times "We have received the first number of the Salt Lake Daily Times, (dated December 24, 1875) edited and published by John C. Graham," says the Utah Evening Mail December 27, 1875. "It declares itself to be independent in all things . . . Music and the drama will be encouraged as a specialty." The Tribune merely mentioned it Saturday, June 29, 1876; and the Provo Enquirer lifted an item from it March 3, 1877. Comes then the Deseret News November 29, 1879, with this reference to "Mr. H. L. A. Culmer, of the Times Printing Office."

  The Directory for 1879-80 shows "Salt Lake Times, J. C. Graham & Company;" and the News of February 26, 1880 mentions its "Change of Base.—J. C. Graham and Company, the enterprising firm of job printers and publishers of the Daily Times (moved)." The Times then submerged for a time, appearing again through the Deseret News of October 1, 1883: "We have received the first issue of a new edition to the ranks of Salt Lake Journalism, the Times, a weekly paper published in this city by the Times Publishing Company (J. C. Graham and Company). The new paper will be issued every Monday, and announces its devotion to business, mining, real estate and commercial interests." Sounds like a reincarnation!

  The Ogden Herald mentions it October 4, 1883: "The first number of Vol. 1, the Times, published every Monday, has reached us. It is a well gotten up publication of 12 pages, devoted to the business interests of Utah." Not until June 17, 1889, do we hear of it again, in the Manti Home Sentinel: "The Salt Lake Times has reached us in its new form. It is a very neat 8-page weekly now." And the Provo Enquirer August 30, 1889: "The Salt Lake Times emerges as an evening daily on the first of October. Then the people will see Nichols in his best role, for he is great on daily paper work."

  The Manti Sentinel November 22, 1889 says: "The editorial management of the Salt Lake Evening Times is now under the control of Mr. F. E. Curry. Mr. C. Sun Nichols, former editor, is Business Manager." And the Provo Enquirer adds April 3, 1890: "The Salt Lake Times has enlarged, and is printed to an 8-page paper on a new perfecting press, similar to those used by the Herald and Tribune." The Park City Record of September 6, 1890, refers to "Theodore A. Davis, Proprietor of the Salt Lake Times." And the Provo Enquirer September 11, 1890 says: "Alfred Sorenson, Manager of the Salt Lake Times, has gone to Butte, to edit the Daily Miner."

"The Salt Lake Times has changed ownership," says the Provo Enquirer October 22, 1890, "and the following prominent Liberals are now the stockholders: Frank Pierce, M. K. Parsons, N. Treweek, George N. Ifft, E. W. Critchlow, George A. Lowe, Arthur Brown, C. E. Allen and George Geoghegan." The Home Sentinel of Manti, October 24, 1890, puts it: "The Salt Lake Times has changed hands, that is, instead of T. A. Davis being sole proprietor, he will share that honor with 34 others—all Liberals." The Brigham Bugler says January 10, 1891: "The Times, a radical anti-Mormon paper of growing influence in Salt Lake, is slashing the soulless Tribune."

The file for 1891-92 is in the Salt Lake Public Library; 7 columns, 8 pages; the Times Publishing Company. The editor sticks his neck out January 12, 1891: "The Times was rash enough to correct the English of that relic of barbarism, the Ogden Standard, and for its pains, it receives nothing but abuse! The Standard is incorrigible in grammar, politics, morals and all. It is too old to learn, too stupid to hearken, too vile to appreciate!"

The Denver News February 2, 1891, says: "The Salt Lake Times is about to erect a handsome new building, which is now required by the increasing business and circulation of that bright and enterprising evening newspaper." And the Provo Dispatch, February 24, 1891: "The Salt Lake Times is a sensible paper. It is doing more to bury dead issues in Utah than all the other Gentile papers combined; and so far as this part of its territory is concerned, it is meeting with the popular approval." The Times editor adds: "Which only shows that a paper can be partisan, and yet fair; aggressive and yet decent!"

On May 4, 1891, we read: "The Times has established a special telegraphic service that will add greatly to its news features." Ayer's Newspaper Annual for 1892 gives: Times, evenings except Sunday, Republican, 8 pages, 18 x 24, $8, circulation 2500, Saturday 8 to 12 pages, $1.50, Times Publishing Company. October 6, 1891: "The Weekly Times will be issued Thursday, October 13 . . . at the low rate of $1.50 per year." No name appeared on the masthead, but on Saturday, April 30, 1892, we find:

"Ring Out The Old, Ring In The New! On Monday morning, Mr. A. L. Pollock will take charge of the Times under a two-year lease, an option on a majority interest. With this issue of the paper, the present management lays down the Faber and covers over the paste-pot! We do so not without regret . . . Mr. Pollock, who will on Monday assume the duties of editor-in-chief, is a thorough newspaper man . . . well known in Salt Lake City." Consequently, on May 2, the masthead shows A. L. Pollock, lessee.

Another change occurred, however, on August 12, 1892: "William E. Smyth, editor, L. R. Britton, Business Manager, A. L. Pollock, lessee," also this statement: "The Times is Republican in its editorial columns, but in the news columns it is unprejudiced and non-partisan." And November 17, 1892: "The Times comes out of the campaign with a magnificent growth of circulation . . . The Times has won great popularity!" But the election was over—and so was the Times! The last issue in the files was dated November 18, 1892; all names were dropped from the masthead, and there was no mention of any expected demise, but the Manti Times Reporter of December 1, 1892, is the voice from the Great Beyond: "The Salt Lake Times has suspended publication. The cause is easily told: The field was covered by other papers!"

The Daily Telegraph, Volume 1, No. 1, Monday, July 4, 1864. T. B. H. Stenhouse, Proprietor and Editor. File, Salt Lake Public Library; some volumes in L. D. S. Church Library and Tribune-Telegram Library. "A journalistic foil to the Vedette was deemed necessary in the city, and Mr. T. B. H. Stenhouse projected the Salt Lake Telegraph," says E. W. Tullidge in his History of Salt Lake City. Also, the Deseret News had frequently referred to the need for a strictly *news*paper, while Stenhouse was working for the News. "Published every morning except Sunday; $10 a year; office opposite the Theater;" about 60-62 East First South Street.

Page 1 was completely filled with business and professional advertising cards, column-width. In the second number, July 5, was this borrowed "Correction.—We presumed that the Prospectus for the Daily Telegraph published in the News on the 15th inst. was sufficiently plain, but we are informed that some have an idea that the proposed Telegraph is to have some connection with the News. This is a mistake, for the Telegraph, as plainly stated in its Prospectus, is altogether a personal enterprise of Mr. Stenhouse, and has nothing whatever to do with the News or News office business."—From the Deseret News, June 29, 1864.

"We are under obligations for the distinctness of the 'Correction' but we cannot permit the opportunity that it presents to pass without acknowledging that we are much indebted to the Proprietor of the News for the accommodations in the use of press, types, etcetera, without which the daily Telegraph could not have made so early an appearance."

There was some telegraphic news, but mostly quoting eastern papers on the progress of the War; also fairly good local news, including one item picked up from the editor's window: "Run-a-way.— Yesterday morning the Salt Lake and Camp Douglas Stage and several passengers were considerably injured by the stampeding of the horses. It occurred opposite the Theater, and was a fine exhibition of lofty and ground tumbling!"

The News says of the Telegraph, July 6, 1864: ". . . On the whole a very tasteful appearance and promising to be both profitable and useful." There were editorials on theatricals, gold standard, the war, morals and religion, apparently supporting the Church; overland mails, emigrant travel, Indian troubles, and the like. There were interests enough to keep the editor minding his own business.

Eastern dispatches were not always available, for example, July 12, 1864 "Nothing was received yesterday over the wires. 'Storm east of Laramie'. We should be obliged if storms would visit less frequently the eastern line." And, Monday, July 18, 1864. — "There was no communication over the eastern line 'till late on Saturday evening. In consequence of a break from accident near the city. The abundance of telegrams since and their general interest force us again to omit other matters." Also, July 26, 1864: "No telegrams were received yesterday from the east. The Indians are 'ugly' below Laramie." Again Friday, July 29, 1864: "Our readers should be pleased this morning with the abundance of telegraphic news. We would prefer more moderate doses!"

On Tuesday, September 6, 1864, the Telegraph was enlarged to 5 columns and this editorial was run: "A few weeks ago we telegraphed to New York for the type necessary for this enlarged edition of the Daily Telegraph. The Indians thought proper to commence their tragic amusements on the direct overland route; the pale faces got terribly frightened; the mail and express stopped, and we failed to get our type. We then telegraphed to San Francisco for some and thought we could be supplied sufficiently early to commence early in a new dress, but 'Providence willed it otherwise', and we are therefore this morning, in our new form, without the new dress we anticipated."

Joining the News, the Telegraph on Monday, September 12, 1864, called for "Rags, Paper. We ask the attention of every housekeeper in the Territory to the advertisement of Mr. Findley, calling for rags . . . President Young brought from the States three years ago a paper mill capable of making all the paper necessary for the use of the Territory. It is a fine piece of machinery and for the quality of its performance we point with some degree of pleasure to the paper on which the Telegraph is published . . . We have not been supplied without some labor on the part of Mr. George Goddard, Mr. Levi Stewart, and Mr. Chas. Robinson, gentlemen whose names are prominently associated with paper and the paper mill.

"In order that there may be an abundance of paper for us all, we respectfully urge upon good housewives and well trained young maidens to be specially careful with the rags. Preserve them and sell them to those who purchase either at your own homes, here, or at the paper mill. We are anxious to have all the rags that can be secured in time to make paper before the frosts of winter close the mill, and shall be obliged to all who help us. Finally we wish it understood that though we are anxious to get all the paper we can for our Daily and for other projects in our programme, we shall not be pleased to receive any such assistance at the expense of any other paper . . ."

Wednesday morning, September 14, 1864: "The wire is still down and we are a second day without dispatches. We regret the frequent interruptions on the Eastern Line, but our regrets have nothing of that accusative asserity so commonly exhibited by some portions of the press towards the specific telegraphic company." The Vedette editor did complain frequently, bitterly—and the army came, ostensibly to guard the Overland Telegraph Line!

Again we read: "We are informed . . . that for the last five months scarcely have 24 hours passed away without a storm somewhere on the plains between this city and Omaha, and terrific thunderstorms were daily occurrences along the banks of the Platte River. But the destruction of poles and the bursting of instruments by the lightning, though of frequent occurrence, were nothing like the evils endured from the actions of malicious and thoughtless emigrants who seemed to consider nothing but the facility of finding the camp firewood from the telegraph line. To replace these poles sometimes a distance of fifty miles had to be traversed by the repairers. On one occasion this season the line was down for three days, from the rather cool attempt of some emigrants to serve themselves with the wire for a ferry cable across the Platte River.

"The Indians, fortunately, have been superstitious concerning the wire; but there are apprehensions that some pale faces among them are instilling into them courage enough to handle it freely. At one time they cut the line in little pieces on the South Pass for a quarter of a mile. At another time they cut it near Willow Springs, and carried off about 150 feet of it for bridle bits and ornaments. Very recently they burned the poles for a short distance near Cottonwood Springs, and at another time cut the line in six or seven places between Laramie and Scottsbluffs . . . The offices range from 35 to 65 miles apart, at which horses are kept in constant readiness to carry off repairers to any scene of disasters. We are indebted to Mr. Ellsworth, the Superintendent of the line between this and Laramie for the facts in the foregoing . . ."

On October 6, 1864 subscription rates rose from $10 to $16. The semi-weekly began Monday, October 10, 1864. Stenhouse was plenty big enough to spread himself over both the large Daily and Semi-Weekly. Thus, sometimes the advertising almost blotted out the news. He tells us Wednesday, October 26, 1864: "This morning's paper is printed in our new building on First South Temple Street, half a block west of Jenning's Emporium. We have now commodious premises built expressly for us, where all business connected with daily and semi-weekly Telegraph will hereafter be transacted." (The offices in which the Mormon Tribune was started.)

We learn what the editor did in his spare time from this, Tuesday, November 22, 1864: "Notice.—The post office has been removed to the first floor of the Daily Telegraph Building, west of meat market . . . T. B. H. Stenhouse, Postmaster." Friday morning, November 25, 1864: "Wood and Coal.—Big piles of wood and heavy loads of coal are in East Temple Street every day now. The possessors are afraid of the coming snows and want to sell off. Two or three companies are now forming in the city for the purpose of rushing in the firing as soon as sleighs can be used.

"Bye-the-bye—You folks at Coalville who have got the Telegraph, please bring in the coal you promised, at your earliest convenience. We require it. We are watching a few gentlemen—not at Coalville—on the subject of promises to pay. Some day they will have a heavy dose. All we ask is for folks to honor their promises—we ask no more."

Saturday morning, November 26, 1864: "The day is bleak and cold, Local is shivering before the expiring embers. He hears the whining tale for the twentieth time: Who in July last was to pay his cord of wood for the Telegraph, but who had a fresh excuse of balderdash every time he was dunned, and now that the wood is three prices, would fain pay the greenbacks and put $20 in his pockets. *Local* is an honorable man, sees through him, is annoyed, and indignation warming proportionately with his pedestals, he looks to *Editor*, 'Shall I give him a dig?'—'Not yet'. *Cash*. 'There is some coal promised from the east! Good we shall ask for it—'Coalville, send on that coal'. The morrow comes; Spriggs . . . innocent of everybody's wishes, announces a fine load of coal on subscription at former rates. 'Spriggs, you are a gentlemen, sir, a scholar and a poet sir . . .' "

No complaining of other papers, no references to them—not even the Vedette. December 24, 1864: "Some friends have wondered that we had not told our readers that the Daily and Semi-weekly Telegraphs are printed on the Valley Tan Press! If we live long enough we will see greater and more marvelous transformations than that . . ."

From the Daily Union Vedette, Saturday morning, January 20, 1866: "A split among the Mormons! Ye Telegraph Editor (The Federal Postmaster of Salt Lake who shortly after taking the oath of office to support the Constitution and laws of the United States, took to himself a 'second wife' in violation of his oath) speaks thus anonymously of some other paper, per adventure of his master's organ, The Deseret News: 'The Institution was brought forth in falsehood, lives upon it, and will perish with it'; and he adds, apparently in boldness, as if his bread and butter rations would be curtailed by the split: 'Any person not satisfied can have back his subscription money'. Satisfied with what? Doubtless his dissatisfaction with his late master's News." It must have irritated the Vedette to have said so much about the Telegraph and gotten so little mention in return.

Saturday morning, July 21, 1865: "In accordance with a generally expressed regret, we have concluded to deliver a paper on Sunday morning instead of Monday." $16 per annum. There was always room for Theatrical and home entertainment news. More and still more news of Indian troubles on the overland route. Mails, Indians and freight. Irrigation and livestock news are played up; Cattle stealing; forming an irrigation company. One could write a book on the overland stage and telegraph lines from the news in these papers. Indian fights are news items, whether in Arizona, Montana, Wyoming or Nebraska. The editor was not prone to rush into the editorial column—frequently left out.

March 17, 1865: "For some days we have had no telegrams and now they are rushing upon us. For them everything else has to be left out." (Except the omnipresent ads). On March 23, 1865: "There is a famine for telegraph news again. The wires have been out of order again for days beyond Omaha—high waters or something else." Eagle Emporium—Wm. Jennings, Proprietor, was the first to break out of the one column advertising fence with a standing advertisement of three column width in March, 1865.

On May 18, 1865: "A rush of telegrams. For some days we were famishing for want of lightning messages; today everything else has to be set aside to give them place. We do not like the style, but we have no choice."

On Sunday, June 4, 1865, the editor soliloquizes: "The Daily Telegraph has entered upon the last month of its first volume . . . The Telegraph, small as it is, engages in the bookkeeping, editorial, composing, printing, carrying and traveling departments, in all 16 persons, and every line of the writing of the original matter, excepting occasional correspondence and the composition of all is paid for. As regards the line of policy we have pursued, we have endeavored to treat all persons with courtesy and where a contrary spirit has been manifested towards us, we have treated it according to its deserts—with silent contempt, and we have the satisfaction of knowing that our course has been very generally approved . . ."

June 21, 1865: "The operator at Sweetwater Bridge, accompanied by eight soldiers, went east this morning to repair the line. They were attacked by Indians and the Operator, Mr. Quinn and one soldier were killed. The line is down again." Again on July 9, 1865: "The Wires.— After a fortnight's silence the wires have again spoken and we are favored with a bit of ancient news about as modern as the mail would have brought us in the ordinary course of things when Indians and whites are on tolerable terms of neighborship . . ."

July 21, 1865: "After a long spell of silence, the wires have again spoken, and this time with a garrulity altogether unprecedented. The dispatches came upon us like an avalanche; and like the man with his elephant, we hardly knew with our limited space what to do with them . . ."

December 6, 1865: "To meet the increased demand for the Telegraph, combined with the requisitions made on us for job work and to release our editorial and business offices from the overcrowding consequent upon the influx of business, we have added a spacious and well lighted new press room to our establishment, where we have in full blast one of Digener's admirably rapid job presses . . . and where also will be found our new Railway Power Press, imported this season, upon which our daily and semi-weekly editions are now being printed. These presses—with the addition of a Roe's Washington Press heretofore used for the Telegraph—will enable us to meet an increase in subscriptions . . ."

December 12, 1865: "We draw the attention of our subscribers . . . to the permanent enlargement of the Semi-weekly Telegraph. It is now the largest sheet published in the Territory . . ." December 30, 1865: "Workingmen who wish to subscribe for the Daily or Semi-weekly Telegraph in this city for the ensuing year, can—during the first week in January—pay for either paper in labor tithing orders."

A masthead change occurred on January 9, 1867: Add T. G. Webber, Business Manager, and John B. Mabin, General Agent. On November 13, 1867 the paper was published on Wednesday morning; no issue the 14th. Changed to evening Friday the 15th. No explanation.

The Frontier Index compliments the Salt Lake Telegraph, April 28, 1868: "Talk of western papers and mountain news, but for general intelligence and matters of universal interest, no paper published in the west can outdo the Telegraph . . . The Telegraph articles are clear, sound, logical and racy. There is no editor of our reputed acquaintance that can excel Mr. S. as a lucid and a fluent writer. We admire his independence and sagacity, to say nothing of his energy and strength of mind . . . Frontier Index."

Out of respect to Heber C. Kimball, June 23, 1868: "From the Editor.—The following telegram dated Cheyenne, Dakota, was received near midnight yesterday from the editor of the Telegraph: 'Drape the Telegraph until the funeral services of President Kimball are over to manifest that we mourn the death of a great man in Israel . . . Let my son, Serge, attend, representing his absent and afflicted father'. No paper tomorrow, in order that the employees of the Telegraph may have opportunity to attend the obsequies . . ."

On September 1, 1868 the paper was enlarged to 8 columns with a longer page and the title was changed to Salt Lake Daily Telegraph and Commercial Advertiser . . . "In order to meet the increase of business that is rushing upon us from home and abroad." There were 25 columns of advertising out of a total of 32 columns. (a princely patronage).

The editor lifts this item on October 2, 1868 from the Reese River Reveille of September 25th: "We had the pleasure of a visit at our office this morning from Mr. T. B. H. Stenhouse, well known as the proprietor and editor of the S. L. Telegraph . . . Mr. Stenhouse has resided in the city of Salt Lake for nine years and his position as editor of the chief paper, devoted to the interests of the Mormon Church and society should render his exposition of those interests valuable. He is a pleasant gentleman . . ."

December 31, 1868: "Will Remain.—For some days past a rumor has been current that the Telegraph establishment was about to remove, soul and body, from this city to Ogden, and many regrets were consequently expressed by friends of the paper that such a movement should occur . . . We take pleasure in assuring our numerous friends and patrons that the Telegraph will continue to be published in this city as usual, with the addition of a weekly edition of the paper commencing next Thursday. Salt Lake City is our place of residence, our home. and we are identified and bound up with its fortunes . . . We propose to commence the publication of a daily newspaper at Ogden as soon as we can get the type and the material there in running order, which will be in a very short time."

Beginning September 2, 1868, this paragraph was placed permanently on the masthead: "The Telegraph is the Pioneer Daily paper in the Territory, has a large circulation in the city and in the settlements, has its subscribers in the mining camps and cities of Colorado, Wyoming, Nevada, Idaho, Montana and Arizona, California, Oregon and in the principal cities of the East. As a popular paper and commercial advertiser in Utah and the mountains, it stands unrivaled."

The American Newspaper Directory for 1869 says of the Telegraph: "Every evening except Sunday, Semi-Weekly, (Mondays and Thursdays), and Weekly; four pages, weekly, eight pages; subscription, daily $10, semi-weekly $7, weekly $5."

Wednesday evening, January 6, 1869: "The Salt Lake Weekly Telegraph's first regular number will be published tomorrow. This will be the largest weekly newspaper published in the Territory . . . Price per year only $5.00—one half year, $3.00." January 9, 1869: "All gone.—So great was the demand for the first number of the weekly Telegraph that a very large edition was all gobbled up in thirty six hours." April 10, 1869: "To Correspondents.—During the absence of Mr. Stenhouse to the East, a large number of letters requiring his personal attention have been left unanswered until his return . . ."

April 24, 1869: "The Telegraph.—In consequence of the decision of the Union Pacific-Central Pacific Railroad Company to locate the junction terminal of the two roads at Ogden or its immediate vicinity and of the recently changed commercial condition of this city, we have determined to move the office of the Salt Lake Telegraph from this city to Ogden, although we do it with some regrets. Everybody is now convinced that Ogden will be the great city of the Great Basin, the commercial center of this and surrounding Territories and States . . . While by our removal of the Telegraph to Ogden, we shall obtain a largely increased circulation in the thriving north, in which direction all eyes are now turned and on the various cities of the line of railroad east and west, we are satisfied that we shall also secure a larger list of paying subscribers in this city and vicinity and in the southern parts of the Territory than we ever have had . . .

"We expect to discontinue the publication of the Telegraph in this city next week, to forthwith remove the material thereof to Ogden, and to issue the paper there as early as possible thereafter. We shall retain our present job office and book bindery in this city, and in addition it is our intention to publish daily the Salt Lake Theatre Program

. . . (distributed gratuitously). To our present prepaid subscribers, the Telegraph will be sent by mail every morning."

There are twenty columns of advertisements in that issue, out of a total of 32—apparently an immense supporting patronage to walk away from! (If it was "real"!) The Deseret News says April 26, 1869 (Monday).—"We notice by Saturday's issue of the Daily Telegraph, that its course in this city is finished, but only to again shortly appear at Ogden, which its editor regards as the future 'Commercial center of this and the surrounding Territory'. We sincerely hope that his fullest anticipations will be realized."

The editor announces Tuesday evening, April 27, 1869: "Salt Lake Telegraph.—After we recommence publication of the Telegraph at Ogden we shall forward the paper by mail to our prepaid subscribers outside of that city. The Telegraph will reach this city within a few hours after its publication in Ogden, and probably within an hour after the few months required for the building of the branch railroad between that city and this. Our subscribers to the semi-weekly and weekly Telegraph will also receive those papers by mail as usual . . .

"We go, we go. This is the last number of the Telegraph which we expect to issue from this city. Tomorrow we shall begin to remove the necessary material of the establishment to Ogden, whence we expect to resume the publication of the paper as early as we conveniently can, and we shall endeavor to occupy no more time than necessary in removing, refitting and getting ready for regular publication, daily, semi-weekly, and weekly at our new headquarters.

"The Telegraph has been a diurnal visitant to the homes of our citizens for the past five years. It enjoys the distinction of being the first daily newspaper published in this city, (He evidently assumes Fort Douglas is not Salt Lake City). Ever devoted to the best interests of the people it has met with a flattering degree of popularity and support which naturally enough induces much regret on our part as well as on that of our friends that circumstances should render it advisable to remove our office of publication from this city to Ogden.

"It is now generally conceded that Ogden will be the principal commercial city in the Territory, owing to the influence of the railroad and consequently the best point for the publication of the leading commercial newspaper in the Rocky Mountains. With our removal there, we shall strive as a matter of course to build up that city. We shall expect to see it rise out of the mud, lengthen its cords, strengthen its stakes, and put on its beautiful garments as scripture says . . . Notwithstanding all this, we shall still regard this city with peculiar affection. It has been the place of our residence so many years. It was the birthplace of The Telegraph. We have here many friends, and we shall continue to maintain here a Publishing Job Office.

"Furthermore, Salt Lake City is the capital of the Territory. It is also the headquarters of the Church or of Mormonism, as the world will have it, and it will ever be the great point of attraction and interest to tourists and visitors from all parts of the world. In these respects, it will continue to be the principal place in the Territory, and in the Rocky Mountain region. If we had our unbiased wish, we should continue to make this city our place of abode and of labor. But it should be remembered that Zion must expand and grow. It cannot be forever limited to one brief spot of earth. Her sons must go forth from the paternal roof tree and build up cities . . . And how can they do it without live newspapers to entertain, instruct and encourage them?"

The Telegraph went to Ogden early in May to give the city a fair trial. By June 15, 1869 there were 26 columns of advertising out of a total of 32. However, the Editor gives up on Wednesday, July 28, 1869: "To Our Patrons.—Circumstances having rendered it advisable to remove the Telegraph back to Salt Lake City, its issue in Ogden will cease with the present number. The reasons for this change have been well considered and are of sufficient importance to fully justify it. Our patrons in this city who have subscribed for the paper will be furnished with it until the term of their subscription expires, as soon as we recommence publication in Salt Lake City. We shall ever take a warm interest in Ogden and its prosperity, and solicit from our friends here a combination of their efforts in behalf of the Telegraph. Agents and others will oblige by publicly announcing the above change."

August 17, 1869 was the next issue, and bore the Salt Lake City date line. Tuesday, November 16, 1869: "A Contradiction.—Several papers east and west have been commenting freely on the alleged defection of the editor of the Telegraph from Mormonism, and his opposition to President Young. We had no thought of noticing the matter . . . But as we find that papers of reputation give credit to it and republish it, we think it time to give the allegation a flat and emphatic contradiction. The files of the Telegraph can be examined from the first issue to the present number, and will show that the course of the editor has ever been to sustain the authorities of the Church and their declared policy."

December 3, 1869 "Gone East.—T. B. H. Stenhouse, Esq. Proprietor of the Telegraph left for the East by yesterday morning's stage." (Incidentally, Mr. Stenhouse "went west" March 7, 1882—died in San Francisco).

On December 22, 1869, the last number in the file, makes no mention of discontinuance. The Millennial Star of February 1, 1870 says: "The Salt Lake Telegraph suspended publication 'temporarily' January 3, 1870." And the Corinne Reporter January 6, 1870 says: "Gone Up.—Our very unworthy contemporary, the Salt Lake Telegraph, has 'passed in its checks'. In other words, has failed, suspended, busted, repudiated its contracts, defrauded its creditors, and taken refuge in that oblivion it so richly deserved,—The Past . . . The Telegraph has long been considered a dead beat." Thus we see, as someone has said, it was Stenhouse's luck to be criticized by the Gentiles and exiled by the Mormons! But the Deseret News says, Monday, March 7, 1870: "The Daily Telegraph.—The Salt Lake Daily Telegraph, M. A. Fuller,

Esq., Editor and Proprietor, today makes its appearance. It has long been favorably known to the public of this territory, and though it has changed hands, as a co-laborer in Zion's cause, we wish it every success."

The Mormon Tribune adds its story March 12, 1870: "The Daily Telegraph.—This well and favorably known paper was reissued on the 7th inst. . . . The Telegraph makes its re-appearance under circumstances, in many respects, much more advantageous than those under which its former enterprising proprietor, T. B. H. Stenhouse, Esq., commenced it and established its reputation; and if Mr. Fuller can steer successfully through the present 'hard times' he may reasonably expect a prosperous future."

The American Newspaper Directory for 1870 says: "Every morning except Sunday, and weekly on Wednesdays; daily, 4-pages, 25 x 37, weekly 8-pages, 28 x 42, daily $8.00, weekly $4.00, M. A. Fuller, editor and publisher. Circulation, daily 1,000; weekly 3,000." Sorry, but we seem to have missed the Telegraph's "second death." L. S. Hills, writing July 26, 1870, in the Millennial Star, says: "The Telegraph has about petered out. It has not been published for some time, and the fixtures are advertised for sale by the U. S. Marshal for debt."

"Mormon Tribune, organ of the Liberal Cause in Utah, devoted to mental liberty, social development, and spiritual progress. Volume 1, Number 1, January 1, 1870. Published every Saturday, $5 per year, currency. Eli B. Kelsey, Advertising and Business Manager; Daniel Camomile, general canvassing agent. Godbe & Harrison, publisher, E. L. T. Harrison, general editor, E. W. Tullidge, assistant editor and W. H. Shearman, assistant editor."

In a feature article on "The Tribunes of The People," Eli B. Kelsey concludes: "In a word the *Tribunes were the defenders of the people.*" "Salutatory . . . less than one year ago the last volume of the Utah Magazine commenced its career . . . A new era has opened upon Zion and prophetic voices are crying to her: 'Arise! Shine! For thy light has come!' To assist her in this great mission, we humbly dedicate the pages of the Mormon Tribune.

"On the occasion of the first issue of the Tribune, it is well that we should re-state our case that the points of issue between us and the ecclesiastical rulers of Utah may be clearly understood. One of the first objects of the Movement is to oppose the undue exercise of priestly authority . . . As we have a considerable number of subscribers to the Mormon Tribune who did not take the Utah Magazine and who consequently may not be aware of the circumstances which have led to the publication of this paper, we present a brief outline of the history of the New Movement . . . The Utah Magazine was published and edited by the publishers and editor of the present paper (who) believing that a newspaper would be a more appropriate medium than a magazine for the expression of their views, and better adapted for general circulation, propose in a few weeks to suspend the publication of the Utah Magazine and publish a large weekly newspaper," according to the Prospectus distributed earlier.

In a "Letter to the Deseret News" which it declined to publish, from W. H. Shearman (in which he states in part) "That Brother Godbe was not influenced to his course by the love of money . . . In obedience to what he believed to be the will of Heaven, he has, as one of the publishers of the Utah Magazine, sunk over $10,000 in sustaining that periodical for the sole benefit of the people of this Territory. He did this with a clear understanding beforehand of the pecuniary loss he would sustain. And now, when there is every probability that the successor of the Utah Magazine—the Mormon Tribune—will eventually become a paying institution, both he and Brother Harrison, still assuming most of the expense and labor necessary to make it a success, voluntarily announce that they will lay the results of their labor at the feet of the New Movement as the property of the people!"

For some time it was more—much more—a propaganda or New Movement organ than a newspaper, although each number did contain a little news. Through the late winter and spring months of 1870 its news service did not expand, nor did its space or fervor diminish in championing the New Movement. One wonders, in looking over the files, if any Movement was ever so weak as to require as much booming as the New Movement got in the columns of the Mormon Tribune! Gradually, however, articles on mines and industries of the State were given space.

"With this the eighteenth number of the Tribune (April 30, 1870) we complete the number of Tribunes due to those who subscribed to the Utah Magazine, Volume 3 for one year". . . The first semi-annual conference of the New Movement and the deliberations of the executives were duly covered in full through several subsequent issues. Thus it will be observed that the Mormon Tribune was far from an Anti-Mormon paper, yet occupying the paradoxical position of aiming to destroy and supplant all other so-called Mormon authorities. It was a religious paper, in fact, throughout; hence the following expression uttered May 7, 1870 concerning:

"The Utah Reporter.—We are glad to notice an improvement in the tone of our contemporary at Corinne . . . The various papers which have been started in this Territory in opposition to what they regard as the errors of Mormonism would have had more influence and success, had their language been more dignified and their tone less bitter . . . We are warring against what we conceive to be wrong principles; but in so doing we do not wish to be regarded as enemies to any people, whether they believe as we do or not!"

Add to the masthead F. T. Perris, general advertising and business agent, and on May 7, 1870: "To Our Friends and Patrons.—Elder Eli B. Kelsey has for some weeks been afflicted with a bodily complaint which has entirely disqualified him for the various and arduous labors devolving upon him . . . He finds however, that repose of body and mind are absolutely essential to his speedy restoration to health, and has decided to retire for a few weeks to his home in Tooele . . . Brother Kelsey has therefore felt it necessary to resign for the present his connection with the Tribune as business manager, and Brother F. T. Perris has kindly consented to act for a few months . . ."

"The Utah Magazine and Mormon Tribune . . . The Mormon Tribune is the people's organ and is sustained by voluntary contribution. The income derived from its publication does not near pay its expenses at present and the burden of its support has hitherto been chiefly borne by a few individuals. Let no one suppose that because we are thus plain in our statements of the financial condition of the Tribune, that it is at all in danger of suspension, as some have hoped and reported. The gentlemen connected with it are pledged to continue its publication until the last vestige of despotism is swept from our Territory.

"Our friends should remember that the Utah Magazine paved the way for the development of those mineral resources which already inspire the minds of our citizens with hope and give promise of speedy financial relief and prosperity. They should also bear in mind that the publishers of this paper have been sacrificed in behalf of the workingmen of this Territory; that they were cut off the Church, turned over to the buffetings of Satan, denounced as the vilest of men, and every effort made to ruin them temporally as they were supposed to be spiritually, for the *terrible crime* of advocating the cause of the laboring classes."

"Valedictory (June 4, 1870).—With this number of the Tribune ends my labor as one of its associate editors . . . I go to cooperate with Neil Warner in the production of the play 'Oliver Cromwell', for which he is bound by contract to pay me for its purchase the sum of $10,000. I also anticipate bringing out my plays of 'Elizabeth' and 'Napoleon'. . . Occasionally I shall doubtless contribute to the Tribune. I pray God's blessing on my dear compeers . . ."—Edward W. Tullidge, whose name was dropped from the masthead in the next issue, June 11, 1870.

(Mr. Tullidge died in Salt Lake City, May 21, 1894, age 65 years. An Englishman by birth, he came to Utah a Mormon convert, but was excommunicated with several other prominent members on October 25, 1869, as a result of his connection with the Utah Magazine, and the socalled Reform Movement in the Church. He was an able writer, and his works occupy a prominent place in Utah literature. In addition to his editorial connection with the Peep O' Day, Utah Magazine, and the Mormon Tribune, he published the Life of Brigham Young in 1876, The Women of Mormondom in 1877, and The Life of Joseph The Prophet, later, which went into its second, revised edition with leanings toward the Reorganized L. D. S. Church, in 1880. Tullidge's Quarterly Magazine of history and literature ran from 1880 to 1884. His best work was The History of Salt Lake City and Her Founders, partly in the Quarterly, and in full as a book in 1886. The Western Galaxy, 4 numbers in 1888, was a purely literary Journal. His History of Northern

Utah appeared in 1889. Tullidge also had some histrionic ability, and wrote several plays that were fairly well received. The widow and five children survived.)

Mormon-Tribune—"Change of Title (June 18, 1870). With No. 27 of this journal—being the first number of our new half yearly volume as a newspaper—we propose to change the title of our journal to that of the Salt Lake Tribune. We consider this title will be less sectional, and more appropriate for the representative paper of a universalian movement . . . The word 'Tribune' means 'the representative of the peoples' rights'." Kenner said later, "The word 'Mormon' was dropped from the title, as well as from friendly consideration!" Accordingly on July 2, 1870, Vol. 2, No. 27:

"Salt Lake Tribune: Organ of the Liberal Cause in Utah, devoted to mental liberty, social development, spiritual progress, published every Saturday by Godbe & Harrison." A change in the masthead occurred October 29, 1870; Shearman's name was dropped, and C. W. Crouch became Managing Editor. In that issue this notice was run, dated October 22: "To The Readers Of The Tribune.—It is now about one year since I identified myself with the Reform, or Zion Movement . . . Last fall I offered my services 'till spring. When spring arrived . . . at their earnest solicitations (Godbe and Harrison), I consented to labor in the editorial department a few months longer . . . I desire it to be understood however, that in withdrawing my name from all official connection with the Tribune, I do not withdraw my interest in it . . . I heartily pray: 'God Bless the Tribune, the editors who write for it, the printers who work upon it, those who read it, and all who labor for its success.—W. H. Shearman'."

Crouch begins meekly enough November 12, 1870. "Retirement Of Our Managing Editor: The Orthodox Body have long said that the publishers of the Tribune were no better than they should be; and at the present moment, we feel as if there was more truth than sentiment, in the assertion!" The advertising patronage through November diminished, and by the 19th only one page remained, coming back to two pages at the close. The last issue of the weekly Tribune was dated December 10, 1870. The American Newspaper Directory for that year says of it; "Saturdays, 8 pages, 28 x 42, $5, E. L. T. Harrison, Editor-in-Chief, Godbe and Harrison, publishers, claims 2000 circulation."

"Salt Lake Daily Tribune and Utah Mining Gazette, Vol. 1, No. 1, Salt Lake City, U. T. Saturday morning, April 15, 1871." 7 columns, 4 pages, one-half advertising. Masthead: "The Daily Tribune; W. S. Godbe, W. H. Shearman, E. L. T. Harrison, O. G. Sawyer and Associates. The Tribune Publishing Company, W. H. Shearman, Business Manager. The Salt Lake Daily and Weekly Tribune are the only newspapers published in Salt Lake City, independent of Church control. The Tribune was the pioneer of the present mineral development."

"Publisher's Notice. — The publishers are happy to inform the public that the columns of the Daily Tribune will be under the editorial supervision of Oscar G. Sawyer, Esquire, late of the New York Herald. Mr. Sawyer has been for over 10 years connected with the New York press." "To The Public: The type intended for the publication of this journal not having arrived, and being unwilling to keep our subscribers longer without it, we have concluded to suspend our weekly for a short time, and publish with such type as we have on hand, sooner than subject the people and ourselves to any further delay . . . This first number of the Daily Tribune issued herewith is sent free of cost to our weekly subscribers, with the hope that they will lend it around to their friends for perusal and forward such subscriptions as they can obtain."

"Our Program.—The Daily Tribune will be a purely secular journal devoted entirely to the presentation of news and to the development of the mineral and commercial interests of the Territory. It will have no sectarian bias, and will be the organ of no religious body whatever. The aim of the publishers will be to make it a Newspaper in every sense of the word . . . The Tribune will be a complete record of mineral facts and statistics, the determination of the publishers being to make it the great mineral paper of the Territory."

"On political and social questions the policy of the paper will be to sustain the Governmental institutions of the country. It will oppose all ecclesiastical interference in civil or legislative matters, and advocate the exercise of a free ballot by the abolition of 'numbered tickets'. . . As a journal the Tribune will know no such distinctions as 'Mormon' or 'Gentile'."

"Editorial Valedictory April 16, 1871: After a period of over three years of arduous editorial toil, with two years of it without a single day's release for rest or recuperation, my health and pressing duties in other departments of the Reform Cause, require that I should have at least an intermission of the closer duties of the sanctum. Having had the gratification of seeing the Weekly Tribune maintain its ground until its popularity and permanence have become settled questions, and having had the further satisfaction of seeing the Daily Tribune to the birth, with every indication of a prosperous future before it, it gives me great pleasure to leave these journals in the hands of their respective editors, and confine my future duties towards them to that of a contributor. The next issue of the Weekly Tribune will be under the supervision of Mr. W. H. Shearman, whose past labors on that journal . . ."—E. L. T. Harrison.

"The 'policies' of the Weekly.—(April 26, 1871) We stated that the Daily Tribune was 'entirely disconnected from the old Weekly and its policies'. What we meant was of course, that as a journal, we were disconnected from its religious and philosophical policies, as indeed we are equally from those of all other parties . . . As all who have read it well know, the Weekly is not simply a religious or more properly speaking, a philosophical organ. It includes all reforms within its scope. We hope that a few days will see it again in the field, working to the same great ends."

The Tribune adds its prayer May 20, 1871: "During our suspension, besides the Daily Tribune, another Daily, the Corinne Journal, has sprung up . , . its only bias being toward Republicanism . . . We devoutly trust we are approaching the grand finale of 'Blood and Thunder', whether in public speeches or the newspaper press of Utah. Nothing is to be gained, but on the contrary, liberty itself is jeopardized by tolerating abusive and threatening language." However, Harrison dropped out, along with his policies, we are to learn.

The Prospectus of "New Daily Paper, The Daily Tribune and Utah Mining Gazette" was first run December 24, 1870, and on May 20, 1871, "Out Again.—For a brief period the Weekly Tribune has been suspended, which as the exponent of the secular policies of the Reform Cause, is now gaining ground every day . . . With a Daily, a Weekly in full blast, and the handsomest Hall in Salt Lake at their control, the Great Cause of political, social and intellectual freedom never looked brighter." The masthead was changed to show E. L. T. Harrison, Editor, W. S. Godbe, Eli B. Kelsey, E. W. Tullidge and F. T. Perris, Corresponding Editors. On May 24, 1871, F. T. Perris became Assistant Business Manager.

On July 25, 1871, the Herald gives us this news item: "The Tribune establishment has moved into the new building recently erected for it on the east side of East Temple Street (between South Temple and First South Streets), ("No. 34"; now No. 33 or 35.), on the site of the old Western Union Telegraph Office. The exterior of the new building presents a fine, handsome appearance, a most desirable addition to the block."

November 18, 1871: "Policy of the Tribune.—As some misunderstanding exists in the minds of the few as to the true spirit and policy of the directors of this journal, we publish the following from their minutes for the information of all interested: Resolved that the daily Tribune shall be conducted as a free, liberal, independent high-toned secular newspaper, devoted to the interests of the entire people of Utah; strong in the support of right, and fearless in exposing wrong; that its columns be open to the public for a free discussion of all questions pertaining to the Territory; that it support so far as consistent with right, a government and its officers, but that it be free to reprove and condemn these when wrong, as well as to criticize the acts of all public men.

"Resolved that it be not the organ of any person, party or sect, religious, political or otherwise, nor that it attack any person, party or sect as such. Resolved that it regard the majority of the Mormon community as an honest but misguided people and that in discussing any question in which they are interested, it be done in moderation and kindness and not in the spirit of attack. Resolved that the daily Tribune shall not express any opinion as to the guilt or innocence of any persons accused of crime until such cases are decided by the Courts . . . The Tribune ignores the hateful distinction of Mormon and Gentile and claims to be solely an American paper . . ."

On March 23, 1872, the Weekly was clearly the companion of the Daily in spirit and in fact, but without a name on the masthead, and containing few editorials of the old Gospel type. Most of the editorials, like the news stories, were lifted bodily from the daily issues. The subtitle "And Utah Mining Gazette" was omitted Monday morning, April 15, 1872, and henceforth.

By August 3, 1872, the advertising patronage became so very poor —7 columns of advertisements out of a 48-column newspaper, 3 columns being patent medicines—one wonders why they ran it, but one does not wonder why no one wanted his name on the editorial masthead! It was in 1872 that J. Bonwick in his book The Mormons And The Silver Mines, said: "The Tribune is the radical fault finder with the Saints and their headship . . . There is spirit, and there is spite about its utterances."

The American Newspaper Directory for 1872 says the circulation was about, daily 1,000, weekly 1,600. This announcement was run Sunday morning, July 27, 1873: "The Tribune.—In accordance with the announcement made in the Tribune of Thursday, we have taken charge of its editorial and business management . . . We have come to Utah to make our permanent home." (But forgot to print his name!)

"Sunday Edition.—The Tribune will hereafter be published on Sunday morning, instead of Monday, as heretofore, and it will at the same time give the attaches of the office an opportunity of properly observing the Sabbath by refraining from work on that day."

"Daily and Semi-Weekly. Notice To Subscribers Of Weekly Tribune. The Directors of the Tribune Printing and Publishing Company beg to inform their subscribers and the public at large, that in consequence of arrangements lately effected for the transfer of their weekly paper to the superintendence of Mr. E. L. T. Harrison, its publication under its present form and title, will cease with the present number. The next issue of this paper, which will be on Saturday next, will be under the title of The Leader, (q.v.) which will be edited and directed by Mr. Harrison. It will be of the same size and price as the Weekly Tribune."

The following is from The Leader, but published in the Tribune October 14, 1873: "Owing to the fact of his having been one of the original projectors of the Salt Lake Tribune, the undersigned has been held responsible in the public mind for the utterances of the present daily paper . . . Within the past few months, the management of the Daily Tribune, as a financial experiment, has been placed in the hands of the present managers, with the understanding that they were to conduct it in consonance with views of the Directors of the company. So far, however, as the writer is concerned, that agreement has not been carried out . . . But as it happens that they write over or under the name of The Tribune Publishing Company, of which he is a member, his sanction is virtually assumed. He will therefore, as a Director of the company, say that they are none of his choosing, while they are in many respects in opposition to his long expressed views from press and platform."—E. L. T. Harrison. After that article, we noticed the Tribune stopped borrowing from the Leader!

The Tribune was a little "high-hatty" at times with the country press, and on December 11, 1873 observes: "Several of the little Mormon papers published in the outskirts, seem to find a peculiar pleasure in barking at the heels of the Tribune." The following news item appeared July 15, 1874: "The Tribune Office has been removed to Second South Street, nearly opposite the foot of Commercial, on the south side of the street."

The Evanston Wyoming Daily Age tells us August 29, 1874, "What enterprise will do.—The Salt Lake Tribune is an instance of what enterprise can and will do. When the present management, Messrs. Hamilton, Prescott and Lockley (took hold), it was truthfully on its last legs. It had long before ceased paying running expenses, and instead, assessments were levied to keep the paper above water. The paper now has a respectable circulation among the liberal Mormons, notwithstanding the heavy blows it is dealing the Mormons of the Church, and denouncing in unmeasured terms the action of the Mormon rulers."

The Tribune may have let go of the New Movement, but if it was thought by anyone that it cuddled up to the Church, these editorial headings might be noted through 1874: An Indiscreet Liar (Herald); Is Brigham Young Insane; Non-Intercourse With Mormons; The Truth Is Not In Them; Brigham Commands Non-Intercourse With Gentiles; Backed Down At Last; The Prophet On His Haunches; Brigham Young Backing Down On Enoch; The Gentile Revelation; Enoch In Provo; Brigham's Failures; United Order Of Euchre; The Poland Bill; The Herald Aghast; Unsound Teaching; Marriage In Utah; Convincing Them Of Their Error; Bamboozling The Heathen; The Lord's Bookkeeper; A Little Of The Creed; The Curse Of Utah, et cetera, et cetera.

"The Corinne Mail says of us (July 2, 1875), 'The Tribune, with all its bitterness, has not said things as severe as the contemptuous utterings of the whole Mormon press'. That's because we don't understand the Deseret alphabet, which is the only thing containing words mean enough to do the matter justice!" The American Newspaper Directory for 1875 adds these data: "Every Morning Except Monday, and Weekly Saturdays; Daily 4 pages, Weekly 8 pages, 28 x 42; Daily $10, Weekly $4, Tribune Publishing Company, circulation, Daily 2,425; Weekly 3,033."

Incidentally, another Tribune appeared for a day; according to the Millennial Star February 19, 1877, borrowing the item from the Salt Lake Herald: "On the morning of November 8th, a new Democratic paper called The Tribune, made its appearance here; but after one issue, subsided, lest it should give offense to someone. Salt Lake City is evidently entitled to the Champion's Belt, as the journalistic extinguisher!"

An extraordinary rich mine of information, or misinformation, according to viewpoint, connected with the political, religious and industrial history of those stirring 1870's, appears in the Tribune. Its pages presented not only the editor's own vigorous views and the outpourings of his reporters, but dozens of persons grasped the vitriolic pen of power, and had ample space accorded them, in the Tribune. For example, the trial of John D. Lee produced many scores of columns on Lee and the Mountain Meadows: No wonder enough was gleaned from its pages, for several books!

The editor tells us July 3, 1877: "Circulation of the Daily Tribune is 4200. It is double that of the combined Mormon press of the Territory, and is constantly increasing. It has a national reputation, by reason of its fearless fight in behalf of the priest-ridden people of Utah, and will undoubtedly double in circulation in the next twelve months." In those days there were no Independents; they were either Mormon or Gentile, and were very positive about it. They had to be; there was no middle ground, for the two forces were very squarely against each other—if we believe all we read in the papers!

Editor Lockley, speaking of the latter part of his term on the Tribune, 1874-1879 says, "the office was over the Walker Brothers department store, corner of Main and Second South streets, West." Oddly enough the Tribune letterheads were printed "1222-1226 West Second South" meaning 22-26, as given in the directories for 1884 and 1887. The 1879-80 directory had showed it without number but at the same address: "North side Second South, between East and West Temple."

The Provo Enquirer May 26, 1880: "Judge C. C. Goodwin, late of the Virginia Enterprise, has assumed editorial charge of the Salt Lake Tribune." "We learn that a fifth interest in the Salt Lake Tribune was sold a few days ago, to O. J. Hollister, for the sum of $10,500 in cash, from J. R. Schupbach," says the Park Mining Record, April 22, 1882. A news item says "The Tribune passed to P. H. Lannan and C. C. Goodwin, September 9, 1883." Colonel Hollister, who owned a one-third interest, declined to sell. And on Saturday, October 27th, 1883, we gather from the Salt Lake Chronicle, "A Bit Of History.—It is announced that Fred Lockley, the former well known and able editor-in-chief of the Salt Lake Tribune, but latterly occupying the same position on the Inter-Mountain of Butte, Montana, is intending to lecture in the East, with Mormonism as his subject. We know of no one more competent for the task. Mr. Lockley was present at the trial and conviction of John D. Lee."

A valued contributor is given due credit in the Chronicle, November 22, 1884: "Mr. Joseph Lippman, for the past year local editor of the Tribune, resigned his position effective tomorrow. Mr. Lippman has done good work for the Tribune. He has worked harder, and gathered more news than any other one man ever connected with that paper. He is temporarily succeeded by J. C. Young, telegraph editor. Mr. Lippman will spend the winter in New Orleans."

Describing one way of gathering "news items," the Salt Lake Evening Democrat, August 3, 1885 says: "Over a dozen local items in Saturday's Democrat were stolen and transferred to yesterday morning's Tribune! What was it the Latin Editor of that paper got off about 'Verbum Sap'?" The Democrat hails a great event April 29, 1886: "The News and Tribune Agree! — That worthless dogs should be killed!" The Provo Enquirer gives the editor a left-handed compliment April 30, 1886: "C. C. Goodwin, editor of the Salt Lake edition of the Police Gazette, otherwise known as the Tribune." On Wednesday morning, August 20, 1890, the Masthead showed C. C. Goodwin, Editor, P. H. Lannan, Manager, the Tribune Publishing Company. The 1890 Directory gives the Tribune address "80 West Second South street," but in 1891 it was 133 South West Temple. Some of the Tribune's clashes struck fire, it is evident from this in the Park Record, October 31, 1891: "Jesse B. Barton's suit for damages against the Tribune Publishing Company for libel, has taken a new lease of life lately."

Also August 3, 1892: "Colonel Nelson, Manager of the Salt Lake Tribune, has been bound over to await the action of the grand jury on the charge of libel." Another left-handed compliment comes from the Manti Times-Reporter December 8, 1892: "Editorial Jots.—And still the Tribune is fighting the Civil War over! We remember hearing Frank Cannon remark, that the Tribune was like an old hag—blind and deaf, mumbling and grumbling, praying for the dawn, when the sun was already shining brightly!" Add, left-handed compliments, from the Park Record of September 16, 1899, quoting the Salina Press: "The Salt Lake Tribune and the Deseret News are covered with War Paint, and are making the welkin ring with their savage cries. They are still pounding away at the same old pile of straw, and indulging in choice expletives. It all helps to sell the respective papers, and so long as the ink-bespattered editors do not resort to dynamite to score a point, the country is safe!"

On Saturday morning, October 19, 1901, the masthead was changed to show Perry S. Heath, publisher and general manager. The day before, this story had appeared: "With this issue of the Salt Lake Tribune, its stock, good will, franchises, machinery, clientele and all its appurtenances pass from the control of its former owners, into the hands of a new management . . . To Mr. P. H. Lannan, who retires after a service covering a period of many years, it bids good speed! . . . To Judge C. C. Goodwin, who retires as editor, whose trenchant pen has given the Tribune a reputation second to no newspaper in the West, nothing we can say can add lustre to a fame so firmly established in the State and community he has served so well. . . ."

"The foregoing explains itself. The men who have been in control of the Tribune for the past 19 years (are leaving). There is not much more to say, except that no self-reproaches are mingled with this parting. With the lights that have been given them, the old managers have performed their work with such ability as they could command, and without ever deviating from what they believed was duty. . .

"In the days of the panic and the hard times, the Tribune, through its friends, was the only paper that paid expenses between the Missouri

River and San Francisco; and today it is more prosperous than it ever has been in its career.

"The memory of those true men and women (friends) is the sweetest one that the managers carry away. Some of the past was very dark. To live in a community, knowing that thousands look upon one as an enemy is a little hard to bear; to live knowing that thousands are praying that misfortune may come to one, is not especially pleasant to that one; but it can be borne if the thought behind the worker is that to those and the children of those who hate and revile, there will be more light and joy, when the night shall be passed and the new morning which is to be, shall dawn."

It was evidently Judge Goodwin speaking. He died August 25, 1920, after a long term of years as Editor of Goodwin's Weekly. He was the Author of The Comstock Club (1891), The Wedge of Gold (1894), and As I Remember Them (1913), books of considerable literary merit. He published The Virginia City (Nev.) Territorial Enterprise 1874-1880 and attracted nation-wide attention as Editor of The Salt Lake Tribune, becoming probably the paper's most noted spokesman. The Tribune moved to 145 Main street, early in 1907, and on July 1, 1938 to 143 Main street.

Taking unto itself a partner, if not an helpmeet, the annual edition for Sunday, December 31, 1911, was titled: The Salt Lake Tribune and Evening Telegram. The sworn ownership and circulation statements first required by the Government, October 5, 1913, show: "Editor Wm. Nelson; Managing Editor, F. P. Gallagher; General Manager, A. N. McKay. Owners, Thomas Kearns, David Keith." In October, 1919 the Kearns Corporation purchased the Keith interests.

Colonel Nelson had served as associate editor for a time with Judge Goodwin. During the flare-up of the Anti-Mormon fight, when the American Party was born in Salt Lake City in 1904, ex-U. S. Senator Frank J. Cannon became associate editor under Colonel Nelson for the period of the Campaign. Of statuesque build,—a handsome face, heavy curly hair which fit him like a halo; an engaging voice, with an extraordinary vocabulary; a remarkable gift of oratory, and a flair for the spectacular, Frank J. Cannon was the William Jennings Bryan of the West! He became Utah's first full term U. S. Senator, (1896) and rounded out his truly meteoric career as Editor of the Rocky Mountain News in Denver, where he died.

Frank P. Gallagher succeeded Colonel Nelson as Editor, but was himself shortly succeeded by E. H. Holden, with the Tribune since 1911 as Telegraph Editor and editorial writer. Holden retired early in 1930, being succeeded by G. B. Heal, who had been managing editor since February 1, 1927. Holden died June 23, 1931. Mr. Heal has continued Editor in chief to date, with Noble Warrum, associate editor since 1934. The masthead has been without a name since Colonel Nelson's day, following the practice of most metropolitan newspapers.

After the Heath regime the names of the owners and managers have likewise been omitted from the editorial page, and changes in personnel were not always considered to be news; consequently only vague memories are available, of Joseph Lippman becoming manager about 1904-5 and Frank I. Sefrit from about 1905 to December, 1910. A. N. McKay took over the management of The Tribune January 1, 1911, continuing to his death, November 18, 1924. Homer F. Robinson, who entered the Tribune's services in 1882, and was business manager under Mr. McKay, succeeded Mr. McKay as General Manager in 1924. J. F. Fitzpatrick represents the Kearns Corporation, as publisher.

Out of the clamor of the crusading press of the heart-sickening Seventies, and the heart-aching Eighties in Utah, there was bound to come a tranquil day of peace and prosperity among newspaper men. And out of that journalistic carnage there was sure to come those that were first to hail the New Dawn, and introduce the New Way to run a newspaper, with policies involving the Golden Rule of human relations. Clearly the latter-day editors, managers, and owners of the Tribune have been keen to perceive, that neither today's news stories, nor tomorrow's fortunes or institutions, are builded so much out of a people's hates and fears and fights and failures, as out of their hopes, their joys, their plans and their successes.

The following figures are presented to show how a typical, well managed metropolitan newspaper can literally outgrow the country. From one daily Tribune, for about every six persons, the circulation density has increased to more than one paper for every three persons in Salt Lake City; and the Sunday Tribune circulation has increased from one paper for every sixty persons in Utah, to about one for every seven. Of course several "Dailies," and a great many "Sundays" go outside the State; but there is one Sunday Tribune sold in its territory for every 1.6 persons in Salt Lake City!

NET PAID CIRCULATION—SALT LAKE TRIBUNE

Year	POPULATION		Daily	Sunday	Persons in Salt Lake City For Every Daily Trib.	Persons in Utah For Every Sun.Trib.
	Salt Lake City	Utah				
1871	12,854	86,786	1,000	1,600*	12.85	54.24
1875			2,425	3,033*		
1880	20,768	143,963	3,200	3,500*	6.49	41.13
1885			5,000	3,000*		
1890	44,843	210,779	6,500	(3,250)*	6.90	64.54
1895			8,000	3,500*		
1900	53,531	276,749	9,128	13,362	5.86	20.71
1905			11,060	16,038		
1910	92,777	373,351	15,975	22,783	5.81	16.34
1915			15,946	35,892		
1920	118,110	449,396	34,909	65,061	3.39	6.91
1925			42,146	68,928		
1930	140,367	507,847	50,763	70,934	2.77	7.16
1935			51,615	73,998		
1938	(150,000)	(532,000)	57,500	92,300	2.61	5.76

* Weekly; No Sunday Edition.

Union Vedette, Volume 1, Number 1, Camp Douglas, near G. S. L. City, U. T., Friday, November 20, 1863, "Published weekly by officers and enlisted men of the California Volunteers." File, Salt Lake Public Library; several volumes in L. D. S. Church Library. Seventy Five cents a month, 4 columns, 4-pages, 11 x 15. On page 3 was this "Correction: Since our first page went to press, it has been deemed advisable to remodel our rates of advertising and subscription. Subscription, 50c a month, advertising, $30 a column (instead of $15)." (The only advertisement run was a 3-inch "Camp Douglas Theatre").

Salutatory: "We are dwelling in the heart of an organized Territory of the U. S. boasting a population of 80,000 souls who possess but one general newspaper from which to gather news . . . This fact . . . has no parallel within the boundaries of the U. S. Secondly, the Gentile (so called) portion of the community—including the military within this district—has no medium of publicity, setting forth its opinions, or communicating its thoughts, correcting mis-apprehension or rebutting misrepresentation . . . The want of a press for these and similar purposes has been sorely felt, since the troops arrived in these valleys, and we propose to supply the want, so far as our ability and limited space will permit."

". . . While as soldiers we came not to make war on this people, neither in this enterprise is it our design to intrude upon their everyday life . . . We have begun our enterprise in the best of feeling, trusting and believing that our language will not be distorted into aught that savors of threat or unkindness, but as the friendly voice of those who seek the good and the prosperity of every man, woman and child in Utah, who have not voluntarily placed themselves beyond the pale of charity and friendship.

"Concerning ourselves.—. . . The Vedette is not designed for a money making institution, and will be published whether it pays or not. We are vain enough to believe that we can do good, extend information, and give pleasure to a large number of readers. Our paper will furnish the means of recreation to our soldiers and our columns contain the effusions of many a facile pen . . . We hope to receive sufficient patronage to repay the absolute outlay required to meet current expenses; but whether we do or not, the Vedette is a fixed fact . . . The editorial columns will be controlled by officers whose aim will be to instruct and please . . .

"We ask an indulgence by our readers for the apparent typography in some portions of our paper. It is not our fault. Some of the fonts of type were put up without a full complement of 'sorts' and we have been obliged 'to turn' in order to supply the deficiency. The difficulty will be obviated by a fresh supply as soon as the type can be forwarded from San Francisco."

The paper contained some official orders, circulars, and notices issued by General Connor, some theatrical and mineral notes and several clippings, but no local news. In the issue for November 27th was an editorial on the "Mines of Utah" and "A Word to Our Farmers"; also some unsigned communications and an advertising professional card, "Dentistry, Dr. Wm. H. Groves, late of San Francisco, California, Surgeon and mechanical Dentist." (Founder of Dr. Wm. H. Groves L. D. S. Hospital).

December 4, 1863: "We present today as the first of the series special telegrams from San Francisco, made up by an agent expressly for the Vedette . . . An interesting and reliable summary of California, events of the preceding week . . . No exertion will be spared on our part to make the Vedette interesting, as well to the soldiers as to the people of Utah. We are gratified at the result of our undertaking . . . Our subscription list is fast rolling up to goodly proportions. Our special thanks are due to our friends at Fort Bridger who have done nobly in the way of subscriptions. We hope other posts in the Territory will send in their subscriptions at an early day . . . Let the people of Utah swell the list; no effort will be left untried to make the Vedette a welcome and instructive visitor to every fireside. . ."

December 25, 1863: "We propose on Monday next, or as soon thereafter as practicable to begin the issue of a daily newspaper from this office . . . The Daily will be entirely distinct from the Weekly and the publication of the latter will be continued as usual . . ." January 1, 1864: ". . . We spell the name Vedette and therein follow both Webster and Worcester." A subsequent editor also explains, August 7, 1865: "The French word Vedette, according to Webster is thus defined: 'A sentinel on horseback; a dragoon or horseman stationed on the outpost of an army to watch an enemy and give notice of danger'." January 14, 1864, publication day of week changed. On December 11, 1863, subtitle changed: "A champion brave, alert and strong, to aid the right, oppose the wrong . . ."

The following refers to Mr. Woolley, a Utah Legislator: "He found the Daily Vedette on his desk long before the telegrams from the other office made their appearance. This morning, as usual, he found the little visitor . . . The House was waiting the slow action of the public printer in order to act intelligently on this bill, but the Vedette laid it before them, printed in full, on clear white paper and in creditable style. He (Mr. Woolley) commended the energy and enterprise of the proprietors of the Vedette and referring to another paper published in Salt Lake City, gave notice that unless greater promptness was shown on its part, he would on Monday next, move to transfer the public printing to the Daily Vedette, printed at Camp Douglas! . . ."

Daily Vedette, January 5, 1864, Tuesday morning, Volume 1, Number 1, 3 columns, 9 x 14 (about).—"We present today the first number of the Daily Vedette, and propose to continue it hereafter with regularity. The delay in issuing has been occasioned by not having received paper sufficient to insure regularity of issue . . . We propose to print the daily telegrams from the East and from the West . . . with such local or foreign matter as will prove interesting to our readers . . . The *Daily* will be entirely separate and distinct from the Weekly, and the latter will not be made up of matter published in the Daily."

While there was a full legislature report, there was news, nearly all of it being telegraphic. January 8, 1864: (The Weekly Vedette) "On account of the non-receipt of our paper from California, we are sorry to announce to our subscribers that we are obliged to suspend the Weekly Vedette which is due this morning. The stormy weather which has delayed the coaches is, of course, beyond our control. We used our best endeavors to get the paper through in time but succeeded in getting only a sufficient amount to issue the Daily, which does not require so much, not having the large circulation that has the Weekly . . . We have decided hereafter to issue the Weekly upon Thursday, instead of Friday, hoping by this change that our mail subscribers will receive their papers with greater regularity than heretofore. . ."

No names appear on the Masthead, but from December 4, 1863, "Mr. Ed Pennington is our authorized agent for the transaction of business in Salt Lake City, office U. S. Quartermaster's storehouse, Main Street." (In spite of advertising patronage being confined almost exclusively to Salt Lake City professional businessmen and houses, there is very little Salt Lake news).

January 22, 1864: "In consequence of the non-arrival of our expected supply of paper we were unable to issue the Weekly Vedette yesterday and are compelled to suspend the Daily for three or four days. We deem this a suitable time to announce to our patrons that we propose to discontinue the Weekly altogether hereafter for the following reasons: We find that a large majority of our subscribers are transferring their subscription from the Weekly to the Daily, seeming to prefer the Daily because it contains all the telegraphic and local news, which it is impossible for us with our limited supply of type, small press, and the scarcity of printers, to furnish in the Weekly, and as we do not propose to compete with large first class offices . . . we think we can give better satisfaction by discontinuing the Weekly and making the Daily more worthy of patronage than it is now . . . We propose in a few days to enlarge the Daily to nearly the former size of the Weekly . . . We have a very limited amount of paper on hand, and that our subscribers may not be without the telegraphic news, extras will be issued to supply their demands until more paper arrives."

Wednesday morning, January 27, 1864, the name was changed to "Daily Union Vedette" and enlarged to 4 columns, about 11 x 15. On February 4, 1864 the story is told that: "A man came into a printing office to beg a paper. 'Because', said he, 'we like to read newspapers very much, but our neighbors are all too stingy to take one'! Some of the neighbors here take the Vedette—from the doorsteps of others."

There was column after column of letters and editorials, complaints, counter complaints, and explanations, concerning non-receipt of newspapers and poor mail service during the winter of 1863-64.

February 29, 1864: "No paper will be issued from this office tomorrow. In consequence of the demands of the public service upon our printers and those engaged in the office for Muster and Review on the last day of each month, we find that it will be impossible for us to issue a paper on the first and last days of each month."

Certainly there was not much news from Salt Lake City or its people, though city advertising patronage was rather generous. There was always a smattering of Fort news and plenty to say about the winter weather! "The officers and enlisted men of this command, for whose benefit this paper was first commenced, will be pleased to know that upon striking a balance sheet of its operations, the result has been found highly satisfactory," the editor says March 30, 1864. "It will be remembered that we commenced this publication as a Weekly; but as it seemed utterly inadequate to the wants of such a community as that of Salt Lake City alone, not to speak of the entire Territory, and the country dependent thereon, we determined promptly to face the risk by publishing the Vedette as a daily paper.

"It will be borne, however, carefully in mind that the paper was not started, is not carried on, and will not be continued for the sake of gain, but for the more noble and glorious purpose of issuing in this community an organ devoted to the Union, as against Native Secessionists and foreign ill wishers . . . as well as for the further purpose of giving to every individual in the Territory or elsewhere a full opportunity of bringing before the community whatever he may deem desirable for his own interests or those of the public; and we are exceedingly misinformed if there be elsewhere any place where the English language is spoken in which such an organ is more needed."

Attempting to explain the dearth of Salt Lake City news items April 4, 1864: "The quest for items.—A search for locals in this 'Saintly Burg' is, of all sublunary pursuits, the most hopeless; and when said quest is undertaken of a Sunday, the results are infinitesimal! For six days of the week the place looks like Sunday anywhere else; and if we except the stream of people tending towards the Tabernacle and homeward twice a day on Sunday, one might imagine the population dead or the city abandoned! A murder or an execution may indeed occur once in awhile, but the steady stream of genuine locals to be found in any other place of half the population is not here to be found. A runaway would on yesterday (Sunday) have been a Godsend!"

A column editorial was run on The Mines in Utah, April 5, 1864, complaining of efforts to suppress the news of important discoveries. Other editorials about this time were: The Teachings of The Tabernacle; Polygamy and Laws Relating Thereto; Is Young Joe Smith a Polygamist?

On Tuesday morning, May 31, 1864 the editor reports: "A visit from Major Bowman, Assistant Inspector General on General Wright's Staff, caused all hands in the office to appear for inspection on Sunday, and as a consequence, since men cannot be in two places at once, they were not in the office, and Monday's paper could not be gotten out. We cannot tell when a similar event may again take place, but have simply to state that whenever it does, there will be no paper issued by the present hands."

"June 11, 1864.—As it is made evident to us from time to time that the object and purpose of our paper are to a considerable extent misunderstood, we propose fairly and squarely to explain the stand we have taken. The reason why we do this is because some people do not seem capable of comprehending the fact that a journal such as The Vedette can be other than an experiment, instituted with a view to making money, and to be dropped, should it appear that the money is not forthcoming.

"This paper was established and has been conducted as to its typographical execution and otherwise, by soldiers—men thoroughly competent in their business, who can command at any time in California at that business the highest ruling prices, who have shown by volunteering at $13 a month that a higher object than mere pecuniary advantage has influenced them, and they all deem as intelligent men, that short of active service in the field (from which circumstances and not their own will will debar them) they cannot better subserve the cause of their country than by thus devoting their time, talent, and energy to the objects above set forth, viz. the propagation of loyal sentiment and the development of a regenerated Utah!

"Our paper is extensively patronized and still more extensively read in the Territory. Understand then, once for all, ye of the rabid persuasion, that you spite not us; suit yourselves in withdrawing your support from the Vedette. This is our stand and the object of our paper. We are successful in it, and not being a Firm, gotten up with a money making view, we can afford to publish the Vedette until all our objects shall have been accomplished. After the accomplishment of which desirable result, we may or may not as suits ourselves, continue the Vedette; but with the publication until that time, nothing that you can do will in the smallest degree interfere. We are above patronage and independent of every consideration, but the consciousness of pursuing faithfully a just and noble cause." (Was he implying the Government was paying the bills?)

"We received on Tuesday (14th) an installment of our supply of paper, consisting of 144 reams (Vedette size)," the editor announces June 16, 1864, "and there are now on the road as per invoices received from the shippers, over 400 reams of the same size of paper. This does not look much like abandoning our post or discontinuing the Vedette. We publish the fact for the information and edification of those who have from the first so kindly predicted for us a discontinuance to be caused, doubtless, by the want of their patronage!"

Mr. L. W. A. Cole succeeds Mr. Pennington on July 25, 1864 as authorized business agent. But "We this day (July 5, 1864) enter upon the second volume of the Daily Vedette. That our views in regard to the increasing demand for the current intelligence of the day, as well as touching the want of a medium of communication with the public, were correct, is sufficiently evidenced by the patent fact of our own success, and by the further fact that where we at first met only the slurs and sneers of the *deadweights* of the community, we now find imitators; and with the honor of being the first daily paper established in the Territory, we claim and deserve the further credit of having started and given an impetus to the demand for information in an almost stagnant community."

July 8, 1864 "A Hint.—We wish to state broadly and explicitly that the office of the Vedette is no place for any man who has not immediate and important business *connected with the paper* to transact with the editor, and that it is no place for such persons one moment after such business is transacted! We had hoped that the cold shoulder, so evidently shown by the editor to all such visitors, might have been sufficient to prevent a repetition of their visits; but as such has not been the case, we make this public announcement, which, if it shall not prove effectual, will be followed in due course by such a tirade of the King's English as will ring in the deafest side of the head of every such 'bore', for there is no other name for the man, who, without urgent business, will enter an editorial room on any other pretext!" (Take that, you snooper!).

"Arrival of New Press and Material, September 16, 1864.—We are very happy to announce to the public the arrival of a new press, and a fresh and large supply of type and other printing material for the Vedette office. In due time we shall enlarge the paper." The editor eats a small piece of humble pie, October 26, 1864: "We are under obligations to the publishers of the Deseret News for their generous loan of news ink until our supply arrives." (That seems to be the first time "Deseret News" was spelled out in the Vedette).

The following is the first mention of the editor's name, and it appeared November 30, 1864 in The Denver News, Personal.—"We had the pleasure today of a call from Captain C. H. Hempstead of Brigadier General Connor's Staff, who arrived here with the General. The Captain, in addition to his military duties at Camp Douglas, Salt Lake City, has been editing and publishing The Vedette, a live and spicy daily paper there for over a year past. The Vedette newspaper has always been a welcome visitor to our office, and its gentlemanly editor was much more so."

In the News for December 5th and 6th, 1864 were long letters signed "H" and entitled Editorial Correspondence, describing the travels of the editor. He evidently travelled far and near, for on December 21, 1864 is this "Valedictory.—With this issue the undersigned relinquishes editorial control of the Daily Union Vedette. For a long time it has been apparent that the pressure of other duties would necessitate this course. He finds that it borders on the impossible, and reaches the impracticable to attempt to edit a Daily paper at a distance of three miles from the place of publication . . . He turns over the editorial conduct of the paper to able and zealous hands and bids them Godspeed in the glorious work.—Chas. H. Hempstead." Three miles? The paper was still dated at Camp Douglas. Some of the numbers, at that, may have been the more safely printed beyond the "three-mile limit!"

The new Salutatory appeared December 22, 1864: "We are instructed by the proprietors, and but express the unanimous sense of all connected with the Vedette, when we return thanks to our predecessor for his past editorial labors. The Vedette was the offspring of his vigorous intellect, and was nourished into life and strength by his unremitting attentions. All regret that he leaves its sanctum. For ourselves we have very little to say. We recognize that the true mission of the Vedette is to combat heresies which oppress the people of Utah, and to be the chronicler of the times in which we live." Incidentally, the bound file of The Vedette in the Salt Lake Public Library was presented by Captain Hempstead.

Editorials continued on such subjects as The Union Cause in The War; The Indian Problem; Polygamy; The Gold Standard; Mines and Mining; The Peep O' Day; Mormonism As We Find It; Who Are The Persecuted; Victims of Polygamy; Opposing the Mormon Church; Sacred To The Memory of Valley Tan; Utah's Mournful Record; The Book of Mormon Versus Polygamy; Beauties of Polygamy; Polygamy and More Polygamy; and The Cause of The Union, Again and Again. (That is where the "Union" originates, in the name "Union Vedette").

The new editor is glad to say, January 19, 1865: "It is evident from the sermon delivered by Elder John Taylor in the Tabernacle last Sunday that the polygamists are becoming constant readers of The Vedette." As indicating the paper's popularity the editor says May 6, 1865: "Some of our city subscribers are complaining that their Vedettes are taken without leave from their doors in the morning. Wonder if it could possibly be some curious Mormon who is forbidden to subscribe for it under the penalty of being cut off from the Mormon (Holy) Church."

The editor misses a cog, and June 3, 1865 says: "We respectfully beg the indulgence of our readers for the unavoidable omission of an issue of the Vedette on Monday next. On Tuesday, June 6, our paper will be issued with double its present size. Its columns will be filled daily. We intend to make it in every sense the newspaper of the plains! On June 6, 1865 the Vedette page was increased to 6 columns, about 13 x 21; the date line was also changed to Great Salt Lake City, U. T., the masthead showing "The Daily Union Vedette, published every morning, Sundays excepted at Salt Lake City, Utah. The large Weekly Vedette will be issued at an early date. (Editorial). "To Our Comrades At Home and Abroad.—We are out, shining with a brand new face. Our little champion so long, 'alert and strong', feels assured of your support. We feel big and don't deny it, and we want the Third Infantry and the Second Cavalry, C. V., and the First Nevada Cavalry to extend to us hearty congratulations by renewed subscriptions. Their little Vedette has grown to a mammoth sheet. Its editorial staff is increased, and the expenses are increased. To meet these extra outlays, the officers and soldiers should come forward and shell out. Take the Vedette and send it to your friends. Soldiers everywhere should subscribe; let's see if they'll do it. (Signed) L." (presumably Fred Livingstone).

"O. J. Goldrick, branch office, Daily Vedette, East Temple Street," is the signature to the list of newspaper agencies. "Prospectus-ly.— Time has both hallowed and abused the custom of saying something Salutatory, when commencing enterprises editorial. The writer has a theory about the matter which differs from the most of his 'illustrious co-temporaries'. It is, that performances — not promises — are more befitting a paper paragrapher, leaving time, which can tell all things, to 'define his position', and display his talents—if he's got 'em!" (Signed) O. J. Goldrick.

Also this "Particular Notice.—Persons receiving the first number of our enlarged issue, and who are not subscribers, are respectfully solicited to become so by return mail, and get their friends to take it also. City residents can order it from our carrier, Mr. (Lucius A.) Billings, or through Mr. Goldrick, at the Branch Office, temporarily in Gray's Book Store, Main Street, North of Theater Street. Subscribers to our large Weekly (containing the news, telegrams, markets, mining and miscellaneous items of the six dailies) will receive the Daily issue until our Weekly size paper reaches it. Resident and transient citizens wishing job work, advertising, or subscription, will be promptly waited upon by applying to O. J. Goldrick at the temporary branch office . . . or at the main office in Camp Douglas, upper part of town." (Thus is Camp Douglas first annexed to Salt Lake City!)

This one is evidently "over the shoulder," June 13, 1865: "One Vedette which we heard of traveled a circuit of say, 15 families—large ones at that—the other morning before breakfast! The only expense that you'll be at if you exgage 'em (circulating mediums) is the cost of some sweet oil, to keep the hinges of their tongues well greased!" The way in was pointed out, June 14, 1865, "City advertising intended for our Daily issue will be promptly published by leaving 'copy' with Mr. Goldrick at the Salt Lake House. This will obviate the necessity of patrons personally taking it up to the Camp Office." The new editor seemed a little less patient and a little more curt than his predecessor —less forgiving, less kind; and there were still numerous Anti-Mormon editorials. He was "against" a lot of things!

Nevertheless he says, July 4, 1865: "Business men in Utah, Idaho and Montana are daily adding to our subscription lists. They want an organ of the right tone—true to the true interests of the enterprise and of the West! We are in favor of settling the Territories with a 'Gentile' element; the development of these mines, the encouragment of capital, and the extermination of Mormon selfishness—and they know it!"

For a successful paper, still another qualification was required (July 15, 1865). "Pay Up.—For months and seasons past our city agent has been easy to a fault with scores of friends and patrons in the matter of collecting. With the present poor facilities for getting paper, ink and printing material from the East, at former freight, and indeed at any figure, we must be *just* before we are *generous*, and put in force our published terms 'invariably in advance' for subscriptions without respect of persons. Every *pound* of this white paper stands us *One dollar and fifty cents*, first cost and coach freight delivered."

Patting himself on the back with the hand of the Virginia, Nevada Enterprise August 12, 1865: "The Union Vedette of Salt Lake is a thorn in the side of Mormonism. It is a Daily journal, published under the guns of Camp Douglas, and the 'Destroying Angels' are not disposed to molest the audacious little sheet. It is the enemy of polygamy, and the effect of its broadsides upon the Tabernacle are beginning to be seen and felt. Were the Federal Troops to be withdrawn from Salt Lake City, the Vedette would not long be permitted to assault the sacred symbols of Mormonism."

The editor was skimping on paper again, August 24, 1865. Explanatory.—"Finding ourselves out of paper and unable to buy, beg or borrow, we saved a part of yesterday's outside edition—intended for the California and Colorado subscribers—and used the inside of the same with yesterday's date, today, in order to lay the news before our home readers one day more." The next paper appeared September 4, 1865.—"With 'joy unspeakable' we greet again our readers in town and country; having received a small portion of our paper by last Overland Stage Coach, with the prospect of a continuance of such favors until our mule team with the bulk of it arrives."

"Personal.—Captain C. H. Hempstead returned here last week from New Orleans. Having doffed the double bars with credit to himself and honor to the service, the worthy gentleman will, for the future, reside among us, resuming the practice of the law." Incidentally, the editor could do with a little more job work (October 7, 1865) "Bill heads, cards, posters, and printing generally, are gotten up at the Vedette, Camp Douglas office, in superior style and at the most reasonable rates. Orders may be left at Room 18, Salt Lake House."

But Wednesday morning, November 22, 1865: "In consequence of moving our office to new quarters in the business part of the city, there will be no issue of this paper tomorrow, nor perhaps the next day." And Saturday, November 25, 1865: "After two days cessation we have the pleasure of issuing this number of the Daily Union Vedette in the heart of the 'Holy City', having removed our office from Camp Douglas, and set down our stakes to remain." But he doesn't say where.

"To officers and soldiers.—Owing to the large outlay and the increase of expenses attendant upon the removal of our office, we are reluctantly compelled to raise the price of their subscription to $2 per month, $5 per quarter, $9 for six months, $16 a year." (The price it had previously been to others). A "Trade Last" appears Wednesday morning, December 13, 1865 from the Gold Hill, Nevada News: "The Union Vedette is a rip-staving paper! We hope that it will live on—despite musterings out." Also one from the Owyhee, Idaho Avalanche: "The Union Vedette has lately removed to the heart of the business portion of Salt Lake City. The Vedette has been heretofore throwing hotshot (at short range) into the Mormons daily, never going into Winter Quarters, nor resting on arms."

"Tomorrow dissolves my connection and association with the Daily Union Vedette," we read December 19, 1865. "In taking leave of my employers . . ." (Signed) Fred Livingstone. Peeping Toms and Mollies, February 12, 1866: "Reading it on the sly! There's a club of 25 Mormon ladies, wives of Saints, who have an old man who furnishes them with weekly files of The Vedette, after it has been read by veritable subscribers. They do this as regularly as the aforesaid carrier comes around and have been so supplied all season. Their fractional hubands have no idea that they ever see the 'horrible Gentile sheet'!"

"Prospectus of the Weekly Union Vedette (Tuesday morning, February 22, 1866). The Daily Vedette has been published now over two years. Cheered by the staunch support of its friends towards the good for which we started and which we are now fast moving, the overthrow of Polygamy, and the one-man power in Utah. We had intended to start a Weekly long ere this, but from various causes, have found it impossible. Now, however, we hesitate not to enter upon the enterprise. The Weekly will be made up to a considerable extent from the original matter contained in the Daily. Its columns will always indicate to the outside world the precise condition of the mortal conflict we are waging with the dominant power here, now fast ceasing to be so, however, thanks to the vigor of our blows, among other potent causes operating for its overthrow. The Vedette is the Wooden Horse entered into the very Troy of Polygamy. The Weekly Union Vedette will be ready for mailing to subscribers East, West, North and South, tomorrow morning." (That paragraph bears evidences of having been composed at the type case).

Another compliment is quoted from the Denver News, March 20, 1866: "The Vedette.—This sprightly Anti-Mormon newspaper, published in the very teeth of the tiger at Salt Lake, comes to us with a new heading, and otherwise improved. The Vedette will soon appear enlarged and on new type, the material having been laying some months in this city awaiting transportation."

The paper was also noticed at home: "As Usual.—The Vedette was made the subject of extended remarks in the Tabernacle on Sabbath morning. One speaker said in substance that 'The vile, dirty, nasty sheet had been tolerated long enough in this community, and that it should be suppressed'. We are of the opinion that the Leaders will have to tolerate The Vedette a little while longer." Incidentally the editor tells us, April 3, 1866: "The past month has been one of the most prosperous in the history of The Vedette. Subscriptions and advertisements have poured in from the north, south, east and west at an unprecedented rate. In the Territory of Montana alone our daily list has increased 97, and the weekly list 117." Here is the reason, from the Montana Post quoted Thursday, April 15, 1866: "Our friend and brother, editor O. J. Goldrick, of the Vedette, has gone over to Helena for the purpose of soliciting subscriptions for his paper." (No objections appeared in Utah, when the editor headed straight for Helena!).

April 11, 1866, "From the Register.—We are the grateful recipient of the first copy of the Weekly Union Vedette, published at Salt Lake City. It is a fine specimen of western journalism. Its typographical beauty is irreproachable, and its editorial matter evidently written by one who knows his duty and dares to perform it. O. J. Goldrick, whose Colorado friends and acquaintances are numbered by the legions, is the local editor, but is now on a canvassing tour through Montana and Idaho."

Riding over them rough-shod, we read, Saturday, May 5, 1866: "A few mornings ago the carrier of the Vedette was fined $10 in the Police Court of this city for riding his horse on the sidewalk of East Temple Street. On Thursday afternoon we witnessed a person riding his horse on the sidewalk of East Temple Street. Starting at the Pacific Telegraph Office, and riding on the sidewalk until he reached Brigham Street. We observed several of the city's Stars nearby, but nothing was said or done in the premises. Perhaps they thought that the horse and rider were not worth collectively $10, and perhaps the true reason was that the rider was neither a Vedette carrier or a 'Chicken Thieving Regenerator'."

They depended a great deal on the wires to the East in those days. May 5, 1866: "Again we are without dispatches. Very heavy storms have been prevailing along the line East during the past few days, and as soon as the line is up in one place, it is down in another."

Saturday, June 2, 1866: "Today the Vedette establishment will be removed to the large and commodious building two doors North of Lee's Provision Store on Main Street.—Enlargement. We have received invoices of two power presses for the Vedette office, one for the newspaper work and the other for job printing. They will be here within sixty days, when the Vedette will be enlarged to a size equal to any paper published between the River and California."

Beginning June 1, 1866 this item appeared regularly: "To Advertisers.—The Vedette is the pioneer newspaper of Utah. Its immense circulation in every mining camp and city of Montana and Idaho (to which it gives the telegraphic dispatches a whole week ahead of the Pacific dispatches) makes it the most advantageous medium for advertising in these four central Territories." The editor had a still wider horizon in his columns, cuttings from the St. Joseph Union on Indian Affairs on the Plains, appearing alongside of the Oregon election in the Oregonian. Also "O. J. Goldrick, traveling solicitor for the Vedette, subscriptions and advertisements through the Pacific States and Territories," was run pretty regularly.

One might wonder if the Vedette paid its rent as often as it moved, for on Saturday, September 1, 1866: "Today the Vedette establishment will be removed to King's Building on Second South Temple Street (sic). The business office will be in the building formerly occupied by the Assay Office of Bohne and Moliter." But they were after him, October 2, 1866, for he says: "Come on.—We hear rumors that the Vedette Office and Billiard Club Rooms will be the next objects of attack by the heroes of the Jordan. We believe you tried cleaning out printing offices in Nauvoo, and if we recollect aright, it didn't pay! But a few of you had better engage your 'wooden overcoats' before making the attempt."

The temporary suspension, however, was for another purpose, October 19, 1866: "The proprietors of The Vedette, having decided to enlarge its pages, it will be necessary to suspend publication one day in order to reset the advertisements. Consequently there will be no paper issued from this office until Monday morning." The new masthead: The Daily Union Vedette, published every morning, Sundays excepted, by P. L. Shoaff and Company. Salutatory: "It will be seen that the Vedette has changed proprietorship and today enters upon a new career. The new proprietors propose to make The Vedette henceforth a live business newspaper. They hope by a proper criticism of public men and public measures, by upholding laws and striking down error whenever or wherever it may show its cloven foot or rear its horrid front, though trebly mailed, to derive the countenance and support of all loyal citizens. Signed P. L. Shoaff." (We shudder to recall what was said by the previous editor about "Heroes of the Jordan," and "Wooden Overcoats!").

However, when the paper changed hands, October 22, 1866, it did not change heart towards the Mormons nor any part of the original text its founders were preaching from. As to the new proprietor personally, the Stockton, California Independent is quoted November 9, 1866: "Mr. S. (P. L. Shoaff) was formerly connected with The Stockton Independent Job Office; is a first class printer, and has had a large newspaper experience."

Why those early Utah editors went incognito and invented nom de plumes is covered November 14, 1866 in this "Explanatory. — While we do not desire to intrude our private affairs on the public, yet in consequence of a misapprehension on the part of many, of which we are only advised by our exchanges, we are disposed to explain the apparent mystified question as to the editorship of The Vedette. At the time of the late kidnapping, which is really the cause of bringing this subject in question, the chair was filled as it had been for sometime previously, by Mr. I. M. Weston, who with other attaches of the paper, were attacked by a band of midnight marauders. The articles in the editorial column had previously been written by such literary gentlemen, whose services we were able to secure. The responsibility of each and every article was assumed by the proprietor."

Sidestepping again, Saturday, November 24, 1866: "As the removal of our publication office may possibly prevent our issue on Monday next, we ask indulgence. We will in future be found on the south side of Second South Street, between East Temple and First East Street, Number 76." But he was able to publish Monday and Tuesday. This compliment appeared December 19, 1866 from the New Mexico Press: "The Salt Lake, Utah Vedette is now owned and ably edited by P. L. Shoaff. Phil is a good man in every respect."

The dearth of news was sometimes itself a cracking good news item. January 5, 1867, Saturday.—"Indians On The Telegraph Line. Last Thursday the operator at Three Crossings (Central Wyoming) started towards Sweet Water Bridge, the next station East, for the purpose of repairing a break in the line. As he neared the latter station he saw a body of about 50 Indians holding a grand Pow Wow over the charred ruins of the Station. He of course took to his heels and made remarkably quick time back to Three Crossings. There were three soldiers and an operator at the Station, whose fate is at present unknown." And on January 8, 1867: "It becomes our painful duty to record the death of Mr. Kelloch, the telegraph operator at Sweet Water Station. The body of Mr. Kelloch was found scalped and otherwise maltreated in the vicinity of the ruins of the station which was burned by the Indians. Of the soldiers, no account is yet received!"

In February and March, 1867 the Vedette was not nearly so *Anti*-Mormon, there being a distinct let up in that form of space filling. Incidentally, there was plenty of railroad news, for the locomotive whistle could almost be heard. On May 9, 1867: "P. L. Shoaff, Publisher," succeeds P. L. Shoaff and Company. The change was confirmed by the Nevada Daily Trespass, Friday, May 24, 1867: "The Union Vedette, Salt Lake, has passed entirely into the ownership of P. L. Shoaff, and been reduced in size." Here also, from the Vedette and the Trespass, is a sample of the stories pioneer newspapermen were always telling on one another: "Correction.—Instead of 'People Are All Very Lousy', in a correspondence letter from Crystal Peak, read 'People Are All Very Busy'. Compositors will make a mistake sometimes!"

However, when Shoaff took sole charge of The Vedette, he did not neglect the Mormons. In fact, according to the Gold Hill News, June 12, 1867: "The Salt Lake Vedette is fearfully and wonderfully written up on the Mormon question. McLaughlin will get scalped or Jordan-ducked if he don't look out!" Also, Brother Shoaff sends himself on a Mission, June 22, 1867.—"Our Mission: We are commissioned not to let up in our laudable and noble efforts until the 'Twin Relic' is abolished in Utah, the mails arrive regularly, and Bingham Canyon is thoroughly explored. When the triple tack shall have been consummated, and we are full of days, we will consent to be gathered to our fathers. So take warning! Abolish polygamy right off! Make schedule time with the mails; and let some enterprising explorers visit Bingham Canyon and test its minerals at once!"

Pretty loud, but evidently they were not all listening, for July 3, 1867: "Notwithstanding the steady effort of two newspapers and several Church dignitaries to ignore the existence of The Vedette; and when whipped and spurred into an admission of its existence, to speak of it as a 'dirty little sheet', it is read with raw relish (secretly by the Mormons)." As a newspaper, however, it was not nearly up to previous standards and there may have thus been other reasons for ignoring it. Beadle says: "During Shoaff's administration, the financial embarrassment of the firm increased to such an extent that all the surplus material was sold," (to the Utah Magazine and the Sweetwater Mines)—(from Life In Utah).

The editor himself reveals a little further August 16, 1867, in quoting "Opinions of the Press.—Since we have assumed editorial charge of The Vedette, its merits and demerits have been freely discussed in this obscure village. To say that it has not been condemned as freely as it has been commended, would not be true. It has its enemies, bitter, unrelenting and vindictive, and friends, generous, faithful and true. Wishy-washy, back-boneless Gentiles, and those reeking with hypocrisy, as well as the advocates and defenders of polygamy, can see everything to blame and nothing to praise in its columns."

Even if it was not popular at home the editor says the world awaited the Vedette for its Utah news. August 21, 1867: " 'Please Exchange'.—We are in daily receipt of papers from Maine to Texas, asking us to exchange. We would be happy to do so, could we afford it; but we can't. It costs a heap of money now to publish The Vedette."

Smaller and smaller grew the pedestal on which The Vedette held its fort, until there was not room for all its personnel. October 7, 1867: "Valedictory.—With this issue of The Vedette, our connection with it as editor ceases. In retiring we desire to say that it is with a view of bettering our financial condition, that we leave the Chair Editorial in the Vedette office, and for no other reason! It would be unmanly to withdraw without at this time correcting some rumors . . . about our life having been threatened, and that we were ordered to leave this city by the Mormons. Nothing could be further from the truth than such fabrication. A residence of nearly a year in this city has not given us one instance of molestation or personal affront . . . and we have traversed the streets at all hours of the day and night, when our business or pleasure required."—(Judge) Daniel McLaughlin. News Item: October 10, 1867: "Daniel McLaughlin, late editor of The Vedette, and his family, took their departure in J. M. Wilson's Mule Train this morning for Cheyenne City."

The Vedette for October 28, 1867 consisted of only two pages, though eight of the twelve columns were advertisements. In a news item, "O. J. Goldrick writes from Fort Union, New Mexico." Also

"We learn that P. L. Shoaff and family arrived in San Francisco from the East on Friday last, and intends leaving for Salt Lake sometime this week." With past and present publishers so far afield, what could we expect would become of The Vedette? One of the boys in charge fills space with these notes: "On account of that drill, we are compelled to issue a half sheet for four days, commencing today.—Today that big drill commenced. There must be a big crowd of troops down near the River Jordan. Two privates armed and equipped as the law demands, and about 50 officers, passed by our office this forenoon."

There is something for consideration at this point in retrospection, in a paragraph published Tuesday, July 2, 1867: "Another new Paper.—We are informed that some parties here are making an effort to establish a new Mormon paper in opposition to the Telegraph. It proposes to be entirely independent of Brigham Young, and treat that amiable soul simply as a human being, and like the rest of the race liable to err . . . Hurry up things, boys, if you are in favor of a 'Free Press'. We can outfit you in The Vedette office and have enough left for our purposes."

The editor had said, September 18, 1867: "The reason why there are no telegraphic dispatches in this morning's Vedette is purely *atmospheric*." It will be equally clear if we say likewise, the reason there are no more Vedettes is "purely atmospheric."

The Utah Grant Vidette. No files and only these notes. (from the Tribune Monday morning, March 24, 1873) "The Utah Grant Vidette.— On Saturday this new weekly newspaper, a claimant for public patronage, made its first appearance. It is under the editorial control of the Reverend Norman McLeod, (Chaplain at Fort Douglas) of this city, and is owned by Mr. Vaughn, the proprietor of the Evanston Age and Council Bluffs, Nonpareil. In size it is about the same as the Weekly Tribune (8 columns, 4-pages), but has a supplement added to it for Sunday reading. In typographical appearance it is fair, and the quality of the paper upon which it is printed is good.

"At first sight it looks like a very creditable, well filled paper, but a close inspection reveals one or two important features about its 'get up', which rather militates against the enterprise of its proprietor, as it leads to the belief that just two thirds of the paper is printed at some point East, possibly Chicago, where they 'do Journalism' for country towns to order. The peculiar magnetism of the supplement and inside of the paper affect us in this way and we cannot help it, more especially when we see telegraphic news which our Dailies have all given about three weeks ago, given with an air of freshness.

"If we read aright, there are about 13 columns and five of advertisements printed here, which is really the *Grant Vidette*. Legitimate journalism is alright and ought to be supported everywhere, but in the paper before us we fail to find any telegraphic news whatever, except the rehash we have named. For the benefit of our readers, we will state that in the East, whole columns of short stories, nice for

'Sunday Reading' are furnished very cheap, being stereotyped for the purpose. We recently had an offer of about 300 columns of it to last a year for the extraordinary price of $100; and we presume the rest of our Dailies here have had similar offers. Lately, however, this plan has been improved on, and people in the West are somewhat accustomed to being humbugged with a newspaper, half of which is printed in the East. With this little digression, an explanation of new styles of journalism, we think that for selected Sunday reading the Utah Grant Vidette can possibly be equalled by subscribing for some of the Eastern periodicals, which cost from $1.50 to $2.00 per annum."

That is how the Tribune received Utah's first readyprint newspaper; and though similar reflections were often cast upon the readyprints for years, practically all of the weekly country newspapers are serviced by readyprints today—they could not exist without them! But it wasn't the readyprint that caused the demise of the Grant Vidette. In fact its passing may have been due to the want of readyprint or any other kind of print! We only know what the Salt Lake Daily Journal, June 23, 1873, says of it: "Suspended Publication.— The Utah Grant Vidette has petered out: Cause, lack of spondulicks to run the machine." The Journal says elsewhere on another subject: "Backed Out.—Since the collapse of the Vidette, Judge Toohy made a bid for the material of that office which was accepted. The Judge, however, has since thought better of the bargain and backed out. How about the Daily Times?"

Utah Magazine, Volume 1, Number 1, January 17, 1868. Elias L. T. Harrison, General Editor, E. W. Tullidge, Dramatic Editor, Prof. John Tullidge, Musical Editor, W. Shires, Advertising and Business Manager. W. S. Godbe and E. L. T. Harrison, Publishers. Twenty-four pages, 8 x 11, $4.50. "The Home Journal of the People, devoted to literature, art, science and education." File, Salt Lake Public Library.

J. H. Beadle (Life In Utah) says that the Utah Magazine plant was obtained by purchase of part of the Vedette plant, after its removal to Salt Lake City. Tullidge, in his History of Salt Lake City, says: "The Utah Magazine was really the offspring of the Peep O' Day, with the same editors, but with a new backing, Wm. S. Godbe being its patron . . . This Magazine ran through two series, and three volumes. The second series signified the period while it was working with a definite mission, bringing forth the 'Godbeite Movement'."

"Prospectus of the Utah Magazine," appears in the Deseret News, November 25, 1867. "The undersigned announces his intention to publish shortly a weekly magazine with the above title to be edited by himself and printed at the office of the Deseret News. This magazine will consist of 12 pages, each page half the size of the Deseret News. No advertisements will be permitted within the portion devoted to reading matter. Four pages in addition for a cover, which is intended to be taken off when the volume is bound and answer in the interim as an advertising medium.

"The magazine will be edited with especial reference to combining instruction with amusement. It will have an educational department devoted to . . . languages and sciences to meet the wants of such as are aspiring to education and cultivation. The magazine will also contain instructions to mechanics and artists. The editorial department will be devoted to the defense of our social system and to essays on the laws of life and health. The cream of the papers clipped, answers to correspondence, entertainments and comments, historical tales, remarkable adventures of travelers, illustrations of individuals, etc. Delivered at the residence of the subscribers, $7 a year. Office: Godbe's Exchange Bldg., G. S. L. City; entrance on East Temple Street, adjoining the large drugstore upstairs.—" E. L. T. Harrison.

In an Editorial Note Mr. Harrison says: "Editorially and typographically, we ask a gentle criticism of our first number. Having been under the necessity of purchasing just such type as could be obtained in Salt Lake City, our selection has of course been limited. It will take the experience of one or two numbers to discover how, with the materials we have on hand, to set up the proposed departments in the greatest possible variety and fullness. The educational, as well as some other divisions, do not yet present all the features we desire. Give us time." That paragraph is from the Daily Telegraph, which adds: "Believing that every periodical published among us cannot fail to do some good to the people, we heartily wish Mr. Harrison success."

The Deseret News favors it November 27, 1867. "The necessity for a paper combining instruction, entertainment and amusement, freed from the objectionable elements which characterize imported articles has been urged for some time. We cordially recommend the Prospectus of the Utah Magazine to our readers for their encouragement and support." And the News welcomes the paper, January 18, 1868: "The first number of the Utah Magazine was laid on our table Monday . . . The Magazine is an enterprise worthy of commendation and support. Annually our people send a large amount of money East for the purchase of serials . . . The Utah Magazine presents a very attractive appearance, more so than could have been expected, considering the difficulties the editor had to encounter in procuring type, etc."

The News further praises, February 15, 1868, "The Utah Magazine.—Number six of this periodical is before us, and is fully equal to any of the previous ones. There is a very good blending of the amusing, entertaining, solid and instructive in it." The Mineral Cactus of St. George says, March 11, 1868: "We find numbers 6 and 7 of this pleasing periodical on our table this morning. Its selections are excellent and spicy, its editorials racy and interesting, and its mechanical status all that could be wished in a weekly."

Then came the transformation, indicated April 28, 1869 by the Deseret News: "The publishers of the Utah Magazine inform us that the first number of the new form will appear in a few days. We had placed in our hands today a specimen page of the new volume, and must confess that in the increase of its size, in the beauty of the type and the superior character of the paper on which it is printed, it is a vast improvement on the previous volume. The News further says May 3, 1869: "The first number of the third volume of the Utah Magazine . . . has come to hand. It should be called number 1, volume 1 of the new series of the Utah Magazine, for it is so thoroughly improved. Among its contributors we notice the names of E. W. Tullidge, E. B. Kelsey and Jabez Woodard . . . The Magazine is not marred by advertisements, while the price per year is reduced from $7.00 to $4.50."

In a few months the Deseret News awakened with a start on discovering the real purpose of the new Utah Magazine. It publishes October 26, 1869: "Our attention has been called of late to several articles which have appeared in the Utah Magazine . . . An examination of them has convinced us that they are erroneous, opposed to the spirit of the Gospel, and calculated to do injury. According to the practice in the Church, teachers were sent to labor with the editor and publishers, to point out to them the evil results which would follow a persistence in the course they are pursuing. This did not have the desired effect, and they have since been tried before the High Council, and after a thorough and patient investigation of the case, it was found they had imbibed the spirit of apostasy to the degree that they could not any longer be fellowshiped and they were cut off the Church.

"The Utah Magazine is a periodical that in its spirit and teachings is directly opposed to the work of God. Instead of building up Zion and uniting the people, its teachings, if carried out, would destroy Zion, divide the people asunder, and drive the Holy Priesthood from the earth. Therefore we say to our Brethren and Sisters in every place, the Utah Magazine is not a periodical suitable for circulation among or perusal by them, and should not be sustained by Latter Day Saints. We hope this will be sufficient, without ever having to refer to it again." (Signed) Your Brethren, Brigham Young, George A. Smith, Daniel H. Wells, Orson Pratt, Wilford Woodruff, George Q. Cannon, and Joseph F. Smith.

On October 2, 1869, the Utah Magazine had carried this "Notice to our Patrons.—As, owing to certain Church requirements, lately made on us, some of our subscribers may fear the suspension of the Utah Magazine! We beg to inform them that, under any circumstances, we intend to see that our issue does not stop for a single number . . . E. L. T. Harrison, W. S. Godbe."

Great, however, as was the Harrison-Godbe-Tullidge triumvirate, there was evidently a still greater, for in the Utah Magazine of December 25, 1869 we find: "The Last.—With this number we close—for the present at least—the publication of the Utah Magazine. It is withdrawn that the labors of the editorial staff may be concentrated upon its successor, The Mormon Tribune, the first number of which we desire to publish on the first day of the coming year. With this issue we present a title page and index so that the volume may be bound . . . Amen.

"The present volume of this magazine was commenced by the publishers with the express purpose of presenting before the people of Utah some of those broad and grand conceptions of God and humanity which they felt themselves called upon to present . . . In the face of special prohibition, by the absolute ecclesiastical authority which has prevailed in this territory, it has run its course, a silent preacher of advanced thoughts . . . and a steady opponent of absolutism in Church and State. It is now withdrawn to make way for a more prominent advocate of the same great principle."

T. B. H. Stenhouse (Rocky Mountain Saints) adds to the above history: "But even with Mr. Godbe's willing hand and ready purse to support it, (the publishers) realized that the effort to establish a purely literary paper in Utah was premature (in its first phase). The career of the Magazine was fast hastening to a close, and by way of rest and recreation, the editor accompanied the merchant (Godbe was the city's leading druggist and merchandiser) to New York. The Magazine that had before this been hastening to an end took a new lease of life and became a brilliant and well conducted paper (with Elder Henry W. Lawrence's support)."

The Journalistic Mortuary in the Deseret News September 29, 1874, says the "Utah Magazine died of too much 'New-Move'. It new-moved until it couldn't move any more!" Incidentally the 1869 Salt Lake City Directory has these listings: "Utah Magazine, office, Exchange Building, (SE) corner First South and East Temple. Edward Tullidge, literateur, 13th Ward. E. L. T. Harrison, Editor Utah Magazine, residence 13th Ward, Third East, corner of Second South."

Valley Tan, Volume 1, Number 1, G. S. L. City, U. T., Friday, November 6, 1858. File Salt Lake Public Library and L. D. S. Church Library both end with February 22, 1860. Kirk Anderson, publisher. In fact the title was "Kirk Anderson's Valley Tan!" Masthead: "Custom has made it necessary, upon the advent of a new paper, that the editor should present himself before the footlights of public opinion and indicate his course and policy.

"Our Christening—Valley Tan.—This name will doubtless excite some curiosity in the 'States' as to what it signifies, and we will therefore make an explanation: Valley Tan was first applied to the leather made in this Territory in contradistinction to the imported article from the States; it gradually began to apply to every article made or manufactured or produced in the Territory, and means in the strictest sense Home Manufactures, until it has entered and become an indispensable word in our Utah vernacular; and it will yet add a new word to the English language. Circumstances and localities form the mint from which our language is coined, and we therefore stamp the name and put it in circulation!

"Our Paper.—We are not disposed, neither do we intend to make an apology for this our first number; circumstances themselves will furnish an explanation, and if need be, a justification. The train containing our materials arrived last Saturday (October 31); boxes had to be opened, materials distributed, press set up, etc.; without stands and short of cases, we used boxes and in some instances the floor, a very uncomfortable condition of things, but which our compositors had the backbone to accomplish, so that it can be readily understood the confusion of affairs we are in and the disabilities we labor under.

"Our frontispiece looks naked and blank, but it is the best we could do, and if its bleakness strikes the eye of the critical observer, let him charitably conclude that we are in the Rocky Mountains, and 'pass our imperfections by'! Our paper is not as large as we have been used to, or as we intended, but our remote distance from the States requires that we should economize.

"Our annual subscription price for the present is as published: Single copies 25c. This may appear high, but it must be recollected that we are in Utah. We shall send several hundred copies to the following persons and will ask the favor that they will act as agents and receive subscriptions for us at Camp Floyd, viz. Messrs. Livingston, Kinkaid & Company; Radford Cabot & Company; R. H. Dyer & Company; C. A. Perry & Company; Gilbert & Gerrish, and Miller & Russell & Company. We trust our friends at the camp will let us hear from them often, and give us such matters of interest as may transpire."

The number contains a long article on the legal aspects of polygamy, and nearly two columns of advertising. Also: "Pay up.—We would remind our readers and subscribers that we expect them to pay in advance. We have been at much trouble and expense in starting this enterprise, and as we intend to pay our employees in *cash*, the necessity of prompt payments will be apparent to our friends." Tullidge, (History of Salt Lake City) says: "Valley Tan originated at Camp Floyd, but was published in Salt Lake City."

December 3, 1858: "The city subscribers will please call at our office and get their papers for the present. The location is convenient; and until we can make other arrangements, we would request this of them." An editorial entitled "Treason" required three columns; it was a big subject! Valley Tan should have been published in Camp Floyd; it would doubtless have been better patronized, for it is evident that most of the circulation was at Camp Floyd. About two columns of advertisements was all the paper could muster. There was usually plenty of Overland Stage news. As to its editorial policy: If the "Danites" had been as vigilant and efficient as Editor Anderson claimed them to be, he would not have lasted through the first two issues!

"The office of the Valley Tan has been transferred to the hands of the Hon. John Hartnett," the announcement reads May 17, 1859. "Considerations of a personal and private character have induced me to take this step. The paper will be continued under his auspices, and as soon as facilities and arrangements can be perfected, it will be enlarged." The "Retrospect and Valedictory" required two columns; to the editor it was a thrilling tale, in part as follows: "It will be seen by this number that we part with Valley Tan. A little Nursling in the mountains and probably endeared to us on account of its very infancy and weakness!

"We had scarcely commenced our publication before the Utah Legislature declared the Valley Tan 'A libelous and scurrilous sheet . . .' Although the resolutions were subsequently repealed . . . The judgment, however, pronounced upon us by a Mormon Senate we most gratutiously accept. Our offense, however, consisted in the establishment of a free press. We can say that our personal relations with 'this people' have been of a friendly kind, and we have no animosity against them. We have warred against the corruptions and crimes that have existed here, against the Church which has protected it . . . We have taken our last 'tag'; we have no apologies to offer, no retractions to make."

It is easy to believe that a Vigilance Committee, alias Danites, may have waited on Kirk, and did not wait long! It would have been so in any community in those days in the West. He asked a freedom of the press sanctuary that he could not have demanded in conversation, for considerations of personal safety! Indeed, we may glance backward to the leading editorial of November 26, 1858 entitled "The Police of Great Salt Lake City."—(nearly two columns) Written to his Honor, the Mayor of G. S. L. City, by John Hartnett and Kirk Anderson, who claimed "that at the corner of East Temple and First South . . . at least eight men in number, armed with guns, and who as we approached within a few feet of them, cocked their guns and placed themselves directly in front of us in a hostile manner . . . One of the number, viz. fired a pistol . . . we desire to enter complaint against certain policemen (the above mentioned eight) for acting contrary to law."

It might show there were "no hard feelings" to indicate a few editorial headings of that period: Cruel murder of deaf and dumb boy; The Danites at Work; Complicity of Mormon Officials; An Incredible Catalog of Crime!

On Tuesday, May 24, 1859, the title was changed to The Valley Tan, John Hartnett, Proprietor. "Today the Valley Tan makes its appearance under a different proprietorship, as may be seen by the above card of Mr. Kirk Anderson, he being on the eve of departing for the States. This is a position not desirable to the present proprietor for many reasons, nor is it his intention to continue the directorship of this paper any longer than he can help; but whilst under his control it will contain only expressions independent, fair and honorable. At present, time forbids our saying more, but if we continue our position much longer we will be better understood."

On Wednesday, June 8, 1859: "By accident this paper shews (sic) different dates on two sides of the paper. At the time of assuming the proprietorship of the Valley Tan we did not expect to have our name at its head for more than the first issue; but failing to accomplish our wishes, this number has to appear as did the last. The next issue must appear in some other party's name and will come in regular time if our arrangements can be perfected.

"Mr. Anderson, who leaves in a few days for the States, takes with him our best wishes. We have known him for many years in many occupations of life, and have ever found him a true gentleman, and a warm friend, and we heartily wish him much success. He can use his talents to a better advantage and in a more agreeable manner in another place; we cannot blame him for the steps he has taken."

On Wednesday, June 22, 1859: "With this number Mr. Thomas Adams takes control of the Valley Tan. It will be under his sole direction. I have full confidence that he will conduct it with ability and independently. How far he will use the rod will soon be seen—I hope always where it belongs!"—John Hartnett. (Editorial) "Having arrived here recently, and finding the editor of the Valley Tan, Kirk Anderson, Esq., on the eve of departing for the States, we have been induced by the solicitations of friends to take charge of the paper for a season, believing that a Journal ought to be published here, independent of the influences . . . Owing to the limited time allowed, we are not able to express ourself as fully as we would wish, but trust that the main object will be understood, as well as though the folios were written—that is, to have an Opposition paper." (Not signed, but presumably by Thomas Adams).

The paper was still Anti-Mormon, but was more conservative, and actually supported the Church candidates for political office. On August 10, 1859 a column-and-a-half-speech of Heber C. Kimball in the Tabernacle appeared. On Wednesday, September 12, 1859: "During my absence, the editorial department of the Valley Tan will be under the control of H. M. Maguire, Esq., until further arrangement is announced."—Thomas Adams.

Editor Maguire's Salutatory appeared September 28, 1859: "By the Valley Tan preceding this, its readers perceived a change in the editorial management. Although young, we are not altogether unaccustomed to the pen." He then proceeds with a three column editorial levelled against the lawyer editors of The Mountaineer and Mormons in general. On October 12, 1859 he explains "Why we accepted our Position: To edit a Republican Journal, a free paper in the midst of a secret and concealed despotism, is anything but an agreeable task . . . It was with the greatest reluctance that we consented to take editorial charge of the Valley Tan; but while we remain here, deport ourselves as best we know how, we are fully convinced that we must submit to the sneers and enmity of 'God's people'.

"We know that a free and untrammeled journal will always stand a sentinel on the watch tower of liberty in Utah— that the dark and bloody influences which have sent many of our countrymen beyond the vale (sic) can *never crush it out;* that whether our present labors be suspended by the hand of violence or by volition, an abler expositor of the insiders and disguised heresies of Mormonism will take the place vacated, and send the ball rolling with accelerated power!" It was his last editorial; evidently the Vigilanties must have "got" either him or his nerve!

The new masthead appearing Wednesday, October 19, 1859 showed Stephen DeWolfe, editor, who says: "Circumstances and not choice have devolved on the undersigned the duty of conducting for a time the editorial department of this paper. I deem it due to make known one fact: an opinion prevails quite extensively in some parts of this territory, and perhaps out of it, that the Valley Tan was established and has been conducted as an organ of a small number of Federal office holders in this Territory. These opinions, I believe, are, in a great measure, erroneous. My connection with it is altogether free and independent." S. DeWolfe.

On October 26, 1859, a news item refers to "Mr. John Hartnett, Secretary of The Territory." Begging the people of Camp Floyd to subscribe, on November 2, 1859 the editor says: "The first volume of The Valley Tan will expire with next issue. With the commencement of the new volume the price of the paper will be reduced to $6.00 per annum to subscribers paying in advance." On February 29, 1860, "With the present number of The Valley Tan, we shall be compelled for the want of paper on which to publish it, to suspend the publication of the paper for some weeks to come. A sufficient quantity of paper to last us during the winter and until more could reach here this spring was purchased last fall in San Francisco, and sent to Placerville, to be forwarded from there by stage; but owing to the financial embarrassments of the Stage Company only a small portion of the paper was brought through by them; and we should in consequence have been without the material for publishing our paper several weeks ago, if the proprietor of the Deseret News had not, in an obliging spirit, supplied us with paper.

"In addition to the want of paper, the foreman of the Valley Tan office, Mr. George Hales, has been forced, through the dictation of a portion of the Church rulers here, to quit the position of foreman in the office which he has filled since the Valley Tan was first established, or be cut off from the fellowship of his associates in the Church. We take pleasure in recommending him to Mormons and Gentiles as a worthy and honorable man. This circumstance in regard to Mr. Hales, illustrates better than any remark that we can make in regard to it the control exercised by the rulers of the Mormon Church over the members of the same."

A two column editorial, February 1, 1860, was entitled To The Public, (that a certain man) "had heard many threats made against me by different persons . . . After being thus officially warned by two of the corporate officers of the city, and indirectly notified of danger by a third . . . (he wrote to Governor Cummings). The threats made against me for making a statement which I, in common with almost every man in this valley not connected with the Mormon Church, believes is true, affords proof . . . of all that I said about the insecurity of life here, to such as fell under the ban of the Church authorities . . .

"The conservatism heretofore practiced is henceforth at an end, and I shall hereafter put in my best licks, and invite all others opposed to the miserable system . . . My position is now defined. I neither fear hierarchal authorities, nor priestly curses . . . Nor will threats and intimidations lead me to shrink from the performance of any known duty." S. DeWolfe. At that, he may have been glad when the print paper gave out!

Kenner, in Utah As It Is, says of Valley Tan: "a rabid Anti-Mormon Weekly; . . . being unable to exude its virus as fast as the same was generated, it passed away through congestion of the spleen . . . 'unhonored, unwept and unsung'. Its editor, Kirk Anderson, had the reputation of being the homeliest man in the Territory. Where Kirk got the name of his paper . . . A distillery manufactured Valley Tan in the valley, but which was named for the other is a sealed secret. They were, however, properly endowed for a name in common, both being long range paralyzers."

Another story gained wide circulation, and traces through the Chronicle, January 19, 1885 to Colonel Clawson in the Ketchum Keystone: "The Valley Tan was certainly not of Gentile extraction. It was issued and disseminated by (members of) the Mormon Church. We remember distinctly of going into the office at Salt Lake City as early as 1863, and purchased a gallon jug full of it to take on the Snake River Plains to circulate among the hostile savages. It killed all who took it, with the exception of one, and it threw him into fits . . . Valley Tan was a tough issue!"

Young Woman's Journal, was launched October 1889, in the interests of the Young Ladies' Mutual Improvement Association, by Mrs. Susa Young Gates, editor. She was succeeded in 1901 by Mrs. May Booth Talmage, in 1902 by Miss Ann M. Cannon and Ellen Wallace, in 1907 by Miss Mary Connelley, in 1923 by Miss Clarissa Beesley, in 1928 by Miss Elsie Talmage Brandley. In 1929 it was merged with the Improvement Era.

*Newspapers, with Brief Accessible History, Mostly Long Discontinued & Without Files

Place	Name of Paper	When Published	Editor and Publisher	Remarks
Altonah	Inter-Mtn. News	Weekly, 1917-1917	Cook and H. Dubendorff	Democratic
American Fork	Republican	Weekly, 1892-1892	Newman A. Mix	Republican
"	World	Weekly, 1896-1897	W. E. and Eva B. Smith	Independent
"	Tri City Times	Weekly, 1903-1903	James T. Jakeman and Gray	Republican
Beaver	County News	Weekly, 1896-1896	"Neat 6-column folio," Vernal Express	
"	County Blade	Weekly, Sept, 1897	M. H. White, mentioned by Wasatch Wave	
"	County Observer	Weekly, 1900-1903	James T. Jakeman (C. T. Stoney), 6 columns, 4 pages	
"	Bulletin	Weekly, 1903-1904	O. A. Whitaker, Beaver Publishing Co.	Non-Partisan
Bingham Canyon	Review	Weekly, 1912-1915	Lester G. Baker	Independent
Brigham City	Box Elder Report	Weekly, 1904-1905	Christenson; B. H. Jones	Republican
"	Bulletin	Tri-Wkly, 1916-17	L. Jorgenson; J. E. Baird	
Cedar City	The Observer	Weekly, 1912-1915	Alex H. Rollo & Co.	Independent
Centerville	Call	Weekly, 1897-1898	E. S. Carroll; Melvie Smith	
Clear Lake	Review	Weekly, 1898-1900	C. W. Aldrach and Barclay John	
Elsinore	S. V. Banner	Weekly, 1912-1912	J. W. Robinson, from State Gazetteer	
Ephraim	Sanpete Democrat	Weekly, 1898-1899	"Two color Xmas number."—Utah County Democrat	
Eureka	Sentinel	Weekly, 1879-1881	Says Ogden Junction & Provo Enquirer	
"	Leader	Weekly, 1881-1881	Mentioned by Park City Record	
"	Tintic Min. Times	Weekly, 1888-1889	Union Printing & Publishing Co.	Republican
Farmington	Davis Co. Argus	Weekly, 1903-1912	D. P. Felt; F. Vernon Felt	
Ferron	Castle Valley Press	Weekly, 1917-1920	Harold Dubendorff (See Altonah)	
Garfield	Messenger	Weekly, 1916-1918		
Garland	Globe	Weekly, 1906-1925	J. A. Wixom (probably others)	
"	Times	Weekly, 1928-date	Roy Wahlen, B. Dale Gibson, V. W. Jones	

* Including a few early magazines; but excluding 21 newspapers in Salt Lake City, and 49 outside of Salt Lake City, launched and suspended since 1918; also excluding about 56 class periodicals launched since 1900, such as school, fraternity, labor, professional, occupational and other group organs.

*Newspapers, with Brief Accessible History, Mostly Long Discontinued & Without Files

Place	Name of Paper	When Published	Editor and Publisher	Remarks
Gold Hill	Standard	Weekly, 1916-1919	L. G. Schwalenberg, Gold Hill Publishing Co.	
Grantsville	Reflex	Weekly, 1912-1917	R. D. Halladay	Republican
"	News	Weekly, 1917-1923	R. D. Halladay; L. E. Kramer	
Ibapah	Deep Creek News	Weekly, 1914-1916	L. E. Kramer, Tooele County Publishing Co.	
Kamas	Courant	Weekly, 1912-1920	R. B. Rand, from State Gazetteer	
Loa	Advice	Weekly, 1898-1899	George H. Crosby, Jr., (See Richfield)	
Logan	Rocky Mtn. Farming	Monthly, 1906-1907	Utah Agricultural Experiment Station—Exten. Div.	
Mammoth	Record	Weekly, 1896-1930	I. E. Diehl, all directories	
"	News	Weekly, 1900-1900	C. F. Spillman, State Gazetteer	
Manti	Sanpete Free Press	Weekly, 1901-1901	L. A. Lauber	Democratic
Marysvale	Optimist	Weekly, 1912-1912	N. H. Felt, from State Gazetteer	
Midvale	Times	Weekly, 1909-1909	J. S. Barlow, C. I. Goff	
"	Messenger	Weekly, 1914-1933	J. L. Ewing, D. M. Clark, Vernon Gray	
"	Ute Sentinel	1937-date	Howard Barrows	
Milford	Index	Weekly, 1897-1897	B. W. Rice, mentioned by Bingham Bulletin	
Monroe	News	Weekly, 1910-1913	G. N. Campbell, Ayer's Newspaper Annual	
"	Record	Weekly, 1916-1917	F. A. Edison, Chas. Shaffer, R. F. Walsh	
Moroni	News-Letter	Weekly, 1898-1898	Joseph Gee	Independent
Murray	Citizen	Weekly, 1914-1914	John G. Weaver, from State Gazetteer	
Myton	Dawn	Monthly, 1915-1915	Dawn Publishing Co.	Socialist
Ogden	Times	Semi-Wkly, 1878-78	Nickum & Smith, in Deseret News	
"	Monday Morning	Weekly, 1890-1890	Intermountain Ptg. & Pub. Co. (Wasatch Wave)	
"	Junction Weekly	Weekly, 1891-1891	Distributed free	Non-Political
"	American X-Ray	Weekly, 1892-1898	S. S. Smith	Populist

* Including a few early magazines; but excluding 21 newspapers in Salt Lake City, and 49 outside of Salt Lake City, launched and suspended since 1918; also excluding about 56 class periodicals launched since 1900, such as school, fraternity, labor, professional, occupational and other group organs.

*Newspapers, with Brief Accessible History, Mostly Long Discontinued & Without Files

Place	Name of Paper	When Published	Editor and Publisher	Remarks
Ogden	Press	Daily, 1893-1897	E. A. Littlefield; B. F. Thomas	Republican
"	Advertiser	Daily, 1895-1895	Matt E. Edsall, In Directory	
"	Review	Semi-Wkly, 1895-95	H. L. Gant; Rev. Pub. Co.	Populist
"	Times	Weekly, 1896-1896	Matt E. Edsall	Society
"	(Danish Language)	Weekly, 1896-1896	Jacobsen, Petersen and Coleman	
"	Commonwealth	Weekly, 1897-1898	J. S. Boreman, in Provo Utonian	
"	Switch	Weekly, 1897-1898	E. A. Littlefield; A. C. Ivins	Society
"	Utah Home	Semi-Mo., 1898-99	F. J. Hendershot, S. H. Hobson	Home & Farm
"	Bi-Metallist	Weekly, 1899-1899	W. H. Curleton, in Directory	
"	Weber Co. Times	Weekly, 1899-1899	Mansfield L. Snow, in Directory	
"	Industrial Utah	Semi-Mo., 1901-04	B. F. Thomas	Agriculture
"	Advance	Weekly, 1912-1913	Frederick Vining Fisher, Advertising Publishing Co.	
"	Japanese News	Daily, 1914-1915	T. Kameyama, in Directory	
Ophir	Examiner	Weekly, 1913-1921	L. E. Kramer (Tooele) Ayer's Newspaper Annual	
Provo	Utah Co. Press	Weekly, 1897-1897	Milton L. Scott, American Newspaper Directory	
"	Utah Industrialist	Monthly, 1887-1888	Wm. M. Egan, Editor; D. P. Felt, Mgr.	
Sandy	Sentinel	Weekly, 1899-1899	Johnson and Jakeman (Wasatch Wave)	
"	Enterprise	Weekly, 1912-1912	W. D. S. Harrington, Sandy and Midvale	
"	Star	Weekly, 1913-1921	J. S. Barlow, Eagle Publishing Co., Murray	
Salt Lake City	Juvenile Instructor	Monthly, 1866-date	G. Q. Cannon, G. D. Pyper, S. M. Tanner	
"	Footlights	Show Nights, 1870-74	John C. Graham; W. T. Harris	Program
"	Women's Exponent	Semi-Mo., 1872-1914	Louisa L. Greene (Richards), Emmeline B. Wells	
"	Utah Posten	Weekly, 1873-1874	P. O. Thomassen, First Foreign Language Paper	Danish
"	Utah Miner	Weekly, 1875-1876	Wm. Lapham & Co.; Dr. A. W. Smith	

* Including a few early magazines; but excluding 21 newspapers in Salt Lake City, and 49 outside of Salt Lake City, launched and suspended since 1918; also excluding about 56 class periodicals launched since 1900, such as school, fraternity, labor, professional, occupational and other group organs.

*Newspapers, with Brief Accessible History, Mostly Long Discontinued & Without Files

Place	Name of Paper	When Published	Editor and Publisher	Remarks
Salt Lake City	The Advocate	Semi-Mo., 1875-76	Henry Snell, Advertising Medium	
"	R. M. Chrstn. Advo.	Monthly, 1876-1878	Rev. G. M. Peirce, Methodism & Mining	
"	W. Min. Gazetteer	Weekly, 1880-1881	Mark W. Musgrove	
"	Mining Reporter	Weekly, 1880-1880	Major Bradley	Agriculture
"	Utah Farmer	Monthly, 1880-1881	A. M. Musser; J. E. Callister; H. Van Dam	Hist. & Gen. Lit.
"	Quarterly Magazine	Quarterly, 1880-84	E. W. Tullidge	
"	Journal of Com.	Semi-Mo., 1881-92	H. L. A. Culmer	Cooperation
"	Z C M I Advocate	Semi-Mo., 1884-85	H. B. Naisbitt	
"	The Refugee	Weekly, 1885-1885	July 4 and 11 in New York Public Library	Literary Jour.
"	Parrys Magazine	Monthly, 1884-1887	J. H. Parry & Co.	Dan.-Norweg.
"	Utah Posten	Weekly, 1885, 4 Mo.	Andrew Jenson, C. A. F. Orlob	Mormon
"	Svenska Harolden	Weekly, 1885-1885	Swedish Publishing Co.	
"	Mirror	Sundays, 1885-1885	Literary, Society, Sporting	Utah Resources
"	Enterprise	Weekly, 1887-1887	Enterprise Publishing Co.	
"	Palantic	Monthly, 1887-1887	A. M. Musser, against Anti-Mormon Press	
"	Baptist Mountaineer	Monthly, 1887-1887	Rev. L. L. Wood, Baptist	Lit. & Art
"	Western Weekly	Weekly, 1888-1889	G. Q. Coray; J. M. Romney	Gen. Lit.
"	Western Galaxy	Monthly, 1888-1888	E. W. Tullidge	
"	Irrigation Age	Semi-Wkly, 1890-92	Wm. E. Smythe; Smythe, Britton & Poore Co.	
"	Korrespondenten	Weekly, 1890-1915	C. V. Anderson, Otto Rydman	Swedish
"	Valkyrien	Weekly, 1890-1890	J. P. Jacobsen	Dan.-Scand.
"	Utah Oddfellow	Monthly, 1890-1892	E. W. Loder; Kelly Co.	Fraternal
"	Inter-Mtn. Educator	Monthly, 1891-1891	Wolfe, Newbern and McKay	Educational
"	The Daily Bee	Daily, Sept. 1893	Mentioned by Wasatch Wave	

* Including a few early magazines; but excluding 21 newspapers in Salt Lake City, and 49 outside of Salt Lake City, launched and suspended since 1918; also excluding about 56 class periodicals launched since 1900, such as school, fraternity, labor, professional, occupational and other group organs.

*Newspapers, with Brief Accessible History, Mostly Long Discontinued & Without Files

Place	Name of Paper	When Published	Editor and Publisher	Remarks
Salt Lake City	Silver Star	Weekly, 1893-1893	Mentioned by Brigham Bugler	Populist
"	Inter-Mtn. Advocate	Weekly, 1894-1897	Warren Foster & N. B. Dresser	
"	New Star	Weekly, 1895-1895	New Star Publishing Co.	
"	Relief Society Mag.	Monthly, 1895-Date	Susa Young Gates; Alice L. Reynolds	
"	Utahnian	Weekly, 1896-1897	Colonel P. Donan	"Silver"
"	Western Recorder	Weekly, 1897-1897	E. S. Carroll, Utah Publishing Co.	
"	Living Issues	Weekly, 1897-1898	Warren Foster; M. V. Wagner; Scott Anderson	
"	Utah Oracle	Weekly, 1897-1897	5 col. 4 pages, politics	"16 to 1"
"	The Bee	Wkly, March, 1898	Noble Warrum, Mentioned by Wasatch Wave	
"	Kinsman	Monthly, 1898-1899	Rev. Wm. R. Campbell	Anti-Polygamy
"	The Journal	Daily, 1899-1899	An evening paper, ran 8 days	
"	Demo. Headlight	Weekly, 1899-1899	J. McPherson; A. B. Douglas; A. H. Grice	
"	Mining Review	Semi-Mo., 1899-Date	Will C. Higgins, L. E. Camomile, B. B. Brewster	
"	Utah Posten	Weekly, 1900-1935	A. L. Dahlquist, J. M. Sjodahl, A. W. Winberg	
"	Goodwin's Weekly	Weekly, 1902-1918	C. C. Goodwin; J. Todwin Goodwin	
"	Tri-City Oracle	Weekly, 1902	Washington, Sellers & Co. (Ogden & Murray)	Negro
"	Deseret Farmer	Weekly, 1904-1912	J. A. Widtsoe, L. A. Merrill, J. E. Taylor	Agriculture
"	Rocky Mtn. Times	Weekly, 1908-1933	Shiro Iida	Japanese
"	Outlook	Monthly, 1908-1909	J. Cecil Alter, Tribune-Reporter Ptg. Co.	Industrial
"	Utah Independent	Weekly, 1909-1909	V. S. Peet	Political
"	Western Monthly	Monthly, 1909-1910	A. N. McKay; Geo. E. Carpenter	Gen. Lit.
"	The Light	Semi-Wkly, 1912-21	A. and Dr. Peter Kassinikos	Greek
"	Progress	Weekly, 1912-1912	Alexander Grannikos	
"	Radicka Obranna	Weekly, 1912-1912	E. and A. Basetich	Slavonian

* Including a few early magazines; but excluding 21 newspapers in Salt Lake City, launched and suspended since 1918; also excluding about 56 class periodicals launched since 1900, such as school, fraternity, labor, professional, occupational and other group organs.

*Newspapers, with Brief Accessible History, Mostly Long Discontinued & Without Files

Place	Name of Paper	When Published	Editor and Publisher	Remarks
Salt Lake City	Gazetta	Weekly, 1912-1923	G. and Wm. Milano, Italian Publishing Co.	
"	Utah Farmer	Semi-Mo., 1912-date	J. M. and J. Arno Kirkham; Stringam A. Stevens	Agriculture
"	Progressive	Weekly, 1914-1916	J. G. Weaver; J. H. Turner; W. D. Livingston	
"	Utah Nippo	Daily, 1916-1933	Uneo Terasawa	Japanese
"	Utah Nederlander	Weekly, 1916-1931	A. L. Peterson; W. J. DeBry	
"	New World	1918-1918	K. Hirasawa	Japanese
Silver City	Star	Weekly, 1897-1903	"Enters its 3rd year."—Park Record	
Silver Reef	So. Utah Times	Weekly, 1886-1887	C. S. King, (see Frisco)	
Spanish Fork	Rocky Mtn. Star	Weekly, 1891-1891	Jos. A. Rees; J. Frank Pickering	Republican
"	Spanish Fork Star	Weekly, 1892-1892	J. T. Jakeman, (printed in Payson)	
Stockton	Sentinel	Weekly, 1899-1915	J. T. Jakeman; J. S. Hollow; F. G. Shelton	
Trenton	Post	Weekly, 1914-1914	F. I. Mortenson	
West Jordan	Chronicle	Weekly, 1904-1904	J. A. Borlase	
Woods Cross	Watchman	Weekly, 1898-1898	Samantha Sessions (pub. Salt Lake City)	Political

* Including a few early magazines; but excluding 21 newspapers in Salt Lake City, launched and suspended since 1918; also excluding about 56 class periodicals launched since 1900, such as school, fraternity, labor, professional, occupational and other group organs.

INDEX

C

H